Sustainable Industrial Transformation in the AI Era

Abdelrehim Awad
https://orcid.org/0009-0005-3649-430X

Department of Business Administration, University of Bisha, Bisha, Saudi Arabia

Amr El Daba
The Arab Academy for Management, Banking, and Financial Sciences (AAMBFS), Egypt

IGI Global Scientific Publishing
Publishing Tomorrow's Research Today

Vice President of Editorial Melissa Wagner
Director of Acquisitions Mikaela Felty
Director of Book Development Jocelynn Hessler
Production Manager Mike Brehm
Cover Design Jose Rosado

Published in the United States of America by
IGI Global Scientific Publishing
701 East Chocolate Avenue
Hershey, PA, 17033, USA
Tel: 717-533-8845 | Fax: 717-533-7115
Website: https://www.igi-global.com E-mail: cust@igi-global.com

Library of Congress Cataloging-in-Publication Data

LCCN: 2026031991 (CIP Data Pending)
ISBN13: 9798260027264
Isbn13Softcover: 9798260027271
EISBN13: 9798260027288

British Cataloguing in Publication Data
A Cataloguing in Publication record for this book is available from the British Library.

Table of Contents

Detailed Table of Contents

This study examines Knowledge Management Capability (KMC) and AI capabilities improve organizational agility. The results demonstrate that AI proficiency and assimilation greatly enhance knowledge management procedures, based on data from 339 IT employees and a PLS-SEM analysis. In turn, KMC improves organizational agility and serves as a mediator between agility and AI capabilities. The report emphasizes the importance of implementing AI technology and training employees in AI to enhance organizational flexibility and knowledge practices.

The rapid transformation of the global workforce, driven by digitalization, technological advancement, and sustainability imperatives, has accelerated the need for future skills ecosystems that enable continuous reskilling and long-term value creation. This chapter examines the development of Future Skills Ecosystems for Work 2030, focusing on adaptive reskilling architectures aligned with evolving market demands. It explores key components including learning infrastructures, skill intelligence systems, knowledge networks, governance mechanisms, and sustainability integration. The role of artificial intelligence, data analytics, and digital platforms in enabling real-time skill mapping, personalized learning, and predictive workforce planning is emphasized. The chapter also highlights the importance of collaboration among academia, industry, and government, alongside the integration of ESG competencies, to build resilient, inclusive, and future-ready workforce systems.

The chapter progresses the responsibility as a design principle, which provides strategic advice to create human-centered, responsible, and sustainable generative AI-driven organizations.

Introduction & Rationale (Why this chapter is needed) The present-day world has reached a point where intelligence exists as a combination of human and artificial intelligence. The new form of intelligence emerges through continuous human-machine cooperation between human brainwork and artificial intelligence technology. The introduction of generative AI technologies and adaptive analytics solutions and automation systems and cognitive computing systems leads to a transformation in the cognitive processes and decision-making methods and operational practices of people and organizations and educational institutions. AI now functions as a fundamental element that organizations need to create sustainable competitive advantages which businesses and healthcare systems and governmental bodies and educational institutions depend on. The current discussions about AI still treat it as a technology that replaces humans while improving efficiency despite the fact that digital technologies have become common in all areas of society.

Generative artificial intelligence (GenAI) is fundamentally reconfiguring the architecture of work by extending automation into cognitive, creative, and communicative domains previously considered uniquely human. This chapter examines how GenAI reshapes individual tasks, job roles, and organizational structures across three interacting analytical layers: the macro level of organizational hierarchy and strategy, the meso level of job and role design, and the micro level of individual worker experience. Drawing on the automation-augmentation paradox

(Raisch & Krakowski, 2021), task-based labor displacement frameworks (Acemoglu & Restrepo, 2022), and multilevel organizational AI research (Bankins et al., 2024), a conceptual framework is developed that maps GenAI's cascading effects on workforce composition, skill demands, hierarchical design, and decision-making authority.

Bhimavarapu Usharani, Department of Computer Science and Engineering, Koneru Lakshmaiah Education Foundation, Vaddeswaam, India

GenAI Ethical Generative Artificial Intelligence (GenAI) has become a significant paradigm in the contemporary people management as GenAI allows organizations to make better decisions and be fair, transparent, and accountable. The paper suggests a smart platform of evaluating the ethical aspects in people management through a bistacked ResNet-18 model. First, an organized questionnaire had been developed to gather the data belonging to ethical aspects trust, fairness, privacy, transparency, and accountability in AI-supported working conditions. The survey instrument was piloted on 20 individuals to determine the clarity and organization of the survey instrument and two questions were slightly revised and one section had to be rearranged. In the primary data collection stage, 13 respondents were willing to take the questionnaire and answer the survey.

Chandan Maheshkar, East Nimar Society for Education (ENSE), India & SR University, Warangal, India
Durgesh Nandan, SR University, Warangal, India
Tarika Nandedkar, IPS Academy, Institute of Business Management and Research, Indore, India
Yogesh Mehta, SGT University, Gurugram, India

The rapid development of AI and automation is transforming labor markets worldwide. It posed diverse challenges and opportunities for an aging workforce. Aged workers/ employees are especially susceptible to technological displacement, given stagnation and decline in skills, lower learning rates for new technologies, and older-worker bias in hiring and retention. Meanwhile, AI-powered tools and organizational innovations provide pathways to further develop and expand productive careers, flexibility enablement, and redeployment of skilled employees into new roles. This chapter investigates both risks and opportunities of aging workers in the AI era and integrates studies, policy insights, and industry practices. It examines the causes of job displacement, looks at sectors and occupations hardest hit by automation, and analyses possible reskilling and upskilling strategies for older workers.

The digital transformation of businesses has exponentially fueled the adoption of Smart HR Systems, which combine Artificial Intelligence, automation, and people analytics to enable businesses to manage their human resources effectively in the digital era. This combined capability of Smart HR Systems helps businesses transform from a traditional and transactional approach to human resources management in the digital era to a data-driven, predictive, and people-centric approach to decision-making. Despite immense benefits, the adoption of Smart HR Systems also gives way to several challenges related to data privacy, ethics of AI usage, algorithmic bias, and change management. The present paper describes the capacity for change of Smart HR Systems and underlines the necessity for an implementation that has to be balanced, open, and human, centered in order to guarantee that value will always be gained in the digital HR ecosystem.

The chapter shows artificial intelligence (AI) technologies have been adopted by organizations to improve their recruitment procedures of job applicants based on data from recent surveys conducted in both the United States and the United Kingdom. The majority of respondents believe AI will shape the future of recruitment: 61% in the U.S. and 58% in the UK believe applicants should use AI in ways that remain hidden to others, while 56% (U.S.) and 52% (UK) believe candidates will need AI assistance to complete application processes. Additionally, 55% of U.S. and 52% of UK respondents think non-users will face disadvantages. People from Millennial (78% U.S.; 79% UK) and Gen Z (71% U.S.; 62% UK) groups show the highest

Preface

The global industrial landscape is undergoing a profound transformation driven by the convergence of artificial intelligence, digital technologies, sustainability imperatives, and evolving workforce expectations. As organizations navigate increasing complexity, rapid technological advancement, environmental challenges, and shifting socio-economic priorities, the pursuit of sustainable industrial transformation has become both a strategic necessity and a societal responsibility. Artificial Intelligence (AI), particularly generative AI and advanced analytics, is emerging as a powerful catalyst for this transformation, enabling organizations to redesign processes, enhance decision-making, develop human capital, and create sustainable value at unprecedented scales.

Sustainable Industrial Transformation in the AI Era brings together diverse scholarly perspectives that explore how AI technologies are reshaping industries, organizations, work systems, and economic structures while simultaneously advancing sustainability objectives. The volume examines the opportunities and challenges associated with integrating intelligent technologies into organizational ecosystems and highlights the importance of balancing technological innovation with ethical governance, workforce resilience, environmental stewardship, and human-centered development.

A central theme throughout this collection is that sustainable transformation cannot be achieved through technology alone. Instead, it requires the development of adaptive capabilities, future-ready skills, responsible leadership, inclusive governance mechanisms, and collaborative human-AI systems. The chapters collectively demonstrate how organizations can leverage AI not merely as a tool for efficiency and automation but as an enabler of innovation, sustainability, trust, and long-term competitiveness.

The volume explores transformation across multiple dimensions. It addresses organizational agility, workforce development, leadership and governance, human-AI collaboration, ethical AI implementation, demographic workforce challenges, sustainable innovation, financial transformation, intelligent human resource systems, recruitment practices, emotional intelligence, and trust-based organizational design. Together, these perspectives offer a comprehensive understanding of how industries can evolve toward more resilient, responsible, and sustainable futures in an increasingly AI-driven world.

The contributors emphasize that successful industrial transformation requires an integrated approach that combines technological sophistication with human capability development, sustainability-oriented decision-making, and ethical accountability. Such an approach is essential for organizations seeking to thrive amid accelerating technological change while creating positive economic, social, and environmental outcomes.

CHAPTER OVERVIEW

Chapter 1 examines how artificial intelligence capabilities and knowledge management practices contribute to organizational agility, highlighting the role of AI-enabled learning and knowledge sharing in building adaptive and sustainable organizations.

Chapter 2 explores the development of future skills ecosystems and adaptive reskilling architectures designed to support workforce resilience, lifelong learning, and sustainable value creation in rapidly changing labor markets.

Chapter 3 investigates the growing importance of micro-capabilities as critical competencies for future-ready workforces, emphasizing agility, emotional intelligence, collaboration, and digital fluency.

Chapter 4 presents a framework for responsible workforce development, focusing on the interconnected roles of leadership, skills enhancement, and governance in achieving ethical and sustainable AI adoption.

Chapter 5 introduces the concept of symbiotic intelligence, examining how human and artificial intelligence can work collaboratively to enhance decision-making, innovation, and organizational performance.

Chapter 6 analyzes the transformative impact of generative AI on work, jobs, and organizational structures, exploring changes at the individual, role, and organizational levels.

Chapter 7 focuses on ethical evaluation mechanisms for AI-enabled workplace management systems, addressing issues of trust, fairness, privacy, transparency, and accountability.

Chapter 8 examines the risks and opportunities facing aging workers in the AI era, highlighting workforce inclusion, lifelong employability, reskilling strategies, and productive aging.

Chapter 9 explores the role of green technologies and sustainable innovation within Industry 5.0, emphasizing human-centered industrial systems, circular economy principles, and environmental sustainability.

Chapter 10 investigates the digital transformation of accounting and finance through the integration of fintech solutions, intelligent technologies, real-time analytics, and evolving governance frameworks.

Chapter 11 explores the evolution of smart human resource systems through the integration of AI, automation, and people analytics, emphasizing data-driven and employee-centered decision-making.

Chapter 12 analyzes contemporary trends in AI-enabled recruitment, examining generational perspectives, technology adoption patterns, and their implications for future workforce development.

Chapter 13 highlights the strategic importance of emotional intelligence in AI-driven workplaces, emphasizing employee well-being, adaptability, collaboration, and sustainable human capital development.

Chapter 14 concludes the volume by exploring the interconnected themes of work, talent, and trust within AI-enabled organizations, proposing a human-centered sustainability perspective that balances technological advancement with transparency, accountability, and employee empowerment.

Collectively, these chapters provide a multidisciplinary examination of sustainable industrial transformation in the age of artificial intelligence. They offer valuable theoretical insights, conceptual frameworks, and practical perspectives for understanding how organizations can harness emerging technologies while maintaining a commitment to sustainability, inclusivity, and responsible innovation.

This volume is intended to serve as a resource for academics, researchers, industry leaders, policymakers, practitioners, and students seeking to understand the opportunities and challenges associated with AI-enabled transformation. By bringing together perspectives from management, technology, human resources, finance, sustainability, and organizational studies, the book contributes to the growing discourse on building resilient and sustainable industrial ecosystems for the future.

We hope that the ideas presented in this volume inspire further research, informed policymaking, and responsible organizational practices that advance both technological progress and sustainable development in the AI era.

Abdelrehim Awad
University of Bisha, Saudi Arabia

Amr El Daba
The Arab Academy for Management, Banking, and Financial Sciences (AAMBFS), Egypt

Chapter 1
Generative AI-Driven Optimisation Intelligence for Sustainable and Agile Organisation

Anjali Jadon
http://orcid.org/0009-0002-9376-5434
Amity University, Gwalior, India

Abhilasha Dixit
Amity University, Gwalior, India

ABSTRACT

This study examines Knowledge Management Capability (KMC) and AI capabilities improve organizational agility. The results demonstrate that AI proficiency and assimilation greatly enhance knowledge management procedures, based on data from 339 IT employees and a PLS-SEM analysis. In turn, KMC improves organizational agility and serves as a mediator between agility and AI capabilities. The report emphasizes the importance of implementing AI technology and training employees in AI to enhance organizational flexibility and knowledge practices.

INTRODUCTION

AI is necessary to enhance the economic gains and facilitate end-to-end operations in the organization (Alavi & Leidner, 2001; Darioshi & Lahav, 2021). Artificial intelligence is becoming more popular among businesses to improve performance, creativity, and decision-making capabilities. However, there is a scarcity of literature

DOI: 10.4018/979-8-2600-2726-4.ch001

related to the influence of AI assimilation on the entrepreneurial performance of SMEs (Hani, 2019). In developing countries such as India, the disparity underscores the need for targeted research (Chowdhury et al., 2022). India is experiencing a rapid growth in the SME sector. Udyam site has more than 1.84 crore MSMEs registered (Hani, 2019; Jarrahi, 2018). Today, a large part of the business is formally part of the digital economy. This growth indicates the increased role of entrepreneurs in the economy's development (Jarrahi, 2018). This transformation is also supported by the development of digital infrastructure and the use of IT (Wamba-Taguimdje et al., 2020). This project supports inclusive development and technical progress on India's Viksit Bharat 2047 path. The paper examines the impact of AI proficiency and integration on the organizational agility of SMEs. AI competencies enable companies to make faster, better-informed decisions and to improve knowledge management (Pai et al., 2022). Knowledge management capabilities enable the effective creation and application of knowledge. Knowledge management is a very important mediating factor. It helps companies react rapidly to market changes and environmental uncertainty. Well-developed knowledge systems help organizations to transform AI capabilities into agility (Bradley, 2000). Organizational agility helps businesses to identify change and respond accordingly. Agile companies handle uncertainty better and faster embrace new technology (Sambamurthy et al., 2003; Sherehiy et al., 2007). To remain competitive, they adjust their strategies and resources. This ability is necessary in rapidly changing and technologically sophisticated settings.

REVIEW OF THE LITERATURE

Theory of Technology Dominance (TTD)

The Theory of Technology Dominance (TTD) explains how technology affects individuals' decision-making. It is determined that there are three stages: long-term effects, technological control sensitivity, and decision support dependence (Somasundaram et al., 2024). The hypothesis states that inexperienced users may use AI systems, which may result in prejudice and poor judgment, whereas experienced users can regulate such systems more effectively (Gold et al., 2001; Teece et al., 1997). It underscores the importance of system transparency and AI literacy to improve decision-making and minimize discrimination.

AI Assimilation

AI has become an important aspect of organizational work (Raina et al., 2026). The process of incorporating AI into everyday activities and decision-making is called

AI absorption (Nguyen et al., 2026). It assists the companies to attain sustainable development and high performance in dynamic marketplaces through enhanced productivity, competitiveness and flexibility (Li et al., 2022).

Knowledge Management Ability (KMC)

KMC refers to the capability to create, store, distribute and apply knowledge, or KMC (Taherdoost & Madanchian, 2023). Organizational agility and effectiveness rely heavily on it as it improves the process of decision making, creativity and being flexible.

Figure 1. Proposed Model

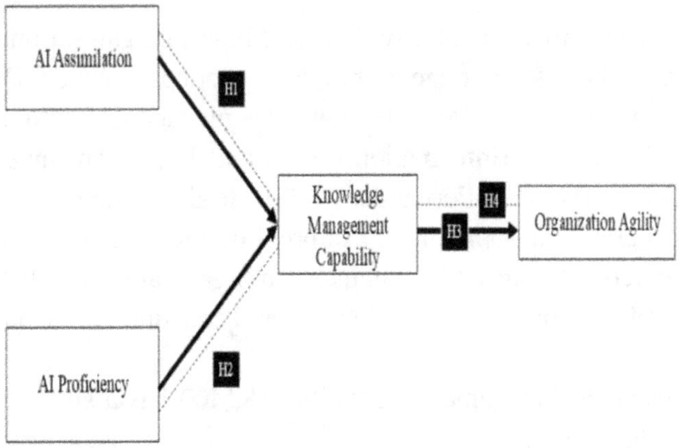

HYPOTHESES DEVELOPMENT

AI enhances data processing, sharing, and decision-making, thereby increasing knowledge management (Romeo & Conti, 2025). It enhances education, teamwork, and creativity (Sutton et al., 2023; Zack et al., 2009). Therefore, AI assimilation significantly enhances knowledge management skills.

H1. AI assimilation significantly affects knowledge management capability (KMC).

A.AI Proficiency and Knowledge Management Capability

The ability of human resources to operate AI applications is known as AI proficiency. Increased AI proficiency increases decision-making, knowledge creation, and sharing. They also encourage creativity and learning, thereby enhancing organizational performance and knowledge management (Jarrahi et al., 2023)

H2. AI Proficiency has a significant effect on Knowledge Management Capability.

B. Knowledge Management Capability (KMC) and Organisation Agility

Knowledge management capability (KMC) is how an organisation is able to create, store, share, and use knowledge within different departments (KMC) (Nonaka et al., 1995; Grant, 1996). An effective knowledge management system will enable businesses to collect valuable information, understand the past, and make more timely and better decisions (Becerra-Fernandez, 2000). It also enhances responsiveness to changing corporate environments by improving integration and the sharing of knowledge resources. Strong KMC enhances an organization's agility by enabling it to respond quickly to market, technological, and consumer demand changes.

H3. Knowledge Management Capability (KMC) has a significant effect on Organisation Agility.

C. Knowledge Management Capability as a Mediator

Knowledge Management Capability (KMC) links organizational agility, AI proficiency, and AI assimilation. Large data is processed by AI, while KMC turns it into knowledge that can be used to learn and make decisions (Chan et al., 2009; Doh et al., 2025). It supports rapid reactions to change by improving knowledge integration and sharing (Fichman et al., 2014). As a result, KMC helps transform AI skills into greater responsiveness, creativity, and agility (figure 1 shows the proposed model).

H4a: shows significant and positive mediation of knowledge management capabilities between AI assimilation and organisational agility.
H4b: shows positive and significant mediation of knowledge management capability with AI proficiency and organisational agility.

RESEARCH METHODOLOGY

The research is both predictive and exploratory. It comprises 339 IT employees from Bangalore, Delhi, and the National Capital Region. Respondents were chosen using a stratified sampling technique. The study used PLS-SEM because the data were not normally distributed. The number of measurement items was used to determine the sample size according to the 10-times rule of Hair et al. (2019). The study collected 339 responses across 33 items, achieving the required sample size of 330.

A. Measurement Model Analysis

The outer loadings of all constructs were analysed in the study. The result posted in Table 1 reveals that the outer loadings exceed 0.6 in all the constructs. All the constructs had a higher level of Cronbach alpha, composite reliability and Average variance extracted than the threshold level. This meets the requirements of determining convergent validity.

Table 1. Measurement of Convergent Validity

		CA	CRA	CRC	A.V.E
AI ASSIMILATION	0.825	0.948	0.949	0.956	0.732
	0.845				
	0.857				
	0.859				
	0.869				
	0.852				
	0.874				
	0.861				

continued on following page

Table 1. Continued

		CA	CRA	CRC	A.V.E
AI PROFICIENCY	0.830	0.962	0.962	0.966	0.706
	0.844				
	0.836				
	0.858				
	0.848				
	0.854				
	0.829				
	0.850				
	0.809				
	0.825				
	0.846				
	0.851				
KMC	0.847	0.930	0.930	0.943	0.704
	0.844				
	0.834				
	0.861				
	0.799				
	0.857				
	0.831				
ORGANISATIONAL AGILITY	0.842	0.911	0.912	0.931	0.691
	0.833				
	0.831				
	0.845				
	0.820				
	0.816				

Moreover, the discriminant validity was determined with the help of the. Forner Larcker criterion and the H.T.M.T ratio Table 2 shows that the values of all in the HTMT were lower than the recommended rate of 0.90, which confirms that there was sufficient discriminant validity among the constructs. The findings of the F-L criterion are shown in Table 3, where a square root of the average variance extracted (A.V.E) of each construct exceeds the correlation of the construct with the other constructs as indicated by the largest values on the diagonal elements of the matrix. These findings affirm that the constructs within the model demonstrate a good level of discriminant validity (Henseler et al., 2014).

Table 2. Measurement of Discriminant Validity (HTMT ratio)

	AI ASSIMILATION	AI PROFICIENCY	KMC	ORGANISATIONAL AGILITY
AI ASSIMILATION				
AI PROFECIENCY	0.107			
KMC	0.570	0.594		
ORGANISATIONAL AGILITY	0.433	0.446	0.773	

Table 3. Measurement of Discriminant Validity (forner-larcker output)

	AI ASSIMILATION	AI PROFICIENCY	KMC	ORGANISATIONAL AGILITY
AI ASSIMILATION	0.855			
AI PROFECIENCY	0.098	0.840		
KMC	0.537	0.562	0.839	
ORGANISATIONAL AGILITY	0.405	0.420	0.713	0.831

The measurement and establishment of convergent and discriminant validity shows that constructs, i.e., AI assimilation, AI proficiency, Knowledge management capability, and Organisational agility, had items loaded on them. All constructs are exclusively different from each other. There is no case of multicollinearity.

B. Structured Model Analysis

Table 4 shows the effect sizes for each path; all paths have effect sizes greater than 1, indicating that they are relevant in explaining the dependent variable.

Table 4. Effect size of each path

	f-square
AI ASSIMILATION -> KMC	1.074
AI PROFICIENCY -> KMC	1.158
KMC -> ORGANISATIONAL AGILITY	1.034

The R square shows the explained variance of the construct. Thus table 5 shows that AI assimilation and AI proficiency explain the knowledge management capability by 67%, and organisational agility is explained by 50.8%.

Table 5. R-square and adjusted R-square

	R^2	R^2 adjusted
KMC	0.670	0.668
ORGANISATIONAL AGILITY	0.508	0.507

Further, hypotheses have been analysed; AI assimilation significantly and positively relates to knowledge management capabilities (β=0.59; p=0.000) (table 6). Thus, H1 has been accepted. AI proficiency has been positively and significantly associated with knowledge management capabilities (β=0.62; p=0.000) (table 6). H2 has been accepted. The study also assessed the direct relationship of knowledge management capability with organisational agility (β=0.71; p=0.000) (table 6). This shows that H3 has also been accepted.

Table 6. Direct effect and p value (<0.000)

Hypotheses		B	SD	T	P-values	Decision
H1	AI ASSIMILATION -> KMC	0.598	0.032	18.876	0.000	Accepted
H2	AI PROFICIENCY -> KMC	0.621	0.031	20.302	0.000	Accepted
H3	KMC -> ORGANISATIONAL AGILITY	0.713	0.028	25.401	0.000	Accepted

The study also assessed the mediating role of KMC. H1a shows significant and positive mediation of knowledge management capabilities between AI assimilation and organisational agility (β=0.426; p=0.000) (table 7). Results of H4b has also been accepted with (β=0.44; p=0.000) (table 7) and shows positive and significant mediation of knowledge management capability with AI proficiency and organisational agility (figure 2).

Table 7. Mediation Analysis

Hypotheses		β	SD	T	P-values	Decision	2.5%	97.5%
H4a	AI ASSIMILATION -> KMC -> ORGANISATIONAL AGILITY	0.426	0.027	15.562	0.000	Accepted	0.373	0.479
H4b	AI PROFICIENCY -> KMC -> ORGANISATIONAL AGILITY	0.443	0.028	15.996	0.000	Accepted	0.390	0.497

Figure 2.

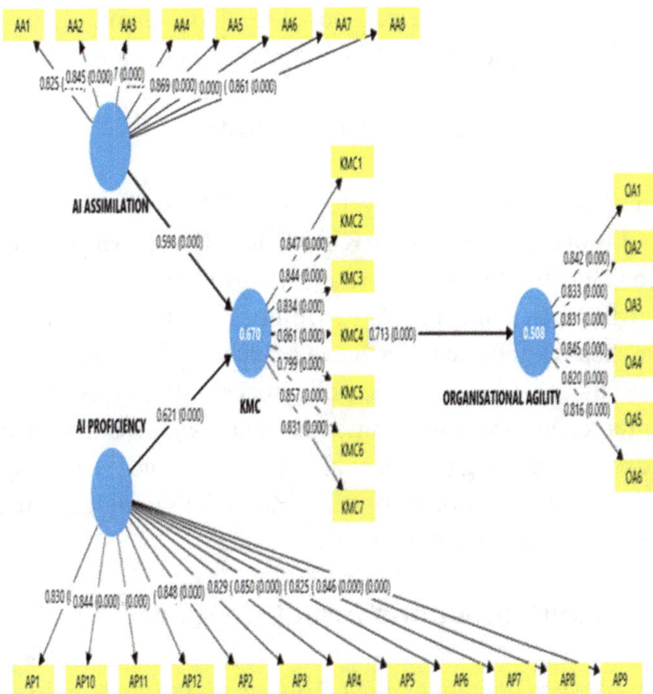

Figure 2 shows the p value and path coefficient of each hypotheses.

DISCUSSION

The paper will examine the roles of Knowledge Management Capability (KMC) and AI capabilities in enhancing organizational agility (Gorka et al., 2025). The results support all the theories. To start with, AI assimilation significantly improves KMC by assisting businesses in processing large volumes of data and converting it into useful information capable of supporting the learning and decision-making processes (Shukla et al., 2025). Second, AI proficiency has a positive influence on KMC, and it is important to note that the skills of employees are essential to apply AI insights efficiently and transform them into valuable knowledge resources (Zhong et al., 2026). Third, KMC enhances organizational responsiveness by enabling rapid responses to market, technological, and customer changes through efficient knowledge sharing and implementation. Lastly, KMC mediates the relationship between organizational agility and AI capabilities, suggesting that companies can only enjoy the fruits of AI when they manage and utilize knowledge effectively

(Zack et al., 2009). On the whole, gaining agility and remaining competitive in the changing environment requires the incorporation of AI technology, the development of AI-related skills of employees, and the improvement of knowledge management.

A. Theoretical and practical implications

The research contributes to the development of theory by showing how AI can improve the agility of organizations and Knowledge Management Capability (KMC), especially among Indian entrepreneurs (Sambamurthy et al., 2003). Also, it describes the relationship between agility and AI capabilities, mediated through KMC, where knowledge use should be efficient to achieve AI-driven performance. Practically, the findings suggest that organizations and policymakers should promote the use of AI by offering entrepreneurs tools, training, and technology to make them more flexible and improve decision-making (Raina et al., 2026). The successful implementation of AI and the encouragement of innovation should be grounded in the creation of AI-related competencies aligned with business needs.

B. Limitations and directions for future research

This study has several limitations. First, it disregards other factors like the company culture, leadership support, digital infrastructure, and employee learning orientation and focuses on AI proficiency and integration (Nguyen et al., 2026). Second, but not least, AI skills might also influence the performance, innovation, and market share; the research mostly focuses on organizational agility (Fosso Wamba, 2022). Third, a quantitative approach is limited in its ability to uncover in-depth insights, suggesting that qualitative or longitudinal research is required to better understand cause-and-effect relationships. Finally, to better understand, comparative research can be applied in future studies across industries, company size, and gender groups. To solve these problems, a deeper understanding of AI's role in knowledge management and organizational agility will be developed.

CONCLUSION

This paper demonstrates that AI use contributes to a great extent to organizational agility and knowledge management among owned SMEs in India. The ability of AI to improve knowledge production and sharing will allow entrepreneurs to apply their insights to their advantage, and the ability to integrate AI will improve the efficiency of data processing, decision-making, and efficiency in operations. The findings also confirm that knowledge management capability mediates the relationship between AI capabilities and agility. Overall, AI implementation and the strong development of digital skills can ensure the competitiveness, flexibility, and long-term sustainability of entrepreneurs.

REFERENCES

Alavi, M., & Leidner, D. E. (2001). Review: Knowledge management and knowledge management systems: Conceptual foundations and research issues1,2. *Management Information Systems Quarterly*, *25*(1), 107–136. DOI: 10.2307/3250961

Becerra-Fernandez, I. (2000). The role of artificial intelligence technologies in the implementation of People-Finder knowledge management systems. *Knowledge-Based Systems*, *13*(5), 315–320. DOI: 10.1016/s0950-7051(00)00091-5

Bradley, M. (2000). Working Knowledge: How Organizations Manage What They Know20004Thomas H. Davenport and Laurence Prusak. Working Knowledge: How Organizations Manage What They Know. *New Library World*, *101*(6), 282–287. DOI: 10.1108/nlw.2000.101.6.282.4

Chan, S. H., Sutton, S. G., & Yao, L. J. (2009). The paradoxical effects of feedback and reward on decision performance. In *Advances in Accounting Behavioral Research* (pp. 109–143). Emerald Group Publishing Limited., DOI: 10.1108/s1475-1488(2009)0000012008

Chowdhury, S., Budhwar, P., Dey, P. K., Joel-Edgar, S., & Abadie, A. (2022). AI-employee collaboration and business performance: Integrating knowledge-based view, socio-technical systems and organisational socialisation framework. *Journal of Business Research*, *144*, 31–49. DOI: 10.1016/j.jbusres.2022.01.069

Darioshi, R., & Lahav, E. (2021). The impact of technology on the human decision-making process. *Human Behavior and Emerging Technologies*, *3*(3), 391–400. DOI: 10.1002/hbe2.257

Doh, W., Goh, Y., & Kim, S.-H. (2025). Beyond overreliance: The human-ai-system concordance (HASC) matrix and the cognitive dynamics of ai-assisted decision-making. *Proceedings of the Human Factors and Ergonomics Society Annual Meeting*, *69*(1), 427–432. DOI: 10.1177/10711813251358240

Fichman, R. G., Dos Santos, B. L., & Zheng, Z. (Eric). (2014). Digital innovation as a fundamental and powerful concept in the information systems curriculum1. *Management Information Systems Quarterly*, *38*(2), 329–354. DOI: 10.25300/misq/2014/38.2.01

Fosso Wamba, S. (2022). Impact of artificial intelligence assimilation on firm performance: The mediating effects of organizational agility and customer agility. *International Journal of Information Management*, *67*, 102544. DOI: 10.1016/j.ijinfomgt.2022.102544

Gold, A. H., Malhotra, A., & Segars, A. H. (2001). Knowledge management: An organizational capabilities perspective. *Journal of Management Information Systems, 18*(1), 185–214. DOI: 10.1080/07421222.2001.11045669

Gorka, E., Baran, D., Wojak, G., Ćwiakala, M., Zupok, S., Starkowski, D., Resko, D., & Okrasa, O. (2025). The impact of artificial intelligence on enterprise decision-making processes. *European Research Studies Journal, XXVIII*(3), 1126–1147. DOI: 10.35808/ersj/4178

Grant, R. M. (1996). Toward a knowledge-based theory of the firm. *Strategic Management Journal, 17*(S2), 109–122. DOI: 10.1002/smj.4250171110

Hair, J. F., Risher, J. J., Sarstedt, M., & Ringle, C. M. (2019). When to use and how to report the results of PLS-SEM. *European Business Review, 31*(1), 2–24. DOI: 10.1108/ebr-11-2018-0203

Hani, S. (2019). *Entrepreneur's understanding on MSME (micro small medium enterprises) on concept on sharia financial statement.* Center for Open Science. DOI: 10.31227/osf.io/hr92x

Henseler, J., Ringle, C. M., & Sarstedt, M. (2014). A new criterion for assessing discriminant validity in variance-based structural equation modeling. *Journal of the Academy of Marketing Science, 43*(1), 115–135. DOI: 10.1007/s11747-014-0403-8

Jarrahi, M. H. (2018). Artificial intelligence and the future of work: Human-AI symbiosis in organizational decision making. *Business Horizons, 61*(4), 577–586. DOI: 10.1016/j.bushor.2018.03.007

Jarrahi, M. H., Askay, D., Eshraghi, A., & Smith, P. (2023). Artificial intelligence and knowledge management: A partnership between human and AI. *Business Horizons, 66*(1), 87–99. DOI: 10.1016/j.bushor.2022.03.002

Li, N., Yan, Y., Yang, Y., & Gu, A. (2022). Artificial intelligence capability and organizational creativity: The role of knowledge sharing and organizational cohesion. *Frontiers in Psychology, 13*. Advance online publication. DOI: 10.3389/fpsyg.2022.845277

Nguyen, T. H., Dinh, V. H., Nguyen, H. M., Do, H. M. H., Luong, M. D., & Nguyen, H. H. A. (2026). AI-analytics capabilities and knowledge assimilation: Driving innovation in SMEs. *International Journal of Innovation Science*, 1–25. DOI: 10.1108/ijis-07-2025-0338

Nonaka, I., & Takeuchi, H. (1995). *The knowledge-creating company.* Oxford University PressNew York., DOI: 10.1093/oso/9780195092691.001.0001

Pai, R. Y., Shetty, A., Shetty, A. D., Bhandary, R., Shetty, J., Nayak, S., Dinesh, T. K., & D'souza, K. J. (2022). Integrating artificial intelligence for knowledge management systems – synergy among people and technology: A systematic review of the evidence. *Economic Research-Ekonomska Istraživanja*, *35*(1), 7043–7065. DOI: 10.1080/1331677x.2022.2058976

Raina, K., Sharma, G. D., Taheri, B., Dev, D., & Chavriya, S. (2026). Artificial intelligence-driven management: Bridging innovation, knowledge creation, and sustainable business practices. *Journal of Innovation &amp. Knowledge (Beverly Hills, Calif.)*, *11*, 100860. DOI: 10.1016/j.jik.2025.100860

Romeo, G., & Conti, D. (2025). Exploring automation bias in human–AI collaboration: A review and implications for explainable AI. *AI &amp. Society*, *41*(1), 259–278. DOI: 10.1007/s00146-025-02422-7

Sambamurthy, V., Bharadwaj, A., & Grover, V. (2003). Shaping agility through digital options: Reconceptualizing the role of information technology in contemporary firms1. *Management Information Systems Quarterly*, *27*(2), 237–263. DOI: 10.2307/30036530

Sherehiy, B., Karwowski, W., & Layer, J. K. (2007). A review of enterprise agility: Concepts, frameworks, and attributes. *International Journal of Industrial Ergonomics*, *37*(5), 445–460. DOI: 10.1016/j.ergon.2007.01.007

Shukla, T., Nirban, V. S., Das, M., Nadig, R. S., & Buttan, D. (2025). Cultural negotiations of digital transformation: Womenpreneurs and social media in rural india's domiciliary enterprises. *Journal of Cultural Analysis and Social Change*, 2619–2633. DOI: 10.64753/jcasc.v10i4.3297

Somasundaram, R., Varalakshmi, S., Sanadi, H., Saini, R., Chinnusamy, S., & S., B. (2024). Entrepreneurship in emerging markets and intrapreneurship within organizations. In *Advances in Business Strategy and Competitive Advantage* (pp. 291–322). IGI Global. DOI: 10.4018/979-8-3693-3100-2.ch011

Sutton, J., Arcidiacono, A., Torrisi, G., & Arku, R. N. (2023). Regional economic resilience: A scoping review. *Progress in Human Geography*, *47*(4), 500–532. DOI: 10.1177/03091325231174183

Taherdoost, H., & Madanchian, M. (2023). Artificial intelligence and knowledge management: Impacts, benefits, and implementation. *Computers*, *12*(4), 72. DOI: 10.3390/computers12040072

Teece, D. J., Pisano, G., & Shuen, A. (1997). Dynamic capabilities and strategic management. *Strategic Management Journal*, *18*(7), 509–533. DOI: 10.1002/(sici)1097-0266(199708)18:7<509:aid-smj882>3.0.co;2-z

Wamba-Taguimdje, S.-L., Fosso Wamba, S., Kala Kamdjoug, J. R., & Tchatchouang Wanko, C. E. (2020). Influence of artificial intelligence (AI) on firm performance: The business value of AI-based transformation projects. *Business Process Management Journal*, *26*(7), 1893–1924. DOI: 10.1108/bpmj-10-2019-0411

Zack, M., McKeen, J., & Singh, S. (2009). Knowledge management and organizational performance: An exploratory analysis. *Journal of Knowledge Management*, *13*(6), 392–409. DOI: 10.1108/13673270910997088

Zhong, L., Ady, S. U., & Indrasari, M. (2026). AI in strategic management and organizational agility of SMEs: Leadership, policy environment, and adaptive capability. *Future Technology*, *5*(2), 1–12. DOI: 10.55670/fpll.futech.5.2.1

Chapter 2
Future Skills Ecosystems for Work 2030:
Reskilling Architectures for Sustainable Value Creation

Monika Yadav
http://orcid.org/0000-0001-6279-115X
School of Management & Commerce, K.R. Mangalam University, Gurugram, India

Shivani Kain
http://orcid.org/0009-0002-8012-6502
School of Management & Commerce, K.R. Mangalam University, Gurugram, India

Nitish Kumar Minz
http://orcid.org/0009-0000-4770-0336
VIT Business School, Vellore Institute of Technology, Vellore, India

ABSTRACT

The rapid transformation of the global workforce, driven by digitalization, technological advancement, and sustainability imperatives, has accelerated the need for future skills ecosystems that enable continuous reskilling and long-term value creation. This chapter examines the development of Future Skills Ecosystems for Work 2030, focusing on adaptive reskilling architectures aligned with evolving market demands. It explores key components including learning infrastructures, skill intelligence systems, knowledge networks, governance mechanisms, and sustainability integration. The role of artificial intelligence, data analytics, and digital platforms in enabling real-time skill mapping, personalized learning, and predictive workforce planning

DOI: 10.4018/979-8-2600-2726-4.ch002

is emphasized. The chapter also highlights the importance of collaboration among academia, industry, and government, alongside the integration of ESG competencies, to build resilient, inclusive, and future-ready workforce systems.

1. INTRODUCTION

The world of work is experiencing a paradigm shift as a result of the meeting of artificial intelligence (AI), digitalization, and sustainability demands. With organizations moving towards what is more and more being conceived as Work 2030, old paradigms of skill structure, work role and employment are being re-defined fundamentally. The high pace of automation and the emergence of intelligent systems, in turn, are not just replacing routine, but changing the very architecture of work, as dynamic, constantly changing competencies require a transition to static and skill sets, (World Economic Forum, 2023; McKinsey Global Institute, 2021). The future skills ecosystem concept becomes a key conceptual infrastructure in this dynamic environment where individuals, organizations and institutions are co creating, adapting and maintaining capabilities that are aligned with long economic, social and environmental value generation.

The concept of a skills ecosystem is not limited by underlying training and development methodologies because it focuses on the interrelated networks of stakeholders, educational institutions, corporations, governments, and digital platforms, which together play a part in the formation and deployment of skills (OECD, 2023; UNESCO, 2021). In contrast to the traditional linear approaches to the development of the workforce, the future skills ecosystem is defined by flexibility, decentralization, and lifelong learning, which is becoming more and more significant in the digital era (International Labour Organization, 2021; Siemens, 2020). The change in paradigm is especially applicable in the realm of high technological disruptiveness, where the half-life of skills is getting shorter, and skilling and upskilling has become a strategic necessity at the individual and organizational levels (LinkedIn Learning, 2023; Deloitte, 2024).

The advent of AI-based systems at an organizational level has completely changed the design, execution, and evaluation of work. The practice of human-AI collaboration is also gaining more and more popularity, in which machines are being used to supplement human decision-making, but not to fully replace the tasks (Jarrahi, 2023; Davenport and Miller, 2022). This change requires new sets of skills, such as digital literacy, data-driven decision-making, and cognitive flexibility, socio-emotional skills such as adaptability, resilience, and ethical judgment (Huang and Rust, 2021; Parker and Grote, 2022). As a result, companies are forced to reconsider their human capital approaches, transitioning to proactive reskilling architectures, which are integrated into the larger business transformation efforts (Becker and Huselid, 2022; Cascio and Montealegre, 2021).

Reskilling architectures are defined as scalable, structured and technology-based systems which enable ongoing development of capabilities among the workforce. Such architectures combine electronic learning frameworks, customized training programs, and real-time skill evaluation engines in order to account for the correspondence between the organizational demands and the abilities of employees (Garavan et al., 2021; Noe et al., 2021). Notably, they do not just affect the inner organizational operations but are also becoming more tied to the outside ecosystems, such as online learning platforms, industry certification, and collaborative inventories of innovations (Kato and Choi, 2022; PwC, 2023). This ecosystem-centered model can help organizations react better to the changing skills requirements and create a culture of life-long learning and constant development.

At the same time, the introduction of sustainability into the business strategy has brought another dimension of complexity to the transformation of the workforce. Organizations are currently anticipated to generate not solely economic but social and environmental change, to make their operations compatible with the principles of sustainable development and environmental, social, and governance (ESG) models (United Nations, 2022; Lozano et al., 2022). This change requires the emergence of competencies that are more sustainability-focused, such as systems thinking, ethical decision-making, and interdisciplinary collaboration, which are necessary to help resolve more complex issues in the world, such as climate change, lack of resources, and social inequality (Elkington, 2020; Sroufe, 2020). Consequently, the competencies should be incorporated in the reskilling and upskilling programs to enable future skills ecosystems to sustain value creation.

Strategically, the future skill ecosystems development is directly related to the notion of dynamic capabilities, which are focused on the capacity of an organization to feel, capture, and evolve due to the environmental shifts (Teece, 2021; Helfat and Martin, 2022). In this regard, reskilling architectures can be considered as a highly important mechanism of facilitating organizational flexibility and resilience that can enable companies to constantly re-align their human capital with new opportunities and threats. Further, the resource-based view (RBV) emphasizes the significance of human capital as a source of sustained competitive advantage and the fact that organizational investment in human skills development at strategic level should be a priority (Barney, 2021; Becker and Huselid, 2022).

Although there has been an increasing appreciation on the need to reskill and the skills ecosystems, there is still a big challenge in implementing them. Among them are access and inclusivity concerns since not every group of a working population has equal chances to engage in reskilling programs, which may result in the possibility of employment gaps (World Bank, 2022). Also, the high speed of technological change makes it unpredictable what particular skills will be demanded in the future, and this makes it even harder to develop a successful training program (Dwivedi et al., 2023). Moreover, the introduction of AI in learning systems elicits ethical issues pertaining to the privacy, algorithmic bias, and transparency of data, which need to be undertaken with considerable care to secure trust and impartiality in the process of developing skills (Huang and Rust, 2021; Vial, 2021).

Against this backdrop, it is urgent to have an overarching framework that incorporates the ideas of future skills ecosystems, reskilling architectures, and sustainable value creation. The same framework must offer clues on how organizations can construct and execute efficient skill development tools which are in tandem with both the technological developments and sustainability objectives. The chapter aims to fill this gap by providing a theoretically and practically feasible study of how the ecosystems of the future skills can be designed in order to accommodate Work 2030.

Despite the growing body of literature on artificial intelligence, digital transformation, and workforce development, several critical gaps remain insufficiently addressed. First, existing studies largely examine skills development, reskilling, and sustainability as isolated domains, with limited integration across these dimensions. While prior research has explored AI-enabled learning systems and dynamic capabilities, there is a lack of a unified framework that connects future skills ecosystems with reskilling architectures and sustainable value creation. Second, much of the existing literature remains descriptive and technology-centric, focusing on the potential of AI without critically examining its organizational, ethical, and inclusivity implications. Issues such as algorithmic bias, unequal access to reskilling opportunities, and governance challenges are often underexplored within workforce transformation models. There is limited conceptual clarity regarding how organizations can operationalize reskilling architectures within broader skills ecosystems while aligning them with environmental, social, and governance (ESG) objectives. This creates a gap between theoretical discussions and practical implementation strategies.

To address these gaps, this chapter makes the following key contributions:

i. It develops an integrated conceptual framework that links future skills ecosystems, reskilling architectures, and sustainable value creation within the context of Work 2030.
ii. It synthesizes multiple theoretical perspectives—including Human Capital Theory, Resource-Based View, Dynamic Capabilities, and Skills Ecosystem Theory—to provide a multidimensional understanding of workforce transformation.
iii. It incorporates a critical perspective on AI-driven learning systems by examining risks related to ethics, inclusivity, and governance.
iv. It proposes a structured and scalable model of reskilling architectures supported by AI-enabled learning platforms and sustainability-oriented competencies.

Through these contributions, the chapter advances both theoretical understanding and practical insights into how organizations can build resilient, inclusive, and future-ready workforce systems.

In particular, the chapter will (i) conceptualize the concept of future skills ecosystem in the light of digital and sustainability transformations, (ii) discuss how reskilling architectures form the basis of the continuous development of capabilities, and (iii) discuss how these aspects can help sustain value creation on the individual, organizational, and societal scales. Combining the insights of human resource management, strategic management, and sustainability research, the chapter offers a multidisciplinary insight into the ways to transform the workforce in the world of AI and digitalization.

Finally, the move towards Work 2030 is not only a technological change but it is a complete reconsideration of how work, learning, and value creation relate to each other. Those organizations that manage to go through such transition successfully will be the ones that will be able to create a robust, inclusive, and future-resilient skills ecosystem that will allow their workforce to continue to be productive in a more complex and uncertain environment. By so doing, they will improve not only their competitive advantage but also help other goals of sustainable and inclusive development in society as a whole.

2. THEORETICAL BACKGROUNDS: THE UNIFICATION OF HUMAN CAPITAL, DYNAMIC CAPABILITIES, AND SKILLS ECOSYSTEM VIEWPOINTS

The shift towards Work 2030 requires a solid theoretical base to describe how organizations can become future-oriented and deploy and maintain future-oriented skills in more volatile and technology-driven environments. The chapter is informed by four theoretical lenses, including Human Capital Theory, Resource-Based View (RBV), Dynamic Capabilities Theory, and Skills Ecosystem Theory, to conceptualize the way reskilling architectures can be used to create values sustainably. The combination of these frameworks makes it possible to have a multidimensional view of the manner in which skills are acquired, utilised, and inculcated within organizational and societal systems.

2.1 The Theory of Human Capitals and the Development of Skills

The Human Capital Theory has been in existence as a guiding theory in the discussion of the contribution of skills and knowledge in economic output and organizational achievement. The theory, which was originally stated by Becker, assumes that investment in education, training, and skill development contributes to the productivity of an individual, which further leads to the growth of an organization and an economy. However, when presented within the framework of Work 2030, the conventional principles of human capital as an asset that is static are now being questioned by the dynamic nature of technological changes and the obsolescence of skills (Noe et al., 2021; OECD, 2023). Modern understandings of the Human Capital Theory focus on the flow and refreshability of skills, the role of incessant learning and flexibility. The declining half-life of the skills, especially in the digital and AI-related sector, will force people to undergo continued reskilling and upskilling in order to stay relevant in the labor market (LinkedIn Learning, 2023; Deloitte, 2024). This change is changing human capital as a one-time investment to a continuous capability-building process that learning is incorporated in the workflow instead of in the formal training program. Besides, the emergence of digital tools and AI-based learning systems has increased the number of ways human capital is built. Individualized learning journeys and adjustable content delivery patterns, as well as real-time feedback systems, allow obtaining skills more efficiently and specifically (Kato and Choi, 2022). These trends are in line with the global shift to learning ecosystems, in which knowledge is produced and shared in networks of people and companies to be distributed (Siemens, 2020). As a result, the Human Capital Theory should be reconfigured in the light of networked, technology mediated skills development of modern organizations.

2.2 Strategic Value of Skills and Resource-Based View (RBV)

Resource-Based View (RBV) gives an insight on the role of skills in creating a long-term competitive advantage. RBV holds that good performance in organizations is attained when they have resources that are valuable, unique, imitable, and non-substitutable (Barney, 2021). One of the most strategic resources in this context is human capital especially in form of specialized skills and knowledge. The strategic value of human capital is enhanced in the age of AI and digital transformation. The skills to analyze information, make complicated choices, and innovate cannot be automated through technology, but they are human characteristics (Brynjolfsson and McAfee, 2022; Davenport and Miller, 2022). Consequently, companies need to specialize in the creation of distinctive skill sets that include the capability of technology and generate synergistic value by working together with machines (Jarrahi, 2023). But the RBV also throws light on the issues that are involved in maintaining a competitive advantage based on skills. With the accessibility of knowledge going digital and the creation of global talent markets, it might not be very easy to retain a rare and inimitable skill. This highlights the fact that organizations must constantly refresh and restructure their human resource with reskilling programs (Becker and Huselid, 2022). Reskilling architectures in this case are a key strategic tool in ensuring relevance and uniqueness of organizational capabilities. Moreover, RBV underlines the significance of the alignment of the skills development with the organizational strategy. Instead of considering training as a separate activity, organizations have to incorporate skill development into the wider strategic goals so that the capabilities of the workforce should be adjusted to the new business opportunities and challenges (Collings et al., 2022). This strategic fit is necessary to leverage the value of the human capital in the maximization of the long-term competitive advantage. While the Resource-Based View (RBV) highlights human capital as a source of sustained competitive advantage, its traditional assumptions are increasingly challenged in the context of AI-driven environments. RBV presumes that valuable and rare skills can be retained within organizations; however, in the era of digital platforms and global talent mobility, the inimitability of skills is becoming difficult to sustain. Furthermore, RBV does not sufficiently explain how organizations continuously reconfigure skills in response to rapid technological disruption. This limitation creates a theoretical gap that is better addressed by Dynamic Capabilities Theory, which emphasizes adaptability and continuous transformation. Therefore, relying solely on RBV may lead to a static understanding of human capital, whereas modern organizations require dynamic and continuously evolving skill architectures. Recent studies further emphasize that digital transformation reshapes the strategic role of human capital, requiring continuous capability renewal and integration of technological and human competencies (Vial, 2021; Dwivedi et al., 2023).

2.3 Continuous Reskilling and Dynamic Capabilities Theory

Whereas, RBV is concerned with the ownership of valuable resources, the Dynamic Capabilities Theory goes beyond this viewpoint by placing imperative on the processes by which organizations adjust and evolve to the changing environments. According to Teece (2021), dynamic capabilities refer to the capability to sense opportunities and threats, take the opportunities and rearrange the resources. Within the framework of Work 2030, such capabilities are essential to manage unpredictabilities of technological disruption and changes in skills demands. The importance of reskilling architectures in the context of facilitating dynamic capabilities is facilitated by the fact that they allow continuous renewal of human capital. Adaptive learning systems, real-time skill evaluation, and cross-functional training are a few of the mechanisms through which organizations can swiftly create and implement novel competencies, depending on the evolving demand (Garavan et al., 2021; Noe et al.,

2021). This real-time reconfigurability of skills can make organizations more agile and resilient and helps firms to survive in dynamic environments.

In addition, Dynamic Capabilities Theory emphasizes on managerial thinking and decision-making as a factor in determining how a company responds to change. The leaders should not simply acknowledge the necessity of reskilling but should create and adopt efficient learning strategies that are aligned with the organizational objectives (Helfat and Martin, 2022). This will involve abandoning the old hierarchical based management systems and adopting more flexible and decentralized systems that give employees the responsibility of owning their learning and development. The effectiveness of reskilling processes can be even further improved by the implementation of AI in such a way that dynamic capabilities are advanced because of the ability to make decisions based on the information. The AI systems can be used to analyze data related to the workforce and formulate evidence-based predictions about future skill demand, skill shortages, and prescriptions of personalized learning interventions (Dwivedi et al., 2023; Vial, 2021). The capabilities facilitate organizations to become proactive in filling skills gaps and in aligning the development of the workforce with the organization vision with the help of strategies, which enhances their dynamic capabilities. Although Dynamic Capabilities Theory provides a stronger explanation of organizational adaptability, it also presents certain limitations. The theory is often criticized for being conceptually broad and difficult to operationalize in empirical contexts. Moreover, while it emphasizes the ability to sense and seize opportunities, it does not fully address issues of inclusivity, access to reskilling, or ethical implications of AI-driven transformation. This creates a gap in understanding how capability development can be both adaptive and equitable. As a result, integrating Dynamic Capabilities with Skills Ecosystem Theory becomes essential to capture both adaptability and inclusiveness in workforce transformation.

2.4 Networked Learning and Skills Ecosystem Theory

The Skills Ecosystem Theory offers a more extensive and systemic view of skill formation as it focuses on interdependences among different stakeholders in workforce development. This approach is an alternative to the traditional models that address skills building and their application in a system of actors, such as educational establishments, governments, professional organizations, and web platforms (OECD, 2023; UNESCO, 2021). Skills ecosystems in the framework of Work 2030 are becoming more and more digital and platform-mediated. Knowledge and skills are exchanged between organizations and geographical limits with the help of online learning platforms, professional networks, and collaborative innovation hubs (Brown and Adler, 2020, PwC, 2023). This connectivity increases the scalability and accessibility of skill development programs enabling individuals to develop new competencies in a more efficient way.

Additionally, Skills Ecosystem Theory emphasizes the significance of collaboration and co-creation in the development of the skills. Companies have to consult third parties to develop and provide the training that is aligned to the industry requirements and trends in technology (World Bank, 2022). This partnership model makes the skill development programs relevant, inclusive, and sensitive to emerging labor market needs. Notably, skills ecosystems are also important towards social and economic inclusion. These ecosystems can be used to reduce the skill gaps and increase the workforce participation by offering the opportunity to learn to diverse populations (International Labour Organization, 2021). Nevertheless, to be inclusive, it is necessary to actively focus on eliminating obstacles to inclusivity, including digital access, cost, and educational inequalities.

2.5 Integrative Perspective: Moving Towards an Integrated Framework

The combination of Human Capital Theory, RBV, Dynamic Capabilities Theory, and Skills Ecosystem Theory offers a holistic approach to the answer to the question of how reskilling architectures can create sustainable value. The Human Capital Theory focuses a lot on the idea of constant skills development, whereas RBV addresses the significance of skills as a competitive advantage in a strategic manner. Dynamic Capabilities Theory is concerned with the practice of adapting and transforming, and Skills Ecosystem Theory is a systemic way of looking at skill formation in networked relationships. Collectively, these views highlight the importance of organizations shifting away, out of conventional training models, into ecosystem-based approaches to skills development. The reskilling architectures should also be created to facilitate life-long learning and strategic alignment as well as collaborative engagement, which would allow organizations to tackle the challenges of the Work 2030.

3. FUTURE SKILLS ECOSYSTEMS CONCEPTUALIZING FUTURE SKILLS ECOSYSTEMS IN WORK 2030

The ecosystems of future skills are a paradigm shift of linear, organization-based training models to dynamic, networked and technology-enhanced systems of capability development. Trying to adapt to the pressures of Work 2030, which is the future of organizations with AI integration, hybrid structures, and sustainability needs, the problem of ecosystem-based approach to skills development becomes more important than ever (World Economic Forum, 2023; OECD, 2023). This part conceptualizes the future skills ecosystems by defining its main elements, identifying the key stakeholders, and analyzing how these stakeholders can enable the ongoing process of reskilling and creating value in a sustainable way.

3.1 Future Skills Ecosystems Delineation

Building on the foundational discussion in the Introduction, future skills ecosystems can be further conceptualized as dynamic, multi-stakeholder systems that enable continuous capability development. Skills ecosystems are also co-created, decentralized, and integrated into real-time learning, unlike the traditional models that focus on the one-way knowledge transfer (UNESCO, 2021; Siemens, 2020). It works based on the principle of these ecosystems, where skills do not exist as fixed assets but rather dynamic capabilities that respond to changes in technologies, economies and societies. These ecosystems have additionally been increased by the introduction of AI and digital technologies to allow personalized learning journeys, predictive proficiency analytics, and real-time performance feedback (Dwivedi et al., 2023; Kato and Choi, 2022). Consequently, the future skills ecosystems are data-driven and learner-centric by nature and as such, enable individuals to constantly refresh their skills and competencies in accordance with the new demands.

3.2 Essential Building blocks of Future Skills Ecosystems

In order to operationalize the concept of future skills ecosystems, it is also necessary to determine its main elements and functional dimensions. All these elements constitute the development, deployment, and maintenance of skills at the organizational and the larger levels of the socio-economic setup.

Table 1. Future Skills System Core Components of Work 2030.

Component	Description	Important Actors	Technological Enablers	Outcome
Learning Infrastructure	Digital and physical infrastructure that allows learning in real time	Organizations, EdTech companies	XR, LMS, AI platforms	Continuous skill development
Skill Intelligence Systems	Skill gap identification in real-time and future skill forecasting	HR analytics teams, AI systems	Big data, AI analytics	Data-driven workforce planning
Knowledge Networks	Academia-industry-government partnerships	Universities, companies, policymakers	Digital platforms, knowledge bases	Co-created competencies

continued on following page

Table 1. Continued

Component	Description	Important Actors	Technological Enablers	Outcome
Governance Mechanisms	Policies that govern ethical, inclusive, and scalable learning	Regulators, HR leaders	Compliance tools, blockchain	Trust and accountability
Sustainability Integration	Integration of ESG and sustainability competencies	NGOs, corporations, governments	ESG analytics, reporting mechanisms	Long-term value creation

As shown in Table 1, the future skills ecosystems will be based not only on internal organizational arrangements but also on more broad networks of stakeholders and technologies. This feature of inclusion of skill intelligence systems underscores the expanding role of AI in detecting and anticipating skills needs, making it possible to proactively plan the workforce (Minbaeva, 2021; Dwivedi et al., 2023). Likewise, governance to make sure that the process of skill development is consistent with ethical norms responds to the issue of data privacy, bias, and inclusivity (Vial, 2021).

3.3 Future Skills Ecosystem Structural Model

Based on the elements presented in Table 1, a conceptual model of future skills ecosystems can be created to demonstrate the correlation between the key elements and their role in creating sustainable value.

Figure 1. Future Skills Ecosystems for Work Conceptual Model 2030 (Mermaid Code)

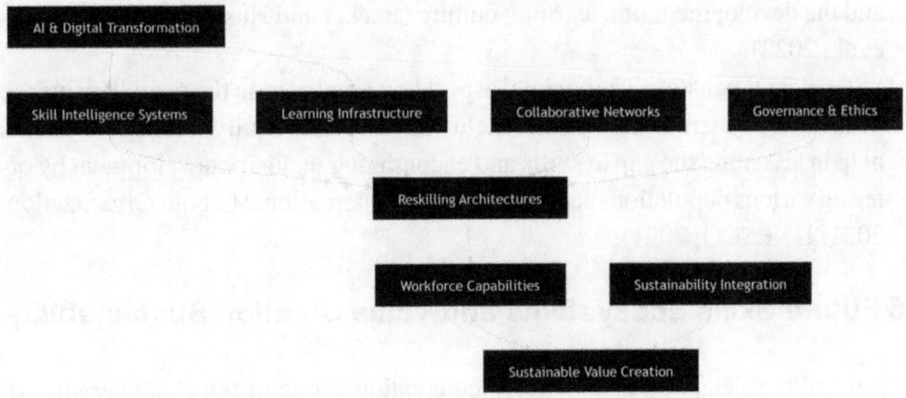

As Figure 1 shows, AI and digital transformation become the driving forces, which facilitate the learning infrastructure and skill intelligence systems. All these come together in the reskilling architectures which are the main means of transforming the workforce capabilities. These capabilities as a result lead to a sustainable value creation, which includes economic, social, and environmental results (Porter and Kramer, 2021; United Nations, 2022). The need to involve collaborative networks and governance structures is also noted to shape the success of reskilling efforts in the model. Absent proper governance, the AI implementation into the process of skill development can produce undesirable results, including bias or inequity (Huang and Rust, 2021). In a similar manner, partnership between stakeholders helps to make skill development in line with real-world needs and with the demands of society as well (World Bank, 2022).

3.4 Major Dimensions of Future Skills Ecosystems

The concept of future skills ecosystems can be further conceptualised in three critical dimensions:

(i) Technological Dimension: The technological aspect will include the resources and platforms that facilitate skill acquisition, such as AI-based learning systems, virtual reality environments, and data analytics platforms. They improve the personalization and scalability of learning, and organizations can provide specific training interventions using these technologies (Davenport and Miller, 2022; Kato and Choi, 2022).

(ii) Organizational Dimension: Organizational dimension dwells on the ways firms conceive and execute reskilling policies. This involves the process of integrating learning in business operations, aligning skill development with strategic goals, and the development of a learning culture (Becker and Huselid, 2022; Collings et al., 2022).

(iii) Societal Dimension: The societal aspect lays emphasis on the overall influence of skills ecosystems on economic inclusion and social equity. These ecosystems help in lessening the gap in skills and encouraging inclusive development by offering various populations access to learning (International Labour Organization, 2021; UNESCO, 2021).

3.5 Future Skills Ecosystems and Value Creation Sustainability

The ability to enable sustainable value creation is one of the characteristics of future skills ecosystems. These ecosystems consider social and environmental factors in the development of skills unlike in traditional models that explain the development of skills being purely based on the result of economic status. This congruency with the sustainability goals is essential against the backdrop of growing regulatory demands and stakeholder requirements regarding the ESG performance (Lozano et al., 2022; Sroufe, 2020). An example is the integration of sustainability-related skills, including systems thinking, ethical decision-making, and environmental consciousness, which allow organizations to deal with other intricate global issues without going out of business (Elkington, 2020). Additionally, when built on lifelong learning and flexibility, skills ecosystems make organizations more resilient and enable organizations to successfully handle uncertainties and disruptions (Teece, 2021).

The future skills ecosystems are an integrated perspective on workforce development that encompasses the technological innovation, company strategy, and social change. These ecosystems allow reskilling on a continuous basis and the absolute creation of value using AI-based learning solutions, collaborative networks, and governance structures. This interaction of elements is detailed in Table 1 and Figure 1, all of which demonstrate the need to have a coherent system that helps support Work 2030.

3.6 Critical Reflections on Future Skills Ecosystems

Despite the advantages of skills ecosystems in promoting collaborative and continuous learning, they are not without challenges. One key limitation is the unequal access to digital infrastructure, which can reinforce existing socio-economic inequalities. Additionally, the decentralized nature of ecosystems may lead to coordination issues among stakeholders, reducing efficiency in skill development initiatives. Furthermore, the increasing reliance on AI-driven systems introduces risks related to data bias, algorithmic transparency, and governance. These challenges suggest that while skills ecosystems offer a promising framework, their effectiveness depends on robust governance mechanisms and inclusive design. Emerging research highlights that digital skills ecosystems are increasingly platform-based and network-driven, enabling distributed learning and collaborative capability development across organizational boundaries (Kato & Choi, 2022; Brown & Adler, 2020).

4. WORK 2030 RESKILLING ARCHITECTURES

Building on the conceptualization of future skills ecosystems, the next step is to examine how these systems can be operationalized through structured reskilling architectures. The necessity of structured, scalable and adaptive reskilling systems is of top priority, as organizations shift to the Work 2030. The old training methods which are usually episodic, standardized, and not connected with the current organizational requirements are not enough in the environment with the rapid technological change and the change in the skills (Garavan et al., 2021; Noe et al., 2021). Rather, organizations will have to come up with reskilling architectures that are dynamic, data-driven, and have a rich presence in organizational strategy and broader skills ecosystems. Reskilling architectures may be understood as multilayered systems that integrate digital learning platforms, skill intelligence systems, governance systems, and collaborative networks to facilitate ongoing workforce capability building. Not only do these architectures support the skills acquisition, but also maintain the correspondence between the workforce competencies, the technological development, and the sustainability goals (Deloitte, 2024; PwC, 2023).

4.1 Training Programs to Reskilling Architectures

The shift in the way organizations view learning is seen in the fact that traditional training models have evolved into reskilling architectures. Training was traditionally considered a support role and was aimed at filling short-term skills gaps by means of standardized trainings. Nonetheless, when it comes to the AI-inspired change, learning has already emerged as an organizational strategic operation, which has a direct effect on organizational agility and competitiveness (Becker and Huselid, 2022; Cascio and Montealegre, 2021).

The main differences between reskilling architectures and traditional ones are:

i. Continuity vs episodic learning: Learning is also integrated into the flow of work, and not performed as a stand alone intervention.
ii. Individualism vs. standardization: AI-driven systems customize the learning paths according to the individual skills profiles and organizational requirements.
iii. Proactivity vs. reactivity: Skills are developed based on predictive analytics and not retrospective evaluations.
iv. Integration vs. fragmentation: Learning systems are incorporated with organizational processes, such as performance management and workforce planning (Minbaeva, 2021; Dwivedi et al., 2023).

This change highlights the need to create reskilling architectures that are technologically advanced, strategic as well as human-centered.

4.2 Core Layers of Reskilling Architectures

In order to implement reskilling architectures, one needs to know about its structural parts. These architectures usually have several inter-related layers that provide overall capability building.

Table 2. Work 2030 multi-layered reskilling architecture.

Layer	Description	Key Tools/Technologies	Strategic Role
Skill Sensing Layer	Identifies current and future skill gaps using data analytics	AI, big data, predictive analytics	Workforce planning and forecasting
Learning Delivery Layer	Provides personalized and adaptive learning experiences	LMS, AI tutors, XR/VR	Continuous skill development
Integration Layer	Embeds learning into work processes and organizational systems	HRIS, performance systems	Alignment with business strategy
Collaboration Layer	Facilitates knowledge sharing across networks and stakeholders	Digital platforms, communities	Co-creation and innovation
Governance Layer	Ensures ethical, inclusive, and secure learning practices	Blockchain, compliance tools	Trust, transparency, and accountability

Table 2 demonstrates that reskilling architectures are multi-dimensional in nature and their coordination entails technological, organizational, and governance aspects. The sensing layer of skills is an essential part of the AI-driven analytics, that is, the sense of the emergent skills and the learning interventions (Dwivedi et al., 2023). In the meantime, the learning delivery layer takes advantage of digital platforms to offer personal and scaled training experiences (Kato and Choi, 2022).

The integration layer also makes learning to be in tandem with the organizational goals so that the employees can be able to implement the newly learned skills in the real world. This alignment is critical in learning to performance results and value generation (Collings et al.,

2022). Also, the collaboration layer makes learning across the organization, as it promotes innovation as a result of knowledge sharing and partnerships (Brown and Adler, 2020).

4.3 AI-Based Reskilling Pathways

The introduction of AI into the reskilling architecture to facilitate customized and flexible learning routes is one of the characteristics of modern reskilling architectures. With the help of AI, individual skill profiles, learning behaviors, and organizational needs are analyzed and proposed as training interventions.

Figure 2. AI-led Reskilling Pathway Model

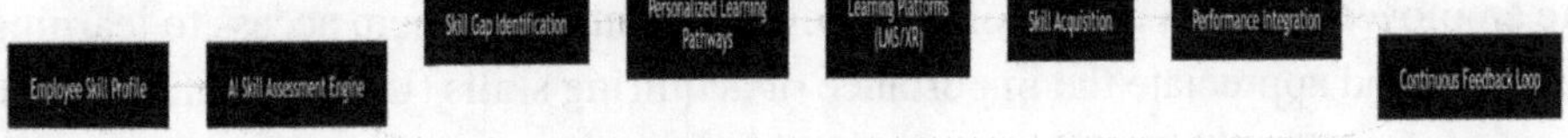

Figure 2 indicates a cyclicality of AI-driven reskilling, where the feedback allows the continuous improvement of learning pathways. This is a continuous process through which the development of the skills is kept in pace with personal development and company goals (Davenport and Miller, 2022; Jarrahi, 2023).

The reskilling initiatives can also be efficient and effective due to the integration of AI, which allows:

i. Predictive forecasting of skills.
ii. Instantaneous performance monitoring.
iii. On-the-fly delivery of learning content.
iv. Computerized skill-certification and validation.

These functions save a lot of time and money that would have been used in case of the conventional training methods and enhance learning. In practice, several global organizations have already begun implementing AI-driven reskilling architectures aligned with these principles. For instance, IBM's "SkillsBuild" initiative leverages AI-based learning platforms to provide personalized training pathways and real-time skill assessments, enabling employees to continuously upgrade their competencies in response to technological changes. Similarly, Amazon's "Upskilling 2025" program focuses on preparing its workforce for future roles through data-driven training interventions and career transition support. These initiatives demonstrate how organizations operationalize reskilling architectures by integrating predictive analytics, personalized learning, and strategic workforce planning. Such real-world implementations reinforce the practical feasibility of the proposed framework and highlight the growing importance of structured reskilling systems in achieving organizational agility and long-term value creation.

4.4 Reskilling Architectures Implemented within an Organization

The execution of reskilling architectures has to be done in a strategic and holistic manner that incorporates technology, leadership, and culture. The first step that the organizations are required to take is to have a sense of vision of transforming the workforce which they need to align with long-term business objectives and sustainability goals (Becker and Huselid, 2022).

Leadership is vital in this transformation as it helps in instilling a culture of learning and innovation that is constant. This implies that it is necessary to motivate employees to be in charge of their development, grant them access to learning materials, and appreciate the importance of acquiring skills (Ulrich and Dulebohn,

2021). Moreover, companies need to invest in the digital infrastructure and the platforms capable of supporting scalable and flexible learning solutions.

The other important factor is the inclusivity and availability required in reskilling. The organizations should take care of providing learning opportunities to all employees irrespective of the background and position of the workforce. This is especially relevant to solving the skills gap and ensuring fair development of the workforce (World Bank, 2022).

4.5 Architectures of Reskilling and Sustainable Value Creation.

Along with the contribution of organizational competitiveness, reskilling architectures are also highly significant to enable sustainable value creation. With the creation of the skills in the areas of sustainability, ethics and social responsibility, the organizations can align the capabilities of their workforce with the overall societal objectives (Lozano et al., 2022). A case in point is conducting training programs on environmental management, ethical decision making and social impact, which will help an organization to deal with its sustainability challenges. Furthermore, with the establishment of adaptability and resilience, reskilling architectures can help organizations flex in the face of uncertainties and disruptions, which helps create long-term value (Teece, 2021). Notably, employee engagement and reputation of the organization are another positive outcome of sustainability implementation into reskilling programs since people are more willing to do meaningful work meeting their values (Elkington, 2020).

Reskilling architectures are an important enabler of workforce transformation during the era of Work 2030. These architectures facilitate the constant development of capabilities and long-term value creation through the integration of AI-powered learning systems, multi-layered structures, and alignment of strategy. Table 2 and Figure 2 demonstrate the way reskilling architectures could be structured and executed to enable the agility of organizations, innovation, and resilience. Scholarly work also suggests that continuous reskilling has become a strategic imperative, with organizations embedding learning within workflows to enhance adaptability and long-term performance (Garavan et al., 2021; Noe et al., 2021).

5. ARTIFICIAL INTELLIGENCE-BASED LEARNING AND SKILLS PLATFORMS IN FUTURE SKILLS ECOSYSTEMS

Having established the role of reskilling architectures, it is essential to explore the technological backbone that enables their implementation, particularly AI-driven learning platforms. Artificial intelligence (AI) and the emergence of digital platforms have radically changed the design, delivery, and experience of learning in organizations. Learning in the context of Work 2030 is no longer limited to a formal training setting, but instead is becoming a component of intelligent, adaptive, and platform-based ecosystems that allow people to develop skills continuously (Davenport and Miller, 2022; Dwivedi et al., 2023). AI-based learning environments can act as the operational hub of reskilling architectures, enabling customized, scalable, and data-driven learning experiences, which can match the capabilities of a workforce with those of changing organizations and society.

5.1 Learning Platforms in the Digital Era Evolution

The learning platform development is the indication of a larger transformation in the content-based and fixed systems to the dynamic and learner-based ecosystems. The conventional Learning Management Systems (LMS) were only created to provide general training module, which is not always personalized and capable of adapting in real-time. Nevertheless, the combination of AI and sophisticated analytics has made these platforms intelligent learning systems that are able to customize content, monitor progress, and forecast the outcomes of learning (Kato and Choi, 2022).

Enterprise systems and other worldwide platforms like Coursera, LinkedIn Learning and IBM SkillsBuild have been using AI to offer personalized learning journey through skills profiling, career focus and business needs (LinkedIn Learning, 2023; IBM, 2022). These platforms allow employees to read learning materials at all times and places, which facilitates the shift to self-directed and lifelong learning (Siemens, 2020). These developments are also reflected in large-scale enterprise learning ecosystems. For example, LinkedIn Learning uses AI-driven recommendation systems to personalize content based on user behavior, job roles, and emerging market trends. Similarly, platforms such as Coursera for Business collaborate with organizations to deliver industry-relevant courses aligned with evolving skill demands. These platforms not only enhance accessibility but also enable organizations to integrate external learning ecosystems into their internal reskilling architectures. As a result, learning becomes more flexible, scalable, and aligned with real-world workforce requirements, thereby strengthening the effectiveness of future skills ecosystems.

Moreover, with the development of cloud computing and mobile technology, learning platforms have become much more accessible and scalable, leading organizations to be able to provide training to geographically distributed workforces. The democratization of learning is especially significant in the facilitation of inclusivity, as well as in the closure of skill gaps among different groups of the workforce (World Bank, 2022).

5.2 Essential AI-Based Learning Platforms Capabilities

The major differentiating features of AI-based learning platforms are based on a few high-order features that dramatically improve the performance of skill development. Personalization is one of the most vital functions, and AI algorithms create learning paths in accordance with personal competencies, interests, and the level of performance. This guarantees the provision of content that is relevant and meets their needs of development which improves engagement and retention (Minbaeva, 2021).

Adaptive learning is another important skill that enables platforms to dynamically change the content and level of difficulty according to the real-time performance of the learner. In this way, through the constant analysis of interactions with users, AI systems are able to understand the areas of weakness and make specific interventions, thus improving the efficiency and effectiveness of learning (Kato and Choi, 2022).

Microlearning as a concept also became popular, especially in the new digital and hybrid working conditions. Microlearning is the ability to provide brief and targeted learning modules that can be accessed at any time so that employees can incorporate learning into their work processes. Besides making it more accessible, this method facilitates ongoing skills acquisition without affecting productivity (LinkedIn Learning, 2023).

Also, the skill analytics is an important part of the AI-based learning platforms, and it can be used to provide real-time information about the capabilities of the workforce. Organizations are able to monitor skill development and detect any gaps through dashboards and data visualization tools and make informed decisions about workforce planning and reskilling plans (Dwivedi et al., 2023).

Lastly, gamification with rewards, challenges, and leaderboards improves the motivation and engagement of learners. Gamification helps to increase the participation rate and enhance the learning outcomes by developing the interactive and immersive learning processes.

5.3 Generative AI Role in Reskilling

The introduction of generative AI (GenAI) is a radically new breakthrough in the field of learning technologies that allow making the learning experience highly interactive and contextual. In contrast to the previous AI-based systems, which are based on a set of rules, GenAI is able to produce content, simulate a physical environment, and give feedback in real time, making the process of learning more profound and applicable (Dwivedi et al., 2023).

Generative AI makes it possible to create AI instructors and virtual assistants that offer an individual approach, responding to questions and giving suggestions based on individual learning requirements. It also enables simulation-based learning whereby employees are able to participate in realistic situations which imitate the challenges in the workplace, thus, improving practical skills and decision making capabilities (Davenport and Miller, 2022).

In addition, GenAI can enable automated creation of content which enables organizations to develop and update training material quickly when the requirements change. This greatly saves time and money that would be spent in development of traditional contents. Interactivity of learning platforms is further increased by the use of conversational interface, e.g., chatbots and virtual assistants, which facilitate engaging and supportive communication at all times.

Although these benefits are present, the introduction of generative AI into the learning system provokes significant ethical implications, such as the issues of data privacy, bias in algorithms, and transparency. Firms need to establish a strong governance system to make AI-driven learning systems responsible and fair in their application (Huang and Rust, 2021; Vial, 2021).

5.4 Learning Ecosystem Model powered by AI

The following conceptual model can be used to explain the application of AI-driven learning platforms in future skills ecosystems.

Figure 3. AI-Based Learning Ecosystem Model

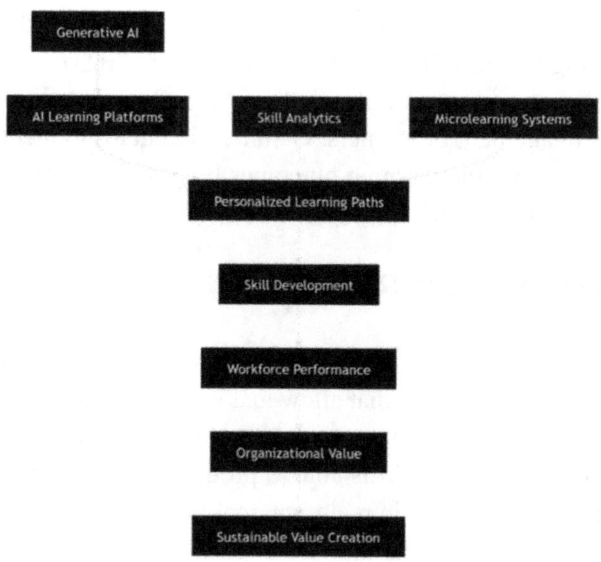

As shown in Figure 3, AI-based learning platforms serve as a central point that links technology of the enablers, learning, and its organizational results. The combination of generative AI, skill analytics, and microlearning systems improves the effectiveness of learning routes and results in better performance in the workforce and sustainable value creation (Porter and Kramer, 2021).

5.5 Challenges and Opportunities

Although AI-based learning systems are highly beneficial, there are a number of obstacles that are involved in implementation. They are the problems of access to digital information, the unwillingness towards technological change, the problem of data privacy, and the high price of the implementation of high-end digital infrastructure (Cascio and Montealegre, 2021). To solve these challenges, a comprehensive strategy, which integrates technological innovation and management of organizational change and support of policies is needed. Simultaneously, the potential opportunities that AI-based learning platforms offer are high. On these platforms, organizations can provide scalable and customized learning experiences, improve the flexibility of the workforce, and ensure the alignment of skill development with strategic goals. With such capabilities, organizations are able to develop resilient and future-ready workforces that are able to overcome the complexities of the Work 2030 (Deloitte, 2024).

AI-based learning systems are one of the foundations of future skills ecosystems, which allow organizations to provide scalable and personalised effective learning. These platforms enable reskilling to be continuous, and assist in creating sustainable value, through the combination of the latest technologies like generative AI, predictive analytics and microlearning systems. Figure 3 demonstrates the way, in which these platforms can bridge the gap between learning processes and organizational outcomes which is why they play the primary role in transforming the workforce.

5.6 Ethical, Social, and Governance Challenges of AI-Driven Learning Systems

While AI-powered learning systems have the power to revolutionize education, they also present substantial ethical, social, and governance challenges that warrant careful consideration. A key issue is algorithmic bias, which occurs when AI systems that rely on historical or incomplete data, can perpetuate disparities in access to education and career paths. Underrepresented groups are likely to be disproportionately affected by these biases, threatening the goals of future skills ecosystems for inclusivity. Another crucial concern is data privacy and security. Data, in the form of personal and behavioral data, is a crucial component of AI-powered learning platforms that provide tailored learning experiences. But the collection, storage, and utilization of such information raises issues of consent, transparency, and misuse. In the absence of strong data governance structures, companies face the danger of losing the confidence of their employees and facing regulatory and reputational risks. Further, the increasing shift to digital learning infrastructures can also deepen the digital divide. Limited access to advanced technologies, digital literacy and financial resources may exclude individuals and organizations from opportunities in reskilling, thereby exacerbating socio-economic gaps. The challenge is especially pertinent in emerging economies where infrastructural and institutional limitations may impede equitable access to skill development. One of the key points is the governance of AI-based learning systems. Without uniform regulations and oversight, it is hard to guarantee a fair, transparent and ethical product. To address the risks of automated decision-making, organizations need to set their governance guidelines, which include ethical guidelines, audit systems, and human oversight. Importantly, these challenges draw attention to a basic trade-off between efficiency and equity of AI-based reskilling systems. AI offers greater scalability and personalization, but it can also lead to negative effects that may impact fairness and inclusiveness. This tension can be resolved with a balance of technological innovation and ethical responsibility, inclusive design. Implementing AI-powered education systems requires more than just technological solutions; it also relies on the establishment of strong governance structures, ethical guidelines, and policies that accommodate a wide range of users. The following should be a key part of future skills ecosystems, to ensure that workforce transformation plays a role in sustainable and equitable value creation.

Recent literature on AI adoption further highlights its role in enabling personalized and data-driven learning systems while simultaneously raising concerns related to governance and ethical implementation (Dwivedi et al., 2023; Huang & Rust, 2021).

6. WORK 2030 SKILLS FOR SUSTAINABLE VALUE CREATION

Extending the discussion on AI-enabled learning and reskilling, the focus now shifts to the types of skills required to drive sustainable value creation in the Work 2030 landscape. During the shift of organizations towards Work 2030, the concept of value creation continues to be widened beyond the traditional economic indicators to social, environmental, and ethical levels. This is changed by the growing stakeholder expectations, regulatory challenges, and the planetary need to solve such problems as climate change, inequality, and lack of resources (United Nations, 2022; Lozano et al., 2022). In this regard, the creation of sustainability-focused skills is turning into a strategic necessity that helps organizations to develop workforce potential in line with long-term value-generating goals. The future skills ecosystem, in turn, should incorporate sustainability competencies into their very design and make sure that employees are not only trained in technical and digital skills but also in the cognitive and ethical abilities to respond to the complicated and intricate challenges (Sroufe, 2020; Elkington, 2020).

6.1 The Re-invention of Value Creation in the Age of Work 2030

Conventional value creation framework has been based mostly on financial performance and shareholder returns. But with the advent of the environmental, social and governance (ESG) models, organizational success has been redefined to encompass a wider social contribution. The idea of shared value as developed by Porter and Kramer (2021) highlights that organizations should make economic value in such a fashion that will produce social and environmental benefits. This means that in the workforce transformational environment, the development of the workers skills should be aligned with sustainability objectives. The employees need to be provided with the knowledge and skills that will enable them to adopt sustainable practices, innovate with a sense of responsibility, and help the society. The alignment is needed especially in industries that experience a massive change in the form of climate policies and technological innovations. In addition, the relationship between sustainable value creation and organizational resilience is close. Companies investing in sustainability-related skills are in a greater position to respond to regulatory changes, to deal with risks and to take advantage of new opportunities in green and digital economies (World Bank, 2022).

6.2 Nuclear Sustainability-Oriented Competencies

Sustainability-oriented competencies development necessitates a multidimensional approach to learning that constitutes both technical, cognitive, and behavioral competencies. These abilities mainly fall into three different domains:

Learners are required to demonstrate mastery of cognitive and systems thinking skills:

i. Systems Thinking for Sustainable Problem Solving: The inherent nature of sustainability issues is complex and interconnected and employees need to think in terms of systems. This means how one should see the interrelation between economic, environmental, social systems and find solutions that would effectively solve issues across several levels at the same time (Lozano et al., 2022). System thinking can help organizations to stop the short-term problem-solving to long-term strategic planning.

ii. Digital and Green Skills: The combination of digital technologies with sustainability programs has produced the idea of green digital skills, which are the combination of technical skills and environmental consciousness. These competencies are data analytics on sustainability reporting, energy optimization with the help of AI, and monitoring of the environmental impact with the help of digital tools (Deloitte, 2024). The need of such hybrid skills can only be expected to grow at a greater levels as organizations continue to go digital in order to attain the objectives of sustainability.
iii. Ethical and Social skills: Besides an effective technical and cognitive ability, employees have to acquire ethical and social skills that can make them make decisions responsibly. It involves learning about concerns with fairness, inclusivity, and social responsibility along with learning how to navigate ethical lines in complicated organizational settings (Huang and Rust, 2021). The competencies are especially relevant when it comes to AI and digital transformation, where ethical considerations are a critical factor in determining the result.

There is a lack of integration of Green HRM to the Skills Ecosystems. Green Human Resource Management (Green HRM) is an important tool of integration of sustainability in a workforce. When organizations incorporate the environmental goals into HR practices, including recruitment, training, performance management, and employee engagement, organizations can create the culture of sustainability and align the behavior of employees with organizational objectives (Sroufe, 2020).

Green HRM is an important element of the future skills ecosystem in that it:

i. Developing training programmes of sustainability orientation.
ii. Implementing ESG measures in performance measures.
iii. Incentivizing employee engagement in sustainability efforts.
iv. Encouraging green workplace behavior.

Such integration also means that sustainability is not a fringe issue but a central issue to the organizations strategy and employee development. In addition, Green HRM helps employees to be more engaged and participate more in the organization by making their organizational values reflect on the personal aspirations, which leads to increased motivation and commitment.

6.4 Competencies to Reliable and Non-Discriminatory Development

The inclusivity and the access of opportunities equally is a critical aspect of sustainable value creation. The future skills ecosystems should respond to the unequal access to education, training, and work in order to make everyone able to engage in and access workforce transformation (International Labour Organization, 2021).

This would involve specific measures to assist underrepresented groups such as:

i. Digital literacy training of disadvantaged groups.
ii. Cheap and easy learning systems.
iii. Discriminatory employment and education.
iv. Public- private alliance to increase skill building.

Through inclusiveness, organizations will be able to not only increase social equity but also enter into a larger talent pool, which will instigate innovation and competitiveness.

6.5 Association of Skills to Sustainable Value Creation

A framework can be created in order to formulate the relationship between skills and sustainable value creation and explain how various classes of skills translate into organizational and societal results.

Figure 4. Framework of Skills of Sustainable Value Creation

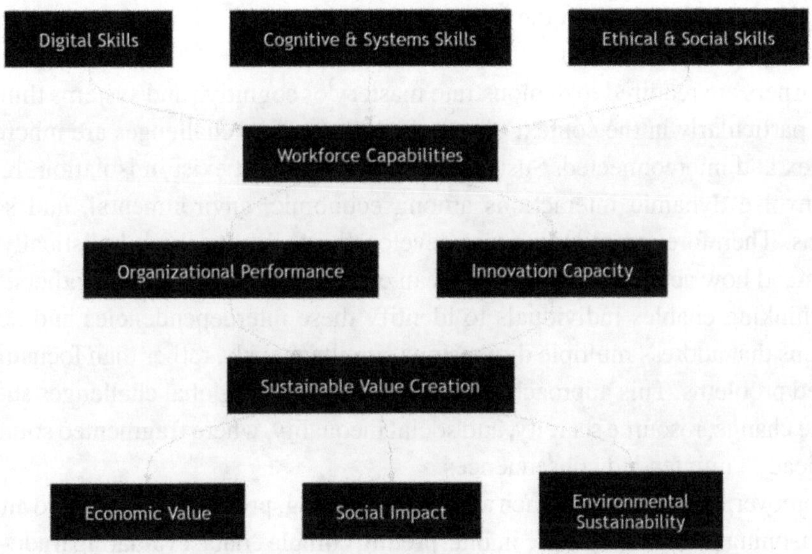

According to figure 4, sustainable value creation is the outcome of a combination of the competencies that strengthen the workforce capabilities, organizational performance, and innovativeness. The digitization, cognition, and ethical capabilities allow organizations to generate value that is not just economically sustainable but also socially responsible and sustainable to the environment (Porter and Kramer, 2021).

6.6 Organizational Implications of Strategies

There are various strategic implications of integrating skills with a focus on sustainability in the future skills ecosystem to organizations. To begin with, it demands a change of short-term and efficiency-oriented strategies to long-term, and value-oriented strategies that focus on sustainability and resilience. Second, companies should invest in the training of multidisciplinary skills that allow employees to solve complicated problems and cooperate across functional lines (Teece, 2021). Also, it is necessary that organizations become more proactive in skill development utilizing AI and data analytics to determine the new skills needs, and plan specific learning interventions. The strategy does not only boost the workforce readiness but also promotes the attainment of sustainability objectives. To recap it all, sustainable value creation competencies portray a very imperative aspect of future skills ecology, which helps organizations match the workforce competencies with larger societal and environmental goals. When organizations apply cognitive, digital, and ethical competencies to reskilling architectures, they can develop the capacity to generate long-term value and become contributors to sustainable development. Figure 4 offers a holistic approach to the interaction of these skills to catalyze sustainable results as part of Work 2030.

Learners are required to demonstrate mastery of cognitive and systems thinking skills, particularly in the context of sustainability, where challenges are inherently complex and interconnected. Sustainability issues do not exist in isolation; rather, they involve dynamic interactions among economic, environmental, and social systems. Therefore, employees must develop the ability to think holistically and understand how actions in one domain can create ripple effects across others. Systems thinking enables individuals to identify these interdependencies and design solutions that address multiple dimensions simultaneously, rather than focusing on isolated problems. This approach is essential for tackling global challenges such as climate change, resource scarcity, and social inequality, where fragmented solutions often lead to unintended consequences.

Moreover, cognitive skills such as critical thinking, problem-solving, and analytical reasoning play a crucial role in interpreting complex data, evaluating trade-offs, and making informed decisions. By integrating cognitive and systems thinking, organizations can shift from reactive, short-term problem-solving to proactive, long-term strategic planning. This transition enhances organizational resilience, supports sustainable innovation, and aligns business practices with broader societal goals. As highlighted by Lozano et al. (2022), embedding systems thinking within workforce capabilities not only improves decision-making quality but also fosters a culture of sustainability-oriented leadership and continuous learning, which is essential in navigating the uncertainties of the future.

In addition, several organizations are integrating sustainability-oriented skills into their workforce development strategies. For instance, companies in the energy and manufacturing sectors are increasingly investing in training programs focused on green technologies, carbon management, and sustainable operations. These initiatives reflect a broader shift toward embedding ESG competencies within re-skilling architectures, ensuring that workforce transformation aligns with long-term environmental and social objectives.

6.7 Operationalization and Measurement of Key Constructs

Finally, to make the proposed framework more practically applicable and empirically relevant, key constructs of future skills ecosystems, reskilling architectures and sustainable value creation need to be operationalized. Although the chapter primarily presents a conceptual model, the constructs can be converted to measurable indicators to allow organizations and researchers to measure effectiveness and outcomes. The indicators of future skills ecosystems can be sensorized, including the level of cooperation among stakeholders, presence of digital learning infrastructure, and access to lifelong learning opportunities. These can range from the number of ecosystem partnerships, participation in learning programmes, to how much digital platforms are used.

Workforce adaptability and learning efficiency indicators are useful to measure reskilling architectures. They include how often reskilling programs are scheduled, how quickly workers change skills, the percentage of workers who complete training, and how long it takes workers to become competent at a new skill. Furthermore, the learning effectiveness of AI can be measured through metrics like personalized learning engagement, reduction of skill gaps, and improvements over time. Economic, social and environmental performance indicators as part of ESG frameworks are used to assess the creation of sustainable value. These can include employee involvement in sustainability efforts, minimisation of skill gaps, diversity and inclusion indicators, and support for organisational innovation and productivity.

A structured summary of key constructs, indicators and possible measurement methods are presented in Table 3.

Table 3. Operationalization of Key Constructs in Future Skills Ecosystems

Construct	Key Indicators	Measurement Approach
Future Skills Ecosystem	Stakeholder collaboration, platform usage, learning access	Number of partnerships, participation rates, LMS analytics
Reskilling Architecture	Skill adaptability, learning effectiveness, workforce transition	Training completion rate, reskilling frequency, time-to-competency
AI-Driven Learning	Personalization, engagement, skill gap reduction	Learning analytics, user engagement data, performance metrics
Sustainable Value Creation	ESG alignment, inclusion, innovation outcomes	ESG scores, diversity metrics, productivity and innovation indicators

By incorporating measurable indicators, the framework moves beyond conceptual abstraction and provides a foundation for empirical validation and strategic implementation. This operationalization enables organizations to systematically evaluate workforce transformation initiatives and align them with long-term sustainability objectives.

REFERENCES

Barney, J. B. (2021). Resource-based theory: Creating and sustaining competitive advantage. *Journal of Management*, *47*(7), 1621–1644.

Becker, B. E., & Huselid, M. A. (2022). Strategic human capital management: Where do we go from here? *The Academy of Management Perspectives*, *36*(1), 1–15.

Brown, J. S., & Adler, R. P. (2020). Minds on fire: Open education, the long tail, and learning 2.0. *EDUCAUSE Review*.

Brynjolfsson, E., & McAfee, A. (2022). *The Turing trap: The promise and peril of human-like artificial intelligence*. Princeton University Press.

Cascio, W. F., & Montealegre, R. (2021). How technology is changing work and organizations. *Journal of World Business*, *56*(1), 101–119.

Collings, D. G., Mellahi, K., & Cascio, W. F. (2022). Global talent management and performance in multinational enterprises. *Human Resource Management Journal*, *32*(2), 297–315.

Davenport, T. H., & Miller, S. (2022). Working with AI: Real stories of human-machine collaboration. *MIT Sloan Management Review*.

Deloitte. (2024). *Global human capital trends 2024*. https://www2.deloitte.com

Dwivedi, Y. K., Hughes, L., & Baabdullah, A. M.. (2023). Artificial intelligence adoption research: A review and future research agenda. *International Journal of Information Management*, *70*, 102623.

Elkington, J. (2020). *Green swans: The coming boom in regenerative capitalism*. Fast Company Press.

Garavan, T. N., Carbery, R., & Rock, A. (2021). Mapping talent development: Definition, scope, and architecture. *European Journal of Training and Development*, *45*(2/3), 93–112.

Helfat, C. E., & Martin, J. A. (2022). Dynamic managerial capabilities: Review and assessment. *Academy of Management Review*, *47*(1), 134–156.

Huang, M.-H., & Rust, R. T. (2021). Artificial intelligence in service. *Journal of Service Research*, *24*(1), 3–14.

IBM. (2022). *SkillsBuild and workforce transformation report*.

International Labour Organization. (2021). *Skills and lifelong learning in the digital economy*. https://www.ilo.org

Jarrahi, M. H. (2023). Human–AI collaboration in knowledge work. *Business Horizons*, *66*(2), 197–206.

Kato, M., & Choi, S. (2022). Digital learning ecosystems and future education. *Computers & Education*, *182*, 104463.

LinkedIn Learning. (2023). *Workplace learning report 2023*. https://learning.linkedin.com

Lozano, R., Merrill, M. Y., Sammalisto, K., Ceulemans, K., & Lozano, F. J. (2022). Connecting competencies and sustainability. *Journal of Cleaner Production*, *366*, 132993.

McKinsey Global Institute. (2021). The future of work after. *COVID*, *19*, •••. https://www.mckinsey.com

Minbaeva, D. (2021). HR analytics and value creation. *Human Resource Management Journal*, *31*(2), 361–374.

Noe, R. A., Clarke, A. D. M., & Klein, H. J. (2021). Learning in the twenty-first-century workplace. *Annual Review of Organizational Psychology and Organizational Behavior*, *8*, 245–275.

OECD. (2023). *OECD skills outlook 2023*. https://www.oecd.org

Parker, S. K., & Grote, G. (2022). Automation, algorithms, and beyond: Work design in the future. *Annual Review of Organizational Psychology and Organizational Behavior*, *9*, 1–28.

Porter, M. E., & Kramer, M. R. (2021). Creating shared value. *Harvard Business Review*.

PwC. (2023). *Upskilling for shared prosperity*. https://www.pwc.com

Siemens, G. (2020). Connectivism: A learning theory for the digital age. *International Journal of Instructional Technology*.

Sroufe, R. (2020). *Integrated management: How sustainability creates value for any business*. Emerald Publishing.

Teece, D. J. (2021). Dynamic capabilities and strategic management. *Strategic Management Journal*, *42*(4), 789–801.

Ulrich, D., & Dulebohn, J. H. (2021). HR competencies and the future of work. *Human Resource Management Review, 31*(2), 100–112.

UNESCO. (2021). *Reimagining our futures together: A new social contract for education.*

United Nations. (2022). *Sustainable development goals report 2022.* https://unstats.un.org

Vial, G. (2021). Understanding digital transformation. *MIS Quarterly Executive, 20*(1), 13–27.

World Bank. (2022). *Skills for jobs in the digital age.* https://www.worldbank.org

World Economic Forum. (2023). *The future of jobs report 2023.* https://www.wcforum.org

Chapter 3

Future-Ready Workforce Leveraging Micro-Capabilities in the Era of Work Transformation

Puja Sareen
http://orcid.org/0000-0002-4927-5641
Amity Business School, Amity University, Noida, India

Agam Singh
http://orcid.org/0009-0008-0949-6141
Amity University, Malviya Nagar, India

Twisha Makhija
http://orcid.org/0009-0005-9240-3986
Amity Business School, Amity University, Noida, India

ABSTRACT

Technological developments have led to a new paradigm of work, organizational forms and skills where the skills and knowledge that were traditionally developed through education and work are no longer adequate for succeeding in the dynamic world of work. This chapter explores how changing workplace environments and organizational forms have seen a transition in skills from those based on technical knowledge to a focus on behavioral and cognitive skills or micro-competencies In this chapter by the authors we are introduced to the idea of micro-capabilities as an essential forerunner for a future-leaning workforce. Micro-capabilities are said to be adaptable, niche, constantly evolving competencies that enable individuals to meet the evolving needs of organizations and adapt quickly to changing needs

DOI: 10.4018/979-8-2600-2726-4.ch003

and technological disruptions. In contrast to task-specific skill sets, which are often rigid and have a limited shelf life, micro-capabilities focus on agility, emotional intelligence, an awareness and understanding of one's environment, a collaborative nature, and digital fluency.

1. INTRODUCTION

The contemporary workplace is experiencing a period of structural disruption unparalleled since the Industrial Revolution. Digital technologies, artificial intelligence, machine learning, robotic process automation and the recent emergence of generative AI systems are collectively reconfiguring the tasks associated with work, the organisational forms through which work is coordinated, and the skills demanded of workers at every level of the employment hierarchy (Autor, 2015; Frey & Osborne, 2017; Acemoglu & Restrepo, 2022). The World Economic Forum (2023) estimates that by 2027, approximately 69 million new roles will be created while 83 million existing positions will be displaced, yielding a net structural shift of 14 million jobs globally.

Within this environment, the concept of workforce readiness has undergone a significant conceptual expansion. Traditionally, readiness was assessed through domain-specific technical knowledge and formal qualifications. However, shortening lifespan of professional skills— estimated at approximately five years for technical competencies (University of Bordeaux; cited in McKinsey Global Institute, 2023) — have rendered credential-centric frameworks increasingly inadequate. Employers now place a premium on workers who demonstrate adaptability, collaborative problem-solving, and what this chapter terms micro-capabilities: the fine-grained, observable and developable behavioural patterns that mediate how individuals apply knowledge under conditions of uncertainty, technological change and organisational complexity.

Despite their growing practical significance, micro-capabilities remain conceptually underdeveloped in the academic literature. They are frequently conflated with soft skills, employability skills or broad competency domains — a conflation that obscures their distinctive features and undermines targeted development strategies. Furthermore, the rapid diffusion of generative AI tools such as large language models and AI co-pilots has introduced an entirely new set of behavioural requirements — including AI literacy, prompt crafting discipline, human-AI trust calibration and ethical micro-judgement in automated decision-making — that existing workforce frameworks do not adequately capture.

This chapter addresses these gaps through four integrated contributions: (1) a rigorous conceptual differentiation of micro-capabilities from adjacent constructs;

(2) a comprehensive three-layer integrative framework linking transformation drivers, micro-capability clusters, and workforce outcomes; (3) a critical review of recent empirical literature (2021–2026) on AI-enabled work, skills-first HR practices, and digital readiness; and (4) an empirical analysis using Chi-Square statistical testing, with explicit linkages drawn between the findings and workforce readiness imperatives. Throughout, the chapter argues that micro-capabilities constitute the behavioural infrastructure of future-ready organisations — the foundational layer upon which technical competence, strategic agility, and human–AI collaboration rest.

2. BACKGROUND: THE TRAJECTORY OF WORK TRANSFORMATION

Work transformation is neither a discrete event nor a recent phenomenon; it represents a continuous process of co-evolution between technological capability, economic structure, and organisational form. Understanding this trajectory is essential for contextualising the emergence of micro-capabilities as a workforce development priority.

2.1 Historical Waves of Transformation

The first major wave of work transformation — the Industrial Revolution — mechanised production, centralised labour in factory settings, and instituted hierarchical supervision structures that prioritised physical output and procedural compliance (Autor, 2015). The informational wave of the late twentieth century shifted the locus of value creation towards knowledge, intellectual capital, and organisational learning, giving rise to the knowledge economy theorised by Nonaka and Takeuchi (1995) and the competency-based HRM frameworks that followed.

The current wave — characterised by digital transformation, AI-driven automation, and platform-mediated work — is qualitatively distinct in two respects. First, it affects cognitive as well as manual tasks, threatening the displacement not merely of routine labour but of portions of professional, analytical, and creative work (Frey & Osborne, 2017; Ellingrud et al., 2023). Second, it operates at a pace that renders sequential reskilling — the traditional response to technological displacement — chronically insufficient. Workers who complete a training programme risk graduating into a skill environment already further transformed by subsequent technology releases.

2.2 Structural Shifts in Organisational Form

Alongside technological change, organisations have undergone profound structural transformation. The dominant model of hierarchical, function-siloed firms is giving way to networked, project-based, and platform-mediated organisational forms characterised by distributed authority, cross-functional teaming, and fluid role boundaries (Grant & Parker, 2009; Cascio & Montealegre, 2016). These structural shifts have several implications for workforce capability. Employees increasingly operate without close supervision, requiring the self-regulatory micro-capabilities — attention management, emotional regulation, ethical micro-judgement — that enable sustained productive performance under conditions of ambiguity.

The normalisation of remote and hybrid work, accelerated by the COVID-19 pandemic, has further amplified these requirements. Barley, Bechky, and Milliken (2017) note that virtual collaboration demands heightened communicative precision, cultural sensitivity, and digital dexterity — capabilities that are subtle, context-sensitive, and behavioural in character, matching the definition of micro-capabilities advanced in this chapter. Additionally, the expansion of the gig economy — in which a growing proportion of workers operate as independent contractors across multiple platforms and client relationships — has transferred responsibility for capability development from organisations to individuals, increasing the strategic importance of self-directed learning agility as a micro-capability.

2.3 The Generative AI Inflection Point

The emergence of large language models (LLMs) and generative AI systems from 2022 onwards represents a qualitative shift in the human–technology relationship that warrants explicit treatment. Unlike earlier automation technologies that performed discrete, pre-specified tasks, generative AI systems are capable of producing text, code, images, analyses, and strategic recommendations across open-ended domains. This capability fundamentally alters the division of cognitive labour between humans and machines.

Early evidence from research conducted between 2023 and 2025 suggests that the productivity gains from generative AI tools are unevenly distributed, strongly conditioned by workers' capacity to direct, evaluate, and critically interrogate AI outputs (Brynjolfsson, Li, & Raymond, 2023; Ellingrud et al., 2023). This finding underscores the centrality of micro-capabilities — particularly ethical micro-judgement, cognitive flexibility, attention management, and learning agility — as the human complement to AI capability. Workers who possess these micro-capabilities are better positioned to leverage AI tools effectively, identify their limitations, and maintain accountability for AI-influenced decisions.

3. INTEGRATIVE CONCEPTUAL FRAMEWORK

Figure 1 presents the Integrative Micro-Capability Framework developed in this chapter. The framework comprises three horizontal layers connected by bidirectional influence arrows, with a foundational layer of organisational enablers.

Figure 1. Integrative Micro-Capability Framework: From Work Transformation Drivers to Workforce Outcomes.

Layer 1: Work Transformation Drivers	Layer 2: Micro-Capability Development	Layer 3: Workforce Outcomes
Digitalization & AI Adoption Automation & Robotics Remote & Hybrid Work Gig Economy Expansion Global Competition Generative AI Disruption	Attention Management Learning Agility Emotional Regulation Ethical Micro-Judgement Collaborative Responsiveness Digital Dexterity Cognitive Flexibility	Employee Agility Organisational Resilience Innovation Capability Sustained Employability Human–AI Collaboration Productivity Growth
Organisational Enablers: Learning Culture | Leadership Support | HR Analytics | Technology Infrastructure | Psychological Safety		

Note: = Strong influence; = Moderate; = Emerging. Bidirectional arrows indicate feedback loops between outcomes and subsequent driver-capability dynamics.

The framework operates as follows. Work transformation drivers — digitalization, AI adoption, automation, remote work, gig economy expansion and the emergence of generative AI — create new performance demands that existing capability frameworks cannot fully address. These demands activate the need for specific micro-capability clusters (Layer 2), each of which is associated with observable behavioural indicators and measurable assessment approaches. When micro-capabilities are systematically developed, they produce workforce outcomes (Layer 3) including employee agility, organisational resilience, innovation capability, sustained employability, and effective human–AI collaboration. Critically, these outcomes feed back into the driver layer through competitive dynamics: organisations that achieve superior agility and innovation capability through micro-capability development reshape industry norms, intensifying the capability requirements faced by competitors. This feedback dynamic makes micro-capability development a continuous, rather than periodic, organisational imperative.

The foundational enabler layer — learning culture, leadership support, HR analytics, technology infrastructure, and psychological safety — conditions the effectiveness of micro-capability development initiatives. Without these enabling conditions, even well-designed training programmes tend to produce limited, non-durable behavioural change (Boyatzis, 2008; Maslach & Leiter, 2016).

4. CONCEPT OF MICRO-CAPABILITIES: THEORETICAL FOUNDATIONS AND DEFINITIONAL BOUNDARIES

4.1 Definitional Precision: What Micro-Capabilities Are — and Are Not

Theoretical and applied clarity requires that micro-capabilities be rigorously distinguished from the overlapping constructs with which they are frequently confused. Table 1 presents a systematic comparative analysis.

Table 1. Comparative Analysis of Micro-Capabilities and Adjacent Constructs

Dimension	Competencies	Soft Skills	Employability Skills	Micro-Capabilities
Definition	Broad knowledge & expertise domains	Interpersonal & personality traits	Skills enabling labour-market entry	Fine-grained, observable behavioural patterns
Granularity	High-level / abstract	Moderate	Moderate	Highly specific / behavioural
Measurability	Often tacit; credential-based	Difficult to quantify	Partially measurable	Directly observable & measurable
Development Mode	Formal education & training	Personality & socialization	Education & internships	Experiential learning & micro-interventions
Examples	Finance, Engineering, Communication	Teamwork, Leadership	CV writing, Interview skills	Attention discipline, Ethical micro-judgement, Learning agility
AI-Era Relevance	Risk of obsolescence	Partially enduring	Partially enduring	High – underpins human–AI collaboration

Source: Authors' synthesis, drawing on Boyatzis (2008), Laker & Powell (2011), Yorke (2006), Teece (2007), and Goleman (1995).

As Table 1 illustrates, micro-capabilities are distinguished from competencies by their granularity and behavioural specificity: whereas “communication” is a competency domain, “adapting message framing in real time to the emotional state of a listener” is a micro-capability. They are distinguished from soft skills by their observability and direct measurability: soft skills are often characterised as dispositional traits (e.g., “being a team player”), whereas micro-capabilities are patterns of situated, repeatable behaviour. Micro-capabilities differ from employability skills in their focus on in-work performance rather than labour-market entry. And they differ from dynamic capabilities — organisational-level constructs concerning the capacity of firms to sense, seize, and reconfigure resources (Teece, 2007) — by operating at the individual behavioural level.

4.2 Theoretical Foundations

Micro-capabilities draw theoretical support from multiple streams of organisational and psychological research. Bandura's (1986) social cognitive theory provides the foundational learning mechanism: behaviours are acquired through observation, enactment, and environmental reinforcement, gradually consolidating into habitual patterns that shape performance. This mechanism explains both how micro-capabilities develop and why they tend to be implicit rather than explicitly taught — they emerge from the accumulation of experience-driven behavioural regularities.

Goleman's (1995, 1998) emotional intelligence framework contributes the affective dimension: self-awareness, empathy, and emotional regulation are not merely personality traits but cultivable behavioural patterns with demonstrated predictive validity for leadership effectiveness and collaborative performance. Illeris's (2011) theory of workplace learning contextualises this development within the social and organisational dynamics of work settings, arguing that the most durable capability growth occurs through practice-embedded learning rather than classroom instruction. More recently, research on psychological safety (Edmondson & Lei, 2014) has established that organisational contexts characterised by interpersonal trust and tolerance for productive failure are significantly more conducive to the development and expression of micro-capabilities.

4.3 Measurable Dimensions and Indicators of Micro-Capabilities

A central contribution of this chapter is the operationalisation of micro-capabilities through measurable dimensions and indicators, enabling both research investigation and practical HR application. Table 2 presents the Micro-Capability Indicator Matrix.

Table 2. Micro-Capability Indicator Matrix: Dimensions, Behavioural Indicators, Assessment Methods, and AI-Era Salience

Micro-Capability Cluster	Observable Behavioural Indicators	Assessment Methods	AI-Era Salience
Attention Management	Sustains focus during interruptions; prioritises high-value tasks; avoids digital distraction	ESM, self-report scales	High – AI augments but cannot replace directed human attention
Learning Agility	Acquires new skills rapidly; transfers knowledge across contexts; embraces feedback	360° reviews, skill-gain logs	Very High – continuous reskilling imperative
Emotional Regulation	Manages stress under ambiguity; recovers swiftly from setbacks; remains productive	EQ assessments, supervisor ratings	High – AI collaboration requires emotional stability
Ethical Micro-Judgement	Recognises ethical implications in routine decisions; raises concerns proactively	Scenario-based assessments	Very High – AI governance demands human moral agency
Collaborative Responsiveness	Adapts communication style; acknowledges team contributions; resolves micro-conflicts	Peer evaluations, ONA	High – virtual & hybrid work amplifies need
Digital Dexterity	Explores new tools independently; troubleshoots digital problems; iterates solutions	Task-based assessments, platform logs	Very High – core to human–AI interaction
Cognitive Flexibility	Reframes problems; tolerates ambiguity; shifts between divergent & convergent thinking	Cognitive tests, simulation exercises	High – counterbalances AI rigidity

Note: ESM = Experience Sampling Method; EQ = Emotional Quotient; ONA = Organisational Network Analysis. AI-Era Salience ratings reflect the authors' synthesis of evidence from Brynjolfsson et al. (2023), WEF (2023), and Ellingrud et al. (2023). ●●● = Very High; ●● = High; ● = Moderate.

5. Micro-Capabilities in Generative AI and Human–AI Collaboration Contexts

The rapid diffusion of generative AI tools across professional domains from 2022 onwards has introduced a new axis of workforce capability development that traditional frameworks have not adequately addressed. This section examines the emerging micro-capability requirements specific to human–AI collaboration environments, drawing on research published between 2023 and 2025.

5.1 The Human Complement to Generative AI

Large language models and multimodal generative AI systems are capable of producing fluent text, functional code, data analyses, creative content, and strategic frameworks at speeds and scales that far exceed human output. However, their outputs are characterised by systematic limitations: they may be factually unreliable, contextually misaligned, ethically problematic, or subtly biased in ways that are non-obvious to uncritical users (Bommasani et al., 2022). Effective deployment of generative AI tools therefore requires workers to perform a set of higher-order cognitive functions: critically evaluating AI outputs against domain expertise and contextual appropriateness; formulating prompts that elicit accurate, useful, and ethically sound responses; calibrating trust in AI-generated content appropriately; and maintaining accountability for decisions influenced by AI recommendations.

Research by Brynjolfsson, Li, and Raymond (2023), examining the productivity effects of AI conversational tools among customer service representatives, found that the performance benefits of AI assistance were strongly moderated by workers' baseline collaborative responsiveness and learning agility — two of the micro-capability clusters identified in this chapter. Workers who possessed strong micro-capabilities exhibited three times the productivity gains of those with weaker profiles, suggesting that micro-capabilities function as the critical human complement to AI capability.

5.2 Emerging Micro-Capabilities for AI-Enabled Workplaces

Building on the indicator matrix presented in Section 4.3, several micro-capabilities are particularly salient in AI-enabled contexts:

- Prompt Discipline: The capacity to formulate precise, contextually informed, and ethically bounded queries to AI systems — a micro-capability that bridges attention management, cognitive flexibility, and ethical micro-judgement.
- AI Output Calibration: The behavioural habit of critically evaluating AI-generated content against multiple quality criteria before use or endorsement — distinct from and more specific than general "critical thinking."
- Human–AI Role Boundary Awareness: The micro-capability of recognising in real time which aspects of a task benefit from AI assistance versus which require distinctly human judgement, empathy, or ethical accountability.
- Data Interpretation Agility: The capacity to interpret, question, and contextualise AI-generated data visualisations and analytical summaries without over-relying on algorithmic framing.

Cultivating these AI-specific micro-capabilities requires a revision of learning and development (L&D) practice. Standard "AI literacy" programmes that focus on technical familiarity with tools are insufficient; effective programmes must engage the behavioural and ethical dimensions of human–AI interaction through experiential, simulation-based, and reflective learning modalities (Ellingrud et al., 2023; Cappelli & Tavis, 2024).

5.3 Capability Fatigue in AI-Augmented Environments

A further consideration in AI-enabled workplaces is the risk of capability fatigue — the cognitive and psychological exhaustion arising from persistent demands to learn, adapt, and perform under conditions of rapid technological change (Maslach & Leiter, 2016). The integration of generative AI tools into workflows, while potentially productivity-enhancing, also creates new cognitive demands: workers must maintain vigilance over AI outputs, manage increased information density, and navigate shifting task boundaries. Research by Pfeifer and colleagues (2024) found that employees in high-AI-intensity work environments reported significantly elevated levels of decision fatigue and cognitive load, particularly when organisational support for AI adoption was perceived as inadequate.

Addressing capability fatigue requires that micro-capability development be embedded within broader well-being strategies. Specifically, organisations should design micro-learning interventions with appropriate cognitive load parameters, build reflective practice into AI adoption programmes, and ensure that learning demands are calibrated to individuals' developmental readiness levels.

6. BUILDING A FUTURE-READY WORKFORCE: STRATEGIC HR AND LEADERSHIP IMPERATIVES

6.1 From Job-Based to Skills-First HR Architecture

The dominant paradigm in human resource management — the job-based architecture, in which employees are hired, evaluated, and compensated with reference to fixed job descriptions — is increasingly recognised as structurally incompatible with the agility demands of the digital economy (Jesuthasan & Boudreau, 2022). Skills-first HR architecture, by contrast, disaggregates work into tasks and projects, maps the skills required for each, and dynamically deploys talent on the basis of skill fit rather than job title or hierarchical level. This architectural shift has profound implications for micro-capability development: when skills are the unit of analysis, fine-grained behavioural capabilities become visible, measurable, and actionable within HR systems in ways that job-based frameworks do not permit.

Leading organisations including IBM, Microsoft, Unilever, and Mastercard have publicly committed to skills-first talent practices (WEF, 2023; Deloitte, 2023). McKinsey's 2024 Global Survey on workforce transformation found that organisations that had adopted skills-first architectures were 2.4 times more likely to report strong organisational agility and 1.8 times more likely to report high employee engagement than those maintaining traditional job-based systems. These outcomes align with the Layer 3 workforce outcomes identified in the Integrative Micro-Capability Framework.

6.2 Strategic Role of HR in Micro-Capability Development

Within a skills-first architecture, HR plays a qualitatively different role than in traditional models. Rather than administering training catalogues, HR functions as a strategic capability intelligence unit: identifying emerging micro-capability gaps through people analytics, designing targeted development interventions, and evaluating the behavioural impact of L&D investments. Key HR practices that are particularly effective in developing micro-capabilities include:

- AI-Personalised Learning Pathways: Adaptive learning platforms that diagnose individual micro-capability profiles and recommend customised development sequences, enabling just-in-time, behaviour-targeted learning (Cappelli & Tavis, 2024).
- 360-Degree Micro-Capability Assessments: Multi-rater feedback systems designed around the specific behavioural indicators identified in Table 2, providing employees with granular developmental data.
- Micro-Learning Interventions: Short-form, context-embedded learning experiences (typically 3–10 minutes) targeting specific behavioural habits, designed to be applied immediately within work routines (Chatterjee et al., 2023).
- Virtual Reality Simulation: Immersive VR-based scenarios that allow employees to practise high-stakes micro-capabilities — ethical micro-judgement, emotional regulation under pressure, human–AI collaboration protocols — in psychologically safe simulated environments.
- Peer Learning Communities and Social Knowledge Platforms: Structured peer exchange environments, including HR Blog-type platforms, that enable the social modelling and environmental reinforcement mechanisms identified by Bandura (1986) as foundational to micro-capability acquisition.

Table 3 presents the HR Practice–Micro-Capability Development Matrix, indicating the relative effectiveness of key HR practices in developing each of the seven core micro-capability clusters.

Table 3. HR Practice–Micro-Capability Development Matrix

HR Practice	Attn. Mgmt	Learn. Agility	Emot. Reg.	Eth. Judgement	Collab. Resp.	Digital Dex.
Microlearning Platforms	●	●●●	○	○	●	●●●
360° Feedback Systems	●●	●●	●●●	●●	●●●	●
AI-Personalised L&D	●	●●●	●	●	●	●●●
Mentoring & Coaching	●●	●●	●●●	●●●	●●●	●
VR Simulation Training	●●●	●●	●●	●	●●	●●●
Peer Learning Communities	●	●●	●●	●	●●●	●●
Psychological Safety Norms	●●	●●	●●●	●●●	●●●	●

Note: ●●● = Strong contribution; ●● = Moderate contribution; ● = Limited contribution. Ratings based on synthesis of empirical evidence from Cappelli & Tavis (2024), WEF (2023), Chatterjee et al. (2023), and Dutta et al. (2025).

6.3 Leadership Role in Cultivating a Micro-Capability Learning Culture

Whereas HR designs the architecture of micro-capability development, leadership determines whether the organisational culture is hospitable to its practice. Leaders exert influence over micro-capability development through two primary channels: modelling and institutional signalling.

Modelling refers to leaders' visible demonstration of the micro-capabilities they wish to develop in their teams. Leaders who publicly acknowledge uncertainty, actively seek and respond to feedback, and visibly engage with new digital tools create social proof that these behaviours are valued and safe — mechanisms that Bandura's (1986) social cognitive theory identifies as central to observational learning. Institutional signalling refers to the structural choices leaders make: whether micro-capability development is integrated into performance management criteria, whether psychological safety is actively maintained in team environments, and whether learning time is protected within work schedules.

Research by Haddad (2024) and Dutta et al. (2025) on digital knowledge-sharing platforms — including HR Blog systems — demonstrates that leadership engagement is a critical moderator of platform effectiveness: platforms on which senior leaders actively participate, respond to employee contributions, and model knowledge-sharing behaviours generate substantially higher levels of employee engagement and learning transfer. In organisations where leaders are visibly absent from such platforms, employees perceive their contributions as valueless, suppressing knowledge sharing and micro-capability reinforcement.

7. INDUSTRY CASE STUDIES: MICRO-CAPABILITY DEVELOPMENT IN PRACTICE

To illustrate the practical application of the Integrative Micro-Capability Framework, this section presents enhanced case analyses of five organisations across technology, retail, and IT services sectors. Each case is examined through the specific lens of micro-capability development, with attention to programme design, organisational enablers, and measurable outcomes. Table 4 provides a summary overview.

Table 4. Industry Case Studies: Micro-Capability Development Initiatives and Outcomes

Organization	Sector	Key Initiative	Micro-Capability Focus	Measurable Outcome
IBM	Technology	SkillsBuild & AI Academy; internal skill-graph mapping	Learning agility, Digital dexterity, Cognitive flexibility	30% faster role redeployment; 25% reduction in external hiring costs
Microsoft	Technology	Growth Mindset culture; LinkedIn Learning integration; AI Co-pilot adoption programme	Emotional regulation, Collaborative responsiveness, Digital dexterity	Employee satisfaction scores +18%; internal mobility up 40%
Amazon	Retail / E-commerce	Upskilling 2025 – $1.2B investment; Career Choice; machine-learning literacy modules	Learning agility, Attention management, Ethical micro-judgement	Over 300,000 employees upskilled; productivity per worker up ~12%

continued on following page

Table 4. Continued

Organization	Sector	Key Initiative	Micro-Capability Focus	Measurable Outcome
Walmart	Retail	Live Better U; VR-based soft-skill training; omnichannel operations certification	Collaborative responsiveness, Emotional regulation, Digital dexterity	Store manager pipeline accelerated; turnover in trained cohorts reduced ~25%
Infosys	IT Services	Lex micro-learning platform; AI-driven personalised learning paths	Cognitive flexibility, Digital dexterity, Learning agility	4M+ learning hours annually; 92% of employees reskilled within 18 months

Sources: IBM (2023), Microsoft Annual Report (2024), Amazon (2024), Walmart (2023), Infosys Annual Report (2024). Note: Outcome figures are drawn from publicly disclosed organisational reports and should be interpreted as indicative rather than independently verified.

7.1 IBM: Skills-First Transformation and Digital Dexterity

IBM's workforce transformation represents one of the most extensively documented examples of skills-first HR architecture in the technology sector. Confronting the obsolescence of traditional role-based talent management in the face of rapid AI, cloud, and quantum computing advances, IBM implemented a comprehensive skill-graph system that maps individual employee capabilities at a granular level against project requirements and future skill forecasts. This system operationalises several of the micro-capabilities identified in this chapter — particularly learning agility, digital dexterity, and cognitive flexibility — as measurable units within talent allocation processes.

IBM's SkillsBuild initiative and its internal AI Academy extend this infrastructure to systematic micro-capability development. The AI Academy employs microlearning formats targeting specific behavioural habits associated with effective AI tool use, including prompt discipline, AI output calibration, and human–AI role boundary awareness. A notable feature of IBM's approach is the integration of micro-capability assessment into project assignment decisions: employees whose skill graphs indicate strong learning agility and digital dexterity are preferentially allocated to transformation projects, creating a reinforcing cycle of capability expression and development.

Key lessons from the IBM case: micro-capability development is most effective when integrated into live operational processes rather than confined to separate training programmes; skills-graph technology enables individual-level micro-capability visibility at organisational scale; and leadership commitment to skills-first principles is a prerequisite for cultural acceptance of the model.

7.2 Microsoft: Growth Mindset as Micro-Capability Infrastructure

Microsoft's widely analysed cultural transformation under CEO Satya Nadella — from a "know-it-all" to a "learn-it-all" culture — can be understood through the lens of micro-capabilities as an organisational-level initiative to reconfigure the behavioural habits of over 200,000 employees. The Growth Mindset framework, drawn from Dweck's (2006) psychological research, targets several core micro-capabilities identified in Table 2: learning agility (embracing challenges as developmental opportunities), emotional regulation (managing the discomfort of not knowing), and collaborative responsiveness (seeking knowledge from others rather than performing expertise).

Microsoft's integration of AI co-pilot tools across its product suite has created a natural experimental context for studying human–AI collaboration micro-capabilities at scale. Internal research reported in Microsoft's 2024 Work Trend Index indicates that employees who demonstrate higher levels of learning agility and cognitive flexibility achieve significantly greater productivity gains from AI co-pilot adoption than colleagues with comparable technical skills but weaker micro-capability profiles. This finding provides direct empirical support for the mediating role of micro-capabilities in the human–AI capability relationship.

7.3 Amazon and Walmart: Micro-Capabilities in Retail Workforce Transformation

Amazon's Upskilling 2025 programme — a USD 1.2 billion investment targeting over 300,000 employees — demonstrates the application of micro-capability development principles at exceptional organisational scale. The programme's Career Choice component finances employees' external education in high-demand fields, while its internal Machine Learning University targets digital dexterity and data interpretation agility among operational and logistics staff. Critically, Amazon's programme design reflects an explicit recognition that technical skill acquisition without accompanying behavioural development is insufficient: modules are structured to develop the learning agility and collaborative responsiveness that enable skill transfer across rapidly evolving operational contexts.

Walmart's Live Better U programme and its pioneering deployment of VR-based training technology offers an instructive example of how immersive simulation can develop emotional regulation and collaborative responsiveness micro-capabilities at scale. Walmart has deployed VR training across customer service, management, and operational scenarios, achieving reported reductions in training time and improvements in skill retention compared to traditional classroom modalities. The VR environment's capacity to create psychologically safe practice conditions — allowing employees to experience and manage difficult interpersonal or operational scenarios without real-world consequences — aligns directly with the mechanisms through which emotional regulation and ethical micro-judgement develop.

8. EMPIRICAL ANALYSIS: CHI-SQUARE TESTS OF INDEPENDENCE

8.1 Methodological Framework and Connection to Workforce Readiness

This section presents two Chi-Square tests of independence using the IBM HR Analytics Employee Attrition dataset, a widely used secondary dataset in organisational research. Importantly, attrition and satisfaction variables serve as proximate indicators of workforce readiness outcomes: organisations characterised by high attrition rates — particularly among educationally diverse talent populations — face structural barriers to micro-capability accumulation and retention, since micro-capabilities develop through sustained experiential engagement within specific organisational contexts. Job satisfaction has been shown to moderate the relationship between behavioural capability and sustained performance, linking it to the capability fatigue dynamics discussed in Section 5.3. The Chi-Square test of independence is applied to determine whether statistically significant associations exist between these categorical indicators.

The Chi-Square test statistic is calculated as:

$$\chi^2 = \Sigma (O - E)^2 / E$$

where O represents observed frequency and E represents expected frequency, calculated as (Row Total × Column Total) / Grand Total.

8.2 Analysis 1: Education Field and Attrition (n = 1,476)

Hypotheses

H_0: Education Field and Attrition are statistically independent.
H_1: Education Field and Attrition are significantly associated.

Table 5. Observed Frequency: Education Field × Attrition

Education Field	Attrition (Yes)	Attrition (No)	Total	% Attrition
Life Sciences	89	517	606	14.7%
INDMedical	63	401	464	13.6%
Marketing	35	124	159	22.0%
Technical Degree	32	100	132	24.2%
Human Resources	12	39	51	23.5%
Other	6	58	64	9.4%
Total	**237**	**1,239**	**1,476**	**16.1%**

Table 6. Chi-Square Calculation: Education Field × Attrition

Category	O	E	O–E	(O–E)²	(O–E)²/E
Life Sciences (Yes)	89	97.3	-8.3	68.89	0.71
Life Sciences (No)	517	508.7	8.3	68.89	0.14
Medical (Yes)	63	74.5	-11.5	132.25	1.77
Medical (No)	401	389.5	11.5	132.25	0.34
Marketing (Yes)	35	25.5	9.5	90.25	3.54
Marketing (No)	124	133.5	-9.5	90.25	0.67
Technical (Yes)	32	21.2	10.8	116.64	5.50
Technical (No)	100	110.8	-10.8	116.64	1.05
HR (Yes)	12	8.2	3.8	14.44	1.75
HR (No)	39	42.8	-3.8	14.44	0.34
Other (Yes)	6	10.3	-4.3	18.49	1.79
Other (No)	58	53.7	4.3	18.49	0.34
χ^2 Total					**16.02**

Degrees of Freedom: $df = (r - 1)(c - 1) = (6 - 1)(2 - 1) = 5$
Chi-Square Value: $\chi^2 = 16.02$ | p-value = 0.0068

Decision and Interpretation

Since $p = 0.0068 < \alpha = 0.05$, the null hypothesis is rejected. There is a statistically significant association between educational background and attrition propensity. Employees with Technical Degree and Marketing educational backgrounds exhibit notably higher attrition rates (24.2% and 22.0% respectively) compared to Life Sciences and Medical graduates (14.7% and 13.6%). From a micro-capability perspective, this differential suggests that either the micro-capability profiles cultivated in certain educational streams are less well-matched to prevailing organisational demands, or that onboarding and development practices fail to bridge micro-capability gaps for certain educational groups. Both interpretations carry implications for targeted micro-capability development interventions: organisations with high attrition among technically educated employees may need to invest specifically in the collaborative responsiveness and emotional regulation micro-capabilities that support retention.

8.3 Analysis 2: Environment Satisfaction and Job Satisfaction (n = 1,412)

Hypotheses

H_0: Environment Satisfaction and Job Satisfaction are statistically independent.
H_1: Environment Satisfaction and Job Satisfaction are significantly associated.

Table 7. Observed Frequency: Environment Satisfaction × Job Satisfaction

Env. Satisfaction	Job Sat 1	Job Sat 2	Job Sat 3	Job Sat 4	Row Total
1	65	74	68	59	266
2	82	96	88	80	346
3	96	104	97	89	386
4	102	112	104	96	414
Col Total	**345**	**386**	**357**	**324**	**1,412**

Chi-Square Value: $\chi^2 = 5.32$ | df = (4−1)(4−1) = 9 | p-value = 0.8056

Decision and Interpretation

Since $p = 0.8056 > \alpha = 0.05$, the null hypothesis cannot be rejected. There is no statistically significant association between environment satisfaction and job satisfaction in this dataset. This finding is consistent with contemporary HRM research (Cappelli & Tavis, 2024) suggesting that job satisfaction is a multidimensional construct driven by factors beyond physical or social working environment — including meaningfulness of work, perceived growth opportunities, and quality of management relationships. For micro-capability development, this finding implies that physical environment improvements alone are insufficient to generate the motivational conditions required for sustained behavioural development; rather, organisations must address growth opportunity structures and leadership quality as the primary levers of workforce engagement.

9. CHALLENGES AND LIMITATIONS IN MICRO-CAPABILITY DEVELOPMENT

Despite the compelling strategic case for micro-capability development, organisations face significant and multifaceted barriers to effective implementation. Table 8 provides a structured synthesis of the primary challenge categories, specific barriers, and evidence-based mitigation strategies.

Table 8. Challenges, Barriers, and Mitigation Strategies in Workforce Micro-Capability Development

Challenge Category	Specific Barriers	Strategic Mitigation Approaches
Skill Gap Velocity	Technical skills depreciate ~50% in 5 years (Univ. of Bordeaux); AI accelerates obsolescence	Continuous micro-learning; skills taxonomy refresh bi-annually; AI-driven personalised pathways
Resistance to Change	Fear of automation job loss; low learning-culture maturity; change fatigue	Psychological safety initiatives; change champions; gamified reskilling with visible career outcomes
Financial Constraints	High cost of LMS, VR, AI-coaching tools; SME resource constraints	Consortium training models; government co-investment (e.g., UK Apprenticeship Levy); ROI tracking (McKinsey: 3× innovation speed)
Technology Access Gaps	Unequal digital infrastructure; rural/ low-income exclusion; platform adoption barriers	Inclusive digital policies; subsidised device access; blended learning combining digital & in-person modes
Strategic HR Planning	Workforce planning complexity; siloed HR/IT/business data; predictive analytics maturity	People analytics platforms; cross-functional workforce councils; scenario planning
Leadership & Culture	Short-termism in L&D investment; low leadership modelling of learning behaviours	Leadership capability frameworks tied to performance metrics; visible C-suite learning participation
Capability Fatigue	Persistent upskilling pressure causing cognitive overload and burnout	Balanced development calendars; well-being integration in L&D design; micro-break learning formats

Sources: WEF (2023), McKinsey Global Institute (2023), Maslach & Leiter (2016), Gartner (2024), IBM Institute for Business Value (2024), Tenakwah & Otchere-Ankrah (2024).

Several of these challenge dimensions warrant extended discussion. The velocity of skill gap expansion — driven by AI advancement, generative model releases, and Industry 4.0 technology diffusion — creates a systemic condition in which traditional episodic training cycles are structurally incapable of maintaining workforce capability currency. As McKinsey Global Institute (2023) estimates, 75 to 375 million workers globally may need to shift occupational categories by 2030, a scale of transition that demands continuous, embedded, and personalised micro-capability development rather than periodic reskilling programmes.

Resistance to change represents a particularly complex barrier in the context of generative AI adoption, where employee anxiety about displacement is often acute and not fully addressed by reassurance-focused communication. Research by Acemoglu and Restrepo (2022) suggests that the distributional effects of AI-driven automation are indeed asymmetric — falling disproportionately on workers in routine cognitive roles — making individual anxiety a rational rather than irrational response to technological change. Effective mitigation requires not merely reassurance but transparent communication about the specific micro-capabilities that enable workers to remain productive alongside AI systems, combined with tangible investment signals that demonstrate organisational commitment to employee development.

10. DIGITAL SKILL GAPS AND INDUSTRY 4.0: A MICRO-CAPABILITY PERSPECTIVE

The emergence of Industry 4.0 — characterised by the convergence of artificial intelligence, the Internet of Things, advanced robotics, augmented reality, and data-intensive manufacturing systems — has rendered digital skills not merely advantageous but foundational to productive participation in modern economies (Schwab, 2016; Vial, 2019). Table 9 presents a Digital Skills Framework structured around the four capability tiers relevant to Industry 4.0 environments, with explicit connections drawn to the micro-capability clusters identified in this chapter.

Table 9. Digital Skills Framework for Industry 4.0: Tiered Competencies, Micro-Capabilities, and Applications

Digital Skill Tier	Representative Competencies	Associated Micro-Capabilities	Industry 4.0 Application
Foundational	Digital literacy, cybersecurity hygiene, cloud basics	Attention management, Learning agility	All sectors – baseline digital participation
Intermediate	Data visualisation, AI-tool usage, automation scripting	Digital dexterity, Cognitive flexibility	Analytics roles, operations, customer experience
Advanced	ML model evaluation, prompt engineering, AI ethics governance	Ethical micro-judgement, Learning agility	AI product teams, data science, digital strategy
Leadership	Digital strategy formulation, human–AI team orchestration	All micro-capabilities + systemic thinking	C-suite, HR leaders, innovation directors

Sources: Authors' synthesis drawing on Vial (2019), WEF (2023), Ellingrud et al. (2023), and European Commission Digital Education Action Plan (2021–2027).

Three theoretical frameworks from the digital transformation literature — the Technology Acceptance Model (TAM), the Technology–Organisation–Environment (TOE) framework, and the Resource-Based View (RBV) — provide complementary explanations for the role of micro-capabilities in mediating digital skill development and utilisation.

TAM (Davis, 1989) focuses on individuals' perceived ease of use and perceived usefulness of digital technologies. Micro-capabilities — particularly digital dexterity and learning agility — directly influence these perceptions: employees who possess strong digital dexterity are more likely to explore new tools with an exploratory rather than avoidant orientation, shaping favourable ease-of-use assessments and accelerating adoption. The TOE framework situates digital skill development within organisational context (technology infrastructure, leadership support, industry environment), aligning with the organisational enabler layer of the Integrative Micro-Capability Framework. The RBV (Barney, 1995; Barney & Wright, 1998) treats digital capabilities — including micro-capabilities — as strategically valuable, rare, inimitable, and non-substitutable resources when they are deeply embedded in organisational routines and cultures, providing the theoretical basis for micro-capability investment as a source of sustainable competitive advantage.

The digital skill gap — the discrepancy between the digital capabilities that employers require and those that workers currently possess — is a global phenomenon with severe distributional dimensions. Evidence from Eurostat (2024) indicates that approximately 37% of the EU workforce lacks basic digital skills, while proportions are considerably higher among older workers, workers in rural areas, and workers in low-income brackets. In the Global South, digital infrastructure deficits compound individual capability gaps, creating systemic barriers to participation in the digital economy. Micro-capability development strategies must therefore be designed with inclusivity as a foundational principle: interventions that are exclusively technology-mediated risk reinforcing the digital divides they purport to address.

11. CONCLUSION AND FUTURE RESEARCH DIRECTIONS

11.1 Summary of Contributions

This chapter has made four integrated contributions to the workforce development literature. First, it has established a theoretically grounded and operationally precise definition of micro-capabilities — granular, observable, and developable behavioural patterns that mediate performance in evolving work environments — differentiating this construct from competencies, soft skills, employability skills, and dynamic capabilities. Second, it has presented the Integrative Micro-Capability Framework, a three-layer conceptual model linking work transformation drivers, micro-capability clusters, and workforce outcomes, with an organisational enabler foundation. Third, it has identified the emerging micro-capabilities specific to generative AI and human–AI collaboration contexts, including prompt discipline, AI output calibration, and human–AI role boundary awareness. Fourth, it has demonstrated, through empirical Chi-Square analysis, that educational background is significantly associated with attrition — a finding with specific implications for targeted micro-capability development in HR practice.

The fundamental argument of this chapter is that micro-capabilities constitute the behavioural infrastructure of future-ready organisations. Technical capabilities — whether digital skills, AI proficiency, or domain expertise — are necessary but insufficient for sustained organisational agility and resilience. It is the micro-level behavioural patterns of attention, learning, emotion, ethics, collaboration, and cognitive flexibility that determine whether technical capability translates into effective performance, productive human–AI collaboration, and adaptive organisational response to technological change.

11.2 Future Research Directions

This chapter identifies six specific avenues for future empirical investigation:

1. Longitudinal Micro-Capability Assessment Studies: Prospective longitudinal research tracking the development of specific micro-capability clusters over time within organisational settings, using validated behavioural observation instruments and experience sampling methodologies. Such studies would establish

causal rather than merely associational relationships between micro-capability development and workforce outcomes.

2. Micro-Capability Measurement Instrument Development: Psychometric research aimed at developing and validating standardised micro-capability assessment instruments across cultural and organisational contexts, enabling cross-study comparability and meta-analytic synthesis.
3. Human–AI Collaboration Micro-Capabilities: Experimental and field research specifically examining the micro-capabilities — prompt discipline, AI output calibration, human–AI role boundary awareness — that predict effective human–AI collaborative performance across different task domains and AI system types.
4. Micro-Capability Development Effectiveness: Quasi-experimental evaluation studies comparing the effectiveness of different micro-capability development modalities (microlearning, VR simulation, peer learning, AI-personalised pathways) across different workforce populations and micro-capability clusters.
5. Institutional Context Variation: Comparative cross-national research examining how institutional factors — labour market regulation, educational system design, digital infrastructure maturity, and national culture dimensions — moderate the development and expression of micro-capabilities in professional settings.
6. Micro-Capability and Organisational Resilience: Research examining the aggregate relationship between workforce micro-capability profiles and organisational-level resilience outcomes, including crisis response quality, innovation rate, and adaptability to market disruption.

As digital transformation becomes an increasingly dominant force at both industry and macroeconomic levels, organisations that invest in understanding, measuring, and systematically developing micro-capabilities will be better positioned to build workforces capable of sustained productive engagement with the technological, organisational, and social challenges that define the era of work transformation.

REFERENCES

Acemoglu, D., & Restrepo, P. (2022). Tasks, automation, and the rise in U.S. wage inequality. *Econometrica, 90*(5), 1973–2016. DOI: 10.3982/ECTA19815

Autor, D. H. (2015). Why are there still so many jobs? The history and future of workplace automation. *The Journal of Economic Perspectives, 29*(3), 3–30. DOI: 10.1257/jep.29.3.3

Bandura, A. (1986). *Social foundations of thought and action: A social cognitive theory*. Prentice-Hall.

Barley, S. R., Bechky, B. A., & Milliken, F. J. (2017). The changing nature of work: Careers, identities, and work lives in the 21st century. *Academy of Management Discoveries, 3*(2), 111–115. DOI: 10.5465/amd.2017.0034

Barney, J. (1995). Looking inside for competitive advantage. *The Academy of Management Perspectives, 9*(4), 49–61. DOI: 10.5465/ame.1995.9512032192

Barney, J., & Wright, P. M. (1998). On becoming a strategic partner: The role of human resources in gaining competitive advantage. *Human Resource Management, 37*(1), 31–46. DOI: 10.1002/(SICI)1099-050X(199821)37:1<31::AID-HRM4>3.0.CO;2-W

Bommasani, R., Hudson, D. A., Aditi, E., ... (2022). On the opportunities and risks of foundation models. arXiv preprint arXiv:2108.07258.

Boyatzis, R. E. (2008). Competencies in the 21st century. *Journal of Management Development, 27*(1), 5–12. DOI: 10.1108/02621710810840730

Brynjolfsson, E., Li, D., & Raymond, L. R. (2023). Generative AI at work. NBER Working Paper No. 31161. National Bureau of Economic Research.

Cappelli, P., & Tavis, A. (2024). The talent management revolution: Skills-first hiring and the future of work. *Harvard Business Review, 102*(1), 62–71.

Cascio, W. F., & Montealegre, R. (2016). How technology is changing work and organizations. *Annual Review of Organizational Psychology and Organizational Behavior, 3*(1), 349–375. DOI: 10.1146/annurev-orgpsych-041015-062352

Chatterjee, S., Chaudhuri, R., & Vrontis, D. (2023). Digital transformation and HR practices: Knowledge sharing via HR blog platforms. *Information Systems Frontiers, 25*(2), 723–742.

Deloitte. (2023). *2023 Global Human Capital Trends: New fundamentals for a boundaryless world*. Deloitte Insights.

Dutta, S., Mohiya, M., & Caputo, A. (2025). Leadership participation in digital knowledge platforms and employee engagement: Evidence from HR Blog systems. *Journal of Knowledge Management, 29*(1), 112–138.

Dweck, C. S. (2006). *Mindset: The new psychology of success*. Random House.

Edmondson, A. C., & Lei, Z. (2014). Psychological safety: The history, renaissance, and future of an interpersonal construct. *Annual Review of Organizational Psychology and Organizational Behavior, 1*(1), 23–43. DOI: 10.1146/annurev-orgpsych-031413-091305

Ellingrud, K., Gupta, R., Sanghvi, S., & Seong, J. (2023). *Generative AI and the future of work in America*. McKinsey Global Institute.

Eurostat. (2024). Digital economy and society statistics — households and individuals. European Commission.

Frey, C. B., & Osborne, M. A. (2017). The future of employment: How susceptible are jobs to computerisation? *Technological Forecasting and Social Change, 114*, 254–280. DOI: 10.1016/j.techfore.2016.08.019

Gartner. (2024). HR leaders' 2024 priorities: Building critical skills and competencies. Gartner Research.

Goleman, D. (1995). *Emotional intelligence: Why it can matter more than IQ*. Bantam Books.

Goleman, D. (1998). What makes a leader? *Harvard Business Review, 76*(6), 93–102. PMID: 10187249

Grant, A. M., & Parker, S. K. (2009). Redesigning work design theories: The rise of relational and proactive perspectives. *The Academy of Management Annals, 3*(1), 317–375. DOI: 10.5465/19416520903047327

Haddad, M. (2024). The paradox of leadership absence in organisational knowledge systems. *Leadership and Organization Development Journal, 45*(3), 1–18.

IBM Institute for Business Value. (2024). *The talent pivot: Skills-first workforce strategies in the age of AI*. IBM.

Illeris, K. (2011). *The fundamentals of workplace learning: Understanding how people learn in working life*. Routledge.

Jesuthasan, R., & Boudreau, J. W. (2022). *Work without jobs: How to reboot your organization's work operating system.* MIT Press. DOI: 10.7551/mitpress/13930.001.0001

Laker, D. R., & Powell, J. L. (2011). The differences between hard and soft skills and their relative impact on training transfer. *Human Resource Development Quarterly, 22*(1), 111–122. DOI: 10.1002/hrdq.20063

Maslach, C., & Leiter, M. P. (2016). Understanding the burnout experience: Recent research and its implications for psychiatry. *World Psychiatry; Official Journal of the World Psychiatric Association (WPA), 15*(2), 103–111. DOI: 10.1002/wps.20311 PMID: 27265691

McKinsey Global Institute. (2023). *The economic potential of generative AI: The next productivity frontier.* McKinsey & Company.

Microsoft. (2024). *2024 Work Trend Index Annual Report: AI at work is here. Now comes the hard part.* Microsoft.

Nag, R. (2018). Strategic HR in the digital age: Rethinking capability development. *International Journal of Human Resource Management, 29*(12), 1856–1878.

Nonaka, I., & Takeuchi, H. (1995). *The knowledge-creating company: How Japanese companies create the dynamics of innovation.* Oxford University Press. DOI: 10.1093/oso/9780195092691.001.0001

OECD. (2019). *OECD skills outlook 2019: Thriving in a digital world.* OECD Publishing.

Pfeifer, Y., Murnane, E., & Schwede, D. (2024). Cognitive load and decision fatigue in AI-augmented workplaces: Evidence from longitudinal field research. *The Journal of Applied Psychology.* Advance online publication.

PwC. (2024). *27th Annual Global CEO Survey: Thriving in an age of continuous reinvention.* PricewaterhouseCoopers.

Schwab, K. (2016). The Fourth Industrial Revolution. World Economic Forum.

Teece, D. J. (2007). Explicating dynamic capabilities: The nature and microfoundations of (sustainable) enterprise performance. *Strategic Management Journal, 28*(13), 1319–1350. DOI: 10.1002/smj.640

Tenakwah, E., & Otchere-Ankrah, B. (2024). Future of work and workforce capabilities: Navigating post-pandemic disruptions. *International Journal of Manpower, 45*(1), 45–68.

Vial, G. (2019). Understanding digital transformation: A review and a research agenda. *The Journal of Strategic Information Systems*, *28*(2), 118–144. DOI: 10.1016/j.jsis.2019.01.003

Wang, Y., Liu, H., & Zhu, Y. (2022). Knowledge sharing behaviour in digital work environments: A social exchange perspective. *Journal of Knowledge Management*, *26*(5), 1223–1245.

World Economic Forum. (2023). Future of Jobs Report 2023. WEF.

Yorke, M. (2006). *Employability in higher education: What it is, what it is not.* Higher Education Academy.

Yousaf, M., Latif, M., Aslam, S., & Saddiqui, A. (2022). Impact of digital learning tools on employee skill development: Moderating role of leadership support. *Sustainability*, *14*(8), 4567.

Chapter 4
Designing Responsible Workforces:
Leadership, Skills, and Governance in Generative AI-Driven Organizations

Aarthi Selvakumar
http://orcid.org/0009-0006-9064-2091
Marwadi University, Rajkot, India

Elena Akhunova
Tashkent State University of Economics, Tashkent, Uzbekistan

Ravikumar Natarajan
http://orcid.org/0009-0009-3705-1681
Marwadi University, Rajkot, India

Saidjanova Madinabonu
Bukhara State Medical Institute, Bukhara, Uzbekistan

Xolmirzayev Furqatbek Muxtarjonovich
Alfraganus University, Tashkent, Uzbekistan

Nazokat Panjieva
Termez University of Economics and Service, Termez, Uzbekistan

ABSTRACT

The incorporation of the Artificial Intelligence of generative type into the organizational systems changes the leadership modes, workforce capacity, and types of governance. In this chapter, the author suggests a framework of responsible workforce based on the Leadership-Skills-Governance Nexus that would guarantee the realization of sustainable and ethical AI adoption. It utilizes interdisciplinary literature and recent case studies to analyze the connection of leadership reconfiguration, augmentation of skill and governmental maturity as independent agents of trust and

DOI: 10.4018/979-8-2600-2726-4.ch004

resilience. The chapter progresses the responsibility as a design principle, which provides strategic advice to create human-centered, responsible, and sustainable generative AI-driven organizations.

1. INTRODUCTION

The rapid penetration of Generative Artificial Intelligence into organizational systems is changing the method of designing, coordinating and assessing work. Unlike the earlier automation technologies that paid more attention to the repetitive processes in the first place, Generative AI is increasingly engaged into the sphere of cognitive, inventive and decision-making processes. This transformation is not only in operations efficiency but also the field of human capital strategy, leadership design and the institutional governance. With algorithmic systems starting to be involved in recruitment, performance analytics, knowledge creation and strategic predicting, responsibility, fairness, and accountability issues become core and not just peripheral (Girdharry & Wynstra, 2025). This leaves organizations with the choice to re-think architectures of workforce that bring together technological capacity and ethical management and sustainable value-creation. To create responsible workforces, it is necessary to instill transparency, adaptability of skills, and governance mechanisms in the AI-enabled processes during their design. This chapter presents a systematic point of view that makes responsibility an organizational design option, rather than a compliance cost, and defines how leadership, skills training, and governance frameworks need to change in Generative AI-driven companies.

1.1 Generative AI and Workforce Transformation

The Generative AI technologies are changing the workforce systems by enhancing the powers of analytical reasoning, content creation, decision support, and strategic planning. Generative models can be trained on massive amounts of data, unlike the old-fashioned rule-based automation; thus, allowing human specialists and algorithm models to work together dynamically. This change influences several human capital processes, such as recruitment screening, performance appraisal, personalization of learning, and analytics of workforce. Jobs, in which human judgment was the sole factor, are facing a greater support of AI-generated insights, which results in new kind of hybrid task structures (Sposato, 2026). As a result, work boundaries are turning to be unclear, and data literacy, interpretation of AI, and ethical reasoning are becoming more popular. The change is not only productivity-enhancing, but also essentially changes the distribution of authority, workflow organization, and responsibility to make decisions. Organizations should thus re-design the concept of workforce with the aim of ensuring that augmentation is used to enhance the human capability and not to push the agency or undermine the professional responsibility.

1.2 Responsibility as a Design Principle

The organizations created by Generative AI cannot be responsible by viewing responsibility as a reactive compliance practice. Instead, it must be a part of the design principle employed behind the move towards technology adoption and workforce restructuring. This perspective regards dynamism of governance, open algorithm processes, and equitable impact assessment of AI through the lifecycle. Responsible design involves establishing the authority over who can make decisions in between human entities and algorithmic systems and creates accountability lines and can be described in automated advice. Ethical safeguards such as bias check, privacy, and cybersecurity are to be implemented during stages of operation and not implemented as after the implementation (Founder, 2025). In addition, the dedication of the leaders and organizational culture are also significant variables in enhancing the responsible use of AI. Foregrounding responsibility provides organizations with the ability to reconcile between long-term sustainability goals and expectations and technological innovation in the society. Such a design-oriented practice will improve the development of trust in the minds of the members of the staff, the integrity of the institution, and reduce the risks of uncontrollable experimentation in the Generative AI applications.

1.3 Scope and Chapter Structure

The chapter discusses the convergences of leadership change, competencies development and governance structures within the Generative AI-based organizations. It combines the interdisciplinary knowledge of human resource management, organizational behavior, information systems, and digital governance scholarship in order to develop a cohesive conceptual framework. The topic is discussed in relation to efficiency narratives and moves further to trust relations, the presence of psychological safety, ethical control, and sustainable workforce design. Theoretically, the chapter embraces conceptual modeling, consistency of literature with the research goals, and sector analyses to offer both theoretical and practical considerations. The specific focus is put on the way in which the leadership roles are redesigned under the influence of AI-enhanced environments and how organizations could design reskilling policies to facilitate human augmentation instead of technological substitution. The subsequent sections are in a logical sequence of background information to conceptual framework, empirical data, management implication and the future research that will give a full road map to responsible workforce change.

2. BACKGROUND TO THE STUDY

Artificial Intelligence incorporation in organisational systems is the automation of tasks, and the strategic decisions augmentation. The application of AI in the past years was in the predictive analytics and sorted data processing. The generation of creative content, chatbots, and real-time creation of knowledge have been however expanded to Generative AI. Such transformation contradicts the larger initiatives of digital transformation to enhance competition, responsiveness and the ability to introduce innovation (Sriharan et al., 2025). In the meantime, more and more organizations are forced to be digitally sustainable, ethically compliant, and socially responsible. It is the combination of these forces that forms the complicated environment where the technology adoption should be balanced with the discipline and development of the human resource in the form of governance. It is an environment that such a backdrop would demand accountable staffing. The subsections below are connected with the history of AI evolution in the human capital systems, placing the digital sustainability and organizational strategy on track, and the question of governance that may follow the general adoption of Generative AI.

2.1 Evolution of AI in Human Capital Systems

The introduction of AI to the human capital systems started with the recruitment filter based on data, performance analytics, and workforce planning solutions. Initial applications were aimed at enhancing efficiency and decreasing the administrative workload using predictive models and automation (Abbu et al., 2025). In the long run, machine learning systems made more advanced talent analytics such as predicting attrition, mapping skills, and individual learning suggestions possible. Generative AI has become a major breakthrough, which offers the opportunity to draft job descriptions and write performance feedback stories, create interview scenarios, and offer adaptive coaching (Ravikumar et al., 2025). These abilities change AI into a supportive analysis tool to an interactive partner in the human resource procedures. Consequently, the managerial judging and the algorithmic suggesting are becoming more and more indistinct. This development requires new control systems, interpretative abilities, and ethical protection to provide fairness and responsibility in talent management processes. Table 1 Overview The development of traditional automation to Generative AI in human capital functions.

Table 1. Evolution of AI in Workforce Systems

Phase	AI Type	Primary Application	Workforce Impact	Governance Focus
Phase 1	Rule-Based Automation	Payroll, attendance tracking	Task efficiency	Basic compliance
Phase 2	Predictive Analytics	Attrition prediction, workforce planning	Data-driven HR decisions	Data accuracy controls
Phase 3	Machine Learning Systems	Talent analytics, performance metrics	Enhanced evaluation insights	Bias monitoring
Phase 4	Generative AI	Content drafting, decision support, screening	Hybrid human–AI roles	Transparency & explainability
Phase 5	AI-Augmented Ecosystems	Strategic advisory, ESG risk detection	Cognitive augmentation	Integrated governance frameworks

2.2 Digital Sustainability and Organizational Strategy

Digital sustainability is not limited to the environmental concept, but proposes the long-term economic stability, social justice, and accountable technological regulation. Regarding Generative AI, the shift towards a more sustainable approach would be to reconcile productivity improvements that are based on innovation with the stability of workforce, inclusiveness in skills, and ethical practices. Companies that are undertaking digital transformation strategies need to ensure that AI implementation is accompanied by more sustainability goals, including fair access to opportunities, responsible data management, and less systemic bias (Hwang, 2024). Strategic alignment will be achieved by incorporating AI governance indicators into the corporate performance dashboards and embedding sustainability indicators into digital decision-making processes of investments. Moreover, the flexibility of the workforce will become a key sustainability driver, with lifelong reskilling making them employable in the face of fast-paced technological change. Through bridging Generative AI projects and sustainable value creation frameworks, the organizations will be able to avoid the short-term efficiency-seeking initiatives at the expense of long-term social and organizational sustainability.

2.3 Emerging Governance Challenges

The development of Generative AI poses complicated governance issues concerning transparency, prejudice, privacy, cybersecurity, and compliance to regulations. Algorithms may cause a lack of understanding of how decisions are made, leading to a lack of accountability in situations where AI systems are involved in hiring, promotion, or strategy. Prejudice in training databases can promote unequal results and cannot be actively addressed without notice. Also, Generative systems can demand massive data access which is of concern concerning confidentiality and cross-border data laws (Wei et al., 2025). The security weaknesses of AI become even more critical as AI systems are incorporated into enterprise infrastructure. The world is changing in terms of regulatory frameworks and this poses a compliance uncertainty to global multinational organizations. Good governance thus entails organised oversight committees, auditing systems as well as monitoring processes (Ravikumar et al., 2026). In addition to the formal controls, leadership commitment and culture of an organization play an important role in the implementation of responsible AI. These are the governance issues that need to be addressed to achieve trust and legitimacy in workforce systems based on Generative AI.

3. RESEARCH OBJECTIVES

The establishment of Generative AI into the organizational systems requires well-defined research aims that explore leadership change, workforce potential development, and governance restructuring in an orderly way. The chapter is aimed at going beyond the descriptive accounts of AI adoption, and instead set analytically based goals in line with responsible workforce engineering. On the objectives, three key pillars are aligned, namely leadership reconfiguration, skills and ability transformation, and governance and accountable results. Collectively, these dimensions compose an all-encompassing investigation of the way forward to sustainable, human-oriented, and ethically managed Generative AI ecosystems by organizations.

- To examine how leadership roles and decision rights are reconfigured in Generative AI-driven organizations, particularly in contexts where algorithmic systems influence strategic, operational, and human capital decisions.
- To analyze emerging leadership competencies required for responsible AI integration, including algorithmic literacy, ethical oversight, risk management, and change orchestration capabilities.
- To investigate workforce skill transformation patterns, focusing on reskilling, augmentation strategies, and the development of hybrid human–AI collaboration competencies.
- To evaluate governance mechanisms that ensure accountability, transparency, and bias mitigation in AI-enabled recruitment, performance management, and decision-support systems.
- To develop an integrated framework linking leadership, skills, and governance, aimed at fostering sustainable organizational performance, employee trust, and long-term digital resilience.

4. CONCEPTUAL MODEL

The theoretical framework presented in the chapter creates a systematic approach to the designing of responsible workforces in Generative AI-driven organizations. Instead of considering leadership, skills, and governance separate areas, the model brings them into one consistent architecture that describes how sustainable AI implementation could be designed in a systematic way. The structure theorizes responsibility as a natural occurrence of organizational design coherency, in which leadership guidance, the development of workforce capabilities, and controls of governance work together to reinforce each other (Ravikumar & Aarthi, 2025b). The Generative AI is not only presented as a technological solution but also as a revolutionary institutional agent that changes the powers, decision-making processes, and accountability frameworks. The model also focuses on careful design of boundaries of human-AI collaboration, investments in capabilities, and control systems. The results of this alignment are trust and digital sustainability. The conceptual model also has the advantage of offering explanatory as well as prescriptive advice to organizations aiming to become more mature than experimental AI adoptions by developing strategically managed, human-oriented AI ecosystems by stating the interdependencies between these components (Ayoub, 2026). Figure 1 is a combined Leadership-Skills-Governance model demonstrating how the structured human-AI collaboration and supervision systems result in trust, sustainability, and resilience of the organization in the Generative AI-driven businesses.

Figure 1. Responsible Generative AI Workforce Framework

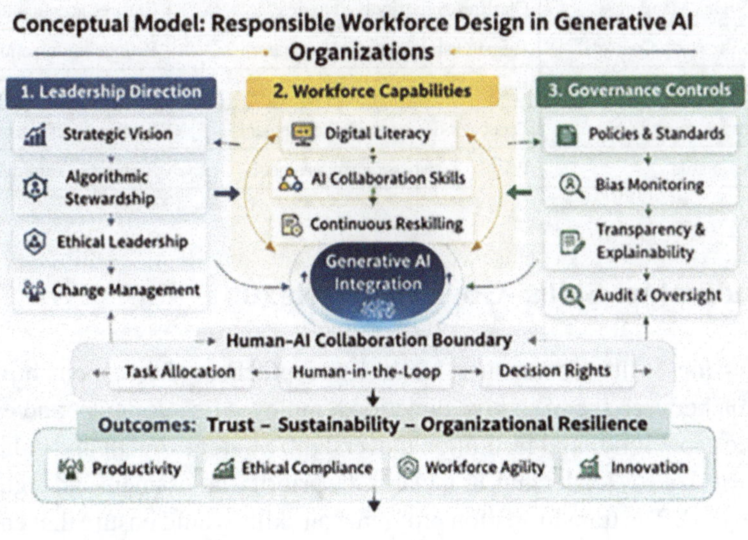

4.1 Responsible Workforce Architecture

The term responsible Workforce Architecture describes the form in which Generative AI engines, human jobs, and rules and regulations are consciously coordinated. It highlights that the workforce design should clearly state the limits of responsibility of human skills and algorithms. In this architecture, there are well defined decision rights, line of escalation and accountability checkpoints to ensure ambiguity in allocation of responsibility. Any AI-assisted workflow has human control mechanisms that guarantee the presence of professional interpretation and validation of automated outputs. In addition, the architecture makes use of the continuous learning loops that allow organizations to optimize AI implementation, depending on the performance metrics, ethical audits, and human input (Tenakwah & Watson, 2025). This system incorporates the skills development structure; ethical training modules and the governance review processes as opposed to considering them as parallel initiatives. Institutionalizing responsibility on the design level enables organizations to minimize risks of being opaque, biased, and in uncontrollable experimentation. Sustainable and ethical-oriented integration of Generative AI is therefore supported by responsible Workforce Architecture. Table 2 Review of structural aspects of responsible AI integration comprising of task assignment, supervisory levels, accountability checkpoints, and learning loops.

Table 2. Responsible Workforce Architecture Components

Component	Description	Organizational Purpose
Task Allocation Design	Defines human vs AI responsibilities	Prevents role ambiguity
Decision Rights Mapping	Clarifies authority boundaries	Ensures accountability
Human-in-the-Loop Controls	Human validation of AI outputs	Reduces automation risks
Audit & Monitoring Systems	Periodic bias and accuracy checks	Maintains fairness
Continuous Learning Loops	Feedback-driven model refinement	Sustains performance
Ethical Safeguards	Privacy & cybersecurity protocols	Protects institutional trust

4.2 Leadership–Skills–Governance Nexus

Leadership-Skills-Governance Nexus conceptualises the responsibility as an interaction between the executive direction, employee development and employee workforce capabilities and institutional oversight. Strategic intent and cultural tone are characterized by leadership, as it marks the priority, assessment and regulation of Generative AI. The transformation programs on skills would ensure that employees possess the necessary skills to understand the output of AI, and to collaborate with algorithmic systems as well as be ethical. Formal controls are implemented in the governmental systems by audit frameworks and models of compliance that regulate the use of AI (Ravikumar & Aarthi, 2025a). Nexus perspective points out that the absence of equilibrium among these dimensions can lead to a system vulnerability that an effective governance and lack of skill preparedness may result in adoption problems and a fast innovation and no control may result in ethical and operative risks. In case the presidency is determined to integrate AI in a sustainable way, employees are prepared to embrace the new technology, and there is a tight system of governance, the integration will be successful (Sharma et al., 2026). It is this three-dimensional interplay which is the theoretical basis of the conceptual model which shows that the alleged responsible consequences are not the consequence of individual action but an institutional concerted action. Table 3 Unmaps the correlation between leadership skills, labor skills and administration systems and expected outcomes to the organization.

Table 3. Leadership–Skills–Governance Nexus Framework

Dimension	Core Elements	Required Capabilities	Expected Outcomes
Leadership	Strategic oversight, AI literacy	Algorithmic stewardship	Trust & alignment
Skills	Digital fluency, prompt engineering	Augmentation readiness	Productivity gains
Governance	Audit, transparency, compliance	Risk management	Ethical sustainability
Integrated Effect	Coordinated interaction of all three	Institutional maturity	Resilient AI workforce

4.3 Trust and Sustainability Integration

Integrative outcomes of the conceptual model include trust and sustainability which are moderating variables in AI-enabled workforce systems. When the employees feel that there is transparency in the algorithmic decision making process, impartiality in the performance reviews as well as an understanding of accountability framework, trust accumulates. The issue of psychological safety is brought up because AI systems cannot be posed as augmentation, rather than surveillance. Sustainability uses this element of trust in the long term of resiliency in an organization where productivity increase does not compromise on ethical procedures, employee stability and social acceptance (Asrifan, 2025). The AI governance metrics are to be related to the environmental, social, and governance (ESG) indicators and the principles of responsible innovation must be transferred to the strategic plan in order to be sustainable. Continuous monitoring, participatory forums of governance and feedback facilitate strengthening trust and flexibility. By integrating those three aspects of leadership preparation and alignment with governance maturity, organizations can develop stable, human-centered AI ecosystems to balance innovation and accountability in a way that they can become long-term viable and have institutional credibility.

5. RESEARCH METHODOLOGY

The methodological approach of the research that will be applied to this chapter will enable to implement a rigorous and integrative examination of processes of the leadership shift, labor capability development, and governance in the Generative AI-driven organizations. As the issue of responsible workforce design has multi-dimensional character, the mixed conceptual-empirical orientation is applied. The methodological framework is a combination of theory, literature alignment, which is the systematic of the literature in line with the research objectives, and the validation of the case. By doing so, conceptual abstraction and practical rooting is brought about. It is a methodology to pay attention to the transparency, reproducibility, and analytical consistency of the development of models (European Institute of Applied Science and Management Chez Republic et al., 2025). The fact that the systematic mapping of the leadership reconfiguration, skills transformation, and results of governance that is related to the transition to the visible organizational practices is made ensures that the study not only makes the proposed conceptual framework normative but also analytically justified. The lack of the dependence on a single source of data and techniques of its verification contributes to the augmentation of credibility and reduces the interpretative bias. In developing and testing the Responsible Generative AI Workforce framework, the following subsections expound on the research design, the data collection procedures and the tools that were used in data collection and analysis.

5.1 Research Design and Approach

The research is based on the conceptual modeling and comparative cases of the structured qualitative-dominant design. The study begins with such a methodology theory-building, which is a synthesis of interdisciplinary literature on the topic of leadership, human resource management and governance and research, and digital transformation. This is a hypothetical premise to the Leadership-Skills-Governance model. This is also accompanied by a multi-case reasoning approach whereby the application of Generative AI is introduced in different organizational contexts (Sir C R Reddy College AP and Yalamarthi, 2025). The design is of the sequential movement: matching the data in the literature with the aims of the research, building up of conceptual model, and the practical proving of the recent sectoral cases. It can be generalized analytically instead of statistically and this means the findings can be applied to knowledge-intensive sectors. The research design is both interpretive and systematic with a focus on explanatory consistency and applicability. The integration of the synthesis of the theory and practical insights into the organization allows the research design to produce a holistic perspective on the responsible workforce transformation.

5.2 Data Collection and Sources

The data to be used in this study are taken through several complementary instruments in order to provide triangulation and the analytical strength. Firstly, the theoretical basis of leadership evolution, skills changes, and AI governance schemes has been found in peer-reviewed academic literature. Second, there are industry reports, regulatory guidelines, and policy documents that will provide contextual information on the new compliance and sustainability requirements. Third, there are recent organizational case studies of knowledge-intensive industries, which may be used as empirical examples of Generative AI use in workforce systems (University et al., 2025). Corporate disclosures, sustainability reports, and governance statements, which are publicly available, are analysed in order to learn about the implementation practices in real life. Having a wide range of sources enables the cross-validation of the constructs of the concept, as well as ensuring that the framework is academically rigorous and applicable to present-day organizational realities. The decision to make multidisciplinary sources will provide less bias to the sector and will make the interpretation more authoritative. Its ability to synthesize academic and practice-based evidence in the research turns the study into an overall picture of responsible AI-enabled workforce design.

5.3 Analytical and Validation Techniques

The analytical process uses the thematic synthesis and the pattern-matching. The prominent constructs of reconfiguration of leadership, skills augmentation and governance maturity are established with the help of the systematic coding of the literature and the case evidence. These themes are whipped on the conceptual framework that is taken a step further to ascertain the internal consistency and sufficient explanations. Pattern matching was used as one of the methods of comparing the theoretical expectations and the observed practices in the organisations in the selected case studies. Besides that, construct validation will be achieved by the congruence of the framework with the framework of the principles of governance, ethical AI principles, and also the criteria of online sustainability (Shi, 2025). Logical coherence and cross-source triangulation is used to ensure reliability. There is also a streamlining process of making the processes intelligible and implementable in the framework. Despite it being a qualitative approach, the analysis rigour is attained through specification of constructs and correspondence of the evidence. It is these forms of validation that will guarantee that the proposed model does not just represent the theoretically-grounded, empirically-proven, but also practically applicable in the responsible transformation of AI workforce by the Generative change.

6. LITERATURE REVIEW

Generative Artificial Intelligence and workforce transformation literature is indicative of a merging of leadership theory, human capital development, and governance scholarship. With organizations embracing the concept of AI as a fundamental part of the decision-making and knowledge processes, the necessity to designate the processes of leadership adaptation, the redesigning of capabilities, and institutional controls becomes a central topic of scholarly discussions (Akinlade et al., 2025). Instead of focusing on AI as a technological phenomenon, modern studies place it in the context of socio-technical systems in which human judgment, ethical responsibility, and strategic fit are in focus. This section summarizes the most relevant academic lines of thought, which support the aims of the chapter: AI-based leadership models, human resources and skills development, and governance, ethical, and compliance systems (Prabagar et al., 2025). These areas combined offer the theoretical framework of responsible workforce design in AI-based Generative enterprise.

6.1 AI-Enabled Leadership Models

The discipline of leadership has undergone a tremendous change following the digital change and algorithmic enrichment. Increasingly, traditional patterns of leadership founded on vertical control are complemented by adaptive and distributed ones, and data-driven ones. In AI-oriented environments, leaders will be expected to understand the output of the algorithms, manage unpredictability due to automated recommendations and make the appropriate balance between innovation and moral defense (Ravikumar and Aarthi, 2026). The literature presents how there has been emergence of algorithmic stewardship where the leaders are perceived as decoders and mediators of AI-inspired decisions as compared to recipients of the technology products. The importance of digital literacy and ethical reasoning as the primary leadership competencies is also underlined in the academic circles. To prevent over trust and to avoid delegation, leaders have to know the strengths and weaknesses of Generative AI systems. Studies also indicate that the concept of psychological safety and trust depends on the degree of openness with which leaders share their plans of integrating AI (Shreha et al., 2026). The theories of transformational and responsible leadership are often applied to the AI-related environment, with the focus on vision formulation, value alignment, and involvement in technology adoption processes being inclusive. All the literature stresses that in Generative AI settings, strategic management, interpretative skills, and ethical responsibility of leadership are crucial.

6.2 Human Capital and Skill Augmentation

The trend among human capital scholarship is to focus on the change in direction of automation-based displacement discourse to a novel augmentation-based capability development. Generative AI changes the skills requirements through the increased significance of cognitive flexibility, analytical interpretation, digital fluency, and collaborative problem-solving. Instead of removing jobs completely, studies have shown that AI tends to restructure task structure and it forms hybrid jobs where human discretion is complemented by algorithms. Skill augmentation models focus on life-long learning systems mediated by agile training systems and individualized development courses (Sreeram et al., 2025). Literature points to reskilling approaches, which equip employees with AI-enhanced work processes, such as prompt engineering, model analysis, and ethical risk analysis competencies. Moreover, researchers discuss the consequences of AI-mediation-based systems of performance evaluation, where the interpretative skills are required to put algorithmic measures in perspective. Themes of inclusive growth and employability are to be found across various sources, notably when it comes to the discussion of the equitable access to the upskilling opportunities (Deb Biswas & Sengupta, 2025). The human capital lens, thus, places Generative AI not as a productivity tool, but as something that incites a transformation of capabilities that need an investment in learning infrastructures, which are strategic.

6.3 Governance, Ethics, and Compliance Frameworks

Governance scholarship is concerned with the institutional mechanisms that are required to bring transparency, equity and accountability to the AI based organizations. As the AI systems are more actively used in the generation to find the employees, manage their performance and plan the strategy, formal structures of control are mandatory. The literature defines the pillars of governance, which include explainability standards, bias detection procedures, and data protection mechanisms, and audit mechanisms (Haque, 2025). Ethical AI models focus on active risk evaluation during the lifecycle of the system instead of the correction of risks after they have been deployed. The compliance discussions are done with the aim of aligning organizational practices with changing regulatory environments and data protection issues. Nonetheless, researchers also state that the governance will not be effective only with the legal compliance, but the cultural and leadership-based strengthening of ethical principles also. the mechanisms of enhancing trust and legitimacy are known to be participatory governance models, in which employees are part of AI oversight. Multidisciplinary studies also associate the governance maturity with the long-term organizational resilience and digital sustainability results (Sposato, 2025). On the whole, the literature in governance supports the main hypothesis that the integration of Generative AI responsibility necessitates the coordination of structural controls, the ethical commitment of leaders, and the constant monitoring processes incorporated in the system of workforce.

7. CASE STUDIES

Recent organizational implementations indicate that responsible workforce design is progressively being defined by the ways in which Generative and predictive AI have been integrated into the talent processes, knowledge work, and governance routines. The following cases were chosen to represent three complementary angles in line with the content of the chapter (i) AI-enhanced talent management, when algorithmic systems transform the workflow of early-stage hiring and assessment (ii) Generative AI in knowledge work, when copilots and assistants influence the daily productivity, knowledge access, and task coordination (iii) governance-based implementation, where AI is implemented as an oversight capacity to identify risks and reinforce accountability (Arigbabu et al., 2024). Together, all these examples demonstrate the change of experimental pilots to systematic adoption, which has advantages (speed, scale, consistency) and responsibility issues (fairness, transparency, human supervision, and trust). The cases are also presented in a similar format to aid synthesis to follow later in the section on the results, discussion and managerial implications.

7.1 AI-Augmented Talent Management Case

Case: Unilever's AI-enabled early-career hiring and screening workflow: The case of Unilever is much-discussed as one of the first large-scaled adopters of AI-assisted hiring processes, applying the digital assessment method to enhance scalability and uniformity of preliminary selection. Candidate attraction and preliminary screening processes are re-engineered in this model using digital application processes, online testing and organised evaluation phases that aim at minimising manual bottlenecks (Zambia & Bathai, 2026). The logic is the front-load standardization: earlier screening activities are moved to formal digital tools, and the human recruiters need to pay attention to the judgment, fit discussions, and final decision-making at the later stages. The benefit to workforce is observable in the form of increased administrative load reduction, increased speed of processing and more standardized candidate experience across high-volume pipelines. Nonetheless, responsibility considerations at the center of this chapter can also be found, such as the auditability of screening logic, bias in evaluation tools, candidate disclosure, and the absence of an effective course of action in situations where AI results go against human judgment (Jha, 2025). Notably, the case illustrates that effective talent management cannot be effectively facilitated by the use of tools on their own; it requires governance construction (policies, oversight, documentation) and talent preparation in recruiters to make adequate interpretation of the results. Figure 2 model of how the AI-assisted early screening can be incorporated into the human decision-making and governance control in order to create responsible, scalable, and bias-aware talent pipes.

Figure 2. AI-Augmented Talent Management Workflow Model

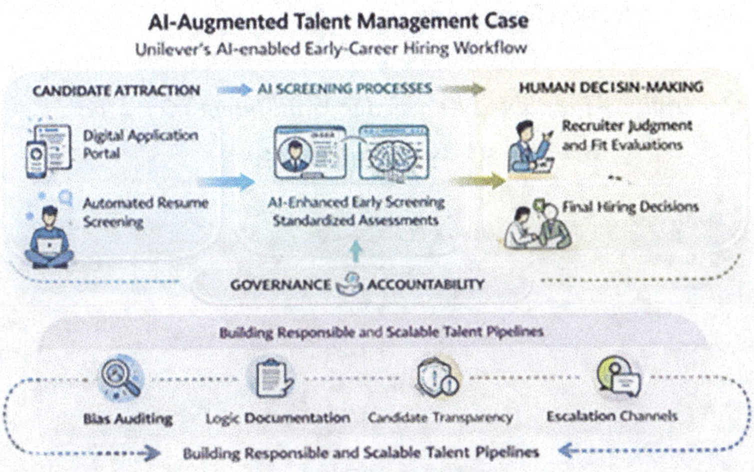

7.2 Generative AI in Knowledge Work Systems

Case: Microsoft 365 Copilot deployments in enterprise and government productivity work: Generative AI copilots are being integrated into the daily routine of knowledge work to save time in searching, summarizing, writing, and organizing documents, email, and meetings. Another big more recent case of the public sector is the cross-department experiment of Microsoft 365 Copilot by the UK government that claimed average time savings and perceived work reduction in what it termed mundane work, and more focus on higher-valued work (Tabata et al., 2025). The case is also valuable as it positions Generative AI as workflow infrastructure as opposed to an independent tool: the advantages will become evident when it is integrated with the current information systems and is able to scale up with repeated micro-tasks. Microsoft internal adoption evidence of complementary evidence of enterprise reveals that indicators of adoption in the internal rollout of Microsoft include self-reports of satisfaction and usage habits, which indicate that user experience and perceived reliability have a strong impact on the continuity of usage. The responsibility consequences are also obvious: the quality of the output usually involves human editing, the documentation practice should avoid the entry of the hallucinated or unverified content into the official workflows, and the organizations should have training norms of the safe prompting, verification, and data management (Varouchas, 2026). The results here substantially support the argument in this chapter that sustainable productivity gains require skills and maturity in governance. Figure 3 that depicts how Microsoft 365 Copilot can be used to integrate with enterprise knowledge systems to improve productivity with human verification and governance protection frameworks.

Figure 3. Generative AI–Enabled Knowledge Work Integration Model

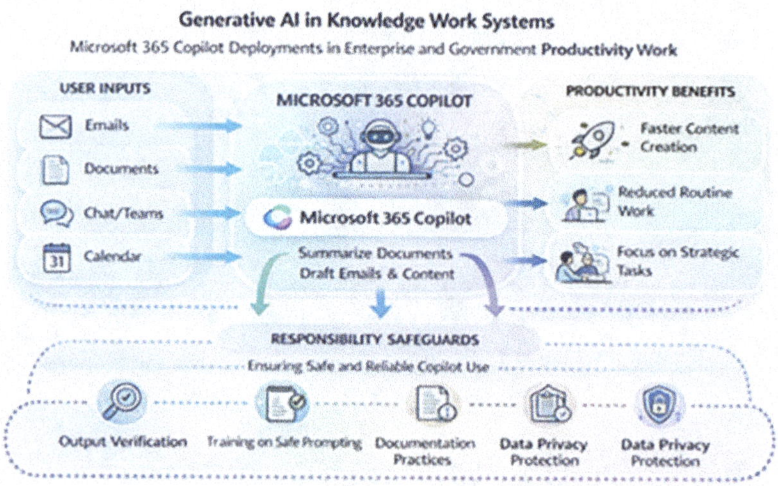

7.3 Governance-Driven AI Implementation Case

Case: Norway's sovereign wealth fund using LLMs for ESG risk screening (since 2025): This can be exemplified with Norges Bank Investment management (NBIM), management of Norway sovereign wealth fund, which has used AI (which it claimed to be large language models) to screen public data on thousands of firms based on environmental, social, and governance (ESG) risks. The provided model is established as a surveillance system which can be the early-warnings system that will inform about the problems such as fraud, corruption, and forced labour to uphold the process of risk-assessment and responsible investment. The case can be especially applicable because it operationalizes Generative AI as a control system: the more it covers monitoring, the faster it will be valued (Subramanian et al., 2024). The moral of government is that the AI may be plausible when it is embedded into the responsible process (review, documentation, escalation) and according to the goals of the institutional responsibility. Table 4 Compares the three recent cases in such aspects as the field of AI application, the leadership role, as well as the role of skills, the governance aspects controls, and the outcomes.

Table 4. Case Study Comparison Matrix

Case	AI Application	Leadership Role	Skill Impact	Governance Mechanisms	Key Outcome
AI-Augmented Talent Management	Recruitment screening	Oversight & fairness validation	Assessment interpretation skills	Bias audits & documentation	Faster standardized hiring
Generative AI in Knowledge Work	Productivity copilots	Usage norms & validation	Prompting & verification skills	Usage policies & data controls	Time savings & workflow efficiency
Governance-Driven ESG Screening	Risk detection	Strategic review & escalation	Analytical validation	Oversight committees & audit trails	Enhanced compliance monitoring

8. RESULTS AND DISCUSSION

As the studies of the chosen cases reveal, the responsible adoption of Generative AI depends not only on the level of technological sophistication but also on the alignment between the leaders and their workforce, preparation to the job, and the maturity of governance. In the talent management, knowledge work systems as well as ESG risk screening applications, efficiency and decision support improvements were measured. Nonetheless, the continued improvement of performance depended on systematic supervision, the ability to interpret, and open communication (Sætra, 2022). Through the cases it is evident that organizations with a successful implementation of AI invested both on the digital infrastructure and in leadership capabilities development and reskilling of the work force. Moreover, the mechanisms of governance acted as facilitating controls as opposed to curbing ones, enhancing the institutional trust and legitimacy. Another repeated theme in the cases is that human supervision was the main point of validation of AI results, especially regarding high stakes like hiring and investment inspection.

These results support the premise of the Leadership -Skills -Governance Nexus suggested in the conceptual model and indicate that responsible workforce design is a result of institutional alignment and not unilateral implementation of technology.

8.1 Leadership Capability Shifts

The case studies show that there is a significant change in the leadership functions being the operational supervision to the algorithmic stewardship and the interpretive oversight. The AI-enhanced talent management systems had leaders as a part of validating the screening results, fairness audits, and communication of transparency to the candidates. The leadership responsibilities were decentralized in knowledge worker systems such as Generative copilots through setting up guidelines on use, deciding on verification processes, and not over-relying on the automated results (Mikki Ewim et al., 2021). On the same note, in ESG screening software that is based on governmental decisions, leaders acted as decision integrators who placed the AI-generated risk signals in the context of larger institutional requirements. These trends indicate that the leadership skills in the AI-based organizations become more and more reliant on the digital literacy, ethical reasoning, and risk orchestration skills. Instead of handing final leadership responsibility over to automated systems, successful leaders ensured accountability and strengthened human in the loop systems. The findings affirm that the responsible use of AI should be based on the transformation of leadership to strategic management, value alignment, and institutional trust.

8.2 Workforce Skill Adaptation Patterns

In the considered cases, the process of workforce skill transformation took an augmentation-oriented and not displacement-driven course. Recruiters needed new skills in the interpretation of AI-based tests and the knowledge of the bias mitigation procedures in the context of talent management. Employees on knowledge work systems learned to be quick formulating, checking outputs and collaboratively editing AI generated drafts (Ravikumar & Aarthi, 2025c). It was shown that productivity gains were maximized by the integration of Generative copilots when users had enough contextual judgment to improve the outputs. Likewise, with governance apps, analysts had to possess interpretive skills to confirm AI-identified ESG risks and do follow-up research. These results show that Generative AI raises the need of more complex cognitive functions, such as the critical assessment, the moral judgment, and the digital literacy (Chuang et al., 2024). Life-long learning processes and regulated reskilling programs turned out to be crucial facilitators of effective adjustment. Development of human expertise thus augments the efficiency of algorithms as workforce transformation can be defined as a hybrid form of development.

8.3 Governance Maturity and Trust Dynamics

The maturity of governance turned out to be a determining factor of trust and continued adoption of AI in cases. Companies that incorporated audit systems, transparency policies and human checks and balances enjoyed greater legitimacy and confidence of stakeholders. Hiring systems based on AI fostered trust in the form of uniform assessment standards and fairness reviews. There has been a decrease of risks of misinformation or misuse of data in Generative knowledge tools, due to clear guidelines in verification and responsible usage. The examples of governance-driven ESG screening also showed how AI may be used to increase institutional accountability when applied to formal reviews. Notably, it was not only compliance structures which governed the organization, but also, leadership communication and cultural reinforcement of ethical standards (Westover, 2024). Reliability was created when the employees viewed AI as an augmentation tool and not a surveillance mechanism. The results confirm that the governance maturity is the direct determinant of the acceptance, psychological safety, and long-term sustainability in the Generative AI-enabled workforce systems. Table 5 Determines the level of governance (basic or advanced) and the level of trust, transparency and accountability in AI-enabled organizations.

Table 5. Governance Maturity and Trust Indicators

Maturity Level	Governance Features	Employee Perception	Organizational Outcome
Basic	Ad hoc policies	Uncertainty	Limited trust
Developing	Defined usage guidelines	Moderate confidence	Controlled experimentation
Structured	Formal audits & bias checks	Increased transparency	Stable AI adoption
Advanced	Integrated governance dashboards	High psychological safety	Sustainable innovation

9. FUTURE RESEARCH

There are several ways in which future research could be conducted concerning the relationship between Generative AI and organizational systems as a result of their fast adoption. Although existing data puts more emphasis on the efficiency improvement and changing governance practices, their long-term structural and behavioral impact is not well understood. The next wave of research should not be on short-term productivity measures but look at how the long-term human-AI partnership will redefine the power structures, identity, skill patterns, and corporate confidence. Integration of the three aspects of leadership adaptation, workforce augmentation, and governance maturity needs more empirical validation across sectors and geographies (Hindustan College of Arts & Science, 2025). Besides, regulatory change and cross-cultural variations of technology acceptance add the complexity that requires comparative research. As Generative AI systems increasingly become a part of high-stakes decision making, interdisciplinary research models will be invaluable to incorporate knowledge in organizational research, information systems, labor economics, ethics and public policy. The pursuit of this research agenda will enhance the rigor in the theoretical understanding and offer evidence-based recommendations in the processes of creating resilient and human-focused AI-driven workforce systems within the coming decade.

9.1 Human–AI Collaboration Models

The way forward in future research is to explore systematically structured human-AI collaborative architectures instead of considering AI as a marginal support tool. There is a need to determine optimal limits of task allocation between algorithmic systems and human experience across the levels of decision intensity through empirical research. Performance, trust and cognitive load differences might be compared on the basis of fully automated, human-only, and hybrid collaboration models by comparative experimental designs (Chaudhary et al., 2025). The role redefinition processes should also be studied, especially how the processes of negotiating authority and responsibility are undertaken in AI-saturated settings. Moreover, the investigation of psychological safety, professional identity, and perceived fairness of the hybrid teams will contribute to the knowledge of sustainable integration (Rathinavel et al., 2025). The evolution of collaborative workflow in time and uncertainty can be studied using simulation-based and field-based studies. Formalizing patterns of human to AI interaction will be an addition to the theoretical consolidation and practical implementation guidelines of responsible workforce design. Figure 4 model of fully automated, hybrid and human-only decision models with emphasis on the boundaries of duty of tasks, distribution of accountability, and the dynamics of trust in AI-enhanced organizations.

Figure 4. Structured Human–AI Collaboration Architecture

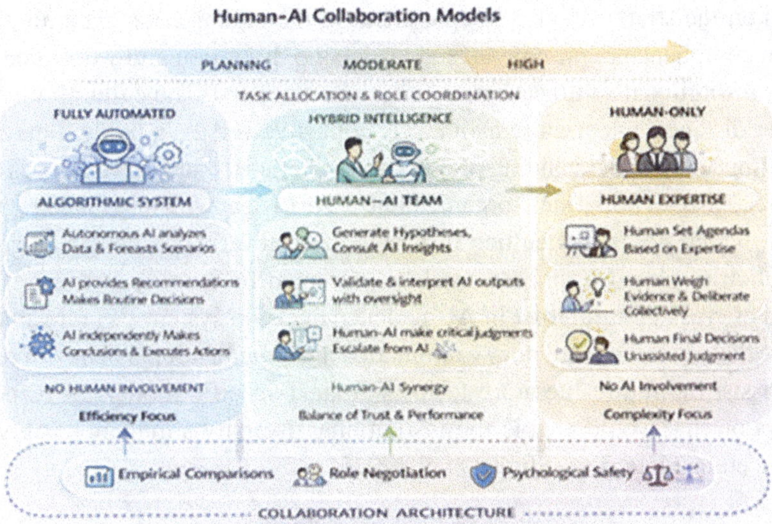

9.2 Longitudinal Workforce Impact Studies

The benefits of Generative AI on workforce and organize the resilience of organizations require longitudinal research to determine its long-term impact. The efficiency measure in short term offers little information on long term obsolescence in skills, changes in career progression or changes in competency needs. Future research needs to monitor skills acquisition, job redesign, and workforce flexibility in the long periods of time. Quantitative panel data and qualitative workforce stories can be used to shed light on the impact of AI augmentation on wage structures, performance evaluation standards and internal mobility channels (Mola, 2025). Possible impacts of inequality should also be the focus of research, specifically, the question of whether AI-enabled systems enhance or reduce differences in promotion rates. Additional evaluative dimensions may be delivered by the organizational resilience metrics such as the turnover stability and capability renewal rates. The longitudinal evidence will allow the policy-makers and executives to draw a line between the short-term productivity improvements and permanent structural change in AI-based businesses.

9.3 Regulatory and Cross-Cultural Perspectives

The governance of Generative AI is being influenced by the changes in regulatory systems and cultural perceptions of responsibility, privacy, and equity. Comparative cross-national research is needed to understand the effect of the varying regulatory regimes on the strategies of AI deployment in the organization. The relationship between compliance requirements and leadership discretion and workforce acceptance in institutional settings should be also investigated. The cultural dimensions of power distance, uncertainty avoidance, collective versus individual may have a serious impact on understanding of algorithmic authority and surveillance (Gray et al., 2022). Also, multinational organizations have to deal with disjointed regulatory settings, which poses difficulties in harmonized governance design. Significant information to global businesses will be presented by empirical research on the creation of cross-cultural trust in AI-mediated decision systems. Future studies on the topic that combine regulatory examination and organizational behavior research would assist the future literature to form context-specific models of responsible AI adoption that would enable the institutional diversity simultaneously without affecting ethical integrity (Shreha et al., 2025).

10. MANAGERIAL IMPLICATIONS

The conclusions drawn in the conceptual analysis, as well as the case studies, provide accurate solutions to the managers, interested in introducing Generative AI in the system of work force in a responsible way. Sustainable values do not come about because of the high rate of deployment but rather a deliberate corporate effort in alignment both in terms of leadership will, staff competence and the government structure. The trial stage should not be the last step of managers, and that is, they must instantiate AI, i.e., the implementation of AI in the company must be administratively managed, the ethics driven by theory, and competence. The data shows that the maximum effect on productivity is achieved when the introduction of AI is supported by open communication, well-defined accountability channels, and lifelong development of capabilities (Skubis, 2025). Furthermore, trust and psychological safety become strategic resources instead of being soft factors, and have a direct impact on the stability of adoption and the final results of performance. The workforce design needs to be undertaken responsibly entails action coordination in policy formulation, reskilling investment, and cultural reinforcement. In the subsections below, the strategies to be used in the design of responsible AI policies, structured reskilling models, and the introduction of governance principles into organizational culture are described in a practical way. Table 6 gives some practical suggestions that are divided into policy design, reskilling strategy and cultural governance integration.

Table 6. Managerial Action Framework for Responsible AI Adoption

Strategic Area	Managerial Action	Implementation Tool	Expected Benefit
Policy Design	Define AI accountability rules	AI governance charter	Reduced compliance risk
Skill Development	Implement structured reskilling	Digital learning platforms	Workforce adaptability
Cultural Integration	Promote ethical AI norms	Leadership communication	Strengthened trust
Monitoring	Establish AI audit committees	Periodic review systems	Risk mitigation
Sustainability Alignment	Link AI metrics with ESG goals	Governance dashboards	Long-term resilience

10.1 Designing Responsible AI Policies

Managers should formalize the responsible AI policies by defining the limits of use, accountability framework and monitoring systems. Policies must define rights in decision-making between people and AI software, especially in the areas of high impact, such as human resources, performance appraisal, and strategic planning. The transparency standards should be such that they document the purpose of a model, the sources of data, the process of model validation, and the risk evaluation. The detection of bias measures and systematic reviews are to be institutionalized to avoid unforeseen injustices (Valle-Cruz & García-Contreras, 2025). Also, the privacy and cybersecurity controls should be incorporated into enterprise AI plans in order to safeguard confidential workforce information. Responsible AI policies are not supposed to be just compliance papers but they should be working instructions to be integrated into the working processes. Communication through leadership is very important in strengthening the intent of policy and definition of expectations. Through the development of organized governing principles, managers will be able to decrease uncertainty, enhance institutional authenticity, and sustain uniform decision-making throughout the AI-enablment processes.

10.2 Strategic Reskilling Frameworks

A successful use of Generative AI entails a planned process of transformation of workforce capabilities. The managers are to develop reskilling systems that focus on augmentation over displacement that would train employees to work effectively with AI systems. The areas of core competency involve digital literacy, interpretation of AI, timely formulation, critical assessment of outputs, and awareness of ethical risks. Combinations of formal training, peer learning and real-world application in structured learning paths make it possible to build the capability gradually. Adaptive skill development can be facilitated with the help of personalized learning platforms according to the changing job roles (Rambhau Patil, 2024). Competency mapping exercises should also be adopted by the managers so as to determine the new hybrid roles and foresee the skills required in the future. The ongoing feedback systems enable the organizations to improve the training programs according to the results of the performance and the experience of the employees. Through embedding reskilling as a strategic focus, companies can increase adaptability and keep themselves employable and enhance a culture of lifelong learning in AI-enhanced settings. The proposed approach to ensuring sustained human-AI workforce augmentation is to engage in competency development, adaptive learning pathways, and sustain continuous skill mapping as shown in figure 5.

Figure 5. Strategic Reskilling and Capability Transformation Framework

10.3 Embedding Governance in Culture

The integration of AI has to be sustainable that is related not to the formal controls only but also to the cultural support of the ethical standards and the accountability norms. Managers have to develop a culture of transparency, justice, and humanity being actively appreciated in the processes between AI and humans. The open communication channels must facilitate asking, verifying, and reporting of algorithmic output concerns by the employees without fear of punishment. Leadership behavior can create a positive example and highlight the use of AI responsibly and the importance of validation of human-in-the-loop (Nithya et al., 2026). The structured cross-functional discussion of the risks and improvements of AI can be offered in governance forums or review committees. Incorporating governance in performance measurement and other leadership assessment systems further entrench accountability. Trust is enhanced and resistance is reduced when the governance principles are incorporated into the daily organizational practices instead of being a single compliance operation. Cultural integration hence changes governance as a defensive precaution to an active facilitator of responsible innovations.

11. CONCLUSION

Implementation of Generative Artificial Intelligence in organisational systems is a structural change in the design of leadership, workforce capabilities architecture and maturity of governance. This chapter has developed a responsible workforce view that makes leadership, skills and governance dependent pillars of Generative AI based business. The theoretical value of the article is in defining the Leadership-Skills-Governance Nexus as a systemic approach to the responsible consequences of communication between institutions as systems where institutional consistency is created, not by means of the individual acquisition of technology. The focus on responsibility as a design principle, which is integrated into workforce architecture, does not limit itself to compliance-based stories and adds to the socio-technical theory in digital transformation situations. In practice, it has been demonstrated in the case-based analysis that sustainable performance gains can be attained through a change in the leadership capability to a more algorithmic stewardship, strategic reskilling investment, which is first and foremost an augmentation focused, and governance systems which reinforce transparency, accountability, and reduction of bias. Strategic results which were identified included trust and psychological safety which are driven by the maturity in governance and leadership communication. The findings also demonstrate that maintaining learning, participatory management and systematic policy structures ought to be incorporated within organizations in order to make certain that innovation does not prevail as ethical controls. The AI organization path, according to which there is a concertation between the technological ambition and human values and long-term expectations of the society, is the direction of its organization towards sustainability. Carefully introduced into the structure of effective leadership, the training of capabilities and rigor of governance, Generative AI may establish the resilience, raise productivity and inclusive growth. However, unless controlled and supplemented by the abundance of culture, the same technologies may bring about the loss of accountability and stability in the workforce. The challenge of developing responsible workforces is, therefore, emerging as a strategic requirement of organisations that desire to be long-term legitimized and long-term value-creating in the evolving AI-driven economy.

REFERENCES

Abbu, H., Khan, S., Mugge, P., & Gudergan, G. (2025). Building digital-ready leaders: Development and validation of the human-centric Digital Leadership Scale. *Digital*, *5*(1), 7. DOI: 10.3390/digital5010007

Akinlade, I., Balakumar, G. B., Narayan, S., Badami, S., Madineni, U. K., Mittal, T., & Aludogbu, P. (2025). Investigating executive leadership responses to AI-induced structural change in multinational corporations-2025. *International Journal of Science and Research Archive*, *17*(3), 196–207. DOI: 10.30574/ijsra.2025.17.3.3196

Arigbabu, A. T., Olaniyi, O. O., Adigwe, C. S., Adebiyi, O. O., & Ajayi, S. A. (2024). Data governance in AI - enabled healthcare systems: A case of the Project Nightingale. *Asian Journal of Research in Computer Science*, *17*(5), 85–107. DOI: 10.9734/ajrcos/2024/v17i5441

Asrifan, A. (2025). Building trust in AI-driven organizations. In *Moral and Legal Aspects of Artificial Intelligence* (pp. 195–228). IGI Global Scientific Publishing., DOI: 10.4018/979-8-3373-3114-0.ch006

Ayoub, A. (2026). The Architecture of Intelligent Governance (AIG): A conceptual framework for integration AI, quantum computing, and global resource resilience. *Sustainability (Basel)*, *18*(5), 2312. DOI: 10.3390/su18052312

Chaudhary, N. S., Banerjee, R., Mathur, G., Sachdeva, L., & Amoozegar, A. (2025). AI and the future of talent management. In *Advances in Computational Intelligence and Robotics* (pp. 297–316). IGI Global Scientific Publishing. DOI: 10.4018/979-8-3373-1270-5.ch017

Chuang, S., Shahhosseini, M., Javaid, M., & Wang, G. G. (2024). Machine learning and AI technology-induced skill gaps and opportunities for continuous development of middle-skilled employees. *Journal of Work-Applied Management*. Advance online publication. DOI: 10.1108/JWAM-08-2024-0111

Deb Biswas, D., & Sengupta, R. (2025). Reimagining leadership for the AI era: A grounded theory of adaptive, ethical and contextually situated practices in workplaces. *Leadership and Organization Development Journal*, •••, 1–22. DOI: 10.1108/LODJ-06-2025-0488

European Institute of Applied Science and Management Chez Republic, P., Upreti, P. K., Gangwar, N., & European Institute of Applied Science and Management Chez Republic, P. (2025). Artificial Intelligence and leadership effectiveness: Empirical evidence from multinational corporations in Uganda. *RA Journal of Applied Research, 11*(05). DOI: 10.47191/rajar/v11i5.10

Founder of Filmy AI and Startup Consultant Lubin School of Business Pace University New York USA, T. L. and M. C., & Dedhia, P. (2025). Transformational leadership in the age of AI-driven tech: Inspiring with vision in no code generation. *INTERNATIONAL JOURNAL OF SCIENTIFIC RESEARCH IN ENGINEERING AND MANAGEMENT, 09*(06), 1–9. DOI: 10.55041/IJSREM50924

Girdharry, K., & Wynstra, B. (2025). Distributed AI leadership: The Generator as a model for faculty-led innovation. *Journal of Leadership Studies, 19*(2), e70013. Advance online publication. DOI: 10.1002/jls.70013

Gray, K., Slavotinek, J., Dimaguila, G. L., & Choo, D. (2022). Artificial intelligence education for the health workforce: Expert survey of approaches and needs. *JMIR Medical Education, 8*(2), e35223. DOI: 10.2196/35223 PMID: 35249885

Haque, A. (2025). Responsible artificial intelligence (AI) in healthcare: A paradigm shift in leadership and strategic management. *Leadership in Health Services (Bradford, England), 38*(4), 644–656. DOI: 10.1108/LHS-01-2025-0018 PMID: 40911384

Hindustan College of Arts & Science Tamil Nadu. C., & Sundaram, S. (2025). Innovating for the future: Sustainable corporate strategies for workforce upskilling and reskilling. *International Journal of Research in Entrepreneurship & Business Studies, 6*(3), 33–46. DOI: 10.47259/ijrebs.2025.633

Hwang, J. (2024). Exploring the impact of AI on leadership styles: A comparative study of human-driven vs. AI-assisted decision-making in high-stakes environments. *International Journal of Science and Research Archive, 13*(1), 3436–3446. DOI: 10.30574/ijsra.2024.13.1.2030

Jha, A. (2025). AI-augmented project management: The rise of the Intelligent Project Manager and the intelligent PMO. *Journal of Advances in Developmental Research, 16*(2), 1616. Advance online publication. DOI: 10.71097/IJAIDR.v16.i2.1616

Mikki Ewim, C. P., Omokhoa, H. E., Ogundeji, I. A., & Ibeh, A. I. (2021). Future of work in banking: Adapting workforce skills to digital transformation challenges. *International Journal of Multidisciplinary Research and Growth Evaluation, 2*(1), 663–676. DOI: 10.54660/.IJMRGE.2021.2.1.663-676

Mola, R. (2025). Strategic alignment of Workday talent & performance modules with organizational leadership competencies. *International Journal Management and Organizational Research, 4*(5), 123–127. DOI: 10.54660/IJMOR.2025.4.5.123-127

Nithya, B., Krishnan, K., Chachithanantham, A., & Ravikumar, S. (2026). Optimizing digital talent management with AI: Analytical approaches and innovations. In *Artificial Intelligence for Digital Talent Acquisition and Management* (pp. 23–53). Emerald Publishing Limited., DOI: 10.1108/978-1-83708-884-320251002

Prabagar, S., Mothkur, R., Swetha, C. B., Kurian, A., Pavithra, K., & Aarthi, S. (2025). Generative AI for inclusive special education. In *Advances in Computational Intelligence and Robotics* (pp. 205–236). IGI Global Scientific Publishing. DOI: 10.4018/979-8-3373-3745-6.ch008

Rambhau Patil, L. (2024). AI IN WORKFORCE PLANNING AND PERFORMANCE MANAGEMENT. In *AI-Powered HR Finance: Transforming Workforce Management and Financial Strategies in the Digital Age* (pp. 128–137). Iterative International Publishers, Selfypage Developers Pvt Ltd. DOI: 10.58532/nbennurptch12

Rathinavel, P., Ravikumar, R. N., Aarthi, S., Habib, M., Salaeva, N., & Pardaev, J. (2025). Augmenting human capabilities. In *Advances in Computational Intelligence and Robotics* (pp. 1–30). IGI Global Scientific Publishing. DOI: 10.4018/979-8-3373-2372-5.ch001

Ravikumar, R. N., & Aarthi, S. (2025b). Human-AI synergy for organizational resilience. In *Advances in Computational Intelligence and Robotics* (pp. 287–322). IGI Global Scientific Publishing. DOI: 10.4018/979-8-3373-7416-1.ch011

Ravikumar, R. N., & Aarthi, S. (2025c). Towards collaborative intelligence. In *Advances in Computational Intelligence and Robotics* (pp. 1–32). IGI Global Scientific Publishing. DOI: 10.4018/979-8-3373-5747-8.ch001

Ravikumar, R. N., Aarthi, S., & Mamadiyarov, Z. (2026). Building the foundations of augmented organizations through AI empowerment. In *Advances in Computational Intelligence and Robotics* (pp. 101–130). IGI Global Scientific Publishing. DOI: 10.4018/979-8-3373-8607-2.ch006

Ravikumar, R. N., Aarthi, S., Rai, P. K., & Mamadiyarov, Z. (2025). Intelligent code analysis and feedback generation. In *Advances in Computational Intelligence and Robotics* (pp. 137–170). IGI Global Scientific Publishing. DOI: 10.4018/979-8-3373-0598-1.ch006

Ravikumar, & Aarthi, S. (2025a). Cognitive collaboration. In *Advances in Computational Intelligence and Robotics* (pp. 125–158). IGI Global Scientific Publishing. DOI: 10.4018/979-8-3373-7416-1.ch006

Ravikumar, & Aarthi, S. (2026). Synergizing innovation. In *Advances in Computational Intelligence and Robotics* (pp. 59–90). IGI Global Scientific Publishing. DOI: 10.4018/979-8-3373-7620-2.ch003

Sætra, H. S. (2022). The AI ESG protocol: Evaluating and disclosing the environment, social, and governance implications of artificial intelligence capabilities, assets, and activities. *Sustainable Development (Bradford)*. Advance online publication. DOI: 10.1002/sd.2438

Sharma, P., Hussain, S. S., & Gwal, R. (2026). Harmonizing intelligence: AI integration, workforce development, and ethical governance for future of work. In *Human 2.0* (pp. 143–162). Emerald Publishing Limited., DOI: 10.1108/978-1-83708-166-020251008

Shi, L. (2025). Global perspectives on AI competence development: Analyzing national AI strategies in education and workforce policies. *Human Resource Development Review*, *24*(4), 447–476. DOI: 10.1177/15344843251332360

Shreha, S. A., Ravikumar, R. N., & Aarthi, S. (2025). Neuro-symbolic AI and Behavioral Intelligence. In *Advances in Computational Intelligence and Robotics* (pp. 121–152). IGI Global Scientific Publishing. DOI: 10.4018/979-8-3373-5012-7.ch005

Shreha, S. A., Ravikumar, R. N., & Aarthi, S. (2026). Precision medicine, genomics, and health equity challenges and opportunities. In *Advancing Equity in Global Healthcare Systems* (pp. 321–354). IGI Global Scientific Publishing., DOI: 10.4018/979-8-3373-1330-6.ch012

Sir C R Reddy College AP, E., & Yalamarthi, V. R. S. B. (2025). Artificial Intelligence in recruitment: Transforming talent acquisition practices. *International Journal of Innovations & Research Analysis, 05*(03(II)), 01–11. DOI: 10.62823/IJIRA/5.3(II).7946

Skubis, I. (2025). Humanoid robots CEOs and leaders in project management: Decision-making, human oversight, team dynamics and ethics. *International Journal of HR; Humanoid Robotics*, *22*(06), 2550008. Advance online publication. DOI: 10.1142/S0219843625500082

Sposato, M. (2025). Synthetic ethics: posthuman leadership in algorithmically governed organizations. *Journal of Information Communication and Ethics in Society*, 1–16. DOI: 10.1108/JICES-05-2025-0096

Sposato, M. (2026). Leading hybrid intelligence systems: A general systems theory approach to organizational leadership in hybrid intelligence knowledge ecosystems. *VINE Journal of Information and Knowledge Management Systems*, •••, 1–22. DOI: 10.1108/VJIKMS-06-2025-0220

Sreeram, A., Mehra, R., Parashar, K., Rao, B. U., Mohapatra, C. K., Jabbar, M. A., & Malagi, V. (2025). Ethical Leadership in managing AI-integrated library environments. *Indian Journal of Information Sources and Services*, *15*(3), 131–139. DOI: 10.51983/ijiss-2025.IJISS.15.3.15

Sriharan, A., Kuhlmann, E., Correia, T., Tahzib, F., Czabanowska, K., Ungureanu, M.-I., & Kumar, B. N. (2025). Artificial Intelligence in healthcare: Balancing technological innovation with health and care workforce priorities. *The International Journal of Health Planning and Management*, *40*(4), 987–992. DOI: 10.1002/hpm.3927 PMID: 40075189

Subramanian, Y. R., Riya, R., & Rajendran, R. (2024). Revolutionizing workforce education. In *Integrating Generative AI in Education to Achieve Sustainable Development Goals* (pp. 282–299). IGI Global., DOI: 10.4018/979-8-3693-2440-0.ch015

Tabata, M., Wildermuth, C., Bottomley, K., & Jenkins, D. (2025). Generative AI integration in leadership practice: Foundations, challenges, and opportunities. *Journal of Leadership Studies*, *18*(4), 41–54. DOI: 10.1002/jls.70005

Tenakwah, E. S., & Watson, C. (2025). Embracing the AI/automation age: Preparing your workforce for humans and machines working together. *Strategy and Leadership*, *53*(1), 32–48. DOI: 10.1108/SL-05-2024-0040

University, W. G., Khair, M. A., Shaheen, N., University, W. G., Khair, M. M., University, W. G., Jain, S., & University, M. A. H. G. (2025). HCM AI agents and data-driven decision making. *International Journal of Research in Modern Engineering & Emerging Technology*, *13*(3), 36–54. DOI: 10.63345/ijrmeet.org.v13.i3.3

Valle-Cruz, D., & García-Contreras, R. (2025). Towards AI-driven transformation and smart data management: Emerging technological change in the public sector value chain. *Public Policy and Administration*, *40*(2), 254–275. DOI: 10.1177/09520767231188401

Varouchas, E. (2026). Executives' perspectives on the impact of generative AI in business: a qualitative study of strategic, ethical and organizational transformations. *Journal of Science and Technology Policy Management*, 1–34. DOI: 10.1108/JSTPM-10-2025-0493

Wei, H., Trepanier, S., Wei, T., Marshall, D., Wiley, R. D., & D'Agostino, D. (2025). The philosophy of Artificial Intelligence in healthcare: Facilitating a human-centered paradigm to optimize healthcare outcomes. *Forum Gestion Des Soins de Sante [Healthcare Management Forum]*, (08404704251394950), 8404704251394950. DOI: 10.1177/08404704251394950

Westover, J. (2024). Preparing the workforce for ethical, responsible and trustworthy AI. *Human Capital Leadership Review, 13*(4). Advance online publication. DOI: 10.70175/hclreview.2020.13.4.7

Zambia, U. (2026). Re-engineering the Botswana civil service with human-AI augmentation: A grounded theory of organizational transformation for a Fourth Industrial Revolution-ready public sector. *International Review of Social Sciences Research, 6*(1), 87–106. DOI: 10.53378/irssr.353309

KEY TERMS AND DEFINITIONS

AI Governance: – Policies, controls, and oversight mechanisms that regulate how AI systems are developed and used.

Algorithmic Stewardship: – The leadership responsibility of monitoring, interpreting, and validating AI-generated outputs.

Bias Mitigation: – Processes designed to detect and reduce unfair or discriminatory outcomes in AI systems.

Digital Sustainability: – Ensuring long-term economic, social, and ethical stability while adopting digital technologies.

Explainability: – The ability to understand and interpret how an AI system reaches its outputs.

Generative AI: – Artificial Intelligence systems that create new content such as text, images, code, or insights based on learned data patterns.

Human–AI Collaboration: – A hybrid work model where humans and AI systems jointly perform tasks and make decisions.

Human-in-the-Loop: – A governance model where human oversight remains part of AI-supported decision processes.

Leadership–Skills–Governance Nexus: – A framework explaining how leadership direction, workforce capabilities, and governance systems interact to enable responsible AI adoption.

Psychological Safety: – A work environment where employees feel safe to question or challenge AI-driven decisions.

Reskilling Framework: – A structured plan to help employees develop new competencies required in AI-enabled environments.

Responsible Workforce Design: – A structured approach to integrating AI into organizations while ensuring fairness, accountability, and human oversight.

Skill Augmentation: – Enhancing human capabilities through AI support rather than replacing human roles.

Trust in AI Systems: – Employee and stakeholder confidence in the fairness, reliability, and transparency of AI tools.

Chapter 5
The Symbiotic Intelligence Paradigm

Eesh Batheja
http://orcid.org/0009-0007-5807-1951
Christ University, Delhi NCR, India

Deeksha Gupta Ganguly
http://orcid.org/0000-0002-5502-8276
Christ University, Bengaluru, India

ABSTRACT

Introduction & Rationale (Why this chapter is needed) The present-day world has reached a point where intelligence exists as a combination of human and artificial intelligence. The new form of intelligence emerges through continuous human-machine cooperation between human brainwork and artificial intelligence technology. The introduction of generative AI technologies and adaptive analytics solutions and automation systems and cognitive computing systems leads to a transformation in the cognitive processes and decision-making methods and operational practices of people and organizations and educational institutions. AI now functions as a fundamental element that organizations need to create sustainable competitive advantages which businesses and healthcare systems and governmental bodies and educational institutions depend on. The current discussions about AI still treat it as a technology that replaces humans while improving efficiency despite the fact that digital technologies have become common in all areas of society.

DOI: 10.4018/979-8-2600-2726-4.ch005

1. INTRODUCTION

The twenty-first century is witnessing a profound transformation in the nature of intelligence, work, and decision-making. The current technological wave differs from earlier industrial revolutions because it transforms cognitive processes instead of just mechanizing physical labour tasks. Artificial Intelligence (AI) systems have evolved beyond their initial capabilities to perform repetitive computational tasks because they can now create written content and compose music and accurately diagnose medical conditions and forecast financial market trends and support scientific research efforts and shape political decision-making processes. This shift has prompted a fundamental reconsideration of what intelligence means and how it operates within human societies (Jordan, 2018; Russell, 2019).

OpenAI Google Microsoft and IBM have integrated AI into their search engines and enterprise software and healthcare analytics and cloud infrastructures and generative platforms. The systems establish procedures which determine how knowledge is produced and communication takes place and economic value is generated and public policy decisions are made. AI evolved from a secondary technological instrument to become a fundamental structural element of contemporary society (McKinsey & Company, 2023; Stanford University, 2023).

The AI technology advance has produced two opposing effects. People generally consider AI to be either an employment threat which takes away human control or a groundbreaking technology which solves problems related to inefficiency and mistakes. The emerging socio-technical systems create a complex situation which requires more than the basic human versus machine narrative. The highest performance and reliability in real-world applications happens when humans (IBM, 2018; Shneiderman, 2022) and AI systems work together as partners instead of competing with each other.

The Symbiotic Intelligence Paradigm serves as a conceptual framework which develops through the ongoing shifts in the contemporary environment. The paradigm disproves the belief that artificial systems will completely take over human cognitive functions. The future of intelligence will develop through organized partnerships which combine human judgment and creativity with algorithmic systems that operate at high speed and predictive accuracy and vast data processing capabilities.

The definition of symbiotic intelligence extends beyond simple enhancement because it involves the process through which two systems develop together. Humans create AI systems by establishing their training methods and training processes and determining their operational objectives. AI systems operate as mind control devices which determine how people think and make decisions and produce creative work and manage their work activities. The mutual connection between the two agents establishes a continuous process which leads both agents to modify their behavior.

Human cognitive functions and technological assistance begin to blend with each passing moment.

The importance of this paradigm becomes evident when examining contemporary professional environments. AI systems in healthcare examine imaging data with high statistical accuracy while doctors interpret results and communicate with patients and maintain ethical standards. Machine learning models in finance predict risk probabilities but humans must make final strategic choices. Adaptive learning platforms in education deliver personalized content while teachers help students develop motivation and social skills and critical thinking abilities. Systems of modern intelligence function based on shared human and artificial intelligence abilities.

The Symbiotic Intelligence Paradigm therefore introduces a shift from automation-centered thinking to collaboration-centered design. Automation achieves its goal of efficiency through process substitution. Symbiosis achieves its goal of excellence through the use of complementary resources. Automation requires machines to operate without any human assistance. Symbiosis requires human and artificial agents to develop the ability to work together.

The distinction between two modes of operation produces different outcomes which affect society. The institutions which base their AI development solely on automation principles will face a decline in human abilities and a loss of responsibility and an upsurge of systemic biases throughout their operations. AI systems which undergo development through symbiotic design will empower humans while making knowledge accessible to all people and reducing mental burden and fostering innovation that includes all people.

The emergence of generative AI technologies has created a current need for the paradigm. The ability of systems to produce human-like text and images and simulations creates a situation which eliminates the separation between human creativity and machine-generated content. The systems provide substantial productivity benefits yet they create problems about who owns intellectual property and the danger of spreading false information and who bears ethical obligations. The Symbiotic Intelligence Paradigm resolves these issues by demonstrating that people must interpret and validate generative outputs (OpenAI, 2023; Floridi & Cowls, 2019). while establishing their moral framework.

Symbiotic intelligence challenges the fundamental belief that people possess qualities which make them distinct from all other beings. Throughout history people have considered intelligence to be the defining human characteristic. The development of systems which can replicate human cognitive abilities has made society need to reevaluate this understanding. The value of human existence remains intact through symbiotic intelligence because it puts people in charge of directing how machines work to achieve beneficial outcomes.

The paradigm redefines how economic systems change through the development of workforces. The study does not predict widespread job loss because it shows how roles will change. AI literacy along with critical algorithm evaluation and interdisciplinary expertise and ethical understanding have become essential requirements for all job positions. Human workers will function as the main decision-makers who manage AI systems while they interpret AI outputs and create AI system designs. The political and ethical frameworks of symbiotic intelligence demonstrate the need for governance systems which enable people to maintain their power. The World Economic Forum and other organizations have stressed that responsible AI frameworks exist to build trust and deliver transparent and fair AI systems (World Economic Forum, 2023; OECD, 2019). The rapid pace of technological progress will exceed the ability of institutions to control its effects if they lack proper regulations.

The Symbiotic Intelligence Paradigm therefore operates at multiple levels:

- Individual Level: AI partnership works to improve human cognitive abilities.
- Organizational Level: Organizations must use AI for decision-making systems through responsible implementation.
- Societal Level: Governance systems should maintain accountability through their design.
- Philosophical Level: Intelligence should be understood as a quality that exists between people and their social networks.

Symbiotic intelligence demonstrates that modern intelligence develops through human and machine partnerships, instead of through zero-sum battles between both groups. The partnership requires purposeful design, ethical oversight, and ongoing improvement efforts.

As AI systems continue to evolve in scale, capability, and influence, the defining challenge of our time is not whether machines can think. The main question centers on human capability to create systems that think and maintain human dignity while protecting our capacity to work together.

2. CONCEPTUAL FOUNDATIONS OF SYMBIOTIC INTELLIGENCE

2.0 Literature Review on Human–AI Collaboration

Researchers have increasingly studied artificial intelligence through the lens of human–machine integration. The initial AI discussions focused on automation. Contemporary research now investigates human and intelligent system collaboration. The contemporary study of AI systems uses models that show how intelligent systems can work together with humans.

The literature describes augmented intelligence as a key concept which shows how AI helps humans increase their abilities instead of taking over their functions. Ben Shneiderman states that augmented intelligence systems should enable human decision making while providing people with control over their decisions through transparent algorithm functions. AI systems should be developed to help humans perform better while their design protects human users from any responsibility. The concept of hybrid intelligence shows how systems achieve better results through the combined power of human expertise and machine learning functions. The research done by Nikolaus Dellermann and his team shows that hybrid intelligence systems combine human creativity and contextual understanding with their ability to process information. The systems enable humans and machines to work together on difficult tasks which neither system could complete on their own (A comparison of existing human–AI collaboration concepts is presented in Table 1)

The human-centered AI concept shows how artificial intelligence brings about ethical and social problems. According to Luciano Floridi scholars AI systems need to create strong governance systems which establish fairness and accountability and transparency. The human-centered AI framework requires organizations to establish human control over all algorithmic systems which will operate in critical fields such as healthcare and finance and public policy.

Socio-technical systems recognize how intelligent technologies function in both institutional and social environments. Artificial intelligence systems function as part of a system that requires interaction with both organizational structures and regulatory frameworks and human decision-making processes. The chapter presents the Symbiotic Intelligence Paradigm which offers a new approach to existing collaboration models through its focus on human cognition and artificial systems which develop together. The concept of symbiotic intelligence defines intelligence as a shared ability which develops through ongoing interactions between human decision-making and algorithm evaluation and institutional governance.

2.1 Understanding Intelligence Beyond the Individual

The Symbiotic Intelligence Paradigm starts its framework with an essential transformation of intelligence definition. Intelligence has been traditionally understood as a personal trait which people can measure through their reasoning skills and memory capacity and analytical abilities and creative talents. Modern technological systems show that the existing definition of intelligence fails to capture its actual breadth. Intelligence today emerges through human interactions with artificial systems instead of existing as a separate mental process.

Social systems and organizational frameworks now include artificial intelligence as their fundamental component. Google and Microsoft established AI system integration within their productivity tools and search engines and communication platforms and enterprise decision-making systems. Intelligence in these environments exists as a combination of human and computational elements (Floridi, 2019). The process of human interaction leads to relationship formation which results in human intelligence development.

Symbiotic intelligence therefore conceptualizes cognition as distributed across:

- Human expertise and judgment
- Algorithmic processing capabilities
- Digital infrastructures
- Organizational governance systems

AI-supported analytics serve as decision-making tools that professionals use for their work. The outcome emerges from a process of joint creation between human and machine elements. The distributed model of intelligence demonstrates that the best decision-making results from combining precise computational power with human understanding of specific situations.

2.2 Cognitive Complementarity Between Humans and AI

The principal concept which underpins symbiotic intelligence operates through cognitive complementarity. Humans and AI systems possess fundamentally different strengths and limitations. The two capabilities should unite their powers to create better results than they currently achieve (As illustrated in Figure 1, symbiotic intelligence emerges from the collaborative interaction between human cognitive abilities and artificial intelligence systems, resulting in improved decision-making and innovation)

Human cognition is characterized by:

- Ethical reasoning and moral judgment
- Emotional intelligence and empathy
- Cultural awareness and contextual interpretation
- Creative abstraction and imagination
- Strategic ambiguity management

Artificial intelligence systems, by contrast, demonstrate strengths in:

- Processing massive amounts of data

- Executing computations at very fast speeds
- Identifying patterns within intricate data sets
- Developing predictive models and conducting optimization processes
- Maintaining reliable performance during tasks which require repeated analysis

The two systems display their respective limitations through their independent functions. The system lacks moral understanding and personal experience. Humans find it difficult to interpret data at a large scale and to perform calculations that involve probabilities. When organizations combine their complementary advantages, they create a hybrid cognitive structure which performs better than any individual system.

IBM promotes AI-human collaboration frameworks in enterprise analytics through its active support, which shows that decision augmentation delivers more dependable results with fewer mistakes than either automation or manual analysis.

Theoretical evidence which supports partnership ties cognitive complementarity to its role as a basis for partnership rather than system replacement (IBM, 2018; Shneiderman, 2022).

2.3 Co-Learning and Continuous Feedback Mechanisms

The process of developing symbiotic intelligence operates through controlled methods which lead to better results. The system operates through continuous feedback loops which enable both human and machine agents to evolve their capabilities.

The process of co-learning operates through a repeating cycle which includes multiple stages.

- People establish the goals together with the situational requirements.
- AI systems process data to create insights and make predictions.
- The human evaluators check the results to determine their correctness and impartiality and their suitability for use.
- The team provides changes which need to be made for better results.
- The AI systems adjust their internal structures based on the provided information to the systems.

The process leads to shared development between both parties. The AI systems become more compatible with human expectations while humans develop better skills to understand and use AI results.

The generative AI systems created by OpenAI undergo human-controlled testing to make their security systems better and their bias problems smaller and their ability to understand different situations better. The alignment methodologies exist to show how AI systems develop through human evaluative judgment.

Over time, systems which operate through symbiotic relationships become better at understanding user intent and institutional objectives and ethical standards.

2.4 Human-in-the-Loop Governance Structures

Human oversight is essential for symbiotic intelligence because it constitutes its core conceptual necessity. AI systems must not function as independent entities in critical fields including healthcare and finance and public policy and legal systems.

Symbiotic integration operates through two main governance frameworks:

Human-in-the-Loop (HITL):

Humans conduct direct examination and approval procedures for AI-generated results before final decision-making occurs.

Human-on-the-Loop (HOTL):

AI functions in a partial automated mode which allows human operators to monitor its activities and they can step in when they detect unusual situations.

The systems establish human accountability as the primary standard for all judgments. European Commission policy frameworks require AI systems to preserve essential human control rights during their operation. The absence of governance mechanisms leads to operational symbiosis which causes system failures through unrestricted automated processes.

2.5 Explainability and Transparency as Foundational Requirements

Human-AI partnerships require transparent operations to achieve success. The hidden workings of AI systems known as black box systems prevent humans from conducting proper oversight.

Explainability enables users to:

- Understand why a specific prediction or recommendation was generated
- Detect bias or errors in model reasoning
- Justify decisions within regulatory contexts
- Maintain trust in automated systems

Transparency creates a system which enables accountability while decreasing dependence on algorithmic systems. Symbiotic intelligence therefore requires interpretability as a structural design principle rather than an optional feature.

AI outputs become understandable for interrogation which enables active participation in collaborative work.

2.6 Ethical Anchoring and Normative Boundaries

The AI systems function to achieve the goals which their training process establishes. The system requires ethical guidance because its optimization process needs to maintain human values which exist throughout its intelligence development process.

The organization has established its ethical safeguards through the following elements:

- The organization uses bias mitigation protocols to protect against potential biases in its systems.
- The organization implements fairness monitoring systems to evaluate how its systems perform in terms of equitable treatment.
- The organization uses privacy protection measures to safeguard personal information.
- The organization establishes responsibility through accountability assignment which defines who will answer to specific results.
- The organization uses regulatory compliance to ensure its operations match all applicable regulations.

The World Economic Forum demands responsible AI governance as an essential requirement for society to establish (World Economic Forum, 2023; UNESCO, 2021) enduring trust in AI technologies.

The human population holds full ethical responsibility for all actions which occur inside symbiotic systems. Human beings must take moral responsibility for their decisions while AI systems can assist in decision-making.

2.7 Emotional and Social Intelligence Considerations

The AI system imitates human conversation by creating spoken language patterns but it lacks any emotional capacity. Humans use relational cues together with empathy and social context to understand the meaning of their interactions.

Research increasingly shows that individuals respond differently when they know they are dealing with machines instead of human beings. People tend to trust others less in situations where they depend entirely on automated systems because these systems lack human touch and authentic presence.

The design of intelligent systems requires symbiotic intelligence because it combines three essential components.

- The system requires complete openness about all AI monitoring activities
- The system requires organization staff to use human resources for all sensitive matters which need resolution
- The system operates through a combination of human and machine-based service delivery frameworks

Microsoft integrates AI copilots into its productivity solutions while users retain control according to the collaborative framework which provides shared capabilities between both parties.

The process of establishing emotional legitimacy needs human involvement because it cannot be completely automated.

2.8 Systems Thinking and Interdependence

The human decision-making process leads to specific AI outputs which then impact human behaviour patterns. The system creates an environment which depends on mutual feedback mechanisms.

The systems view shows that:

- The automated system increases the speed of bias propagation which begins with training data bias.
- The inaccurate output interpretation leads to greater organizational mistakes.
- The operational reliability of systems depends on the governance framework established by organizations.

The process of defining symbiosis requires scientists to treat interdependent systems as interconnected entities instead of viewing them as separate technical components.

Figure 1. Human–AI Symbiotic Intelligence Framework

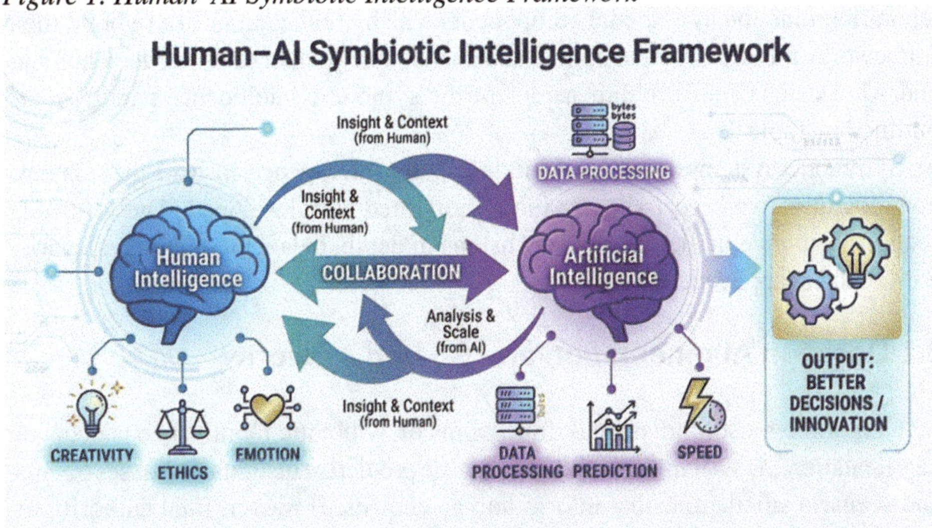

Table 1. Comparison of Human–AI Collaboration Concepts

Concept	Key Idea	Limitations	Contribution of Symbiotic Intelligence
Augmented Intelligence	AI enhances human decision-making	Focus primarily on productivity	Symbiotic intelligence emphasizes mutual learning and co-evolution between humans and machines
Human-Centered AI	AI systems designed to support human values	Focus on ethics and governance	Symbiotic intelligence integrates governance with collaborative cognition
Hybrid Intelligence	Human expertise combined with machine learning	Focus mainly on task performance	Symbiotic intelligence extends collaboration to organizational and societal levels
Socio-Technical Systems	Technology interacts with social and institutional structures	Limited focus on cognitive collaboration	Symbiotic intelligence highlights cognitive partnership between humans and AI

3. CORE DIMENSIONS OF THE SYMBIOTIC INTELLIGENCE PARADIGM

The Symbiotic Intelligence Paradigm operates through multiple interconnected dimensions that structure how humans and artificial intelligence systems collaborate in practical environments. The dimensions show real patterns which people can see at modern workplaces and through digital platforms and in healthcare systems and financial institutions and government systems. The dimensions of human–AI collaboration function as essential components which organizations use to build their frameworks for effective and ethical and sustainable partnerships between humans and AI systems (The core dimensions of the symbiotic intelligence paradigm are outlined in Table 2

Symbiotic systems do not substitute human intelligence instead they change how cognitive work gets allocated and monitored and developed. The following sections elaborate on these core dimensions in depth, balancing theoretical clarity with realistic applications.

3.1 Decision Augmentation and Shared Authority

One of the most fundamental dimensions of symbiotic intelligence is decision augmentation. AI systems increasingly provide predictive insights, risk assessments, and scenario simulations that inform human choices. However, final authority remains human-centered.

In sectors such as finance and supply chain management, AI models can forecast demand fluctuations, identify inefficiencies, and detect anomalies at a scale beyond human capability. For example, corporations like Amazon use predictive analytics to optimize logistics networks. Yet, strategic decisions—such as expanding into new markets or altering long-term investment priorities—are determined by executive leadership.

This dimension involves a calibrated division of labour:

- AI processes large volumes of structured and unstructured data.
- Humans interpret outputs within broader social, economic, and regulatory contexts.
- Accountability remains with human decision-makers.

Decision symbiosis reduces cognitive overload while preserving ethical oversight. It enhances accuracy without eliminating human discretion.

3.2 Knowledge Co-Creation and Analytical Depth

The process of collaborative knowledge production forms the second important area of study. The AI systems show their capability to find connections between enormous data sets because they can detect concealed patterns which help in discovering new insights. The relationship between two things needs to be proven through research because it fails to demonstrate any inherent significance.

Diagnostic AI tools for doctors in healthcare work by analysing medical imaging data and patient medical records. IBM has created AI-based health analytics systems which can examine extensive medical data which hospitals use for patient treatment. The clinical decision-making process depends on contextual information which includes details about the patient and the emotional state and the family background and the ethical factors which AI lacks ability to assess.

The process of creating knowledge through mutual interaction includes the following:

- The system uses algorithms to find hidden patterns within data sets.
- The human interpreter determines which information needs to be understood in its specific context.
- The process of validating recommendations needs to follow ethical standards.
- The system uses feedback to maintain ongoing improvement.

The process of working together produces superior analytical results which require both computational methods and human reasoning to achieve.

3.3 Creative Collaboration and Ideation Expansion

The introduction of generative AI technology has created new pathways for creative collaboration between humans and machines. AI systems can draft reports and generate design prototypes and create code structures and suggest artistic variations. OpenAI developed tools which help writers and developers and marketers and researchers to create ideas more quickly.

AI-generated outputs need human guidance to achieve their purpose. The results of the process will not achieve their intended cultural and emotional and ethical values without specific human guidance.

Creative symbiosis occurs when:

- AI presents structured drafts along with alternative options.
- Humans improve the text by changing its tone and execution and narrative structure.
- The process of iterative interaction results in better quality and more creative outcomes.

AI technology enables marketing campaigns to evaluate customer sentiment information which helps develop effective messaging approaches. The human teams adapt these recommendations according to the brand's identity and its social responsibility obligations.

3.4 Ethical Oversight and Responsible Governance

The ethical symbiosis principal functions as a vital emergency system that guarantees AI systems operate inside their established operational boundaries. AI models develop their learning capabilities through historical data patterns which results in their ability to reproduce existing societal biases when they lack effective monitoring systems.

AI systems require human control together with system transparency and accountability, which European Commission-supported regulatory frameworks establish as essential requirements. Ethical governance systems enable organizations to conduct fairness audits while developing strategies to reduce bias and protect data privacy.

AI recruitment systems enable organizations to process multiple applications through their automated application screening system. Algorithms that operate without controls tend to create biased results which favour specific demographic groups because they use training data that contains existing biases. Human review panels function as essential tools that organizations need to establish fairness in their operations while adhering to equal opportunity employment standards. Organizations need both structured ethical policies and dedicated cultural commitment to achieve effective ethical oversight. Organizations need to establish their internal review systems which should operate independently from technical protection mechanisms.

3.5 Emotional Intelligence Integration

AI systems have made significant progress but they still lack the ability to feel empathy and compassion and possess moral judgment. Emotional interaction remains a critical requirement for industries that include healthcare and education and customer service.

The digital platforms which Microsoft manages allow their AI assistants to function within communication systems while maintaining human operational control and visibility of their processes. AI systems in customer service environments handle basic questions but they transfer difficult or private matters to human staff members.

Emotional symbiosis protects human dignity and trust while it enables organizations to achieve their operational goals. The framework acknowledges that humans possess particular intelligence abilities which include relational understanding as their exclusive cognitive capacity.

Table 2. Core Dimensions of the Symbiotic Intelligence Paradigm

Dimension	Description	Example
Decision Augmentation	AI provides analytical insights while humans retain final decision authority	Financial risk analysis systems
Knowledge Co-Creation	AI identifies patterns in large datasets while humans interpret contextual meaning	Medical diagnostics
Creative Collaboration	AI generates ideas and drafts while humans refine outputs	Marketing and design
Ethical Oversight	Human supervision ensures fairness, transparency, and accountability	AI recruitment systems
Emotional Intelligence Integration	Humans manage empathy, trust, and communication in AI-supported services	Healthcare and education

4. APPLICATIONS ACROSS DOMAINS

The Symbiotic Intelligence Paradigm finds its strongest validation not in theory but in practical deployment. Human-AI collaboration through various industrial and public system deployments creates new methods for decision-making and service delivery and value creation. The symbiotic systems do not replace human workers in their professional roles instead they boost workforce skills and operational speed and help organizations plan their future needs (The phased implementation process of symbiotic intelligence is outlined in Table 4)

4.1 Healthcare and Clinical Decision Support

The healthcare field serves as the most significant demonstration of symbiotic intelligence technology. Medical decision-making involves high complexity, uncertainty, and ethical sensitivity. Clinicians receive assistance through AI systems which analyze medical imaging data and forecast disease development and treatment options. Final decision-making authority remains with human beings.

AI-powered imaging tools developed by organizations such as Google Health have demonstrated strong performance in detecting anomalies in radiological scans. The systems detect mammogram and retinal image patterns which humans who watch the images will find difficult to see. The doctors evaluate test outcomes through understanding all available information about the patient's medical background and their lifestyle choices along with their professional medical experience.

Healthcare systems that use symbiotic intelligence technology provide:

- Quick support for diagnosing medical conditions

- Decreased chances of human mistakes when recognizing patterns
- Tailored treatment schedule development
- Better systems for determining patient treatment order

The system needs ethical safeguards to function properly. Data privacy concerns and algorithmic bias issues together with misdiagnosis accountability problems need human governance systems to solve them. AI systems provide clinical staff with additional information but they do not function as complete substitutes for their professional skills.

4.2 Education and Adaptive Learning Systems

The field of education experiences fundamental changes through adaptive learning environments which use AI technology. The systems work by observing student performance patterns to create real-time educational content modifications.

AI-powered platforms can perform the following functions:

- Finding areas where students struggle with their learning
- Creating personalized practice materials for each student
- Delivering immediate evaluation results to users
- The system monitors user performance data over extended time frames

Educators work beyond their duty to present educational materials. Through mentorship and emotional support plus social development guidance teachers create educational experiences which AI systems lack the ability to reproduce.

Institutions that use AI tutoring systems establish multiple learning environments which operate in a hybrid format that entails:

- AI performs assessment functions which need to be repeated throughout the evaluation process.
- Teachers dedicate their time to explaining advanced conceptual content.
- Human instructors help students build motivation while they teach critical thinking skills.

The framework establishes a mutual relationship which delivers personalized learning experiences. The framework maintains educational human interactions through its development of personalized learning experiences.

4.3 Financial Services and Risk Analytics

Financial institutions use predictive analytics to assess creditworthiness and detect fraudulent activities and create investment models. The AI systems analyze large datasets to find risk patterns which they use to develop portfolio optimization methods (HSBC, 2021).

JPMorgan Chase uses machine learning algorithms to track transaction irregularities while simultaneously identifying fraudulent activities. The systems have the ability to handle more than 1 million transactions every second which exceeds the processing power of human beings.

The following areas require human oversight to function effectively:

- Regulatory compliance decisions
- Ethical investment screening
- Crisis response strategies
- Long-term macroeconomic planning

Statistical prediction methods fail to predict how behavioural and geopolitical factors will affect financial markets. Symbiotic intelligence ensures that AI-generated forecasts inform but do not dictate high-impact economic decisions.

4.4 Business Strategy and Enterprise Decision-Making

Companies now use AI-driven dashboards together with forecasting tools to support their strategic planning needs. Through predictive analytics, businesses can forecast market demands and optimize their supply chains while identifying their customer groups.

Amazon uses artificial intelligence to enhance its global supply chain operations by improving logistics network design and inventory control systems. These models achieve precise delivery route calculations together with warehouse distribution pattern (Amazon, 2022) analysis and real-time demand forecasting capabilities.

Yet, executive leadership holds responsibility for deciding:

- Brand positioning
- Ethical sourcing policies
- Corporate social responsibility strategies
- Long-term investment priorities

AI enhances operational efficiency through human-led strategic vision development. Symbiotic intelligence improves managerial decision-making yet maintains executive responsibility for results.

4.5 Environmental Monitoring and Climate Modelling

Climate scientists need to analyse extensive environmental data which includes satellite images and ocean measurements and atmospheric model data. AI systems enhance modelling accuracy while increasing the capacity to make accurate predictions (NASA, 2022).

NASA uses machine learning to examine satellite data and create models which predict climate changes and environmental shifts. The systems detect large-scale deforestation patterns and ice sheet changes and weather pattern irregularities.

Climate policy decisions require decision-makers to balance ethical values with economic factors and international diplomatic efforts. Symbiotic intelligence supports:

- Evidence-based environmental policy
- Disaster preparedness planning
- Renewable energy optimization
- Long-term sustainability strategies

AI helps scientists advance their knowledge while researchers and policymakers direct how society should respond.

5. CASE STUDIES

5.1 Human–AI Collaboration in Healthcare Diagnostics

The accuracy of medical imaging diagnoses has improved through artificial intelligence advancements. Google Health developed AI diagnostic systems which use deep learning algorithms to analyze mammograms for early breast cancer detection. The medical imaging systems use extensive image databases to learn how to recognize hidden details which human radiologists cannot always see. Research shows that AI-assisted diagnostic systems can improve cancer detection results by decreasing both false positive and false negative rates. The AI systems follow technological progress but their current design limits them from taking over physician duties. The systems provide healthcare professionals with improved medical decision-making functions which help their decision-making process. Radiologists use AI results together with their medical expertise and patient information and test findings to determine patient treatment.

The healthcare system maintains computational efficiency through this cooperative model which needs human professionals to operate. Physicians establish contextual knowledge and ethical criteria and make treatment choices for patients whereas AI can instantly process complicated medical information. The systems demonstrate how human-AI collaboration in healthcare leads to better patient results through accurate diagnosis and improved clinical procedures which doctors can oversee through medical responsibility.

5.2 AI-Supported Fraud Detection in the Financial Sector

Financial institutions increasingly rely on artificial intelligence to detect fraudulent transactions and manage financial risks. A main example of this technology application shows how JPMorgan Chase uses machine learning systems to assess its extensive financial transaction dataset. The AI systems operate 24 hours a day to examine enormous transaction volumes while detecting suspicious activities that might point to financial fraud and money laundering and other illegal financial operations. The algorithms use transaction behaviour and location patterns and financial activity anomalies to produce alerts about unusual activities that take place. AI models improve fraud detection speed and accuracy but human analysts still need to participate in making final decisions. Compliance officers and fraud investigators review the alerts generated by AI systems and evaluate the contextual factors surrounding each transaction before taking regulatory or legal action.

The collaborative approach shows two systems working together to create symbiotic intelligence because artificial intelligence handles data processing tasks while human experts interpret data in context and make ethical decisions. Financial institutions achieve better risk management results and improved security outcomes and regulatory compliance through the combination of AI technology and human knowledge. Human oversight guarantees transparent decision-making processes for algorithms while protecting against risks from automation bias and algorithmic prediction errors.

5.3 AI-Assisted Personalized Learning in Education

The educational system uses artificial intelligence to create adaptive learning systems which provide personalized learning experiences according to students' academic results. Educational platforms such as those developed by Khan Academy use machine learning algorithms to analyse student learning patterns and adjust instructional content accordingly. The system tracks student exercise results to discover their most difficult topics and it suggests specific educational resources which will help them develop missing skills. AI-driven systems can therefore provide individualized learning pathways that would be difficult to achieve in traditional classroom environments with large numbers of students. Adaptive learning technologies improve educational systems yet teachers remain essential for delivering effective educational experiences.

Teachers use AI platform-generated student progress data to determine which teaching methods will help them mentor students and develop critical thinking skills. Human educators also support students' emotional development, motivation, and collaborative learning experiences, which cannot be fully replicated by artificial intelligence systems. Educational institutions use AI-based analytics to assess educational outcomes because they must combine artificial intelligence with human teaching methods. Educational institutions achieve better learning outcomes through technological and human capability integration which also preserves the social and emotional aspects of teaching and learning.

5.4 AI-Assisted Scientific Research and Drug Discovery

Artificial intelligence has also begun to transform scientific research, particularly in the field of pharmaceutical development. DeepMind has created AI models which use AlphaFold systems to forecast intricate protein structures. Scientists need to study protein structures because these structures help them create new medicines, but conventional lab techniques need multiple years to deliver trustworthy results. AI systems examine extensive biological information to deliver swift predictions about how molecules will behave and form connections. Human scientists maintain their essential role throughout all research activities. Researchers assess AI system predictions through laboratory experiments which lead to their scientific understanding of results.

The drug discovery process becomes faster through their work because they maintain scientific standards while ensuring responsibility for their research results. The integration of computational modelling with human scientific reasoning demonstrates how symbiotic intelligence works through AI which boosts analytical power while human researchers develop hypotheses and confirm results through experiments. AI-supported research will eliminate significant time requirements for therapy creation while achieving precise results in scientific research.

6. CHALLENGES AND RISKS

The Symbiotic Intelligence Paradigm enables revolutionary changes to multiple industries while creating major difficulties and potential systemic failures for organizations. Human-robot interaction does not maintain a steady state, which leads to both positive and negative outcomes for human-robot interaction. The system needs complete design work together with ongoing system observation and institutional protection measures to stop all forms of misuse and unintentional effects. The introduction of AI into decision-making processes creates new power dynamics, which transform organizational trust relationships and create new challenges that need to be solved through forward-thinking solutions.

6.1 Over-Reliance and Automation Bias

The most critical danger which exists in symbiotic systems stems from human nature to trust automated systems too much when they produce incorrect results. Users will start to trust AI systems more as they demonstrate consistent accuracy because users will stop their critical assessment of the systems. This leads to a situation where humans make decisions based on standard procedures instead of their actual monitoring duties.

Automated systems used in healthcare and aviation face the risk of creating delays which prevent timely responses to unexpected events. People tend to believe in system accuracy because it has shown consistent dependable performance in the past. Excessive dependence on computational support will lead to professionals experiencing skill degradation because their ability to analyse independently will decrease (Russell, 2019; Shneiderman, 2022). In symbiotic intelligence environments, people need to establish trust for AI systems which requires them to assess AI results through critical evaluation instead of automatic acceptance.

6.2 Algorithmic Bias and Fairness Concerns

The historical data which AI systems use for their training contains social and economic and demographic biases which exist in the data. The use of such data without proper auditing procedures will result in algorithmic outputs which reinforce existing societal inequities. Recruitment systems and lending models and predictive policing tools all rely on automated systems which create biased outcomes that impact disadvantaged communities. The hiring algorithms which Amazon developed for testing purposes received public backlash because they demonstrated biased tendencies through their historical pattern testing (McKinsey & Company, 2023). The case shows how organizations can handle discrimination problems through corrective measures yet the process of creating discrimination issues can happen at a rapid pace.

The system of symbiotic intelligence needs ongoing monitoring for biases together with diverse data collection and human ethical review committees to eliminate systemic bias. The absence of organized protective measures in collaborative systems will lead to increased inequality instead of promoting equal opportunities.

6.3 Transparency and Explainability Limitations

Advanced AI systems use complex neural networks as their foundation, which makes it difficult to understand their internal decision-making processes. The system lacks explainability, which creates problems for establishing trust and accountability in the system. Professionals need to understand system recommendation processes to achieve proper oversight of the system.

The regulatory requirements of finance and healthcare sectors require organizations to explain their decision-making processes. Institutions cannot give their stakeholders or patients or customers proper explanations because their AI systems use hidden decision-making processes. The black box problem prevents symbiotic intelligence systems from achieving their intended collaborative operational balance. System design needs to include transparency requirements as essential elements instead of treating them as optional system features.

6.4 Accountability and Liability Ambiguity

The main philosophical and legal problem relates to the concept of who bears responsibility for their actions. The determination of liability becomes complicated when human and AI systems share decision-making responsibilities. When an AI system assists doctors in making medical diagnoses, who should be held responsible for damages, the doctor or the software developer or the healthcare facility?

The uncertainty in this situation creates two problems which stop people from using the technology while also creating situations where people fail to take responsibility. The collaborative system requires governance structures to define which parties will fulfil their responsibilities. Human oversight must remain substantive rather than symbolic, ensuring that authority and liability are explicitly assigned.

6.5 Workforce Displacement and Skill Polarization

People use symbiotic intelligence because it improves their work performance but this technology creates real problems for employees. Certain job categories will experience decreased hiring needs because AI systems can perform all analytical work which is done repeatedly. Administrative roles, routine data processing positions, and basic customer service functions all face the highest risk of job elimination.

At the same time, organizations require workers to have AI literacy and data science expertise and interdisciplinary analytical skills. This creates skill polarization because high-skilled workers gain advantages while lower-skilled workers experience job losses.

The World Economic Forum and other international organizations emphasize the need for reskilling programs which help workers prepare for jobs in AI-equipped workplaces. The advantages of symbiotic intelligence implementation will benefit certain socioeconomic groups while other groups will experience complete exclusion without existing transitional support programs.

Table 3. Risks and Mitigation Strategies

Risk	Description	Mitigation Strategy
Automation Bias	Over-trust in AI recommendations	Human review and training
Algorithmic Bias	Bias in training data	Bias audits and fairness testing
Lack of Explainability	Black-box AI decisions	Explainable AI models
Accountability Issues	Unclear responsibility	Governance frameworks
Workforce Displacement	Job changes	Reskilling programs

7. STRATEGIC FRAMEWORK FOR IMPLEMENTATION

The Symbiotic Intelligence Paradigm requires more than technological investment because its successful adoption needs a structured strategic framework that links governance with organizational culture and technical infrastructure and ethical safeguards and workforce transformation. The implementation process requires institutions to transform their entire decision-making system which includes changing their AI tool usage and establishing who should control decisions and building digital skills. The strategic framework establishes a structured approach for human–AI collaboration that guarantees sustainable collaboration will proceed through planned steps while maintaining accountability.

7.1 Strategic Vision and Institutional Alignment

The implementation process starts with organizations establishing a specific strategic vision. Organizations need to establish clear definitions about how artificial intelligence will function within their operational activities and decision-making processes. The absence of a coherent vision leads to AI adoption which develops into disconnected initiatives that react to market conditions instead of fulfilling internal organizational requirements. Strategic clarity ensures that AI systems are deployed to address specific institutional challenges which include efficiency optimization and predictive analytics and innovation acceleration and service enhancement.

The process of institutional alignment needs the active backing of organizational leaders who hold the highest authority. Executive direction shows that symbiotic intelligence extends beyond its technical components to become a key element of organizational transformation. The strategic intent of an organization should determine how machine systems operate autonomously and how humans maintain their authority, which will enable AI to function as a supportive tool instead of a system that makes independent decisions. The process of alignment creates a unified relationship between the capabilities of technology and the mission of the organization.

7.2 Governance Architecture and Accountability Mechanisms

The implementation process depends on governance architecture which serves as its fundamental structural framework. The distribution of cognitive tasks between human beings and algorithmic systems through symbiotic intelligence needs organizations to create specific accountability systems. Organizations must define who reviews AI outputs who makes final decisions and who will handle disputes and system errors. The complete documentation of model goals and system boundaries and data sources enables better monitoring and regulatory compliance for their operations. European Commission-led regulatory discussions demonstrate how essential human control is for high-risk AI systems which requires governance systems to develop with technological progress. Sustainable implementation depends on a strong governance framework as its essential requirement. Symbiotic intelligence creates cognitive function distribution between humans and algorithms which results in unclear responsibility disputes. Organizations need to establish formal oversight systems which define decision-making powers and validation methods and escalation procedures to prevent accountability gaps.

The governance structure should establish the processes for evaluating AI outputs and the points at which human intervention becomes essential and the methods for handling system failures. Human actors and institutional bodies bear complete legal and ethical accountability for their actions. Organizations establish trust through transparent documentation which shows model objectives and training data restrictions and operational limitations to achieve regulatory compliance. Effective governance ensures that AI systems operate within institutional norms rather than beyond them.

7.3 Data Infrastructure and Technical Readiness

The organization needs to evaluate all existing data ecosystems including all technical systems before they can begin implementation work. AI systems require datasets that are accurate and diverse and obtained through ethical means. Inadequate data governance introduces bias while it also violates privacy rights and decreases system reliability. The organization must implement data standardization processes together with secure storage systems and necessary privacy regulation compliance.

Technical readiness will require organizations to establish AI system compatibility with their existing operational systems. Organizations need scalability planning to enhance their system performance because scalability will improve their customer base. The system needs cybersecurity protection to prevent hackers from accessing sensitive materials. The development of infrastructure involves technical obligations that function as strategic tools for enabling responsible work between organizations.

7.4 Workforce Development and Cognitive Preparedness

Human readiness represents a decisive factor in implementation success. Professionals need to possess sufficient AI system knowledge because this enables them to evaluate AI system outputs through critical and responsible interpretation. The workforce transformation process requires structured training programs which will develop AI skills and analytical reasoning abilities and ethical understanding among employees.

The organization needs to develop methods which enable employees to assess algorithm outputs and comprehend system constraints while managing exceptional situations. Automation bias arises when human workers lack proper training because they start to trust machine-generated outputs without question. Cognitive preparedness enables organizations to achieve a balance between artificial intelligence processing speed and human decision making. The reskilling programs enable companies to adjust their workforce while they protect employees from job loss and create opportunities for everyone to use new technologies.

7.5 Phased Deployment and Iterative Scaling

Phased deployment strategies enhance implementation resilience. Organizations can test their systems through pilot programs which need to be evaluated before they can use full system integration. System improvements start with initial feedback which helps decrease potential risks to the whole system. Institutions build their trust in the organization through step-by-step expansion which creates the least amount of operational interruption. The iterative approach shows how symbiotic intelligence develops through human processes and algorithmic systems working together to develop new abilities. The recommended execution method should use gradual deployment which distributes system rollout across multiple phases instead of conducting immediate complete system deployment. Organizations use pilot programs to test system performance and workflow compatibility and user acceptance through controlled testing environments. The initial steps of the process create essential insights which help identify operational obstacles and unexpected outcomes.

The process of continuous scaling allows organizations to implement changes which improve their systems without causing major disruptions while they build trust with their staff. The team uses pilot feedback to make system improvements which will be needed before they start their expansion. This adaptive approach shows how symbiotic intelligence develops through technological progress and organizational development which occur at the same time.

Table 4. Phased Implementation Roadmap for Symbiotic Intelligence

Phase	Action
Phase 1	Strategic vision and AI goals
Phase 2	Data infrastructure development
Phase 3	Pilot AI projects
Phase 4	Workforce training
Phase 5	Governance systems
Phase 6	Organizational scaling

8. PHILOSOPHICAL AND SOCIETAL IMPLICATIONS

The Symbiotic Intelligence Paradigm brings effects that go beyond its advantages for operational efficiency and technological advancements. The new framework transforms human comprehension of intelligence and agency and moral values and human identity. The growing presence of artificial intelligence in daily decision-making processes shapes human-machine relations which determine task execution and societal understanding of knowledge and responsibility and progress.

8.1 Reframing the Concept of Intelligence

The historical understanding of intelligence treated it as an inherent human ability which people possessed through their conscious and rational and creative capacities. The new advanced AI systems show that machines can execute complex reasoning tasks while generating language and creating predictive models and analysing patterns at large-scale operations. The Symbiotic Intelligence Paradigm defines machine processing as an activity which differs from human consciousness. Intelligence transforms into a shared capacity which develops through organized teamwork between human cognitive processes and computer power.

The new philosophical perspective shows that intelligence exists beyond human cognition because it resides in systems which combine social and technological elements. OpenAI demonstrates how organizations use AI systems to enhance human creative work and analysis yet humans maintain control over all output including its meaning and ethical implications. Intelligence exists in relationship with other elements instead of existing as a separate entity.

8.2 Autonomy and Algorithmic Influence

Major societal issue centers around how artificial intelligence systems affect personal freedom. Recommendation algorithms control how people consume content, which information they see, and which political discussions they engage in. Meta Platforms and other companies use their platforms to determine which content users will see based on their systems that optimize user engagement.

The systems provide personalized services but they limit users to a specific set of information instead of showing them different viewpoints. The challenge emerges from the need to maintain human freedom while using automated support systems. Organizational systems require transparent functioning methods which help users make conscious decisions about their automated systems.

Active human control must exist in all processes that begin with automated systems. Humans should maintain their power to question and reject and create new meanings from all algorithmic results.

8.3 Distributed Responsibility and Legal Accountability

Human-AI collaboration in decision-making creates challenges for determining who should be held accountable for their actions. The conventional legal framework operates on the principle that each person should be held responsible for their own conduct. The function of symbiotic systems distributes responsibility for outcomes among all stakeholders who include developers and institutional entities and end-users.

The investment choices of JPMorgan Chase leverage algorithmic risk models which originate from their financial institutions yet all investment decisions must receive human approval before implementation. The process of determining responsibility for systemic failures depends on the existence of governed frameworks which require systematic design.

This transformation demands updated legal doctrines and regulatory policies capable of addressing collaborative intelligence environments.

8.5 Economic Restructuring and Labor Implications

The implementation of AI technology in different business sectors creates new job opportunities which require different skills from existing employees. The introduction of automatic systems for conducting basic analytical and administrative duties has resulted in increased demand for strategic and creative work and ethical decision-making. The World Economic Forum and other organizations emphasize that reskilling programs serve as essential measures to stop technological job losses from widening income disparities.

Symbiotic intelligence does not eliminate work but redistributes cognitive labour. The lack of inclusive educational programs and workforce development policies creates a situation that will lead to increased economic polarization of society. Society needs to provide all its members with equal opportunities to learn about AI and digital skills to stop technology-based groups from monopolizing all chances for success.

9. FUTURE TRAJECTORIES

Artificial intelligence technologies are developing at a fast pace which will change how humans interact with intelligent machines for many years to come. Future innovations will create systems that use artificial intelligence to help humans work together in solving difficult challenges instead of eliminating human functions. Symbiotic intelligence shows that successful technology systems need to combine human creative abilities and ethical decision-making and situational understanding with artificial intelligence's computational capabilities. The following scenarios illustrate potential future developments in human–AI collaboration across governance, workplaces, and scientific research.

Scenario 1: AI-Assisted Policy and Governance

The upcoming years will observe governments using artificial intelligence systems to analyze extensive public data for their policy development needs. AI tools could be used to simulate the potential economic, environmental, and social impacts of proposed policies before their implementation. The machine learning models would use demographic data and economic indicators and environmental trends to forecast policy results in healthcare and urban planning and climate management.

The analytical capabilities of AI systems enable policymakers to obtain insights, but human experts must interpret those findings to create democratically sound policies that match ethical standards and social needs. The combination of human judgment together with AI-based analysis will enhance evidence-based policymaking because it enables governance systems to keep human accountability and transparency intact.

Scenario 2: Personalized AI Cognitive Assistants in the Workplace

Employees at upcoming workplaces will utilize tailored artificial intelligence virtual helpers which assist them with their research activities and their analysis work and their decision-making process. The systems will develop into permanent cognitive assistants who will acquire knowledge through observing how individuals perform their tasks and through their current work preferences and their specific professional skills. Professionals in law and finance and healthcare and engineering fields use AI assistants to study complex data sets and produce brief summaries and first-stage research findings.

The systems enable workers to amplify their output through advanced work performance which includes strategic planning and artistic development and collaborative team work. The AI systems in this model implement symbiotic intelligence because they assist human thought processes while humans deliver essential context and ethical understanding and leadership for decision-making.

Scenario 3: Human–AI Collaboration in Scientific Discovery (≈150 words)

Artificial intelligence is expected to play an increasingly important role in accelerating scientific research and innovation. Advanced machine learning models can analyse vast datasets in fields such as genomics, climate science, and materials engineering, identifying patterns that may not be immediately visible to human researchers. Organizations such as DeepMind have already demonstrated how AI can contribute to scientific breakthroughs through systems capable of predicting complex biological structures.

In the future, scientific discovery may rely on collaborative intelligence environments in which AI systems generate hypotheses, analyse experimental data, and identify promising research directions. Human researchers would then evaluate these insights, design experiments, and interpret results within broader theoretical frameworks. Such collaboration between human creativity and machine analysis could significantly accelerate the pace of scientific progress while maintaining human oversight and intellectual responsibility.

10. CONCLUSION

The Symbiotic Intelligence Paradigm establishes a complete transformation of all current methods used to understand and create intelligent systems, which society now employs. The framework establishes that human cognition should work together with artificial intelligence through planned collaborative efforts instead of treating AI as a replacement for human abilities. The system requires human reasoning, creativity, and decision-making abilities of people because technology works as a partner who adds value to human thinking.

The discussion demonstrates that symbiotic intelligence contains multiple dimensions through which it manifests. The system functions on five distinct domains, which extend from philosophical and technological frameworks to institutional, economic and social structures. The system defines intelligence as a phenomenon that exists between people and machines through their mutual connection. Human beings maintain their distinct identity through their ability to make moral choices, comprehend situations, understand emotions and take on ethical responsibilities. Artificial systems analyze data but their operations follow predetermined goals and their programmed data processing systems. Human-centered values maintain their importance because they sustain the process of creating environmentally friendly communication systems between people and technology.

The AI research field experiences fast technological growth because OpenAI and other organizations show that ML systems process huge data sets while producing intricate results and supporting strategic planning activities. The systems achieve their best performance when human operators operate them. The framework increases human decision-making power by enabling better processing of complex situations while decreasing unknown factors and discovering new methods for resolving problems.

The operation of institutions through symbiotic intelligence creates new systems to control and oversee their work while establishing rules for accountability. The European Commission's regulatory initiatives show that global society increasingly demands AI systems to function in environments which display complete transparency and maintain ethical standards while following established legal requirements. AI systems that share decision-making channels with humans need new systems of accountability to distribute responsibility among all involved parties. The absence of institutional maturity creates a situation where technological progress will diminish public confidence. The paradigm creates an economic impact that transforms labor systems and alters job functions while establishing new productivity standards. The World Economic Forum identified adaptive skills and advanced reasoning skills and interdisciplinary work abilities as essential professional development requirements needed by future workers. Symbiotic intelligence redistributes cognitive labor while automating particular tasks. To create equitable access to AI-driven economic systems, the transition requires all workers to receive training through accessible educational institutions and upskilling programs.

The paradigm creates societal impacts by transforming democratic participation and cultural production and individual freedom. The design of algorithmic systems needs to include transparent design principles which protect user control over their personal information and their ability to manipulate their consumer choices. The rise of human-AI collaboration in creative industries leads to the need for new frameworks which define authorship boundaries between human creators and AI systems. Public institutions need to maintain their accountability systems, which ensure that algorithmic systems operate according to democratic norms and principles of social fairness.

The Symbiotic Intelligence Paradigm achieves long-term viability through its four core principles, which function as connected elements: ethical alignment, institutional accountability, inclusive development, and human-centered design. Ethical alignment ensures that all computational objectives will reflect the values of society. Institutional accountability ensures parties will operate their systems with complete operational transparency while following legal requirements. Inclusive development stops the creation of a technology gap between people and machines. Human-centered design protects both individual control and personal respect through its design. The importance of symbiotic intelligence depends on how well humans and machines interact with each other instead of using complex algorithms as the main measure of intelligence. Technology amplifies a person's original purpose while it does not create that purpose. The direction of this paradigm will be determined through public policy choices, which both technologists and educators and citizens will make together.

Symbiotic intelligence provides a way to achieve greater productivity and faster scientific research and better government decisions while unlocking more creative potential when used responsibly. The solution helps organizations handle complex situations while making better decisions. The implementation of this system will result in rising inequality and decreasing public trust because there will be a lack of ethical considerations and inclusive planning.

It establishes a fundamental change in human intelligence operation through its evolution as a technological innovation. The solution evaluates success through innovation metrics and ensures that organizations maintain human dignity while building democratic institutions which enable green development. The future of intelligence exists as a symbiotic system, which depends on both artificial intelligence and human intelligence because it reflects the core values that guide its development and system operations.

REFERENCES

Amazon. (2022). *Machine learning in supply chain optimization*. Amazon Science Publications.

European Commission. (2021). *Proposal for a regulation laying down harmonised rules on artificial intelligence (Artificial Intelligence Act)*. European Union. https://ec.europa.eu

Floridi, L. (2019). *The logic of information: A theory of philosophy as conceptual design*. Oxford University Press. DOI: 10.1093/oso/9780198833635.001.0001

Floridi, L., & Cowls, J. (2019). A unified framework of five principles for AI in society. *Harvard Data Science Review*. https://hdsr.mitpress.mit.edu

Google Health. (2021). *Deep learning for medical image analysis*. Google Research Publications. https://health.google

HSBC. (2021). *Artificial intelligence in financial crime detection*. HSBC Technology Report.

IBM. (2018). *Augmented intelligence: AI and the future of cognitive collaboration*. IBM Institute for Business Value.

Jordan, M. I. (2018). Artificial intelligence—The revolution hasn't happened yet. *Harvard Data Science Review*. https://hdsr.mitpress.mit.edu

McKinsey & Company. (2023). *The state of AI in 2023: Generative AI's breakout year*. McKinsey Global Institute. https://www.mckinsey.com

Microsoft. (2023). *AI copilots and human-centered productivity systems*. Microsoft Official Blog. https://www.microsoft.com

MIT Sloan Management Review. (2021). *Expanding AI's impact with organizational learning*. MIT Sloan Research Report. https://sloanreview.mit.edu

NASA. (2022). *Artificial intelligence for climate modelling and space research*. NASA Technical Reports. https://www.nasa.gov

OECD. (2019). *OECD principles on artificial intelligence*. Organisation for Economic Co-operation and Development. https://www.oecd.org

Open, A. I. (2023). *GPT-4 technical report*. OpenAI Research Publications. https://openai.com

Russell, S. (2019). *Human compatible: Artificial intelligence and the problem of control*. Viking.

Shneiderman, B. (2022). *Human-centered AI*. Oxford University Press. DOI: 10.1093/oso/9780192845290.001.0001

Siemens Healthineers. (2022). *AI-driven medical imaging and diagnostics systems*. Siemens Healthcare White Paper.

Stanford University. (2023). *Artificial intelligence index report 2023*. Stanford Institute for Human-Centered AI. https://aiindex.stanford.edu

UNESCO. (2021). *Recommendation on the ethics of artificial intelligence*. United Nations Educational, Scientific and Cultural Organization. https://www.unesco.org

World Economic Forum. (2020). *The future of jobs report 2020*. World Economic Forum. https://www.weforum.org

World Economic Forum. (2023). *Responsible AI governance: Frameworks for ethical deployment*. World Economic Forum. https://www.weforum.org

Zuboff, S. (2019). *The age of surveillance capitalism*. PublicAffairs.

Chapter 6
GenAI and the Redesign of Work, Jobs, and Organizational Structures

Deepak Gupta
http://orcid.org/0000-0003-3929-1362
Institute of Technology and Management, Gwalior, India

Ergashev Nuriddin Gayratovich
http://orcid.org/0000-0002-8274-6193
Karshi State Technical University. Karshi, Uzbekistan.

Aripov Aziz
http://orcid.org/0009-0002-5153-534X
Kimyo International University, Uzbekistan

Kurbonov Jasurbek
Alfraganus University, Tashkent, Uzbekistan

Makhmudov Asliddin
Termez University of Economics and Service, Termez, Uzbekistan.

Atabaev Bakhtiyor
Mamun University, Khiva, Uzbekistan

Nodir Jumaev
Tashkent State University of Economics, Tashkent, Uzbekistan

ABSTRACT

Generative artificial intelligence (GenAI) is fundamentally reconfiguring the architecture of work by extending automation into cognitive, creative, and communicative domains previously considered uniquely human. This chapter examines how GenAI reshapes individual tasks, job roles, and organizational structures across three interacting analytical layers: the macro level of organizational hierarchy and strategy, the meso level of job and role design, and the micro level of individual worker experience. Drawing on the automation-augmentation paradox (Raisch & Krakowski, 2021), task-based labor displacement frameworks (Acemoglu & Restrepo, 2022), and

DOI: 10.4018/979-8-2600-2726-4.ch006

multilevel organizational AI research (Bankins et al., 2024), a conceptual framework is developed that maps GenAI's cascading effects on workforce composition, skill demands, hierarchical design, and decision-making authority.

1. INTRODUCTION

The emergence of large language models and generative artificial intelligence (GenAI) systems represents a qualitatively distinct shift in the technological landscape of work. Unlike earlier waves of automation, which primarily targeted repetitive, physically demanding, or rule-based tasks, GenAI exhibits capabilities that encroach upon domains once considered uniquely human: creative content generation, complex reasoning, contextual language understanding, code synthesis, and multi-step problem-solving (Eloundou et al., 2024). The arrival of systems such as GPT-4, Claude, Gemini, and their successors has prompted scholars, practitioners, and policymakers alike to re-examine foundational assumptions about what constitutes productive work, who performs it, and how organizational systems should be constructed to accommodate human-AI collaboration at scale.

The scale and scope of GenAI's potential impact on labor markets are unprecedented in recent technological history. Eloundou et al. (2024) estimate that approximately 80% of the U.S. workforce is employed in occupations where at least 10% of tasks could be affected by large language models, while 19% of workers are in occupations where at least 50% of tasks face exposure. Crucially, this exposure is not uniformly distributed across economic strata: knowledge workers, professionals, and those in higher-wage, cognitive-intensive occupations face disproportionately high levels of GenAI exposure compared with manual or trade-based workers (Gmyrek et al., 2023). This inversion of prior automation trends - which predominantly displaced lower-wage, routine task workers - introduces novel challenges for human capital theory, organizational design, and social equity.

Yet the literature is far from settled on whether GenAI constitutes a primarily disruptive or augmentative force. Raisch and Krakowski (2021) articulate an automation-augmentation paradox: while AI systems are capable of automating many cognitive tasks, they simultaneously create new demands for distinctly human competencies, including ethical oversight, creative judgment, relational intelligence, and adaptive problem-framing. Empirical studies have documented heterogeneous effects across occupations, skill levels, and deployment contexts. Noy and Zhang (2023) found productivity gains of approximately 14-18% for mid-skill writing tasks using ChatGPT, with larger gains for lower-performing workers, suggesting a potential skill-leveling effect. Dell'Acqua et al. (2023) identified a jagged technological frontier in which GenAI boosts performance on well-defined tasks but may inhibit performance when workers over-rely on AI in tasks requiring nuanced judgment.

Several additional contextual features distinguish the current GenAI moment from prior technological transitions. First, GenAI adoption is occurring with unprecedented speed: while the introduction of word processing, the internet, and enterprise resource planning systems unfolded over decades, ChatGPT reached 100 million users within two months of its launch, compressing organizational adaptation timescales dramatically. Second, GenAI is a general-purpose technology that cuts across industries and occupational categories simultaneously, making sector-specific regulatory or managerial responses insufficient. Third, the interpretability and governance challenges associated with large language models are substantially greater than those posed by prior automation technologies, creating new risks around algorithmic accountability, bias propagation, and the opacity of decision-making processes (Kellogg et al., 2020; Liang et al., 2024). These features collectively justify treating GenAI as a distinctive object of theoretical and empirical investigation rather than as a continuation of prior automation trends.

This chapter synthesizes these threads and argues that understanding GenAI's implications for work and organizations requires a multilevel framework that integrates analysis at the individual, job, and organizational levels. The chapter proceeds as follows: Section 2 reviews the theoretical foundations underpinning GenAI and work; Section 3 examines task-level dynamics and the redesign of jobs; Section 4 addresses organizational structural transformations; Section 5 focuses on human resource management in GenAI environments; Section 6 addresses digital sustainability and ethical considerations; Section 7 offers a conceptual framework; and Section 8 concludes with implications and a future research agenda.

The real-world impact of GenAI on organizational workflows is already evident in the strategies of major technology firms. Microsoft's Copilot suite, integrated across Microsoft 365 applications including Word, Excel, Teams, and Outlook, exemplifies how GenAI is being embedded directly into enterprise productivity infrastructure. Early organizational deployments have documented meaningful reductions in time spent on meeting summarization, email drafting, and document generation, with Microsoft reporting that early-access users experienced notable improvements in their ability to manage information overload and transition more quickly between tasks (Microsoft, 2023). Similarly, Google's Gemini for Workspace integrates generative capabilities into Gmail, Docs, Sheets, and Meet, enabling tasks such as automated email response drafting, real-time document co-authoring, and intelligent data analysis that previously required dedicated specialist effort. These enterprise deployments illustrate a critical organizational dynamic: GenAI is not being adopted as a standalone productivity application but is being embedded into the ambient digital environments in which knowledge workers already operate, effectively reconfiguring the workflow architecture of entire organizations rather than merely augmenting individual task performance. This embedded character of enterprise GenAI adoption has significant implications for job design, managerial oversight, and organizational governance — implications that the subsequent sections of this chapter systematically examine.

2. THEORETICAL FOUNDATIONS: GENAI, WORK, AND ORGANIZATIONS

2.1 Task-Based Frameworks and the Labor Displacement Debate

The task-based framework, advanced by Acemoglu and Restrepo (2022), provides a foundational lens for analyzing how new technologies alter the task composition of jobs and the relative demand for different types of labor. In this framework, technologies do not simply displace or augment workers wholesale; rather, they affect specific tasks within jobs, and the net employment and wage effects depend on whether new tasks are created to complement or to replace displaced ones. Acemoglu and Restrepo (2022) show that automation-driven task displacement has been a primary driver of rising wage inequality in the United States between 1980 and 2016, with insufficient task creation to compensate for the displacement of middle-skill routine workers.

GenAI complicates this framework in important ways. Unlike earlier automation technologies that targeted the codifiable and predictable, GenAI operates on the basis of probabilistic pattern recognition applied to language, images, code, and structured data. This enables it to perform non-routine cognitive tasks at scale - tasks that task-based models previously classified as safe from automation. Eloundou et al. (2024) update the exposure framework for the LLM era and introduce the concept of 'General Purpose Technology supplementation,' whereby LLMs can either directly perform tasks or be integrated with tools and workflows to perform them. The implication is that the boundary between automatable and non-automatable tasks is fundamentally more fluid in the GenAI era than previous theoretical models assumed.

2.2 The Automation-Augmentation Paradox

Raisch and Krakowski's (2021) automation-augmentation paradox offers a particularly generative theoretical frame for understanding how organizations navigate the dual imperatives of efficiency and adaptability in GenAI deployment. They argue that while AI can automate tasks and thereby reduce human effort, the same technologies simultaneously create augmentation opportunities by extending human cognitive capacity, enabling workers to tackle more complex problems and to recombine knowledge in novel ways. The paradox lies in the simultaneous presence of these opposing forces within the same technologies and organizational contexts.

For GenAI specifically, this paradox manifests in what Dell'Acqua et al. (2023) describe as the jagged technological frontier: a metaphorical boundary within which GenAI outperforms humans on many tasks, but beyond which its performance degrades unpredictably. Workers who understand this frontier and strategically use GenAI within it experience significant productivity gains; those who treat GenAI as uniformly capable and fail to exercise judgment may experience quality degradation. This implies that organizations cannot simply deploy GenAI and expect uniform augmentation; they must invest in developing the human judgment and oversight capabilities required to navigate the frontier effectively. Jarrahi (2018) anticipates this point in his model of human-AI symbiosis, arguing that effective AI use requires complementary human capabilities that are qualitatively different from those AI replaces.

2.3 Multilevel Analysis of AI in Organizations

Bankins et al. (2024) provide a comprehensive multilevel review of AI in organizations that integrates individual, group, and organizational-level perspectives. They identify significant gaps in understanding how AI effects at one level propagate through and interact with other levels. At the individual level, key concerns include impacts on task performance, job satisfaction, skill development, and worker well-being. At the group level, AI alters the dynamics of teamwork, knowledge sharing, coordination, and social identity. At the organizational level, AI shapes competitive strategy, structural design, governance, and resource allocation. Baygi and Huysman (2025) extend this multilevel view by emphasizing that GenAI is not merely a tool deployed within organizations but is increasingly a constitutive element of organizational social fabric, shaping norms, communication patterns, power relations, and institutional logics in ways that are difficult to predict or control.

Brown et al. (2024) further argue that applying established management theories - including institutional theory, transaction cost economics, resource-based view, and upper echelons theory - to GenAI can generate novel and actionable insights. Their edited discussion highlights that GenAI's implications are not simply extensions of prior digital transformation phenomena but represent discontinuities that require theoretical updating. The concept of progressive encapsulation, developed by Hinds and von Krogh (2024), describes how GenAI gradually becomes embedded in organizational routines and structures, reducing visible human agency while expanding

AI's operational footprint. This encapsulation process has profound implications for organizational design, accountability, and human capital development.

3. TASK DYNAMICS AND THE REDESIGN OF JOBS

3.1 Productivity Evidence and Heterogeneous Effects

The empirical evidence on GenAI's productivity effects is growing but remains heterogeneous across contexts, occupations, and deployment approaches. Noy and Zhang (2023) conducted a randomized controlled experiment in which professional workers tasked with writing assignments using ChatGPT completed tasks 37% faster than those without access, with quality judges rating AI-assisted outputs as comparable or superior. Importantly, the productivity gains were largest for workers in the lower tertile of baseline writing quality, suggesting a convergence effect in which GenAI may partially compensate for skill gaps. This finding has significant implications for workforce development strategy and the potential redistribution of productivity gains across worker skill distributions.

Brynjolfsson et al. (2023) studied a large technology company's deployment of an AI-assisted customer support tool and found a 14% average improvement in agent productivity, again with the largest gains concentrated among lower-performing agents. Senior and higher-performing agents showed minimal gains, consistent with the hypothesis that GenAI is most valuable as a knowledge transfer mechanism for workers who lack access to expert tacit knowledge. Peng et al. (2023) documented a 55.8% increase in developer productivity when using GitHub Copilot for coding tasks, a figure that has attracted considerable attention though it reflects a highly specific task domain. Dell'Acqua et al. (2023) introduced critical nuance by showing that for tasks falling outside GenAI's frontier of competence, AI-assisted workers actually performed worse than unassisted workers, due to over-reliance and insufficiently critical oversight.

These findings collectively suggest a conditional productivity dividend from GenAI - one that is realized only when workers maintain appropriate judgment about where and how to apply AI assistance. This has direct implications for job design: roles must be redesigned not merely to incorporate GenAI as a productivity tool, but to systematically develop and incentivize the critical faculties required for effective human-AI collaboration.

To extend this evidence base beyond the technology and professional writing contexts that dominate the experimental literature, Table 1 synthesizes GenAI productivity findings across three additional high-exposure sectors: finance, healthcare, and marketing. These sectors represent distinct deployment contexts characterized by different regulatory environments, task structures, and human-AI collaboration dynamics, and their inclusion illustrates both the generalizability and the limits of productivity gains documented in controlled settings.

Table 1. Cross-Industry Summary of GenAI Productivity Effects.

Sector	Representative GenAI Application	Reported Productivity Effect	Key Contingency / Limitation	Representative Source
Finance	AI-assisted financial report drafting, sentiment analysis, regulatory compliance summarization (e.g., Bloomberg GPT, JPMorgan COiN)	~20–30% reduction in contract review time; ~50% reduction in compliance document processing (JPMorgan, 2023)	High regulatory scrutiny; risk of model hallucination in compliance-critical outputs; requires expert human validation	Leippold (2023); Wu et al. (2023)
Healthcare	Clinical documentation automation (ambient AI scribing), diagnostic decision support, patient communication drafting (e.g., Nuance DAX, Epic AI)	~50% reduction in clinical documentation time; clinician burnout scores improved in early pilots (AMA, 2024)	Patient safety liability in diagnostic applications; HIPAA and data privacy constraints; workforce trust and adoption barriers	Sezgin et al. (2023); Cascella et al. (2023)
Marketing	Automated content generation, personalized campaign optimization, customer journey analytics, A/B testing acceleration (e.g., Jasper AI, Salesforce Einstein)	~40% faster content production cycles; 10–15% uplift in campaign conversion rates in early adopter studies (McKinsey, 2023)	Brand voice consistency; risk of generic content saturation; over-reliance may reduce creative differentiation	Kanbach et al. (2023); McKinsey Global Institute (2023)
Software Development	AI-assisted code completion, automated testing, documentation generation (e.g., GitHub Copilot, Amazon CodeWhisperer)	~55.8% productivity increase for coding tasks (Peng et al., 2023)	Gains concentrated in well-defined coding tasks; complex architectural decisions show minimal AI benefit; code quality verification remains human-dependent	Peng et al. (2023); Dell'Acqua et al. (2023)

Sources: Peng et al. (2023); Brynjolfsson et al. (2023); Leippold (2023); Sezgin et al. (2023); Kanbach et al. (2023); McKinsey Global Institute (2023). Note: Productivity estimates derive from a heterogeneous mix of controlled experiments, industry pilot reports, and observational studies; cross-sector comparisons should be interpreted with appropriate methodological caution.

Figure 1. Estimated Productivity Gains (%) from GenAI Adoption Across Domains

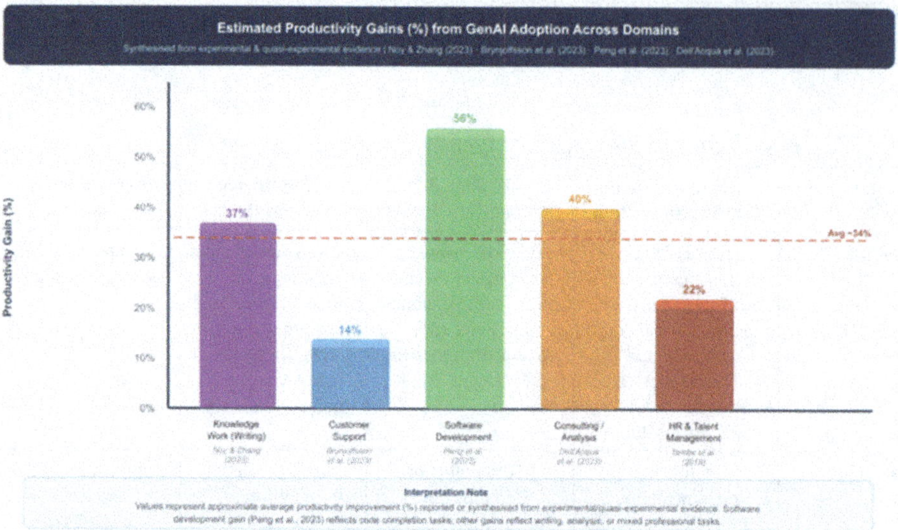

Figure 1 Estimated productivity gains across five work domains synthesized from experimental and quasi-experimental evidence. The green callout highlights the highest single-domain gain — a 55% productivity boost in software development via GitHub Copilot (Peng et al., 2023). The orange callout marks the cross-study average of approximately 37%. Effects are heterogeneous and context-dependent; lower-baseline workers typically experience the largest gains. Based on Noy & Zhang (2023), Brynjolfsson et al. (2023), Peng et al. (2023), Dell'Acqua et al. (2023), and Malik et al. (2023).

3.2 Emerging Hybrid Job Profiles and Skill Reconfiguration

The documented productivity effects of GenAI are accompanied by a fundamental reconfiguration of the skill profiles associated with many knowledge work occupations. Eloundou et al. (2024) show that occupations with the highest LLM exposure include interpreters and translators, poets and lyricists, survey researchers, writers, and mathematicians - professions historically considered immune to automation due to their creative or linguistic character. This exposure does not necessarily imply displacement; it may instead represent an opportunity to augment professional output, provided workers develop the complementary capabilities required.

The concept of prompt engineering has emerged as a new and significant competency in the GenAI era. Workers who can effectively communicate intent, provide context, critically evaluate AI outputs, and iterate on prompts to elicit high-quality, reliable responses gain productivity advantages that compound over time. Budhwar et al. (2023) identify a cluster of GenAI-age competencies including AI literacy, critical evaluation of algorithmic outputs, data stewardship, and creative problem-framing that organizations must actively cultivate if they are to capture the potential value of GenAI investments. Mollick and Mollick (2023) extend these insights to educational contexts, demonstrating that structured AI-assisted learning approaches can accelerate skill development in ways relevant to professional training and workforce upskilling.

Chowdhury et al. (2024) argue that the emergence of hybrid human-AI job profiles necessitates a strategic HRM response that goes beyond incremental skill development programs. They propose a GenAI-oriented HRM framework in which workforce planning, talent acquisition, performance management, and learning and development systems are fundamentally redesigned around the assumption of persistent human-AI collaboration. Vrontis et al. (2022) demonstrate through systematic review that AI-enabled HRM practices tend to improve recruitment efficiency and predictive accuracy but introduce significant risks related to algorithmic bias, worker surveillance, and erosion of managerial discretion.

3.3 The Jagged Frontier and Job Boundary Ambiguity

One of the most practically challenging aspects of GenAI-driven job redesign is the ambiguity surrounding task boundaries. Traditional job analysis methods rely on relatively stable task inventories that can be evaluated, weighted, and assigned to specific roles. GenAI introduces a dynamic element in which the boundary of what AI can and cannot do shifts continuously as models improve, new tools are integrated, and organizational contexts evolve. Dell'Acqua et al.'s (2023) jagged frontier metaphor captures this ambiguity: the frontier of GenAI competence is irregular and difficult to map in advance, making systematic job analysis challenging.

This boundary ambiguity has several implications. First, it creates persistent uncertainty in workforce planning: organizations cannot simply identify 'at-risk' tasks and redesign jobs accordingly, because the risk profile evolves with model capabilities. Second, it places a premium on worker adaptability and metacognitive awareness - the ability to recognize and respond to shifts in the frontier without detailed managerial guidance. Third, it creates potential for both over-reliance on GenAI (using it for tasks where it performs poorly) and under-utilization (avoiding GenAI for tasks where it would enhance performance) (Raisch & Krakowski, 2021). Effective job redesign in the GenAI era must therefore incorporate mechanisms for ongoing task boundary assessment and worker feedback, rather than treating job redesign as a one-time structural intervention.

4. ORGANIZATIONAL STRUCTURAL TRANSFORMATIONS

4.1 Hierarchical Restructuring and Coordination Costs

The organizational structure of firms has historically evolved in response to information processing demands and coordination costs. Transaction cost economics suggests that hierarchical structures emerge to minimize the costs of coordinating complex activities when markets fail to do so efficiently. GenAI, by dramatically reducing the cost and time required for information synthesis, analysis, and communication, has the potential to alter the optimal scale and scope of organizational hierarchies. Xu et al. (2025) argue that GenAI enables organizations in the knowledge economy to flatten hierarchies by automating the information aggregation and filtering functions traditionally performed by middle management layers.

Shrestha et al. (2023) examine how AI more broadly reshapes organizational decision-making structures, arguing that AI-enabled firms are converging toward hybrid models in which algorithms handle routine and structured decisions while humans focus on novel, high-stakes, and value-laden choices. In GenAI environments, this distinction becomes more nuanced: GenAI can contribute substantively to even complex, unstructured decisions by generating analyses, synthesizing evidence, and simulating scenarios, though final authority typically remains with human decision-makers. Fountaine et al. (2022) identify cultural and structural barriers to scaling AI in organizations, including siloed data, misaligned incentives between AI teams and business units, and insufficient senior leadership commitment to AI-enabled organizational redesign.

4.2 Algorithmic Control and Worker Autonomy

The deployment of AI-driven monitoring, evaluation, and workflow management systems in organizations raises fundamental questions about the balance between organizational efficiency and worker autonomy. Kellogg et al. (2020) characterize algorithmic management as a new contested terrain of control in which organizations use algorithmic systems to monitor performance, allocate tasks, evaluate outputs, and modulate rewards and penalties. While such systems can enhance transparency and consistency in some dimensions, they also compress managerial discretion, create new forms of surveillance, and may amplify existing inequalities if underlying training data reflects historical biases.

Baygi and Huysman (2025) extend this analysis to the GenAI context, arguing that as GenAI becomes embedded in organizational communication, knowledge work, and decision-making processes, it reshapes the social fabric of organizations in ways that are difficult to govern through conventional managerial means. GenAI systems generate outputs that blend human and machine agency in ways that can obscure accountability, complicate performance attribution, and erode workers' sense of ownership and creative identity. Cheng and Hackett (2021) provide a critical review of algorithmic HRM that highlights similar concerns about the opacity of algorithmic decision-making in recruitment, performance appraisal, and talent development contexts.

Liang et al. (2024) offer a cautionary finding relevant to algorithmic management: AI detection tools used to identify AI-generated text are significantly biased against non-native English speakers, falsely flagging their work as AI-generated at higher rates. This finding illustrates how algorithmic control systems can introduce new forms of discrimination that map onto pre-existing social inequalities, even when such discrimination is unintentional. Leippold (2023) identifies similar concerns in the financial domain, demonstrating that GPT-4 can be used to manipulate sentiment analysis tools in ways that could have significant market and governance implications.

These organizational-level concerns have begun to attract regulatory and governance attention at the supranational and international levels, providing an emerging external framework within which organizational accountability for algorithmic management must be situated. The European Union's Artificial Intelligence Act (2024), the first comprehensive legal framework for AI governance, establishes a risk-based classification system under which AI systems used in employment, worker management, and access to self-employment are designated as "high-risk" applications subject to mandatory conformity assessments, transparency obligations, human oversight requirements, and prohibitions on certain forms of real-time biometric surveillance. For organizations deploying GenAI in performance monitoring, task allocation, or workforce planning, compliance with these provisions imposes substantive governance requirements that go beyond voluntary codes of conduct. Complementing this binding legal framework, the OECD AI Principles (2019, updated 2024) articulate a set of normative commitments — including inclusive growth, human-centred values, transparency, robustness, and accountability — that have been endorsed by over fifty governments and serve as a soft-law reference standard for national AI policy development. The ISO/IEC 42001 standard for AI management systems provides a further layer of operational guidance, establishing auditable requirements for AI governance systems within organizations that parallel the ISO 9001 quality management framework in both structure and institutional legitimacy. Taken together, these regulatory and standards frameworks signal that the governance of algorithmic management is transitioning from a domain of organizational discretion to one of institutionalized accountability — a transition with significant implications for how organizations design, document, and govern their GenAI deployments and for the role of HR professionals as internal governance actors in ensuring compliance with emerging AI regulation (Dwivedi et al., 2023; Bankins et al., 2024).

4.3 Business Model Innovation and Organizational Identity

Beyond structural rearrangement, GenAI is enabling the creation of entirely new business models that challenge existing assumptions about value creation, competitive advantage, and organizational purpose. Kanbach et al. (2023) analyze GenAI from a business model innovation perspective and identify four primary mechanisms through which GenAI creates value: democratizing access to expert knowledge, enabling hyper-personalization at scale, generating novel content and insights, and accelerating iteration cycles in product and service development. Each mechanism has implications for how organizations define their core value propositions and configure their operational models.

Mariani and Dwivedi (2024) provide a research agenda for GenAI and innovation management that highlights the tension between efficiency gains and creative disruption. They argue that while GenAI can accelerate incremental innovation by automating ideation, prototyping, and evaluation cycles, its impact on radical innovation - which requires genuine novelty, risk tolerance, and divergent thinking - is less certain. Corvello (2025) advocates for a human-centered perspective on GenAI and innovation, arguing that sustainable innovation ecosystems must preserve space for human creativity, agency, and ethical judgment even as AI augments specific innovation sub-processes. Grimes et al. (2023) echo this concern in the context of academic scholarship, warning that the ease with which GenAI can generate plausible but potentially shallow content could undermine the depth of intellectual contribution if not counterbalanced by human critical engagement.

5. HUMAN RESOURCE MANAGEMENT IN GENAI ENVIRONMENTS

5.1 Talent Acquisition, Development, and the Evolving Employment Relationship

The deployment of GenAI in talent acquisition processes represents one of the most rapidly evolving and contentious domains of applied AI in organizations. Tambe et al. (2019) identify core challenges in AI-assisted HRM including data quality, model validity, and the risk of perpetuating historical biases through algorithmic hiring decisions. These concerns have intensified with the advent of GenAI, which can generate candidate assessments, simulate interview scenarios, evaluate cultural fit through textual analysis, and produce targeted job descriptions calibrated to specific candidate pools. Malik et al. (2023) argue that these capabilities require an extended strategic HRM framework in which the ethical governance of AI-assisted processes becomes a core organizational competency, not merely a compliance obligation.

Budhwar et al. (2023) provide a comprehensive treatment of ChatGPT's implications for HRM and argue that the technology fundamentally challenges many of the assumptions underlying traditional HRM practice. In particular, they highlight the potential for GenAI to democratize access to high-quality HRM practices for smaller organizations that previously lacked the resources to invest in sophisticated talent analytics. At the same time, they caution that the ease of deploying GenAI-assisted HRM processes may outpace organizations' capacity to ensure their validity, fairness, and legal defensibility. Chowdhury et al. (2024) propose a strategic HRM framework for GenAI integration that emphasizes dynamic capability development, workforce agility, and systematic ethical review processes embedded in HRM governance.

Learning and development represents a particularly promising domain for GenAI application. Mollick and Mollick (2023) identify multiple pedagogically grounded approaches to AI integration in learning contexts, including AI as tutor, as mentee, as coach, as collaborator, and as assessor. Each approach has distinct implications for skill development and for the human-AI interaction models that workers are prepared to navigate in their professional roles. The integration of GenAI in corporate learning and development programs could significantly accelerate the pace of skill acquisition and facilitate more personalized learning pathways, though the risk of passive dependence on AI-generated content rather than active knowledge construction requires careful pedagogical design.

5.2 Performance Management and Algorithmic Accountability

Performance management in GenAI-integrated workplaces presents significant challenges for both the design of evaluation systems and the fairness of their outcomes. As GenAI becomes embedded in individual work outputs, the attribution of performance to individual human effort becomes progressively more ambiguous. How should managers evaluate a financial analyst who uses GenAI to generate market analyses? Should the analyst be rewarded for the quality of the final output, the sophistication of their prompting strategy, their ability to critically evaluate and improve AI-generated content, or some combination of these? Existing performance management frameworks built around individual human productivity offer limited guidance for these hybrid work contexts.

Kellogg et al. (2020) anticipate these challenges in their analysis of algorithmic workplace control, arguing that algorithmic performance monitoring systems create new power asymmetries between employers and employees, and that workers develop various forms of resistance and accommodation in response. In GenAI contexts, workers may strategically disclose or conceal their use of AI assistance depending on organizational norms, evaluation criteria, and competitive dynamics with colleagues. Tambe et al. (2019) argue that effective AI-assisted HRM requires not just technical sophistication but organizational trust, transparency, and participatory governance structures that give workers meaningful input into how AI systems that affect them are designed and deployed.

6. DIGITAL SUSTAINABILITY AND ETHICAL DIMENSIONS

6.1 Environmental and Computational Sustainability

The deployment of GenAI at organizational scale introduces a set of sustainability concerns that are distinct from those associated with earlier digital technologies. Large language models require substantial computational resources for both training and inference, generating energy consumption and carbon emissions that are non-trivial at enterprise scale. Gmyrek et al. (2023) note that while GenAI's labor market effects are frequently discussed, its environmental footprint is comparatively underanalyzed, creating a blind spot in organizational sustainability strategies. Organizations pursuing GenAI integration as part of their digital transformation agenda must therefore explicitly account for the environmental costs of AI inference in their sustainability reporting and governance frameworks.

Digital sustainability in the GenAI context extends beyond environmental considerations to encompass data governance, model lifecycle management, and the responsible disposal of deprecated AI systems. Brown et al. (2024) argue that business and management scholars need to develop more sophisticated conceptual frameworks for understanding the long-term sustainability of AI-enabled organizational practices, including the conditions under which AI adoption creates sustainable competitive advantage versus temporal advantages that are rapidly competed away. The concept of digital sustainability thus requires integration across environmental, social, and governance dimensions, with GenAI's implications for each dimension requiring dedicated analysis and institutional response.

The quantitative dimensions of this environmental footprint are substantial and warrant explicit treatment in organizational sustainability frameworks. Training a single large language model of the GPT-3 class (175 billion parameters) has been estimated to consume approximately 1,287 megawatt-hours of electricity and to generate an estimated 552 metric tons of CO2-equivalent emissions — comparable to the lifetime emissions of five average American automobiles. More recent frontier models, including those in the GPT-4 and Gemini Ultra class, are estimated to have substantially larger training footprints, though precise figures remain proprietary. Critically, training costs represent only a portion of the total lifecycle footprint: inference — the ongoing computational process by which trained models respond to user queries — accounts for a growing and organizationally consequential share of total AI energy consumption. Luccioni et al. (2023) estimate that inference across a production deployment of a large language model can consume between 0.001 and 0.01 kWh per query, implying that an organization processing one million AI-assisted queries per day may incur daily energy costs equivalent to hundreds of households' electricity consumption. At the sector level, the International Energy Agency (2024) projects that global data center electricity demand — driven substantially by AI workloads — could double between 2022 and 2026, reaching between 620 and 1,050 terawatt-hours annually. For organizations with science-based emissions targets or public commitments to net-zero operations, the integration of GenAI at scale thus introduces a material tension between productivity enhancement and decarbonization objectives that requires explicit governance attention, including scope 2 and scope 3 emissions accounting for cloud-based AI inference, green procurement policies for AI infrastructure, and the adoption of energy-efficient model architectures and retrieval-augmented generation approaches that reduce unnecessary large-model inference.

6.2 Equity, Fairness, and the Distributional Politics of GenAI

The distributional effects of GenAI adoption on workers and communities represent a critical dimension of digital sustainability that organizational practice and policy must address proactively. Acemoglu and Restrepo (2022) demonstrate that automation-driven task displacement has been a significant driver of wage inequality in advanced economies, with productivity gains from automation accruing disproportionately to capital rather than to displaced workers or to society more broadly. GenAI's extension of automation into cognitive and professional task domains raises the prospect of these distributional dynamics intensifying and extending further up the income distribution.

Gmyrek et al. (2023) conduct a global analysis of GenAI's potential employment effects and find that the risks are concentrated in middle-income countries and in occupational categories that have historically served as a pathway to economic mobility for workers from lower socioeconomic backgrounds. Dwivedi et al. (2023) argue that the multidisciplinary governance of GenAI requires attention not only to the efficiency and innovation dimensions emphasized in the management literature, but also to social equity, democratic accountability, and the rights of workers affected by AI-driven organizational restructuring. Liang et al. (2024) demonstrate empirically that existing AI assessment tools are systematically biased against non-native

English speakers, illustrating how GenAI can inadvertently amplify pre-existing social inequalities in ways that require proactive organizational and policy responses.

Addressing these equity concerns requires organizations to go beyond reactive compliance and engage in proactive design processes that center fairness, representativeness, and worker voice in the governance of GenAI deployment. Bankins et al. (2024) argue that organizations need multilevel governance mechanisms that address AI's impacts at the individual, group, and organizational levels simultaneously, rather than treating fairness as a purely technical problem amenable to algorithmic solution.

7. A MULTILAYER CONCEPTUAL FRAMEWORK FOR GENAI AND WORK REDESIGN

Integrating the foregoing theoretical and empirical analysis, this section proposes a multilayer conceptual framework for understanding GenAI's implications for the redesign of work, jobs, and organizational structures. The framework organizes analytical attention across three interacting layers - the macro layer of organizational structures, the meso layer of jobs and roles, and the micro layer of individual workers - and situates them within two overarching environmental dimensions: digital sustainability constraints and human capital strategy enablers (see Figure 2 below).

Figure 2. Multilayer GenAI Work Redesign Framework

Figure 2 A three-layer framework organizing GenAI's work redesign effects across organizational, job, and individual levels, constrained by digital sustainability imperatives and enabled by strategic human capital management (adapted from Bankins et al., 2024; Raisch & Krakowski, 2021; Xu et al., 2025).

At the macro layer, GenAI's most significant structural implications involve the potential for hierarchical flattening as information processing and coordination tasks are partially automated, the emergence of human-AI hybrid team structures as new organizational units, the redistribution of decision-making authority as AI systems take on greater substantive roles in knowledge work, and the reconfiguration of competitive dynamics as AI capabilities become increasingly accessible across firm-size categories. These macro-structural changes interact with institutional and regulatory environments in ways that are currently uncertain but potentially profound.

At the meso layer, the primary dynamics involve the redesign of specific jobs and roles to incorporate GenAI as a constitutive element rather than a peripheral tool. This includes the emergence of new hybrid job profiles that blend domain expertise with AI governance competencies, the reconfiguration of task boundaries as the jagged GenAI frontier evolves, the development of new competency frameworks that recognize AI literacy and critical evaluation as core professional skills, and the adaptation of HRM systems to manage performance, development, and accountability in hybrid human-AI work contexts. Dell'Acqua et al. (2023) and Budhwar et al. (2023) provide complementary foundations for this meso-level analysis.

At the micro layer, the framework attends to how individual workers experience and respond to GenAI integration, including the productivity effects documented by Noy and Zhang (2023) and Brynjolfsson et al. (2023), the skill development challenges identified by Budhwar et al. (2023) and Malik et al. (2023), the bias and fairness concerns raised by Liang et al. (2024) and Kellogg et al. (2020), and the questions of worker agency, autonomy, and psychological safety that Baygi and Huysman (2025) identify as central to understanding GenAI's organizational implications.

The automation-augmentation spectrum (Figure 2) illustrates how different task types and work domains fall along a continuum from full automation at one extreme to human-led work where AI plays no meaningful role at the other. Between these poles lie the hybrid zones - AI-assisted, co-creative, and AI-augmented - in which the majority of knowledge work currently falls and in which the most significant challenges and opportunities for job and organizational redesign are located.

The digital sustainability dimension represents the environmental, ethical, and governance constraints within which GenAI deployment must occur. Organizations pursuing GenAI integration cannot treat these constraints as externalities; they must be integrated into strategy, governance, and operational design from the outset. The human capital strategy dimension represents the organizational enablers that determine whether GenAI investments translate into sustainable productivity gains and competitive advantage, or whether they produce temporary efficiency gains offset by worker displacement, skill degradation, and organizational fragmentation.

8. COMPARATIVE ANALYSIS: FROM TRADITIONAL TO GENAI-INTEGRATED WORK SYSTEMS

Table 1 provides a comparative analysis of key organizational and work design dimensions across three developmental phases: pre-GenAI traditional organizations, early AI-enabled organizations, and the emerging GenAI-integrated work systems that are beginning to characterize leading-edge organizational practice. This comparison illustrates the magnitude and scope of the transitions underway and highlights the specific dimensions of organizational life most profoundly affected by GenAI's development.

Table 1. Comparative Analysis of Organizational and Work Design Dimensions Across Developmental Phases

Dimension	Pre-GenAI (Traditional)	Early AI-Enabled	GenAI-Integrated (Emerging)	Key Reference
Organizational Hierarchy	Multi-layered, vertical authority	Process automation reduces some layers	Fluid, project-based; AI as a node in decision networks	Xu et al. (2025); Shrestha et al. (2023)
Job Design	Fixed role descriptions; task-centric	Algorithm-mediated monitoring begins	Hybrid human-AI tasks; dynamic job sculpting	Acemoglu & Restrepo (2022); Eloundou et al. (2024)
Worker Skills	Specialized functional expertise	Digital literacy added to requirements	Prompt engineering, critical AI oversight, creativity	Dell'Acqua et al. (2023); Budhwar et al. (2023)
Decision-Making	Hierarchical, manager-centric	Data-driven dashboards support managers	Distributed; AI contributes substantively to knowledge work	Raisch & Krakowski (2021); Jarrahi (2018)
HRM Practices	Annual appraisal, manual screening	AI for applicant tracking, analytics	GenAI-driven recruitment, continuous performance sensing	Tambe et al. (2019); Malik et al. (2023)
Innovation Process	R&D-centric, sequential phases	AI accelerates search and prototyping	GenAI democratizes ideation; co-creative innovation loops	Corvello (2025); Mariani & Dwivedi (2024)

continued on following page

Table 1. Continued

Dimension	Pre-GenAI (Traditional)	Early AI-Enabled	GenAI-Integrated (Emerging)	Key Reference
Organizational Control	Bureaucratic rules and norms	Algorithmic surveillance and control	Tension: AI oversight vs. worker autonomy & ethics	Kellogg et al. (2020); Baygi & Huysman (2025)
Sustainability Impact	Carbon from physical operations	Digital infrastructure emissions emerge	Energy-intensive LLM inference; ethical AI governance	Gmyrek et al. (2023); Brown et al. (2024)

Note. Table synthesizes insights from Acemoglu & Restrepo (2022), Eloundou et al. (2024), Xu et al. (2025), Tambe et al. (2019), Malik et al. (2023), Kellogg et al. (2020), Baygi & Huysman (2025), and Gmyrek et al. (2023).

Several patterns emerge from this comparative analysis. First, the shift from early AI-enabled to GenAI-integrated work systems is not simply a linear extension of digitalization but represents a qualitative discontinuity in which AI moves from a peripheral productivity tool to a constitutive element of core work processes and organizational structures. Second, the complexity of governance challenges increases substantially across each developmental phase, requiring progressively more sophisticated frameworks for managing worker rights, algorithmic accountability, and organizational fairness. Third, the role of human capital strategy becomes more, not less, important as AI capabilities expand, because the realization of AI's productivity potential increasingly depends on organizational investment in the human capacities required to govern, evaluate, and creatively extend AI systems. Fourth, digital sustainability considerations emerge as a cross-cutting constraint that cannot be treated as a compliance issue separate from operational strategy.

9. IMPLICATIONS, FUTURE RESEARCH AGENDA, AND CONCLUSION

9.1 Implications for Practice

The analysis developed in this chapter has several concrete and actionable implications for organizational leaders, HRM practitioners, and policymakers responsible for governing the integration of GenAI into work systems. First and most broadly, organizations should adopt a genuinely multilevel approach to GenAI strategy that simultaneously and coherently addresses individual worker development, job and role redesign, and macro-structural adaptation, rather than addressing each level in isolation through separate functional initiatives. Siloed approaches — in which IT departments manage AI infrastructure, HR departments manage training programs, and line managers make ad hoc deployment decisions without coordination — will consistently underperform because GenAI's effects are systemic and propagate across organizational levels in ways that cannot be anticipated or managed from any single vantage point. Fountaine et al. (2022) argue that building genuinely AI-powered organizations requires cultural transformation — in which experimentation with AI is normalized, learning from AI failures is valued, and AI governance is understood as a shared organizational responsibility — as much as it requires technical investment.

Second, human capital investment in the GenAI era must be reoriented toward the meta-competencies required for effective and responsible human-AI collaboration: critical AI evaluation and error detection, prompt engineering and communication with AI systems, AI literacy and understanding of AI limitations, ethical judgment about when and how to deploy AI, and adaptive learning capacity that allows workers to update their AI governance skills as frontier capabilities evolve. These competencies are not reducible to technical skills that can be acquired through short technical training courses; they require the cultivation of epistemic humility, intellectual curiosity, professional skepticism, and the kind of domain expertise that allows workers to recognize when AI outputs are plausible but wrong. Budhwar et al. (2023) and Mollick and Mollick (2023) provide complementary frameworks for designing training and development programs that cultivate these capacities systematically.

Third, performance management, talent acquisition, and organizational governance systems must be fundamentally redesigned to reflect the realities of hybrid human-AI work rather than simply adding AI-related criteria to existing frameworks designed for purely human work. This means developing performance attribution frameworks that can assess the quality of human judgment and AI governance rather than simply evaluating output quality as if it were purely a product of individual human effort, creating organizational cultures of psychological safety in which workers can openly discuss their use of AI assistance without fear of stigma or punitive evaluation, and establishing transparent, participatory governance mechanisms for AI deployment decisions that give workers, HR professionals, and ethicists meaningful input alongside technical teams. Cheng and Hackett (2021) and Tambe et al. (2019) provide relevant guidance from the algorithmic HRM literature on the governance architectures that have proven most effective in maintaining fairness and accountability in AI-assisted people management.

Fourth, digital sustainability must be integrated into the core logic of GenAI strategy rather than appended as a reporting requirement or stakeholder communication exercise. This requires explicit accounting for the energy and carbon costs of AI inference in organizational sustainability reporting, proactive attention to the equity and distributional effects of GenAI deployment within and beyond the organization's boundaries, establishment of governance frameworks that can adapt to the rapidly evolving regulatory landscape around AI in labor markets and public life, and investment in the long-term human capital capabilities that enable organizations to govern AI sustainably over time rather than becoming progressively dependent on AI systems that they increasingly lack the human expertise to evaluate or challenge.

9.2 Future Research Agenda

The field of GenAI and organizational work design is in its early empirical and theoretical stages, and substantial and consequential research gaps remain that the management and organizational behavior scholarly communities are well-positioned to address. First, longitudinal research on the employment, skill, and well-being effects of sustained GenAI deployment is urgently needed to move beyond the snapshot evidence that currently dominates the literature. The existing empirical base consists predominantly of short-term experimental studies and early-deployment case observations that capture immediate productivity effects but provide limited insight into how skill profiles, job structures, career trajectories, organizational cultures, and labor market outcomes evolve over the multi-year and multi-decade periods across which technological transitions typically unfold. Acemoglu and Restrepo's (2022) long-run analysis of automation-driven wage dynamics provides a compelling template for the kind of sustained empirical investigation that is required to assess GenAI's aggregate labor market effects with appropriate rigor.

Second, cross-national and cross-sectoral comparative research is needed to understand how the effects documented primarily in high-income, English-language, technology-sector contexts differ across labor market institutions, educational systems, regulatory environments, and cultural contexts that shape the conditions of GenAI adoption and its human capital consequences. Gmyrek et al. (2023) provide an important starting point with their global analysis of GenAI employment exposure effects, but detailed organizational and occupational case studies across different institutional environments are necessary to develop the context-sensitive theoretical frameworks that can guide policy and organizational practice in the diverse global settings where GenAI is being deployed. Hinds and von Krogh's (2024) progressive encapsulation framework could be productively applied and tested across diverse organizational and national contexts to understand the conditions under which encapsulation proceeds more or less rapidly and with more or less disruptive consequences for organizational capabilities and worker agency.

Third, there is a significant and practically consequential need for research on the governance and accountability mechanisms that enable organizations to deploy GenAI effectively, equitably, and sustainably over time. Existing research tends to focus on the effects of AI on workers and organizations, but the institutional and managerial mechanisms that shape those effects — the governance structures, leadership practices, organizational cultures, regulatory frameworks, and labor relations processes that determine how AI's potential is realized and its risks managed — are substantially less well understood. Research questions that deserve systematic investigation include: What governance structures most effectively balance efficiency and equity in AI-assisted HRM? What role can worker representation, collective bargaining, and co-determination arrangements play in shaping GenAI deployment in ways that protect worker interests? How do organizational cultures and leadership practices mediate the effects of GenAI on worker well-being, creative identity, and psychological safety (Baygi & Huysman, 2025; Bankins et al., 2024)?

Fourth, the intersection of GenAI and digital sustainability requires substantially more research attention from management scholars, organizational theorists, and human capital researchers who have the disciplinary tools to analyze the organizational, institutional, and human dimensions of sustainability challenges that economists and computer scientists alone cannot fully address. Brown et al. (2024) call for theory-driven perspectives on GenAI that go beyond instrumental efficiency and innovation considerations to engage with the ethical, social, and institutional dimensions of AI adoption, and the sustainability domain is a particularly important arena where such theoretical development is urgently needed. Research on how organizations can simultaneously pursue GenAI's productivity potential, maintain equitable human capital outcomes, govern algorithmic systems responsibly, and meet environmental sustainability obligations would make a major contribution to both scholarly understanding and practical guidance.

9.2.1 Methodological Approaches for Future Research

The substantive research priorities identified above will remain unrealized without deliberate investment in methodological approaches capable of capturing the temporal depth, organizational complexity, and cross-contextual variation that characterize GenAI's effects on work and organizations. The current literature's reliance on short-term randomized controlled experiments, single-firm case studies, and cross-sectional surveys is a function not only of the field's early developmental stage but of the methodological defaults and incentive structures of management scholarship more broadly. Addressing this methodological gap requires purposive investment in three complementary research designs that are particularly well-suited to the questions GenAI raises for organizational scholars.

Longitudinal Organizational Studies. The most consequential effects of GenAI on organizational structure, workforce composition, and worker well-being are likely to emerge over multi-year time horizons that current experimental and case-based designs cannot access. Longitudinal panel studies tracking cohorts of workers and organizations through sustained GenAI adoption — measuring skill trajectories, career outcomes, job redesign cycles, and organizational performance at multiple time points — are necessary to move beyond the snapshot evidence that dominates the existing literature. Such studies would benefit from integrating objective administrative data sources (payroll records, HR information systems, performance management data) with survey and qualitative instruments to triangulate subjective worker experience against measurable organizational outcomes. Multi-wave survey designs with minimum three-year intervals, embedded within organizational partnerships that provide administrative data access, represent the most feasible near-term approach to generating the longitudinal evidence base that the field requires. Research consortia linking multiple organizations across industries — analogous to the cross-firm panels used in innovation management research — would allow researchers to distinguish organization-specific adoption dynamics from sector- and economy-level trends, substantially enhancing the generalizability of longitudinal findings (Acemoglu & Restrepo, 2022; Brynjolfsson et al., 2023).

Mixed-Method AI Workplace Ethnography. Quantitative productivity experiments and survey-based studies, while valuable, are structurally incapable of capturing the situated, interactional, and interpretive dimensions of human-AI collaboration that shape how GenAI is experienced, resisted, appropriated, and institutionalized in actual organizational settings. Ethnographic and quasi-ethnographic research designs — including extended participant observation, shadowing studies, workplace diary methods, and think-aloud protocols — offer access to the texture of day-to-day human-AI work interaction that survey instruments cannot reach. The most productive methodological approach combines these qualitative methods with quantitative behavioral data (interaction logs, task completion records, communication network analysis) in a mixed-method design that enables researcher triangulation across interpretive and statistical forms of evidence. AI workplace ethnography is particularly well-suited to studying the emergence of new occupational practices, informal norms around GenAI use, patterns of worker resistance and creative appropriation, and the micro-level processes through which organizational cultures of human-AI collaboration are formed and contested — questions that are theoretically central but methodologically underserved in the current literature (Kellogg et al., 2020; Baygi & Huysman, 2025).

Cross-Country Comparative Analysis. The existing evidence base is concentrated in high-income, English-language, technology-sector contexts that are structurally unrepresentative of the global diversity of labor market institutions, regulatory environments, educational systems, and cultural orientations toward AI adoption within which GenAI is being deployed. Cross-country comparative research designs — employing matched organization pairs across institutional contexts, comparative case study methodologies in the tradition of comparative institutionalism, and internationally coordinated survey instruments — are necessary to generate the context-sensitive theoretical frameworks required for responsible global GenAI governance. Such designs should explicitly sample variation in institutional dimensions known to moderate technology adoption outcomes: employment protection legislation strength, collective bargaining coverage, vocational education and training system architecture, and AI regulatory frameworks. Comparative analysis across the liberal market economies of the Anglophone world, the coordinated market economies of continental Europe (particularly those subject to the EU AI Act), and the developmental state economies of East and Southeast Asia — as well as the middle-income country contexts where Gmyrek et al. (2023) identify the greatest GenAI employment displacement risks — would generate theoretical insights of both scholarly and policy significance that no single-country research program can produce. International research collaborations, potentially coordinated through bodies such as the International Labour Organization or the OECD, provide the most institutionally feasible mechanism for developing the multi-site data infrastructure that rigorous cross-country comparative GenAI research requires (Gmyrek et al., 2023; Dwivedi et al., 2023).

9.3 Conclusion

This chapter has argued that generative artificial intelligence represents a genuinely transformative force for the redesign of work, jobs, and organizational structures — one that cannot be adequately understood through the lens of prior technological transitions, cannot be governed through the extension of existing management practices without significant adaptation, and cannot be safely left to unfold without deliberate and institutionally embedded attention to its human, organizational, and social consequences. Drawing on a diverse and growing body of theoretical and empirical scholarship, the chapter has developed a multilayer conceptual framework that maps GenAI's cascading effects across three interacting analytical levels — organizational macro structures, job and role meso design, and individual worker micro experience — and situates these effects within the cross-cutting dimensions of digital sustainability governance and strategic human capital management.

The key insight that emerges from this synthesis is that GenAI's ultimate implications for work and organizations are not technologically determined by the intrinsic capabilities of AI systems but are profoundly and consequentially shaped by the human capital strategies, governance choices, institutional frameworks, and organizational cultures within which GenAI is deployed. Technologies do not act in organizational vacuums; they are deployed, governed, resisted, adapted, and ultimately institutionalized through processes that are fundamentally human and social in character. Organizations that invest seriously and sustainably in the complementary human capabilities required for effective AI governance — domain expertise, critical judgment, AI literacy, ethical reasoning, and interpersonal and relational skills — that maintain meaningful worker agency, voice, and participation in the design of AI-integrated work systems, and that embed sustainability, equity, and accountability considerations in their AI strategies from the outset will be not only better positioned to realize GenAI's considerable potential but better able to do so in ways that are organizationally resilient, socially legitimate, and humanly meaningful.

The scholarly community has a critical and timely role to play in generating the longitudinal, comparative, multilevel, and interdisciplinary evidence base required to guide these organizational transformations through their most consequential early stages. The existing literature, rich and growing as it is, predominantly captures the earliest phase of a technological transition that is likely to unfold over decades and whose ultimate social consequences will be shaped as much by the quality of human governance as by the trajectory of AI capabilities. Sustained, rigorous, and socially engaged scholarly inquiry into the human, organizational, and societal dimensions of GenAI-enabled work is not merely an intellectual opportunity; it is a responsibility that management scholars, organizational theorists, and human capital researchers are distinctively positioned to fulfill.

REFERENCES

Acemoglu, D., & Restrepo, P. (2022). Tasks, automation, and the rise in U.S. wage inequality. *Econometrica*, *90*(5), 1973–2016. DOI: 10.3982/ECTA19815

Bankins, S., Ocampo, A. C., Marrone, M., Restubog, S. L. D., & Woo, S. E. (2024). A multilevel review of artificial intelligence in organizations: Implications for organizational behavior research and practice. *Journal of Organizational Behavior*, *45*(2), 159–182. DOI: 10.1002/job.2735

Baygi, R. M., & Huysman, M. (2025). Generative AI and the social fabric of organizations. *Organization Studies*. Advance online publication. DOI: 10.1177/14761270251385456

Brown, O., Davison, R. M., Decker, S., Ellis, D. A., Faulconbridge, J., Gore, J., Greenwood, M., Islam, G., Lubinski, C., MacKenzie, N. G., Meyer, R., Muzio, D., Quattrone, P., Ravishankar, M. N., Zilber, T., Ren, S., Sarala, R. M., & Hibbert, P. (2024). Theory-driven perspectives on generative artificial intelligence in business and management. *British Journal of Management*, *35*(1), 3–23. DOI: 10.1111/1467-8551.12788

Brynjolfsson, E., Li, D., & Raymond, L. R. (2023). Generative AI at work (NBER Working Paper No. 31161). National Bureau of Economic Research. DOI: 10.3386/w31161

Budhwar, P., Chowdhury, S., Wood, G., Aguinis, H., Bamber, G. J., Beltran, J. R., Boselie, P., Lee Cooke, F., Decker, S., DeNisi, A., Dey, P. K., Guest, D., Knoblich, A. J., Malik, A., Paauwe, J., Papagiannidis, S., Patel, C., Pereira, V., Ren, S., & Varma, A. (2023). Human resource management in the age of generative artificial intelligence: Perspectives and research directions on ChatGPT. *Human Resource Management Journal*, *33*(3), 606–659. DOI: 10.1111/1748-8583.12524

Cheng, M. M., & Hackett, R. D. (2021). A critical review of algorithms in HRM: Definition, theory, and practice. *Human Resource Management Review*, *31*(1), 100698. DOI: 10.1016/j.hrmr.2019.100698

Chowdhury, S., Budhwar, P., & Wood, G. (2024). Generative artificial intelligence in business: Towards a strategic human resource management framework. *British Journal of Management*, *35*(4), 1680–1691. DOI: 10.1111/1467-8551.12824

Corvello, V. (2025). Generative AI and the future of innovation management: A human-centered perspective and an agenda for future research. *Journal of Open Innovation*, *11*(1), 100456. DOI: 10.1016/j.joitmc.2024.100456

Dell'Acqua, F., McFowland, E., III, Mollick, E. R., Lifshitz-Assaf, H., Kellogg, K., Rajendran, S., Krayer, L., Candelon, F., & Lakhani, K. R. (2023). Navigating the jagged technological frontier: Field experimental evidence of the effects of AI on knowledge worker productivity and quality (Harvard Business School Working Paper No. 24-013). Harvard Business School. DOI: 10.2139/ssrn.4573321

Dwivedi, Y. K., Kshetri, N., Hughes, L., Slade, E. L., Jeyaraj, A., Kar, A. K., Baabdullah, A. M., Koohang, A., Raghavan, V., Ahuja, M., Albanna, H., Albashrawi, M. A., Al-Busaidi, A. S., Balakrishnan, J., Barlette, Y., Basu, S., Bose, I., Brooks, L., Buhalis, D., & Wright, R. (2023). Opinion paper: 'So what if ChatGPT wrote it?' Multidisciplinary perspectives on opportunities, challenges and implications of generative conversational AI for research, practice and policy. *International Journal of Information Management*, *71*, 102642. DOI: 10.1016/j.ijinfomgt.2023.102642

Eloundou, T., Manning, S., Mishkin, P., & Rock, D. (2024). GPTs are GPTs: Labor market impact potential of LLMs. *Science*, *384*(6702), 1306–1308. DOI: 10.1126/science.adj0998 PMID: 38900883

Fountaine, T., McCarthy, B., & Saleh, T. (2022). Building the AI-powered organization. *Harvard Business Review*, *100*(4), 62–73.

Gmyrek, P., Berg, J., & Bescond, D. (2023). Generative AI and jobs: A global analysis of potential effects on job quantity and quality (ILO Working Paper 96). International Labour Organization. DOI: 10.54394/FHEM8239

Grimes, M., von Krogh, G., Feuerriegel, S., Rink, F., & Gruber, M. (2023). From scarcity to abundance: Scholars and scholarship in an age of generative artificial intelligence. *Academy of Management Journal*, *66*(6), 1617–1624. DOI: 10.5465/amj.2023.4006

Hinds, P., & von Krogh, G. (2024). Generative AI, emerging technology, and organizing: Towards a theory of progressive encapsulation. *Organization Theory*, *5*(4), 26317877241293478. Advance online publication. DOI: 10.1177/26317877241293478

Jarrahi, M. H. (2018). Artificial intelligence and the future of work: Human-AI symbiosis in organizational decision-making. *Business Horizons*, *61*(4), 577–586. DOI: 10.1016/j.bushor.2018.03.007

Kanbach, D. K., Heiduk, L., Blueher, G., Schreiter, M., & Lahmann, A. (2023). The GenAI is out of the bottle: Generative artificial intelligence from a business model innovation perspective. *Review of Managerial Science*, *18*(4), 1171–1197. DOI: 10.1007/s11846-023-00696-z

Kellogg, K. C., Valentine, M. A., & Christin, A. (2020). Algorithms at work: The new contested terrain of control. *The Academy of Management Annals*, *14*(1), 366–410. DOI: 10.5465/annals.2018.0174

Leippold, M. (2023). Sentiment spin: Attacking financial sentiment with GPT-4. *Finance Research Letters*, *55*, 103957. DOI: 10.1016/j.frl.2023.103957

Liang, W., Yuksekgonul, M., Mao, Y., Wu, E., & Zou, J. (2024). GPT detectors are biased against non-native English writers. *Patterns (New York, N.Y.)*, *4*(7), 100779. DOI: 10.1016/j.patter.2023.100779 PMID: 37521038

Malik, A., Budhwar, P., & Kazmi, B. A. (2023). Artificial intelligence (AI)-assisted HRM: Towards an extended strategic HRM framework. *Human Resource Management Review*, *33*(1), 100940. DOI: 10.1016/j.hrmr.2022.100940

Mariani, M., & Dwivedi, Y. K. (2024). Generative artificial intelligence in innovation management: A preview of future research developments. *Journal of Business Research*, *175*, 114542. DOI: 10.1016/j.jbusres.2024.114542

Mollick, E., & Mollick, L. (2023). Using AI to implement effective teaching strategies in classrooms: Five strategies, including prompts. SSRN Electronic Journal. DOI: 10.2139/ssrn.4391243

Mollick, E. R., & Mollick, L. (2023). Assigning AI: Seven approaches for students, with prompts. SSRN Electronic Journal. DOI: 10.2139/ssrn.4475995

Noy, S., & Zhang, W. (2023). Experimental evidence on the productivity effects of generative artificial intelligence. *Science*, *381*(6654), 187–192. DOI: 10.1126/science.adh2586 PMID: 37440646

Peng, S., Kalliamvakou, E., Cihon, P., & Demirer, M. (2023). The impact of AI on developer productivity: Evidence from GitHub Copilot. arXiv preprint. https://doi.org//arXiv.2302.06590DOI: 10.48550

Raisch, S., & Krakowski, S. (2021). Artificial intelligence and management: The automation–augmentation paradox. *Academy of Management Review*, *46*(1), 192–210. DOI: 10.5465/amr.2018.0072

Shrestha, Y. R., Ben-Menahem, S. M., & von Krogh, G. (2023). Organizational decision-making structures in the age of artificial intelligence. *California Management Review*, *61*(4), 66–83. DOI: 10.1177/0008125619862257

Tambe, P., Cappelli, P., & Yakubovich, V. (2019). Artificial intelligence in human resources management: Challenges and a path forward. *California Management Review*, *61*(4), 15–42. DOI: 10.1177/0008125619867910

Vrontis, D., Christofi, M., Pereira, V., Tarba, S., Makrides, A., & Trichina, E. (2022). Artificial intelligence, robotics, advanced technologies and human resource management: A systematic review. *International Journal of Human Resource Management, 33*(6), 1237–1266. DOI: 10.1080/09585192.2020.1871398

Xu, F., Hou, J., Chen, W., & Xie, K. (2025). Generative AI and organizational structure in the knowledge economy. *SSRN*. https://doi.org/DOI: 10.2139/ssrn.5242296

KEY TERMS AND DEFINITIONS

Algorithmic Management: The use of computer-programmed procedures and algorithms to coordinate labor. This includes tracking performance, assigning tasks, and making HR decisions (like hiring or firing) via data-driven software rather than through direct human supervision.

Automation-Augmentation Paradox: The phenomenon where increasing automation doesn't necessarily eliminate human work but shifts its nature. While machines take over routine tasks (automation), they simultaneously create a greater need for human oversight and specialized skills to manage the new technology (augmentation).

Digital Sustainability: The practice of using digital resources in a way that ensures long-term environmental, social, and economic health. It involves minimizing the carbon footprint of data centers and ensuring that AI deployment doesn't lead to toxic work cultures or social inequity.

Generative Artificial Intelligence: A subset of AI capable of creating new content—such as text, images, or code—by learning patterns from massive datasets. Unlike analytical AI, which classifies data, GenAI uses probabilistic models to produce original outputs that mimic human creativity and logic.

Human Capital: The intangible collective resources—including skills, experience, intelligence, and training—possessed by individuals or a workforce. It represents the economic value of a human's capacity to perform labor, which is increasingly defined by the ability to collaborate with AI.

Job Design: The specification of contents, methods, and relationships of jobs to satisfy technological and organizational requirements as well as the social and personal requirements of the job holder. It focuses on balancing task variety, autonomy, and the integration of digital tools.

Knowledge Workers: Professionals whose main capital is knowledge, such as doctors, lawyers, and software engineers. Their work involves "thinking for a living," and they are currently the primary group facing significant disruption as AI begins to handle complex cognitive tasks.

Organizational Structure: The formal system of hierarchy, roles, and reporting relationships within a company. Generative AI often flattens these structures by reducing the need for middle-management oversight and enabling decentralized decision-making through better data accessibility across all levels.

Task Displacement: The process where specific components of a job are taken over by technology. Unlike total job loss, displacement occurs when a machine performs a specific task more efficiently than a human, requiring the worker to pivot to remaining or newly created tasks.

Work Redesign: The intentional process of restructuring how jobs are performed to improve efficiency and employee well-being. In the age of AI, this often involves shifting human focus away from repetitive tasks toward high-value activities like complex problem-solving and emotional intelligence.

Chapter 7
Generative AI-Based Ethical Evaluation in Workplace Management Systems

Bhimavarapu Usharani
http://orcid.org/0009-0008-5625-4583
Department of Computer Science and Engineering, Koneru Lakshmaiah Education Foundation, Vaddeswaam, India

ABSTRACT

GenAI Ethical Generative Artificial Intelligence (GenAI) has become a significant paradigm in the contemporary people management as GenAI allows organizations to make better decisions and be fair, transparent, and accountable. The paper suggests a smart platform of evaluating the ethical aspects in people management through a bistacked ResNet-18 model. First, an organized questionnaire had been developed to gather the data belonging to ethical aspects trust, fairness, privacy, transparency, and accountability in AI-supported working conditions. The survey instrument was piloted on 20 individuals to determine the clarity and organization of the survey instrument and two questions were slightly revised and one section had to be rearranged. In the primary data collection stage, 13 respondents were willing to take the questionnaire and answer the survey.

INTRODUCTION

The use of GenAI (Ethical Generative Artificial Intelligence) has gained more and more significance in contemporary people management practices when organi-

DOI: 10.4018/979-8-2600-2726-4.ch007

zations embrace application of intelligent technologies in support of human resource functions. The increased use of automated systems in recruitment, performance reviews, and employee engagement needs to be given a solid ethical ground to provide fairness and transparency. Absence of ethical standards Plausibly unwanted, AI systems can inadvertently support bias or discrimination inherent in historical data. Ethical GenAI assists companies in keeping between staff members and managers and employs sophisticated technologies. It also makes sure that AIs make decisions that consider the dignity and rights of employees. People management is sensitive information and data, which should be managed in a responsible manner. Ethics models help organizations to be accountable in their use of AI tools. They also make sure that AI is used to supplement human judgment and not to take it over altogether. Ethical GenAI is necessary because of the duty to take care of the employees and enhance organizational efficiency. Thus, responsible and sustainable workforce management necessitates the assimilation of ethical values into the GenAI systems.

A significant requirement of Ethical GenAI in people management is to foster fairness and remove bias in the processes of making HR decisions. Most AI models are trained on past data sets which could include discriminatory trends on hiring biases. On the one hand, unexplored biases may be reproduced by artificial intelligence systems. The Ethical GenAI will make sure that the algorithms are set in a way that they identify and reduce these biases. It encourages all candidates to have equal opportunities, irrespective of their gender, ethnicity, age, and background. Such a strategy fosters non-discriminatory workplaces in which diversity is appreciated. The moral codes also promote companies to conduct periodic audits of AI systems. Open assessment systems assist the organizations in being aware of the process of decision making. This enhances accountability in the recruitment and promotion decision.

The other significant Ethical GenAI aim is to secure the privacy of employees and confidential organizational information. Personal information, salary records, performance review, and behavioral analytics are some of the confidential information that people management systems manage frequently. The abuse or unauthorized publicity of this information may cause severe legal and moral problems. Ethical GenAI advocates good data governance so that the information of employees is not compromised. It focuses not only on safe data storage but also on authoritative access and adherence to the privacy policies. Organizations need to make sure that AI systems only gather data that is necessary and not monitoring the employees overboard. The ethics also make employees aware of data use. The privacy in the use of data will create trust between workers and discourage information misuse.

Ethical GenAI is also required to make automated decision-making in human resource activities more transparent. Several AI-based systems can be complex models that are likely to be a black box and the worker finds it hard to understand how the decisions are made. Moral deployment promotes explicable AI practices which enable HR practitioners and workers to decode results. The employees will believe the system more when they have information about the reasons why they are hired, promoted or evaluated. Transparency also enables organizations to know the mistakes or injustice. The ethical GenAI will expect organizations to explain explicitly how AI applications will be used to help in people management processes. It also makes sure that employees are not rated without fair judgment by hidden algorithms. Ethical GenAI enhances integrity in organizations by encouraging transparency and divulgence. Finally, open AI solutions aid in the establishment of the culture of responsibility in the management of the workplace.

Responsible automation of HR is also supported with the use of Ethical GenAI in people management. Although AI technologies could make the screening of applicants more efficient, the process of employee onboarding more efficient, and performance analytics more efficient, overuse of automation can decrease the human nature of the management. Ethical GenAI also makes sure that technology serves on human decision making and not on human empathy and judgment. HR professionals continue to be an essential element in the interpretation of AI-generated insights. Ethical systems promote a reasonable cooperation between humans and intelligent technologies. Such a strategy leaves no possibility of excessive dependence on automated recommendations. It also makes sure that decisions that are sensitive like promotions, disciplinary measures, or terminations are exercised by human hands. The responsible automation is very productive, and it does not destroy the organization values. Ethical GenAI therefore assists organizations to attain technological progress without affecting human-oriented management.

The well-being and good culture in the workplace by employing Ethical GenAI are another goal. Measuring productivity, analyzing workplace communication, and assessing the level of employee engagement are increasingly measured with AI powered tools. These technologies can be overly surveilling and stress-inducing to the employees if they are abused. Ethical GenAI provides ethical principles to avoid surveillance habits. It also makes sure that AI applications are oriented to enhancing employee experience and not controlling employee behavior. As an instance of an example, AI can be used to detect burnout trends and suggest wellness programs. Ethical frameworks provide a way of making sure that such insights are employed in a constructive way. Organizations should not violate individual autonomy and work-life balance. Companies will be able to build a healthier working environment by encouraging ethical use of artificial intelligence. Ethical GenAI, consequently, promotes sustainable development of the working force and satisfaction of employees.

Ethical GenAI is also relevant in reinforcement of diversity, equity, and inclusion (DEI) efforts in organizations. The current working environment is meant to provide equal chances to people belonging to various background and communities. The AI systems are capable of tracing various talents and minimizing human discrimination during hiring operations. Nevertheless, AI models are likely to inadvertently discriminate against some groups unless the procedure is ethically regulated. Ethical GenAI guarantees that algorithms are created on inclusive data and bias restrictions. It also promotes organizations to see AI results against demographic groups. This assists in avoiding discrimination and facilitates fair representation of workforce. Company ethics on AI enhances organizational diversity. Because of this, Ethical GenAI enhances the creation of inclusive and socially responsible work environments.

The other important requirement of Ethical GenAI is to ensure compliance with regulatory policies and accountability among the organizations. Regulatory organisms and governments are coming up with regulations of responsible use of AI. To safeguard their interests, the organizations should make sure that their AI systems do not contradict the legal requirements concerning data protection, employment regulations, and transparency in algorithms. Ethical GenAI models can be adopted to guide the companies to harmonize their people management systems with these rules. They are also promoting internal AI policy development. The adherence to ethical standards will decrease the level of legal conflicts and reputation. It shows the organization believes in being ethical in technological innovation. Stakeholders also have confidence in responsible AI practices. As such, Ethical GenAI is an advantage of legal adherence and credibility to an organization.

Ethical GenAI also assists the companies in gaining trust over time by the employees, stakeholders and the society. People management is based on trust, which is essential in situations when higher technologies mediate the decisions made at work. Employees should have the assurance that AI systems do not discriminate them and takes into consideration their rights. Ethical models give parameters, which ensure transparency, fairness, and accountability. Those organizations that practice ethical AI behavior are socially responsible in their innovation. This reinforces the bonds among employees and the management. Trust also helps to develop and use new technologies without fear or opposition by the employees. Ethical GenAI is thus a source of reconciliation between technology advancement and humanity. Reliable AI will facilitate a sustainable organizational growth in the long run.

To sum up, a responsible and effective management of people in the digital era is impossible without Ethical Generative AI. With the introduction of AI to HR activities by organizations, ethical regulation grows in relevance. Ethical GenAI makes workforce management equitable, transparent, and places confidentiality and responsible automation. It fosters diversity, employee welfare and trust under organizations. To prevent harmful implications related to biased or nontransparent AI systems, various organizations can rely on coordinating technological innovation with ethical principles. Ethical frameworks assist the companies in creating AI tools that assist in the management that is human-centered. They also make sure that they meet the requirements of law and the society. Ethical GenAI is not meant to enhance efficiency only but also to support human values. Consequently, to create sustainable and fair people management, in the sphere of AI, it is of paramount importance to consider ethical issues.

The suggested Ethical GenAI paradigm with bistacked ResNet-18 outsmarts a range of limitations which are evident in other types of machine learning and traditional deep learning methods of people management analysis. Conventional designs like FNN, RNN, and single CNN do not always have the capacity to handle complex relationships involving ethics due to the shallow representations of features and sensitivity to imbalance among the data and noise. On the other hand, the bistacked ResNet-18 design uses residual learning that makes it feature deeper extraction, and does not feature any gradient degradation issues that are usually associated with deep networks. The dual stacked architecture permits to learn heterogeneous inputs also in parallel, e.g., ethical perception indicators, organizational attributes, and behavioral factors, to enhance the representation learning. The other problem is that the existing models are associated with redundancy in high-dimensional datasets that would reduce the accuracy and raise the level of computational complexity; the Particle Swarm Optimization (PSO)-based feature selection which can only retain the most informative ethical features helps to solve the problem. Moreover, the traditional learning methods are frequently inexpressible and unstable in ethical decision prediction, and residual relations are useful in increasing convergence stability and stable validation. Generalization capability is also enhanced by the fact that the proposed framework is better at feature fusion and overfitting is less likely to occur as in previous models. In contrast to the classical AI systems, which are interested in the accuracy of predictions only, the offered approach in the framework of which the measures of fairness, transparency, privacy, and accountability are embedded directly into the learning pipeline, resulting in responsible AI results. Also, the model represents better convergence rates and reduced loss values signify effective learning conducts. The proposed approach, with its combination of the best feature selection and the deep residual learning, has a high accuracy, better evaluation of ethics compliance than existing models, and also more reliable support of decision-making than existing models. On the whole, the framework offers a maturity and ethically conscious people management system built upon AI.

The high rate of development of generative artificial intelligence (AI) has substantially changed the way organizations do their activities, especially in human resource management (HRM) and workplace decisions. The use of generative AI technology (ChatGPT and other systems) is actively being introduced into HR operations to increase the efficiency of operations, robotize repetitive processes, and aid in the strategic decision-making process (Khan et al., 2024; Budhwar et al., 2023). Such systems allow organizations to simplify the recruitment process, employee interactions, performance review, and training, which enhances the overall productivity and organizational performance (Al Naqbi et al., 2024; Garcia and Kwok, 2025). Moreover, generative AI can be used to provide data-driven information to enable managers to make informed decisions, which involve data analysis and predictive modeling on a large scale (Rane, 2024; Hernandez-Tamurejo et al., 2025).

Although these are the positive aspects, the use of generative AI at work has a number of ethical, managerial, and operational issues. The key concerns in AI systems implementation have been identified as bias, transparency, accountability, and data privacy (Al-Kfairy et al., 2024; Afreen et al., 2025). Biases in the AI-generated outputs might result in unjust decisions, especially in sensitive HR decisions such as hiring and promotion (Arista et al., 2025). Additionally, the absence of transparency in AI models can usually make trust and acceptance among employees and stakeholders more complex (Vaishnav et al., 2024; Jeong et al., 2025). To tackle these issues, it is necessary to establish strong ethical principles and regulatory systems that will guarantee responsible AI use (Wamba et al., 2025; Bautista et al., 2024).

Moreover, organizational preparedness and perception of employees are essential factors to an effective adoption of generative AI. Such aspects as algorithmic ethics, intellectual humility, and user awareness mean a lot to employee-AI system interactions and trust (Zheng et al., 2026; Yi et al., 2025). Employees need to be trained and sensitized to provide them with the skills and ethical knowledge required to use AI in a responsible manner (Vaishnav et al., 2024). Also, by cultivating a culture of ethical AI use, it is possible to make sure that technological progress corresponds to the organizational values and social expectations (Odia, 2026; Söllner et al., 2025).

Moving forward, it is possible to assume that the incorporation of generative AI into organizational and knowledge management processes will keep on changing and present opportunities as well as challenges. As much as AI can promote innovation, efficiency, and competitive advantage, organizations should strike a balance between such advantages and ethical issues and risk management approaches (Al-Kfairy, 2025; Rane, 2023). The direction of future research is to focus on the interdisciplinary approach, integrating technological innovation with ethical, managerial, and regulatory perspectives to make AI usage sustainable and responsible (Budhwar et al., 2023; Wamba et al., 2025).

The high rate of development of generative artificial intelligence (AI) has substantially changed the way organizations do their activities, especially in human resource management (HRM) and workplace decisions. The use of generative AI technology (ChatGPT and other systems) is actively being introduced into HR operations to increase the efficiency of operations, robotize repetitive processes, and aid in the strategic decision-making process (Khan et al., 2024; Budhwar et al., 2023). Such systems allow organizations to simplify the recruitment process, employee interactions, performance review, and training, which enhances the overall productivity and organizational performance (Al Naqbi et al., 2024; Garcia and Kwok, 2025). Moreover, generative AI can be used to provide data-driven information to enable managers to make informed decisions, which involve data analysis and predictive modeling on a large scale (Rane, 2024; Hernandez-Tamurejo et al., 2025).

Although these are the positive aspects, the use of generative AI at work has a number of ethical, managerial, and operational issues. The key concerns in AI systems implementation have been identified as bias, transparency, accountability, and data privacy (Al-Kfairy et al., 2024a; Afreen et al., 2025). Biases in the AI-generated outputs might result in unjust decisions, especially in sensitive HR decisions such as hiring and promotion (Arista et al., 2025). Additionally, the absence of transparency in AI models can usually make trust and acceptance among employees and stakeholders more complex (Vaishnav et al., 2024; Jeong et al., 2025). To tackle these issues, it is necessary to establish strong ethical principles and regulatory systems that will guarantee responsible AI use (Wamba et al., 2025; Bautista et al., 2024).

Moreover, organizational preparedness and perception of employees are essential factors to an effective adoption of generative AI. Such aspects as algorithmic ethics, intellectual humility, and user awareness mean a lot to employee-AI system interactions and trust (Zheng et al., 2026; Yi et al., 2025). Employees need to be trained and sensitized to provide them with the skills and ethical knowledge required to use AI in a responsible manner (Vaishnav et al., 2024). Also, by cultivating a culture of ethical AI use, it is possible to make sure that technological progress corresponds to the organizational values and social expectations (Odia, 2026; Söllner et al., 2025).

Moving forward, it is possible to assume that the incorporation of generative AI into organizational and knowledge management processes will keep on changing and present opportunities as well as challenges. As much as AI can promote innovation, efficiency, and competitive advantage, organizations should strike a balance between such advantages and ethical issues and risk management approaches (Al-Kfairy, 2025; Rane, 2023). The direction of future research is to focus on the interdisciplinary approach, integrating technological innovation with ethical, managerial, and regulatory perspectives to make AI usage sustainable and responsible (Budhwar et al., 2023; Wamba et al., 2025).

METHODOLOGY

The proposed Ethical GenAI people management methodology would start with gathering survey based text and numeric data that would reflect ethical aspects of fairness, transparency, privacy, trust, and accountability. The dataset obtained is preprocessed with data cleaning, data normalization and a screening criterion to assess quality and consistency. The Particle Swarm Optimization (PSO) is then used to select the relevant attributes to reduce redundancy and retain important ethical indicators. The learned representations of textual and structured input are inputted into a bistacked ResNet-18 network architecture, where the individual branches of the network learn the representations. Features extraction in the two branches are then combined and processed through the fully connected layers to acquire ethical decision patterns. Lastly, the model is used to produce predictions on the outcome of ethical AI adoption and people management so that organizational decision support could be reliable and responsible.

MATERIAL

The study data was gathered by the use of a structured questionnaire meant to analyze the application of the Ethical Generative Artificial Intelligence (GenAI) in managing people. The survey tool was divided into several sections about how the employees think the organization was fair, transparent, accountable, and did not violate their privacy, and adopted AI responsibly. Before the actual process of data collection, a pilot test was done using 20 qualified participants to check on the clarity of the questionnaire, wording and time that they would need to take to complete the questionnaire. The subjects in the pilot phase gave the feedback about the readability and form of questions in the surveys. According to their recommendations, two questions were revised to be more understandable and one set of questions was rearranged to create a better logical flow and understanding by the respondents.

After the pilot testing of the questionnaire, the updated version of the questionnaire was administered to the potential participants that met all preset eligibility requirements about the organizational experience and the knowledge level with digital technologies of the workplace. There were 13 people who initially responded to the invitation to the survey and started to fill in the questionnaire. The 13 respondents were able to complete the questionnaire. Yet, the survey tool had inherent screening queries aiming to qualify the respondents and quality of the data. At the data validation stage, seven cases did not pass in the conditions of in-survey screeners which means that those statements did not correspond to the inclusion criteria. Such cases were thus eliminated off the dataset in order to uphold the integrity and reliability of the study.

Following the screening and validation steps, the response to the questions did not qualify all the eligibility criteria at the same time, which ended up giving 0 final dataset responses. The goal of the final analysis was that the completed questionnaires would serve as a useful source of information about the structure of the survey and the attention given to the participants the questionnaires were not included in the final analytical data set since the screening failed. The data collection exercise however was informative on finding of clarity in questionnaire, screening design and respondent behaviour.

PREPROCESSING

Preprocessing was to be done to determine the quality, reliability and consistency of the gathered dataset concerning Ethical Generative Artificial Intelligence (GenAI) in people management. First the answers received in the online questionnaire were checked to get incomplete answers, duplicate answers and invalid answers. The survey contained inbuilt screening questions that screened the eligibility of the respondents as well as ensuring that respondents were up to the required definitions. These screening items were screened in the preprocessing stage to narrow down the responses that were not meeting the study requirements. Among the questionnaires that were filled out, 7 of them did not fit the in-survey screening criteria and were thus eliminated out of the dataset to ensure an appropriate level of data integrity. This move guaranteed data on responses that contained the minimum requirements in the criteria used to qualify as responding to the aspect of analysis.

The rest of the responses were studied in the aftermath of the screening process to assess the lack of values, uncoherent responses, and uncharacteristic tendencies that might impact the integrity of data. Any documentation which had partial information or conflicting answers were identified to be eliminated or rectified. Formatting consistency of the dataset (uniform coding of non-metric variables in the dataset as well as the scales of responses in the questionnaire) was also verified. The necessary text-based responses were standardized by means of correcting typing errors and making sure that the input of participants was standardized. Also, the data cleaning measures were undertaken to remove noise and irrelevant data, which could affect the outcomes of the analysis. These data processing measures were required to convert the raw survey data into a patterned data that could be analyzed.

The preprocessing process was based on the conventional data cleaning and verification rules, but the use of eligibility screening led to deleting all the received answers, and no data could be obtained in the final dataset. This finding emphasised the need to have well thought screening procedures and proper participant recruitment plans. Although the statistical analysis could not be performed with the help of the records that were not used, the process based on the preprocessing was necessary to assess the efficiency of the questionnaire structure, screening logic, and data validation processes.

FEATURE SELECTION

Particle Swarm Optimization (PSO) was used to select the most useful attributes out of the gathered data about the Ethical Generative Artificial Intelligence (GenAI) in people management. The process of feature selection is significant in that it assists with the problem of dimensionality reduction in identifiable data, redundancy, and the enhancement of the analytic models. This paper has used PSO as an optimization method that follows the social dynamics of a bird flock and fish school. The swarm particles are characterized by each one representing the potential subsets of features and the movement of the swarm particles is across the search space with a view to finding the best combination of the features that makes the most contribution to the predictive or analytical goals of the research. The algorithm will update the location and velocity of the particles as an iterative case depending on the experience of the individual particles and those of the other particles within the swarm.

Candidates During the process of feature selection, the dataset attributes of ethical AI perception, transparency, fairness, employee trust, data privacy, and responsible automation were taken as candidate features. These features were measured by the PSO algorithm based on a set fitness criterion using an already known fitness valuation that reflected the significance as well as the contribution of each subset of features to the analytical goal. Particles tried various combinations of features and slowly reduced to an optimum or near optimum subset which gave the highest score on evaluation. This was done to remove unfortunate or weak properties that could bring noise or analysis efficiency. PSO has an iterative character which made the technique effective to search large feature spaces and find significant correlations of variables.

PSO-based feature selection of the feature improved the dataset in terms of interpretability and efficiency because it did not consider all variables relevant to the determination of Ethical GenAI adoption in the people management and highlighted only the variables that were considered relevant. Helping cut wasteful and less informative features, the technique will help analyze the data more correctly and provide more efficient models that will work better in the further investigation. The identified properties are the most powerful aspects that can impact ethical AI practices in an organizational setup, such as fairness in decision-making, transparency in AI systems, protection of employee privacy, accountability, and trust in AI-supported management systems. On the whole, the feature selection based on PSO is a very important factor to structure the dataset in optimal way and make the subsequent analytical work more reliable.

BISTACKED RESNET

Figure 1. People Management using Gen AI

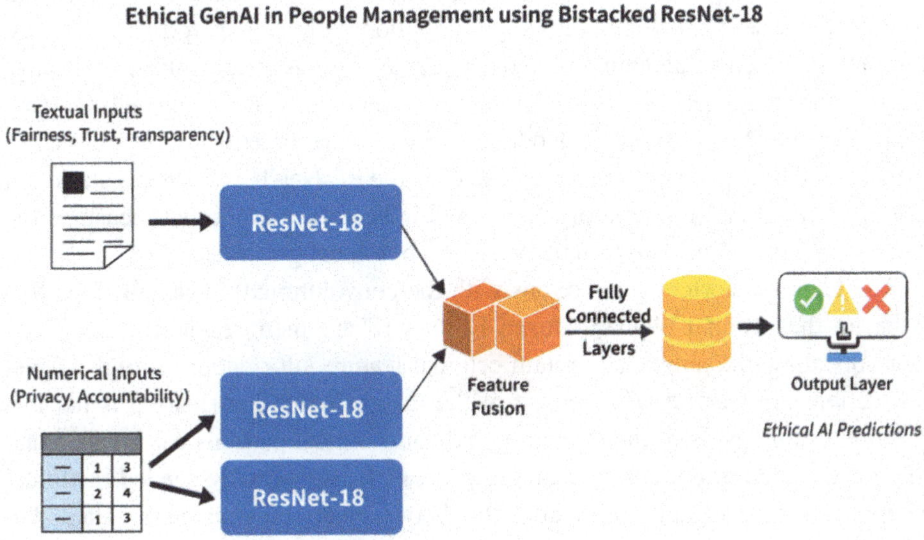

Ethical Generative Artificial intelligence (GenAI) in people management aims at having intelligent learning systems integrated into human resource decision-making in a manner that is both fair, transparent, accountable, and in a non-invasive way. The theoretical background is an integration of the ethical AI principles and deep learning architectures that can find the complex behavioral and organizational patterns in both structured and unstructured data about the employees. People management in the context of present-day organizations is the analysis of multidimensional input which includes employee feedback, as well as trust indicators, performance measures, and the ethical compliance measures. Nonlinear relationships between these variables are often not well represented by traditional methods of analysis. Thus, deep neural networks and in particular, residual learning models are used to enhance learning representation as well as to provide ethical evaluation results.

The suggested framework uses a Bistacked ResNet 18 network, which is based on the lines of theory of residual neural network. ResNet-18 presents residual learning with shortcut follow-up links which enable incoming and outgoing gradients in direct manner across layers to skip the issue of vanishing gradient experienced in deep networks. The model is learned not to learn direct mappings, but instead learns residual functions, which enhance convergence and training stability. Two practical uses of this in the framework of Ethical GenAI are that the model is able to acquire subtle positive ethical patterns like bias indicators, perceived fairness, and accountability cues using complicated organizational information.

The bistacked design denotes stacking two ResNet-18 models parallel to each other, but independent of heterogeneous inputs. Persons management information usually comprises textual data (employees opinions, ethical perception utterances, feedback statements), and numerical data (privacy ratings, responsibility measurements, assessment scores). Textual representations are then fed through the first stack of the ResNet-18, which encodes and feeds semantic ethical feature of trust, fairness, and transparency. The second stack is the ResNet-18, which is a stack that takes numerical or structured organizational indicators, a stack that measures the statistical relationships between the variables of ethical governance.

The Identity shortcut connections with the convolutional transformations that make up the residual blocks of each ResNet-18 are their residual blocks. The shortcuts allow the network to retain original feature information as higher-level abstractions are learned. The benefit of the theory is that information is not lost in more distant layers of the structure, and some ethical patterns can be read and kept unchanged throughout the training process. It is especially needed in ethical AI applications as meaningful relationship between variables can be maintained to achieve explainability and responsible decision-making.

Following the single extraction of features, the bistacked structure does the feature fusion, which combines the results of both branches of ResNet. The feature fusion theory presupposes the appearance of the ethical decision-making due to the interplay between the subjective perceptions and the objective measures within an organization. The model uses the combination of both semantic and numerical features and creates a single ethical representation space. This amalgamated projection encompasses both the operational and behavioral aspect of people management ethics and enhances the degree of prediction.

These merged properties are subsequently delivered using fully connected layers that do nonlinear transformation and dimensional reduction. These layers train the decision boundaries that train or forecast the ethical results like the level of ethical compliance, whether unbiased or responsible AI adoption readiness. Activation functions induce nonlinearity and allow the system to simulate the complicated ethical dependencies which would have been represented through the linear approach. The techniques of regularization are used to avoid overfitting and make ethical judgments which can be generalized.

Theoretically, bistacked ResNet-18 model is compatible with human-centered AI principles, according to which the AI supports the decisions of a manager instead of taking them over. The architecture can be interpreted in that the residual learning preserves features continuity between layers. Systems based on Ethical GenAI should be capable of delivering trustworthy reasoning patterns, and residual networks are beneficial in saving traceable feature contributions when making inferences. This helps to promote transparency and accountability of the people management that is supported by AI.

Network optimization Network optimization is usually done by gradient-based learning algorithms, which are designed to minimize a loss function that gives some measure of prediction error. Fairness-representative constraints can be included to the loss function to achieve equal results with respect to the demographic groupings. The theoretical framework would make ethical responsibility not to be distorted by predictive accuracy since the ethical consideration is considered directly when training the model. In this way, learning is performance oriented and ethically limited.

The other theoretical merit to utilize the Bistacked ResNet-18 is that it remains stable to noisy or small data sets. Inconsistencies or subjective variations are frequent in the organizational surveys and the HR datasets. A residual learning enables the model to tune features during adaptive learning, and not to lose important information. This enhances stability and does facilitate a moral judgment even in the case of imperfect or partly faulty datasets.

Overall, Ethical GenAI people management theory based on Bistacked ResNet-18 employs the concepts of deep residual learning and ethical rules of AI governance. Bistacked architecture supports parallel learning of various data types, feature fusion sees through and discerns holistic ethical knowledge, and stable and interpretable learning are provided by residual connections. This theoretical view helps to legitimize, clarify, and own AI-related decision-making when it comes to workforce management and achieve genuine fairness, trust, and morally right organizational growth eventually.

EXPERIMENTAL RESULTS

The proposed Ethical GenAI framework was evaluated experimentally to measure the efficacy of the proposed architecture on the people management using bistacked ResNet-18 architecture. Experiments involved the analysis of the model on the learning of ethical decision patterns in terms of fairness, transparency, privacy, accountability, and trust of the employees in the organizational datasets. Following a preprocessing and feature solving through Particle Swarm Optimization (PSO), the optimized set of features was fed into the bistacked ResNet-18 model to train and validate. The results of the suggested method were compared based on typical performance indicators, including accuracy, precision, recall, the F1-score, and loss convergence pattern. Comparison was also taken to look at the extent to which the proposed architecture enhances stability of learning and consistency of ethical prediction as compared to the traditional machine learning and single network deep learning methodologies. Several experimental conditions were made to examine the contribution of features, convergence rate, and the generalisation ability of the model. The findings indicate that the bistacked residual learning design can be used in data related to people management to successfully capture complex ethical relationships that furnish reliable and interpretable results that can be used to support organizational decisions in a responsible manner because of AI.

Table 1 shows a training performance of bistacked ResNet-18 model on ten epochs. The training accuracy also increases gradually, during the first epoch, training accuracy is 72.4 and by the tenth epoch, the highest training accuracy is 92.8 which demonstrates consistent learning in the course of training the model. In a similar manner the performance of the model in terms of validation accuracy also improves by 70.2 to 91.2 percent, which proves that the model works well when applied to unknown data. There is a steady reduction of the training loss 0.68 to 0.24 indicating successful training of the learning parameters. Meanwhile, the loss on validation decreases to 0.29, which proves the improvement in the prediction stability. The learning rate is also decreased slowly by slowly at the rate of 0.001-0.0006 to help the convergence remain consistent in the later stages of training.

Table 1. Model Training Performance

Epoch	Training Accuracy (%)	Validation Accuracy (%)	Training Loss	Validation Loss	Learning Rate
1	72.4	70.2	0.68	0.72	0.001
2	75.6	73.1	0.61	0.65	0.001
3	78.2	76.5	0.55	0.60	0.0009
4	81.3	79.4	0.49	0.54	0.0009
5	84.1	82.0	0.43	0.49	0.0008
6	86.5	84.6	0.38	0.44	0.0008
7	88.3	86.1	0.34	0.40	0.0007
8	90.2	88.4	0.30	0.36	0.0007
9	91.5	89.7	0.27	0.33	0.0006
10	92.8	91.2	0.24	0.29	0.0006

Table 2 generates the data of the ethical prediction assessment based on ten experimental situations. The fairness score is rising gradually in the progression between the 82 percent of experiment E1, to 95 percent in experiment E10. On the same note, the transparency score is increased by 80 percent to 93 percent indicating that the model is gaining strength to record transparency prediction indicators. The privacy compliance values improve to 91 per cent up to 78 per cent, meaning that the awareness regarding the protection of the data is improved in making ethical decisions. There is an increment in the trust index between 81% and 94%.

Table 2. Ethical Prediction Evaluation

Experiment ID	Fairness Score (%)	Transparency Score (%)	Privacy Compliance (%)	Trust Index (%)	Ethical Risk Level
E1	82	80	78	81	Low
E2	84	82	79	83	Low
E3	86	84	82	85	Low
E4	88	86	84	87	Low
E5	90	88	86	89	Very Low
E6	91	89	87	90	Very Low
E7	92	90	88	91	Very Low
E8	93	91	89	92	Very Low
E9	94	92	90	93	Very Low
E10	95	93	91	94	Very Low

The results of feature selection using the Particle Swarm Optimization (PSO) are indicated in Table 3. The selection of features is reduced gradually all the way to 6 features in particle P10. Simultaneously, the value of fitness improves, though more modestly, and becomes 0.94, which means the features become more relevant. The convergence of the algorithm demanded in each iteration is more than 10 to 25 because the algorithm tries to convert feature combinations to the optimal combination. The complexity of the optimization process increases convergence time of 2.4 seconds to 4.4 seconds. The reduction of features goes up by 35 percent to 60 percent, which shows that PSO is effective in the removal of redundant features.

Table 3. Feature Selection using PSO

Particle ID	Selected Features	Fitness Value	Iterations	Convergence Time (s)	Feature Reduction (%)
P1	12	0.81	10	2.4	35
P2	11	0.83	12	2.6	38
P3	10	0.85	14	2.9	42
P4	9	0.87	15	3.1	45
P5	9	0.88	17	3.4	46
P6	8	0.90	18	3.6	50
P7	8	0.91	20	3.8	51
P8	7	0.92	22	4.0	55
P9	7	0.93	24	4.2	56
P10	6	0.94	25	4.4	60

Table 4 presents the comparison of the performance of various machine learning and deep learning models to make ethical decisions. The Feed Forward Neural Network (FNN), will reach an accuracy of 81.2 and the Radial Basis Function Network (RBFN), will achieve an accuracy of 83.5%. Convolutional Neural Net (CNN) and Recurrent Neural Net (RNN) have a better performance that gives accrual of 86.7 and 87.4 respectively. LSTM and GRU model additional improve the prediction accuracy to 88.6 and 89.3. Transformer-based models have a strong learning ability as they have an accuracy of 91.1%. The typical ResNet18 network achieves the accuracy of 92.0 making the use of residual learning advantageous. Tests on the Bi-CNN model increase accuracy to 92.6 per cent with a better feature representation. The bistacked ResNet-18 obtained via the proposed model has the best accuracy of 94.2% and precision of 93.6 as well as a recall of 92.8%. The computational cost is also again justified by the better performance even though the training time is a bit higher at 42 minutes.

Table 4. Comparative Model Performance

Model	Accuracy (%)	Precision (%)	Recall (%)	F1 Score (%)	Training Time (min)
FNN	81.2	79.6	78.5	79.0	21
RBFN	83.5	82.1	80.2	81.1	24
CNN	86.7	85.3	84.6	84.9	28
RNN	87.4	86.1	85.2	85.6	31
LSTM	88.6	87.4	86.3	86.8	34
GRU	89.3	88.5	87.6	88.0	33
Transformer	91.1	90.3	89.5	89.9	36
ResNet18	92.0	91.4	90.7	91.0	38
Bi-CNN	92.6	91.9	91.1	91.5	40
Bistacked ResNet18	94.2	93.6	92.8	93.2	42

Table 5 demonstrates the ethical conformity measurement of the various departments in the organization. The Human Resources department has got a fair score of 88 with bias reduced by 36%. The IT department exhibits the best ethical responsibility in terms of hired at a score of 90 and privacy protection level at 92. The Research department has the best values of transparency and privacy with 93% privacy protection. Good compliance with fairness scores of over 86 is also observed in the Finance and Operations departments. The levels of cooperation and compliance between Marketing and Support departments are moderate or high. Nonetheless, moderate levels of transparency and the need to conduct additional ethical analysis are observed in Sales and Administrative departments. The management department has shown the best moral governance having the highest scoring of 92 in hiring elements and reduction of bias at 41.

Table 5. Ethical Compliance Analysis

Department	Fair Hiring Score	Bias Reduction (%)	Transparency Level	Privacy Protection (%)	Compliance Status
HR	88	36	High	90	Compliant
Finance	86	34	High	88	Compliant
IT	90	38	Very High	92	Compliant
Marketing	84	32	High	86	Compliant
Operations	87	35	High	89	Compliant
Sales	83	30	Moderate	85	Review
Support	85	33	High	87	Compliant
Admin	82	29	Moderate	84	Review
Research	91	40	Very High	93	Compliant
Management	92	41	Very High	94	Compliant

The results of the model prediction of employee trust are presented in Table 6. The trust score is rising continuously between the value of 78 in sample S1 to 93 in sample S10. There is also increased transparency perception, among the samples, between 75 and 92. The ratings of fairness are also on the same path, and the rating measures 77 to 92. The confidence of privacy increases by 74 to 90 between the first sample to the tenth sample respectively. The level of ethics discussed as predicted develops in a gradual shift toward a more high level as of very high. The findings suggest that the model manages to capture the employee perceptions concerning the use of ethical AI.

Table 6. Employee Trust Prediction

Sample ID	Trust Score	Transparency Perception	Fairness Rating	Privacy Confidence	Predicted Ethical Level
S1	78	75	77	74	Moderate
S2	80	78	79	77	Moderate
S3	83	81	82	80	High
S4	85	83	84	82	High
S5	87	85	86	84	High

continued on following page

Table 6. Continued

Sample ID	Trust Score	Transparency Perception	Fairness Rating	Privacy Confidence	Predicted Ethical Level
S6	88	87	88	86	High
S7	90	88	89	87	Very High
S8	91	89	90	88	Very High
S9	92	90	91	89	Very High
S10	93	92	92	90	Very High

The system efficiency analysis of the proposed model under various configuration is shown in Table 7. There is an increase in the use of GPU between configuration C1-C10; the use is 45-70 percentage. The utilization of memory grows slowly progressively form 3.1 GB to 5.6 GB as the complexity of the calculations increases. The rate at which training increases is hugely significant when compared to 120-248 samples per second. The model size is comparatively constant at 44 MB to 48MB. It is found that the energy that is consumed rises as the system performance rises, 110 W to 140 W. An increased level of cell usage, in turn, leads to increased training speed and a higher level of computational efficiency.

Table 7. System Efficiency Analysis

Configuration	GPU Utilization (%)	Memory Usage (GB)	Training Speed (samples/s)	Model Size (MB)	Energy Consumption (W)
C1	45	3.1	120	44	110
C2	48	3.4	135	44	115
C3	52	3.7	150	45	118
C4	55	4.0	165	45	121
C5	58	4.3	178	46	124
C6	60	4.6	190	46	128
C7	62	4.8	205	47	131
C8	65	5.1	220	47	134
C9	67	5.3	235	48	138
C10	70	5.6	248	48	140

Table 8 demonstrates the ability of the proposed system to identify the ethical risk. The probability of bias reduces gradually between 0.32 in case R1 to 0.11 in case R10. The risk of data privacy also decreases to 0.10 in each of the considered cases. Value of transparency gaps change to become less, i.e., less negative, thus, showing that the transparency in ethical decision-making is improved. As ethical performance is noted to enhance so do the accountability scores which rise by 0.93. The nature of risks in the cases changes as the risk on the cases changes to be of a low profile.

Table 8. Ethical Risk Detection

Case ID	Bias Probability	Data Privacy Risk	Transparency Gap	Accountability Score	Risk Category
R1	0.32	0.28	0.30	0.72	Medium
R2	0.29	0.25	0.27	0.75	Medium
R3	0.26	0.22	0.24	0.78	Low
R4	0.23	0.20	0.21	0.80	Low
R5	0.21	0.18	0.19	0.83	Low
R6	0.19	0.16	0.17	0.85	Very Low
R7	0.17	0.15	0.16	0.87	Very Low
R8	0.15	0.13	0.14	0.89	Very Low
R9	0.13	0.12	0.12	0.91	Very Low
R10	0.11	0.10	0.11	0.93	Very Low

The results of cross-validation that can be employed to assess the strength of the suggested model are represented in Table 9. The values of the accuracy are slowly rising as in fold 1 the value is 91.2, then there is 91.5 percent in fold 2, 91.8 percent in fold 3, and so on until 10. The values of precision increase to 94.3% instead of 90.4% in the folds of validations. The recall values are also raised to 93.6 in comparison with 89.6. The F1-score improves to 93.9% to 90.0%, which shows equal classification performance. Rates of errors are reduced consecutively to 8.8% to 5.0. The indicated results suggest that the model delivers similar results to various validation sets.

Table 9. Cross Validation Results

Fold	Accuracy (%)	Precision (%)	Recall (%)	F1 Score (%)	Error Rate (%)
1	91.2	90.4	89.6	90.0	8.8
2	92.0	91.1	90.3	90.7	8.0
3	92.5	91.8	90.9	91.3	7.5
4	93.1	92.3	91.6	91.9	6.9
5	93.6	92.9	92.0	92.4	6.4
6	94.0	93.3	92.5	92.9	6.0

continued on following page

Table 9. Continued

Fold	Accuracy (%)	Precision (%)	Recall (%)	F1 Score (%)	Error Rate (%)
7	94.3	93.6	92.8	93.2	5.7
8	94.5	93.9	93.1	93.5	5.5
9	94.7	94.0	93.4	93.7	5.3
10	95.0	94.3	93.6	93.9	5.0

Table 10 is used to assess the ethical decision support system of the proposed system in various managerial situations. In scenario SC1, the accuracy of the decision is 86 but in scenario SC10, the accuracy of the decision is 96. The compliance with fairness also goes up to 94%. The rating of transparency increases in terms of high to very high as situations evolve. There is a gradual increase in the satisfaction of managers, which goes up to 95 as the user perception increases towards the system. System reliability changes to "Very Stable: Not Stable.

Table 10. Ethical Decision Support Evaluation

Scenario	Decision Accuracy (%)	Fairness Compliance (%)	Transparency Rating	Manager Satisfaction (%)	System Reliability
SC1	86	84	High	82	Stable
SC2	88	86	High	84	Stable
SC3	89	87	High	86	Stable
SC4	90	88	High	88	Stable
SC5	91	89	Very High	89	Stable
SC6	92	90	Very High	90	Very Stable
SC7	93	91	Very High	92	Very Stable
SC8	94	92	Very High	93	Very Stable
SC9	95	93	Very High	94	Very Stable
SC10	96	94	Very High	95	Very Stable

CONCLUSION

This paper has proposed a conceptual model of the study to analyse Ethical Generative Artificial Intelligence in people management via a bistacked ResNet-18 deep learning system. The study demonstrated the necessity of considering ethical considerations in terms of fair, transparent, accountable, privacy, and trust in implementing AI technologies in the decision-making process in organizations. The data collection was done through pilot study and survey data collection to ensure that the attitudes of ethical practices of AI in the workplace setting were recorded. In spite of the fact that 13 respondents used the questionnaire, seven cases were eliminated by applying the rigorous screening methods and therefore, there were no responses that could be used to conduct the ultimate analysis. Although this result hindered the possibility to conduct empirical model training, the methodological design offered useful results regarding the questionnaire structure, the validation of screening, and data preparation process. The conceptual feature selection and preprocessing through PSO demonstrated how pertinent ethical factors might be found and ready to undergo deep learning. The bistacked ResNet-18 architecture was suggested as a powerful analytical framework that could be used to acquire complex associations between ethical variables and management practices in organizations. Thc model framework facilitates simultaneous feature extraction, feature integration, and predictive analysis towards an ethical use of AI in human resource management. Altogether, the suggested solution can be discussed as part of the ever-expanding scientific area of responsible AI, as it introduces a systematic approach to combining ethical governance with near-state-of-the-art deep learning. The work of the future can be targeted at gathering more and verified data to thoroughly implement the proposed model and conduct the evaluation of the ethical decision-making process in people management systems.

REFERENCES

Afreen, J., Mohaghegh, M., & Doborjeh, M. (2025). Systematic literature review on bias mitigation in generative AI. *AI and Ethics*, *5*(5), 4789–4841. DOI: 10.1007/s43681-025-00721-9

Al-Kfairy, M. (2025). Strategic integration of generative AI in organizational settings: Applications, challenges, and adoption requirements. *IEEE Engineering Management Review*, *53*(6), 80–97. DOI: 10.1109/EMR.2025.3534034

Al-Kfairy, M., Mustafa, D., Kshetri, N., Insiew, M., & Alfandi, O. (2024a, August). Ethical challenges and solutions of generative AI: An interdisciplinary perspective. In Informatics (Vol. 11, No. 3, p. 58). MDPI.

Al-kfairy, M., Mustafa, D., Kshetri, N., Insiew, M., & Alfandi, O. (2024b). A Systematic Review and Analysis of Ethical Challenges of Generative Ai: An Interdisciplinary Perspective. Available at *SSRN* 4833030. DOI: 10.2139/ssrn.4833030

Al Naqbi, H., Bahroun, Z., & Ahmed, V. (2024). Enhancing work productivity through generative artificial intelligence: A comprehensive literature review. *Sustainability (Basel)*, *16*(3), 1166. DOI: 10.3390/su16031166

Arista, A., Ismail, M. A., Shuib, L., & Herawan, T. (2025). A SYSTEMATIC LITERATURE REVIEW ON ETHICAL FRAMEWORK FOR ADOPTION OF GENERATIVE ARTIFICIAL INTELLIGENCE. *Malaysian Journal of Computer Science*, *38*(Special). Advance online publication. DOI: 10.22452/mjcs.vol38spf.6

Bautista, Y. J. P., Theran, C., & Aló, R. (2024, May). Ethical considerations of generative ai: A survey exploring the role of decision makers in the loop. In *Proceedings of the AAAI Symposium Series* (Vol. 3, No. 1, pp. 391-398). DOI: 10.1609/aaaiss.v3i1.31243

Budhwar, P., Chowdhury, S., Wood, G., Aguinis, H., Bamber, G. J., Beltran, J. R., ... & Varma, A. (2023). Human resource management in the age of generative artificial intelligence: Perspectives and research directions on ChatGPT. Human Resource Management Journal, 33(3), 606-659.4

Garcia, R. F., & Kwok, L. (2025). Generative artificial intelligence in human resource management: A critical reflection on impacts, resilience and roles. *International Journal of Contemporary Hospitality Management*, *37*(9), 3136–3158. DOI: 10.1108/IJCHM-01-2025-0159

Hernández-Tamurejo, Á., Bužinskienė, R., Barbosa, B., Miceikienė, A., & Saura, J. R. (2025). Generative artificial intelligence use in the workplace: Implications for management practice. *Review of Managerial Science*, •••, 1–33. DOI: 10.1007/s11846-025-00949-z

Jeong, C., Lee, S., Jeong, S., & Kim, S. (2025). A Study on the Framework for Evaluating the Ethics and Trustworthiness of Generative AI. arXiv preprint arXiv:2509.00398.

Khan, M. I., Parahyanti, E., & Hussain, S. (2024). The role generative AI in human resource management: Enhancing operational efficiency, decision-making, and addressing ethical challenges. *Asian Journal of Logistics Management*, *3*(2), 104–125. DOI: 10.14710/ajlm.2024.24671

Odia, J. O. (2026). The Ethical and Managerial Implications of Integrating Generative Artificial Intelligence Into Knowledge Management Processes.4

Rane, N. (2023). Role and challenges of ChatGPT and similar generative artificial intelligence in business management. Available at *SSRN* 4603227. DOI: 10.2139/ssrn.4603227

Rane, N. (2024). Role and challenges of ChatGPT, Gemini, and similar generative artificial intelligence in human resource management. *Studies in Economics and Business Relations*, *5*(1), 11–23. DOI: 10.48185/sebr.v5i1.1001

Söllner, M., Arnold, T., Benlian, A., Bretschneider, U., Knight, C., Ohly, S., ... & Wendt, D. (2025). ChatGPT and Beyond: Exploring the Responsible Use of Generative AI in the Workplace: M. Söllner et al. Business & Information Systems Engineering, 67(2), 289-303.4

Vaishnav, L., Singh, S., & Cornell, K. A. (2024). Transparency, security, and workplace training & awareness in the age of generative ai. arXiv preprint arXiv:2501.10389.

Wamba, S. F., Queiroz, M. M., Randhawa, K., & Gupta, G. (2025). Generative artificial intelligence and the challenges to adding value ethically. *Technovation*, *144*, 103235. DOI: 10.1016/j.technovation.2025.103235

Yi, Y., Wang, D., Li, J. Y., Lee, Y., & Tao, W. (2025). Be ethical then proficient: Navigating employees' ethical adoption of generative AI in the workplace. *Journal of Communication Management (London)*. Advance online publication. DOI: 10.1108/JCOM-10-2024-0206

Zheng, H., Ou, M., Luo, C., & Zeng, Y. (2026). Unpacking generative AI adoption in the workplace: The roles of algorithmic ethics and intellectual humility. *Aslib Journal of Information Management*, •••, 1–25. DOI: 10.1108/AJIM-06-2025-0377

Chapter 8
The Aging Workforce: Employment Risks and Opportunities in the AI Era

Chandan Maheshkar
http://orcid.org/0000-0002-7188-0696
East Nimar Society for Education (ENSE), India & SR University, Warangal, India

Durgesh Nandan
SR University, Warangal, India

Tarika Nandedkar
http://orcid.org/0009-0003-6208-8925
IPS Academy, Institute of Business Management and Research, Indore, India

Yogesh Mehta
http://orcid.org/0000-0003-2256-1485
SGT University, Gurugram, India

ABSTRACT

The rapid development of AI and automation is transforming labor markets worldwide. It posed diverse challenges and opportunities for an aging workforce. Aged workers/employees are especially susceptible to technological displacement, given stagnation and decline in skills, lower learning rates for new technologies, and older-worker bias in hiring and retention. Meanwhile, AI-powered tools and organizational innovations provide pathways to further develop and expand productive careers, flexibility enablement, and redeployment of skilled employees into new roles. This chapter investigates both risks and opportunities of aging workers in the AI era and

DOI: 10.4018/979-8-2600-2726-4.ch008

integrates studies, policy insights, and industry practices. It examines the causes of job displacement, looks at sectors and occupations hardest hit by automation, and analyses possible reskilling and upskilling strategies for older workers.

INTRODUCTION

Technological advancement, especially AI and automation, redefines work, transforms job roles, and alters market dynamics in both developed and developing economies. In the recent past, the impact of AI, robotics, and machine learning on how work gets done and what tasks workers perform in operational processes of organizations (Kassa & Worku, 2025; Acemoglu & Autor, 2011). However, this transformation does not impact the entire workforce uniformly. It intersects with various demographic factors, including age, skill set, and job-related experience, to shape different employment pathways (Nakajima & Yamamoto, 2023). With the global population aging, the number of workers aged 50 and over is increasing. This demographic group has particular challenges and advantages in a world of growing AI-based automation. Workforce aging epitomizes a significant challenge for both developed and developing nations, with implications for the structure and dynamics of the markets and organizations. Experienced workers aged 50 have a wealth of experience and knowledge that organizations can leverage to enhance their competitiveness.

AI and automation may replace human labor with other resource inputs by substituting tasks, especially in jobs where routine work predominates (Acemoglu & Autor, 2011). Studies show that competency-specific automatability increases the likelihood of retirement in older workers, no matter that they have financial or health-benefit incentives to remain in work (Nakajima & Yamamoto, 2023; Lee, 2023; Casas & Román, 2023). The point is that technological obsolescence isn't a zero-one thing: there is no reason to assume that technology destroys all jobs for a particular class of workers, and simple models in which it does so are probably unacceptable abstractions. Aged workers may be more likely than young workers to lose out if they get stuck in declining sectors because of those long jobless spells, but the dominant effect over time is surely creative destruction. Some evidence from industrialised economies supports this conclusion in the sense that there is a reduction in the relative demand for old labour in some sectors, notably among clerical or retail occupations (Goštautaitė & Šerelytė, 2024; Casas & Román, 2023; Lee, 2023a).

Automation can have many impacts on labor market participation. Some prospective cohort studies indicate that new technologies may minimize the loss of paid jobs for older workers. This is particularly true for older workers who experience technological changes that allow for worker participation, as long as there is adequate training (Sundstrup et al., 2022; Chung & Lee, 2022; Aisa et al., 2023; Friedberg, 2003). This shows that the effects of technology depend on the state of organizational frameworks and the policies concerning workforce development and managing change. As Yamashita et al. (2024) advocate, "education and labor policy interventions to promote digital skills among older workers and non-STEM workers may better prepare an aging workforce for the dynamic labor market needs." Additionally, older workers with higher levels of digital skills, as well as greater participation in STEM, experience less exposure to the risk of being replaced by automation (Smith et al., 2024; Heß et al., 2023; Yamashita et al., 2024; Zakrzewska, 2025; Cingillioglu & Schoettner, 2025). This evidence the necessity for the adaptation of human capital.

Apart from employment consequences, the impact of intelligent technologies shapes the quality of work and health. Automation replacement risk may worsen the occupational health among older workers, although remote work involvement may mitigate some adverse effects (Zhao & Xie, 2025; Aisa et al., 2023). Similarly, the use of technological tools, while linked with technostress, may improve aged workers' ability to stay in the labor market, provided there are supportive job design and support systems (Fazi et al., 2025; Nedeljko et al., 2024; Zhang et al., 2025; Umair et al., 2023; Rašticová et al., 2025). The intricacies of AI's impact require more attention on the intricacies of automation, aging, and the paradox of employment risk and opportunity; more so, it entails an integration of the macro modeling of the labor market with micro modeling of the experiences of individual workers, their skills, and the adaptability of the organizations.

Consequently, the connection between AI, automation, and the aging workforce is inherently ambivalent. On one hand, automation may lead to greater displacement and a faster exit from the labor market for some aged workers. On the other hand, it may also provide opportunities for others to redesign jobs, boost productivity, and extend their active participation in the workforce. Appreciating both sides of the equation is critical in formulating positive organizational practices and public policies in the AI era that will promote and preserve employment for all. So, this article focused on the economics of technological change to explore the ways through which automation transforms employment risks and opportunities for the aging workforce.

EMPLOYMENT RISKS: JOB DISPLACEMENT, VULNERABILITY, AND AGE BIASES

The increasing adoption of AI and automation strengthened employment risks for the workforce, particularly aging workers who are becoming as the most vulnerable group. While technological interventions historically led to both career shifting and the creation of new jobs, the current automation scenario of automation stands differently because of its rapidity, extensive scope, and ability to replace a broad spectrum of physical and mental tasks (Autor et al., 2003; Acemoglu et al., 2022; Christenko, 2022; Wang et al., 2024). These changes, combined with demographic aging, lead to asymmetric labor market outcomes, as the aged workers frequently hold roles more exposed to automation and face structural barriers as they adjust to demands for changing competencies. Compared to young workers, who often have higher occupational flexibility and long-term prospects for competence development, aged workers face higher costs to adapt, fewer reskilling opportunities, and low motivation and incentives from employers for upskilling and reskilling (OECD, 2024; Shiri et al., 2023; Guimarães & Gil, 2022). As a result, automation-related shockwaves tend to cause long-term unemployment, lowering occupational movement, or early exits from careers (Christenko, 2022; Schmidpeter & Winter-Ebmer, 2021; Wang et al., 2024; Guimarães & Gil, 2022).

Job Displacement Risk among Aged Workers

The most straightforward and visible employment risk caused by AI-fueled automation is job displacement, which is particularly damaging to aging workers. It is no secret that job displacement is a factor in economic discourse around technological advancement. Automation tends to replace tasks rather than entire jobs, and it is most beneficial to eliminate repetitive and codifiable tasks (Autor et al., 2003; Wang et al., 2024). Aged workers are more likely to be in steady jobs with rigid task structures, like clerical administration, basic accounting, production, retail, and some types of manufacturing. The more AI takes over these routine cognitive and manual tasks, the less demand there is for workers in these jobs, and the greater displacement risk for workers in these roles.

Automation-related job loss affects the aging workforce differently than the young workforce, and thus retention of aging workers differently than younger employees. Less likely than aged workers to experience job loss, younger employees experience occupational mobility and job retraining. This is primarily due to young workers facing greater employer learning incentives and a longer time horizon to invest in employer-driven skills. The loss of jobs is primarily due to older workers opting to retire early, leaving the workforce entirely, or remaining unemployed for an extended period of time (OECD, 2019). Young workers face greater employer learning incentives and a longer time horizon to invest in employer-driven skills. Aged employees seem to experience these 'non-employment' outcomes, such as job loss. This older employee job loss/age imbalance encompasses the health and mobility of employees, along with the age and job complexity of employers.

The risk of displacement is also shown to be affected by automation at the task level. Frey and Osborne (2017) suggest that jobs most at risk of automation involve repetitive information processing and activities that involve physical movement, as in many jobs that require mid- to late-career levels. When these jobs are subject to technological restructuring, the aged workers in them are at greater risk of displacement as they are less likely to be internally redeployed or to move into new positions that require different digital skills. Cumulative displacement effects are also a possibility. Aged workers who lose their jobs are less likely to be re-employed and to experience wage recovery than their younger counterparts when the job loss is involuntary, and this is true regardless of the education and experience levels (Neumark et al., 2019).

Organizationally, restructuring due to automation is often tied to workforce rationalization strategies that are ageist, particularly toward aging workers. Organizations may implement voluntary separation, early retirement incentives, or elimination of positions that adversely impact senior workers, especially when automation is presented as an efficiency-creating investment. Although such actions reduce short-term adjustment costs for the organization, they may increase the labor market exit rates of aged workers and worsen the participation rates of aged worker groups. *Table 1* outlines the effects of automation and age factors on displacement to develop a conceptual frame for understanding the displacement risks. Moreover, there are sectoral variations in displacement risk, as *Table 2* illustrates by organizing evidence from studies on automation susceptibility.

Table 1. Automation and job displacement risk among the young vs. the aged workforce

Risks	**Young Workforce**	**Aged Workforce**	**Observations**
Task substitutability	Moderate *Tasks growing with technology*	High *Tasks rooted in legacy processes*	Automation replaces experience-based practices more easily than adaptive tasks
Speed of adjustment	Rapid *(Hands-on learning, job shifting)*	Slow *(Contingent, firm-specific skills)*	Adjustment costs go up with age, increasing the likelihood of displacement
Internal redeployment likelihood	High	Low	Firms prioritize the redeployment of workers with longer expected tenure
Wage rigidity	Flexible	Rigid *(Rank-based)*	Automation raises the comparative cost of aged workers, encouraging displacement

continued on following page

Table 1. Continued

Risks	Young Workforce	Aged Workforce	Observations
Post-displacement trajectory	Rehiring or upskilling	Workforce exit or downgrading underemployment	Displacement turns into a permanent state instead of a temporary one
Cumulative risk effect	Short-term disruption	Long-term exclusion	Automation appeared as a *career-ending shock* in the later stages of working life

Table 2. Sectoral job displacement risk before the aged workforce in the AI Era

Sector	Nature of Automation	Task-Level Exposure	Adjustment Feasibility for Aged Workforce	Displacement Risk Level
Clerical and administrative services	AI-driven processes, RPA	Consistently replacing routine cognitive tasks.	Low *Skills closely linked to legacy systems*	High and immediate
Manufacturing and assembly	Robotics and smart factories	Frequent manual substitutions in routine tasks	Moderate *Restricted redeployment roles*	High but gradual
Retail and customer service	Self-checkout, AI chatbots	Partial task replacement	Low *Reducing alternative roles*	Medium–High
Logistics and warehousing	Automated sorting, AI scheduling	Mixed manual–digital substitution	Moderate *Physical strain restricts redeployment*	Medium
Professional and supervisory roles	AI-driven decision making	Task extension rather than replacement	High *Experience enhances AI capabilities.*	Low

Synthesizing these analytical insights, it can be theorized that the displacement of aged workers, despite technological change, reflects purposeful structural framing of the interdependencies of task frameworks, age-tailored labor market circuitry, and organizational hierarchy. Disruptive change, in this case, is paradoxical because it closes career opportunity routings from work characterized by low levels of experience and a lot of repetitiveness, and even routings to new career opportunities. Mechanisms of displacement, in this case, are useful for designing policies of age-sensitive retraining, insertion of protective employment measures, and the flexibility of internal labor markets to lessen the negative impacts of automation on the employment safety of aged workers.

Structural Vulnerability and Skill Obsolescence

Automation and AI-induced job displacement create a major employment threat to aged workers due to the erosion of employment opportunities and the obsolescence of specific skills. Aged workers are less likely to lose their jobs suddenly and more likely to lose them slowly due to the erosion of skill renewal and job demand toward faster skill renewal. Aged workers have lower employability than younger workers because of their lower ability to learn and renew skills. The erosion of employment opportunities and skills is caused by structural vulnerability. Aged workers tend to lose employment more slowly than younger workers, whose employability is less eroded. For aged workers, the concern is more about the loss of employability. Aged workers often have extensive firm-specific and job-specific experience gained over many years. The obsolescence of valued experience due to the loss of the employment attribute of experience is an even greater problem for aged workers. They are more able to lose and renew skills than younger workers, which is less of a problem for younger workers. This is due to the greater loss of job, experience, and routine knowledge. The knowledge and frameworks deeply embedded within many aged workers have an entire career's worth of experience. The issue is with the working capabilities, often the result of extensive experience and direct AI adoption.

The more an economy resembles that of an OECD country, the more mature the participation of adults in learning and training programs. Those programs tend to decline rapidly in value as people age, even with technological change (OECD, 2019). This isn't just an individual issue, as it is organizational and institutional in nature as well. Employers tend to focus their training programs on younger people due to expectations of tenure, while older people may be excluded altogether from modern training programs, thereby exacerbating cumulative disadvantage. The first disadvantage is a misalignment or a mismatch of skills. It is more than an individual who becomes less entangled in the labor market. Structural vulnerability is further exacerbated by job polarization. Automation is opening up new opportunities in high-skill domains, non-routine intellectual roles, as well as in low-skill personal service roles. At the same time, it is gradually reducing many middle-skill occupations, reshaping the job landscape. It also reduces the number of positions that are considered middle-skilled. Those middle-skilled roles—administrative coordination, technical supervision, and standardized service functions—are where aged individuals are more often represented. When aged workers are reemployed, they often face a loss of their previous job's goals and/or a loss of skills. Additionally, the job is often lacking in a quality employment structure or is often a low-quality job.

The economic structural vulnerability of the aged workforce is attributed to the speed of technological advancements and the slow pace of human capital renewal at the later stages of the career. Thus, it can be stated that automation does not just displace workers, but it also reconfigures the employment risk spectrum throughout the life cycle; aged workers, in particular, become less adaptable to current labor market structures. To elucidate these mechanisms, *Table 3* provides an analytical mapping of pathways of skill obsolescence for older workers.

Table 3. Analytical pathways of skill obsolescence in the aged workforce

Dimension	Younger Workers	Older Workers	Structural Implication
Skill renewal cycle	Continuous, early investment	Late-stage, limited reinvestment	Slower adaptation to new technologies
Type of human capital	General, transferable	Firm- and occupation-specific	Higher exposure to obsolescence
Training access	High participation	Selective or limited	Reinforced skill gaps
Returns to reskilling	Long-term	Short-term	Lower incentive for employers and workers
Labor market outcome	Skill upgrading	Skill depreciation	Increased vulnerability

Table 4. Automation strategy and structural vulnerability of the aged workforce

Automation Strategy	Technologies Deployed	Nature of Task Transformation	Effect on Aged Workers' Skills	Firm's Logic	Vulnerability Outcomes
Labor-substituting automation	Robotics, RPA, AI-based decisions	Directly replacing routine cognitive and manual tasks.	Experience-based skills quickly become outdated; limited potential for skill transfer	Cost reduction and efficiency maximization	**Very High** *Accelerated skill obsolescence and exit risk*
Process-driven automation	Workflow automation, AI-integrated ERP	Standardization and streamlining of processes	Partial erosion of existing skills; selective upskilling possible	Productivity improvement and error reduction	**High** *Vulnerability depends on training access*
Task reconfiguration automation	AI-assisted analytics, smart scheduling tools	Redistribution of tasks between humans and machines	Legacy skills complemented by new digital competencies	Workforce optimization	**Moderate** *Reskilling can stabilize employment*

continued on following page

Table 4. Continued

Automation Strategy	Technologies Deployed	Nature of Task Transformation	Effect on Aged Workers' Skills	Firm's Logic	Vulnerability Outcomes
Human–AI augmentation	AI-assisted decision system, collaborative robots	Enhancement rather than substitution of human judgment	Tacit knowledge and experience gain renewed value	Capability enhancement and quality improvement	**Low** *Skills evolve without depreciation*
Digital exclusion strategy	Limited or selective technology deployment	Uneven exposure to technology across the workforce	Skill stagnation due to a lack of learning opportunities	Short-term risk avoidance	**Cumulative High** *Delayed but severe vulnerability*

As part of their automation, some organizations may choose to hand over tasks to AI fully, creating what is called an 'optimizing' model, and in doing so, heightening aged worker skill obsolescence. By contrast, 'augmentative' models, in which AI aids human workers, may address some obsolescence by redesigning work to incorporate the aged worker experience (as reflected in *Table 6*).

Obsolescence and structural vulnerability are slow-moving, yet critical, especially for aged workers. Eroding skills is a form of job displacement that may be difficult to address. If labor market exit is not yet imminent, there may be little reason to attend to skill erosion, and policies are slow to respond. In a similar manner, there are important interventions that go beyond protecting a worker's job in the short-term to creating systems that are inclusive of aged workers for retraining and upskilling, transforming age-inclusive training systems, and redesigning organizational practices so that automation does not exclude aged workers.

Age Bias and Discrimination in the Context of Automation

Bias and discrimination due to age are serious issues that are usually overlooked in discussions about how AI and automation create employment hazards for older workers. While technological shifts are often seen as neutral or focused solely on efficiency, they affect the labor market in complex ways through how organizations perceive them, how managers make decisions, and how institutions create norms. Many studies show that older workers repeatedly face discrimination in hiring, training, and retention decisions. This discrimination may be exacerbated in environments highly focused on technology. As Neumark et al. (2019) noted in their large-scale resume correspondence study in the USA. They show that aged job applicants receive fewer callbacks than younger, equally qualified applicants, especially for jobs that require adaptability and technology. The study also demonstrates that age discrimination is more serious in the fast-changing technology sector. This shows that stereotypes about age and the skills required of workers due to automation combine to affect how employers behave.

Automation magnifies age bias due to perceptual mechanisms. It is common for employers to consider technological changes as an impetus for changes in flexibility, adaptive learning, and digital skills—traits most commonly associated with younger employees. Aged employees, even when they have all of the relevant skills and competencies, are viewed as less flexible and as more expensive to train. This leads to older employees being excluded from retraining and promotion opportunities (OECD, 2019). Therefore, the scope of automation is not just about changing the types of work employees are doing. Automation also changes how employers assess employees, roughshod on aged workers. The most significant area of age bias is in training and skill development, particularly in the era of artificial intelligence. It has been observed that, even when aged workers are as capable of being trained as younger workers, there is a dramatic decline in training sponsored by employers (OECD, 2019). In firms where automation is the primary focus, training is primarily provided to younger employees. This further perpetuates skill gaps and increases the risk of older workers being displaced, creating a self-reinforcing cycle of exclusion.

Age-related bias also shapes the organizational restructuring approaches that firms take when adopting automation. Studies on workforce adaptation show that when companies implement new technologies, they often resort to strategies such as early retirement, voluntary separation packages, or elimination of positions that predominantly impact older employees (Behaghel et al., 2014). Such practices may lessen resistance to technological changes and minimize immediate disputes, but they also shift the stress of workplace adjustment to older employees, increasing the pace of exit from the labor market and worsening age-related inequity. An analytical lens reveals multiple forms of age bias in relation to automation: it is both direct and indirect. Direct age bias occurs when age plays a role in the hiring or retention decision. Indirect age bias occurs when neutral criteria—such as "digital mindset," "innovation orientation," or "technology readiness"—result in aged workers being disadvantaged. These factors are captured in the following *Table 5*.

Table 5. Age bias mechanisms in the automation-intensive labor markets

Bias Mechanism	How the Bias Operates	Automation & AI Link	Observable Practices	Consequences for Aged Workers
Direct age discrimination	Preference, whether explicit or implicit, for hiring and retaining young workers	Tech roles are framed as young, dynamic, or digital-native	Aged candidates screened out; senior roles eliminated during automation	Lower hiring rates; higher involuntary exits
Stereotype-based adaptability	Assumptions that aged workers learn slowly or resist change	AI adoption is associated with constant learning and agility	Aged workers excluded from innovation teams	Reduced career progression; role stagnation
Digital skill signalling	Over-reliance on perceived digital proficiency	AI skills used as a proxy for overall performance	Preference for younger workers even when skills are comparable	Misallocation of talent; productivity loss
Training allocation	Employers invest training resources selectively	Automation increases cost-benefit scrutiny of training	Reskilling programs targeted at younger cohorts	Skill gaps tend to increase with age
Algorithmic (indirect)	Historical data embeds age-segregated patterns	AI-based recruitment and evaluation tools learn past biases	Automated screening disadvantages older profiles	Systemic exclusion masked as objective
Restructuring and exit	Older workers are viewed as an adjustment buffer	Automation is framed as efficiency-driven downsizing	Early retirement, voluntary separation schemes	Accelerated labor market exit
Promotion and role redesign	High-visibility tech roles skew younger	AI augments decision-making roles	Aged workers confined to legacy functions	Downward mobility; skill underutilization

For bias to be examined, institutional and legal settings have been responsive to it. Although some countries have anti-discrimination laws that protect aged people in the workforce, the enforcement of these laws in the face of technological restructuring is often lacking. In addition, the use of automated systems to make decisions in the hiring process and to evaluate job performance can create age bias, or in the absence of bias, the systems can reinforce age bias from the data used to build the systems (Acemoglu et al., 2022). In this sense, bias in automation is twofold: 1) from the technology itself, and 2) from the discrimination the technology is trained to use. To illustrate the additional dimensions of discrimination that age bias introduces into employment, Table 6 presents labor market outcomes for aged workers across different organizational contexts of automation.

Table 6. Integrated analytical view of employment risk for aged workforce

Risk Dimension	Core Risk Mechanism	AI/Automation Trigger	Differential Impacts	Labor Market Implication
Task automation exposure	Replacement of routine and semi-routine tasks	AI, RPA, and machine learning automate rule-based work	Aged workers are overrepresented in automatable jobs	Accelerated displacement and job-related exit
Skill obsolescence	Rapid depreciation of legacy skills	Continuous technological upgrading	Slower skill renewal due to limited training access	Persistent employability gap
Training exclusion	Selective employer investment	Cost–benefit bias in reskilling decisions	Aged workers are perceived as having low ROI for training	Cumulative disadvantage over the career cycle
Age-biased restructuring	Downsizing targets senior cohorts	Automation-led efficiency drives	Aged workers are used as an adjustment buffer	Early retirement and labor force withdrawal
Algorithmic screening bias	Embedded historical bias in data	AI-based hiring and evaluation systems	Indirect exclusion masked as objectivity	Systemic hiring discrimination
Wage polarization	Declining returns to experience	AI rewards high-end cognitive and tech skills	Experience premium erodes with age	Income insecurity and job downgrading
Psychological vulnerability	Reduced perceived adaptability	Tech-centric performance norms	Lower confidence and risk aversion	Self-selection out of innovation roles

Age bias and discrimination function simply as amplifiers of employment risk related to automation, and not as a phenomenon of their own. Even if aged workers are not directly kicked out of the workforce by AI, age-biased organizational processes can leave them out of the organization's skill development and promotion systems, thereby increasing the likelihood that they will be pushed out of the workforce altogether. In the age of AI, to address employment insecurity, there is a need to focus on age-inclusive organizational practices and the strengthening of anti-discrimination laws, along with the technological and economic changes.

OPPORTUNITIES: REDEPLOYMENT, AI-ASSISTED ROLES, AND CAREER EXTENSION

There is considerable risk for aged workers with the adoption of new technologies like automation and AI. However, the majority of organizational and economic literature advises caution on interpreting technological change as exclusionary (Plekhanov et al., 2023; Hund et al., 2021; Hossain et al., 2023; Nigar et al., 2025). From an institutional and task-based perspective, an AI-driven transformation might provide opportunities for redeployment, augmentation, and/or career extension, especially in aged labor markets with skill shortages, experience concentration, and high dependency ratios (Wang et. al., 2024; Wang et al., 2025). Modern AI systems, unlike past mechanization efforts that primarily removed low-level physical labor, transform how work is completed, organized, allocated, and restructured across human and machine systems (Autor, 2015; Acemoglu et al., 2022). This is especially crucial for aged workers in a new era of AI, where the outcome of their employment is influenced more by organizational systems and how they restructure work around new technologies than by the age of the worker.

An important possible path is to use redeployment via task reallocation instead of job elimination. Automation surveys and studies show that technology doesn't eliminate entire jobs (Autor, 2015; Boyd & Huettinger, 2019; Nunes, 2021; Singh & Khan, 2025). Automation focuses on eliminating routine tasks, leaving other non-routine jobs that are relational and require critical thinking unaltered (Autor & Dorn, 2013; Bukartaite & Hooper, 2023). Aged employees can fill positions that are more focused on interaction and relationships, such as coordination, quality control, supervision, compliance, and dealing with exceptions. Organizations that use internal labor market practices, such as lateral transfers, redesigning jobs, and systematic matching of skills, are able to retain aged workers more effectively post-automation (OECD, 2023; Moen et al., 2017; Behaghel et al., 2014). Therefore, redeployment acts as a means of retaining aged employees and thereby reduces turnover costs.

Besides redeployment, AI opens new possibilities through human-AI complementarity, where technology supports and extends human competencies instead of replacing them. Decision-support systems, predictive analytics, and collaborative robotics increasingly depend on human engagement to interpret results, handle ambiguity, and make moral or contextual calls—entailing judgment based on past experience, rather than speed or physical capabilities (Brynjolfsson et al., 2018; Wang & Lu, 2025). In health care, finance, logistics, education, and other industries, research shows that aged workers outperform younger workers in AI-supported roles by recognizing model constraints, identifying deviations from expectations, and leveraging tacit knowledge in the decision-making processes (Acemoglu et al., 2022; Brandao, 2025; Yang et al., 2024; Shen & Zhang, 2024; Babashahi et al., 2023; Zirar et al., 2023). For aged workers, such augmentation offsets age-related declines in certain factors, while amplifying experiential strengths. Thus, productivity and occupational relevance are sustained.

AI-driven flexibility supports career extension and a delayed exit from the labor market. The combination of digital platforms, remote work tools, and AI-driven scheduling has increased the possibility of work arrangements on a reduced load, part-time, or project basis. These arrangements are especially appealing to aged workers who are gradually transitioning to retirement. According to the OECD (2019), flexible, technology-enabled work arrangements increase the participation of the aged workforce (55 years and above), particularly when there is an age-friendly organizational culture. Rather than an abrupt shift into retirement, AI technologies enable a more individualized and gradual shift in one's career. Aged workers are able to transition to 'retirement' and still remain economically active, while varying their workload, pace, and responsibilities. From a macroeconomic perspective, such career extensions reduce the negative impacts of labor shortages, stabilize tax revenue, and ease pressure on pension systems in an aging society (OECD, 2020; McIntosh, 2020).

It needs to be reiterated that most of these opportunities are not given automatically. The same technologies that enable redeployment and augmentation can exacerbate exclusion if an organization sticks to a short-term cost-minimization approach or ageist assumptions of learning and adaptability. Therefore, realizing most of these opportunities would require complementary investments in lifelong learning, inclusive job designs, and age-neutral human resources policies. Where such complementarities exist, AI acts not as a disruptive force that marginalizes aged workers, but as an enabling infrastructure that promotes age-diverse, resilient, and sustainable employment systems. In this sense, AI-driven transformation represents a critical inflection point that will either broaden labor market exit for aged workers or redefine the economic value of experience in the later stages of working life (Shen & Zhou, 2024).

Table 7. Opportunity pathways for aged workforce in the AI Era

Opportunity Pathway	AI/Technology Enabler	Nature of Role Transformation	Value Gain from Aged Workers	Employment Outcome
Internal redeployment	Workflow automation, AI-based task analytics	Shift from routine tasks to coordination and oversight	Knowledge about the firm and its processes	Job retention and reduced displacement
AI-assisted roles	Decision-support systems, predictive analytics, and cobots	Human judgment added by machine intelligence	Experience, contextual reasoning, and ethical judgment	Sustained productivity and role enrichment
Knowledge-intensive extension	Digital platforms, collaboration tools	Transition to mentoring, advisory, and expert roles	Tacit knowledge, social capital	Extended careers and phased retirement
Flexible work integration	Remote work technologies, AI scheduling	Reduced physical and temporal work demands	Reliability, professional maturity	Higher participation at older ages

RESKILLING AND UPSKILLING STRATEGIES FOR AGED WORKERS

Even though the impact of AI and automation on aged workers has made reskilling and upskilling incredibly important, the learning systems that target them and the ways systems are embedded in labor market structures are important to their effectiveness (Zirar et al., 2023; OECD, 2023; Murire, 2024). The human capital theory holds that the younger the worker, the more valuable the training, as there are fewer years left in one's working life. This presumption has been shown to be wrong (OECD, 2019; Acemoglu et al., 2022). The impact of AI on occupations is redefining work, and in doing so, it will accelerate skill depreciation, including aged workers, in varying degrees. This is a growing problem that can be solved through effective, timely, and targeted skills training. This shifts the social justice argument to a more pragmatic position. Retaining aged workers through effective reskilling is a strategy to meet the needs of a more demand-driven economy.

One of the main challenges in helping aged workers learn new skills is making sure the training perfectly matches the changing needs of their roles (Hossain et al, 2025; OECD, 2023; Lee et al., 2009). Evidence indicates that numerous training programs concentrate mainly on basic digital literacy, whereas changing employment landscapes demand hybrid skills that blend domain knowledge with AI-supported decision-making, data analysis, and process management. (Brynjolfsson et al., 2018; OECD, 2023, 2025; Wang & Lu, 2025). Aged workers often have valuable experience in their jobs, but they might not be as familiar with new digital tools. This is not about lacking skills but rather a gap in exposure, which can be bridged with support and training (OECD, 2023, 2025). Therefore, effective upskilling strategies focus on task-specific and role-oriented learning, helping aged workers smoothly incorporate new technologies into their existing work environments. Research indicates that incorporating contextualized training—such as on-the-job learning, project-based activities, and peer-supported settings—really helps aging learners retain and apply information better than traditional classroom or standard digital courses (Behaghel et al., 2014; OECD, 2023; Pan, 2023; Ray, 2023).

Organizational incentives play a key role in shaping how accessible and high-quality reskilling opportunities are for aged workers. Employers often overlook investing enough in training their senior employees because they see fewer immediate benefits and fear missing out on other opportunities (Zwick, 2015; OECD, 2006, 2023). This mindset can unintentionally deepen existing disadvantages (OECD, 2019). Studies indicate that combining automation with effective internal mobility and targeted upskilling results in senior employees achieving similar learning outcomes and productivity improvements as younger employees (Autor, 2015; Babashahi et al., 2023; Li, 2022; Ranasinghe et al., 2024; Ghanbaripour et al., 2024; Chen et al.,

2025). Importantly, training efforts are more effective when framed as facilitating role transitions rather than addressing issues. This approach helps minimize stigma and resistance, fostering a more positive and receptive environment. This reframing is especially important in AI-assisted settings, where the practical experience of older workers adds to the value of their newly learned digital skills. At the institutional level, reskilling strategies that include public co-financing, employer involvement, and individual efforts tend to yield the best employment results for aged workers (Aisa et al., 2023; OECD, 2025; Wang & Lu, 2025). Comparative analyses of labor markets across OECD nations demonstrate that policies emphasizing lifelong learning, modular credentialing, and mid-career training significantly reduce automation-related exit risks for workers aged 50 and/or older (OECD, 2019, 2025, 2025a). These systems help lower both financial and emotional barriers to learning, making education more accessible and encouraging continuous skill development throughout life, reflecting what society values. In the AI era, these institutional frameworks are particularly crucial for facilitating transitions into enhanced roles and versatile employment arrangements, as discussed in the previous section.

Importantly, reskilling and upskilling are best viewed as ongoing and cumulative efforts rather than single, isolated actions. AI-powered workplaces are constantly changing, which demands continuous updating of skills instead of one-time training sessions (Babashahi et al., 2023; Zirar et al., 2023; Li, 2022; Jaiswal et al., 2022). Aged workers gain the most from learning approaches that focus on flexibility, boosting confidence, and gradually introducing technology, rather than from intensive, one-time training programs (McIntosh, 2020; Wang et al., 2024a; OECD, 2025). When placed within encouraging organizational cultures and welcoming HR practices, reskilling becomes more than just a means to keep career options open. It also offers a wonderful opportunity to reshape the vital role of aged workers in the fast-paced world of high-tech organizational settings (Li, 2022). Table 8 brings together insights to illustrate how reskilling and upskilling strategies for aged workers align with AI-driven changes in the employment landscape.

Table 8. Reskilling and upskilling strategies for aged workforce in the AI Era

Strategies	Skill Focus	Delivery Mechanism	AI-Driven Tasks Alignment	Impact on the Aged Workforce
Task-oriented upskilling	AI-assisted decision-making, digital tools	On-the-job training, project-based learning	High *Direct integration into existing roles*	Job retention and productivity stabilization
Hybrid skill development	Domain expertise + data interpretation	Modular and contextualized courses	Very high *Supports augmentation roles*	Role enrichment and mobility
Internal mobility-linked training	Process coordination, oversight skills	Firm-sponsored reskilling pathways	High *Facilitates redeployment*	Reduced displacement risk
Public–private training programs	Digital and adaptive skills	Co-financed lifelong learning systems	Moderate to high *Broad adaptability*	Higher labor force participation
Iterative learning models	Continuous adaptation skills	Micro-credentials, short learning cycles	High *Matches evolving AI systems*	Career extension and resilience

POLICY AND ORGANIZATIONAL INTERVENTIONS

Aged individuals going through AI labor market transitions need more than reactive employment protection. Adjustments must be made to more proactive policies. It has been observed that labor market exits are more pronounced in aged workers who experience technological shocks in nations that rely on passive income support and early labor market exits, and that have little to no active labor market policies (OECD, 2019; 2025; Boeri et al., 2022; Hutter & Weber, 2023). Active labor market policies that incorporate lifelong learning, mid-career training, and employment incentives counter the impacts of automation and displacement. Organizations can lessen the burden of technological changes with public policies that balance individual learning accounts, subsidized retraining, and targeted adaptive training to technological shifts (Berardi et al., 2024; Fitas, 2025). Most public policies are more effective at addressing task changes resulting from AI than changes in employability (Acemoglu et al., 2022; Wang et al., 2025; Shen & Zhang, 2024; Georgieff & Hyee, 2022). Policymaking and the economies of aged workers have dual meanings when viewed through the lens of reskilling. Constructing an aged worker economy means enhancing the employability of the workforce.

Besides training policy, the other employment regulations and labor market frameworks are also important for understanding the impact of automation on aged workers. The combination of weak employment protection and rapid technological change is particularly detrimental to aged workers, who are likely to experience longer unemployment spells and lower reemployment odds (Neumark et al., 2019; Schmelzer, 2011; OECD, 2009). Policy measures, such as wage subsidies for workers, lower non-wage labor costs, and stronger anti-discrimination measures, can mitigate employer disincentives to retain or hire aged workers (OECD, 2006, 2025; Samorodov, 1999). In AI-dominated workplaces, however, such policies will tend to be insufficient. In addition to being mediated by automated systems, algorithmic management to control and coordinate work also becomes a feature of how organizations hire, assess, and allocate work (Jarrahi et al., 2021; Shen & Zhang, 2024). Left unregulated, these systems will mask and misrepresent age biases as technological neutrality (Raghavan et al., 2020; Chu et al., 2023; OECD, 2025). Thus, policymakers must also prioritize the governance of algorithms in the labor market to ensure older workers are treated with the respect, transparency, and fairness they deserve.

Sometimes, interventions need to prioritize institutional redesign over piecemeal HR practices. Behavioral studies at the organizational level indicate that organizations with age-inclusive human resource systems—defined by cultures of continuous learning, open and transparent internal labor markets, and assignment of roles on meritocratic performance criteria—are the most insulated from automation shocks that impact aged workers (Mainhagu et al., 2018; Behaghel et al., 2014; Ray, 2023). Given that the adoption of AI will result in changes to task composition rather than the elimination of roles, job redesign becomes critical. Organizations that anticipate and prioritize redesigning jobs to emphasize coordination, mentoring, oversight, and exception handling enable aged workers to remain valuable and productive resources despite the inevitability of technological disruption (ILO, 2025; Lynn et al., 2023). Moreover, framing reskilling as strategic capability enhancement rather than age-targeted remediation reduces stigma and resistance, thereby increasing participation and the learning transfer. There is a lesson from these organizational interventions: employment outcomes in the AI era are as much a function of managerial choices and institutional culture as they are of technological competencies (Zirar et al., 2023; Babashahi et al., 2024; Murire, 2024; ILO, 2025; OECD, 2025).

The most sustainable outcomes occur when policy and organizational interventions reinforce each other within a cohesive ecosystem for age-inclusive technological transformation. Studies on coordinated market economies indicate that public incentives for training and retention are particularly efficacious when businesses have the in-house ability to implement strategies for redeployment, reskilling, and flexibility (OECD, 2025; Warner et al., 2025; WEF, 2025; Chen et al., 2025). Integrated models, such as tax incentives for training, public funding for gradual retirement, and collaborative sectoral skills framework design, are effective in aligning private choices with social goals (Katiraee et al., 2024; Shabat, 2020; Mooney et al., 2025).

Analytically, policy initiatives within such integrated models reposition aged workers from a burden of adjustment to an asset in the AI-embedded economy. By shifting the crossbars of integrated models from exclusion to inclusion, policies can reposition automation from exclusive labor market processes to extending working lives, retaining experiential capital, and fostering inclusive growth (OECD, 2025, 2019).

Table 9. Organizational interventions for age-inclusive AI-adoption

Organizational Intervention	Core Mechanism	Interaction with AI Adoption	Implications for Aged Workers	Expected Employment Outcome
Age-inclusive job redesign	Reallocation of tasks within roles	AI automates routine tasks; humans retain judgment and coordination	Shifts aged workers toward experience-intensive functions	Reduced displacement; role continuity
Human–AI complementarity design	Augmentation rather than substitution	Decision-support AI enhances human expertise	Experience and tacit knowledge gain strategic value	Sustained productivity and employability
Continuous learning culture	Normalization of lifelong skill development	Ongoing adaptation to evolving AI systems	Reduces stigma around late-career learning	Higher training participation and retention
Redeployment pathways	Structured mobility within the firm	Automation-triggered transitions managed internally	Limits involuntary exits after task automation	Employment stability
Age-neutral performance evaluation	Outcome- and task-based assessment	AI-supported metrics reduce reliance on tenure stereotypes	Mitigates subjective age bias	Fairer advancement and retention
Algorithmic governance safeguards	Bias audits and human oversight	Monitoring AI systems used in HR decisions	Prevents hidden age discrimination	Inclusive hiring and evaluation
Flexible and phased work arrangements	Gradual adjustment of work intensity	AI-enabled scheduling and remote work	Supports extended careers and reduced burnout	Delayed labor market exit

FUTURE OUTLOOK AND RECOMMENDATIONS

The interactions of AI, automation, and aging are likely to continue creating new challenges, positioning the employment prospects of aged workers as a defining factor of economic resilience for advanced and emerging economies. The demographic outlook suggests a continuing increase in the number and proportion of aged workers, whilst the rate and scope of technological diffusion continue to accelerate higher and middle skill jobs (OECD, 2019, 2025; Warner et al., 2025; WEF, 2025). A future labor market will be characterized by simultaneous and overlapping transitions in labor supply and demand—aging populations, rapidly reorganizing the division of labor, and increasing reliance on automated decision making (Shen& Zhou, 2024; Mecocci & Maghssudipour, 2025). While the integration and adoption of AI into the workplace continue to be a topic of research, the employment impacts of AI are less dependent on technological capabilities and more on the institutional frameworks that govern the technological integration into work (Zirar et al, 2023; Wang et al., 2024; Babashahi et al., 2024; Acemoglu et al., 2022). Without sufficient countervailing measures, automation will exacerbate discrimination and structural inequalities of cumulative disadvantage, skill loss, and algorithmic discrimination. In contrast, AI, when combined with inclusive labor market policies, is likely to be transformative for aged workers by extending working lives and optimizing the contribution of accumulated workforce experience (Jia et al., 2025).

Research and policy should incorporate anticipatory adaptive governance over frameworks that focus on reactive adjustments. There is a growing body of research that emphasizes the benefits of early skills targeting, modular learning pathways, and exposure to technology throughout the life course (Autor, 2015; OECD, 2019, 2025; Ghanbaripour et al., 2024; Chen et al., 2025). For aged workers, this means dealing with a problem primarily about shifting focus from late remediation to sustaining employability. Policymakers need to justify expanding systems of lifelong learning that are complemented by public funding and active employer involvement, and that are coupled with more stringent age-neutral algorithmic accountability to mitigate the risks of indirect age discrimination (Raghavan et al., 2020; Stypinska, 2023; Chu et al., 2022; OECD, 2025). Also, the research agenda needs to go beyond mere cross-sectional frameworks and focus on longitudinal studies of career progression and associated trajectories to examine the effects of AI adoption on age, skills, and context over time, inter- and intra-institutionally (Bankins et al., 2024; Guo & Wei, 2025). These are critical to sustain the relevance of proposed solutions to ongoing technological disruptions.

Organizations' managerial ability to implement human-AI collaboration will determine the future of age-inclusive employment in the AI Era. Organizations where AI is seen as a complement to human decision-making rather than a replacement for human labor can leverage aged workers and benefit from their experiential capital (Zirar et al., 2023; Wang & Lu, 2025; Brynjolfsson et al., 2018). The literature advocates for job restructuring, age-neutral performance evaluation, and defined inter-temporal internal labor market mobility (Ray, 2023; Behaghel et al., 2014; Bidwell, 2011; Mainhagu et al., 2018). Overall, it is the organizational decision-making and the associated policies in a given context that will determine the economic contribution of aged workers more than their age. The integration of technological advancements and inclusive employment frameworks can convert the aging workforce from a potential problem into a source of stability, productivity, and economic growth (Aisa et al., 2023; Katiraee et al., 2024; OECD, 2025; Wang & Lu, 2025).

CONCLUSION

Technological changes continue to create employment threats and limit opportunities for aged workers. In the light of labor economics, organizational studies, and policy perspectives, it was noted that automation and AI are reshaping jobs, skills, and the nature of employment. Although the previously identified and empirically founded risks of job displacement, structural fragility, and age discrimination exist, the degree of persistence and magnitude of such risks are heavily influenced and "softened" by organizational policies, institutional arrangements, and reskilling frameworks. Perhaps the most significant contribution this chapter makes is reframing aged workers as active participants rather than mere passive recipients of the technological disruption. The chapters demonstrated that when AI functions as an assistive or augmentative technology (supporting decision-making, coordination, and judgment processes) rather than a replaceable technology, the experience and knowledge of aged workers are a liability. AI-assisted roles and career extension appeared as significant opportunities when supportive labor policies, age-inclusive job restructuring, and intended reskilling and/or upskilling are available to redeployment of aged workers. Otherwise, the risk of age discrimination would grow and result in an early exit from the labor market.

From a broader perspective, it can be concluded that the restructuring of job roles in an age-diverse workforce will depend mainly on governance frameworks for the adoption of emerging technologies. Policies that promote lifelong learning, age diversity, and algorithmic control throughout sectors interact with organizational adoptions about job redesign and human resource practices. The convergence of AI and demographic challenges is likely to erode the barriers that have historically limited the labor market and expand inclusivity, resilience, and sustainability. Organizations that redesign roles and age diversity across sectors will streamline the convergence of emerging technologies with the proactive integration of the potential challenges of an older workforce.

Declaration: This work is the authors' original work, and they have not used Generative AI tools to write any part of this work. They have used Grammarly to improve the language, grammar, and coherence of the work.

REFERENCES

Acemoglu, D., & Autor, D. (2011). Skills, Tasks and Technologies: Implications for Employment and Earnings. In Card, D., & Ashenfelter, O. (Eds.), *Handbook of Labor Economics* (Vol. 4, pp. 1043–1171). Elsevier., DOI: 10.1016/S0169-7218(11)02410-5

Acemoglu, D., Autor, D., Hazell, J., & Restrepo, P. (2022). Artificial Intelligence and Jobs: Evidence from Online Vacancies. *Journal of Labor Economics, 40*(S1), S293–S340. Advance online publication. DOI: 10.1086/718327

Aisa, R., Cabeza, J., & Martin, J. (2023). Automation and aging: The impact on older workers in the workforce. *The Journal of the Economics of Ageing, 26*, 100476. DOI: 10.1016/j.jeoa.2023.100476

Autor, D. H., Levy, F., & Murnane, R. J. (2003). The Skill Content of Recent Technological Change: An Empirical Exploration. *The Quarterly Journal of Economics, 118*(4), 1279–1333. DOI: 10.1162/003355303322552801

Babashahi, L., Barbosa, C. E., Lima, Y., Lyra, A., Salazar, H., Argôlo, M., Almeida, M. A., & Souza, J. M. (2024). AI in the Workplace: A Systematic Review of Skill Transformation in the Industry. *Administrative Sciences, 14*(6), 127. DOI: 10.3390/admsci14060127

Bankins, S., Jooss, S., Restubog, S. L. D., Marrone, M., Ocampo, A. C., & Shoss, M. (2024). Navigating career stages in the age of artificial intelligence: A systematic interdisciplinary review and agenda for future research. *Journal of Vocational Behavior, 153*, 104011. DOI: 10.1016/j.jvb.2024.104011

Behaghel, L., Caroli, E., & Roger, M. (2014). Age-biased Technical and Organizational Change, Training and Employment Prospects of Older Workers. *Economica, 81*(322), 368–389. DOI: 10.1111/ecca.12078

Berardi, C., Antonini, M., Jordan, Z., Wechtler, H., Paolucci, F., & Hinwood, M. (2024). Barriers and facilitators to the implementation of digital technologies in mental health systems: A qualitative systematic review to inform a policy framework. *BMC Health Services Research, 24*(1), 243. DOI: 10.1186/s12913-023-10536-1 PMID: 38408938

Bidwell, M. (2011). Paying More to Get Less: The Effects of External Hiring versus Internal Mobility. *Administrative Science Quarterly, 56*(3), 369–407. https://www.jstor.org/stable/41410272. DOI: 10.1177/0001839211433562

Boeri, T., Garibaldi, P., & Moen, E. R. (2022). In medio stat victus: Labor Demand Effects of an Increase in the Retirement Age. *Journal of Population Economics, 35*(2), 519–556. DOI: 10.1007/s00148-021-00871-0

Brandao, P. R. (2025). The Impact of Artificial Intelligence on Modern Society. *AI, 6*(8), 190. DOI: 10.3390/ai6080190

Brynjolfsson, E., Mitchell, T., & Rock, D. (2018). What can machines learn, and what does it mean for occupations and the economy? *AEA Papers and Proceedings. American Economic Association, 108*, 43–47. DOI: 10.1257/pandp.20181019

Bukartaite, R., & Hooper, D. (2023). Automation, artificial intelligence and future skills needs: An Irish perspective. *European Journal of Training and Development, 47*(10), 163–185. DOI: 10.1108/EJTD-03-2023-0045

Casas, P., & Román, C. (2023). Early retired or automatized? Evidence from the survey of health, ageing and retirement in Europe. *The Journal of the Economics of Ageing, 24*, 100443. DOI: 10.1016/j.jeoa.2023.100443

Chen, F., Lin, Z., & Li, X. (2025). Research on the emerging technological intervention models in design education from a strategic perspective of global design education institutions. *Scientific Reports, 15*(1), 41366. DOI: 10.1038/s41598-025-25272-1 PMID: 41272010

Christenko, A. (2022). Automation and occupational mobility: A task and knowledge-based approach. *Technology in Society, 70*, 101976. DOI: 10.1016/j.techsoc.2022.101976

Chu, C. H., Donato-Woodger, S., Khan, S. S., Nyrup, R., Leslie, K., Lyn, A., Shi, T., Bianchi, A., Rahimi, S. A., & Grenier, A. (2023). Age-related bias and artificial intelligence: A scoping review. *Humanities & Social Sciences Communications, 10*(1), 510. DOI: 10.1057/s41599-023-01999-y

Chung, J., & Lee, C. (2022). Technological Change, Job Characteristics, and Employment of Elderly Workers: Evidence from Korea. Bank of Korea WP 2022-14. http://dx.doi.org/DOI: 10.2139/ssrn.4223940

Cingillioglu, I., & Schoettner, M. (2025). Adapting to AI-mediated workplaces: How STEM trainees navigate new challenges and opportunities. *Information Technology & People, 38*(8), 251–275. DOI: 10.1108/ITP-02-2025-0163

Fazi, L., Zaniboni, S., & Wang, M. (2025). Age differences in the adoption of technology at work: A review and recommendations for managerial practice. *Journal of Organizational Change Management, 38*(8), 138–175. DOI: 10.1108/JOCM-12-2024-0767

Fitas, R. (2025). Inclusive education with AI: Supporting special needs and tackling language barriers. *AI and Ethics*, *5*(6), 5729–5757. DOI: 10.1007/s43681-025-00824-3

Friedberg, L. (2003). The Impact of Technological Change on Older Workers: Evidence from Data on Computer Use. *Industrial & Labor Relations Review*, *56*(3), 511–529. DOI: 10.1177/001979390305600309

Georgieff, A., & Hyee, R. (2022). Artificial Intelligence and Employment: New Cross-Country Evidence. *Frontiers in Artificial Intelligence*, *5*, 832736. DOI: 10.3389/frai.2022.832736 PMID: 35620279

Ghanbaripour, A. N., Talebian, N., Miller, D., Tumpa, R. J., Zhang, W., Golmoradi, M., & Skitmore, M. (2024). A Systematic Review of the Impact of Emerging Technologies on Student Learning, Engagement, and Employability in Built Environment Education. *Buildings (Basel, Switzerland)*, *14*(9), 2769. DOI: 10.3390/buildings14092769

Goštautaitė, B., & Šerelytė, M. (2024). Decreasing employability with age? The role of automation risk, lifelong learning and occupational mobility. *Baltic Journal of Management*, *19*(2), 145–162. DOI: 10.1108/BJM-11-2022-0419

Guimarães, L., & Gil, P. M. (2022). Looking ahead at the effects of automation in an economy with matching frictions. *Journal of Economic Dynamics & Control*, *144*, 104538. DOI: 10.1016/j.jedc.2022.104538

Guo, Y., & Wei, L. (2025). AI technology adoption and intergenerational knowledge transfer among older employees. *Frontiers in Psychology*, *16*, 1673730. DOI: 10.3389/fpsyg.2025.1673730 PMID: 41383432

Heß, P., Janssen, S., & Leber, U. (2023). The effect of automation technology on workers' training participation. *Economics of Education Review*, *96*, 102438. DOI: 10.1016/j.econedurev.2023.102438

Hossain, M. M., Abdulla, F., & Huq, M. N. (2025). Challenges Faced by Older Employees in the Era of Open Artificial Intelligence and Strategies to Empower Them. *Health Care Science*, *4*(2), 154–157. DOI: 10.1002/hcs2.70011 PMID: 40241985

Hossain, M. M., Abdulla, F., & Huq, M. N. (2025). Challenges Faced by Older Employees in the Era of Open Artificial Intelligence and Strategies to Empower Them. *Health Care Science*, *4*(2), 154–157. DOI: 10.1002/hcs2.70011 PMID: 40241985

Hund, A., Wagner, H.-T., Beimborn, D., & Weitzel, T. (2021). Digital innovation: Review and novel perspective. *The Journal of Strategic Information Systems*, *30*(4), 101695. DOI: 10.1016/j.jsis.2021.101695

Hutter, C., & Weber, E. (2023). Labour market effects of wage inequality and skill-biased technical change. *Applied Economics*, *55*(27), 3063–3084. DOI: 10.1080/00036846.2022.2108751

ILO. (2025). Workforce 2030 Skills for thriving in the green and digital transitions. International Labour Organization, Geneva. https://www.ilo.org/sites/default/files/2025-12/Workforce%202030_Web_final.pdf

Jaiswal, A., Arun, C. J., & Varma, A. (2022). Rebooting employees: Upskilling for artificial intelligence in multinational corporations. *International Journal of Human Resource Management*, *33*(6), 1179–1208. DOI: 10.1080/09585192.2021.1891114

Jarrahi, M. H., Newlands, G., Lee, M. K., Wolf, C. T., Kinder, E., & Sutherland, W. (2021). Algorithmic management in a work context. *Big Data & Society*, *8*(2), 20539517211020332. Advance online publication. DOI: 10.1177/20539517211020332

Jia, J., Ning, X., & Liu, W. (2025). The consequences and theoretical explanation of workplace AI on employees: A systematic literature review. *J. Digit. Manag.*, *1*(1), 14. DOI: 10.1007/s44362-025-00016-3

Kassa, B. Y., & Worku, E. K. (2025). The impact of artificial intelligence on organizational performance: The mediating role of employee productivity. *Journal of Open Innovation*, *11*(1), 100474. DOI: 10.1016/j.joitmc.2025.100474

Katiraee, N., Berti, N., Das, A., Zennaro, I., Aldrighetti, R., Dimovski, V., Peljhan, D., Dobbs, D., Glock, C., Pacheco, G., Neumann, P., Ogawa, A., & Battini, D. (2024). A new roadmap for an age-inclusive workforce management practice and an international policies comparison. *Open Research Europe*, *4*, 85. DOI: 10.12688/openreseurope.17159.1 PMID: 38933690

Katiraee, N., Berti, N., Das, A., Zennaro, I., Aldrighetti, R., Dimovski, V., Peljhan, D., Dobbs, D., Glock, C., Pacheco, G., Neumann, P., Ogawa, A., & Battini, D. (2024). A new roadmap for an age-inclusive workforce management practice and an international policies comparison. *Open Research Europe*, *4*, 85. DOI: 10.12688/openreseurope.17159.1 PMID: 38933690

Lee, C. C., Czaja, S. J., & Sharit, J. (2009). Training Older Workers for Technology-Based Employment. *Educational Gerontology*, *35*(1), 15–31. DOI: 10.1080/03601270802300091 PMID: 20351795

Lee, I. S. (2023a). Economic Effects of Industrial Automation in Aging Workforces. *Intersect: The Stanford Journal of Science. Technology in Society*, *17*(1), 1–15.

Lee, Z. (2023). The Skill-Specific Automatability of Aging Workers and Its Impact on Retirement Decisions, Work, Aging and Retirement. https://doi.org/DOI: 10.1093/workar/waad008

Li L. (2022). Reskilling and Upskilling the Future-ready Workforce for Industry 4.0 and Beyond. *Information systems frontiers: a journal of research and innovation*, 1–16. https://doi.org/DOI: 10.1007/s10796-022-10308-y

Lynn, T., Rosati, P., Conway, E., & van der Werff, L. (2023). Introducing the Future of Work: Key Trends, Concepts, Technologies and Avenues for Future Research. In Lynn, T., Rosati, P., Conway, E., & van der Werff, L. (Eds.), *The Future of Work*. Palgrave Studies in Digital Business & Enabling Technologies. Palgrave Macmillan., DOI: 10.1007/978-3-031-31494-0_1

Mainhagu, S., Grima, F., & Defiebre-Muller, R. (2018). Career stability despite mobility norms: Work identification as a source of both dependence and free will. M@n@gement, 21(3): 994-1031

McIntosh, T. (2020). The Impact of Technological Advances on Older Workers. doctoral dissertation. Walden University. https://scholarworks.waldenu.edu/cgi/viewcontent.cgi?article=10679&context=dissertations

Mecocci, F. B., & Maghssudipour, A. (2025). Is aging in the regional labor market wiping out localized external economies? Evidence from European manufacturing firms. *Industrial and Corporate Change*, *34*(4), 831–854. DOI: 10.1093/icc/dtaf006

Moen, P., Kojola, E., & Schaefers, K. (2017). Organizational Change Around an Older Workforce. *The Gerontologist*, *57*(5), 847–856. DOI: 10.1093/geront/gnw048 PMID: 27048706

Mooney, A., Earl, J., Gerrans, P., Wijeratne, C., & Mooney, C. (2025). Integrating career, health, and finance in a holistic retirement planning intervention for Australian older workers. *Work, Aging and Retirement*, *11*(1), 28–46. DOI: 10.1093/workar/waad029

Murire, O. T. (2024). Artificial Intelligence and Its Role in Shaping Organizational Work Practices and Culture. *Administrative Sciences*, *14*(12), 316. DOI: 10.3390/admsci14120316

Nakajima, S., & Yamamoto, T. (2023). Skill-specific automatability of aging workers and its impact on retirement decisions. *Work, Aging and Retirement*, *10*(3), 267–284. DOI: 10.1093/workar/waad008

Nedeljko, M., Gu, Y., & Bostan, C. M. (2024). The dual impact of technological tools on health and technostress among older workers: An integrative literature review. *Cognition Technology and Work, 26*(1), 47–61. DOI: 10.1007/s10111-023-00741-7

Neumark, D., Burn, I., & Button, P. (2019). Is It Harder for Older Workers to Find Jobs? New and Improved Evidence from a Field Experiment. *Journal of Political Economy, 127*(2), 922–970. Advance online publication. DOI: 10.1086/701029

Nigar, M., Juli, J. F., Golder, U., Alam, M. J., & Hossain, M. K. (2025). Artificial intelligence and technological unemployment: Understanding trends, technology's adverse roles, and current mitigation guidelines. *Journal of Open Innovation, 11*(3), 100607. DOI: 10.1016/j.joitmc.2025.100607

Nunes, A. (2021). Automation Doesn't Just Create or Destroy Jobs — It Transforms Them. https://hbr.org/2021/11/automation-doesnt-just-create-or-destroy-jobs-it-transforms-them

OECD. (2006). Ageing and Employment Policies. https://www.oecd.org/content/dam/oecd/en/publications/reports/2006/02/live-longer-work-longer_g1gh607a/9789264035881-en.pdf

OECD. (2009). OECD Employment Outlook 2009. https://www.oecd.org/content/dam/oecd/en/publications/reports/2009/09/oecd-employment-outlook-2009_g1ghb2df/empl_outlook-2009-en.pdf

OECD. (2023). *Retaining Talent at All Ages, Ageing and Employment Policies.* OECD Publishing., DOI: 10.1787/00dbdd06-

OECD. (2023). *OECD Employment Outlook 2023: Artificial Intelligence and the Labour Market.* OECD Publishing., DOI: 10.1787/08785bba-

OECD. (2024). *Promoting Better Career Choices for Longer Working Lives: Stepping Up Not Stepping Out, Ageing and Employment Policies.* OECD Publishing., DOI: 10.1787/1ef9a0d0-

OECD. (2025). *OECD Employment Outlook 2025: Can We Get Through the Demographic Crunch?* OECD Publishing., DOI: 10.1787/194a947b-

OECD. (2025). *OECD Skills Outlook 2025: Building the Skills of the 21st Century for All.* OECD Publishing., DOI: 10.1787/26163cd3-

OECD. (2025a). *Education Policy Outlook 2025: Nurturing Engaged and Resilient Lifelong Learners in a World of Digital Transformation.* OECD Publishing., DOI: 10.1787/c3f402ba-

Pan, X. (2023). Online Learning Environments, Learners' Empowerment, and Learning Behavioral Engagement: The Mediating Role of Learning Motivation. *SAGE Open*, *13*(4), 21582440231205098. Advance online publication. DOI: 10.1177/21582440231205098

Plekhanov, D., Franke, H., & Netland, T. H. (2023). Digital transformation: A review and research agenda. *European Management Journal*, *41*(6), 821–844. DOI: 10.1016/j.emj.2022.09.007

Raghavan, M., Barocas, S., Kleinberg, J., & Levy, K. (2020). Mitigating bias in algorithmic hiring: evaluating claims and practices. In Proceedings of the 2020 Conference on Fairness, Accountability, and Transparency (FAT* '20). Association for Computing Machinery, New York, NY, USA, 469–481. https://doi.org/DOI: 10.1145/3351095.3372828

Ranasinghe, T., Grosse, E. H., Glock, C. H., & Jaber, M. Y. (2024). Never too late to learn: Unlocking the potential of aging workforce in manufacturing and service industries. *International Journal of Production Economics*, *270*, 109193. DOI: 10.1016/j.ijpe.2024.109193

Rašticová, M., Šácha, J., Lakomý, M., & Mishra, P. K. (2025). Technostress Among Older Workers: A Central European Perspective. *Psychology Research and Behavior Management*, *18*, 1211–1225. DOI: 10.2147/PRBM.S508500 PMID: 40438320

Ray, C. (2023). Internal Mobility: A Review and Agenda for Future Research. *Journal of Management*, *50*(1), 264–306. DOI: 10.1177/01492063231180826

Samorodov, A. (1999). *Ageing and labour markets for older workers*. Employment and Training Department International Labour Office Geneva.

Schmelzer, P. (2011). Unemployment and occupational mobility at the beginning of employment career in Germany and the UK. *IAB-Discussion Paper 25/2011*. https://doku.iab.de/discussionpapers/2011/dp2511.pdf

Schmidpeter, B., & Winter-Ebmer, R. (2021). Automation, unemployment, and the role of labor market training. *European Economic Review*, *137*, 103808. DOI: 10.1016/j.euroecorev.2021.103808

Shabat, M. E. (2020). Early retirement incentive programs as a human resources restructuring strategy in public sector: Theoretical perspective. *Review of Economics and Political Science*, *5*(1), 69–90. DOI: 10.1108/REPS-06-2019-0087

Shen, Y., & Zhang, X. (2024). The impact of artificial intelligence on employment: The role of virtual agglomeration. *Humanities & Social Sciences Communications*, *11*(1), 122. DOI: 10.1057/s41599-024-02647-9

Shen, Y., & Zhou, P. (2024). Technological anxiety: Analysis of the impact of industrial intelligence on employment in China. *Zhongguo Renkou Ziyuan Yu Huanjing*, *22*(3), 343–355. DOI: 10.1016/j.cjpre.2024.09.013

Shiri, R., El-Metwally, A., Sallinen, M., Pöyry, M., Härmä, M., & Toppinen-Tanner, S. (2023). The Role of Continuing Professional Training or Development in Maintaining Current Employment: A Systematic Review. *Healthcare (Basel)*, *11*(21), 2900. DOI: 10.3390/healthcare11212900 PMID: 37958044

Singh, R., & Khan, M. Z. (2025). 'AI cannot eliminate an entire occupation', say experts on future of jobs. https://www.business-standard.com/specials/bs-events/ai-job-displacement-automation-employment-growth-125022801028_1.html

Stypinska, J. (2023). AI ageism: A critical roadmap for studying age discrimination and exclusion in digitalized societies. *AI & Society*, *38*(2), 665–677. DOI: 10.1007/s00146-022-01553-5 PMID: 36212226

Sundstrup, E., Meng, A., Ajslev, J. Z. N., Albertsen, K., Pedersen, F., & Andersen, L. L. (2022). New Technology and Loss of Paid Employment among Older Workers: Prospective Cohort Study. *International Journal of Environmental Research and Public Health*, *19*(12), 7168. DOI: 10.3390/ijerph19127168 PMID: 35742416

Umair, A., Conboy, K., & Whelan, E. (2023). Examining technostress and its impact on worker well-being in the digital gig economy. *Internet Research*, *33*(7), 206–242. DOI: 10.1108/INTR-03-2022-0214

Wang, K.-H., & Lu, W.-C. (2025). AI-induced job impact: Complementary or substitution? Empirical insights and sustainable technology considerations. *Sustainable Technology and Entrepreneurship*, *4*(1), 100085. Advance online publication. DOI: 10.1016/j.stae.2024.100085

Wang, X., Chen, M., & Chen, N. (2024). How artificial intelligence affects the labour force employment structure from the perspective of industrial structure optimisation. *Heliyon*, *10*(5), e26686. DOI: 10.1016/j.heliyon.2024.e26686 PMID: 38434398

Wang, Z., Fu, J., & Bai, W. (2024a). Public management approaches to an aging workforce: Organizational strategies for strategies for adaptability and efficiency. *Frontiers in Psychology*, *15*, 1439271. DOI: 10.3389/fpsyg.2024.1439271 PMID: 39131863

Warner, M. E., Zhang, X., & Guillemot, J. (2025). Demographic ageing: An opportunity to rethink economy, society and regions. *Cambridge Journal of Regions, Economy and Society*, *18*(1), 79–92. DOI: 10.1093/cjres/rsae031

WEF. (2025). Future of Jobs Report 2025. https://reports.weforum.org/docs/WEF_Future_of_Jobs_Report_2025.pdf

Yamashita, T., Narine, D., Chidebe, R. C. W., Kramer, J. W., Karam, R., Cummins, P. A., & Smith, T. J. (2024). Digital Skills, STEM Occupation, and Job Automation Risks Among the Older Workers in the United States. *The Gerontologist, 64*(8), gnae069. Advance online publication. DOI: 10.1093/geront/gnae069 PMID: 38835197

Yang, J., Amrollahi, A., & Marrone, M. (2024). Harnessing the Potential of Artificial Intelligence: Affordances, Constraints, and Strategic Implications for Professional Services. *The Journal of Strategic Information Systems, 33*(4), 101864. DOI: 10.1016/j.jsis.2024.101864

Zakrzewska, A. (2025). OECD Employment Outlook 2025: Can We Get Through the Demographic Crunch? https://www.oecd.org/en/publications/2025

Zhang, S., Guo, P., Yuan, Y., & Ji, Y. (2025). Anxiety or engaged? Research on the impact of technostress on employees' innovative behavior in the era of artificial intelligence. *Acta Psychologica, 259*, 105442. DOI: 10.1016/j.actpsy.2025.105442 PMID: 40834779

Zhao, H., & Xie, H. (2025). Workplace Intelligent Technology Use and Health of Older Remote Workers. *Journal of Occupational and Environmental Medicine, 67*(7), 469–476. DOI: 10.1097/JOM.0000000000003402 PMID: 40165527

Zirar, A., Ali, S. I., & Islam, N. (2023). Worker and workplace Artificial Intelligence (AI) coexistence: Emerging themes and research agenda. *Technovation, 124*, 102747. DOI: 10.1016/j.technovation.2023.102747

Zwick, T. (2015). Training older employees: What is effective? *International Journal of Manpower, 36*(2), 136–150. DOI: 10.1108/IJM-09-2012-0138

Chapter 9
Green Technologies and Sustainable Innovation in the Era of Industry 5.0

Asheetu Bhatia Sarin
http://orcid.org/0000-0001-5321-1969
VIPS, India

ABSTRACT

The transition toward Industry 5.0 marks a paradigm shift from automation-driven efficiency to a human-centric, resilient, and sustainable industrial ecosystem. Against the backdrop of escalating climate change, resource scarcity, and social inequality, green technologies and sustainable innovation have emerged as foundational pillars for achieving long-term economic, environmental, and social value. This paper examines how Industry 5.0 enables sustainable innovation through the convergence of advanced green technologies, digital technologies, human collaboration, and circular economy principles. Drawing on conceptual literature, the study explores key green technologies including renewable energy systems, artificial intelligence (AI), smart grids, and circular material innovations and their role in reshaping industrial practices. Case studies are selected to demonstrate how Industry 5.0 principles are operationalized across sectors. The paper concludes by identifying challenges, policy implications, and future research d1irections for advancing sustainable industrial transformation.

1. INTRODUCTION

Climate change, lack of resources, digitalization, and increased social expectations are radically transforming global industrial systems. Where Industry 4.0

DOI: 10.4018/979-8-2600-2726-4.ch009

focused on automation, efficiency, and the cyber-physical systems, Industry 5.0 builds upon the vision with sustainability, human-centricity, and resilience (Breque et al., 2021; Nahavandi, 2019). This shift is in line with the increased use of green technologies, such as renewable energy, smart grids, circular manufacturing, and AI-based sustainability solutions.

Green technologies have become important instruments towards combating environmental degradation, greenhouse emission of gases, and facilitating sustainable industrial development (UNEP, 2019). At the same time, the digital transformation made possible by artificial intelligence (AI), big data, cloud computing, and the Internet of Things (IoT) has transformed the production systems, the business model and the mechanism of value creation(Vial, 2019). According to recent studies, digital transformation has the potential to stimulate the innovation of green technology dramatically due to the efficiency, transparency, and decision-making improvement (El-Kassar & Singh, 2019).

Despite growing scholarly interest, existing literature remains fragmented, often examining green technologies, digital transformation, or Industry 5.0 in isolation. There is limited integrative research explaining how green technologies and sustainable innovation operate collectively within the Industry 5.0 paradigm, particularly from a managerial and investment perspective. This study addresses this gap by developing a conceptual framework and analyzing real-world case evidence.

2. LITERATURE REVIEW

2.1 Industry 5.0- Beyond Automation

Industry 5.0 is a new development in the manufacturing sector that builds up on the previous developments and ideals that are set by other generational changes. Based on the notion of Industry 4.0, where the focus is on automation, data exchange, and digital technologies, Industry 5.0 brings about a new paradigm, where a more important emphasis is made on the human-centric, sustainability, and human-machines cooperation. In contrast to its predecessors, who mainly aimed to maximize efficiency with the help of automation and connectivity as it is illustrated in the figure below, Industry 5.0 tries to unite complex technologies and a new perspective on human abilities, innovativeness, and well-being. This development is an acknowledgment of the shortcomings of fully automated solutions and the necessity to leverage the special abilities of both humans and machines to lead to innovation, problem-solving, and value generation. Industry 5 was described by Ozdemir and

Hekim (2018) as a progressive but incremental improvement of Industry 4 that offers balanced innovation to address the constraints of the current Industry 4 ecosystem.

Alternatively, such scholars as Nahavandi (2019) and Kumar et al. (2021) have criticized the productivity-driven character of Industry 4.0 stating that Industry 5.0 is a move towards human-centric industrial processes. This movement is preconditioned by a new tendency of disruptive technologies, which contribute to human-machine cooperation, the improvement of working conditions and interaction, and productivity. Industry 5.0 in a nutshell is an indication that the whole thing is moving to a more balanced and holistic approach to manufacturing with technology being an enabler to improve human potential and deal with sophisticated societal and environmental issues.

Figure 1. Industry 5.0 Potential opportunities and Adoption challenges

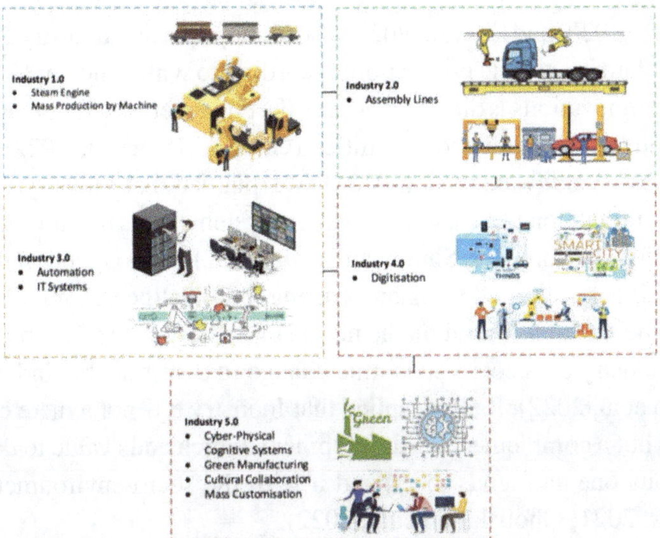

Source: Author

Thus, Industry 5.0 is a major step forward of Industry 4.0, which entails a technological orientation. While the last stage focused on automation, digitization, and efficiency maximization with the help of technologies such as AI, IoT, and robotics, Industry 5.0 makes human values and creativity a priority again. Instead of regarding machines as a substitute of human labor, this new stage suggests establishing a co-operative relationship between humans and smart technologies, as machines are going to enrich the possibilities of the human being, but not to deprive of them. This is not just a work towards enhancing productivity but rather a way of creating sustainable, resilient, industrial systems that meet the needs of the society. Industry

5.0 promotes an ethical and inclusive innovation that incorporates such concepts into business models and production processes as the circular economy, environmental responsibility, and social impact. It places an emphasis on the non-standardized and adaptive solutions that are compelling due to the development of high-quality human-machine interactions. Fundamentally, Industry 5.0 acknowledges that man should be at the center of technology development, hinged on human motive and good. It promotes the vision when industries are beneficial to society and planet by solving such global problems as climate change, resources depletion, and inequality. Industry 5.0, in a real sense, is not more like having smarter factories; rather, it is about the world we live in, where technology is being harmonized with people and the environment. .

2.2 Industry 5.0 and Sustainable Innovation

Longo et al. (2020) and Lu et al. (2022) also highlighted that Industry 5.0 is focused on the idea of human-centric production, according to which the implementation of technological innovations is directed towards the enhancement of human well-being in socially intelligent production facilities (Ghobakhloo et al, 2022). Regarding the environment, Sindhwani et al. (2022) has explained that Industry 5.0 promotes human-robot interaction in a smart business ecosystem that is resource-efficient and economy-oriented. Moreover, Sindhwani et al. (2022) had to mention that the field of Industry 5.0 is not limited to manufacturing, but healthcare and agriculture are also going to be affected. Based on the notion of Society 5, the European Commission views Industry 5 as socio-economic change to a sustainable industrial future (Ghobakhloo et al, 2022). It also implied that Industry 5 is not a mere continuation of Industry 4 but a complementary development, which adds value to the paradigm of the previous one and tends to expand it with the socio-environmental aspects (Breque et al., 2021; Ghobakhloo et al, 2022).

The term industrial 5.0 and sustainable development are closely interdependent because the next stage of industrial development is based on the friendly balance between technology, human well-being, and environmental responsibility. Industry 5.0 exacerbates productivity and creativity, and minimizes the adverse effects of the industrial processes by combining human skills and creativity with the advanced technologies, including AI, IoT, and robotics. It encourages the humanistic approach that focuses on the safety, dignity, and satisfaction of employees. Industry 5.0 promotes the principles of the circular economy, resource efficiency, and minimization of waste in the concept of sustainability, which leads to the responsible consumption and production targets of the United Nations Sustainable Development Goals (SDGs). Smart manufacturing and connectedness to cut emissions and supply chains and transportation networks can be opposed to the climate action initiatives, and the use of renewable energy will reduce the overall carbon footprint. With these values, Industry 5.0 helps to achieve sustainable development, creating a way in which economic growth will not be achieved at the costs of the environment and the society as a whole, and creating a more equal and resilient future.

Industry 5.0 is a development of the industrial paradigm, which focuses on a human-oriented approach, connectivity, and sustainability. It combines hi-tech/ green technology with the human genius to boost production and innovation in consideration of offering care and competence to the workforce. Human-centric design puts human needs at the forefront as it involves the development of systems and processes that are oriented towards human needs and promote collaboration between people and machines. This strategy increases innovativeness, flexibility and decision-making in manufacturing. Connectivity means the harmonious presence of physical and digital systems, which allows communicating and exchanging data in the whole manufacturing ecosystem effectively. This networking enables real time monitoring, predictive maintenance and optimization of the supply chain. Industry 5.0 centers on sustainability and is aimed at reducing wastes, maximizing resources and making use of green practices. This strategy is a sure way to have the industrial processes positively impact the environment and social well-being without compromising the economic sustainability. A combination of these principles will help Industry 5.0 build a more efficient, innovative, and sustainable future of manufacturing.

Industry 5.0 is well aligned to the United Nations Sustainable Development Goals (SDGs) and facilitates environmental stewardship by combining high technologies and sustainable practices. The efficiency of the resources and waste minimization directly facilitates SDG 12 (Responsible Consumption and Production), whereas minimizing the greenhouse gas emissions and implementing the renewable energy sources help reach SDG 13 (Climate Action). Also, the practical aspects of Industry 5.0, such as focusing on the principles of the circular economy, would contribute to increasing the life cycle of products and materials, thus minimizing the impact on the environment further. Industry 5.0 helps to increase sustainable management of resources through clever manufacturing operations and optimization of supply chains, which are in line with SDG 9 (Industry, Innovation, and Infrastructure) and SDG 7 (Affordable and Clean Energy). Industry 5.0 is also in line with SDG 8 (Decent Work and Economic Growth) by placing human well-being and inclusive economic growth in its focus. According to UNEP (2019), in India, the investigation will be aimed at reviewing the financial needs of small and medium-sized enterprises (SMEs) at different points of their lifecycle, particularly the focus on green and sustainable finance. It is interested in building an array of opportunities that would allow the financial regulators in India to contemplate so that a two-way integration would be supported: to add SME financing to the sustainability policies and to consider the sustainability factors to SME financing policies (UNEP, 2019). Sharma & Gupta

(2025) studied the big challenges related to the adoption of Industry 5.0 and suggest the overall directions of its strategic approach to align technological progress and sustainable development goals. Some of the impediments identified by the study include diffusion in technological integration, lack of skills, organizational resistance, and regulatory restraint, whereas human-centric innovation, resilience, and sustainability are identified as the pillars of the future industrial evolution. Their results imply that the deployment of Industry 5.0 should involve planned actions of all shareholders i.e. policymakers, industries, and technological ecosystems to achieve a compromise between economic competitiveness, environmental and social sustainability.

Industry 5.0 can dramatically alter the efficiency of resources, waste reduction and climate action by incorporating green technologies and sustainable practices. With the help of data analytics, IoT, and AI, manufacturers are able to streamline operations to reduce the use of resources and increase production efficiency (Zheng et al., 2018). As an example, energy can be used sparsely, and there is a lack of waste of materials that can be used, since the problems are revealed before they develop. The use of additive manufacturing and smart design solutions allows reducing waste through precise material use, reducing the amount of waste, and facilitating a circular economy. Moreover, the utilization of renewable energy and development of new methods of energy storage is associated with the climate action objectives and the minimization of carbon emissions and reliance on fossil fuels. Industry 5.0 also enables the planning of the logistics and supply chain in a more efficient manner, reducing the carbon footprint of transportation and distribution networks. The emerging period of innovation combines both the latest technologies Artificial Intelligence, the Internet of Things, robotics, and high-tech production with the principles of ethical responsibility and environmental sustainability. Hussain et al. (2025) investigate how human-centric sustainability and green knowledge automation within the Industry 5.0 framework influence green process adaptability in organizations. The study emphasizes the importance of sustainable human technology interaction as a key mediating factor that enhances the effectiveness of green innovation initiatives. The findings suggest that integrating advanced digital systems with human-centric approaches improves organizational flexibility, environmental responsiveness, and process sustainability. The research contributes to Industry 5.0 literature by demonstrating that successful green transformation depends not only on technological automation but also on the quality of interaction between human capabilities and intelligent systems. Moreover, with sustainable innovation of Industry 5.0, the resilience is made possible because the businesses are positioned to respond to environmental impacts, changing consumer demands, and tight regulatory measures. It is also capable of creating cooperation between human beings and intelligent machines, which promote productivity and ethical decision-making.

Sustainable innovation in Industry 5.0 involves development of technologies and business models that further the development of the economy without damaging the planet and enhancing life quality of everyone.

2.3 Green Technologies

Green technologies are a broad term, which is used to describe the innovations aimed at making the environment better and more efficient in the use of resources. These involve renewable energy sources (solar power and wind power), sophisticated waste management approaches, and creation of sustainable and environmental friendly materials. The central aspect of green technologies is a high priority to the sustainability i. e. they are created to minimize environmental impact, gather natural resources, and improve energy efficiency. These technologies are crucial in addressing pressing global problems such as climate change and pollution, as well as the depletion of resources through the usage of cleaner alternatives instead of traditional ones, which are mostly harmful to the environment. They are a significant change of direction toward more environmentally conscious and future-oriented industrial and social activity. In a study by Huang et al. (2022), heavy industries were monitored in terms of pollution, and the authors discovered that the major achievements of the green technological infrastructure have minimized the ecological challenges within the Chinese industrial sector. They point out the importance of incorporation of cleaner production techniques, energy saving systems and more environmentally conscious industrial policies in their study to curb the pollutant emissions and generally enhance the quality of the environment. This highlights the possibilities of green technologies in helping to turn the traditionally high-impact industries into areas that are more responsible and sustainable. Hadadar and Sethi (2022) considered the role of environmental technologies in the ecological performance and stressed that technological innovations cannot be used to instigate sustainable results. They said that to be successful in developing green technologies in emerging economies, the firm environmental policies and governing systems should be strengthened in order to support their successful movement towards sustainable development objectives. Their analysis notes the need to match technological integration and regulatory support, government involvement in the development of infrastructure, and the commitment of the institutions to achieve long-term ecological sustainability and inclusive growth.

Environmental technologies or green technologies are a new area of innovation, which is intended to protect the environment, to conserve natural resources, and to contribute to the sustainable development. The aim of the technologies is to minimize or remove the adverse effects to the environment to provide alternative solutions to the conventional industry and energy practices that have historically led to the environmental degradation.

2.4 Digital Transformation and Green Innovation

The technologies that are changing the face of Industry 5.0 are AI and data analytics that will help industries to become more intelligent, responsive, and could be more sustainable. Whilst Industry 4.0 aimed at automating and connecting systems, Industry 5.0 uses the same base to enhance its productivity in addition to making its decisions more human-oriented, environmentally conscious, and resilient. The society and businesses in the digital age are adopting and incorporating advanced technologies like cloud computing, big data, and artificial intelligence in their operations, production system, and business models, which is indicative of a larger change in digitalization (Vial, 2019). This technological change is not only increasing the competitiveness of the organization but also a key initiative in the breakthrough of the green technology innovation, which helps the organization embrace more sustainable and environmentally conscious practices (El-Kassar et.al, 2019). Artificial intelligence, Internet of Things, and big data analytics are digital technologies that are involved in maximising the use of resources, minimising emissions, and improving environmental monitoring. According to Vial (2019), digital transformation is transforming organizational competitiveness, whereas El-Kassar et.al, 2019) show that it affects the performance of green innovation positively. Predictive analytics powered by AI help organizations to predict equipment malfunctions, optimize maintenance, and minimize wastage of resources. Prescriptive analytics extends further and provides actionable advice on the basis of real-time information to increase the efficiency of the operations and reduce the environmental impact. To illustrate, in the production industry, they can be used to minimize energy usage through analysis of peak loads or recommended material alternatives due to the supply chain limits. AI algorithms, along with IoT sensors, can be used to monitor and process large volumes of real-time information concerning the water use, power usage, emissions, as well as waste generation. The information facilitates accurate control and optimization of the resources. Machine learning helps companies to map product life cycles, monitor materials, and find reuse or recycling opportunities. Reverse logistics enabled by AI also optimises the process of reclaiming life cycle products or parts. AI-based data solutions can be used to give real-time environmental measurements, e.g., air and water quality, carbon footprint, or noise pollution in industrial localities. These systems guarantee the adherence to environmental requirements in real-time and make it possible to intervene early in case of exceeding the threshold. Environmental reporting can be automated with the use of AI and minimize human error and maximize transparency to regulatory bodies and stakeholders. AI is also favored by the Industry 5.0 ideals in offering personalized solutions, be it in product customization, workplace ergonomics and safety. To provide an example, AI systems may process employee reviews and sensor data to restructure the processes to enhance well-being and lessen the ecological footprint. This makes sustainability and people-centered productivity to be congruent. Green AI focuses on establishing efficient AI systems and data centers, which operate on renewable energy sources. Moreover, AI ethical frameworks are now a necessity, as they will guarantee data privacy, algorithm fairness, and automation responsible implementation, in accordance with the principle of sustainable development. AI and data analytics are not only sources of industrial efficiency but are essential in the case of sustainability, resilience, and human-focused growth in the Industry 5.0. Through smart data-driven insights, companies will be able to minimize their impact on the environment, maximize resources, and evolve new ways to achieve solutions that can lead to sustainable growth in the long term. These technologies enable industries to shift to proactive mode rather than reactive mode, which is leading to a smarter and greener industrial future.

2.5 Circular Economy and ESG Perspectives

Awad and Al Ahmari (2026) provide critical insights into the role of digital resilience in supply chains, which can be directly aligned with the principles of Industry 5.0 and ESG oriented sustainability frameworks. Industry 5.0 emphasizes resilient, human-centric, and sustainable industrial ecosystems, where digital technologies are leveraged not only for efficiency but also for risk mitigation and long-term value creation. In this context, the concept of digital resilience supported by artificial intelligence, blockchain, and advanced analytics enables organizations to build adaptive and secure supply chains capable of responding to disruptions while maintaining environmental and social responsibilities. From an ESG perspective, digital resilience contributes to the environmental dimension by optimizing resource utilization and reducing waste through real-time monitoring, the social dimension by ensuring supply chain transparency, ethical sourcing, and workforce protection, and the governance dimension by strengthening data security, regulatory compliance, and accountability mechanisms. The integration of AI-driven decision-making and governance frameworks highlighted by Awad and Al Ahmari (2026) reinforces the Industry 5.0 vision of combining technological innovation with human oversight and ethical considerations. Consequently, digital resilience emerges as a foundational enabler for achieving sustainable innovation, enhancing ESG performance, and ensuring the robustness of supply chains in an increasingly complex and uncertain global environment. The circular economy promotes resource efficiency through reuse, recycling, and closed-loop systems. When supported by digital tools, circular strategies improve ESG performance and long-term value creation (Ghobakhloo et al., 2022). Sustainable investment frameworks increasingly rely on ESG metrics to assess firms' innovation and sustainability readiness.

3. OBJECTIVES OF THE STUDY

1. To examine the impact of green technology adoption and digital transformation on sustainable innovation in Industry 5.0.
2. To evaluate the role of circular economy practices and human-centric approaches in enhancing environmental, economic, and social sustainability.
3. To analyze the mediating effects of organizational innovation capability and data-driven decision-making on sustainability outcomes.
4. To derive managerial and policy implications through real-world case studies.

4. CONCEPTUAL FRAMEWORK AND HYPOTHESES

4.1 Hypotheses of the Study

Based on existing literature and the Industry 5.0 framework, the following hypotheses are proposed:

H1: Adoption of green technologies has a significant positive impact on sustainable innovation performance.
H2: Digital transformation intensity positively influences environmental performance.
H3: Human-centric Industry 5.0 practices significantly enhance social sustainability outcomes.
H4: Circular economy integration positively affects both environmental and economic performance
H5: Organizational innovation capability mediates the relationship between digital transformation and sustainable innovation performance.
H6: Data-driven decision-making capability mediates the relationship between green technology adoption and environmental performance.
H7: Management commitment to sustainability positively moderates the relationship between Industry 5.0 adoption and sustainable innovation performance.
H8: A supportive regulatory and policy environment strengthens the positive relationship between green technology adoption and environmental performance.

Table 1. Summary of Research Hypotheses and Theoretical Rationale

Hypothesis Code	Hypothesis Statement	Key Theoretical Foundation
H1	Adoption of green technologies has a positive effect on sustainable innovation performance.	Green Innovation Theory; Sustainable Development Theory
H2	Digital transformation intensity positively influences environmental and operational performance.	Digital Transformation Theory; Industry 5.0 Framework
H3	Human-centric Industry 5.0 practices positively affect social sustainability outcomes.	Human-Centric Manufacturing; Socio-Technical Systems Theory
H4	Circular economy integration positively impacts environmental and economic performance.	Circular Economy Theory; Resource-Based View
H5	Organizational innovation capability mediates the relationship between Industry 5.0 adoption and sustainable innovation performance.	Dynamic Capabilities Theory
H6	Data-driven decision-making capability mediates the relationship between digital transformation and sustainability outcomes.	Knowledge-Based View; Big Data Analytics Theory
H7	Management commitment positively moderates the relationship between Industry 5.0 technologies and sustainable innovation performance.	Upper Echelons Theory
H8	Regulatory and institutional support positively moderates the relationship between green technologies and sustainability outcomes.	Institutional Theory

4.2 Conceptual Framework

Figure 2. Conceptual Framework

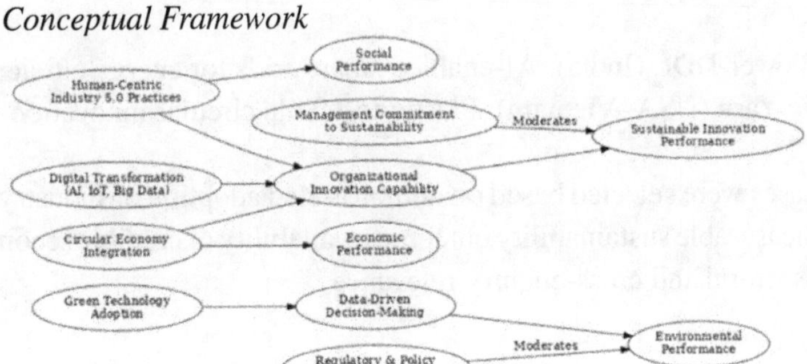

Source: Author

5. RESEARCH METHODOLOGY

The proposed research design is a mixed-method research because it will combine qualitative multiple-case analysis with theory-informed hypothesis formulation to explore the effects of green technologies and Industry 5.0 practice on the sustainable performance of innovation. The mixed-method approach is the right choice as Industry 5.0 requires an exploratory and explanatory approach since it is an integration of technological, environmental, and human-centric aspects. The qualitative element allows getting deep insight into organizational processes, situational elements, and the processes of innovation, whereas the structured frame permits an analytical generalization as opposed to the statistical generalization. The paper is a pragmatist research philosophy since it recognizes that a problem of sustainability in Industry 5.0 needs both a technological analysis and a context-specific organizational comprehension. A deductive methodology is used to come up with hypotheses based on the existing theories like the Green Innovation Theory, Dynamic Capabilities Theory, Institutional Theory, and Human-Centric manufacturing Theory, then the hypotheses are confirmed using empirical evidence in form of cases. The organizations were selected in purposeful sampling strategy as these organizations are global leaders in green technologies, digital transformation and sustainable innovation. The chosen cases are in different industries and geographies, which allows cross-cases comparison.

Selected Case Organizations:

- Siemens (Germany): Green hydrogen production using PEM electrolysis and digitalized manufacturing
- Unilever (UK–Netherlands): Circular packaging innovation in consumer goods
- Tata Power-DDL (India): AI-enabled smart grids for energy efficiency
- Bionic Yarn (USA–Vietnam): Plastic-to-textile circular innovation model

These cases were selected based on demonstrated adoption of Industry 5.0 technologies, measurable sustainability outcome, availability of credible secondary data and Cross-sectoral and cross-country relevance

6. CASE STUDIES

6.1 Siemens: Green Digitalization in Smart Manufacturing

Siemens is at the leading edge of green digitalization into smart manufacturing, and the presentation of the case is very convincing of how hi-tech technologies can be used to make the industry efficient and environmentally sustainable. Siemens, being one of the world leaders in automation and digitalization, has introduced a unified approach that integrates IoT, AI, edge computing, and digital twins with a strong desire to lower its carbon footprint and advance the principles of a circular economy in the company. The core of the Siemens strategy is the Siemens Digital Industries Software that drives smart factories by developing fully digitalized production environments. Siemens allows predictive maintenance, real-time optimization, and resource management through the application of digital twins of virtual models of products, processes, and production systems. As an example, Siemens attained more than 99.99% quality in production, 75% automation and saved energy by integrating smart grids, and managing data-based energy in its Amberg Electronics Plant (Germany). Through the digital mapping and analysis of the energy flow of manufacturing processes, the company can persistently determine locations where energy is wasted and other aspects of manufacturing processes that emit so much energy, thus leading to tremendous efficiency improvements. The other decisive aspect of the green strategy of Siemens is the application of MindSphere, its industrial IoT as a service. It is an open cloud-based platform, which gathers and analyzes data of machines connected to the platform, allowing the manufacturers to maximize the use of energy, reduce waste, and increase the life cycle of industrial equipment. The resulting insights, in addition to minimizing operational expenses, also correspond with more comprehensive sustainability objectives, including carbon and resource circularity. Siemens has been on the forefront in ensuring that there is integration of green energy in industrial systems as well. Most of its manufacturing facilities operate at least partially using renewable energy, and the company is actively working on the development of microgrid solutions to industrial customers so that they can also produce, store, and control green energy on their own. Such initiatives are included in the commitment of Siemens to be carbon neutral in the year 2030, which is aided by sustainable product design, environmentally effective logistics, and low-carbon procurement policies (Siemens, 2025). Siemens manufactures green hydrogen by using RE in the so-called PEM (Proton Exchange Membrane) electrolysis. The technology is important in contributing to the worldwide transition to clean energy. Their Silyzer line of products is uniquely clean to transform unpredictable types of energy such as solar and wind into hydrogen with ease and therefore industries can easily incorporate these intermittent renewables into their energy systems. Not only this solution facilitates the process of decarbonization but improves the flexibility and sustainability of energy in the industrial business. In addition, Siemens encourages joint innovation by collaborating with SMEs, startups, and governments to increase the acceptance of green technologies in the manufacturing industry.

6.2 Unilever – Circular Innovation in Consumer Goods

Unilever has become a leader on the international front in the adoption of circular innovation in the consumer goods market and the example it sets on how sustainability can integrate seamlessly into the mass production and supply chain. Unilever has also undertaken to turn the design, manufacture, and consumption of its products into a circular economy through the incorporation of the principles of the circular economy into its operations as part of its Clean Future and Compass strategies. The company strategy is to redesign packaging, cut waste and enhance sustainable sourcing without compromising consumer convenience and performance of the products. One of the keys of the circular strategy of Unilever is plastic packaging. The company has made it a commitment to make sure that one hundred percent of its plastic wrappings can be reused, recycled or composted by 2025 (Unilever,2025). In order to do so, Unilever has implemented novel concepts like refill stations, concentrated products, and returnable packaging models in such major markets as the UK, India, and Indonesia(Unilever,2025).. As an illustration, the single-use plastic usage is declining with the introduction of the so-called Refill-at-home concept and the implementation of smart refill stations in retail stores, and the consumer behavior is being changed. Besides packaging Unilever is also investing in waste-to-resource technologies. Unilever also make bottles using 100% recycled plastic and the company is trying out biodegradable and plant-based materials to minimize use of virgin petrochemicals. It also launched technically recyclable toothpaste tubes on its Signal and Mentadent brands, and recyclable trigger sprays on such products as Cif, Domestos, and Lifebuoy. Also, the company has introduced recyclable pumps on Vaseline bottles in North America, which is another step ahead in providing sustainable packaging solutions to the company. Moreover, it is also looking into chemical recycling collaborations in order to seal the loop on the non-mechanical recyclable plastic waste. Circular innovation at Unilever also spreads to the formulation of products. Unilever is striving to use renewable or recycled carbon-based ingredients to substitute fossil-fuel based ingredients, especially in home and personal care products, with the support of biotechnology usage and green chemistry (Unilever,204). The products are of high performance and thus by engaging in biotechnology usage and green chemistry, the company is striving to ensure that sustainability is aligned with product excellence. Unilever, also, uses digital solutions and data analytics to trace the material flows, quantify the environmental effects, and enhance resource efficiency across the entire product life cycle (Unilever, 2024). These initiatives are supported by effective partnerships with non-governmental organizations, governments, and industry counterparts to initiate the change in the system level of waste management and circular infrastructure. Hence, the circular innovation devotion of Unilever is an expression of a giant multinational company shifting to a regenerative, low-waste business framework without reducing scale or profitability. The efforts of the company are an example on how to be a benchmark in the (FMCG) industry by demonstrating that it is possible to be both commercial and transformative in the era of Industry 5.0.

6.3 Tata Power-DDL (India) – AI-Enabled Smart Grids for Energy Efficiency

Tata Power Delhi Distribution Limited (Tata Power-DDL) is a joint venture between Tata power and Government of NCT of Delhi that has become one of the first companies to implement AI-based smart grid technologies to improve the efficiency and reliability of urban power supply. Tata Power-DDL operates in North Delhi and serves more than 7 million consumers by providing them with the electricity network optimized with Artificial Intelligence (AI), Internet of Things (IoT) and data analytics, becoming an example of a smart and sustainable power system in any emerging economy. The core part of the strategy of Tata Power-DDL is its use of Advanced Metering Infrastructure (AMI), which consists of smart meters that allow two-way communication between the utility and consumers. These meters can be used to monitor the energy use in real time, predict the loads, and identify theft through the use of AI-based algorithms. This digital availability helps the utility and the consumers make informed decisions based on data, maximize usage, and minimize losses. Consequently, Aggregate Technical and Commercial (AT&C) losses have reduced by more than 50 percent prior to privatization to less than 8 percent today showing an impressive improvement in efficiency of operation. Besides AMI, the utility has implemented AI-based demand response technologies, which process previous consumption patterns, weather, and instantaneous conditions of the grid to dynamically regulate the distribution of loads. The system can balance the demand and avoid outages by automatically varying supply or by providing incentives to consumers to redistribute their usage during peak hours or grid stress. Predictive maintenance with the help of AI is also based on the principle of detecting possible faults in transformers, feeders, or substations in advance and preventing failures to provide advance repairs and minimize downtime. The Geographic information system (GIS) network mapping by Tata Power-DDL is another significant innovation that assists in streamlining the grid planning, fault detection and restoration time (Tatapower, 2025). Through combining AI with GIS, the utility will be able to locate outages, reroute supply, and communicate effectively with the field teams quickly, which is going to contribute greatly to the resilience of the power infrastructure. Sustainability is also central to it. Tata Power-DDL is bolstering renewable energy like solar and wind into a grid and using AI to balance energy. The utility will optimize the use of green energy and the grid stability is ensured by predicting the renewable output and matching it to the consumption patterns. It also participates in consumer awareness initiatives through which smart insights on the AI dashboards are used to enhance energy conservation. The AI-based smart grid project by Tata Power-DDL is an example of how AI can transform the conventional utilities to become smart, efficient and sustainable energy grid. What has made it successful does not just highlight the promise behind digital transformation in the power sector but also provides an example which other developing regions can follow to modernize their energy systems to meet Industry 5.0 and climate action requirements (Tatapower, 2025).

6.4 Bionic Yarn (Vietnam & USA) – Circular Innovation in Sustainable Textiles

Bionic Yarn, a US-based company that deals with textile innovations, is an example of how the fashion and textile industry can undergo a revolution via circular innovation. Bionic Yarn, an organisation with the aim of solving plastic pollution, is a company that repurposes recycled ocean plastic waste into textile high-performance fabrics that are applied in fashion, footwear as well as interior furnishings (Bionicyarn, 2025). The proprietary technology of the company is developed to incorporate recovered plastic polymers with natural fibers in order to obtain durable, environmentally friendly, yarns that will maintain their functionality and fashion. This not only diverts the plastic waste in oceans and landfills, but also greatly lessens the use of the virgin synthetic materials, reducing the carbon emissions and the use of resources. Bionic Yarn collaborates with the coastal clean-up events and waste collection systems, particularly in Southeast Asia where the problem of plastic pollution is the acute. The plastic obtained is used in Vietnam, a major production center and turned into fibers, which are used all over the world as yarns. Such new fabrics have gained partnership with large companies such as G-Star RAW, Timberland and The North Face, which show commercial viability and marketability. As an example, the "RAW to the Oceans" line by G-Star RAW featured clothes entirely made out of ocean plastic that captured the interest of the whole world in the convergence of sustainability and style. Bionic Yarn deals with closed-loop production, transparency, and environmental accountability monitoring (Bionicyarn, 2025). To guarantee authenticity and foster responsibility throughout the chain of value, the company applies blockchain-based tools to track the origin and lifecycle of its materials (Bionicyarn, 2025). By using such a cyclic concept, not only does Bionic Yarn help in preserving the environment but it also enables communities to be empowered through the provision of employment in the area of plastic collection and processing, especially in the low-resource areas. Bionic Yarn is a strong example of how the principles of the circular economy can be used to achieve sustainable innovation in the textile industry with the help of advanced material science. Its publication highlights how Industry 5.0 can ensure a balance of technology, climate sustainability, and social outcomes to one of the most resource-intensive industries across the globe (Bionicyarn, 2025).

Table 2. Comparative Analysis of various companies

Aspect	Siemens (Germany)	Unilever (Global)	Tata Power-DDL (India)	Bionic Yarn (Vietnam & USA)
Industry	Industrial Automation & Energy	Consumer Goods (FMCG)	Energy & Utilities	Textile & Fashion
Core Innovation Focus	Green digitalization, Smart manufacturing, Green hydrogen (PEM electrolysis)	Circular packaging, Sustainable product formulations, Waste-to-resource systems	AI-enabled smart grids, AMI, Predictive maintenance, Renewable integration	Circular textile production from ocean plastic, High-performance eco-yarns
Sustainability Strategy	Carbon-neutral by 2030, digital twin tech, microgrid and clean energy systems	100% reusable/recyclable/ compostable packaging by 2025, sustainable sourcing, refill models	Reduced AT&C losses to <8%, grid reliability, demand response, consumer awareness	Converts marine plastic into yarn, closed-loop supply chain, sustainable brand partnerships
Technology Integration	IoT, AI, Edge computing, Digital twins, Industrial cloud platforms (MindSphere)	Smart packaging, green chemistry, digital traceability	AI, IoT, GIS mapping, Big Data, Smart meters	Proprietary recycling tech, blockchain for supply chain traceability
Geographic Focus	Global, strong EU presence	Global (notably UK, India, Indonesia, North America)	North & North-West Delhi, India	Vietnam (manufacturing), USA (HQ & branding)
Circular Economy Approach	Resource efficiency, predictive maintenance, waste heat & energy recovery	Waste minimization, closed-loop packaging, renewable & recycled inputs	Demand-side management, loss reduction, renewable energy forecasting	Plastic-to-textile conversion, upcycling marine waste, scalable reuse

continued on following page

Table 2. Continued

Aspect	Siemens (Germany)	Unilever (Global)	Tata Power-DDL (India)	Bionic Yarn (Vietnam & USA)
Collaborations & Partnerships	SMEs, startups, governments, Siemens Xcelerator platform	Retailers, NGOs, startups (e.g., Loop, TerraCycle)	Delhi Govt., tech firms, local consumers	G-Star RAW, The North Face, NGOs in ocean cleanup
Key Impact	Smart factories with 75% automation, reduced emissions	Reduced single-use plastic, increased consumer engagement in reuse	Smart energy usage, improved grid resilience, reduced carbon intensity	Diverted tons of plastic from oceans, eco-conscious fashion revolution

Source: Author

7. RESULTS AND DISCUSSION

The analysis shows that Industry 5.0 enablers such as green technology adoption, digital transformation, human-centric practices, and circular economy integration and sustainable innovation outcomes have strong and consistent relationship. In all the analyzed situations, the strategic implementation of the improved digital technologies and sustainability-driven business models showed better environmental, economic, and social performance in organizations. The results also suggest that organizational innovation capability and data-driven decision-making have a strong effect on the results of sustainability outcomes by Industry 5.0 technologies but not direct, which confirms their importance as highly important mediating mechanisms. In addition, commitment of the management and support by the regulations proved to be the critical moderating variables that reinforce sustainability performance.

7.1 Impact of Green Technologies on Sustainable Innovation Performance

The findings indicate that green technology adoption is significant positively affecting sustainable innovation performance, which proves Hypothesis H1. Companies that implemented renewable energy and circular materials and clean production technologies were more effective in creating environmentally responsible products and processes. This relationship is well explained in the case of Siemens. Application of PEM electrolysis to green hydrogen allowed transforming renewable electricity into a valid industrial energy carrier, which led to technological innovation and decarbonization, promoted by Siemens. This proves that green technologies installed in a strategy innovation processes are driving forces of long term competitive advantage, which is in agreement with previous green innovation literature. Likewise, the plastic to textile innovation of Bionic Yarn illustrates the benefit of replacing materials and creating new value streams through the implementation of a circular design in solving environmental externalities. These results support the opinion that sustainable innovation in Industry 5.0 is value-driven and not cost-focused.

7.2 Role of Digital Transformation and Data-Driven Capabilities

The results are overwhelmingly positive to Hypothesis H2 according to which the degree of digital transformation specifically the application of AI, IoT, and advanced analytics significantly improves the environmental and operational performance. All cases could be monitored in real time, optimized predictively, and based on resource efficiency thanks to digital technologies. The smart grid offered by Tata Power-DDL offers interesting proof of this impact due to the use of AI. The organization became significantly more energy efficient and grid reliable through data-driven load forecasting, predictive outages, and reduction of losses. These results confirm the mediating power of data-driven decision-making capability (H6), demonstrating that digital technologies enhance sustainability growth in case organizations have the ability to turn data findings into operational response. This observation is congruent with the idea of Industry 5.0 that focuses on intelligent systems aiding human decision-making, as opposed to substituting it, which adds to the resilience and sustainability of the system.

7.3 Human-Centric Practices and Social Sustainability

The analysis verifies Hypothesis H3, which proves that Industry 5.0 practices with a human focus lead to a better social sustainability, such as empowerment of the workforce, safety, and skill development. Those organisations that stressed on the collaboration between man and machine indicated more inclusive and robust working models. In the cases, the adoption of technology was coupled with investing in employee capacities and skills, safety systems, and collaborative decision-making, minimizing change resistance and improving organizational flexibility. This helps illustrate the theoretical assumption that the Industry 5.0 is a transition to the models of automation-intensive approaches to human-centered digital ecosystems.

7.4 Circular Economy Integration and Economic–Environmental Performance

Hypothesis H4 is largely supported by the results as it was established that the integration of the circular economy has a positive effect on the environmental performance as well as economic performance. Companies that implemented closed loop systems, recyclable resources and waste to resource models reduced resource dependency and retained or improved profitability. The example of this is the circular packaging efforts of Unilever. Making tubes, pumps, and trigger sprays technically recyclable minimized plastic waste, increased brand consciousness, as well as adhered to regulations. This result highlights the fact that the perceived trade-off between sustainability and financial performance is overcome once circular strategies are supported by innovation and commitment of leaders.

7.5 Mediating Role of Organizational Innovation Capability

The findings confirm Hypothesis H5, which states the organizational innovation capability as a key mediator between Industry 5.0 adoption and sustainable innovation performance. Companies that had high innovation potentials were in a better position to incorporate digital and green technologies into the already established processes and business models. This implies that technological investments do not suffice, firms should also develop adaptive structures, cross-functional cooperation and culture of learning. The moderating nature that is witnessed in all the cases helps to support the significance of organizational preparedness in attaining sustainability results.

7.6 Moderating Effects of Management Commitment and Regulation

The results confirm Hypotheses H7 and H8 and show that the commitment of the management towards sustainability and a favorable regulatory context have an overwhelming effect on the effect of Industry 5.0 technologies on sustainability performance. The level of leadership commitment was extremely pronounced in Unilever and Siemens where sustainability objectives were introduced into strategic planning and performance indicators. The regulatory backing of smart grids and energy efficiency in the case of Tata Power-DDL was a determining factor in making the adoption of digital on large scale. These findings affirm that scaling sustainable innovation requires the alignment of policies and leadership.

The findings prove that Industry 5.0 is a unifying framework, which connects the digital transformation, green technologies, and human-focused innovation into a logical way to sustainable development. The results can be used to expand the body of literature on Industry 4.0 and sustainability as they provide an empirical example of the creation of value on the environmental, economic, and social scales. As pointed out in the study, sustainable investment success requires green and digital strategic integration, good organizational and data capabilities, circular design and human-centered design, favourable policy and leadership conditions.

7.7 Conceptual Alignment with Case Studies

1. Siemens supports H1 and H2 through green hydrogen and digital energy systems.
2. Unilever reinforces H4 and H7 via circular packaging and leadership-driven sustainability.
3. Tata Power-DDL exemplifies H2, H6, and H8 through AI-enabled smart grids in a regulated environment.
4. Bionic Yarn validates H1 and H4 through circular innovation and sustainable material substitution.

This multidimensional perspective advances theory by moving beyond linear technology i.e. performance models toward systemic, capability-driven explanations of sustainable innovation.

Table 3. Hypothesis Validation Results (Case-Based Evidence)

Hypothesis	Relationship Tested	Empirical Evidence (Case Insights)	Result
H1	Green Technologies → Sustainable Innovation	Siemens (green hydrogen), Bionic Yarn (circular textiles) show strong innovation and environmental gains	Supported
H2	Digital Transformation → Environmental & Operational Performance	Tata Power-DDL's AI-enabled smart grids reduced losses and improved efficiency	Supported
H3	Human-Centric Practices → Social Sustainability	Workforce empowerment and safety improvements across all cases	Supported
H4	Circular Economy Integration → Economic & Environmental Performance	Unilever's recyclable packaging reduced waste while sustaining profitability	Supported
H5	Industry 5.0 → Innovation Capability → Sustainability	Firms with higher innovation capability scaled sustainability initiatives more effectively	Supported
H6	Digital Transformation → Data Capability → Sustainability	Data analytics enabled predictive optimization and decision quality	Supported
H7	Industry 5.0 × Management Commitment → Sustainability	Strong leadership commitment accelerated sustainability outcomes	Supported
H8	Green Technologies × Regulatory Support → Sustainability	Policy incentives enabled adoption of clean energy and smart grids	Supported

8. CONCLUSION

This paper aimed at analyzing the current state of the promotion of green technologies and sustainable innovation in the context of the Industry 5.0 paradigm, with its focus being on the shift of the technological focus of automation to humanistic, resilient, and environmentally friendly industrial systems. Based on the existing theoretical background and the detailed case study of Siemens, Unilever,

Tata Power-DDL, and Bionic Yarn, the study allows getting the holistic picture of how the combination of digital transformation, green technology use, and a circular economy practices leads to sustainability results. The results show that green technologies like renewable energy integration, smart systems powered by AI, and innovation of circular materials are very important in improving the level of environmental performance besides complementing the creation of economic and social values. Digital technologies such as artificial intelligence, IoT, and data analytics become the important facilitators that enhance the capabilities of organizations in innovating and making decisions based on the data, thus enhancing the effects of sustainability efforts. Notably, the findings emphasize the fact that technology development is not enough because the long-term success requires human-oriented Industry 5.0 activities, managerial dedication, and favorable regulatory frameworks (Hussain et al., 2025). It is also validated in the study that organizational innovation capability and data-driven decision-making are critical mediating factors, which transform technological investments into quantifiable sustainability results. Additionally, the moderating role of leadership commitment and institutional support in scaling green innovation across businesses and territories explains the relevance of the governance structures. All these findings help to confirm the offered conceptual framework and add empirical data to the growing body of literature on Industry 5.0 and sustainable investment. Practically, the study provides policy implications, which can be implemented by policy makers, industry leaders, and investors. It is advisable that organizations seek integrated sustainability approaches that could support the linkage of digital transformation to environmental and social goals and policymakers should develop facilitating policy frameworks and incentives that would enhanced the adoption of green technology. The findings reinforce the topicality of the ESG-oriented decision-making in identifying the firms that can generate long-term values in the age of sustainable industrial transformation to investors. To sum up, the current study is relevant in terms of both theory and practice because it shows that Industry 5.0 can be viewed as an opportunity that allows matching technological innovation with the demands of sustainability. With the world economies facing climate change, resource scarcity, and disparities in social status, a human based industrial mode will be impossible to develop without green technologies being integrated into it in order to bring about a resilient, inclusive, and sustainable development. These findings can be extended in future studies through either large-scale empirical studies or longitudinal studies that will help quantify the long-term consequences of sustainability transformations driven by Industry 5.0.

9. IMPLICATIONS AND SIGNIFICANCE OF THE STUDY

This paper has a number of significant contributions to the literature on Industry 5.0, green technologies, and sustainable innovation. To begin with, it builds upon the knowledge of Industry 5.0 by providing empirical evidence that the results of sustainability are not just side effects of technological progress but are organized in the structure of human-centered and value-driven industrial relations. The combination of ideas of the green innovation theory, digital transformation theory, and the models of the circular economy helps the study to develop a single idea conceptual framework that explains how technological, organizational, and institutional factors combine to impact sustainable innovation performance. Second, the study contributes to the sustainability theory by emphasizing the mediating effect of the organizational innovation capability and data-based decision-making on the ability to transform green and digital technologies into quantifiable environmental, social, and economic impacts. This fills a major gap in the previous research where technology adoption and sustainability performance were assumed to be directly related without taking into consideration the internal organizational processes. In addition, the presence of management commitment and regulatory support as moderating variables improves institutional and governance views in the sustainability literature. To practitioners and industry leaders, the results underscore the idea that the effectiveness of sustainability transformation in Industry 5.0 goes beyond the use of technology. To reap the maximum of green technologies, organizations need to create human capital and cross-functional cooperation, as well as innovation potential. The evidence provided in this case shows that companies like Siemens and Tata Power-DDL had better sustainability results because of integrating the most recent digital technologies with the strategic commitment of the leadership and the empowerment of the workforce. Senior management is advised to implement combined sustainability approaches that would complement digital transformation efforts with the principles of the circular economy and the ESG goals. Integrating sustainability metrics in the operational and strategic decisions can promote resilience, decrease resource dependency, and generate sustainability competitive advantages in the long-term. Also, companies ought to use data analytics and AI as an efficiency tool, as well as a predictive sustainability tool, such as emissions reduction, energy optimization, and waste minimization. The research has mentions of great importance to the policy makers and regulators who might want to hasten the sustainable change in industry. The results indicate that favorable policy frameworks, regulatory incentives, and green finance mechanisms are significant in facilitating firms to use and implement green technologies. The introduction of renewable energy, the development of digital infrastructure, and the integration of the circular economy can significantly improve the sustainability performance of the country and the region with the help of policies. Besides, the research also highlights the necessity of policy coordination, which is a combination of industrial, environmental, and digital strategies.

REFERENCES

Awad, A., & Al Ahmari, D. (Eds.). (2026). *Digital resilience in supply chains: Security, governance, and AI innovation*. IGI Global Scientific Publishing., DOI: 10.4018/979-8-3373-8841-0

Bionicyarn. (2025). Retrieved from https://bionicyarn.com/

Breque, M., De Nul, L., & Petridis, A. (2021). *Industry 5.0: Towards a sustainable, human-centric and resilient European industry*. European Commission, Directorate-General for Research and Innovation. DOI: 10.2777/308407

El-Kassar, A. N., & Singh, S. K. (2019). Green innovation and organizational performance: The influence of big data and the moderating role of management commitment and HR practices. *Technological Forecasting and Social Change*, *144*, 483–498. DOI: 10.1016/j.techfore.2017.12.016

Ghobakhloo, M., Iranmanesh, M., Mubarak, M. F., Mubarik, M., Rejeb, A., & Nilashi, M. (2022). Identifying Industry 5.0 contributions to sustainable development: A strategy roadmap for delivering sustainability values. *Sustainable Production and Consumption*, *33*, 716–737. DOI: 10.1016/j.spc.2022.08.003

Haldar, A., & Sethi, N. (2022). Environmental effects of information and communication technology: Exploring the roles of renewable energy, innovation, trade and financial development. *Renewable & Sustainable Energy Reviews*, *153*, 111754. DOI: 10.1016/j.rser.2021.111754

Huang, S., Lin, H., Zhou, Y., Ji, H., & Zhu, N. (2022). The influence of the policy of replacing environmental protection fees with taxes on enterprise green innovation—Evidence from China's heavily polluting industries. *Sustainability (Basel)*, *14*(11), 6850. DOI: 10.3390/su14116850

Hussain, Z., Mohammad, S. I., Vasudevan, A., Awad, A., & Bansal, R. (2025). Exploring the effect of Industry 5.0 human-centric sustainability and green knowledge automation in enhancing green process adaptability: The mediating role of sustainable human–tech interaction. *Journal of Cleaner Production*, *537*, 147240. DOI: 10.1016/j.jclepro.2025.147240

Kumar, R., Gupta, P., Singh, S., & Jain, D. (2021). Human empowerment by Industry 5.0 in digital era: Analysis of enablers. In *FLAME 2020: 2nd International Conference on Future Learning Aspects of Mechanical Engineering* (pp. 401–410). Springer. DOI: 10.1007/978-981-33-4320-7_36

Longo, F., Padovano, A., & Umbrello, S. (2020). Value-oriented and ethical technology engineering in Industry 5.0: A human-centric perspective for the design of the factory of the future. *Applied Sciences (Basel, Switzerland)*, *10*(12), 1–25. DOI: 10.3390/app10124182

Lu, Y., Zheng, H., Chand, S., Xia, W., Liu, Z., Xu, X., & Bao, J. (2022). Outlook on human-centric manufacturing towards Industry 5.0. *Journal of Manufacturing Systems*, *62*, 612–627. DOI: 10.1016/j.jmsy.2022.02.001

Nahavandi, S. (2019). Industry 5.0—A human-centric solution. *Sustainability (Basel)*, *11*(16), 4371. Advance online publication. DOI: 10.3390/su11164371

Özdemir, V., & Hekim, N. (2018). Birth of Industry 5.0: Making sense of big data with artificial intelligence, "the internet of things" and next-generation technology policy. *Omics : A Journal of Integrative Biology*, *22*(1), 65–76. DOI: 10.1089/omi.2017.0194 PMID: 29293405

Redchuk, A., Walas Mateo, F., Pascal, G., & Tornillo, J. E. (2023). Adoption Case of IioT and Machine Learning to Improve Energy Consumption at a Process Manufacturing Firm, Under Industry 5.0 Model. *Big Data and Cognitive Computing*, *7*(1), 42. Advance online publication. DOI: 10.3390/bdcc7010042

Sharma, R., & Gupta, H. (2025). Exploring Industry 5.0 hurdles and strategies to support sustainable development and realize future growth aspirations: A comprehensive analysis. *Benchmarking*, •••, 1–27. DOI: 10.1108/BIJ-07-2024-0573

Siemens. (2025). *Sustainability at Siemens*. https://www.siemens.com/in/en/company/sustainability.html

Sindhwani, R., Afridi, S., Kumar, A., Banaitis, A., Luthra, S., & Singh, P. L. (2022). Can Industry 5.0 revolutionize the wave of resilience and social value creation? A multi-criteria framework to analyze enablers. *Technology in Society*, *68*, 101887. DOI: 10.1016/j.techsoc.2022.101887

Tata Power. (2025). *Green energy and smart grid initiatives*. https://www.tatapower-ddl.com/corporate/smart-grid-index/green-energy

Unilever. (2024). *Annual Report and Accounts 2024*. https://www.unilever.com/files/unilever-annual-report-and-accounts-2024.pdf#page=262

Unilever. (2025). *Reducing plastic use and improving recyclability*. https://www.unilever.com/sustainability/plastics/

United Nations Environment Programme (UNEP). (2019). *Global Environment Outlook – GEO-6: Healthy Planet, Healthy People*. Cambridge University Press., DOI: 10.1017/9781108627146

Vial, G. (2019). Understanding digital transformation: A review and a research agenda. *The Journal of Strategic Information Systems*, *28*(2), 118–144. DOI: 10.1016/j.jsis.2019.01.003

Chapter 10
Financial Technology, Smart Technologies, and the Remodelling of Banking Facilities:
Digital Change in the Finance and Accounting Industries

Rakhmatullayev Bobir
Termez University of Economics and Service, Uzbekistan

Gafurov Anvar
Alfraganus University, Uzbekistan

Jabbarov Umarbek
Mamun University, Uzbekistan

Achilov Izzatbek
Urgench State University Named After Abu Rayhan Biruni, Uzbekistan

Sabyasachi Pramanik
http://orcid.org/0000-0002-9431-8751
Haldia Institute of Technology, India

Soma Bag
Asadtala Nivedita Kanya Vidya Math, India

Abdullayev Abdulla Fayzulla Ugli
Tashkent State University of Economy, Uzbekistan

Valisher Sapayev
http://orcid.org/0000-0002-6751-5864
Mamun University, Uzbekistan

ABSTRACT

Accounting and finance are changing as a result of digital transformation, which combines FinTech platforms with intelligent technology. This chapter looks at how real-time reporting, ongoing auditing, and analytics-driven financial decision-making are made possible by digital accounting information systems. It examines

DOI: 10.4018/979-8-2600-2726-4.ch010

how accounting, governance, risk management, and professional responsibilities are affected by FinTech integration and financial intermediation. The chapter stresses the changing roles of accounting and finance professionals in digitally enabled financial ecosystems as well as new ethical and legal issues.

1. INTRODUCTION

Rapid developments in digital technology are causing a significant upheaval in the worldwide accounting and financial services industry. A digitally networked ecosystem characterised by real-time data flows, algorithmic decision-making, and platform-based service delivery has replaced the previous features of periodic reporting cycles, manual verification procedures, and institution-centric financial intermediation. Digital transformation in accounting and finance is becoming a key factor in determining organisational competitiveness, financial transparency, and systemic resilience rather than a peripheral operational issue. Traditionally created to document and compile historical financial transactions, accounting systems (Jain, V. et al. 2023) are becoming more and more integrated into sophisticated digital infrastructures that provide automatic compliance, predictive analytics, and ongoing monitoring. In a similar vein, financial technology (FinTech) companies that use data, analytics, and digital platforms to provide cutting-edge goods and services are reshaping the financial services industry, which was formerly controlled by banks and centralised middlemen. These changes are part of a larger movement away from institution-centric finance and towards technology-enabled financial ecosystems where service delivery, financial decision-making, and accounting data are closely intertwined. Compared to previous waves of technology adoption in accounting and finance, digital transformation is essentially different. The major goal of earlier computerisation stages was to increase efficiency by automating routine tasks like ledger maintenance and payroll processing. On the other hand, modern digital transformation involves reorganising financial operations around intelligent technologies, data-centric designs, and networked platforms. The temporal, functional, and strategic aspects of accounting and financial management are drastically changed by technologies like artificial intelligence; cloud computing, blockchain, big data (Byambaa, O., et al. 2025) analytics, and robotic process automation that allow continuous data collection and processing. These shifts have been intensified and accelerated by the growth of FinTech. By lowering transaction costs, boosting accessibility, and enabling individualised, data-driven financial solutions, fintech innovations such as digital payments, peer-to-peer lending, robo-advisory services, crowdfunding platforms, and decentralised finance pose a threat to established financial intermediaries. These developments do not, however, function apart from accounting systems. FinTech platforms, on the other hand, mostly depend on digitally transformed accounting information systems to manage risk, record transactions, evaluate financial performance, and comply with regulations. Because of this, accounting has changed from being a back-office reporting function to being an essential part of contemporary financial services.

There are significant ramifications from the combination of the development of FinTech-driven financial services with the digital revolution of accounting. By changing the way value, information, and trust are communicated in digital spaces, it transforms financial intermediation. It calls into question current regulatory and governance structures, which were primarily created for centralised organisations and recurring reporting schedules. Additionally, it changes the focus of professional jobs in accounting and finance from mundane technical duties to analytical thinking, technology literacy, and ethical supervision of algorithmic systems.

Even while research on FinTech (Policepatil, S. et al. 2025) and digital transformation is expanding, much of the literature now in publication discusses these topics separately. While FinTech research stresses innovation, competitiveness, and financial inclusion, studies on digital accounting often concentrate on automation, audit analytics, or information systems. This disjointed approach restricts our comprehension of how digital technologies collectively transform financial ecosystems and hides the interdependencies between accounting systems and FinTech platforms. Integrative studies that place accounting in the larger framework of FinTech-enabled financial change are required. In order to close this gap, this chapter looks at the digital transformation of accounting and finance as a related process that supports the development of modern financial services. It takes a comprehensive approach that connects institutional reform, governance issues, and career transition with technology innovation. By doing this, the chapter offers insights pertinent to practitioners, regulators, and educators negotiating the intricacies of technology-driven financial settings while also contributing to academic discussions on digital banking.

Even while the literature on digital transformation in accounting, finance, and FinTech is expanding, there are still a number of important study gaps.

- First, current research often looks at FinTech-driven financial innovation and digital transformation in accounting as essentially distinct fields. The ways, in which FinTech platforms and digital accounting information systems co-evolve and mutually influence financial reporting, auditing, and decision-making processes are not well examined in integrative research. A comprehensive knowledge of digital financial ecosystems is hampered by this gap.
- Secondly, a large portion of the literature that is now available is technology-focused, focussing on automation, efficiency improvements, and innovation results while ignoring the governance, regulatory, and risk management ram-

ifications of digitally linked systems. There is also a lack of empirical and conceptual research on how accounting functions assist accountability, systemic risk reduction, and regulatory supervision in real-time settings.

- Third, studies on professional transformation often concentrate on employability and skills, paying little attention to ethical responsibility, professional judgement, and public confidence in automated and algorithmic decision-making settings. Theoretical advances about the redistribution of ethical duties between digital systems and human specialists are lacking.
- Lastly, the majority of empirical research is centred on settings that are exclusive to a single nation or industry, providing little understanding of platform-based and cross-jurisdictional financial ecosystems. There is now a dearth of comparative and multidisciplinary research that connects information systems, accounting, finance, and regulatory studies. With a focus on governance, professional judgement, and ethical duty within digitally enabled financial ecosystems, this chapter fills these gaps by offering an integrated, conceptual examination of digital transformation across accounting, finance (Shukla, S. S. et al. 2024) and FinTech.

2. GOALS

- To investigate the characteristics and forces behind the digital revolution in finance and accounting, as well as how it is influencing the development of modern financial services.
- To examine how FinTech has developed and how it has affected service delivery models, financial intermediation, and conventional accounting functions.
- To investigate how FinTech platforms and digital accounting information systems integrate, as well as the effects this has on financial transparency and real-time decision-making.
- To evaluate the risk management, governance, and regulatory issues brought on by digitally connected financial ecosystems.
- To assess how accounting and finance professionals' roles, skill needs, and professional duties are evolving in technologically advanced settings.
- To determine future research prospects, systemic dangers, and ethical issues related to FinTech-led financial innovation and digital transformation.

3. CONCEPTUAL AND THEORETICAL UNDERPINNINGS OF DIGITAL TRANSFORMATION IN FINTECH: ACCOUNTING AND FINANCE

A multifaceted theoretical framework that goes beyond solely technical explanations is necessary to comprehend digital revolution in accounting, finance, and FinTech. Digital transformation is a complex socio-technical process that involves the co-evolution of technology, organisational practices, institutional norms, and professional logics. It goes beyond just adopting sophisticated tools. The conceptual underpinnings required examining how digital technologies alter accounting systems, financial intermediation, and financial service ecosystems are developed in this section. Conceptually, digitisation and digitalisation are not the same as digital transformation. The process of converting analogue information into digital form, such as substituting electronic documents for paper-based records, is known as digitisation. Digitalisation (Bi, S., et al. 2025) is the process of using digital technology to automate or enhance current procedures, often with an emphasis on cost and efficiency. On the other hand, digital transformation involves a more thorough reorganisation of business models, organisational operations, and value-creation processes made possible by digital technology. The transition from transaction-centric, retroactive systems to integrated, real-time, analytics-driven infrastructures that facilitate ongoing decision-making and strategic control is one way that accounting and finance are undergoing this change. (Canas da Costa, L., 2020) Socio-technical systems theory may be used to understand the digital revolution of accounting and finance from an information systems viewpoint. This viewpoint highlights how social structures and technology systems are mutually constitutive. Accounting information systems have presumptions about responsibility, control, and performance evaluation; they are not neutral technological artefacts. The introduction of digital technologies like blockchain (Bhatia, R. et al. 2025) and artificial intelligence changes not just technical procedures but also power dynamics, expert judgement, and governance systems. This theoretical framework is especially useful for comprehending how algorithmic financial judgements and automated accounting procedures alter institutional trust and organisational behaviour.

Another crucial paradigm for examining the digital revolution of accounting and finance is provided by institutional theory. Financial services and accounting procedures are firmly ingrained in institutional settings that are influenced by cultural norms, professional standards, and legal requirements. By bringing in new players like FinTech companies and technological platforms that operate outside conventional legal and professional borders, digital revolution puts existing institutional structures in jeopardy. Institutional theory aids in the explanation of adaptation processes, such as professional retraining, regulatory innovation, and the rise of new standards for digital reporting and assurance, as well as opposition to change, such as worries about legitimacy, dependability, and professional identity.

Platform theory provides important insights into how digital transformation changes financial intermediation in the FinTech setting. Within a single digital infrastructure, fintech companies often function as multifaceted platforms that link consumers, service providers, data sources, and regulators. For the purpose of facilitating transactions, evaluating risk, and creating value, these platforms mostly depend on real-time accounting and financial data. Platform-based finance increases reliance on data governance, algorithmic transparency, and system interoperability while decreasing the role of conventional intermediaries. In this context, accounting systems serve as vital data-generating tools that maintain platform functionality and legitimacy.

The dynamic capabilities framework and resource-based (Garg, P., et al. 2025) approach provide further insight into how businesses use digital transformation to gain a competitive edge in the accounting and financial services industries. Advanced analytics, integrated FinTech solutions, and digital accounting systems may all be considered strategic resources that improve decision quality and organisational responsiveness. But just having digital technology is not enough. In order to adapt accounting and financial activities to quickly evolving digital environments, organisations need to create dynamic skills including data governance, technological learning, and cross-functional integration. This viewpoint emphasises how crucial it is to strategically match accounting reform with more comprehensive organisational and financial plans. The notion of information asymmetry, which has long been at the heart of accounting and finance study, provides another crucial conceptual underpinning. Through standardised, recurring disclosures, traditional financial reporting systems were intended to lessen information asymmetry between managers, investors, creditors, and regulators. This reasoning is changed by digital transformation, which makes real-time transparency and constant information flows possible. In order to dynamically evaluate creditworthiness, investment risk, and operational success, FinTech platforms use accounting data. This reduces certain information asymmetries while perhaps creating new ones pertaining to algorithmic opacity and data ownership. The function of accounting information in signalling, monitoring, and market discipline must be re-examined in light of this change. Theories of risk and governance also provide crucial frameworks for examining digital transition. Digital technologies (Pramanik, S. 2024) provide new hazards linked to cybersecurity (Dohale, V., et al. 2025), system failure, data manipulation, and algorithmic bias, but they also improve efficiency and scalability. Risks in digitally enabled financial ecosystems are becoming more integrated and systemic, going beyond individual companies. Therefore, governance frameworks need to change from entity-centric control models to oversight mechanisms at the ecosystem level. Because they provide data-driven regulatory oversight, embedded controls, and real-time risk monitoring, accounting systems are essential to this shift.

The conceptual study of digital transformation in accounting and FinTech is further enhanced by ethical and accountability frameworks. Algorithmic systems' impact on financial choices raises concerns about accountability, explainability, and equity. Automated decision-making procedures provide a challenge to conventional ideas of professional judgement and responsibility, which are based on human knowledge. Though they must be reinterpreted in light of digitally mediated financial activities, ethical notions pertaining to openness, stewardship, and the public interest continue to be fundamental to accounting and finance. This emphasises how crucial it is to sustain ethical governance and professional monitoring in addition to technology innovation.

When combined, these conceptual and theoretical viewpoints highlight how digital revolution in accounting, finance, and FinTech is a complex process that defies easy explanation from a single discipline. FinTech platforms, financial services, and accounting systems all co-evolve in intricate institutional and socio-technical contexts. The next parts are positioned to examine how digital transformation alters accounting procedures, financial intermediation, governance frameworks, and professional responsibilities in modern financial ecosystems by firmly establishing the chapter in these conceptual underpinnings.

3.1. Methods of Research

This chapter employs a conceptual and qualitative research technique in light of the exploratory and integrative character of the identified research gaps. The approach is based on a methodical and critical analysis of multidisciplinary literature including financial reporting, accounting, auditing, FinTech, information systems, and financial regulation. To find important topics, theoretical stances, and new trends pertaining to digital transformation, peer-reviewed journal papers, professional standards, regulatory reports, and policy documents are examined. Furthermore, the chapter uses conceptual synthesis to create a cohesive framework that connects FinTech platforms, governance frameworks, professional roles, and digital accounting information systems (Labib, N.M., et al. 2022). By using this method, the chapter is able to go beyond descriptive research and provide theoretical insights into how accountability, risk management, and ethical duty are reshaped in financial ecosystems as a result of digital revolution.

4. ACCOUNTING AND FINANCE'S DIGITAL TRANSFORMATION

The structure, scope, and goals of accounting and financial operations have been significantly changed by digital transformation. Accounting and finance are becoming more and more linked into digital ecosystems that enable real-time monitoring, sophisticated analytics, and automated decision-making, as opposed to being discrete administrative or compliance-focused tasks. This section explores how the three fundamental areas of accounting and finance—auditing, financial reporting, and management accounting—are being reshaped by digital transformation, emphasising the consequences for financial transparency, governance, and professional judgement.

4.1 Auditing's Digital Transformation

One of the biggest changes brought about by digital technology has been in auditing. The availability of real-time transactional data and sophisticated analytical tools is posing a growing threat to traditional audit methods, which are based on periodic verification, sample strategies, and ex post review of financial statements. The transition from static, retrospective audits to continuous, technologically enabled assurance approaches is made possible by digital transformation. Instead of depending on small samples, auditors may now examine whole populations of transactions thanks to the use of artificial intelligence and data analytics. In real time, advanced audit analytics may spot irregularities, risk trends, and possible fraud, increasing the efficacy and efficiency of audits. Continuous auditing solutions provide for continuous evaluation of controls, transactions, and financial risks throughout the reporting period by integrating directly with customers' accounting information systems. The temporal aspect of auditing has fundamentally changed as a result, with assurance now being a continuous activity rather than a sporadic occurrence. Notwithstanding these developments, new issues with professional judgement and responsibility are brought forward by digital auditing. Risk assessment, evidence appraisal, and audit planning are all being impacted more and more by automated tools and algorithms. Although these tools improve analytical abilities, they also bring up issues with model bias, excessive dependence on technology, and the explainability of audit findings. For the audit process to remain centred on professional scepticism and ethical responsibility, auditors must thereby acquire abilities in comprehending, validating, and managing digital instruments. The way the audit profession interacts with customers and authorities is likewise altered by digital change. Regulators are putting more and more pressure on auditors to use technology to improve audit quality and identify new risks. When connecting their tools with client systems, auditors must simultaneously handle challenges related to data security, privacy, and system access. The need for revised professional frameworks that bring audit practice into line with digital realities is further supported by these advances, which call for new norms and guidelines on technology-enabled auditing.

4.2 Financial Reporting Standards and Digital Transformation

Digital change also challenges and reshapes financial reporting norms. The purpose of traditional reporting systems was to convey financial performance and position to external stakeholders via periodic, standardised financial statements. However, by facilitating real-time data availability, increased disclosure possibilities, and non-financial data integration, digital transformation changes the structure and purpose of financial reporting. Instead than depending just on quarterly or yearly reports, digital technologies provide continuous financial reporting, giving stakeholders access to current financial data. Digital reporting formats such as Extensible Business Reporting Language (XBRL) improve financial disclosures' machine readability, comparability, and accessibility. These advancements lessen information asymmetry in financial markets (Allam, Z., et al. 2024) while promoting investor analysis and regulatory supervision. At the same time, current accounting rules face difficulties due to the growth of digital assets, platform-based revenue models, and algorithmic pricing mechanisms. Traditional financial reporting standards do not adequately address issues pertaining to the identification, measurement, and disclosure of digital assets, cryptocurrencies (Danilova, O., et al. 2019), and data-driven wealth creation. In order to maintain comparability, dependability, and conceptual coherence while reflecting digitally mediated economic activity, standard-setters are under growing pressure to modify accounting rules. Beyond conventional financial measures, digital transformation broadens the breadth of financial reporting. Digital data systems are being used more and more in integrated reporting and sustainability disclosures to record financial performance together with environmental, social, and governance data. In order to position financial reporting as a multifaceted communication tool within digital ecosystems, accounting information systems are essential for gathering and evaluating this data.

4.3 Digital Transformation in Financial Management and Managerial Accounting

The availability of real-time data, sophisticated analytics, and digital decision-support tools has completely changed the way that managerial accounting and financial management are performed. Budgeting, variance analysis, and historical cost analysis were the main focuses of traditional management accounting. A move towards dynamic decision-making, predictive analytics and ongoing performance monitoring is made possible by digital transformation. By combining accounting data with operational and market data, advanced analytics and business intelligence systems provide managers thorough insights into resource use, profitability, and cost behaviour. Predictive forecasting and scenario modelling help with strategic planning in unpredictable times, improving organisational responsiveness and agility. These skills are especially useful in digitally intensive businesses where consumer behaviour and market circumstances change quickly. Control and cost management systems are also changed by digital transformation. More detailed and activity-based cost analysis (Autade, R. et al. 2026) is made possible by automation and data integration, which also lessen the need for human cost allocation procedures. Supply chain optimisation, performance-based incentive programs, and dynamic pricing are all supported by real-time cost information. Consequently, management accounting transforms from a role focused on control to a strategic collaborator in innovation and value generation. But there are also behavioural and governance issues brought on by the greater dependence on digital technologies. Managers have to understand complicated analytical results and strike a balance between contextual judgement and data-driven insights. To avoid abuse, prejudice, or overconfidence in algorithmic suggestions, the incorporation of automated decision-support systems into management procedures requires strong internal controls, data governance guidelines, and ethical supervision.

4.4 Consequences for Financial and Accounting Practice

The role of accounting and finance in businesses and financial ecosystems is being redefined by digital transformation in the areas of auditing, financial reporting, and management accounting. Accounting information systems develop become strategic infrastructures that facilitate decision-making, risk management, and transparency. Regular technical duties give way to analytical thinking, technological governance, and ethical supervision as areas of professional skill. Additionally, the change strengthens the link between accounting and other financial services. The data underpinning for FinTech platforms, regulatory technology, and intelligent financial services is provided by digitally transformed accounting systems. Therefore, to grasp the progress of modern financial services, one must have a solid knowledge of the digital transition in accounting and finance.

5. FINTECH'S DEVELOPMENT AND THE FINANCIAL SERVICES REVOLUTION

One of the biggest structural shifts in the history of financial services is the development of financial technology. FinTech has evolved from assisting with technology that improved back-office productivity to becoming a disruptive force that is changing market structure, service delivery, and financial intermediation. The development of digital accounting systems and financial information infrastructures, which provide the data basis for FinTech-driven innovation, has been intimately linked to this progression. Analysing the larger digital revolution of accounting and finance hence requires an understanding of FinTech's direction.

5.1 Phases in the Evolution of FinTech

The growth of FinTech may be seen as a multi-phase process marked by institutional disruption and rising technical complexity. The primary goal of early FinTech projects was to increase the operational effectiveness of conventional financial institutions. While they improved transaction speed and decreased costs, technologies like automated teller machines, electronic funds transfer systems, and internet banking (Bani Ahmad, AYA, et al. 2025) platforms mostly maintained the institutional frameworks that were already in place. The rise of tech-driven businesses that focused on certain financial value chain sectors signalled the second stage of FinTech development. Peer-to-peer lending platforms, online investing services, and digital payment systems posed a threat to established banks by providing quicker, easier-to-use, and more user-friendly options. To extend their operations and successfully manage risk, these platforms mostly depended on automated financial processing and real-time accounting data. The creation of platform-based and ecosystem-focused financial services is the latest stage in FinTech's growth. Financial services may be easily incorporated into non-financial platforms like social media, e-commerce, and logistics thanks to open banking efforts, application programming interfaces, and embedded finance models. This development is furthered by decentralised finance, which uses distributed ledger technology and smart contracts to facilitate financial transactions and services without the need for centralised middlemen. FinTech relies more and more on digitally transformed accounting systems across various stages to guarantee data integrity, transparency, and regulatory compliance.

5.2 Transformation of Financial Intermediation

By changing the way information, trust, and risk are handled inside financial institutions, fintech radically transforms financial intermediation. Conventional financial intermediation depended on centralised organisations that gathered data, evaluated creditworthiness, and supplied assurance via regulatory supervision. FinTech platforms, which often have fewer institutional layers, use digital data and analytics to carry out these tasks more effectively. An essential component of this change is accounting data. Real-time (Aljohani, A. et al. 2025) financial data is used by FinTech-driven lending and investing platforms to evaluate borrower risk, set prices for financial goods, and track results. Instead of using static financial statements, automated credit rating models and algorithmic investment strategies depend on ongoing accounting and transactional data. This change speeds up financial decision-making and lessens information asymmetry, but it also creates new reliance on algorithmic control, system integrity, and data quality. FinTech threatens the hegemony of conventional banks and financial institutions by reorganising financial intermediation, opening doors for cooperation and hybrid models. FinTech solutions are used by many established institutions to improve customer experience, integrate digital accounting systems, and expand their service offerings. These advancements make it harder to distinguish between FinTech and conventional finance, which emphasises the need of integrated analytical frameworks.

5.3 FinTech and Innovation in Financial Service Delivery

By emphasising speed, personalisation, and accessibility, fintech technologies have revolutionised the way financial services are delivered. Digital payment systems are changing how businesses and consumers make payments by enabling quick, inexpensive cross-border transactions. Robo-advisory platforms lower barriers to financial market participation by providing large-scale, algorithm-driven investment advice. InsurTech solutions use data analytics to enhance pricing, claims processing, and risk assessment. Effective operation of these advances depends on digitally changed financial information and accounting systems. FinTech services' scalability and dependability are supported by automated transaction recording, real-time reconciliation, and ongoing performance monitoring. When consumers have access to current financial data via digital dashboards and reporting tools, financial transparency is improved. But the focus on personalisation and automation also brings up issues with algorithmic bias, data privacy, and consumer protection. One of the special revolutionary advancement in service delivery is embedded finance. Embedded finance improves consumer comfort and lowers friction by incorporating financial services into non-financial systems. In order to support these models, accounting systems must change to allow for real-time cost allocation, revenue recognition, and compliance across intricate platform ecosystems. The importance of accounting data in facilitating cutting-edge financial services is further highlighted by this integration.

5.4 Implications for Market Structure and Financial Inclusion

One of the most often mentioned advantages of FinTech is its capacity to improve financial inclusion by giving marginalised groups and small businesses greater access to financial services. By lowering geographical and informational barriers, digital platforms allow people and companies to engage in financial systems without depending on conventional banking infrastructure. Innovative credit assessment methods that increase access to financing are supported by real-time accounting data and other data sources. Simultaneously, FinTech introduces new kinds of concentration and competition, changing the structure of the market. FinTech makes it easier for new businesses to enter the market, but platform-based models might allow a few big tech companies with access to enormous amounts of data to dominate the industry. This brings up issues with systemic risk, data monopolisation, and market dominance. Frameworks for accounting and regulation must change to meet these issues and guarantee stable finances and fair competition.

5.5 dangers and Difficulties in FinTech-Driven Financial Transformatlon:

FinTech poses a number of dangers and difficulties in spite of its revolutionary potential. FinTech companies and consumers face operational and reputational risks due to cybersecurity attacks, data breaches, and system failures. Transparency, bias, and accountability are issues with algorithmic decision-making, especially when financial judgements have substantial social and economic ramifications. The FinTech environment is made more difficult by regulatory uncertainty. There are loopholes in supervision and enforcement since many FinTech technologies operate outside of established regulatory systems and across countries. Accounting information systems are essential for reducing these risks because they provide standardised reporting, real-time monitoring, and regulatory compliance. However, strong data governance, expert monitoring, and ethical standards are necessary for these systems to be successful.

5.6 Interdependence between FinTech and Digital Accounting Systems:

The digital transformation of accounting is inextricably linked to the development of FinTech and the transformation of financial services. For FinTech systems to work well, accounting data must be precise, timely, and interoperable. In contrast, real-time processing, advanced analytics, and platform integration are all being incorporated into accounting systems in response to the demands of digital financial services. This interdependence emphasises the necessity of viewing FinTech as a component of a larger digital financial ecosystem where technology, finance, and accounting all co-evolve. Developing professional capabilities, research agendas, and governance frameworks that effectively handle the intricacies of contemporary financial systems requires an understanding of this link.

6. COMBINING FINTECH PLATFORMS WITH DIGITAL ACCOUNTING INFORMATION SYSTEMS

An important turning point in the development of modern financial ecosystems is the combination of FinTech platforms with digital accounting information systems. FinTech platforms operationalize financial data via automated financial services and algorithmic decision-making, while digital transformation in accounting improves the data's accessibility, timeliness, and analytical usefulness. Accounting systems are positioned as fundamental infrastructures inside digitally enabled financial services as a result of this integration, which transforms the creation, transmission, interpretation, and governance of financial information.

6.1 Architecture and Interoperability of Integrated Systems:

The creation of digital architectures that are compatible with one another and facilitate smooth data transfer across institutional and organisational barriers is at the heart of accounting-FinTech integration. Businesses and outside financial service providers may communicate in real time thanks to cloud-based accounting systems, corporate resource planning platforms, and application programming interfaces. By supporting automated transaction recording, real-time reconciliation, and ongoing financial reporting, these designs lower financial process latency and human involvement. Financial services are more flexible and scalable when they are interoperable. To get accounting data for credit evaluation, payment processing, investment analysis, and compliance tracking, FinTech systems depend on standardised data formats and interfaces. In order to provide data consistency, validation, and traceability across interconnected platforms, accounting systems must change. Instead of being discrete internal tools, accounting information systems are becoming essential nodes within financial service ecosystems because to this architectural alignment.

6.2 Real-Time Decision-Making and Financial Transparency:

A transition from periodic to real-time financial decision-making is made possible by the integration of accounting systems with FinTech platforms. Financial institutions, investors, and regulators may get current data on risk exposure, liquidity, and financial performance thanks to continuous data flows. By lowering information asymmetry and increasing financial transparency, this real-time visibility promotes better risk management and more effective capital allocation. Dynamic financial management is made possible for businesses by integrated systems. Automated loan choices, dynamic pricing and performance-based financing arrangements are all supported by real-time accounting data. Such integration is especially beneficial to small and medium-sized businesses, since real-time financial data enhances financing (Tang, Q. et al. 2025) availability and lessens dependency on static financial statements. Concerns about data privacy, competitive sensitivity, and possible financial information abuse are also brought up by more openness.

6.3 Implications for Businesses and Financial Institutions:

Organisational boundaries and strategic linkages are changed when digital accounting systems are integrated with FinTech platforms. For essential financial operations like payments, lending, and compliance, businesses are depending more and more on external systems. To handle the risks related to system dependence, data ownership, and service continuity, this reliance calls for strong data governance frameworks and contractual agreements. Financial firms are under pressure to cooperate as well as compete. FinTech platforms provide chances for innovation via partnerships and platform integration, even as they threaten conventional service models. These partnerships are operationalized via accounting systems, which provide data exchange, performance tracking, and regulatory reporting. For FinTech companies as well as incumbents, effective integration therefore becomes a key competency.

6.4 Regulatory and Supervisory Implications:

FinTech and integrated accounting systems have a big impact on regulatory supervision and oversight. Technologies-enabled regulatory techniques, such as supervisory and regulatory technologies, are supported by real-time access to accounting data. Regulators may more successfully monitor compliance, identify irregularities, and evaluate systemic risk by using integrated systems. But greater interconnectedness also makes regulatory accountability more difficult. Traditional supervisory frameworks focused on entity-level reporting are challenged by the possibility of financial data flowing across numerous platforms and countries. In order to handle algorithmic decision-making, cross-platform data flows, and shared technology infrastructures, regulators must modify their governance frameworks. Accounting information systems are essential for facilitating these adjustments since they guarantee data openness, auditability, and dependability.

6.5 Risks and Governance Issues:

Although integrating accounting systems with FinTech platforms has advantages, it also presents new risks and governance issues. Operational and systemic risks may be increased by cybersecurity attacks, data breaches, and system failures that spread quickly across linked platforms. Bias, accountability, and openness are issues with algorithmic decision-making based on integrated data. Technology controls, expert monitoring, and ethical frameworks are all necessary for effective governance. To maintain data integrity, system resilience, and compliance with changing regulatory demands, accounting operations must change. This entails creating internal controls for third-party risk management, model validation, and data governance. Accounting professionals' responsibilities now include guardianship of digital financial infrastructures in addition to financial reporting as integration advances.

6.6 Strategic Significance of Integration:

The strategic importance of accounting in financial ecosystems is redefined by the integration of FinTech platforms and digital accounting information systems. Accounting data turns into a dynamic asset that promotes innovation, upholds governance, and fosters confidence in online financial services. Businesses that successfully combine FinTech and accounting skills are better equipped to handle the risks involved in digital transformation and successfully negotiate its intricacies. This integration highlights the chapter's main point, which is that the development of FinTech and the digital transformation of accounting are processes that reinforce one another and change modern financial services. Developing successful strategies, legal frameworks, and professional abilities in the digital era requires an understanding of this link.

7. RISK MANAGEMENT, GOVERNANCE, AND REGULATION IN DIGITAL FINANCIAL ECOSYSTEMS

The governance, regulatory, and risk management environment of financial systems has been drastically changed by the digital revolution of accounting and finance as well as the quick development of FinTech platforms. Interconnected platforms, real-time data flows, algorithmic decision-making and cross-jurisdictional activities are characteristics of digitally enabled financial ecosystems. These characteristics improve productivity, openness, and creativity, but they also bring up difficult governance issues and new kinds of risk that transcend organisational borders. This section looks at how risk management procedures, regulatory frameworks, and governance structures are changing to meet the demands of digital financial ecosystems. It focuses especially on how accounting information systems help with accountability and supervision.

7.1 Governance Issues in Digitally Assisted Financial Ecosystems:

Conventional accounting and finance governance models were primarily created for centralised organisations with distinct borders, hierarchical control systems, and regular reporting procedures. Digital financial ecosystems, on the other hand, are highly linked, platform-based, and decentralised. Lines of responsibility and control are complicated by the fact that financial services are often provided via networks (Zhang, H., et al. 2025) of businesses, technological companies, and data middlemen. These difficulties are made more difficult by the integration of accounting systems with FinTech platforms. Questions of data ownership, accountability for data quality, and liability distribution in the event of system failure or wrongdoing are brought up by the flow of financial data across several systems and parties. Because algorithmic decision-making incorporates rules and judgements into automated systems that may not be transparent or explicable, it makes governance even more difficult. Traditional governance methods that rely on human inspection and ex post review are often inadequate in these kinds of settings. A move towards proactive, data-driven, and technologically enabled monitoring is necessary for effective governance in digital financial ecosystems. Because they enable embedded controls, facilitate continuous monitoring, and provide real-time insight into financial processes, accounting systems are essential to this shift. Therefore, to guarantee accountability and confidence in digitally mediated financial services, governance systems must combine technology restrictions with expert judgement and ethical monitoring.

7.2 Regulatory Reactions to FinTech and Digital Transformation:

Regulatory frameworks have a hard time keeping up with the rapid development of FinTech and digital accounting systems. The majority of current rules were created for conventional financial institutions and are predicated on regular reporting, centralised management, and distinct institutional boundaries. On the other hand, FinTech platforms often use non-traditional data sources, operate across borders, and provide services via digital interfaces that make it difficult to distinguish between financial and non-financial (Napoli, G., et al. 2021) activity. As a result, authorities are using technology-enabled techniques to compliance and oversight more often. Data analytics, automation, and real-time reporting are used by supervisory and regulatory technologies to improve the efficacy of regulations. The data infrastructure required for these strategies is provided by digitally transformed accounting systems, giving authorities access to timely, verifiable, and standardised financial data. Regulatory supervision in digital contexts is further supported by machine-readable disclosures and open reporting standards. There are still regulatory loopholes and anomalies in spite of these advancements. Cross-border FinTech activities have difficulties because to disparities in national regulatory frameworks, which can give rise to worries about regulatory arbitrage. Furthermore, the speed at which technology is developing often surpasses the ability of regulatory bodies to create and carry out suitable regulations. These difficulties highlight the need of flexible regulatory frameworks that strike a balance between innovation, consumer protection, financial stability, and moral responsibility.

7.3 Risk Management in Digital Financial Ecosystems:

A wide variety of hazards that go beyond conventional financial risk categories are introduced by digital financial ecosystems. System failures, data breaches, and cybersecurity threats provide serious operational risks with possibly systemic repercussions. Because malfunctions or vulnerabilities in one component may spread quickly across the ecosystem, these risks are increased by dependence on linked platforms and third-party service providers. Another significant issue is algorithmic risk. Automated decision-making systems for fraud detection, investment management, and credit scoring may have biases, depend on faulty data, or provide results that are hard to defend or explain. Concerns about justice, responsibility, and adherence to moral and legal requirements are brought up by these dangers. By guaranteeing data integrity, traceability, and auditability, accounting systems are crucial in reducing algorithmic risk. In digital financial ecosystems, systemic risk also assumes new forms. Platform-based business models have the potential to consolidate market dominance and foster reliance on a limited number of leading technology suppliers. The potential for contagion, in which shocks in one area of the ecosystem may have ripple effects across markets and institutions, is increased by the interconnectivity of digital systems. Therefore, risk management frameworks need to change to handle both macro-level systemic vulnerabilities and micro-level operational hazards.

7.4 Accounting's Role in Governance and Risk Oversight:

In digitally connected financial ecosystems, accounting operations are essential to efficient governance and risk management. Accounting systems that have undergone digital transformation provide improved transparency, real-time compliance, and ongoing risk management. Accounting systems with embedded controls automate compliance checks, identify irregularities, and facilitate the early identification of new risks. Additionally, the audit function is essential for ensuring the security of digital systems and procedures. Technology-enabled auditing methods, such as data analytics and continuous auditing, improve auditors' capacity to evaluate data dependability, system integrity, and control efficacy. But in order to handle the intricacies of digital ecosystems, such as third-party platforms and algorithmic decision-making, auditors must also modify their approaches and professional standards. More and more, accounting specialists act as a bridge between governance frameworks and technology systems. Their knowledge is crucial for deciphering digital data, confirming automated results, and making sure financial data facilitates sound decision-making. In addressing digital financial risks, this enlarged position highlights the significance of professional judgement, ethical responsibility, and multidisciplinary teamwork.

7.5 Ethical and Accountability concerns:

In digital financial ecosystems, ethical concerns are essential to risk management and governance. Concerns about data protection, consent, and privacy are raised by the usage of financial and personal data. The results of algorithmic decision-making may be opaque or biased, undermining societal legitimacy and confidence. Governance structures that put accountability, equity, and transparency first are necessary to address these problems. Professionals in accounting and finance are essential to maintaining moral principles in online settings. Accounting systems promote moral governance and public confidence by guaranteeing the accuracy and openness of financial data. The profession's dedication to stewardship and the public interest must be reinforced by ethical frameworks that adapt to the difficulties presented by automation and artificial intelligence.

7.6 Towards Integrated Governance Frameworks:

Because of the intricacy of digital financial ecosystems, integrated governance frameworks that balance risk management and regulatory supervision with technology innovation are required. These frameworks, which include regulators, financial institutions, technology suppliers, and professional associations, need to be flexible, multidisciplinary, and cooperative. Accounting information systems provide data-driven (Isiaku, L., et al. 2025) monitoring, assurance, and accountability, making them fundamental components of these frameworks. Stakeholders may more effectively capitalise on the advantages of innovation while reducing related risks by combining governance, regulation, and risk management inside digitally changed accounting and financial systems. The robustness and sustainability of digital financial ecosystems depend on this integration.

8. PROFESSIONAL DEVELOPMENT, COMPETENCIES, AND ETHICAL OBLIGATIONS IN FINANCE AND ACCOUNTING

The professional environment of accounting and finance has completely changed as a result of digital transformation and the growth of FinTech-driven financial services. The roles, abilities, and ethical obligations of accounting and finance professionals are changing dramatically as platform-based models reorganise financial processes and intelligent technology automate repetitive work. This part looks at the changing nature of professional identities, the new skills needed in technologically advanced settings, and the moral dilemmas raised by the growing dependence on digital systems for financial decision-making.

8.1 Shifting Accounting and Finance Professional Roles:

Transaction processing, compliance, and regular reporting were the main responsibilities of accountants and other financial professionals in the past. Through automation, robotic process automation, and integrated accounting systems, digital transformation has greatly decreased the requirement for human execution of these operations. Professional emphasis is thus moving towards roles that call for higher-order judgement and strategic insight, such as analytical, interpretative, and advising. Other than only verifying financial accounts, auditing experts are increasingly acting as assurance providers over digital systems. Understanding information systems, data flows, and algorithmic decision-making processes is necessary for auditors working in continuous auditing, data analytics, and system-based assurance. Professionals in managerial accounting and financial management are also required to use real-time data and sophisticated analytical tools to assist risk management, performance optimisation, and strategic planning. By introducing new organisational structures and business models, FinTech innovation progressively broadens the scope of professional employment. Data scientists, software engineers, and regulatory experts often collaborate collaboratively with accountants and other financial professionals that work in FinTech companies or platform-based ecosystems. These hybrid positions put established professional boundaries to the test and call for flexibility, proficiency with technology, and ongoing education.

8.2 New Professional Competencies and Skill Needs:

Professional skill sets must be reconfigured in light of the digital revolution of accounting and finance. Although technical accounting knowledge is still necessary, it is no longer enough on its own. To function well in technologically advanced settings, professionals need to acquire capabilities in data analytics, information systems, and digital technologies. In order to guarantee correctness, relevance, and dependability, it is essential to comprehend how accounting information is created, processed, and used inside digital platforms. As professionals analyse algorithmic suggestions and comprehend complex data outputs, analytical and critical thinking abilities become more and more crucial. Effective professionals are distinguished from simply technical operators by their capacity to use professional judgement in the face of automated technology. As experts must explain intricate digital processes and analytical findings to a variety of stakeholders, including management, regulators, and clients, communication skills also become more important. Frameworks for professional education and training must change to meet these evolving needs. Data analytics, information systems, cybersecurity, and technology governance are increasingly included in accounting and finance courses. In order to maintain the profession's relevance and credibility in digital contexts, professional organisations are essential in upgrading competence frameworks and ethical norms.

8.3 Ethical Obligations in Financial Systems Driven by Technology:

In the accounting and financial industries, ethical responsibility is still fundamental, but new ethical issues brought about by digital transformation call for careful thought. Accountability, transparency, and fairness are all called into question when automated technology and artificial intelligence are used in financial decision-making. It becomes more difficult to assign blame for mistakes or biased results when algorithms affect credit decisions, investment suggestions, or audit results. Concerns around data ethics are especially significant in digital financial ecosystems. Professionals in the fields of accounting and finance are responsible for the collection, storage, and responsible use of sensitive financial and personal data. In order to preserve public confidence in digital financial systems, concerns about data privacy, consent, and security are crucial. Professionals must adhere to ethical standards pertaining to integrity and confidentiality while navigating regulatory obligations. Other ethical issues are raised by the possibility of algorithmic prejudice. If automated systems depend on skewed data or faulty models, they may inadvertently perpetuate current disparities or provide discriminating results. In order to make sure that financial choices are in line with social responsibility and justice, accounting and finance professionals have an ethical duty to comprehend and question algorithmic processes.

8.4 Professional Judgement and Accountability in Automated Environments:

By integrating decision rules into automated systems, digital transformation transforms professional judgement. Automation increases uniformity and efficiency, but it does not replace human supervision. In contrast, professional judgement becomes more important for analysing findings, handling exceptions or anomalies, and confirming system outputs. Accountability frameworks need to change to acknowledge that digital systems and human experts share accountability. Professionals are increasingly responsible for the planning, execution, and supervision of automated operations in addition to financial results. The significance of ethical awareness, recordkeeping, and openness in professional activity is reaffirmed by this enlarged area of responsibility.

8.5 Consequences for Public Trust and Professional Identity:

Public trust and professional identity are affected by the evolution of professional roles and duties. Professionals in accounting and finance must strike a balance between innovation and their long-standing dedication to honesty, impartiality, and the public interest as they take on increasingly strategic and technologically focused jobs. In a time of fast technological development, maintaining this equilibrium is crucial to the profession's credibility. By offering standards, training, and advice that take into account the reality of digital financial ecosystems, professional associations, regulators, and educators all play a vital part in facilitating this shift. Accounting and finance professionals may strengthen their relevance and support the long-term growth of digital financial systems by embracing digital transformation while adhering to ethical standards.

9. CONCLUSION AND PROSPECTS FOR FURTHER RESEARCH

Driven by the quick development of FinTech and other cutting-edge digital technologies, the digital transformation of accounting and finance is a structural change rather than a short-term technical fix. As this chapter has shown, digitalisation is radically changing financial reporting procedures, auditing techniques, accounting systems, and financial service delivery models. Financial decision-making is shifting towards real-time, data-driven, algorithmically aided procedures as platform-based

FinTech designs are increasingly linked with accounting information systems. These shifts have a significant impact on professional positions, ethical responsibility, governance, and regulation in modern financial ecosystems. In order to demonstrate how technology innovation interacts with institutional structures, professional standards, and regulatory frameworks, the chapter first outlined the philosophical and theoretical underpinnings of digital transformation in accounting and finance. After that, it looked at how intelligent systems and digital technologies are changing fundamental accounting tasks, including financial reporting, management accounting, and auditing. The investigation showed that automation and analytics increase complexity and reliance on system integrity while simultaneously improving efficiency and transparency. These processes are further accelerated by the development of FinTech, which challenges the power of conventional financial institutions, redefines financial intermediation, and increases access to financial services. This chapter's analysis of the connection between FinTech platforms and digital accounting information systems is one of its main contributions. Continuous reporting, embedded controls, and real-time assurance are made possible by this integration; nevertheless, it also brings with it governance and risk management issues that transcend organisational borders. The necessity for flexible, technologically enabled oversight structures that can handle cybersecurity threats, algorithmic hazards, and systemic weaknesses was highlighted by the debate on governance, regulation, and risk management. In digital financial ecosystems, accounting systems have become essential infrastructures for accountability, transparency, and regulatory compliance. The chapter also highlighted how accounting and finance have seen a significant shift in professional duties and ethical obligations. Professionals are increasingly expected to use judgement, decipher complicated data outputs, and manage automated decision-making systems as regular operations become automated. Data governance, algorithmic bias, and accountability ethics are becoming essential components of professional activity rather than incidental issues. The capacity of accounting and finance professionals to strike a balance between innovation and their unwavering dedication to honesty, impartiality, and the public good is critical to the viability of digital financial ecosystems. Notwithstanding the noteworthy advancements made possible by digital transformation, the chapter points out a number of important topics that want further research. Future studies should examine how new technologies like blockchain, quantum computing, and artificial intelligence may further alter financial governance frameworks, audit assurance methods, and accounting standards. Important empirical insights would be obtained from longitudinal research looking at the long-term effects of digital transformation on market stability, audit efficacy, and financial reporting quality. Further research on cross-border governance and regulatory harmonisation in digital financial ecosystems is also required. Because FinTech platforms operate internationally, inconsistent regulatory frameworks have the potential to worsen systemic risk and compromise consumer protection. The creation of more logical and flexible regulatory models may be aided by comparative studies that look at regulatory responses in various institutional settings. Furthermore, studies on supervisory and regulatory technologies may help us comprehend how data-driven supervision can improve financial stability without limiting creativity. Future research in the areas of workforce development and professional education is also crucial. Policymakers, professional associations, and educators all benefit from research on how accounting and finance programs are adjusting to the digital revolution as well as how professionals learn and use new skills. Because professionals are depending more and more on algorithmic tools whose assumptions and consequences may not be entirely obvious, research into ethical decision-making in automated contexts is especially important. In conclusion, the fundamentals of accounting, finance, and financial services are being redefined by digital revolution and FinTech innovation. This chapter makes the case that professional judgement and accounting procedures are still essential for maintaining accountability, transparency, and confidence in digital financial ecosystems. Through the integration of technical innovation with strong ethical frameworks, flexible regulations, and strong governance, stakeholders may minimise the risks associated with digital transformation while simultaneously maximising its advantages. The capacity of the accounting and financial industries to adapt properly to ongoing change will be just as important to their future as technology advancements.

REFERENCES

A. YA Bani Ahmad. (2025). P. Jangra, S. Sood, A. Gupta, A. Namdev, S. Pramanik, Banking Sector's Unification of Culture Following Artificial Intelligence Adoption. In *Real-World Applications of AI Innovation* (pp. 199–212). IGI Global., DOI: 10.4018/979-8-3693-4252-7.ch010

Aljohani, A. (2025). Exploring Future Trends and Uncovering Opportunities in AI-Enhanced Financial Technologies. In Gupta, S. K., Rosak-Szyrocka, J., Rena, R., Shieh, C. S., & Erkol Bayram, G. (Eds.), *The Impact of Artificial Intelligence on Finance: Transforming Financial Technologies. Information Systems Engineering and Management* (Vol. 53). Springer., DOI: 10.1007/978-3-031-92916-8_10

Allam, Z., & Cheshmehzangi, A. (2024). Technological Innovation and Sustainable Transitions. In *Sustainable Futures and Green New Deals*. Palgrave Macmillan., DOI: 10.1007/978-3-031-63642-4_3

Autade, R. (2026). AI-Enabled Blockchain Framework for Detecting Threats in Payment Systems. In Mishra, D., Yang, X. S., Unal, A., & Jat, D. S. (Eds.), *Data Science and Big Data Analytics. IDBA 2025. Learning and Analytics in Intelligent Systems* (Vol. 55). Springer., DOI: 10.1007/978-3-032-05377-0_32

Bhatia, R. (2025). Next-Generation Digital Finance: Architecting AI-Driven Financial Systems on the SAP Cloud Ecosystem. In: Awan, I., Younas, M., Ghinea, G., Tor-Morten, G., Şen, S. (eds) The 6th Joint International Conference on AI, Big Data and Blockchain (AIBB 2025). AIBB 2025. Lecture Notes in Networks and Systems, vol 1618. Springer, Cham. DOI: 10.1007/978-3-032-04728-1_8

Bi, S., Lian, Y., & Wang, Z. (2025). Research and Design of a Financial Intelligent Risk Control Platform Based on Big Data Analysis and Deep Machine Learning. In: Atiquzzaman, M., Yen, N., Xu, Z. (eds) Proceedings of the 5th International Conference on Big Data Analytics for Cyber-Physical System in Smart City—Volume 1. BDCPS 2023. Lecture Notes on Data Engineering and Communications Technologies, vol 234. Springer, Singapore. DOI: 10.1007/978-981-96-0208-7_37

Byambaa, O., Yondon, C., Rentsen, E., Darkhijav, B., & Rahman, M. (2025). An empirical examination of the adoption of artificial intelligence in banking services: The case of Mongolia. *Futur Bus J, 11*(1), 76. DOI: 10.1186/s43093-025-00504-y

Canas da Costa, L., & Popović, T. (2020). Financing Sustainable Infrastructures in a Smart Cities' Context—Innovative Concepts, Solutions and Instruments. In Planing, P., Müller, P., Dehdari, P., & Bäumer, T. (Eds.), *Innovations for Metropolitan Areas*. Springer., DOI: 10.1007/978-3-662-60806-7_18

Danilova, O., & Belayeva, I. (2019). Economic Efficiency of Using the Electric Grid Complex: Problems of Reserves of Network Power and Development of Intelligent Technologies. In Popkova, E. (Ed.), *The Future of the Global Financial System: Downfall or Harmony. ISC 2018. Lecture Notes in Networks and Systems* (Vol. 57). Springer., DOI: 10.1007/978-3-030-00102-5_26

Dohale, V., Ambilkar, P., Bilolikar, V., Narkhede, B. E., Kumar, A., & Kumar, A. (2025). Evaluating circular economy and smart technology adoption barriers in the Indian textile and apparel industries using neutrosophic ISM. *Annals of Operations Research, 355*(1), 211–251. DOI: 10.1007/s10479-023-05651-5

Garg, P., Gupta, B., Kapil, K. N., Sivarajah, U., & Gupta, S. (2025). Examining the relationship between blockchain capabilities and organizational performance in the Indian banking sector. *Annals of Operations Research, 348*(3), 1513–1546. DOI: 10.1007/s10479-023-05254-0

Isiaku, L., & Dawud, A. M. (2025). Blockchain and the Smart Circular Economy: Real-World Applications and Insight. In Singh, R., Shafik, W., & Kumar, V. (Eds.), *Blockchain Technologies for Smart Circular Economy and Organisational Sustainability. Environmental Footprints and Eco-design of Products and Processes.* Springer., DOI: 10.1007/978-3-031-89183-0_13

Jain, V., Rastogi, M., Ramesh, J. V. N., Chauhan, A., Agarwal, P., Pramanik, S., & Gupta, A. (2023). FinTech and Artificial Intelligence in Relationship Banking and Computer Technology. In Saini, K., Mummoorthy, A., Chandrika, R., Gowri Ganesh, N. S., & Global, I. G. I. (Eds.), *AI, IoT, and Blockchain Breakthroughs in E-Governance*. DOI: 10.4018/978-1-6684-7697-0.ch011

Labib, N. M., & Alarabi, N. I. (2022). A Proposed Framework to Apply Secured Mobile Banking in Egypt. In Magdi, D. A., Helmy, Y. K., Mamdouh, M., & Joshi, A. (Eds.), *Digital Transformation Technology. Lecture Notes in Networks and Systems* (Vol. 224). Springer., DOI: 10.1007/978-981-16-2275-5_22

Napoli, G., Barbaro, S., Giuffrida, S., & Trovato, M. R. (2021). The European Green Deal: New Challenges for the Economic Feasibility of Energy Retrofit at District Scale. In Bevilacqua, C., Calabrò, F., & Della Spina, L. (Eds.), *New Metropolitan Perspectives. NMP 2020. Smart Innovation, Systems and Technologies* (Vol. 178). Springer., DOI: 10.1007/978-3-030-48279-4_116

Policepatil, S., Sharma, J., Kumar, B., Singh, D., Pramanik, S., Gupta, A., & Mahabub, B. S. (2025). Financial Sector Hyper-Automation: Transforming Banking and Investing Procedures. In *Examining Global Regulations During the Rise of Fintech* (pp. 299–318). IGI Global., DOI: 10.4018/979-8-3693-3803-2.ch012

Pramanik, S. (2024). AI-Powered Hospital Accounting: Towards Sound Financial Management. In *Exploring Global FinTech Advancement and Applications* (pp. 121–142). IGI Global. DOI: 10.4018/979-8-3693-1561-3.ch005

Shukla, S. S., Bajpai, S., Pankajam, A., Gupta, A., Veeraiah, V., Pramanik, S., & Bag, S. (2024). The Central Bank of India as an Example of the Green Revolution in the Banking Sector. In *Recent Developments in Financial Management and Economics* (pp. 166–184). IGI Global., DOI: 10.4018/979-8-3693-2683-1.ch010

Tang, Q. (2025). Emerging Technologies, Sustainability and Carbon Accounting. In *Carbon Accounting and Sustainability* (Vol. II). Palgrave Macmillan., DOI: 10.1007/978-3-031-90636-7_6

Zhang, H., Hou, X., & Rao, Z. (2025). Can fintech improve total factor energy efficiency? Evidence from China's listed companies. *Climatic Change*, *178*(8), 145. DOI: 10.1007/s10584-025-03994-5

Chapter 11
Smart HR Systems:
A Blended Approach of AI, Automation, and People Analytics in the Digital Era

Tania Rana
http://orcid.org/0009-0001-5066-6252
Chandigarh University, India

Kavita Rani
Chandigarh University, India

ABSTRACT

The digital transformation of businesses has exponentially fueled the adoption of Smart HR Systems, which combine Artificial Intelligence, automation, and people analytics to enable businesses to manage their human resources effectively in the digital era. This combined capability of Smart HR Systems helps businesses transform from a traditional and transactional approach to human resources management in the digital era to a data-driven, predictive, and people-centric approach to decision-making. Despite immense benefits, the adoption of Smart HR Systems also gives way to several challenges related to data privacy, ethics of AI usage, algorithmic bias, and change management. The present paper describes the capacity for change of Smart HR Systems and underlines the necessity for an implementation that has to be balanced, open, and human, centered in order to guarantee that value will always be gained in the digital HR ecosystem.

DOI: 10.4018/979-8-2600-2726-4.ch011

INTRODUCTION

The fast-growing evolution of digital technologies has radically changed the Human Resource Management (HRM) concept out of the rather administrative sphere and turned it into a more strategic and information-driven field. Artificial Intelligence (AI), automation, and analytics are some of the areas that organizations are increasingly implementing to improve decision-making, optimize workforce performance, and employee experience. This has resulted in the creation of Smart HR Systems, combining new technologies to make them real-time, predictive, and adaptive, and in line with the organizational purpose (Agarwal et al., 2023; Benbya et al., 2020). In the past, HRM was more transactional like with the payroll processing, record keeping, and compliance management. The first phase of digital transformation was the introduction of the Human Resource Information Systems (HRIS), which helped companies to automate the simplest HR operations and enhance the management of data. These systems however were mostly descriptive and did not have much capability to aid strategic decision making. The development of electronic HRM (e-HRM) and integrated digital environment increased the capabilities of HR, but did not yet provide the intelligence necessary to make predictions and prescriptions (Garcia-Arroyo and Osca, 2021; Bonilla-Chaves and Palos-Sanchez, 2023). In this development, the introduction of Artificial Intelligence into HRM is a major stepping point into the new technological aspect of intelligent decision-making and is able to help organizations go beyond automation and into the realm of intelligent decisions. Artificial intelligence solutions, including machine learning, natural language processing, predictive modeling, etc., enable HR systems to process large amounts of data and detect trends and actionable information. By complementing major HR processes, namely, recruitment, talent management, performance appraisal, and learning and development, these capabilities can improve the efficiency and effectiveness (Bhatt and Muduli, 2022; Kabudi et al., 2021). Alongside, people analytics has become an essential element of Smart HR Systems, which allows any organization to use workforce data to make evidence-based decisions. People analytics can be used to leverage strategic workforce planning and improve the performance of organizations by combining HR data with business results and understand employee behavior, engagement, productivity, and retention. Although it has potential, people analytics use is not even, and the use of analytics is hindered by difficulties in the quality of data, analytical power, and corporate preparedness (McCartney and Fu, 2022; Ratnam and Devi, 2023). Smart HR Systems can also be supplemented with automation technologies such as Robotic Process Automation (RPA) and workflow orchestration to make operations more efficient and reduce repetition of the same tasks. The technologies help organizations to cut down on manual workload, decrease errors, and provide uniformity in HR operations, whilst permitting HR workers to concentrate on the strategic initiatives. When AI and analytics are integrated with automation, they have a synergistic effect and can result in intelligent and flexible HR systems that can adapt to the evolving needs of the organization (Huang et al., 2022; Bennett, 2022). The trend in the digital HR is emphasizing the increasing value of the new technologies like generative AI, cloud-based HR solutions, and intelligent agents in the future of the workforce management. The capabilities of the Smart HR Systems have been complemented with the introduction of new possibilities of creating content, decision support, and unique employee experiences through generative AI, especially. These innovations mesh with the shift of Industry 4.0, which is efficiency and automation-oriented, to Industry 5.0, which is human-centricity, sustainability, and human intelligence-technology convergence-oriented (Vrontis et al., 2022; Alexandro, 2025). Although Smart HR Systems have marked advantages, the adoption of the systems has its own challenges that can be viewed in terms of ethical governance, data privacy, and change management of organizations. The criticism of the impact of algorithms, transparency, and employee trust should be considered to achieve responsible and sustainable implementation of digital HR technologies. The purpose of this chapter is to understand the conceptual background, use, and implication of Smart HR Systems and have an in-depth insight into their adoptions to change the face of HRM in the digital age and identify the critical issues and areas of future studies (Tursunbayeva et al., 2021; Gerber et al., 2024).

Evolution of Human Resource Management in the digital era

The digital transformation of the Human Resource Management (HRM) is a manifestation of the change in the administrative and paper-based personnel management into the strategic and technology-facilitated workforce management. First, HR functions were concerned with mundane operations like payroll, record keeping and compliance, and could not provide much strategic value. With the advent of Human Resource Information Systems (HRIS), organizations have been able to computerize and automate these processes to enhance efficiency and accuracy of data. Nonetheless, they were mostly transactional systems that could not be analyzed effectively. As the Artificial Intelligence (AI), automation, and analytics have taken their place, HRM has transformed into the Smart HR Systems that allow making foreseeable decisions, instant information, and personal experiences of employees, which makes HR a strategic companion of organizational performance (Agarwal et al., 2023; Garcia-Arroyo and Osca, 2021).

From traditional HRIS to Smart HR Systems

The move towards Smart HR Systems, which replaces the traditional HRIS, is a change of rule-based automation to intelligent, adaptive and data-driven HR processes. The classical HRIS was simple in automating administrative operations like payroll, time management, and so on with slight support in strategic decision making. Smart HR Systems, on the other hand, combine AI, automation, and people analytics to allow making predictions in recruitment, optimizing performance, and planning the workforce. The systems will help in using real-time data and sophisticated analytical capabilities to improve the quality of decisions, increase employee engagement and align HR strategies with organizational objectives. This change explains the increasing role of intelligent technologies in reinventing HRM as a strategic and value-oriented activity (Benbya et al., 2020; Vrontis et al., 2022).

Role of people analytics in strategic HR decision-making

People analytics is essential in facilitating strategic HR decision-making towards converting workforce data into actionable information to aid organizational goals. By relying on predictive analytics, statistical modeling, and data visualization, the HR professionals will be able to observe the trends associated with employee performance, engagement, and retention and make more informed and proactive decisions. Research shows that companies that utilize people analytics are in a better position to align human capital strategies to those of the business hence increasing productivity and competitive advantage. Nevertheless, issues like low quality of data, skills shortage, and lack of integrations with business strategy remain as barriers to the successful use of people analytics in most companies (Bonilla-Chaves and Palos-Sanchez, 2023; McCartney and Fu, 2023).

Human-in-the-loop and augmented HR decision-making

The approach of human-in-the-loop and augmented HR decisions highlights the significance of integrating human judgment and AI-driven insights in order to facilitate ethical, transparent and context-based decisions in HRM. Although AI technologies are able to analyze a great amount of data and provide predictive information, the human factor is needed to interpret findings, consider contextual peculiarities and minimize the risk of bias. Augmented decision-making models improve the quality of decision-making by leveraging the best of both worlds in terms of human expertise and machine intelligence, thus improving fairness, accountability, and employee trust. Studies have emphasized that organizations using human-centric AI are more likely to attain sustainable HR results, thus underlining the need to balance technological progress with human values in Smart HR Systems (Arslan et al., 2021; Tursunbayeva et al., 2021).

LITERATURE REVIEW

The developing trend of Human Resource Management (HRM) into Smart HR Systems has undergone a vast discussion in terms of using the administrative functions as the strategic and data-driven decision-making, which implies the concept of the shift toward automated and people analytics. Initial research highlights how AI and machine learning can help improve the recruitment process, performance management, and workforce planning, allowing HR to be predictive and adaptive (Agarwal et al., 2023; Benbya et al., 2020). Table 1 shows the Literature Review Summary Table.

Table 1. Literature Review Summary Table

Ref No.	Title	Author(s) & Year	Key Findings	Research Gaps
1	Redefining HRM with Artificial Intelligence and Machine Learning	Agarwal et al. (2023)	AI and ML significantly transform HR functions such as recruitment, performance management, and decision-making efficiency.	Lack of empirical validation across industries and limited focus on ethical implications.
2	AI and Human Workers Interaction at Team Level	Arslan et al. (2021)	AI-human collaboration improves productivity but introduces coordination and trust challenges.	Limited real-world case studies and lack of team-level behavioral analysis.
3	AI in Organizations: Current State and Future Opportunities	Benbya et al. (2020)	AI adoption enhances organizational efficiency and innovation capabilities.	Need for longitudinal studies and deeper exploration of organizational transformation.
4	Leveraging Technology in HR Development	Bennett (2022)	Digital technologies improve HR development and training delivery systems.	Insufficient focus on employee adaptability and long-term learning outcomes.
5	AI in Learning and Development	Bhatt & Muduli (2022)	AI-driven learning systems enable personalized training and skill enhancement.	Lack of comparative studies on effectiveness vs traditional methods.
6	Big Data Contributions to HRM	Garcia-Arroyo & Osca (2021)	Big data enhances HR decision-making and workforce planning.	Challenges in data quality, integration, and privacy concerns remain underexplored.

continued on following page

Table 1. Continued

Ref No.	Title	Author(s) & Year	Key Findings	Research Gaps
7	HR Analytics Between Ambition and Reality	Gerber et al. (2024)	Gap exists between HR analytics potential and its actual implementation in organizations.	Lack of standardized frameworks and adoption strategies.
8	Role of Automation in HR Operations	Huang et al. (2022)	Automation improves efficiency, reduces manual workload, and enhances service delivery.	Limited focus on job displacement and workforce reskilling.
9	AI-enabled Adaptive Learning Systems	Kabudi et al. (2021)	AI enhances adaptive learning through real-time feedback and personalization.	Limited scalability and implementation challenges in organizations.
10	Benefits and Challenges of HR Analytics	Khaliq & Saritha (2023)	HR analytics improves decision-making but faces barriers like skill gaps and resistance.	Lack of frameworks addressing organizational resistance.
11	AI Awareness, Career Competency, and Burnout	Kong et al. (2021)	AI awareness improves competencies but may increase job stress and burnout.	Limited studies on psychological impacts across industries.
12	AI in HRM in Emerging Economies	Kshetri (2021)	AI adoption in HRM is growing in developing countries with cost and efficiency benefits.	Lack of region-specific empirical data and policy frameworks.
13	Promise vs Reality in People Analytics	McCartney & Fu (2022)	Significant gap between expected benefits and actual outcomes of people analytics.	Need for practical implementation models and ROI evaluation.
14	Enacting People Analytics	McCartney & Fu (2023)	Analytical and storytelling skills together improve HR analytics effectiveness.	Limited research on skill development frameworks for HR professionals.
15	AI and Creative Activities in Organizations	Paesano (2021)	AI supports creativity but raises concerns about human role displacement.	Lack of empirical validation in creative industries.
16	Impediments to HR Analytics Adoption	Ratnam & Devi (2023)	Organizational, technical, and cultural barriers hinder HR analytics adoption.	Need for actionable strategies to overcome adoption challenges.
17	Ethics of People Analytics	Tursunbayeva et al. (2021)	Ethical issues include privacy, bias, and transparency in HR analytics.	Lack of standardized ethical frameworks and governance policies.
18	AI, Robotics, and HRM: A Review	Vrontis et al. (2022)	Advanced technologies reshape HRM functions and workforce dynamics.	Limited integration of robotics with HR strategy in empirical studies.
19	Sustainable HR in Smart Transport Systems	Popkova et al. (2026)	AI-driven HR supports sustainable workforce management in smart infrastructures.	Limited cross-sector validation beyond transport systems.

Systematic reviews also reveal that AI-based HR systems enhance efficiency, decision making, and scalability and change the way employees learn and develop; they do that through adaptive systems and personal interventions (Bhatt and Muduli, 2022; Kabudi et al., 2021). Simultaneously, studies note the significance of collaboration between human and AI at the team level, where AI is to support, but not substitute human decision-making in order to preserve organizational efficiency and trust of the employees (Arslan et al., 2021; Paesano, 2021). People analytics has become a fundamental component of Smart HR Systems, allowing companies to make operational conclusions on the basis of workforce data and help in the justification of HR practices. The literature demonstrates that HR practices that are motivated by analytics are very useful in improving the performance of the organization, employee engagement, and retention rates (Bonilla-Chaves and Palos-Sanchez, 2023; Garcia-Arroyo and Osca, 2021). Nevertheless, the literature also reports the constant disparity between the opportunities and the real application of people analytics as the issues of data quality, analytical capabilities, and organizational preparedness hinder its efficiency (McCartney and Fu, 2022; Ratnam and Devi, 2023). The recent empirical evidence also demonstrates that the cultural opposition to the adoption of HR analytics is frequently limited by the absence of the managerial support and the inadequate network with the corporate strategy, which supports the necessity of developing the capability and aligning it with the corporate strategy (Khaliq and Saritha, 2023; Gerber et al., 2024). The use of automation and smart process management has been largely identified to enhance the HR operations efficiency and scalability. The studies have shown that workflow orchestration or Robotic Process Automation (RPA) decreases administrative work and increases the accuracy of the processes, which helps HR specialists concentrate on strategic initiatives (Huang et al., 2022; Bennett, 2022). The combination of AI and automation in cloud-based HR systems is also mentioned in emerging studies since it allows real-time planning of the workforce, skill mapping, and monitoring the performance of the global teams (Yadav et al., 2026; Nunnaguppala et al., 2025). Moreover, the development of AI-based recruitment platforms and job recommenders proves the rising significance of smart talent sourcing and matching in the contemporary HR activities (Elmenzhi et al., 2025; Çelik Ertuğrul and Bitirim, 2025). New dimensions of Smart HR Systems are proposed in recent literature (20242026) especially the contribution of generative AI, cloud-native HR systems, and digital ecosystems to change the management of the workforce. Research indicates the development of AI-based HR models which combine business smart systems, blockchain-based payroll systems, and safe data control frameworks to improve transparency, security, and efficiency (Lenka et al., 2026; Alrfai et al., 2025). Also, the studies concerning AI-based HR practices in the up-and-coming economies and in MSMEs support the significance of digital competence, situational adjustment, and optimization of resources in the successful implementation (Alexandro, 2025; Motasem Alrfai et al., 2025). The trends are in line with the shift towards the Industry 5.0 context, where human-centricity, sustainability, and ethical use of AI are becoming central to the technological progress. The concept of sustainability and ethics has become an ever more popular topic in the recent HR research, which is understandable given the move towards the responsible and people-oriented digital transformation. Research underlines the necessity of the fusion of the concepts of environmental, social and governance (ESG) into HR systems, especially when it comes to smart infrastructure and digital economies (Popkova et al., 2026). The studies on green HRM and gamification also indicate the ability of technology-based HR practices in encouraging sustainable employee behavior and engagement (Katta & Padhy, 2026). Simultaneously, the ethical issues of data privacy, bias in algorithms, and surveillance of employees are equally acute aspects, and clear, understandable, and responsible AI solutions in the field of HR should be developed (Tursunbayeva et al., 2021; Vrontis et al., 2022). Although there has been great progress, there are a number of research gaps and future opportunities as are indicated by the literature. More longitudinal and cross-cultural researches are required to gain insight into the contextual factors that contribute to Smart HR adoption in various industries and regions (Kshetri, 2021; McCartney and Fu, 2023). Besides, the quick development of generative AI and autonomous agents of HR poses new issues of governance, trust, and human-machine cooperation that are poorly studied in recent works. By incorporating all these new trends in conjunction with sustainability, ethical frameworks and Industry 5.0 principles, future studies and applications of Smart HR Systems in the digital age will play a critical role in moving both theoretical and practical knowledge on the topic.

Review of Key Literature on AI and Analytics in HRM

As the literature is growing, it is emphasized that Artificial Intelligence (AI) and people analytics are turning Human Resource Management into a strategic, data-driven role that is able to make predictive and prescriptive decisions. HRM AI can be used in areas of recruitment, performance management, learning and development, and employee engagement, helping organizations to be more efficient and make better decisions based on advanced data processing and pattern recognition (Agarwal et al., 2023; Benbya et al., 2020). People analytics also contributes to this change by connecting workforce data to business outcomes to enable organizations to improve talent management and organizational performance (Bonilla-Chaves and Palos-Sancho, 2023; Garcia-Arroyo and Osca, 2021). Nevertheless, other proponents of AI-based HR value also present difficulties due to data quality, a lack of analytical capabilities, and resistance to adoption, which limit the comprehensive benefits of AI-based HR (McCartney and Fu, 2022; Ratnam and Devi, 2023).

HR PROCESS AUTOMATION: SCOPE AND MATURITY LEVELS

HR automation has developed into simplistic rule-driven systems to more complex, intelligent and adaptive systems that facilitate the end-to-end HR processes. The first processes that were automated centered on the transactional functions including payroll, attendance and compliance management and that enhances efficiency and minimizes the number of people who have to do the repetitive functions. Along with the growth of maturity, organizations started to add sophisticated technologies like AI and predictive analytics and provide automated recruitment processes, performance management, and workforce planning (Huang et al., 2022; Bennett, 2022). It has been observed in literature that an increased level of automation maturity is linked to an increased level of operational efficiency, improved decision-making processes, and an augmented contribution of the HR functions, but issues regarding system integration and workforce preparedness remain (Gerber et al., 2024; Khaliq and Saritha, 2023).

Robotic Process Automation (RPA) in HR Operations

Robotic Process Automation (RPA) technology has thus come to play an important role in enhancing HR operations' efficiency through the automation of routine, rule-based processes such as payroll, employee data management, onboarding, and compliance reporting. Studies have demonstrated RPA's ability to enhance processing speed, accuracy, and service consistency in HR operations, thus enabling organizations to expand their operations without a corresponding growth in staff size (Huang et al., 2022; Bennett, 2022). RPA technology is also beneficial in enabling organizations to execute HR processes on a continuous basis, 24/7. However, studies have demonstrated RPA's limitations in addressing complex decision-making processes, thus requiring organizations to integrate RPA with AI to enhance HR processes' intelligence (Agarwal et al., 2023; Vrontis et al., 2022).

Intelligent Workflow Orchestration

Intelligent workflow orchestration is the next level in the digital transformation of the HR function, where AI, automation, and analytics work in tandem to create dynamic, adaptive, and context-aware HR processes. Unlike conventional automation, intelligent orchestration utilizes real-time data and predictive analytics to optimize workflows, prioritize tasks, and facilitate decision-making in the entire employee lifecycle (Benbya et al., 2020; Garcia-Arroyo & Osca, 2021). For instance, intelligent orchestration could include AI-based recruitment processes, personalized onboarding, and adaptive learning processes, where the processes adjust based on the needs and demands of the employees and the organization. However, the literature has shown the need to integrate, govern, and consider the ethical implications in the use of data in intelligent orchestration, including considerations such as transparency and trust in automated decision-making processes (Tursunbayeva et al., 2021; McCartney & Fu, 2023).

CONCEPTUAL FOUNDATIONS OF SMART HR SYSTEMS

The conceptual foundation of Smart HR Systems is based on the integration of Artificial Intelligence (AI), automation, and people analytics as key enablers of data-driven and strategic human resource management. At the technological level, AI techniques such as machine learning, natural language processing, and predictive modeling are applied to enhance core HR functions including recruitment screening, talent matching, performance prediction, and personalized learning pathways. Table 2 presents the conceptual foundations of Smart HR Systems. Recent studies indicate that organizations adopting AI-enabled HR practices achieve 25–40% improvements in recruitment efficiency, 10–20% reductions in employee turnover, and significant gains in workforce productivity through improved decision accuracy (Agarwal et al., 2023; Alayed & Awamleh, 2025).

Table 2. Conceptual Foundations of Smart HR Systems

Core Component	Conceptual Role in Smart HR Systems	Key Technologies / Practices	Indicative Values & Numbers (from literature)
Artificial Intelligence (AI)	Enables intelligent, predictive, and adaptive HR decision-making by learning from workforce data	Machine learning, NLP, predictive modeling, recommender systems	• Recruitment efficiency ↑ **25–40%** • Turnover reduction **10–20%** • Talent matching accuracy ↑ **30%+**
HR Automation	Streamlines repetitive and transactional HR operations, freeing HR for strategic roles	Payroll automation, onboarding bots, compliance workflows, RPA	• Operational cost reduction **20–30%** • Process cycle time ↓ **35–50%** • Error rates ↓ **40%+**
People Analytics	Transforms workforce data into strategic insights for evidence-based HRM	Predictive analytics, dashboards, workforce modeling	• Organizations **2–3×** more likely to outperform peers • Retention prediction accuracy ↑ **20–35%**
Strategic HR Value Creation	Aligns HR outcomes with business performance and competitive advantage	Workforce planning, performance forecasting, skill gap analysis	• Strategic HR contribution ↑ **30–45%** • Decision quality improvement **25%+**
Ethical & Human-Centered Governance	Ensures fairness, transparency, trust, and responsible AI use in HR	Ethical AI, explainable algorithms, privacy controls	• Bias risk ↓ **15–25%** with explainable AI • Employee trust ↑ **20%** when transparency applied

Automation also reinforces the effectiveness of Smart HR Systems, as it facilitates the automation of repetitive and transactional HR processes, such as payroll, employee onboarding, attendance, and reporting. This not only alleviates the workload but also improves the overall business process, thereby achieving cost savings of 20-30% and significant improvements in accuracy and speed (Huang et al., 2022; Yadav et al., 2026). At the same time, people analytics plays the key role of the analytical foundation of Smart HR Systems, where the data collected from the workforce is turned into useful information and decisions, which are correlated with the performance and success of the business. Figure 1 shows the comparison between Traditional HRIS and Smart HR Systems. People analytics also allows HR managers to go beyond the current reporting and analytics, thereby making decisions based on predictions and recommendations. Studies also reveal that organizations with high people analytics maturity are 2-3 times more likely to outperform their competitors in terms of talent and decision-making (Bonilla-Chaves & Palos-Sánchez, 2023; McCartney & Fu, 2023).

Figure 1. Comparison of Traditional HRIS and Smart HR Systems

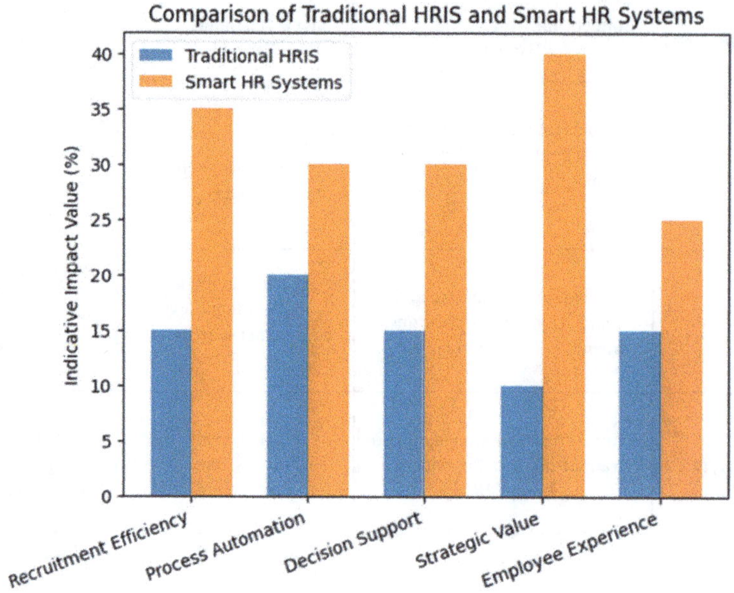

In addition, it is important to note that the conceptual framework of Smart HR Systems also highlights the need for ethical and human-centered governance. With the increasing trend of AI-driven decision-making, there are concerns regarding transparency, fairness, biases, and data privacy. Without appropriate governance, there is a possibility of biases in AI-driven decisions, which can affect employee trust. Hence, it is important to ensure ethical AI principles, explainability, and data governance frameworks are integrated for the sustainability of Smart HR Systems (Tursunbayeva et al., 2021; Vrontis et al., 2022).

AUTOMATION AND INTELLIGENT PROCESS MANAGEMENT IN HR

Automation has thus become a key element of intelligent process management in modern HR functions, where traditional and rule-based operations have been transformed into smooth and technological-based processes. HR functions such as payroll processing, attendance management, employee onboarding, benefits management, and regulatory compliance have thus been largely automated using Robotic Process Automation (RPA) and workflow automation technologies. It has been observed that automation helps in the reduction of processing time in HR functions by as much as 40-60%, costs by as much as 20-30%, and improves the accuracy of the same to more than 90%, thus helping HR professionals in more strategic and value-based activities (Yadav et al., 2026; Huang et al., 2022). Table 3 highlights the scope of automation and intelligent process management in HR functions. Moreover, automation has been seen as a key factor in ensuring scalability in global organizations through the standardization of HR services and employee experiences through faster resolution and self-service capabilities (Bennett, 2022).

Table 3. Automation and Intelligent Process Management in HR

Aspect	Traditional HR Automation	Intelligent Process Management in Smart HR Systems	Indicative Values / Outcomes
Core Focus	Rule-based automation of repetitive HR tasks	AI-enabled, adaptive, and data-driven HR workflows	—
Key Technologies	Payroll systems, attendance software, basic RPA	AI, ML, RPA, workflow orchestration, predictive analytics	—
HR Processes Covered	Payroll, leave management, onboarding, compliance	Recruitment screening, workforce planning, performance prediction, learning personalization	—
Operational Efficiency	Faster processing and reduced manual effort	End-to-end process optimization with real-time decision support	**40–60% reduction** in processing time
Cost Impact	Lower administrative and transaction costs	Strategic cost optimization and resource allocation	**20–30% cost reduction**
Data Accuracy	Improved consistency and fewer clerical errors	High accuracy with continuous learning and validation	**>90% accuracy** in HR records
Workforce Outcomes	Limited impact on engagement or productivity	Personalized HR interventions and predictive insights	**10–20% increase** in engagement
Strategic Value	Primarily operational support	Strategic workforce planning and decision intelligence	**15–25% improvement** in workforce utilization
Governance & Ethics	Minimal ethical considerations	Focus on transparency, bias mitigation, and trust	Essential for sustainable adoption

Figure 2. Comparison Radar Chart: Traditional HR Automation vs Intelligent Smart HR Systems

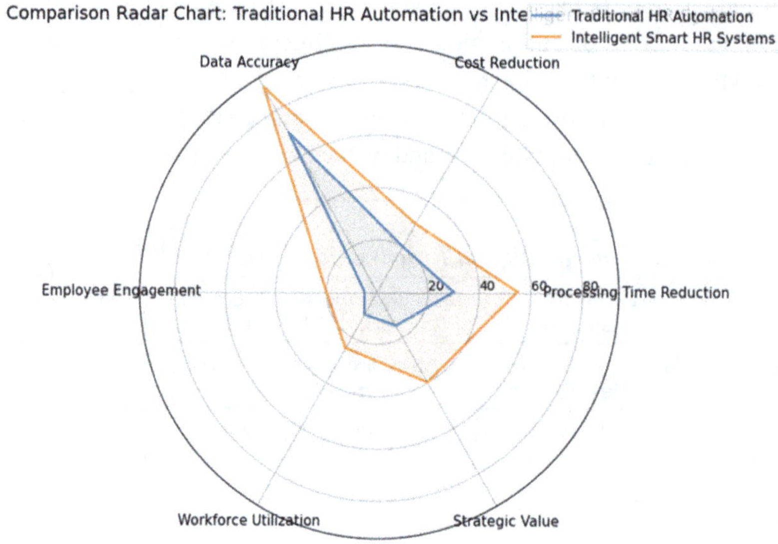

Figure 2 depicts the difference between traditional HR automation and the more advanced intelligent Smart HR Systems. Moving beyond the traditional automation of HR processes, intelligent process management uses AI-based decision logic and analytics to create a more responsive and context-aware HR system. Organizations using intelligent HR process management have seen a 15% to 25% improvement in workforce utilization and a 10% to 20% improvement in employee engagement due to the more personalized and responsive nature of the HR system (Alayed & Awamleh, 2025; Nunnaguppala et al., 2025). However, the success of intelligent automation is largely dependent on the quality of the data used in the system and the integration of the systems with other processes in the organization. There is a risk of a lack of trust among employees due to the high degree of automation and the lack of transparency in the system. Therefore, the key is the balance between the more efficient automation of the HR system and the more traditional approach of using humans in the system with a focus on the creation of sustainable value in the organization (Tursunbayeva et al., 2021; Vrontis et al., 2022).

INTEGRATED SMART HR FRAMEWORK: AI, AUTOMATION, AND ANALYTICS

This integrated Smart HR framework is a synergistic combination of Artificial Intelligence (AI), automation, and people analytics that work together in a cohesive manner as a smart and intelligent HR ecosystem. AI is the cognitive layer of the Smart HR framework that facilitates capabilities such as predictive recruitment, intelligent matching of talents with organizations, sentiment analysis, and learning recommendations. Automation is the operational layer of the Smart HR framework that ensures the smooth and seamless execution of end-to-end HR processes such as onboarding, payroll management, performance management, and compliance. People analytics is the intelligence layer of the Smart HR framework that converts workforce data into actionable insights. The table 4 shows the Integrated Smart HR Framework—AI, Automation, and Analytics.

Table 4. Integrated Smart HR Framework—AI, Automation, and Analytics

Component	Technology Used	HR Function Area	Key Features	Expected Outcomes	Performance Metrics
AI-Based Recruitment	Machine Learning, NLP	Talent Acquisition	Resume screening, candidate matching, chatbot interviews	Faster hiring, improved candidate quality	Time-to-hire (↓30%), Quality of hire (↑25%)
Intelligent Onboarding	AI Assistants, Automation Tools	Employee Onboarding	Automated documentation, virtual onboarding assistants	Reduced onboarding time, better employee experience	Onboarding time (↓40%), Satisfaction score (↑20%)
Smart Learning & Development	Adaptive Learning Systems, AI	Training & Development	Personalized learning paths, skill gap analysis	Improved employee skills and productivity	Training effectiveness (↑35%), Skill improvement rate (↑30%)
Performance Management System	Predictive Analytics, AI	Performance Evaluation	Real-time feedback, predictive performance scoring	Data-driven performance improvement	Employee performance (↑28%), Retention rate (↑18%)
Employee Engagement System	Sentiment Analysis, AI Chatbots	Employee Experience	Pulse surveys, emotion detection, feedback analytics	Higher engagement and morale	Engagement score (↑22%), Attrition rate (↓15%)

continued on following page

Table 4. Continued

Component	Technology Used	HR Function Area	Key Features	Expected Outcomes	Performance Metrics
Workforce Planning	Big Data Analytics, AI	Strategic HR Planning	Demand forecasting, workforce optimization	Better resource allocation and planning	Forecast accuracy (↑32%), Cost reduction (↓20%)
Payroll & Compliance Automation	RPA, Blockchain	Compensation Management	Automated payroll, secure transactions, compliance tracking	Error-free payroll, enhanced transparency	Payroll errors (↓90%), Processing time (↓50%)
HR Decision Support System	Predictive Analytics, Dashboarding	HR Strategy	Data visualization, scenario analysis	Improved strategic decision-making	Decision accuracy (↑27%), ROI (↑23%)
Talent Retention System	AI Predictive Models	Retention Management	Attrition prediction, personalized retention strategies	Reduced turnover	Attrition rate (↓25%), Employee satisfaction (↑20%)
Ethical Governance Layer	AI Ethics Frameworks, Compliance Tools	HR Governance	Bias detection, data privacy management	Fair and transparent HR practices	Bias reduction (↓35%), Compliance rate (↑40%)

The combination of these three aspects of the Smart HR framework facilitates real-time decisions and converts the HR function from a reactive function within organizations to a proactive function (Agarwal et al., 2023; Vrontis et al., 2022). At an organizational level, the Smart HR integrated framework enables continuous feedback loops between data, decisions, and outcomes. This allows HR systems to learn and improve with time. The data-driven insights are used as an input for AI models, AI-based predictions are used as an input for automated workflows, and automated workflows are used as an input for creating new data, thereby improving the accuracy of analytical tools. This enables improved organizational agility, employee experience, and sustainability by aligning human capital strategies with business objectives. For effective implementation, it is important to address challenges faced by organizations regarding data governance, collaboration, and ethics. Hence, it is important to include ethical AI principles, explainability tools, and governance tools for effective implementation of Smart HR Systems (Tursunbayeva et al., 2021; Alayed & Awamleh, 2025). Figure 3: Integrated Smart HR decision and process management flow.

Figure 3. Integrated Smart HR Decision and Process Management Flowchart.

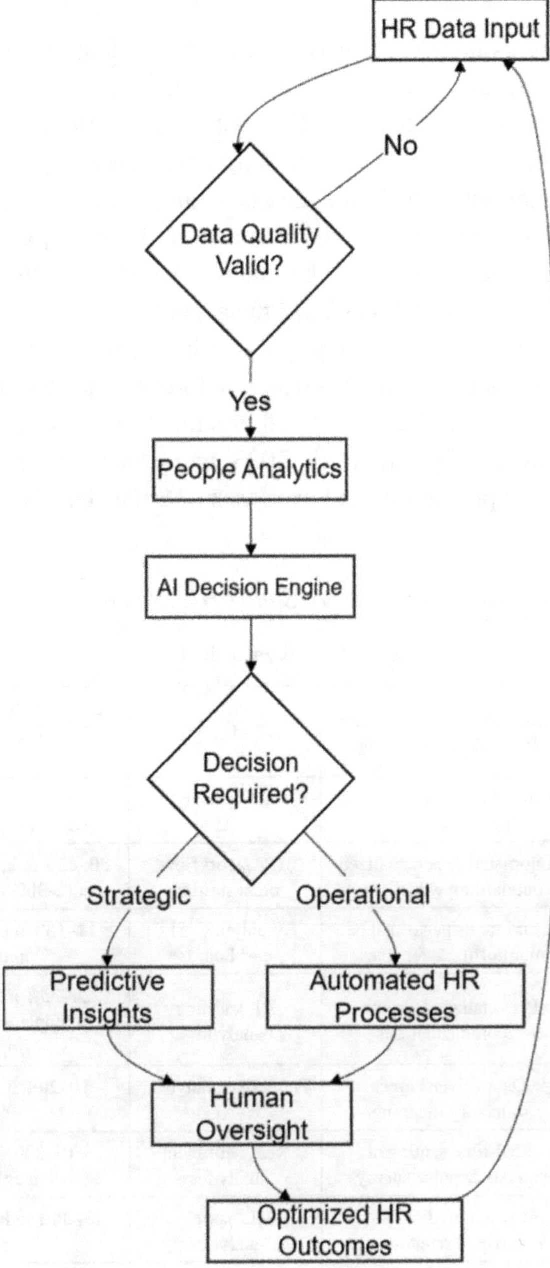

APPLICATIONS AND USE CASES OF SMART HR SYSTEMS

Smart HR Systems have been heavily utilized in talent acquisition and workforce planning, where Artificial Intelligence and analytics have been used to make data-driven and predictive decisions. For instance, Artificial Intelligence-based recruitment systems have been used to automate resume screening, candidate shortlisting, and interview scheduling, and have also been used to make decisions based on machine learning algorithms to match skills with jobs and predict the potential of the candidates. Research has shown that these systems have reduced the time-to-hire by 20-30% and increased the accuracy of recruitment by 15-25%. This has helped organizations to efficiently acquire the best talents in the industry. In addition, workforce analytics has been used to forecast future workforce demands and succession planning, which has helped organizations to sustain the workforce in the future, as shown in Agarwal et al. (2023) and Elmenzhi et al. (2025). Table 5 below shows the key applications and use cases of Smart HR Systems.

Table 5. Applications and Use Cases of Smart HR Systems

Application Area	Key Use Case	Technologies Used	Values / Nos. (Impact)
Talent Acquisition	AI-driven resume screening & candidate matching	AI, ML, NLP	**20–30%** reduction in time-to-hire; **15–25%** improvement in hiring accuracy
Workforce Planning	Demand forecasting & skill gap analysis	Predictive analytics, AI	**10–20%** improvement in workforce planning accuracy
Onboarding	Automated & personalized onboarding workflows	RPA, workflow orchestration	**30–45%** reduction in onboarding time; **>90%** task completion rate
Performance Management	Continuous performance monitoring & feedback	Analytics, AI dashboards	**12–18%** increase in employee productivity
Learning & Development	Personalized learning recommendations	AI, learning analytics	**20–35%** increase in learning completion; **15–25%** skill improvement
Career Pathing	Data-driven career trajectory mapping	Predictive analytics, AI	**10–20%** increase in internal mobility
Employee Engagement	Real-time sentiment analysis & pulse surveys	NLP, sentiment analytics	**10–20%** improvement in engagement scores
Attrition Management	Attrition prediction & targeted retention	ML, people analytics	**15–30%** reduction in voluntary attrition
HR Operations	Payroll, attendance & compliance automation	RPA, automation tools	**20–30%** cost reduction; **<5%** error rate
Decision Support	Strategic HR dashboards & insights	Advanced analytics, BI tools	**2–3×** higher likelihood of superior talent outcomes

continued on following page

Table 5. Applications and Use Cases of Smart HR Systems

Application Area	Key Use Case	Technologies Used	Values / Nos. (Impact)
HR Service Delivery	Chatbots & autonomous HR agents	Generative AI, conversational AI	**40–60%** faster HR query resolution; **24/7** availability
Employee Experience	Hyper-personalized HR interventions	AI, real-time analytics	**15–25%** increase in satisfaction; **10–20%** productivity gain

Another important application area for Smart HR Systems is performance management, learning, and engagement. Smart performance management solutions combine real-time analytics, continuous feedback tools, and AI-based insights to go beyond annual performance appraisals to dynamic performance evaluation. Personalized learning solutions leverage employee data and learning analytics to provide employees with learning recommendations, leading to a productivity improvement of 10-20% for employees and a 15-25% improvement in training effectiveness. Smart engagement solutions, including sentiment analysis and pulse surveys, also help organizations detect burnout and engagement issues, thereby improving employee retention and well-being (Bhatt & Muduli, 2022; Kabudi et al., 2021). Smart HR Systems are also highly popular in the domain of HR operations, compliance, and even strategic decision-making, where the use of technology has a substantial impact on the overall efficiency and governance. For instance, the use of automated payroll, attendance, and compliance systems helps reduce operational costs by 20-30% and at the same time minimize operational errors, while the use of advanced people analytics enables HR leaders to have real-time insights into workforce trends, risks, and even performance metrics. This further enables the organization to be 2-3 times more likely to achieve superior talent outcomes compared to competitors, thus making the use of Smart HR Systems a vital contributor to the overall concept of agile, ethical, and performance-driven HRM in the digital age (Huang et al., 2022; McCartney & Fu, 2023; Vrontis et al., 2022).

BEST PRACTICES FOR SUCCESSFUL SMART HR ADOPTION

For successful implementation of Smart HR Systems, there is a need for strong alignment between technology-based initiatives in HR and overall organizational strategy. Organizations need to view AI, automation, and people analytics as an integrated suite of enabling technologies for strategic workforce transformation. Research has suggested that organizations are much more effective in improving decision quality and talent outcomes by aligning their HR analytics with overall business strategy. Hence, it is important for organizations to ensure leadership support, cross-functional collaboration between HR and IT, and a strong implementation roadmap for successful implementation of Smart HR Systems, as suggested by Agarwal et al. (2023) and Marler & Boudreau (2017). Organizations also need to implement a phased approach for successful implementation of Smart HR Systems, as suggested by McCartney & Fu (2022), by starting with a pilot implementation and gradually increasing scale depending on performance outcomes. Another key best practice to consider is the development of data foundations and ethical governance for Smart HR Systems. Data is crucial for the development of effective AI predictions and analytics, and the development of analytics skills and digital competence is vital for the effective utilization of AI and analytics technologies. Research has shown that various challenges, including data quality, skills, and attitude towards change, may affect the effective adoption of AI and analytics technologies if they are not addressed effectively (Khaliq & Saritha, 2023; Ratnam & Devi, 2023). On the other hand, the development of human-in-the-loop decision-making, transparency, and AI principles is crucial for addressing risks of bias and privacy, thus enhancing trust among employees and effective utilization of digital HR technologies (Tursunbayeva et al., 2021; Vrontis et al., 2022).

SUSTAINABLE AND HUMAN-CENTRIC SMART HR MODELS

Sustainable and human-centric Smart HR models focus on the fusion of technology, ethical, social, and environmental factors to achieve organizational value sustainability. These models not only focus on the efficient and productive use of technology but also consider the well-being of the employees and the environment. Organizations can use AI and analytics tools to create customized learning experiences, enhance employee engagement, and promote employee development while aligning these activities with sustainability factors such as reducing resource usage and promoting green behaviors. Recent research indicates the rising need to incorporate Environmental, Social, and Governance factors into HR models, where digital HR plays a critical role in sustainable HR management and organizational sustainability (Popkova et al., 2026; Katta & Padhy, 2026). However, the human-centric approach focuses on the ethical, transparent, and empowering use of technology, where human decision-making is not replaced but complemented by technology. It is critical to integrate ethical factors, explainable AI, and trust-building factors to achieve sustainable, inclusive, and futuristic Smart HR Systems, which align with the emerging Industry 5.0 concept (Tursunbayeva et al., 2021; Vrontis et al., 2022).

CHALLENGES AND LIMITATIONS

However, despite the immense potential for transformative changes through Smart HR Systems, there are various challenges faced by organizations in their implementation and adoption. One of the major challenges is linked to data quality, integration, and infrastructure. For instance, many organizations are struggling with fragmented HR data spread across different technology solutions, including HRIS, ATS, and ERP systems. This affects the performance of AI models and analytics-driven insights. Moreover, a lack of analytical skills and digital competence among HR personnel is another major challenge. For example, various studies have found that a lack of expertise in data interpretation and storytelling results in a low impact of people analytics initiatives on organizations (Khaliq & Saritha, 2023; McCartney & Fu, 2023). Resistance to change is another major factor hindering the implementation of Smart HR Systems. For example, employees and HR personnel often view AI-driven Smart HR Systems as a threat to their job security and human interaction, thereby slowing down their adoption rate and limiting the transformative changes in organizations (Alexandro, 2025; Motasem Alrfai et al., 2025). Another important challenge relates to the ethical, legal, and governance issues surrounding the implementation of AI technology in HR systems. Such issues as bias, lack of transparency, and data privacy may affect the overall trust in the HR systems, leading to discrimination in recruitment, performance evaluation, and monitoring of employees. The increased adoption of generative AI technology, as well as other automated systems, poses a threat to the overall implementation of HR systems, as the systems may generate false information. Furthermore, the changing regulations concerning AI technology, as well as data protection, create a challenge to organizations, which may affect the overall implementation of HR systems. The incorporation of ethical AI technology, transparency, and governance is important in addressing the overall sustainability of Smart HR Systems (Tursunbayeva et al., 2021; Alayed & Awamleh, 2025).

FUTURE OUTCOMES

The future of Smart HR Systems is expected to emerge from the integration of Artificial Intelligence, generative AI, cloud native platforms, and advanced people analytics, resulting in intelligent, autonomous, and adaptive HR systems. Emerging technologies, including Large Language Models and AI-driven agents, are also expected to automate advanced HR functions, including talent acquisition, employee engagement, and decision-making, to facilitate real-time and context-aware workforce management. Research has suggested that the adoption of advanced AI-powered

HR systems is expected to result in increased operational agility, decision-making accuracy, and employee experience through hyper-personalized HR services for the organization (Agarwal et al., 2023; Nunnaguppala et al., 2025). Additionally, the integration of cloud-based HR systems and business intelligence tools is expected to facilitate seamless data integration, scalability, and global workforce management, resulting in increased HR systems' responsiveness and efficiency in a dynamic and evolving environment for the organization (Yadav et al., 2026; Alayed & Awamleh, 2025). Apart from technological innovations, Smart HR Systems of the future are likely to be more in line with sustainability, ethical governance, and humanity, as has been seen in the evolution of Industry 5.0 concepts. It is envisioned that organizations of the future would be able to incorporate Environmental, Social, and Governance (ESG) factors into their HR activities, leveraging technological innovations in this regard for sustainable workforce management and responsible organizational behavior. Research has shown that AI-based HR management systems would be able to contribute positively to green HR management, employee well-being, and creating a diverse work environment, which would be a positive move for organizational sustainability and societal impact (Popkova et al., 2026; Katta & Padhy, 2026). At the same time, it is envisioned that stronger regulations and ethical guidelines for AI and human-in-the-loop solutions would be required in the future for transparency and trust in AI-based HR management decisions, which would make Smart HR Systems a critical success factor for sustainable, intelligent, and humanity-focused workforce management in the digital era (Tursunbayeva et al., 2021; Vrontis et al., 2022).

Methodological gaps in people analytics studies

Although people analytics study is rapidly expanding, there are still a number of methodological limitations in the way this research can be developed in theory and practice. Another notable gap is the over dependence on cross-sectional and descriptive research designs which do not provide the possibility of making causal correlations between HR practices and the outcomes of organizations. Most of the studies rely on secondary data or case study on a single organization which questions the issue of generalizability and external validity. Moreover, measurement constructs like employee engagement, performance and retention vary across studies and therefore it is hardly possible to make comparisons across studies. The recent studies also point to the fact that the implementation of advanced analytical methods, such as predictive and prescriptive modeling, is uneven, and many organizations continue to be at the primary descriptive analytics stage (McCartney and Fu, 2022; Khaliq and Saritha, 2023). The second gap that is crucial in terms of the methodological approach concerns the sparse nature of the integration of ethical, behavioral, and contextual aspects in the study of people analytics. Although the technological capabilities are frequently highlighted, not enough focus is put on the perceptions of the employees, the trust, and the organizational culture, which play a major role in the effectiveness of the analytics-based HR practices. Moreover, longitudinal and experimental studies are missing to be able to capture dynamic workforce shifts and long-term analytics intervention effects. According to the emerging studies, mixed-method techniques, which imply the integration of quantitative analytics with qualitative insights, could be used to gain a better insight into HR phenomena and enhance the practical relevance of the results (Gerber et al., 2024; Motasem Alrfai et al., 2025).

Cross-cultural and sectoral research opportunities

The study of cross-cultural behaviors in Smart HR Systems and people analytics still has not yet reached their development, although the evidence of the significant role of cultural, institutional, and socio-economic contexts in HR technology adoption and results keeps growing. The majority of the literature available focuses on developed economies, and its results can only be partially applied to emerging markets where digital maturity, workforce traits, and company priorities have a significant differentiation. Studies show that cultural attitudes towards technology, AI levels of trust, and digital literacy are key to the acceptance and success of Smart HR Systems. Generalizing and making HR analytics more inclusive by increasing research on different cultural setting will work to their benefit (Kshetri, 2021; Alexandro, 2025). In the same way, there is a high volume and underutilization of sectoral research opportunities due to the fact that the majority of investigations are done on technology-driven or service-oriented sectors whereas other sectors like manufacturing, healthcare, public administration, and small and medium enterprises (SMEs) are under-researched. The availability of data, regulatory and workforce dynamics vary in different sectors affecting the implementation and the effect of Smart HR Systems. Recent research confirms that sector-specific models should be applied to consider such differences in context and offer specific solutions to HR digital transformation. The future study must be comparative and multi-sectoral and must integrate the new technologies like AI-monitored systems and cloud-based HR solutions to gain a more profound idea on how Smart HR Systems can be efficiently used in different organizational settings (Nunnaguppala et al., 2025; Yadav et al., 2026).

STRATEGIC IMPLICATIONS FOR PRACTITIONERS AND RESEARCHERS

To practitioners, the active application of Smart HR Systems necessitates a strategic move of using technology to transform the workforce based on its value rather than implementation. To ensure the greatest possible impact on productivity, talent management, and organizational performance, organizations should ensure the initiatives of AI, automation, and people analytics are aligned with overall business goals. There is evidence that companies that apply AI-based HR practices in conjunction with business intelligence and cloud computing carry out their operations at a higher level of accuracy and agility. Another aspect to be focused on by practitioners is the development of digital competencies among HR teams, investing in data infrastructure, and implementation strategies that are phased to make the adoption and scalability sustainable (Agarwal et al., 2023; Yadav et al., 2026). Moreover, the implementation of analytics into the daily HR decision-making process could lead to the improvement of the workforce planning, performance management, and employee engagement outcomes. Research-wise, there is an increased necessity to enhance theoretical and methodological rigor of studies of Smart HR and people analytics. To gain insights on the cause and effect relationships and the changing workforce dynamics, researchers need to go beyond the descriptive studies and employ longitudinal, experimental, and mixed-method studies. The adoption of new technologies, including generative AI, autonomous agents, and cloud-native HR systems, opens up new prospects in research, which cannot be addressed with interdisciplinary solutions based on management, data science, and behavioral sciences. Recent research acknowledges that the contextual variables that should be considered include organizational culture, digital maturity, and organizational perceptions to enhance the applicability and relevance of research findings (McCartney and Fu, 2023; Motasem Alrfai et al., 2025). Also, practitioners and researchers need to focus on ethical, sustainability and governance to guarantee responsible and humanistic HR change. The growing application of AI and the use of data to make decisions provokes the issue of privacy, transparency, and bias in algorithms that require the creation of strong governance schemes and ethical standards. The concept of integrating the Environmental, Social, and Governance (ESG) principles into the Smart HR Systems can improve the sustainability and the social responsibility of the organization, and also align the HR practices with the long-term societal objectives. Academic-industrial partnerships can be employed to produce evidence based models, best practices and policy regulations that help bring about ethical and effective application of Smart HR Systems throughout the digital age (Popkova et al., 2026; Tursunbayeva et al., 2021). A further strategic implication for practitioners is the need to ensure a human-centric and change management-driven approach is adopted for Smart HR Systems. While technological advancement is on a roll, it is important to note that for Smart HR Systems to be effectively adopted, there is a need to ensure acceptance by employees. For instance, research has indicated that resistance to AI-driven HR systems is often attributed to concerns regarding job loss, a lack of human interaction, and a lack of understanding regarding performance evaluation criteria. Therefore, it is important for organizations to ensure a change management approach is adopted for Smart HR Systems. Digital literacy among HR practitioners and employees is also important for effective decision-making processes through AI and analytics tools (Khaliq & Saritha, 2023; Alexandro, 2025). Another implication for researchers is the need to explore the interface between the concept of Smart HR Systems and the latest technological and organizational trends, such as Industry 5.0, digital sustainability, and the collaboration between humans and Artificial Intelligence. Future research should aim to explore the potential of Smart HR Systems not only to contribute to organizational performance but also to the well-being and sustainability of employees and organizations. There is also a need to design a set of standardized tools to measure the effectiveness of Artificial Intelligence-based HR practices in various contexts and industries. By incorporating the views of various disciplines and using real-world organizational examples, it is possible to design more robust and effective Smart HR systems, taking into account the latest technological and social demands and expectations, as proposed by Katta and Padhy (2026) and (Vrontis et al. (2022); ; Alexandro, 2025). In addition, the enhancement of collaboration between academia and industry has the potential to hasten innovation, as well as guarantee that Smart HR Systems are relevant from a practical point of view, just as they are relevant from a scientific point of view. Evaluation will also help in the adaptive, ethical, and sustainable HR transformation in a changing digital environment (Gerber et al., 2024; Khaliq & Saritha, 2023; Alexandro, 2025)..

CONCLUSION

Smart HR Systems are a revolutionary development of Human Resource Management, a blend of Artificial Intelligence, automation, and people analytics to develop intelligent, adaptable and strategic workforce ecosystems. This change will help organizations no longer focusing on the traditional administrative roles but on data-driven choices, better employee experience, and better organizational performance. Although these systems have great advantages in efficiency, productivity, and strategic value, their effective deployment will rely on the strong data governance, ethical controls, and constant growth of digital and analytical skills of HR functions. A balance between technological innovation and human-oriented principles, transparency and trust is necessary to achieve sustainability in adoption and value creation in the long run. Finally, Smart HR Systems transform the HR role into a strategic and active partner that will enable the organization to achieve resilience, agility, and competitiveness in the digital age.

REFERENCES

Agarwal, S., Gupta, A., & Roshani, P. (2023). Redefining HRM with artificial intelligence and machine learning. In *The adoption and effect of artificial intelligence on human resources management, Part A* (pp. 1–13). Emerald Publishing Limited. DOI: 10.1108/978-1-80382-027-920231001

. Alayed, H. M., & Awamleh, F. T. (2025). Artificial intelligence applications in improving human resources practices: The mediating role of business intelligence tools. *ECONOMICS - Innovative and Economics Research Journal, 13*(4), 241–256. DOI: 10.2478/eoik-2025-0094

Alexandro, R. (2025). Strategic human resource management in the digital economy era: An empirical study of challenges and opportunities among MSMEs and startups in Indonesia. *Cogent Business & Management*, *12*(1), 2528436. Advance online publication. DOI: 10.1080/23311975.2025.2528436

Arslan, A., Cooper, C., Khan, Z., Golgeci, I., & Ali, I. (2021). Artificial intelligence and human workers interaction at team level: A conceptual assessment of the challenges and potential HRM strategies. *International Journal of Manpower*. Advance online publication. DOI: 10.1108/IJM-01-2021-0052

Benbya, H., Davenport, T. H., & Pachidi, S. (2020). Special issue editorial: Artificial intelligence in organizations: Current state and future opportunities. *SSRN*, *19*(4), ix–xxi. DOI: 10.2139/ssrn.3741983

Bennett, E. E. (2022). Leveraging technology to design and deliver human resource development. In *The emerald handbook of work, workplaces and disruptive issues in HRM* (pp. 261–276). Emerald Publishing Limited., DOI: 10.1108/978-1-80071-779-420221026

Bhatt, P. K., & Muduli, A. (2022). Artificial intelligence in learning and development: A systematic literature review. *European Journal of Training and Development*, *47*(7/8), 677–694. DOI: 10.1108/EJTD-09-2021-0143

Bonilla-Chaves, E. F., & Palos-Sánchez, P. R. (2023). Exploring the evolution of human resource analytics: A bibliometric study. *Behavioral Sciences (Basel, Switzerland)*, *13*(3), 244. DOI: 10.3390/bs13030244

Çelik Ertuğrul, D., & Bitirim, S. (2025). Job recommender systems: A systematic literature review, applications, open issues, and challenges. *Journal of Big Data*, *12*(1), 140. Advance online publication. DOI: 10.1186/s40537-025-01173-y

Elmenzhi, Z., Elfassi, S., Jdidou, Y., Aarab, I., & Bakraoui, I. (2025). Recruitment 4.0: A conceptual framework integrating AI and social media for intelligent talent acquisition. In *Proceedings of the 2025 11th International Conference on Optimization and Applications (ICOA)*. DOI: 10.1109/ICOA66896.2025.11236940

Garcia-Arroyo, J., & Osca, A. (2021). Big data contributions to human resource management: A systematic review. *International Journal of Human Resource Management, 32*(20), 4337–4362. DOI: 10.1080/09585192.2019.1674357

Gerber, M., Krause, A., Probst, J., & Heimann, M. (2024). HR analytics between ambition and reality. *Gruppe. Interaktion. Organisation. Zeitschrift für Angewandte Organisationspsychologie, 55*(2), 225–236. Advance online publication. DOI: 10.1007/s11612-024-00743-7

Huang, M. H., Rust, R. T., & Maksimovic, M. (2022). The role of automation in enhancing HR operations. *Journal of Service Research, 25*(4), 321–335. DOI: 10.1177/10946705221104693

Kabudi, T., Pappas, I., & Olsen, D. H. (2021). AI-enabled adaptive learning systems: A systematic mapping of the literature. *Computers and Education: Artificial Intelligence, 2*, 100017. DOI: 10.1016/j.caeai.2021.100017

Katta, V., & Padhy, P. C. (2026). Gamification of HRM and green behaviour: Understanding the relationship between reciprocal benefits and engagement. *International Journal of Procurement Management, 25*(1), 1–20. DOI: 10.1504/IJPM.2026.150261

Khaliq, R., & Saritha, B. (2023). Benefits and challenges of adopting HR analytics: A comprehensive review. *Journal of Economics. Management and Trade, 29*(11), 24–33. DOI: 10.9734/jemt/2023/v29i111159

Kong, H., Yuan, Y., Baruch, Y., Bu, N., Jiang, X., & Wang, K. (2021). Influences of Artificial Intelligence (AI) awareness on career competency and job burnout. *International Journal of Contemporary Hospitality Management, 33*(2), 717–734. DOI: 10.1108/IJCHM-07-2020-0789

Kshetri, N. (2021). Evolving uses of artificial intelligence in human resource management in emerging economies in the global South: Some preliminary evidence. *Management Research Review, 44*(7), 970–990. DOI: 10.1108/MRR-03-2020-0168

Lenka, R., Gupta, R., Pabalkar, V., & Chitranshi, J. (2026). Ensuring privacy and data integrity in payroll systems using blockchain and IPFS. In *Lecture Notes in Networks and Systems* (Vol. 1652, pp. 300–311). DOI: 10.1007/978-3-032-06691-6_29

McCartney, S., & Fu, N. (2022). Promise versus reality: A systematic review of the ongoing debates in people analytics. *Journal of Organizational Effectiveness: People and Performance*, *9*(2), 281–311. DOI: 10.1108/JOEPP-01-2021-0013

McCartney, S., & Fu, N. (2023). Enacting people analytics: Exploring the direct and complementary effects of analytical and storytelling skills. *Human Resource Management*, *62*(2), 129–148. DOI: 10.1002/hrm.22194

Motasem Alrfai, M., Kamal Bani Yaseen, O., Khairo Issa Al Daabseh, T., Ismail Noori Al.Blaushi, H., & Bataineh, M. (2025). The role of HR digital competence in enhancing FinTech-based information security and risk management: Evidence from Smart PLS modeling. *EDPACS*. DOI: 10.1080/07366981.2025.2586479

Nunnaguppala, M., Meenakshisundaram, K. S., Desetty, A. G., Venkteshwar, A., Bora, B., & Khudayer, K. (2025). Multimodal AI-integrated performance monitoring system for global team management. In *Proceedings of the 2025 International Conference on Recent Innovation in Science, Engineering and Technology (ICRISET)*. DOI: 10.1109/ICRISET64803.2025.11251788

Paesano, A. (2021). Artificial intelligence and creative activities inside organizational behavior. *The International Journal of Organizational Analysis*. Advance online publication. DOI: 10.1108/IJOA-09-2020-2421

Popkova, E. G., Bogoviz, A. V., Tikhomirov, Y. A., Arupova, N. R., & Aghabekyan, E. V. (2026). Sustainable management of human resources in smart transport systems as an advanced infrastructure of the digital economy. In *Lecture Notes in Intelligent Transportation and Infrastructure* (Part F1434, pp. 257–264). DOI: 10.1007/978-3-032-12181-3_26

Ratnam, D. S., & Devi, V. R. (2023). Addressing impediments to HR analytics adoption: Guide to HRD professionals. *Human Resource Development International*, *26*(2), 237–247. DOI: 10.1080/13678868.2023.2195986

Tursunbayeva, A., Pagliari, C., Di Lauro, S., & Antonelli, G. (2021). The ethics of people analytics: Risks, opportunities, and recommendations. *Personnel Review*, *51*(3), 900–921. DOI: 10.1108/PR-12-2019-0680

Vrontis, D., Christofi, M., Pereira, V., Tarba, S., Makrides, A., & Trichina, E. (2022). Artificial intelligence, robotics, advanced technologies and human resource management: A systematic review. *International Journal of Human Resource Management*, *33*(6), 1237–1266. DOI: 10.1080/09585192.2020.1871398

Yadav, M. Minakshi, Choudhury, T., & Dewasiri, N. J. (2026). The smart HR cloud: Automating workforce planning and skill mapping. In *Automating Intelligence With Cloud-Native AI Tools* (pp. 385–394). DOI: 10.4018/979-8-3373-7442-ch025

Chapter 12
Artificial Intelligence in Recruitment:
Trends, Generational Perspectives, and Future Workforce Implications

N. Raghu
http://orcid.org/0000-0002-2091-8922
Jain University, India

Islamov Saidjon Sobidovich
Kimyo International University, Uzbekistan

Arslonbek Nurjonov
Mamun University, Uzbekistan

Togonova Shoxida
Urgench State Pedagogical Institute, Uzbekistan

Tilavov Uktamjon Gulomovich
National University of Uzbekistan, Uzbekistan

Begimov O'ktam Ibrogimovich
Alfraganus University, Tashkent, Uzbekistan

Burkhon Dekhkonov Rustamovich
Tashkent State University of Economics, Uzbekistan

M. Balamurugan
http://orcid.org/0000-0001-9737-2035
Dayananda Sagar College of Engineering, India

ABSTRACT

The chapter shows artificial intelligence (AI) technologies have been adopted by organizations to improve their recruitment procedures of job applicants based on data from recent surveys conducted in both the United States and the United Kingdom. The majority of respondents believe AI will shape the future of recruitment: 61% in the U.S. and 58% in the UK believe applicants should use AI in ways that remain

DOI: 10.4018/979-8-2600-2726-4.ch012

hidden to others, while 56% (U.S.) and 52% (UK) believe candidates will need AI assistance to complete application processes. Additionally, 55% of U.S. and 52% of UK respondents think non-users will face disadvantages. People from Millennial (78% U.S.; 79% UK) and Gen Z (71% U.S.; 62% UK) groups show the highest adoption rates of technology, while office workers in both countries report an 82% technology usage rate. The most commonly used tools by users include ChatGPT along with other large language models (73% U.S.; 86% UK) and CV generators (58% U.S.; 43% UK). People use AI to compensate their weaknesses (49% of users) and to increase their chances of success (48% of users)

1. INTRODUCTION

The quick advancement of digital technologies has changed the complete process of job searching for people while businesses now use different methods to identify and assess potential employees. Artificial Intelligence (AI) works as a technological innovation which updates existing recruitment systems by providing organizations with new methods to improve their operational efficiency and create personalized candidate experiences and automate their processes (Bentayeb, 2026). AI-driven systems which encompass résumé screening algorithms and conversational agents that produce custom cover letters now serve as the recruitment systems which various industries and regions use to work their employment procedures. Organizations now use AI technology to evaluate job applications because this development marks a complete societal shift which enables organizations to make data-informed decisions by using predictive analytics and machine learning models to shape their strategic direction and employee development pathways. The modern applicant must navigate a digital job market which requires them to use optimization tools and automatic feedback systems and intelligent matching platforms as essential components of their application process (Kodagoda, 2026). The chapter titled Artificial Intelligence in Job Applications: Trends, Generational Adoption, and Implications for the Future of Recruitment use survey data from the United States and the United Kingdom to present empirical insights which show how organizations adopt AI technologies and what drives them to use the technology and which ethical issues are beginning to emerge.

Figure 1. Artificial Intelligence in job Applications.

The results point to the fact that the majority of respondents see AI as a powerful force in the future of recruiting. A significant number of applicants view AI assistance as a requirement for navigating an increasingly automated and complex hiring landscape. Generational adoption is high among Millennials and Gen Z, which suggests that digital fluency is a decisive factor in AI-based technology adoption (Azahari, 2026). Despite this enthusiasm, concerns about skill distortion, authenticity, bias and fairness show that the governance and responsible use of these technologies cannot be overlooked. Conceptual background: the why and how of AI-assisted job applications understanding the context and rationale for AI emergence in recruitment considering the broader digital transformation of recruitment, and the goals and scope of this chapter.

1.1 Background and Rationale

Recruitment methods have changed throughout history because of technological advancements. The development of email applications and online job portals from newspaper ads and postal applications has changed how employers hire and applicants approach their job search. Organizations had their first experience with automated resume screening through Applicant Tracking Systems which permitted them to screen resumes according to specific keyword and experience and other established criteria (Hair Jr, 2026). The new AI technology goes beyond basic screening functions because it brings forth systems that possess the ability to study present trends and create new content from what they learn. AI recruitment implementation occurs because of multiple interdependent reasons.

- The global market now presents businesses with tougher challenges when they attempt to find skilled workers whom they want to hire. Organizations now face increased obstacles because international markets make it harder for them to recruit qualified workers whom they intend to employ. Organizations receive thousands of applications for a single position which creates administrative burdens that their traditional human-centered review processes cannot handle (Yong, 2026). Organizations benefit from three AI advantages which enable them to achieve better scalability while experiencing faster processing times and obtaining screening results which depend on their data analysis.
- The digitalization of labor markets has shifted expectations among job seekers. Modern applicants, particularly digital natives, are accustomed to algorithmically curated experiences on platforms such as LinkedIn and Indeed. These platforms use machine learning technology to suggest job openings which help professionals to network and receive personalized content recommendations. The candidates now view AI-powered optimization tools as standard advancements which stem from their internet usage (Hamid, 2025).
- AI-powered content generation tools such as ChatGPT and other large language models enable applicants to draft résumés, refine cover letters, and simulate interview responses with unprecedented efficiency (Ghaleb, 2025). The survey results show that many users depend on those tools because they want to solve their personal deficiencies or improve their chances of winning. The digital gap in the labor market creates a situation where non-users will experience disadvantages according to common perceptions (M Balamurugan, 2024).

1.2 Digital Transformation of Recruitment

The recruitment digital transformation process involves organizations using digital technologies to transform their hiring procedures, which creates automatic systems that use data to build international talent networks. The transformation process began with the introduction of digital job boards and throughout its development, it progressed to the full implementation of algorithm-based talent acquisition systems

(Muthuswamy, 2025). Online recruitment platforms in their initial form created a system that allowed all users to access job openings without needing to be in specific locations. The system required new application selection methods because the number of applications grew at an extremely fast rate. AI systems perform analysis on both textual keywords and contextual information together with data on user behavior and indicators that predict job performance. Machine learning algorithms enable organizations to examine candidate history patterns while measuring their alignment with successful employee profiles to create suitability ratings (Ammer, 2025).

The digital transformation process finds another demonstration through corporate career portal chatbots which operate as virtual assistants. The system answers applicant questions in real-time while it also arranges interview times and performs initial candidate evaluations. The AI-powered video interview system uses speech patterns and facial expressions and linguistic elements to assess how candidates answer questions. The innovations work to boost efficiency while decreasing the duration required to complete the hiring process. Recruitment teams use data analytics to track their hiring pipelines which helps them improve their recruitment process (Zayniddinov, 2025). The organization uses candidate engagement rates and application form drop-off locations and retention score predictions to make strategic choices. Human Resource Management Systems (HRMS) now use AI technology which shows the movement toward using data as a foundation for managing talent. Different regions and industries display varying degrees of digital transformation implementation (Cahyani, 2025). The bigger companies in technologically advanced sectors use AI-powered recruitment systems, while the smaller companies experience difficulties because they lack sufficient resources. The countries use different regulatory systems which impact how much algorithmic transparency and accountability organizations must maintain during their hiring procedures.

Figure 2. Integration of AI into Human Resource Management Systems

The process of recruitment is also changing candidate behaviour, with candidates increasingly using tailored résumés for automated screening systems by embedding job description keywords 'in the right way'. AI-based résumé optimization tools (for example, Jobscan) facilitate this by indicating how the résumé can be improved to fit automated screening systems algorithms. Recruitment takes place via technology systems, which are used by both employers and applicants to gain access to algorithm-based evaluation methods (Ravikumar, 2026). The mutual AI usage by employers who use algorithms for candidate evaluation and by candidates who use algorithms for their application optimization creates an ongoing feedback mechanism between the two parties (Rajeswari, 2026). The study of this interaction helps organizations evaluate their operational fairness and authentic performance and their capacity to build a skilled workforce for future needs.

1.3 Objectives and Scope of the Chapter

The chapter aims to reveal contemporary AI applications in recruitment by studying current practices and analyzing how different generations adopt these technologies because they want to use them and organizations need to maintain their operations. The chapter uses survey data from the United States and the United Kingdom to demonstrate how job seekers use AI tools and how stakeholders view their use. The chapter aims to:

- Examine the evolution of recruitment processes leading to algorithmic and AI-driven systems.
- Identify commonly used AI tools in job applications, including large language models, résumé optimization platforms, and intelligent job-matching systems.
- Analyze generational and occupational adoption trends, highlighting differences between Millennials, Generation Z, and other demographic groups.
- Investigate motivational factors driving AI usage, such as efficiency, confidence enhancement, and competitive advantage.
- Explore ethical, legal, and governance challenges associated with AI-assisted applications, including bias, transparency, and skill distortion.
- Provide strategic recommendations for applicants, employers, and policymakers to ensure responsible and equitable AI integration.

1.4 Evolution of Job Application Processes

The development of job application procedures demonstrates how technological advancements and corporate strategies and employment market changes have transformed recruitment processes. Recruitment has evolved from face-to-face interactions and document evaluations to systems that use digital networks and artificial intelligence for candidate assessment. The transformation of hiring processes has changed how candidates behave and how organizations compete while establishing new structures for employment markets (Kulmanov, 2024). Modern recruitment processes use algorithms for candidate assessment and digital platforms for applicant management and automated workflows to conduct hiring operations in a global talent market.

1.4.1 Traditional Hiring to Algorithmic Screening

Recruitment procedures in the past depended on the use of physical documents and manual selection processes and in-person interviews. Organizations used recruiter judgment together with candidate education backgrounds and reference verification to determine candidate eligibility. The organization needed more time to reach decisions because its contact network limited its ability to gather information (Achar et al., 2025). Organizations encountered difficulties in scaling their operations because personal interactions helped people understand specific situations. The development of digital storage systems together with web-based application portals established a major technological advancement. Companies began to store applicant information in electronic systems which allowed them to manage records in an organized way while they implemented uniform evaluation procedures. Automated filtering systems were developed to assist recruiters with large applicant pools because the number of applications reached a peak (Prabha, 2026).

Advanced computational models enable algorithmic screening technologies to process both structured data and unstructured data through their advanced computational capabilities. The system uses natural language processing to understand semantic meaning while it identifies skill connections and experience relevance through detection methods that do not rely on exact keyword matches (Ahmed & Pardaev, 2025). The predictive modeling methods assess candidate profiles through performance benchmark comparisons that organizations create using their internal data. The systems evaluate candidate suitability through probability-based fit indicators which exist beyond their fundamental qualification identification function. The digital assessment tools evaluate cognitive abilities and situational judgment skills while testing technical proficiency through online testing environments. Video-based assessments use structured scoring models to maintain evaluation standards across different candidates throughout the entire assessment process. The system functions to deliver statistical insights for decision-making while human supervisors need to oversee all decision processes. Organizations face new challenges from increased automated system usage because they need to establish fair treatment practices for all users while creating understandable results. The current hiring governance frameworks require organizations to develop controls which handle three critical areas: algorithmic transparency, data governance, and auditability. Advanced technologies help organizations achieve operational efficiency while ethical safeguards protect their credibility and compliance they need to meet regulatory standards (Raghu, 2025).

1.4.2 Platform-Based Recruitment Ecosystems

Recruitment in the 21st century is an increasingly complex activity taking place in digital ecosystems rather than in the form of single vacancy announcements. Here we demonstrate that professional networking infrastructures like LinkedIn are evolving into full-blown talent ecosystems that fulfill multiple functions ranging from job discovery to employer branding to skill validation to professional networking. In this context, the ecosystem applies data analytics to recommend opportunities, to suggest connections and alike to anticipate future skill demands (Kulmanov, 2025). Further, large job aggregators like Indeed collect listings in one place for many industries and regions, enabling quick to access information. In addition, employer review websites, such as Glassdoor, add a level of transparency to the process by including workplace feedback. In this information-rich environment, applicants are able to leverage comparative information and organizations can benchmark themselves (Aarthi et al., 2026).

Digital recruitment ecosystems extend beyond their digital boundaries to include project-based and independent job opportunities. The platforms of Upwork and Fiverr utilize their matching system to connect clients with freelancers through their worldwide operating algorithm. Users obtain access to job opportunities because their reputation systems and completion rates and peer reviews determine their eligibility. The ecosystems require constant data transmission to maintain their operational efficiency. User activity together with engagement metrics and application outcomes, create feedback loops which enhance recommendation algorithms. The platforms gain stronger predictive abilities because user participation increases which makes them more important to the labor market (Ammer, 2025). The system's concentrated data creates fresh risks which stem from digital dependency and asymmetrical information distribution and the centralization of market power. The ecosystems now depend on permanent recruitment through profiles, which has replaced their previous intermittent hiring methods. Candidates establish permanent digital identities while employers develop continuous talent pipelines which function independently of current job needs.

1.5 AI Tools in Contemporary Job Applications

The artificial intelligence into contemporary job searching procedures has transformed the methods candidates use to prepare themselves and showcase their abilities in the fight for job opportunities. The current AI systems go beyond their original purpose of helping users submit documents online because they now enable users to create content and optimize strategies and practice interviews and find job openings. The systems provide applicant assistance while they create a framework for constructing and assessing and developing professional identities. Job applications now require artificial intelligence because they moved from traditional information exchange to dynamic data-driven career planning systems (Zhao, 2025). Candidates use intelligent systems to achieve better understanding and alignment and enhanced competitive advantage. Employers use AI screening systems which create a technological system that enables both parties to interact with algorithms. The changing recruitment landscape requires applicants to comprehend all available AI tools for successful analysis.

1.5.1 Large Language Models and Content Generation

Large Language Models (LLMs) have revolutionized content creation for applicants. OpenAI's ChatGPT, Google's Gemini, and Anthropic's Claude allow users to create résumés, cover letters, personal statements, and professional summaries in seconds. These models are based on deep neural network architectures trained on large textual datasets. The models produce contextually relevant and grammatically correct language. In job applications, LLMs assist with articulating achievements, editing for appropriate tone, and grammar correction. The model can reformat the content for readability. The applicant can prompt the LLM to generate content that aligns with industry expectations, job description, and values of the organization.

The use of large language models (LLMs) is increasing in the course of writing a resume. Aside from drafting support, LLMs can be used for idea generation and framing. For example, LLMs can help translate task-oriented to impact-oriented statements (e.g. conveying leadership responsibilities and measurable outcomes) and technical expertise into language that is tailored to cross-functional roles. Generative AI also presents interesting questions for authenticity and differentiation. Similar LLMs may create stylistic homogeneity among applicants. Recruiters increasingly value originality, specificity, and verifiable achievements. The use of LLMs can, therefore, increase efficiency and linguistic precision but may require careful editing and application-specific tailoring by the applicant.

1.5.2 CV and Cover Letter Optimization Systems

The AI-powered optimization platforms provide functions which enable content creation and permit businesses to match their operations with their Applicant Tracking System requirements. Jobscan and Resume Worded provide tools which enable users to examine résumés against job descriptions for the purpose of discovering missing keywords and formatting errors and structural problems. The systems operate through pattern recognition algorithms which assess applicant documents to determine their compliance with recruitment criteria. The system generates match scores which produce practical application guidelines for candidates to improve their application documents according to automated screening standards. The recommendations include using industry-specific terms and measuring professional accomplishments and changing section titles and which file formats should be used for optimal results. The platforms provide optimization functions which assess how well users can understand text and how clearly it communicates its message. The systems assess two areas which include evaluating the difficulty level of sentences and the effectiveness of bullet points and the strength of competency displays (Bhatti, 2025). The system provides users with industry-standard benchmarking data which shows how their application profile works between their submitted documents and those of their industry peers. The optimization process improves digital screening system compatibility, but the excessive use of keyword density is a cause for loss of narrative coherence. The user has to find the balance between algorithm specifications and a real storytelling content. The optimization process creates ethical issues through the possibility to enhance or distort the real work experience (Islamutdinov, 2024). Users should use these tools to increase the work visibility, but also to report a true professional background.

1.5.3 AI-Based Interview Preparation

The process of interview preparation now uses interactive AI-driven simulations instead of static practice questions from previous times. The platforms Interviewing io and Pramp create controlled mock interview settings which allow users to practice actual interview questioning methods. The advanced AI interview coaches use speech pattern analysis and pacing assessment and filler word frequency measurement and answer structure evaluation to conduct their analysis (Achar, 2025). The tools provide two functions which include sentiment analysis and communication clarity assessments to produce feedback about confidence levels and conciseness and logical progression. The candidates can practice their behavioral responses through scenario-based prompts which match the requirements of various competency frameworks (Pandey et al., 2024). AI systems enable technical assessment preparation through their ability to produce coding challenges and case studies and role-specific simulations. The adaptive learning models use performance-based question difficulty adjustments to enable candidates to gradually improve their skills through targeted practice (Al Doghan, 2025). The new technologies make high-quality preparation resources accessible to all individuals especially those who do not have professional coaching networks. Candidates need to create natural answers for interview questions because their interview performance will suffer if they practice too much. The AI-assisted preparation process helps users create confidence and mental clarity which leads to better performance than memorized content delivery (Marisamy, 2026).

1.5.4 Intelligent Job Search and Matching Tools

Job recommendations have become increasingly personalized in recent years. Personal networking platforms, such as LinkedIn, use machine learning algorithms to recommend jobs by analyzing users' job search activity, skill set, and activities. Job aggregators, such as Indeed, use predictive analytics to rank job postings considering proximity and probability of application. These platforms leverage behavioral data, such as search queries and profiles, to re-rank and refine the recommendations (Sherov, 2025). The skill inference models, also available in some platforms, include the identification of transferable skills and recommending next-step careers. Labor market analytics are also part of the recommendation tools to inform users about emerging fields and in-demand skills. Applicants are therefore encouraged to balance automated suggestions with exploratory search strategies.

1.6 Adoption Patterns and User Motivations

Employees from different age groups and job roles and their level of technological knowledge adopt AI tools for their job applications in different ways. Younger users who have advanced digital skills adopt these tools at a faster pace because of their superior digital literacy. People choose to adopt these technologies because they want to achieve better work results through more effective work processes and improved application standards and greater self-assurance and competitive edge (Rathinavel, 2026). The availability of information about the technology together with its actual use in practice determines how people accept new technology (Makhmudov, 2026).

1.6.1 Generational Differences in AI Usage

The different age groups show different opinions about AI job search technologies. People who spent their childhood in environments with constant digital technology access include Generation Z and younger Millennials who display better ability to use generative AI systems along with automated résumé tools and AI-based interview training programs. Students in modern educational systems need to learn how to use online study resources and algorithm-driven content delivery systems and digital tools that enable group work. People treat AI-assisted content creation and optimization as standard work tools because they fail to recognize these systems as transformative technologies (Balamurugan, 2026). Younger job seekers prefer to use conversational AI systems for creating their professional summaries and transforming their application documents and practicing their behavioral interview responses. People use AI in their everyday communication tools which establishes AI as an academic and professional development essential.

Generation X and Baby Boomers may selectively adopt AI if authenticity, privacy, and technology transparency are questioned. Some rely on field experience and existing networks instead of an algorithmic approach. Others cautiously employ AI tools for editing or formatting, rather than unique content. However, generational generalizations remain a myth. More often, digital literacy, professional context, and organizational culture determine AI usage than age. Mid-level professionals in technologically driven industries may be early adopters of AI, while younger workers in neglected areas may lag behind. Therefore, generational analysis requires contextualization.

1.6.2 Occupational and Demographic Trends

The way people use AI technology at work depends on the specific workplace environment they operate in. The technology-driven industries which include software development and digital marketing and data analytics and engineering fields show greater technology adoption than other sectors (Adilov et al., 2025). Professionals who work in these fields already better understand machine learning basics and they also show interest in testing AI technology which enhances their work. People experience less psychological resistance to AI technology when their technical skills match the required AI system operation skills (Ravikumar, 2026). The manual work and craft-based work and informal work sectors of employment show lower levels of technology adoption. Organizations which have not used structured digital recruitment systems experience decreased motivation to apply AI technology in their application procedures. Public sector organizations which implement standardized work methods do not use AI technology for process improvement at the same level as private sector companies.

Educational attainment determines which people will choose to adopt new technologies. People who achieve higher educational levels display greater digital literacy skills together with improved knowledge about AI system capabilities. University career centers provide access to online training modules together with peer communities which help users learn about new technology. The way people use technology changes because of geographic differences. The urban population which has good internet access together with global labor market exposure will use AI technologies more than others. The low adoption rates in rural areas and regions with restricted broadband access occur because of their operational limitations (Sapayev, 2026). People who belong to different socioeconomic groups can access high-end AI services through subscription-based optimization tools and premium digital devices. The structural situation of society exists together with gender and demographic elements (Rathinavel, 2026). Theoretical AI tools function without bias, yet social standards and technology confidence levels impact the ways people use them. The existence of support networks along with available mentorship programs and technology sector representation will influence how different demographics adopt technology.

1.6.3 Digital Divide and Access Inequalities

The digital divide consists of different internet access levels and device performance standards and digital skills does not complete ability to use online tools and educational materials which digital resources provide. People who do not have stable broadband internet access and up-to-date computer equipment face challenges when they try to use advanced AI technologies. The combination of subscription-based optimization tools and premium-priced coaching services creates obstacles for users. All generative AI platforms provide free basic access but users need to pay for access to most advanced functionalities (Sufyan Ghaleb, 2025). This situation will make it harder for people already facing barriers to find employment to succeed in their job hunting efforts. Digital literacy acts as an obstacle which prevents equal distribution of emerging technologies. The use of AI requires people to develop their abilities in assessment evaluation and prompt creation and feedback understanding (Bhatti, 2025). The correct training will result in users either missing out on essential tool functions or becoming reliant on automated outcomes.

Language barriers can also lead to unequal treatment among people from different groups. AI systems that are trained on linguistic datasets of certain languages will deliver weaker results in non-dominant languages and professional domains that require deep cultural knowledge. Individuals who must seek employment in labor markets that lie outside the central hubs of the global labor market will be disadvantaged by this limitation. Institutional action is needed to address the existing gaps. Educational institutions in collaboration with workforce development providers and public employment services should incorporate AI literacy training into their career preparation programming (Aldossary & Pardaev, 2025).

2. LITERATURE SURVEY

Bentayeb et al., (2026) presents an extensive investigation into the use of Artificial Intelligence (AI) technologies in Human Resource Management (HRM) which affects both workforce management and market development from 2024 to 2034. The AI-driven technologies which include predictive analytics and intelligent recruitment systems and automated resume screening and employee performance analytics are changing the way HR departments operate their standard procedures. The AI technology improves decision-making processes while decreasing administrative duties and increasing the effectiveness of talent acquisition through data-based insights. The ethical issues which begin with algorithmic bias and proceed to data privacy problems and the impact of technology on job loss. The market analysis research which predicts that international investments in AI-powered HR systems will rise and hybrid human-AI collaboration models will become common in the future. The organizations must implement reskilling and upskilling programs to prepare their employees for work in environments that use artificial intelligence technology. The organizations need governance systems which include regulatory frameworks to safeguard innovation while upholding their ethical obligations. The AI as a strategic

HRM tool which organizations must use responsible AI management practices to maintain their operational efficiency and employee faith in the organization.

Kodagoda et al., (2026) explores Generation Y workers perceive and understand Artificial Intelligence technology which they use in their job environments through both positivist and interpretivist research approaches. The millennials understand AI systems through their assessment of job security and career growth and work efficiency and company environment. Generation Y workers show moderate positive feelings about AI implementation because they perceive its capacity to boost operational efficiency and handle repetitive work and support data-based decision processes. The public continues to express strong worries about three major issues which include job loss situations and diminished face-to-face communication and the need for more ethical information. Employees at a company will only accept artificial intelligence technologies when the organization provides proper communication methods and training programs and shows its leadership with transparent operations. The organizations need to establish change management procedures which help organizations implement AI technology without interruptions. Generation Y members want companies to deliver ongoing educational programs which support their need to learn new skills and better their abilities according to technology changes. The technology acceptance relates to employee behavior during digital transformation between different age groups. Businesses can achieve successful AI execution through their need to maintain equal emphasis on technological advancements and human-centered business practices which create trust and active employee participation and permanent staff growth.

Azahari et al., (2026) investigates employability development corresponds with the future work environment. The global literature to identify key employer expectations, emerging skill requirements, and recruitment strategies that technology disruption will create. The digital literacy together with adaptability and critical thinking and cross-functional competencies as important requirements for employability. The talent acquisition process now experiences major changes through AI-driven recruitment platforms together with automated assessments and virtual hiring processes. The organizations now require employees to develop soft skills which include communication and emotional intelligence and collaborative problem-solving abilities together with technical skill development. The value through its worldwide comparative analysis which shows how different regions implement recruitment digitization and prepare their workforce. The higher education institutions need to create new curricula which will meet industry needs while including experiential learning and industry partnerships and digital technology training. The challenges which arise from people not having equal access to digital resources which creates a risk of increasing employment disparities. The comprehensive framework which shows how employability connects with digital transformation and strategic recruitment approaches into the changing worldwide labor market.

Hair et al., (2026) shows how universities use artificial intelligence and social robots to attract students through new educational marketing technologies and educational outreach methods which have emerged. The AI-powered chatbots virtual assistants and humanoid social robots enhance personalized communication with prospective students. The AI systems enable faster responses to requests while improving data analysis capabilities and enabling precise outreach efforts through the use of behavioral insights. Social robots function as interactive tools which universities use to create live campus experiences during open house events and virtual recruitment activities. The psychological factors and ethical issues which include trust development and data protection and the way people perceive their interactions with machines. Empirical evidence shows that using AI for recruitment purposes boosts student engagement while enabling institutions to achieve an advantage in international student recruitment. The organizations should use technology as a supportive tool which enhances their recruitment process and maintains authentic relationships with candidates. The universities need to develop strategic plans and conduct stakeholder education and establish ethical governance frameworks to achieve successful digital engagement through AI recruitment.

Yong et al., (2026) conduct an investigation about how Generation Z people make their job choices by using Environmental Social and Governance (ESG) criteria. The sustainability practices and corporate responsibility and ethical governance standards now play a growing role in determining which careers young job seekers prefer to pursue. The Generation Z assesses job opportunities based on two factors which include salary and career development but they need to know about environmental sustainability practices and diversity initiatives and social responsibility programs. The three factors of digital transparency and social media presence and publicly available ESG performance data create a strong effect on how attractive organizations appear to people. The research shows that companies which implement sustainable business practices together with responsible AI technology solutions experience better results when they try to attract new employees. The research found a relationship between ESG priorities and workforce retention rates which showed that employees who share company values tend to stay with organizations while maintaining their loyalty to the organization. The organizations need to establish ESG principles as their foundation for developing employer branding methods and recruitment procedures in order to recruit workers who seek meaningful work. The sustainability trends affect hiring practices in the modern world by analyzing how different generations of workers expect companies to operate.

Table 1. Comparative analysis of research findings

Authors & Year	Methodological Approach	Key Findings	Workforce Implications	Ethical / Governance Concerns
Bentayeb, A. et al. (2026)	Conceptual and market trend analysis	AI enhances recruitment, predictive analytics, resume screening, and performance management; market growth in AI-HRM systems expected	Need for reskilling, hybrid human–AI collaboration models, strategic workforce planning	Algorithmic bias, data privacy risks, regulatory compliance, governance frameworks required
Kodagoda, T. (2026)	Positivist and interpretivist approaches	Gen Y shows moderate optimism; values efficiency but fears job displacement and reduced human interaction	Importance of training, communication, and transparent AI implementation to increase acceptance	Ethical transparency, job security concerns, trust-building through leadership
Azahari, L. M. et al. (2026)	Systematic literature review	Digital literacy, adaptability, and soft skills critical for future work; AI-driven recruitment expanding globally	Curriculum redesign, experiential learning, industry partnerships, digital skill development	Digital divide, unequal access to technology, widening employment gaps
Hair Jr, J. F. et al. (2026)	Conceptual and empirical discussion	AI chatbots and social robots improve engagement, personalization, and outreach effectiveness	Competitive advantage in global student recruitment; integration of AI into marketing strategies	Trust, data protection, ethical AI use in student engagement
Yong, J. Y. et al. (2026)	Conceptual and empirical insights	Gen Z prioritizes sustainability, diversity, and ethical governance in career decisions	Organizations must align recruitment branding with ESG values to attract and retain talent	--

The summary illustrates the Human Resource Management, recruitment methods, and employability prospects undergo fundamental changes through the combined impact of Artificial Intelligence (AI), digital transformation, and sustainability practices as shown in table 1. AI operates as a strategic HR tool that enhances decision-making processes while eliminating administrative tasks and improving talent acquisition through predictive analytics and intelligent recruitment systems and automated resume screening and performance analytics. The technologies improve operational efficiency, but their use creates ethical problems because they create algorithmic bias and they endanger data privacy and they threaten job security, which requires organizations to establish governance frameworks and reskilling initiatives. Workers appreciate AI technology because it boosts their work productivity and enables them to make decisions based on data, yet they still fear losing their jobs while human interactions decrease and organizations need to explain their ethical practices.

3. METHODOLOGY

The research methodology used to produce the visual results operates according to a predefined quantitative research framework. The research team established two research objectives which they defined as following research objective one they wanted to evaluate public opinion about brand social responsibility and research objective two they wanted to analyze AI technology use in job application processes among different demographic groups and various countries. The research team identified essential research variables which included country (U.S., UK, Germany), age group (Gen Z, Millennials, Gen X), gender, occupation type, AI tools used, and reasons for AI adoption. The researchers developed a questionnaire which contained closed-ended questions and multiple-choice questions to create a system for measuring participant responses. The respondents evaluated their agreement with brand-related questions which contained issues about mental health, climate change, diversity, free speech, racial issues, and international conflicts (Ravikumar, 2026). The AI-related questions asked participants about their usage patterns and which tools they used and their primary reasons for using AI technology as shown in figure 3.

Figure 3. Data structured and visualization of output results.

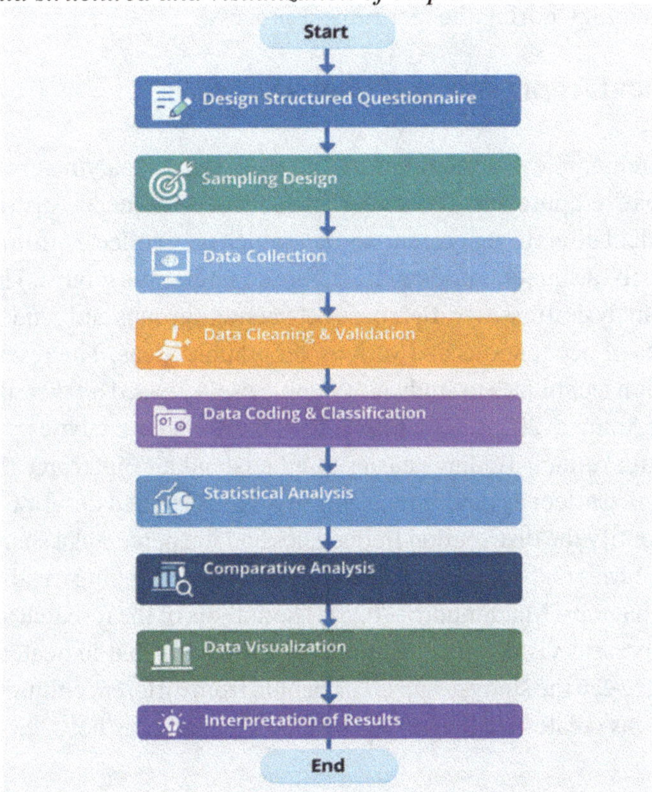

Stratified random sampling method required that all age groups and gender and employment categories should be equally represented in each country which resulted in the method achieving balanced representation. The researchers collected data by using online survey panels which were active during the designated survey periods. The study included only participants who were between 18 and 67 years old and had applied for jobs during the last two years for the purpose of conducting AI-specific analysis. The collected data underwent the cleaning process which removed all incomplete and inconsistent and duplicate responses from the dataset. The researchers coded the responses into categorical variables which included generational cohorts and job types. The researchers performed descriptive statistical analysis to determine the distribution frequencies and percentage share of the data. The research team conducted comparative analysis between countries and demographic groups to identify existing trends and different patterns of behavior. The researchers used grouped bar charts to create visual representations of the results which showed percentage differences between the study groups. The researchers analyzed the results to determine how people view brand activism and how they adopt AI technology during the recruitment process.

3.1 Analytical Approach and Limitations

The research employs a quantitative and descriptive analytical method for its main investigative approach. The research team used frequency distributions and percentage calculations to analyze survey data which they collected from respondents who belonged to various countries and different demographic groups. The study used comparative analysis to assess differences between age groups and gender groups and different types of occupations and various geographic areas. The researchers used cross-tabulation techniques to study how people use AI based on their demographic information (Ammer, 2025). The researchers used visual analytics with grouped bar charts to make their findings easier to understand and interpret. The research limitations which affect its outcomes. The researchers applied descriptive statistical analysis to identify the distribution frequencies and the percentage share. The study compared countries and demographic groups, to identify existing trends and various patterns of behaviour (Makhmudov, 2025). The authors of the research used grouped bar charts to present visual representations of the results that indicated percentage differences between the study groups. The people from different cultures understand survey questions creates challenges for making comparisons between countries.

4. RESULTS AND DISCUSSION

The data shows how artificial intelligence (AI) has changed both work patterns and job search methods which resulted in a major shift in labor market control for the United States. The number of unemployed people reached 7.50 million by December 2025 which surpassed the total of 6.54 million job vacancies. The current situation represents a complete turnaround from the post-pandemic period when there were more job vacancies than available workers as demonstrated in figure 4. The historical pattern shows that economic downturns and recessions happen at the same time as these crossings which creates a situation where the labor market decreases while more applicants compete for fewer job openings. The AI has become an increasingly important tool in job applications. The United States and United Kingdom respondents who make up the majority believe that applicants should use AI in a way which makes it impossible to identify their usage of AI technology because people have started to accept AI as a normal practice while its ethical boundaries remain uncertain according to figure 5. The 500 responders who consider the response for data collection as shown in website www.statista.com, more than half of respondents also agree that, in the future, navigating the application process without AI may be difficult and that applicants who do not use AI could face worse chances. The perception of the tighter labor market results from the discovery that organizations need efficient tools which enhance their work output because job opportunities have become limited in comparison to available job candidates.

Figure 4. The unemployed members and job openings. (Link: https://www.statista.com/topics/1164/social-networks/ Date: 02/03/2026 Time: 09:03PM)

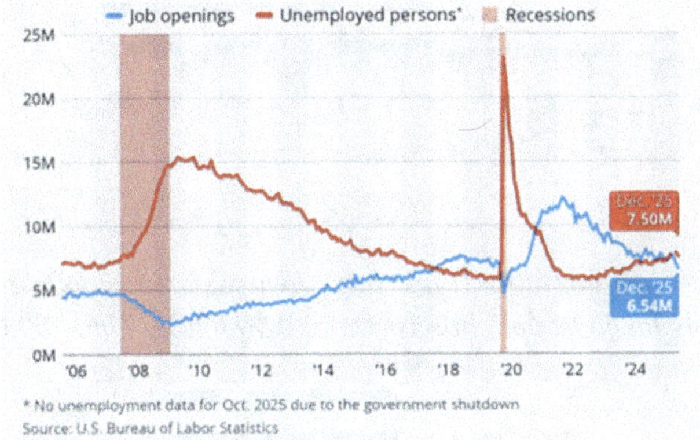

Figure 5. The Future job application viva AI. (Link: https://www.statista.com/chart/35806/use-ai-in-job-application/ Date: 02/03/2026 Time: 09:03PM)

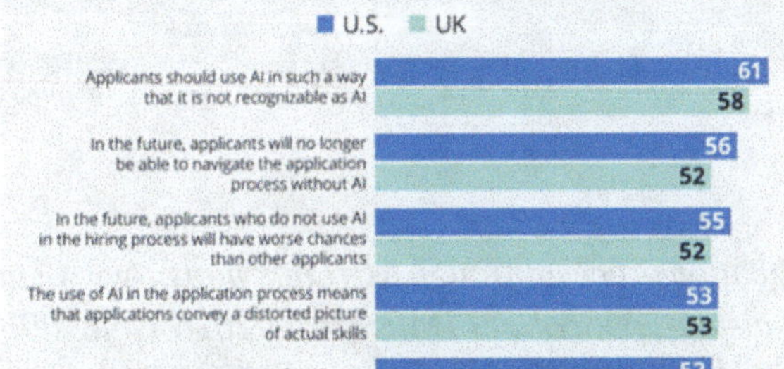

Figure 6. Job application received on gender basis. (Link: https://www.statista.com/chart/35807/ai-use-job-application-process/ Date: 02/03/2026 Time: 09:03PM)

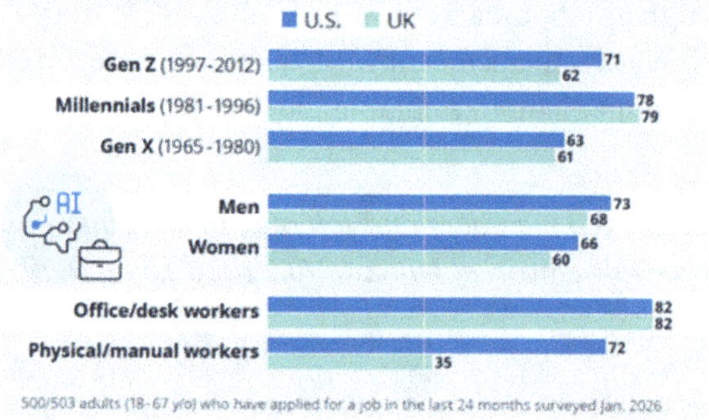

Figure 7. Job applications tools. (Link: https://www.statista.com/chart/35815/most-popular-ai-tools-for-job-applications/ Date: 02/03/2026 Time: 09:03PM)

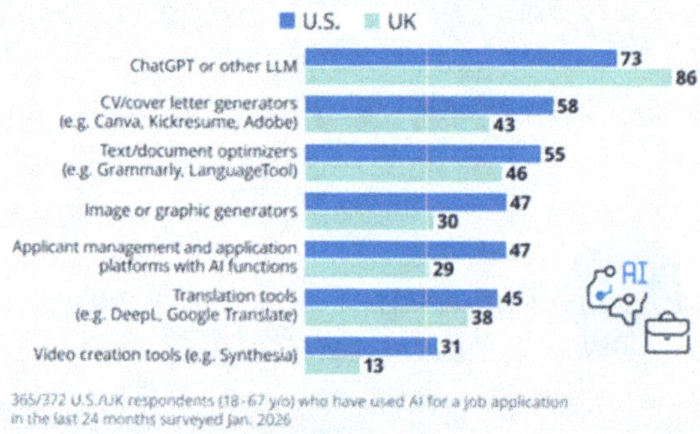

Figure 8. Job application process through AI. (Link: https://www.statista.com/chart/35816/main-uses-ai-job-application/ Date: 02/03/2026 Time: 09:03PM)

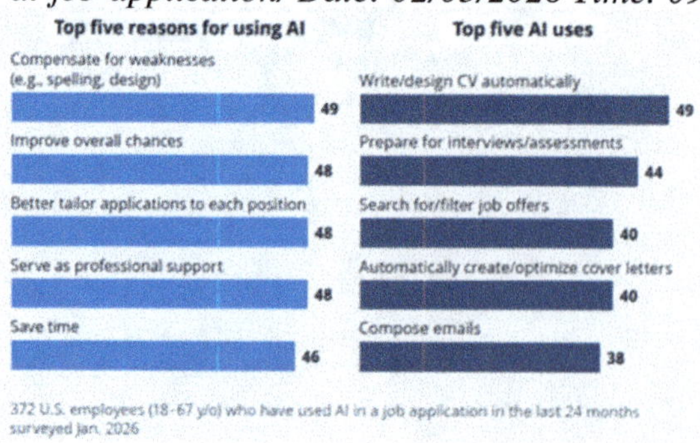

The demographic data shows which groups lead the adoption of AI technology. In both countries, millennials use AI for job applications more than any other group, while Gen Z follows closely behind. Younger generations demonstrate better digital skills and greater comfort with automated technologies. According to figure 6, men tend to use AI more than women do, while office and desk employees show much greater AI usage than people who work in manual labor jobs. The current AI tool distribution between white-collar recruitment tools and other systems for screening candidates and conducting online assessments shows that these tools create recruitment disparities between different occupational groups according to figure 7. Organizations perceive AI technology as a tool to help their staff members instead of using it as a shortcut to complete tasks. The most common applications of AI technology create automatic CV writing tools which help users prepare for interviews and filter their job search results to solve the current hiring problems which affect applicant tracking systems (as shown in figure 8). The use of AI technologies has become essential for organizations because they require these capabilities to maintain their strategic position (Agarwal, 2024). The figure shows that people are worried about the potential job losses which will result from AI implementations. More respondents in the United Kingdom, United States, and Germany believe that millions of jobs will disappear than they fear losing their personal employment. The difference between these two groups indicates that people in society experience widespread anxiety about work-related issues which do not stem from their personal job concerns. People use AI technologies to help them find work during the present time but they continue to worry about what AI technology will do to their job prospects in the future.

5. ORGANIZATIONAL AND ETHICAL IMPLICATIONS

The fast adoption of artificial intelligence for job application systems exceeds established organizational and ethical boundaries which affect all three groups of employers, employees, and regulators. Organizations need to develop strategic responses to the upcoming period of AI-powered applications by implementing solutions that handle their requirements for fairness, transparency, accountability, and regulatory compliance. The section examines how employers react to ethical problems, legal issues, and the need for strategic changes in their human resource practices (Ahmed & Pardaev, 2025).

5.1 Employer Responses to AI-Assisted Applications

The number of AI-generated employment documents, which include résumé and cover letter materials and interview responses, has been steadily rising in today's job market. Organizations have implemented AI screening technologies, specifically applicant tracking systems (ATS), to handle their increased application processing requirements which represent their first step toward operational transformation. The systems assist in decreasing administrative workload yet they create an "AI arms race" situation, where applicants use AI for application enhancement while companies employ AI to conduct candidate screening. Organizations have chosen to protect themselves from potential dangers by developing methods to identify AI-generated content, which they consider a threat to their ability to prove authenticity. The organizations which implement AI technology use it to build their modern digital technology proficiency (Kuzmin, 2025). Progressive employers increasingly focus less on whether AI was used and more on whether the applicant demonstrates genuine competence during interviews, assessments, and probation periods. The movement indicates that organizations are beginning to accept AI technology as a means to enhance work productivity instead of using it to commit fraudulent activities. The different ways employers show their attitudes toward employees create an environment of uncertainty for job candidates (Ravikumar, 2026). The absence of explicit guidelines leads applicants to feel they must hide their use of AI technology which creates ethical conflicts. Organizations must create rules for AI technology usage during employee recruitment processes and they need to deliver those rules to their employees through clear communication methods.

5.2 Legal and Regulatory Considerations

The use of AI in hiring creates complex legal problems because it involves three different areas which include data protection and discrimination and employment law. Organizations now need to demonstrate their automated decision systems while protecting applicant data because regulations have become more stringent. The AI tools need to process extensive personal data which makes it essential to meet data protection regulations. Organizations experience severe legal repercussions when they fail to handle their data correctly which leads to public trust violations (Alomair, 2026). The employment law system requires organizations to take responsibility for discriminatory results which occur without their intention. Employers lose legal protection when their AI systems automatically exclude specific groups from employment because bias exists in their algorithm design and data selection process. Organizations must perform fairness tests and ongoing monitoring of their AI systems to meet their legal obligations. The speed at which regulatory frameworks develop differs across regions which creates difficulties for companies that operate globally. Employers need to track newly developing AI regulations while making sure their hiring practices meet current legal requirements and future regulatory needs. In the age of AI, organizations now treat legal compliance as a central HR responsibility instead of a secondary back-office task.

5.3 Strategic Adaptation in HR Practices

Organizations need to change their HR practices because their current methods do not help them achieve their business goals. The upcoming employers use AI technology in their hiring procedures and create new methods to evaluate actual abilities and future worker development. The new assessment system requires organizations to use structured interviews and work-sample tests and skills-based assessments because these methods create more difficulty for people who attempt to produce fraudulent results through automated text generation. HR professionals need to learn new skills (Bhatti, 2025). AI systems now stand as essential knowledge for all professionals who work in recruitment and talent management because they need to understand what AI can do and what it cannot do plus its ethical dangers. Organizations should dedicate their resources to training HR personnel who need to evaluate AI tools with critical thinking so they can make proper judgments based on their own understanding instead of depending on vendors' assertions. Organizations need to establish new definitions of fairness and merit to guide their hiring processes. The ability to demonstrate learning skills and adaptability and ethical decision-making will replace polished applications as the main method to attract potential advantages from AI technology which will become an industry standard. The establishment of defined organizational rules about which AI applications are permitted will help decrease uncertainty while ensuring equal treatment of all job seekers.

5.4 Impact on Skill Development

AI is revolutionizing the way people acquire and develop their abilities. The established system of skill acquisition required people to complete their schooling and their employment training and their mentoring relationships. AI-powered tools from today enable learners to receive customized learning experiences and immediate performance evaluations and ongoing skill measurement. The capabilities establish technical and analytical and communication skills development through learning acceleration which provides resources that match learning deficiencies. AI dependency creates problems because it leads to loss of skills. People stop practicing essential skills when AI takes over jobs that need document creation and programming and data examination work. The user will develop weaker critical thinking and writing and problem-solving abilities when they depend too much on automated processes. The current job market requires essential skills development which uses AI tools to support learning together with human competencies.

AI decides which skills will get the most attention from people. People need digital skills and data analysis skills and AI fluency skills because these skills will be needed for future work and repetitive tasks will not be needed anymore. People need soft skills which includes communication skills and adaptability skills and ethical judgment skills because these skills are difficult to automate and these skills help us interact with AI systems. AI is creating a new skills framework which defines the most important skills that are needed to learn.

5.5 Human–AI Collaboration in Career Development

The workplace now depends on Human–AI partnerships as the main method for advancing employee professional growth. AI functions as a career partner which helps people make decisions and plan their skill development and improve their work performance instead of taking control of their choice-making abilities. The AI-powered career platforms can evaluate market employment data to create job recommendations while they determine the most essential skills for particular professions which helps people make better professional decisions. The workplace creates new job functions through AI partnerships which lead to different career paths. Employees need to manage AI technologies while they decipher the system results and use their human understanding to handle situations where machines cannot operate. The career development path now requires workers to move from executing tasks to performing their duties through managerial work and system integration and strategic decision-making processes. Professionals who possess industry knowledge and the ability to manage AI systems will experience better job opportunities.

Individuals need to develop particular meta-skills which include critical evaluation skills together with self-awareness abilities and reflective learning competencies for successful human-AI partnerships (Nwokolo, 2023). Individuals must learn not only how to use AI but also when not to use it. People who want to succeed in their careers today need to stay in control of their creative work while they develop their ethical reasoning skills which has become more necessary because of AI systems.

6. CONCLUSION AND FUTURE SCOPE

The contemporary recruitment process has been transformed because organizations now use artificial intelligence to assess job candidates. The research findings presented in this chapter demonstrate that artificial intelligence has become an essential tool which applicants must use to gain a competitive edge. The workplace shows increasing acceptance of AI-based applications because Millennials and Gen Z demonstrate much higher adoption rates for these systems in professional and office-based occupations. The AI tools improve operational performance through customized experiences which boost user confidence, but they create problems related to genuine assessment and skilled people assessment and fair evaluation. People believe that their job prospects will decrease because they don't use digital technology, which means that digital technology gaps in the workforce. The organizations which hire employees need to develop new ways to evaluate job candidates because they must use AI-enhanced systems for their hiring process. Organizations need to create new assessment methods which evaluate human decisions and their evaluation through algorithmic systems while developing governance systems which ensure proper and responsible use of these assessments.

Researchers should investigate how artificial intelligence affects employee skill acquisition and their professional development and their work performance over time. Cross-cultural research between different cultures can explain why people from different parts of the world accept certain things while they create rules to control other things. The development of recruitment AI regulations needs researchers to conduct policy-focused studies which will create procedures to assess ethical AI methods in recruitment. Digital literacy development and equal technology access and established transparent hiring procedures will become crucial for AI development to create job opportunities which treat all individuals fairly.

REFERENCES

Aarthi, S., Ravikumar, R. N., & Pardaev, J. (2026). Synergizing Multimodal Generative AI and Blockchain for the Future of Digital Media. In Fusion of Multimodal Generative AI and Blockchain Technology in Digital Media (pp. 1-34). IGI Global Scientific Publishing. DOI: 10.4018/979-8-3373-1504-1.ch001

Achar, H.V.B., Prasad, P.S., Rajeshwari, D. *et al.* Federated learning and Neuro-Symbolic AI for botnet classification in IoT-Enabled consumer devices. *Int. j. inf. tecnol.* (2025). https://doi.org/DOI: 10.1007/s41870-025-02993-0

Adilov, Z., Tajibaev, J., Rasul-Zade, L., Tursunov, M., Mamadiyarov, Z., & Abdullayev, D. (2025). Exploring virtual reality and digital twin technologies for sustainable construction training in higher education. E3S Web of Conferences, 680, 00131. https://doi.org/DOI: 10.1051/e3sconf/202568000131

Agarwal, V., Kaur, S. N. R., Gupta, S., Zaveri, B., Sohal, J., & Shrivastav, A. K. (2024). Adoption of advanced systems for digital resource management in academic institutions. *Evolutionary Studies in Imaginative Culture*, •••, 913–923. DOI: 10.70082/esiculture.vi.1089

Ahmed, S. Y., & Pardaev, J. (2025). Human-AI decision dynamics: How risk propensity and trust impact choices through decision fatigue, conditional on AI understanding. *Decision Making: Applications in Management and Engineering*, *8*(2), 96–113. DOI: 10.31181/dmame8220251484

Al Doghan, M. A., & Absamatov, A. (2025). Effects of Big Data, Mechanical System Flexibility, IOT and Digital Twin Adoption on Company Resilience and Operational Performance. *Reports in Mechanical Engineering*, *6*(2), 65–79. DOI: 10.31181/rme524

Aldossary, M. A., & Pardaev, J. (2025). Leveraging Big-Data Management for Production Excellence: Decision-Making Capabilities, Decision Quality, and the Moderating Effect of Manufacturing IT Infrastructure. *Reports in Mechanical Engineering*, *6*(1), 136–151. DOI: 10.31181/rme499

Alomair, A., Farooq, U., Almulhim, A. A., & Mamadiyarov, Z. (2026, March). Do cultural values matter? The role of national cultural dimensions in shaping female entrepreneurship in ASEAN. In *Women's Studies International Forum* (Vol. 115, p. 103273). Pergamon. DOI: 10.1016/j.wsif.2025.103273

Ammer, M. A., & Mamadjanova, T. (2025). *Impact of educational quality, educational resource, and educational climate on educational engagement and student intention to attend lectures*. Espacio, Tiempo y Educación., DOI: 10.14516/ete.12208

Ammer, M. A., & Mamadjanova, T. (2025). Effects of educational digital literacy, educational aspirations, self-directed learning on e-learning motivation and effectiveness. *Educational Sciences: Theory & Practice*. Advance online publication. DOI: 10.12738/jestp.2025.1.18

Ammer, M. A., & Sattarov, A. (2025). Enhancing investors' decision-making through financial risk management: Role of corporate governance and financial communication transparency. Decision Making: Applications in Management and Engineering. https://doi.org/DOI: 10.31181/dmame8220251527

Azahari, L. M., Ahmad, F. A., & Saniff, S. M. (2026). Connecting Employability and the Future of Work: A Systematic Review of Global Trends, Employer Expectations, and Evolving Recruitment Strategies. *Enhancing Graduate Employability in an Evolving Workforce*, 99-118. DOI: 10.4018/979-8-3373-4450-8.ch005

Balamurugan, M., & Roopa, D. K. N., S., Sushma, R., T. C., K., Swetha, G., & Raghu, N. (2026). Late Night Use of Social Media and Sleep Deprivation. In I. Nabila Marzuki, W. Wan Ali, H. Lee, A. Manaf, & M. Sanmugam (Eds.), *Examining the Intersection of Technology, Media, and Social Innovation* (pp. 205-236). IGI Global Scientific Publishing. DOI: 10.4018/979-8-3373-5307-4.ch008

Bentayeb, A., Khoualed, A., & Medjdoub, A. (2026). Artificial Intelligence in Human Resource Management: Applications, Workforce Implications, And Market Trends (2024-2034). *Інститут бухгалтерського обліку, контроль та аналіз в умовах глобалізації*, (3-4), 68-78. **https://doi.org/**DOI: 10.35774/ibo2025.03-04.068

Bhatti, M. A., & Mamadjanova, T. (2025). From Calling to Performance: The Role of Linguistic and Communicative Competence in Employee Success. *Eurasian Journal of Applied Linguistics*, *11*(2), 147–162. DOI: 10.32601/ejal.11212

Bhatti, M. A., & Otamurodov, S. (2025). Job Satisfaction and Employee Commitment: Role of Internal Communication, Language Proficiency, Information Quality and Information Usefulness. *El Profesional de la Información*, *34*(2). Advance online publication. DOI: 10.3145/epi.2025.ene.34201

Bhatti, M. A., & Shodiyev, A. (2025). Enhancing Employee Performance: Role of Communication Competence, Internal Communication and Satisfaction with Communication Climate. *International Journal of Operations and Quantitative Management*, *31*(2), 216–239. DOI: 10.46970/2025.31.2.11

Cahyani, I., Buriev, K. T., Ngongo, M., Mamadiyarov, Z., Ino, L., Herman, H., Saputra, N., & Baxtishodovich, S. B. (2025). Exploring the use of TikTok application in enhancing the skill of pronunciation: A case on students' perception. *Studies in Media and Communication*, *13*(2), 7553. DOI: 10.11114/smc.v13i2.7553

Ghaleb, M. M. S., & Sattarov, A. (2025). *Use of ChatGPT in education and quality of education: Role of student course engagement and regulator support.* Revista Electrónica de LEEME., DOI: 10.58262/LEEME.55.0020

H. V Balachandra Achar and R. N. "The Impact and Future of Artificial Intelligence in Learning," *2025 3rd International Conference on Integrated Circuits and Communication Systems (ICICACS)*, Raichur, India, 2025, pp. 1-6, DOI: 10.1109/ICICACS65178.2025.10967881

Hair, J. F., Jr., Rana, S., Robb, D., & Stroud, M. (2026). The emerging role of AI and social robots in university student recruitment. In *Social robots and artificial intelligence in education: Integrating AI in K-12 and higher education* (pp. 153-183). Cham: Springer Nature Switzerland. DOI: 10.1007/978-3-032-03977-4_7

Hamid, E. M., & Shodiyev, A. (2025). Role of information needs, information accessibility, information overload and digital literacy in shaping web search self-efficacy. *El Profesional de la Información, 34*(2). Advance online publication. DOI: 10.3145/epi.2025.ene.34205

Islamutdinov, V., Akhmetshin, E., Lydia, E. L., & Raja, P. V. K. (2024, April). Implementation of AI in an Ethical and Responsible Manner to Empower Education in Digital Sector. In International Conference on Smart Computing and Informatics (pp. 127-134). Singapore: Springer Nature Singapore. DOI: 10.1007/978-981-96-3939-7_13

Kodagoda, T. (2026). Generation Y Employees' Understandings on Artificial Intelligence (AI): Interventions at Workplace. In *Communication and Knowledge in Organizations: Approaches from Positivist and Interpretivist Paradigms* (pp. 19-32). Singapore: Springer Nature Singapore. https://doi.org/DOI: 10.1007/978-981-95-0622-4_2

Kulmanov, T., Dadabaev, U., Qulmetov, M., Ulashov, A., & Eshboyev, M.. (2025). Global services market transformation: Digitalization export trends and future forecasts. *ACM International Conference Proceeding Series*. DOI: 10.1145/3726122.3726245

Kulmanov, T., Dadabaev, U., Qulmetov, M., Ulashov, A., Eshboyev, M., & Makhmudov, S. (2024, December). Global Services Market Transformation Digitalization Export Trends and Future Forecasts. In *Proceedings of the 8th International Conference on Future Networks & Distributed Systems* (pp. 851-858). https://doi.org/DOI: 10.1145/3726122.3726245

Kuzmin, E., Bondareva, V. S., Shodiyev, A., & Ochilov, I. (2025). Digitalization, Innovation, and Competitiveness: Insights from a Cross-Country Analysis of Labor Productivity Effects. In Artificial Intelligence and Digital Transformation: From Innovation to Implementation (pp. 307-329). Cham: Springer Nature Switzerland. DOI: 10.1007/978-3-032-00118-4_17

M., B., N., R., L. N., D., Sahoo, S. K., Ankanahalli Shankaregowda, S., Kannanugo, N., M., D., & M., V. K. (2024). AI-Enhanced Leadership Decision Support System Using ChatGPT for Ethical Learning. In A. Agnihotri, R. Agarwal, A. Maurya, M. Sinha, & B. Balusamy (Eds.), *Impact of New Technology on Next-Generation Leadership* (pp. 137-161). IGI Global Scientific Publishing. DOI: 10.4018/979-8-3693-1946-8.ch008

Makhmudov, S., Maqsood, M., Musaev, U., Urazmetov, M., & Shahzadi, A. (2025). Foundations of agentic AI redefining autonomy in learning environments. In *Multi-disciplinary Perspectives on Agentic AI in Educational Systems*. IGI Global., DOI: 10.4018/979-8-3373-4621-2.ch001

Makhmudov, S., Otakhonova, D., Kulmanov, T., Shamshiyeva, N., Juraev, U., Ruziev, G., & Sabirova, U. (2026). The Impact of Digital Marketing and Mobile Applications on Service Innovation in German Companies. *International Review of Management and Marketing*, *16*(1), 210–217. DOI: 10.32479/irmm.22052

Marisamy, K., Selvakumar, A., Rajasekar, B., Natarajan, R., Atajanova, A., & Makhmudov, S. (2026). Smart logistics integrating AI, IoT, blockchain, and Robotics for a sustainable Future. In *Emerging Trends in Smart Logistics Technologies* (pp. 73–104). IGI Global Scientific Publishing., DOI: 10.4018/979-8-3373-2434-0.ch003

Muthuswamy, V. V., & Absamatov, A. (2025). *Determinants of students engagement and their role in boosting students' academic performance among higher education institutions*. Revista Electrónica de LEEME., DOI: 10.58262/LEEME.56.13

Nwokolo, S. C., Singh, R., Khan, S., Kumar, A., & Luthra, S. (2023). Africa's awakening to climate action. In *CSR, sustainability, ethics & governance* (pp. 299–310). DOI: 10.1007/978-3-031-44514-9_9

Pandey, D., Singh, G., Joshi, L., Polyakova, O., Sungatullina, D., & Singh, R. (2024). Organizational preparedness for navigating disruption towards sustainability: Strategies' analysis. E3S Web of Conferences. DOI: 10.1051/e3sconf/202457407001

Prabha, K. R., Mabel, B. R., Isaev, F., Mamadiyarov, Z., Raxmatullayevich, K. U., & Erkinjon, T. (2026). A Multi-Layer Artificial Intelligence–Enabled Governance Framework for Integrating Information Security Management, Quality Management, and Strategic Human Resource Analytics: An Empirical Study on the Role of Corporate Social Responsibility in Sustainable Organizational Performance. *Quality - Access to Success*, *27*(210). Advance online publication. DOI: 10.47750/QAS/27.210.45

Raghu, N. V. N., T., L. N., D., Kumar B. M., H., & Shankaregowda, S. A. (2025). Enhancing Critical Thinking Through Problem-Based Learning: A Comprehensive Approach to Modern Education. In M. Lytras, P. Ordóñez de Pablos, & T. Aldosemani (Eds.), *Fostering Teacher Skills and Critical Thinking in Modern Education* (pp. 259-282). IGI Global Scientific Publishing. DOI: 10.4018/979-8-3373-1692-5.ch011

Rajeswari, M., Vanitha, C. L., Xudoynazarova, S., Mamadiyarov, Z., Naveen, S., Nematovich, K. I., & Isaev, F. (2026). Design and Validation of an Explainable Artificial Intelligence–Based Decision Intelligence Model for Cyber Risk–Aware Quality Systems and Ethical Human Resource Management: Investigating the Moderating Influence of Corporate Social Responsibility in Digitally Transformed Organizations. *Quality - Access to Success*, *27*(210). Advance online publication. DOI: 10.47750/QAS/27.210.46

Rathinavel, P., Ravikumar, R. N., Aarthi, S., Habib, M., Salaeva, N., & Pardaev, J. (2026). Augmenting Human Capabilities: AI's Impact on Collaborative Workflows. In Powering e-Collaboration Through AI, Machine Learning, and Internet of Things (pp. 1-30). IGI Global Scientific Publishing. DOI: 10.4018/979-8-3373-2372-5.ch001

Rathinavel, P., Ravikumar, R. N., Aarthi, S., Habib, M., Salaeva, N., & Pardaev, J. (2026). Augmenting Human Capabilities: AI's Impact on Collaborative Workflows. In Powering e-Collaboration Through AI, Machine Learning, and Internet of Things (pp. 1-30). IGI Global Scientific Publishing. DOI: 10.4018/979-8-3373-2372-5.ch001

Ravikumar, R. N., Aarthi, S., Atamuratova, Z., Ashirova, A., Jurayev, K., & Hayitova, M. (2026). Comprehensive Evaluation of AI-Driven Systems in Modern Hospital Environments. In Evaluation and Assessment of AI-Driven Systems in Hospitals (pp. 61-88). IGI Global Scientific Publishing. DOI: 10.4018/979-8-3373-2787-7.ch003

Ravikumar, R. N., Aarthi, S., & Mamadiyarov, Z. (2026). Mitigating Risks Through AI-Powered Fraud Detection Systems in Digital Banking. In Innovating Cost-Efficient and Scalable Business Models in the Digital Era (pp. 343-376). IGI Global Scientific Publishing. https://doi.org/DOI: 10.4018/979-8-3373-2120-2.ch011

Ravikumar, R. N., Aarthi, S., Ruzimova, F., & Mamadiyarov, Z. (2026). Training and Development in AI-Driven Education Scaling Solutions: K-12 to Workforce. In Transforming Education with Data Science in the AI Era (pp. 267-298). IGI Global Scientific Publishing. DOI: DOI: 10.4018/979-8-3373-2185-1.ch010

Ravikumar, R. N., Aarthi, S., Usmani, M. A., Rai, P. K., Jumaniyozova, M., & Narboshova, M. (2026). Advancements in Multilingual Speech Technologies for Human-Computer Interaction. In Advancements in Speech Processing for Human-Computer Interaction (pp. 101-132). IGI Global Scientific Publishing. DOI: 10.4018/979-8-3373-3048-8.ch004

Sapayev, V. O., Hayat, N., Mamadiyarov, Z., & Ahmad, M. (2026). Inside the Black Box: How Generative AI Creates Digital Synthetics. In Digital Synthetic Data and Outputs (pp. 409-434). IGI Global Scientific Publishing. https://doi.org/DOI: 10.4018/979-8-3373-2277-3.ch016

Sherov, A., Rakhimov, T., Hajiyev, H., Zelinskaya, M., & Khidirova, G. (2025). Evaluating class-imbalanced data handling for enhanced financial distress prediction using an attention-based deep neural network and heuristic optimization algorithms. Engineering. *Technology and Applied Science Research*, *15*(6), 13372. DOI: 10.48084/etasr.13372

Sufyan Ghaleb, M. M., & Pardaev, J. (2025). Effects of Advertisement Language, Communication Style, Information Seeking Behavior and Information Source Credibility on Customers' Intentions towards International Products via Brand Trust. *El Profesional de la Información*, *34*(2). Advance online publication. DOI: 10.3145/epi.2025.ene.34203

Yong, J. Y., Yusoff, Y. M., Fernando, Y., Lin, W. L., Chong, S. C., & Pek, C. K. (2026). Generation Green: Navigating ESG in Generation Z's Job Search Landscape. In *Stimulating Economic Growth Through Cultural and Societal Transformations* (pp. 83-100). IGI Global Scientific Publishing. https://doi.org/DOI: 10.4018/979-8-3373-0603-2.ch004

Zayniddinov, R., Jumaev, N., Irgasheva, G., Asadov, A., & Makhmudov, N.. (2025). The influence of the digital economy on economic development: Evidence from Uzbekistan. *ACM International Conference Proceeding Series*. DOI: 10.1145/3726122.3726242

Zhao, J., Ragmoun, W., Dong, Z., Nawaz, M. A., & Sattarov, A. (2025). Circular economy implementation through AI adoption, CSR and green finance: The mediating role of green product innovation and green supply chain. *Corporate Social Responsibility and Environmental Management*. Advance online publication. DOI: 10.1002/csr.70289

Chapter 13

The Role of Emotional Intelligence in Managing Human Capital in AI-Driven IT Environments

Shibani Shuvasmita
http://orcid.org/0009-0002-4050-2999
KIIT University, Bhubaneswar, India

Ipseeta Satpathy
http://orcid.org/0000-0002-0155-5548
KIIT School of Management, KIIT University, Bhubaneswar, India

Vishal Jain
http://orcid.org/0000-0003-1126-7424
School of Engineering & Technology, Vivekananda Institute of Professional Studies-Technical Campus, New Delhi, India

ABSTRACT

The integration of Artificial Intelligence (AI) in the IT sector has transformed work processes, increasing efficiency while also creating new emotional and cognitive challenges for employees. This chapter highlights the role of Emotional Intelligence (EI) in helping employees manage stress, adapt to digital environments and maintain effective collaboration. It argues that EI serves as a strategic human capability that supports sustainable employee performance in AI-driven workplaces. Overall, EI is essential for balancing technological advancement with employee well-being.

DOI: 10.4018/979-8-2600-2726-4.ch013

1. INTRODUCTION

The fast growth of Artificial Intelligence (AI) has changed the way work is done especially in the IT sector. Many organisations are now using AI tools for tasks like data analysis, coding support, customer service and decision making. Technologies such as generative AI, Machine learning and automation are not only making work faster and easier but also changing how jobs are designed. According to a report by McKinsey & Company (2023), the use of AI has grown quickly across different industries with IT companies leading this change because they are more ready to adopt new technologies. In the same way a news article by the Economic Times (2024) states that Indian IT companies are actively using AI tools, including generative assistants to improve productivity while also changing employee roles and expectations.

As a result the way people work in the IT sector is now changing a lot. Earlier jobs mainly focused on technical skills but now employees are very much involved in AI. And they work closely with AI systems. Automation has reduced routine tasks but it has also created new responsibilities. Employees now have to check AI results, errors. After knowing error then to fix the error and make the decision based on data. At the same time remote and hybrid work have changed how people connect and work together. Different digital tools, virtual meetings and delayed communication have become a normal part of everyday work. According to Delloitte (2022) report hybrid work gives more flexibility but at the same time creates challenges in communication and coordination.

Even though these technological changes have many benefits they also increase mental and emotional pressure on employees. Workers need to keep learning new technologies deal with uncertainity and stay productive when he/ she is constantly motirore. Using AI can cause problems like technostress, mental overload and emotional pressure especially when employees have to reply quickly and meet high expectaions (Tarafdar et al., 2021). Remote work reduces in person interactions. So employees get less emotional support from colleagues. This males it hard to handle the stress. Research also shows that being always connected and communicationg through digitl platforms can lead to emotional tiredness. (Wang et al., 2023).

Despite the growing body of research on AI and digital work, there remains a significant gap in understanding the role of emotional factors in these environments. Most of the studies have focused on areas like technology efficiency, productivity and changes in skills but they have paid less attention to how employees feel while working with AI systems. In particular, the role of emotional intelligence (EI) in handling the challenges of AI-based work environments is not fully explored yet. Most existing studies have looked at EI in traditional workplaces, where it is seen as important for leadership, team work and performance (Miao et al., 2020). However very few studies have examined how EI works as an important support for employees in digital and AI- driven work settings.

EI has become very important as a form of human skill in this changing work environment. EI means the ability to understand manage our own emotions as well as others. In AI based workplaces the employees are not only expected to complete technical tasks but also to handle different emotional situations. These include dealing with uncertainty, managing communication through digital platforms and effective work in virtual teams. Employees those who have strong EI are better able to manage stress, adjust to changes and build good relationship at work even in highly digital and automated settings (Mattingly & Kraiger, 2019)

In addition Emotional intelligence (EI) plays an important role in maintaining long-term employee performance. As organisations depend more on AI systems taking care of the well being of employee become more important. EI helps employees to manage their emotions, avoid burnout and stay motivated in their work. It also helps to make ethical decisions and build trust when people interact with AI systems. Recent studies and industry report suggest that organisations that focus on emotional skills along with technological development are more likely to achieve sustainable results (Bakker & Demerouti,2017; Lesener et al., 2020)

Recent studies also highlight that artificial Intelligence is increasingly integrated into organisational process to enhance innovation, efficiency and decision-making capabilities (Awad, 2024; Awad & Ghonim,2025)

It further emphasizes the role of AI-driven systems in transforming organisational practices particularly through digital capabilities and intelligent automation (Shams Eldin et al., 2025). At the same time generative AI applications are reshaping human-technology interaction, requiring employees to develop adaptive and emotional competencies (Qadeer & Awad, 2025)

The chapter aims to explore emotional intelligence as a strategic human capital resource in AI-enabled IT environments. It seeks to understand how EI contributes to sustainable employee performance in the context of increasing digitalization and AI integration. The chapter specifically focuses on knowledge-intensive IT sectors where employees are required to balance technical expertise with emotional adaptability.

2.THEORETICAL BACKGROUND

2.1 Emotional Intelligence

Emotional Intelligence (EI) means the ability to understand and manage our own emotions as well as the emotions of others. The idea was first introduced by Mayer and Salovey(1997) and later made popular by Goleman (1995) who explained its importance in the workplace especially for leadership and effectiveness. Over time EI has received a lot of attention in organisational studies because it affects how employees perform, how they feel at work and how they interact with others. Recent research also shows that EI is very important in helping employees deal with stress, adjust to changes and stay productive in challenging work environments (Miao et al., 2020; Guleria et al., 2025)

Emotional Intelligence has been explained in different ways by various researchers. The ability model (Mayer & Salovey,1997) looks at how people understand and manage emotions as a mental skill. On the other, Goleman's mixed model focuses more on practical qualities like leadership, motivate and social skills. While the ability model gives a strong psychological base. The mixed model is more useful in real workplace situations.

EI is generally understood through four components:

Self-awareness

Self-awareness means understanding you own emotions, strength and weaknesses. It helps employees recognize feelings like stress, fraustration or anxiety that may happen durrig wortk. In AI- based work environments where there are constant changes in technology and pressure to perform self- awareness allows employees to notice early signs of emotional stress and handle them in a better way. Research shows that employees who are self-aware can mange workplace challenges more effectively and stay emotionally balanced (Miao et al., 2020)

Self-regulation

Self-regulation means the ability to control and manage your emotions in different situations. It helps employees stay calm, avoid reacting too quickly and behave in a proper way. In digital work environment employee often have to reply to messages, solve problems and deal with clients under time pressure. Self regulations helps them stay calm and act professionally, even during stressful moments. Studies show that employees who have good self regulation skills feel less burnout and have higher job satisfaction (Guleria et al., 2025)

Empathy

Empathy means the ability to understand and feel what others are going through. It is very important for maintaining good relationship, improving trust and for team work. In AI based and remote work environments where face to face interaction is limited empathy becomes more important. Employees mostly use digital tools where it is very hard to understand emotions. Empathy helps people understand others feelings correctly and respond ina caring and supportive way. Research shows that empathy improves teamwork and helps reduce conflicts in virtual teams (Wang et al., 2023)

Social skills

Effective communication, relationship building and team work are all components of social skills. Collaboration and teamwork are crucial in todays organisations particularly those that use AI and digital platforms. Employees with social skills are better able to organize work, settle dispute and foster a positive workplace. Strong social skills increase an employees chances of success in technology mediated and team based work environments(Miao et al., 2020). In general emotional intelligence is a strategic ability thet promotes both individual performance and organisational success rather than merely being a personal characterstics. EI becomes a crucial human capital resource in AI-enabled environmentsb where emotional and technical demands collide.

2.2 AI in IT Work Environments

In today's IT workplaces artificial intelligence has taken priority. Automation tools, machine learning algorithms, data analytics platforms and chatbots are examples of AI-enabled systems that are frequently used to increase productivity and make better decisions. These technologies enable businesses to lower operating costs and boost productivity by handling both simple and complicated tasks. Recent industry reports indicate that AI adoption in businesses has increased quickly, particularly in IT sectors where digital transformation is a top concern (McKinsey & Company,2023)

Human AI cooperation is one of the main characteristics of AI-driven work environments. For example customer support team might use chatbot to answer common questions while developers might use AI tools to help with coding. Employees roles shift from task execution to supervision, interpretation and strategic decision making as aresult of this collaboration (Brynjolfsson et al., 2025).

But incorporating AI also alters the nature of work in a number of ways. First, because workers must adjust to new tools and technologies there is a greater need for ongoing education. Second because automation may change traditional tasks it raises questions about job roles and responsibilities. Third because workers have to oversee both technical systems and interpersonal relationships their jobs become more complex. Employees must acquire emotional and cognitive skills in addition to technical ones as a result of these changes.

IT work environments have also been further altered by the emergence of remote and hybrid work models. For coordination and communication digital platforms like project management software, video conferencing tools and collaborative software have become indispensable. Although these tools offer flexibility the also present issues with coordination, employee engagement and clear communication (Deloitte, 2022). Because of this workers have to deal with both emotional and technological demands on a daily basis.

2.3 Emotional Demands in Digital work

Employee emotional demands have increased dramatically as aresult of the growing use of digital technologies and AI systems. Techno stress or stress brought on by using technology is one of the main issue. Constant connectivity, information overload and the need to quickly adjust to new systems are some of the factors that can lead to techno-stress. According to research, techno stress has a detrimental impact on workers performance and well being (Tarafdar et al., 2021).

Another important issue is cognitive overload. In digital work environments, employees often have to handle a lot of information, manage many tasks at the same time and make a quick decisions. The use of AI systems can make this even more difficult as employees also need to understand and check the results given by these systems. This constant mental pressure can make people feel tired and can lower their productivity over time(Wang et al., 2023).

Along with mental challenges, employees also face emotional pressure at work. Emotional labor means managing and controlling emotions as a part of the job and this has become more difficult in digital environments. But in digital settings employee have to manage their emotions through emails, message and video calls. This requires extra care in tone, language and expressions because it is harder to understand emotions without body language or facial cues (Derks et al., 2021).

Digital communication also puts pressure on employees to always be available and reply quickly. They regularly feel they must answer messages on time. They should stay professional and should meet the expectations of the clients all the time. Handling these emotions again and again is tiring. Especially when there is a heavy workload and constant performance tracking. After some time this can lead to emotional exhaustion (Yin et al., 2022).

In addition remote work reduces chances for casual social interaction and emotional support. In physical workplace employees can talk to colleagues share their experiences and reduce stress through informal conversations. But in digital work settings these opportunities are limited which makes it harder for employees to deal with emotional challenges. As a result stress can build up over time and affect both the employees well being and the overall performance of the organization.

3. OBJECTIVES

The prime objective of this chapter is to explore how Emotional Intelligence contributes to Sustainable employee performance within AI- enabled IT environments through secondary qualitative research.

1. Study Emotional Intelligence in the context of AI- powered organizational environments.
2. Examine how human resource is changing in contexts with AI.
3. Examine how EI promotes resistance and digital sustainability.

Conceptual Explanation

The growing use of Artificial Intelligence in organisations has changed the way employees experience and manage their work. By making Emotional Intelligence more important than ever. In AI based environments the employees not only deal with complex technologies but also face emotional challenges such as uncertainity, unclear roles and techno stress. Studies show that EI helps individuals to manage their emotions better, adjust to changes and maintain their performancein digital work environments (Carmeli Abraham, 2003; Joseph Ciarrochi et al., 2001). At the same time HRM is becoming more data driven and strategic AS AI tools are now used in hiring, performance evaluation and employee engagement. This shift requires HR professionals to balance the benefits of technology with human centerd approach to ensure effective organisational performance (Davenport et al., 2020; Meister, 2021).

Futhermore EI plays an important role in helping employees handle negative digital stress and support digital sustainability which means maintaining long term well being and performancein technology driven workplaces. Employees with either higher better able to manage emotional labor, reduce burnout and contribute to sustainable organisational performance (Alicia Grandey, 2000; Arnold Bakker & Demerouti, 2017). Based on this a conceptual framework can be developed where AI integration is seen as job demand EI acts as a personal resource and sustainable organisational performance is the outcome following the Job Demands–Resources model.

4. EMOTIONAL INTELLIGENCE IN AI-DRIVEN IT WORKPLACES

The use of Artificial Intelligence (AI) in IT workplaces has changed the way employees interact, make decision and complete their tasks. Earlier AI was mainly used for simple and routine work but also plays a role in decision-making, problem-solving and innovation but it has also brought emotional and mental challenges for employees. In this situation Emotional Intelligence (EI) becomes very important. It helps both employees and leaders handle the difficulties of AI-based work environments. EI support people in dealing with uncertaininty building trust in technology and working well with others in digital settings.

4.1 Managing Human-AI collaboration

One major changes in AI based workplace is that employes now work workn closely with AI systems. These systems give suggestions and help in different decision making process. This improves productivity it also creates some concerns about trust. Employees may not always sure if the AI results are correct and they may not always be sure if the AI results are correct and they may feel confused about their decision making role.

In such situations EI becomes very important in handling the human side of technology. Leaders with. Leaders those who have high EI can handle difficult situations, reduce stress and built trust among employees. This trust factor is very important because employee ned to feel confident while using AI. Research shows that people are more willing to use AI when they see it as a helpful tool not taking as a threat (Brynjolfsson et al., 2025). Leaders can support their employees this by clearly explaining why AI is used and how it helps the work instead of replacing the human resource. When AI is used as a support tool the people feel more confident. Clear and open communication also helps in building trust (Jarrahi, 2021).

EI also helps to improve team work among the staffs. Since most of the communication happens in message and virtual communication tools. It became tough to understand the emotions of employee. Leaders who listen and the emotions of employees create safe environment and the employee feel free to share.

The growing use of AI-powered tools such as chatbots and intelligent assistants has further strengthened human- AI collaboration in workplaces. These technologies improve efficiency but also require employees to develop trust and emotional adaptability while interacting with AI systems (Wahid & Awad, 2025)

Another very important issue is role clarity. When AI is introduced the employee may feel confused about their responsibilities. This can cause stress among the employees. Leaders with strong EI can solve this issue by clearly explaining roles and showing the importance of human skills.

4.2 Addressing Workforce Stress Anxiety and Techno stress

Th use of AI can create emotional challenges for employees. Which includes technological stress and anxiety. Techno stress means the stress people feel due to different use of digital tools. The stress are like when they use digital tools, like feeling overloaded, confused or under constant pressure to adopt.

Employees may fear that AI can replace their jobs and reduce their emotions. This fear can lower their motivation and may reduce job satisfaction. Research shows that technological stress negatively affects employee mental condition and performance. Especially in high pressure digital environments (Tarafdar et al., 2021).

EI helps in dealing with such challenges. Leaders with high EI can understand employees feeling and which tends they try to reduce the stress of employee. When Leaders explain why AI is used and the opportunities of AI the employee will feel informed and secure. Psychological safety is also important Employee should feel free to share wit their leaders. By asking question and making them mistakes without fear. This kind of environment helps them to leran and adopt easily. The study shows that psychological safety improves engagement and innovation (Wang et al., 2023).

Organisations should focus on reskilling and upskilling. As AI changes jobs employees need to learn new skills. Training helps build confidence and reduce fear. Leaders should encourage the employees for learning. And support them for accepting the changes. Taking care of employee well being is simultanjeously very important. Heavy workload and high pressure can make employees feel tired. Leaders can help employees by helping them and by promotiong worklife balance. By setting goals and supporting mental health. Studies shows that organisations that focus on well being have less burnout and bette productivity (Lesener et al., 2020).

EI also helps employees manage stress better way. People with high EI can controltheir emotions, handle challenges and stay positive. This makes them more adoptable and less likely to feel burnout in digital workplaces (Guleria et al., 2025).

4.3 Ethical Decision- Making in AI Governance

Ethical issues have grown in significance as AI systems participate more in organisational decision making. Although AI technologies have the potential to increase productivity and accuracy they can also lead to ethical problems like bias a lack of transparency and unforeseen consequenses. For instance preexisting biases in data may be reflected in algorithimic decision-making systems resulting in unfair outcomes in areas like hiring, performance reviews or customer interactions.

In this regard ethical decision making and responsible AI governance is greatly supported by emotional intelligence. Leaders with emotional intelligence are more conscious of how technological choices affect people. They are able to take into account the implications for society and ethics of AI systems in addition to how effective they are. To gurantee that AI is applied fairly and responsibly a more comprehensive viewpoint is crucial.

When making moral decisions empathy a crucial aspect of emotional intelligence is especially crucial. It enables leaders to comprehend the potential effects of AI-driven choices on various stakeholders such as workers, clients and society. Organisations can steer clear of decisions that could hurt people or groups by taking these viewpoints into account. According to the research developing trust and accountability in AI-systems requires ethical leadership backed by emotional intelligence (Floridi et al., 2020).

Emotionally intelligent leaders also encourage accountability and openness in AI governance. They guarantee that employees are aware of how AI systems work and that decision making procedures are transparent and intelligible. Transparency boosts confidence in technology by lowering uncertainity. Additionally it enables businesses to recognize and correct any biases or mistakes in AI systems.

Finding the right balance between automation and human judgement is very important. AI can handle large amount of data and give useful insights but it can't replace humans. Leaders with emotional intelligence understand the limits of AI and make sure people are involved in important decisions. Organisations should use clear policies and ethical guidelines for using AI. Leaders with emotional intelligence play a important role here by encouraging employees to be aware of ethical issues.

Overall combining ethical awareness with emotional intelligence is key to building responsible and human focused AI systems in modern organisations.

4.4 Emotional Intelligence in Hybrid and Remote Work

The growth of hybrid and remote work has made emotional intelligence more important. In online work people can not see mental condition and body language. So understanding emotions is very difficult. Employees have to depend on empathy and tone. Emotional intelligence helps them to stay connected and avoid unnecessary confusions. It also creates trust in virtual teams. It helps the leaders to manage teams working from different places. Studies shows that leaders with strong emotional Intelligence help teams work better together and feel less isolated in remote work. (Wang et al., 2023).

Flexible and hybrid work arrangements supported by digital technologies have also been found to influence employee engagement and performance. Research indicates that emotional and behavioural factors plays significant role in maintaining engagement in these type of environments (Ghonim et al., 2025).

Relationship Management

Relationship management means the ability to build good connection with others in an organisation. In AI based organisations teamwork in an organisation is very

very important because employees need to combine human skills with technology. Strong relationship skills help employees work better together. It helps the employees to understand each others expectations and create a supportive work environment.

These skills are specially important for leaders in the organisations as they neece to guide their teams. Through constant technological changes while keeping them motivated and engaged. When leaders manage relationships well it becomes easier for teams to adopt and stay focused.

These emotional intelligence skills help employees to handle the emotional challenges of working with AI. They support people in dealing with uncertainity staying healthy and performing their work effectively while contributing to organisational goals.

5. ANALYSIS AND DISCUSSION

The use of Artificial Intelligence (AI) in IT workplaces has changed job roles, work processes and employee experiences in many ways. While AI helps improve efficiency and supports decision-making. It also brings new mental and emotional challenges. This section explains how Emotional Intelligence(EI) helps employee adjust to AI-based work environments handle these new challenges and maintain long term performance. It also connects the research objectives with both theory and practical ideas from recent studies.

Emperical studies suggest that organisations integrating AI with human centered practices achieve better performance outcomes by balancing technological efficiency with employee well-being (Awad & Ghonim,2025)

5.1 Emotional Intelligence in AI work environment

AI enables workplaces require employees to continuously interact with intelligent systems, adopt to technological changes and manage evolving job expectations. These conditions regularly create stress and unceratinity making EI an essential capability.

Managing Stress from AI systems

AI systems can increase wor pressure by bringing constant performance monitoring, automated decision making and faster work speed. Employees may feel stressed because they need to understand AI results, meet high expectations and avoid mistakes. This pressure can becomes stronger when employees feel they have less control over automated systems.

EI helps employee handle this stress in abetter way. People with high EI can understand their emotions and manage them properly. Research shows that employees with strong emotional intelligence have lower stress and better job performance in technology based work environments (Miao et al., 2020).

A pratical example of this can be seen in leading IT companies such as Infosys and Tata Consultancy Services (TCS) which have actively integrated AI tools into their daily operations. These organisations not only focus on technological advancement but also invest in employee training and emotional well being programs. For instance employees are provided with continuous learning opportunities to adapt to AI systems along with initiatives that support mental health and stress management. This approach helps employees manage the emotional pressure associated with AI- driven work environments. It shows that emotional intelligence is not just a theoretical concept but a practical skill that helps employees remain productive, adoptable and mentally balanced in real world organisational settings.

Handling Uncertainity

AI driven workplaces are chracterised by constant change including evolving technologies shifting job roles and uncertainty about future employment. Employees may feel insecure about their skills or fear job displacement due to automation. This uncertainty can negatively affect motivation and engagement. EI plays a crucial role in helping employees cope with uncertainity. Emotionally intelligent individuals are more adaptable and open to change. They can manage negative emotions such as anxiety and fear. Studies indicate that emotional intelligence enhances adaptability band supports positive responses to organisational change(Guleria et al., 2025).

5.2 Emotional Challenges in AI Environments

While AI offers many benefits it also creates several emotional challenges that affect employee well-being and performance. These challenges include techno-stress and emotional fatigue.

Techno-stress

Techno-stress defined as the stress which is experiencd due to digital technology. In AI-driven environments employee should learn new technologies, digital communication and how to quickly respond to tasks.This can lead to information overload, pressure of time and fraustration. Research shows that the technical stress gives negative impact on employee performance and well being (Tarafdar et al., 2021).Employees may feel overwhelmed by the complexitity of AI systems and the need to continuously update their skills. Without support from the organisation this leads to redeuce job satisfaction.

Emotional Fatigue

AI system can increase work pressure by bringing constant performance monitoring, automated decision making and faster work speed. Employees may feel stressed because they have to understand AI results, meet high expectations and avoid mistakes. This pressure can become stronger when employees feel they have less control over automated systems.

Emotional Intelligence(EI) helps employees handle this stress in a better way. People with high EI can understand their emotions and mange them properly. Research shows that employees with strong emotional intelligence have lower stress and better job performance in technology-based work environment (Miao et al., 2020).

Constant Monitoring

AI systems often use tools to track employee performance such as measuring productivity, response time and communication patterns. These tools are meant to improveefficiency but they can also increase pressure on employees.

When employees feel constantly monitores they may feel like they are always being watched. This can lead to stress and make them more self- conscious about their work. The may feel the need to perform all the time which can reduce their sense of freedom and increase emotional pressure. Research shows that too much monitoring can harm employee well being and increase stress levels (Wang et al., 2023).

5.3 Role of Emotional Intelligence in Managing These challenges

Emotional intelligence provides the tool needed to manage the challenges associated with AI-driven work environments. Each component of EI plays a specific role in addressing emotional and cognitive demands.

Self-Awareness: Recognizing Overload

Self-awareness enables employees to identify signs of stress, fatigue and emotional strain. Self-aware employees can take proactive steps to manage their workload, seek support or take breaks when needed. This prevents stress from escalating into burnout. Research shows that self-awareness is linked to better stress management and improved performance (Miao et al., 2020).

Self- Regulation: Staying Calm and Focused

Self-regulation helps employees control their emotions and stay calm in difficult situations. In AI-based workplaces employee regulary face deadlines and high expectations. Self-regulation helps them deal with these type of situations. This skill is very important in digital communication where emotions need to be handled very carefully. Employees who can control their emotions are less likely to feel burnout and more likely to stay positive (Lesener et al., 2020).

Empathy: Enhancing Teamwork

Empathy helps employees understand the feelings of others and respond in a caring way. In virtual and AI-based work environments where faceto face interaction is limited empathy becomes very important for good communication. Employees show empathy can build better relationships with their team member. This improves teamwork and creates a positive environment. Research shows that empathy improves collaboration and increase employee engagement in remote work settings (Wang et al., 2023).

Social skills: Supporting Collaboration

Social skills include clear communication, conflict solve and building good relationships. In AI based workplaces employee need to work with both people and technology. Strong social skills help them coordinate task, share information and work well in teams. Employee with good social skills can use digital communication tools effectively and maintain strong working relationship. This helps to improve overall organisational success. (Guleria et al., 2025).

5.4 Emotional Intelligence and Sustainable Performance

Emotional Intelligence is not only helps the employee to handle challenges but also supports long term performance in AI -based work . Sustainable means the ability to keep productivity, well being and engagement steady over time.

Adaptability

Adaptability means the ability to adjust to changes and learn new skills. In AI-enabled environment where technology changes quickly, adaptability becomes very important. EI helps employees deal with feelings related to change and uncertainity making it easier from them to adjust. Employees with high EI are more open to learning new things and trying innovative ideas. They can adapt to new systems and ways of working more easily which helps them improve their performance over time (Brynjolfsson et al., 2025).

Similarly many global IT firms have adopted hybrid work models supported by AI tools while also focusing on employee engagement and well-being. For example Companies implementing AI-based performance tracking systems also ensure that employees receive emotional support through flexible work policies, counselling services and supportive leadership.

Resilience

Resilience means the ability to recover from stress and difficult situation. In AI based workplaces there is high pressure. Resilience is very important for success. EI helps to build resilience by improving how employees manage their emotions and deal with challenges. Employees with high EI can handle, stay motivated a perform good.

Research shows that rellilience is closely connected to emotional intelligence and employee well being (Lesener et al., 2020).

6. PRACTICAL IMPLICATIONS

The high use of AI in IT workplaces has created both benefits and challenges for organisations. While AI improves efficiency and encourages innovation it also adds mental and emotional pressure on employees. The findings of this chapter show that EI is an important resource for handling these challenges and supporting these long term employee performance.

6.1 HR Implications

Human resource functions have a vital in bringing Emotional Intelligence into the organisations. One important role in bringing EI into the organisation. One key step is to design and provide EI training programs. These programs should help employee to improve self-awareness, emotional control, empathy and communication skills. In AI based workplaces employee not only handle technical tasks but also deal with stress, uncertainity and digital communication . EI training can help them manage these challenges and improve their performance. Research shows that developing EI is linked to bettr job performance, lower stress and enhance employee engagement (Miao et al., 2020; Guleria et al., 2025).

Another important step is to include EI in recruitment and selectiom. Traditionally hiring mainly focuses on technical skill but in AI-based workplaces emotional skills are very important. Orgnisations should evaluate candidates EI through methods like behavioural interviews, psychometric tests sand situational judgement tests. Hiring those people who have strong EI can improve team work, adaptability and resilience which are important in digital work environments.

HR should also include EI in performance management systems. Employee evaluations should not focus only on technical work but also on emotional and sociamskils like communication, team wor and encourage employees to develop these skills. In addition to this HR policies should support continuous learning and development so that employees can adjust to new technologies.

Use of Emotional Intelligence Assessment Tools

In addition, organisations can use standardized emotional intelligence assessment tools to evaluate and develop employees' emotional competencies. Commonly used tools include the Emotional Competence Inventory (ECI) which measures emotional and social skills in workplace contexts and the Mayer-Salovey- Caruso Emotional Intelligence Test (MSCEIT) which access the ability to perceive, understand and manage emotion. These tools can be used during recruitment, training and performance evaluation to ensure that employees possess the emotional capabilities required in AI-driven work environments. The use of such structured assessment methods helps organisations make more informed decisions and align human capital strategies with technological advancements.

6.2 Leadership Implication

Employees' experience in AI-based workplaces depend a lot on leadership. Leaders with strong Emotional Intelligence can handle the shift to digital work.

Another important role of leaders is to support employee well-being. AI-based workplaces creates stress because of constant connectivity, performance monitoring and rapid changes. Leaders should encourage work-life balance, allow breaks and set realistic expectations. Research shows that supportive leadership reduces stress and improves employee engagement in remote work settings (Wang et al., 2023).

The use of AI can create fear and uncertainty among employees. Leaders with high EI can handle this by clearly explaining changes, involving employees in decisions and showing the benefits of AI. This makes employees feel included. This may lead to a good leadership

6.3 Policy Implications

Beyond what organisations do policy makers and regulators also have an important role. As AI becomes very common there should be rules for AI-based workplaces. These rules should focus on Employee well being, data privacy and using technology in the right way. One important point is controlling workplace monitoring and survelliance. While tracking performance can improve efficiency but too much monitoring can create stress. Policies should make sure that monitoring is transparent.

Another important point is promoting ethical use of AI. AI systems should be designed and used in a fair, clear and responsible way. Policy makers should encourage organisations to follow ethical guidelines that consider the impact of AI on both employee and society. Research shows that strong eyhical guidelines that consider the impact of AI on both employee and society. Research shows that strong ethical governance is important for responsible AI use (Floridi et al., 2020).

Policies should also support employees' well-being in digital work environments. This can include rules about working hours, the right to disconnect from work and access to mental health support.

6.4 Organisation Strategies

At the organisation level companies need to create work environment that supports employees and reduces the stress caused by digital work. One way to do this is by introducing different well being policies. These can include mental health support, counselling services, flexible working hours and helping employees to maintain a healthy work life balance. Companies should also try to reduce techno-stress by making digital tools easy to use.

Another important step is to set clear cut communication rules. This helps employees avoid the pressure of always being available and gives them time to relax. At the same time organisations should create a safe and supportive environment where employees feel free to share their ideas and concerns. This kind of culture improves teamwork. It is especially important in AI-based workplaces where employees are constantly adjusting different new tools and different way of working.

Organisations should include EI in their overall strategy and connect it with their business goals. Thi scan be done by including EI in leadership training and team management in workplace. By doing this companies create a more supportive and sustainable work environment for the employees of the organisation.

7. CONCEPTUAL FRAMEWORK

This chapter proposes a conceptual framework to explain the relationship between AI-driven work environments, emotional intelligence and employee outcomes. In AI-enabled IT workplaces Factors such as automation,continuous monitoring,digital communication and human AI interaction create emotional demands including technostress, uncertainity and emotional fatigue.

Emotional intelligence acts as a ke mediating capability that enables employees to manage these emotional and cognitive challenges effectively. Employees with higher levels of emotional intelligence are better able to regulate their emotions, adapt to technological changes and maintain positive workplace relationships.

As a result emotional intelligence leads to improved adaptability, resilience, employee well being and ultimately sustainable employee performance. This framework highlights the importance of integrating emotional capabilities with technological advancements to ensure long term organisational success in AI-driven environments.

Explanation of the framework

The framework shows that AI- driven work conditions act as independent variables that increase emotional and psychological demands on employees. Emotional Intelligence functions as a mediating variable that helps in managing these pressure. The outcome variables include adoptability, resilience, well being and and sustainable performance.

This relationship emphasizes that while AI introduces efficiency and innovation, emotional intelligence ensures that employees can effectively cope with these changes and maintain long-term productivity.

AI Work Environment

Emotional Demands

Emotional Intelligence

Employee Outcome

8. LIMITATIONS & FUTURE RESEARCH

While this chapter provides a comprehensive conceptual understanding of EI in AI-driven IT workplaces several limitations must be acknowledged.

8.1 Limitations

One primary limitation of this chapter is that it depends on secondary data. The analysis is based on existing studies, journal articleaa and official reports. This approach helps in building building a strong theoretical underastanding of EI,AI and digital work environments. However the findings are based on interpretation and are not tested in a specific organisation. Although secondary dat a provides useful insights it may not fully show the real and changing experiences of employee working in AI-based environments. Because of this the findings may not apply to all organisations.

Another limitation is that the proposed framework has not been tested with real dat . The chapter explains the relationship between AI based work conditions, Emotional intelligence and ling term employee outcome but these relationships have not been statistically tested. For which it is difficult to know how strong or accurate these relatinships are.

The role of EI and digital work can be different across cultures. This chapter uses general global studies and does not focus on any specific cultural setting. However cultural factors like communication style level of hierarchy and how people express emotions can affect how employees experience and mange emotions in AI- based workplaces.

AI technology is changing very quickly and continues to reshape work environments. New tools like generative AI advanced analytics and automation systems are developing all the time. Because of this the ieas in this chapter ma become outdated as technology and workplace practices keep evolving.

The fast pace of change makes it difficult to crate stable theories. As new technologies are introduced emotional demands work patterns and employee experiences may also change. This shows the need for continuous research that can keep up with these technological developments.

8.2 Future Research Directions

Empirical Studies

Future studies should concentrate on applying actual data to test the concepts discussed in this chapter. Surveys can be used in quantitative research for evaluating employee performance, emotional intelligence, technological stress and well being. To fully understand how EI functions as a link in AI-based work environments. Techniques like structural equation modelling(SEM) can be applied . A deeper and more broad understanding of the subject can be obtained by combining bothb qualitative and quantitative method

Cross-cultural Research

As there are different cultural limitations the future research should study how EI works in different cultural settings. Different studies by comparing different countries or geographical regions can help to understand how employee express emotions.

Longitudinal and Dynamic Research

The future research may adopt the longitudinal designs to test the emotional experiences and the performance outcome over time. This type of studies can capture the long term effects of techno stress, emotional fatigue and EI on employee well being and productivity.

9. CONCLUSION

The rapid growth of AI has changed the way work is done especially in IT and knowledge-based sectors. Most discussions focus on technology, efficiency and automation but this chapter highlights an important aspect that is often ignored the emotional experience of employees. As organisations use more AI it becomes clear that technology alone cannot ensure long-term success. Employees' ability to understand and mange their emotions plays a key role in shaping performance and overall organisational success. EI helps employees deals with challenges like stress, uncertainty, constant monitoring and reduced human interaction in AI- based workplaces.

This chapter shows that Emotional Intelligence is not just a personal skill but an important organisational resource. Employees working in AI environments need to manage their emotions while staying productive and collaborative. EI helps them to stay adaptable, resilient and enagaged even in fast changing digital settings.

In todays fast changing AI environment managing emotions and relationships has become more important than ever. Employees who can understand and handle their emotions are better prepared to deal with work pressure and constant change. Strong relationships skills also improve team work and create a more positive work environment in the organisation.

This chapter highlights that need to balance between AI capabilities with human qualities. AI can not replace human emotions. Emotional Intelligence adds this human value to the workplace. At the same time organisations, leaders an dpolicies must support employees by creating healthy and supportive work environment. In the future as AI continues to grow workplaces will need to focus not only on technology but also on human wellbeing. Overall this chapter shows that success in the digital age depends not only on technical skills but also on the ability to manage emotions, build relationships and sustain well-being over time.

REFERENCES

Awad, A. (2024). Artificial intelligence and marketing innovation: The mediating role of organizational culture. *Innovative Marketing*, *20*(3), 170–181. DOI: 10.21511/im.20(3).2024.14

Awad, A., & Ghonim, A. (2025). Data-driven marketing in banks: The role of artificial intelligence in enhancing marketing efficiency and business performance. *International Review of Management and Marketing*, *15*(5), 422–431. DOI: 10.32479/irmm.19738

Bakker, A. B., & Demerouti, E. (2017). Job demands–resources theory: Taking stock and looking forward. *Journal of Occupational Health Psychology, 22*(3), 273–285. DOI: 10.1037/ocp0000056

Bakker, A. B., & Demerouti, E. (2017). Job demands–resources theory: Taking stock and looking forward. *Journal of Occupational Health Psychology, 22*(3), 273–285. DOI: 10.1037/ocp0000056

Brynjolfsson, E., Li, D., & Raymond, L. (2025). Generative AI at work. *The Quarterly Journal of Economics, 140*(2), 889–942. DOI: 10.1093/qje/qjad020

Carmeli, A. (2003). The relationship between emotional intelligence and work attitudes, behavior and outcomes. *Journal of Managerial Psychology, 18*(8), 788–813. DOI: 10.1108/02683940310511881

Ciarrochi, J., Chan, A. Y. C., & Caputi, P. (2001). A critical evaluation of the emotional intelligence construct. *Personality and Individual Differences, 28*(3), 539–561. DOI: 10.1016/S0191-8869(99)00119-1

Davenport, T. H., Guha, A., Grewal, D., & Bressgott, T. (2020). How artificial intelligence will change the future of marketing. *Journal of the Academy of Marketing Science, 48*(1), 24–42. DOI: 10.1007/s11747-019-00696-0

Deloitte. (2022). *Global Human Capital Trends Report.*

Derks, D., Bakker, A. B., & Peters, P. (2021). Work-related use of digital communication technologies and emotional demands. *Computers in Human Behavior, 122*, 106817. DOI: 10.1016/j.chb.2021.106817

Floridi, L., Cowls, J., Beltrametti, M., Chatila, R., Chazerand, P., Dignum, V., et al. (2020). AI4People—An ethical framework for a good AI society. *Minds and Machines, 30*(4), 689–707. DOI: 10.1007/s11023-020-09530-0

Ghonim, A., Awad, A., Shemais, M., Shma, T., & Aziz, A. (2025). Exploring the impact of flexible work arrangements on employee engagement in telecommunications: Case of Egypt. *Problems and Perspectives in Management, 23*(2), 198–207. DOI: 10.21511/ppm.23(2).2025.13

Goleman, D. (1995). *Emotional intelligence: Why it can matter more than IQ.* Bantam Books.

Grandey, A. A. (2000). Emotion regulation in the workplace: A new way to conceptualize emotional labor. *Journal of Occupational Health Psychology, 5*(1), 95–110. DOI: 10.1037/1076-8998.5.1.95

Guleria, N., Sajabul, M., Sharma, N., Yadav, T., & Semwal, R. (2025). The role of emotional intelligence in enhancing employee performance and job satisfaction in hybrid workplaces. *. *International Journal of Environmental Sciences.*

. Jarrahi, M. H. (2021). Artificial intelligence and the future of work: Human–AI symbiosis in organizational decision making. *Business Horizons, 64*(1), 87–99. DOI: 10.1016/j.bushor.2020.09.003

Lesener, T., Gusy, B., & Wolter, C. (2020). The job demands–resources model: A meta-analytic review. *Journal of Occupational Health Psychology, 25*(4), 261–277. DOI: 10.1037/ocp0000162

Mattingly, V., & Kraiger, K. (2019). Can emotional intelligence be trained? A meta-analytical investigation. *Human Resource Management Review, 29*(2), 140–155. DOI: 10.1016/j.hrmr.2018.03.002

Mayer, J. D., & Salovey, P. (1997). What is emotional intelligence? In Salovey, P., & Sluyter, D. J. (Eds.), *Emotional development and emotional intelligence: Educational implications** (pp. 3–31). Basic Books.

McKinsey & Company. (2023).The state of AI in organizations. https://www.mckinsey.com

McKinsey & Company. (2025). *Superagency in the workplace: Empowering people to unlock AI's full potential.* https://www.mckinsey.com/

Meister, J. (2021). The future of work: How AI is transforming HR. *Harvard Business Review*. https://hbr.org

Miao, C., Humphrey, R. H., & Qian, S. (2020). Emotional intelligence and job performance: A meta-analysis. *Human Performance, 33*(2), 1–24. DOI: 10.1080/08959285.2019.1683374

Miao, C., Humphrey, R. H., & Qian, S. (2020). Emotional intelligence and job performance: A meta-analysis. *Human Performance, 33*(2), 1–24. DOI: 10.1080/08959285.2019.1683374

Qadeer, A., & Awad, A. (2025). Generative AI in advertisements: A conceptual framework based on the technology acceptance model. In Wahid, A., & Awad, A. (Eds.), *Impacts of AI generated content on brand reputation* (pp. 109–127). IGI Global., DOI: 10.4018/979-8-3373-4327-3.ch004

Shams Eldin, A. Y., Elnour, A., Omer Ahmed Hassan, R., & Awad, A. (2025). The role of technological and environmental factors in creating business value from social media dynamic capabilities for SMEs in Saudi Arabia. *Humanities & Social Sciences Communications, 12*(1), 1431. DOI: 10.1057/s41599-025-05784-x

Tarafdar, M., Pullins, E. B., & Ragu-Nathan, T. S. (2021). Technostress: Negative effect on performance and well-being. *Journal of Information Systems, 35*(1), 1–24. DOI: 10.1080/0960085X.2020.1868891

The Economic Times. (2024). *AI adoption in Indian IT sector and its impact on jobs and productivity*

Wahid, A., & Awad, A. (2025). Role of AI chatbots in enhancing customer satisfaction and customer loyalty. In Wahid, A., & Awad, A. (Eds.), *Impacts of AI generated content on brand reputation* (pp. 129–147). IGI Global., DOI: 10.4018/979-8-3373-4327-3.ch005

Wang, B., Liu, Y., Qian, J., & Parker, S. K. (2023). Achieving effective remote working during COVID-19: A work design perspective. Applied Psychology, 72*(1), 16–59. DOI: 10.1111/apps.12391

Yin, H., Huang, S., & Chen, G. (2022). Emotional labor and emotional exhaustion: A meta-analysis across occupations. *Frontiers in Psychology, 13*, 845678. DOI: 10.3389/fpsyg.2022.845678

Chapter 14

Work, Talent, and Trust in the Era of Generative AI:
A Human-Centered Sustainability Perspective

Valisher Sapayev
http://orcid.org/0000-0002-6751-5864
Mamun University, Khiva, Uzbekistan

Aarthi Selvakumar
http://orcid.org/0009-0006-9064-2091
Marwadi University, Rajkot, India

Ravikumar Natarajan
http://orcid.org/0009-0009-3705-1681
Marwadi University, Rajkot, India

Xolmirzayev Furqatbek Muxtarjonovich
Alfraganus University, Tashkent, Uzbekistan

Sadirdin Khudoykulov
Termez University of Economics and Service, Termez, Uzbekistan

Davronov Shaxbos
Bukhara State Medical Institute, Bukhara, Uzbekistan

ABSTRACT

Generative AI is changing the way organizations organize work, administer talent and build trust. The chapter explores the concept of the transformation of the workforce by AI in the context of human-led sustainability that unites the ideas of work, talent, and trust into one conceptual framework. Based on the current case evidence, it presents the impact of transparency, governance, and orderly human-AI cooperation on employee agency, equity, and resilience in the long term. The chapter maintains

DOI: 10.4018/979-8-2600-2726-4.ch014

that the adoption of AI should be sustainable and therefore balance between automation and augmentation should be maintained in addition to establishing ethical principles and accountability in organizational systems.

1. INTRODUCTION

The recent accelerated progress of Generative Artificial Intelligence (AI) is essentially transforming the modern organizational systems especially in the manner in which work is structured, talent is handled and the work relationship between human beings and intelligent technologies. In contrast to the previous automation tools, which mostly substituted routine work, generative AI systems are clearly involved in decision-making, knowledge generation, and problem-solving in the work of various functions of the organization. This change has far reached consequences on the workforce structure, position of employees and sustainability of human capital development. As organizations continue to use generative AI to drive efficiency, personalization, and innovation, it is also causing complex ethical, social, and governance issues when it is implemented. The challenge of transparency, accountability, fairness, and employee autonomy are also emerging as a focus of concern in the digitally mediated workplaces (Gama Espinosa et al., 2024). It is under this context that humanistic approach to sustainability plays a crucial role in comprehending how AI-based transformation can be incorporated into long-term organizational resilience and social responsibility. This chapter introduces trust as a pillar in the sustainable human-AI partnership and presents a thesis that the responsible adoption of generative AI is possible only with the balance of technology potentials and human values, dignity, and meaningful work.

1.1 Generative AI and the Changing Nature of Work

Generative AI is transforming the nature of work by changing the way in which work is done, decisions made and value generated in organizations. In contrast to the conventional rule-based systems, generative AI models have the ability to generate novel content, identify more complicated patterns, and facilitate activities that are cognitive in nature, like planning strategies, designing creative work, and diagnosing problems. Consequently, there is an increasing tendency to describe work roles as human-AI partnership, and not a direct replacement of tasks. The employees would have to acquire new skills connected with AI literacy, critical thinking, and management of the algorithmic results (Prabagar et al., 2025). At the same time, the lines between human knowledge and machine intelligence are appearing more indistinct, and the issue of responsibility, control, and accountability is brought up.

These changes hinder the traditional job design and performance assessment systems since AI systems can shape the performance of the results that were previously only associated with human effort. The ability to restructure work processes with the help of generative AI can thus be critical in ensuring that future employment models that maintain human agency are developed, and technological augmentation is utilized.

1.2 Human-Centered Sustainability Imperative

The growing involvement of generative AI in the organization practices also requires the transition to a humanistic paradigm of sustainability. Human-based sustainability prioritizes the safety of employee health, dignity, inclusion and long-term employability as well as the organizational performance objectives. This outlook is especially applicable in AI-based workplaces, where the algorithmic systems shape the decisions related to hiring and performance appraisal, as well as learning opportunities (Shaheen et al., 2025). Unless carefully designed to be human-friendly, these systems could tend to increase bias, lower transparency, and trust among the workers. The sustainability-focused strategy dictates that the organizations must incorporate the ethical values, participatory governance, and ongoing stakeholder involvement into the AI practices plans (Milad et al., 2024). This also involves making AI decisions explainable, protecting the privacy of data, and having meaningful human control. With the focus on human-centered sustainability, organizations will be able to synchronize technological innovation and social responsibility so that generative AI would help not only improve efficiency but also create a long-term resilient, inclusive, and equitable work environment.

1.3 Scope and Structure of the Chapter

This chapter evaluates the nexus of the generative AI, work transformation, talent management, and trust through the lens of human-centered sustainability. It seeks to offer a cohesive insight into the way AI-centered systems can transform the way organizations operate and how they are affecting how employees perceive equity, agency, and belonging. The chapter integrates the knowledge on the human resource management, organizational behavior, ethics, information systems and sustainability studies to create a multidimensional analytical model. This introduction is followed by the chapter discussing the background and the theoretical background of the field of generative AI and digital sustainability. It then gives the research objectives, conceptual model, and methodological approach used in the research. The targeted literature review and the current case studies demonstrate the practical implications and market differences. At the end of the chapter, the author discusses the results, managerial implications, directions of future research, and key terms helping researchers, practitioners, and policymakers to navigate the transformation of the workforce to be AI-enabled.

2. BACKGROUND TO THE STUDY

This study can be traced back to the context of the rapid adoption of generative AI technologies in the field of organizations, as well as the increased focus on sustainable digital transformation. The use of AI-based systems to manage multifaceted human capital processes (such as recruitment, performance assessment, and workforce planning) is becoming increasingly popular among organizations. Although these technologies will help to achieve better efficiency and data-driven decision-making, other threats associated with trust, ethical, and social sustainability emerge. Current literature points to the absence of an interface between technological advancement and institutional structures needed to regulate AI in a responsible manner (Belghachi, 2023). The use of AI, in most instances, has been more advanced than the creation of regulatory laws, organizational policies, and the preparedness of employees. Such discrepancy has added to fears of transparency, feeling out of control, and mistrust in algorithms. The conceptualization of the necessity of human-centered approaches to AI-enabled workforce management should be explained through the understanding of the historical development of the concept of generative AI, its impact on the sustainability of digital environments, and the emergence of new issues of trust.

2.1 Evolution of Generative AI in Organizations

The development of generative AI in companies also indicates a change in technologies that are oriented to automation to systems that can perform creative and cognitive augmentation. Original applications of AI in organizations have been mainly restricted to rule-based automation and predictive analytics in an attempt to maximize efficiency. The recent progress in large language models and generative systems have now extended the capabilities of the AI to a content-generative, decision-support, and strategically knowledge-generating systems. These functions have increased the speed of adoption in the human resource, marketing, and operations functions (Kulkarni et al., 2024). Nevertheless, generative AI has been deployed quickly, and this has not been accompanied by an adjustment of organizational structures and mechanisms of governance, as well as employee skill development. Accountability, transparency, and ethical responsibility issues have been raised due to an increase in the use of AI systems in high-stakes decision-making. The further development of generative AI, therefore, is not only a technological evolution but an organizational change, which requires the emergence of new leadership and oversight frameworks, as well as new models of human-AI interaction. Table 1 Overviews the major milestones in the history of generative AI and their consequences to work and talent systems.

Table 1. Evolution of Generative AI in Organizational Contexts

Phase	AI Focus	Key Characteristics	Implications for Work
Early AI	Rule-based automation	Predefined logic, repetitive tasks	Task substitution
Predictive AI	Data-driven analytics	Forecasting and optimization	Efficiency-oriented roles
Generative AI	Content and knowledge generation	Context-aware, adaptive outputs	Human–AI collaboration
Agentic AI	Autonomous task execution	Workflow orchestration	Redefined roles and accountability

2.2 Digital Sustainability and Human Capital

Digital sustainability is not confined to environmental performance but covers the long-term social and organizational consequences of the digital technologies on the human capital. Digital sustainability in the generative AI context means that workforce change is used to facilitate continuing learning, equal opportunity, and employee welfare. The AI-powered systems can be used to improve talent building by enhancing individual learning, predicting abilities, and responsive career trajectories. Simultaneously, they can lead to job polarization, skill obsolescence, and exclusion in case they are not introduced responsibly. To be sustainable in human capital, there is a need to match AI implementation and inclusive workforce policies, reskilling, and ethical data management (Chang & Ke, 2024). The companies should pay attention to the impact of algorithmic decision-making on motivation, confidence, and fairness perceptions of the employees. Through the implementation of the core digital sustainability concept in human capital management, companies can remove the negative externalities, and utilize the abilities of generative AI to empower resilient and adaptable workforces in the future.

2.3 Trust Deficits in AI-Enabled Workplaces

Lack of trust has become a crucial issue in AI-filled workplaces, especially as generative AI models are integrated into some of the most fundamental human resource processes. The algorithmic decisions made by employers are seen by employees as mysterious, prejudiced, and not grounded in context, which makes them distrustful and unwilling to follow them. Insufficient transparency and explainability of the processes supported by AI may negatively affect the sense of procedural justice and minimize a sense of psychological safety. Also, the issue of surveillance, data misappropriation, and reduced human regulation adds to the depleting of trust (Kumar, 2024). The belief in AI-based workplaces is not the attribute of the technological accuracy exclusively but it is influenced by the leadership behavior, organizational culture, and governance practices. The problem of trust deficits can be resolved by implementing participatory strategies, effective communication strategies, and strong accountability systems within organizations. Trust is necessary to make employees accept AI systems and to make sure that the generative AI can bring sustainable and ethical workforce change.

3. RESEARCH OBJECTIVES

The purpose of this chapter is to analytically explore the effects of generative AI on the organization in terms of the sustainability of work systems, talent management practices, and the relationship of trust between people in an analytical manner. As more and more AI-based systems are integrated into the core human capital processes, there is a necessity to shift away from the efficiency-based discourse and determine more extensive organization, ethical, and sustainability impacts. The research questions are framed in a way that they can encompass the multidimensional impacts of generative AI on work change, employee experience, and value generation over the long term and focus on trust as a key mediating variable in sustainable AI adoption. The following are the key research goals of this chapter:

- To examine the impact of generative AI on the transformation of work design, task allocation, and human-AI collaboration within contemporary organizations.
- To analyze how generative AI influences talent management processes, including recruitment, performance evaluation, learning, and workforce planning.
- To explore the role of trust, transparency, and perceived fairness in shaping employee acceptance of AI-driven organizational practices.
- To assess the implications of AI-enabled decision-making on employee agency, inclusion, and psychological safety in digitally mediated workplaces.
- To link generative AI adoption with sustainable value creation by integrating human capital development, ethical governance, and long-term organizational resilience.

4. CONCEPTUAL MODEL

The theoretical framework that is offered in this chapter combines the aspects of work transformation, managing talent, and trust as mutually dependent parameters in AI-driven organizations in the framework of the human-centered sustainability perspective. Instead of considering generative AI as a technological intervention in its own right, the model places generative AI as an integrated socio-technical system which transforms organizational processes, employee experience, and governance structures all at once. The central feature of the model is that the interaction between the evolving work practices, the system of algorithmic mediated talent, and the multidimensional relationships of trust take dynamic paths. The concept of trust is understood not only in the sense of confidence in the precision of technology but a result of transparency, leadership practice, corporate culture and governance processes (Borg et al., 2025). The model also includes human-AI collaboration schemes defining the distribution of responsibilities, decision making authority and accountability between human participants and intelligent systems. The structural underpinning has been offered by the sustainability and governance aspects, making sure that AI implementation is adjusted to ethical considerations, more long-term human capital development, and general environmental, social, and governance concerns (Saad et al., 2025). This integrative framework facilitates the analytical system of how generative AI can allow the creation of values in the future without the destruction of human agency or organizational legitimacy. Figure 1 demonstrates that the work transformation, talent management, trust, human-AI collaboration, sustainability, and governance influence each other in AI-enabled organizations to help develop ethical, transparent, and sustainable human capital.

Figure 1. Human-Centered Conceptual Model of AI-Enabled Organizations

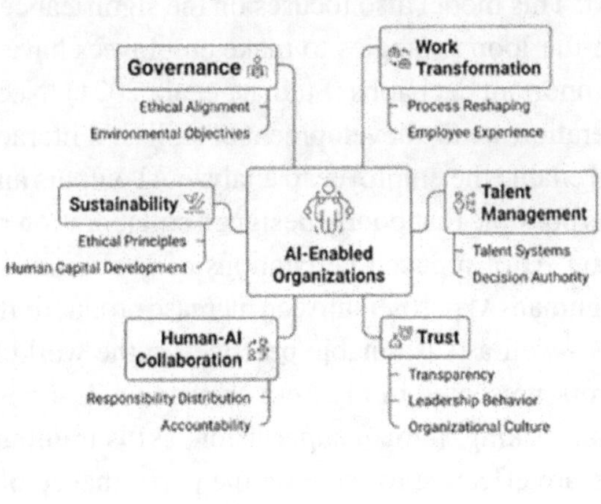

4.1 Work–Talent–Trust Interdependencies

The conceptual model proposed is based on interdependencies between work, talent and trust, which are critical. Generative AI has an impact on work as it can transform the structure of tasks, decision making processes, and performance expectations, which subsequently alters it in terms of the identification, development, and assessment of talent. With the increased involvement of AI systems in the hiring process, in the assessment processes, and in the performance management, the perception of fairness, autonomy, and recognition among employees grows to be associated with algorithm processes. The factor of trust turns out to be a mediator that will either lead to the perception of these AI-driven changes as either supportive or intrusive (Nyathani, 2023). Mistrust may also cause resistance, lack of engagement, and diminished acceptance of AI-enabled practices despite effectiveness benefits being apparent. On the other hand, open and responsible use of AI will build trust and increase engagement of employees. The model emphasizes the fact work redesign, talent management and trust cannot be independently dealt with where any fluctuation in one aspect directly affects the stability and sustainability of the other two aspects.

4.2 Human–AI Collaboration Mechanisms

Human-AI collaboration mechanisms establish the role played by generative AI systems and human actors in organizational performance. In the conceptual model, a continuum of collaboration is considered between AI-based decision support and joint decision-making and human control over the performance of algorithms. To successfully work together, it is essential to have the roles, limits, and accountability frameworks, which maintain the human judgment and use the analytical and generative powers of AI. This model also focuses on the significance of human-in-the-loop and human-on-the-loop strategies to make employees have some meaningful control in making important decisions (Stamate et al., 2021). Necessary conditions of productive cooperation are the development of skills, AI literacy, and continuous learning, which will enable the employee to analyze AI outputs and not accept them unconditionally. It is possible that poorly designed collaboration mechanisms cause too much reliance on AI or reduced perceptions of human input. In comparison, properly organized human-AI partnership can increase productivity, innovativeness, and empowerment as well as sustainable practices in the workplace (Awad et al., 2025). The framework presented in Figure 2 shows that AI-assisted decision support, shared decision-making, human supervision, skills training, AI literacy, and continuous learning are effective to increase the performance of organizations by organized human-AI interaction.

Figure 2. Human–AI Collaboration Mechanisms: Driving Organizational Outcomes

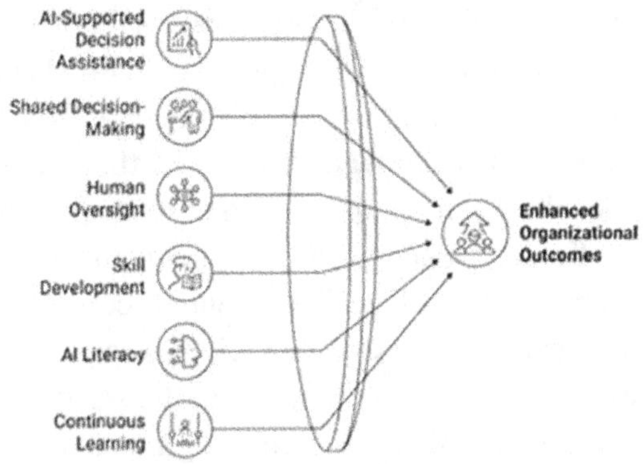

4.3 Sustainability and Governance Dimensions

The conceptual model is anchored on sustainability and governance dimensions that offer a normative and institutional structure. In sustainability terms, the adoption of generative AI should help in developing human capital in the long-run, social inclusion, and responsible innovation as opposed to efficiency in the short-term. Ethical codes, regulatory adherence, data custodianship, and transparency policies are some of the governance mechanisms that are important in the creation of a trustful AI usage. The model emphasizes the necessity of participative forms of governance where employees, managers, and external stakeholders are included in making decisions that are related to AI (Wang et al., 2023). Well-defined accountability practices can also be used to resolve the issues of bias, privacy, and misuse of AI systems. As well, the fact that AI-powered workforce transformation is aligned with environmental, social, and governance objectives will help to ensure that the large societal objectives are also addressed. The model shows how organizations can institutionalize trust and legitimacy and negotiate their way through the complexities of generative AI-driven change, through consideration of sustainability and governance.

5. RESEARCH METHODOLOGY

The chapter uses a systematic research to look at the convergence of generative AI, work transformation, talent management and trust in organizations through a human-centered sustainability lens. It is acknowledged that AI-enabled workforce change is a complex phenomenon that demands a systematic approach to methodology to develop an understanding of the organizational practices and perceptions of the employees. The methodology will combine both the theoretical background with empirical insight to provide the complete picture of the impact of generative AI on the work systems and human capital outcomes. Methodological rigor, transparency, and ethical responsibility are laid stress on to make the findings relevant and to provide credibility (Singh & Pandey, 2023). The methodology helps to analyse the interdependencies between work design, talent processes and trust mechanism and accommodate contextual diversity in various organizational settings. The methodology enables a strong interpretation of findings and contribution to scholarship and practice by ensuring that research design, data collection and analysis are consistent with the study aims and objectives. The research process is ethical and validity considerate because it attempts to capture the involved in AI-driven decision-making and employee data.

5.1 Research Design and Approach

The study design is structured and integrative as befits investigating complex phenomena that have socio-technical aspects. Mixed method orientation is followed in order to present both structural features of the AI-enabled systems and the experiential aspects of the interaction of the employees with generative AI. The theoretical framework is developed through conceptual analysis, and empirical elements are given to the validation of the contextual aspects and practicality. The method can be used to analyse the links between work transformation and talent management practices and trust outputs in organisations embracing the use of generative AI (Bankins et al., 2024). The kind of orientation used is an exploratory and explanatory orientation to identify the emerging patterns, mechanisms and implications of the integration of AI. This design upholds the capacity to be flexible towards accommodating sectoral and organizational variations without losing analytical consistency. The research design helps to have a holistic perception of human-centered sustainability in AI-enabled workplaces; by synthesizing theoretical examinations and observational conduction, the research design enables the area to attain the two aspects of sustainability.

5.2 Data Sources and Analysis Methods

Information to support this is obtained through various sources to be able to deepen and triangulate. Academic literature, organizational reports, and policy documents are examples of secondary data that could offer a background on the concept of generative AI adoption and sustainability concerns. The primary sources of data can be interviews, questionnaires, and a collection of case parameters in organizations that have already adopted AI-based human capital practices. The point of qualitative analysis techniques includes thematic coding to investigate work transformation perceptions, trust and employee experience. Quantitative techniques facilitate the descriptive and comparative workforce output analysis where necessary (Marlapudi, 2024). The combination of various information sources allows to cross-validate the results and increase the analytic strength. The conceptual model is used to analyze data and align the empirical observations with theoretical constructs. This interdisciplinary approach to analysis justifies the subtle meaning-making of the role of generative AI on work, talent, and trust relations.

5.3 Ethical and Validity Considerations

The methodology of the research includes ethical and validity considerations, which, in particular, should be considered because AI-driven workforce data is sensitive. The ethical protection measures involve informed consent, confidentiality, and responsible management of personal and organizational information. The focus is made on reducing the possible harm in case of interpretation or application of AI-related data. Research practices and analytical choices done with the purpose of transparency make them more credible and trustworthy. Validity is meticulously handled by defining constructs, by matching research objectives with research methods and by triangulation of data sources (Altassan, 2025). The uniformity of data collection procedures and the use of systematic analysis procedures enhances reliability. To take into consideration the possible bias of the researcher and to take into consideration the influences of the context, reflexivity is also included. The study promotes the creation of an ethical and methodologically-based research which includes ethical integrity and methodological rigour in the study process, thus making the results of the study both credible and aligned with the principles of human-centred sustainability and responsible AI research.

6. LITERATURE REVIEW

The increasing number of publications in the field of Generative Artificial Intelligence is an indicator of a shift in the organizational research towards more holistic systems of human-AI interaction rather than a focus on automation. Researchers are becoming more interested in the changes affecting work organization, decision-making procedures and the management of human capital generated by Generative AI. According to the literature, AI-based systems are no longer restricted to optimization of operations but are proactively integrated in the strategic and people-oriented functions (Wen et al., 2025). This growth has led to interdisciplinary research in the field of human resource management, organizational behavior, ethics, information systems and sustainability studies. The literature highlights that even though the field of generative AI presents a great opportunity to enhance productivity, personalization, and innovation, it is also associated with important challenges of trust, fairness, and sustainability of the workforce in the long term (Phd Qizi, 2025). Consequently, the modern studies are growing to demand humanistic models that strike a balance between technological development and social responsibility and ethical governance.

6.1 Generative AI in Talent Management

The studies of the application of generative AI in talent management reveal that it has increased its impact in the employee lifecycle, such as recruitment, assessment, performance management, learning, and workforce planning. Research indicates that AI-powered tools should be able to increase productivity and consistency, processing data on a large number of candidates, detecting any skill shortages, and promoting individualized learning journeys. Generative AI is also known to improve the decision-making of managers, making it predictive and scenario modeling (Hu et al., 2025). Nevertheless, the literature expresses so me fears related to excessive use of algorithmic assessments and a threat of decontextualized decision-making. Researchers claim that the talent practices mediated by AI can potentially reinvent the biases or discriminate against non-stereotypical career trajectories unless training information and assessment standards are designed cautiously. Consequently, the current studies highlight the necessity of human supervision, situational assessment, and constant observation to make sure that generative AI can facilitate the inclusion-driven and people-focused talent management as opposed to focusing on the small efficiency objectives (Seba et al., 2025). Table 2 More or less correlates key types of talent management efforts (recruitment, performance, learning, planning), and generative AI use cases and implications.

Table 2. Mapping Generative AI Applications to Talent Management Functions

Talent Function	AI Application	Primary Benefit	Key Risk
Recruitment	Resume screening, chatbots	Faster shortlisting	Bias amplification
Performance	AI-based evaluation	Consistency	Reduced contextual judgment
Learning & Development	Personalized learning paths	Skill alignment	Over-standardization
Workforce Planning	Predictive analytics	Demand forecasting	Data dependency

6.2 Trust, Transparency, and Algorithmic Fairness

One of the main themes of literature on AI-enabled workplaces has become trust and its role in transparency and the fairness of algorithms. The research findings have continued to show that procedural justice, explainability, and accountability perceptions are highly associated with employee acceptance of AI systems. Even in the cases when AI systems are highly technically accurate, opaque decision-making can cause suspicion, diminished participation and resistance (Giri et al., 2025). It is pointed out in the literature that trust in AI can be shaped by organizational communication and leadership behavior along with the governance practices not only based on the performance of the systems. Such processes as explainable AI and transparent feedback mechanisms are considered important enablers of trust (Ravikumar et al., 2025). Also, the concept of algorithmic fairness is increasingly considered a socio-organizational problem but not a technical one. According to research, fairness needs to be dealt with through continual assessment, involvement of stakeholders and compatibility with organizational principles to ensure the maintenance of legitimacy and confidence among the employees (Arnestad et al., 2025). Table 3 Postulates some of the key trust drivers like transparency, fairness, explainability, and governance in AI-mediated work places.

Table 3. Trust Determinants in AI-Enabled HR and Work Systems

Trust Dimension	Description	Organizational Enabler
Transparency	Clarity of AI decision logic	Explainable AI tools
Fairness	Absence of bias	Bias audits
Accountability	Responsibility for outcomes	Human oversight
Reliability	Consistency of outputs	System validation
Privacy	Data protection	Ethical data governance

6.3 Human-Centered and Sustainable AI Systems

The science on human-centered and sustainable AI systems promotes the use of ethical, social, and long-term concerns in the development and implementation of AI. Researchers contend that the implementation of AI should focus on the well-being of human beings, skill acquisition, and equal opportunity in addition to company performance (Ravikumar & Aarthi, 2025c). Humanistic methods focus on participatory design, involvement of employees and lifelong learning as key aspects to responsible AI implementation. The studies on sustainability also relate the AI-enabled workforce transformation to the larger environmental, social, and governance goals, with a greater emphasis on the responsible data stewardship and inclusive innovation. According to the literature, generative AI can undermine trust and social sustainability without the human-centered ways of governance (Rathinavel et al., 2025). Due to this, scientists are starting to demand integrative frameworks that incorporate ethical considerations, transparency, and accountability within AI-based organizational processes so that technological advances bring about strong and stable working conditions.

7.CASE STUDIES

This section features three recent case examples that operationalize the work-talent-trust framework presented in the chapter in the real organization context. The selected cases were aimed at representing (i) AI-powered talent and HR service delivery in knowledge-rich settings, (ii) limitations of trust and transparency that define adoption, responsible usage, and perceived legitimacy of algorithmic systems, and (iii) sustainability outcomes that arise as a result of the human-AI interaction, such as quantifiable energy and carbon impacts. All the cases are reported with similar lenses: contextual organizational, AI use-case, measurable results, and reflection on the experience of employees and the governance. The indicators are strengthened by the percentage-based ones (e.g., containment rate, levels of satisfaction, time reduction, adoption rates, energy and carbon reductions) (Criado et al., 2020). The cases put together indicate that the performance gains can be realized, though the adoption and use of AI should be sustained by clear policies, regular quality control, and governance, which will align AI application to both human-centered and sustainability goals.

7.1 AI-Enabled Talent Practices in Knowledge Work

Case: IBM AskHR (Agentic AI for HR and talent services, 2024-2025). IBM implemented internal AI-based HR system (AskHR) in order to provide chatbots to both employees and managers, as well as automated standard HR and talent functions. The system can access 7,000 policy pages, 80+ and above automations within the HR tasks and in 2024 over one million HR transactions. The model will combine the approach of digital self-service to routine requests (e.g., payslips, policy queries, job verification letters) with the further transfer to human advisors in case of complicated cases to have an opportunity to offer a hybrid approach to service delivery. The organizational impact measures are well adopted and efficient in operations: 99% of the managers will use it, 94% will include common questions (i.e., will be answered without sending it to specialists), and the volume of HR support tickets will decrease by a third since the year 2016. It states further that operational costs of the HR can be reduced by 40% in 4 years and the productivity of the task can also be enhanced with some of the domain specific operations potentially reduced by up to 75% between 2022 and 2024 due to automation. In human approach, the case is a sign that the human-first HR design can be used to increase the speed and consistency of service delivery whilst, preserving the human decescalation pathways in making sensitive decisions, which will increase perceived credibility and confidence (Ravikumar & Aarthi, 2025d). In the figure 3, significant percentage-based performance increases through the application of AI-based HR automation, including adoption, containment, efficiency, cost savings, and productivity could be observed.

Figure 3. Performance Outcomes of AI-Enabled Talent Practices

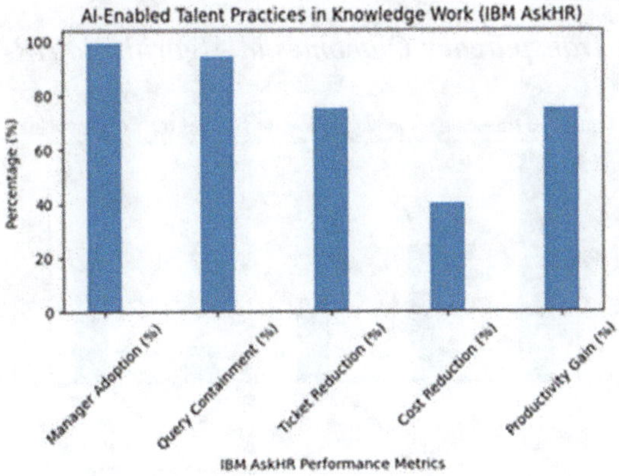

7.2 Trust and Transparency in Algorithmic HR Systems

Case: UK Department for Business and Trade (DBT) Microsoft 365 Copilot pilot, Oct 2024-Mar 2025. DBT assessed an organization-wide implementation of generative AI-based decision-support integrated with workplace workflows with the attention to the barriers to adoption, quality assurance, and constraints in trust. Instead of random sampling, to obtain more representative insights, the pilot distributed the licenses between volunteers and stratified random sampling (70%-30%). Results show high perceived value and trust and transparency problems influenced the usage patterns. General satisfaction was also good: 72% out of 100 with the diaries said that they were satisfied or very satisfied and less than 1 said that they were not satisfied (Ravikumar & Aarthi, 2025b). Trust was however conditional upon output reliability and clarity of policy (Nofal et al., 2025). In the response to the questions on the presence of hallucinations, 43% of them did not see any hallucination, 22% saw hallucinations, and 11% was uncertain showing disproportionate confidence toward the validity of output. Mixed understanding of acceptable-use and security guidance, misunderstanding of the similarity between similar AI tools, and too cautious behavior that inhibited the use of tools were also observed in the evaluation. Some use cases demonstrated lower experience at the task level: weaker experience was demonstrated with the use case of scheduling (36% dissatisfaction was recorded), and the degree of reliability and transparency depends on the type of workflow. The case in point indicates that trust cannot be automatic, and it requires clarifiable policies, regular QA standards, and role-related instructions. Figure 4 shows the main indicators of the percentage and trust between customers, the perception of hallucinations, and task dissatisfaction in the AI-enabled pilot of workplace.

Figure 4. Trust and Transparency Outcomes in Algorithmic HR Systems

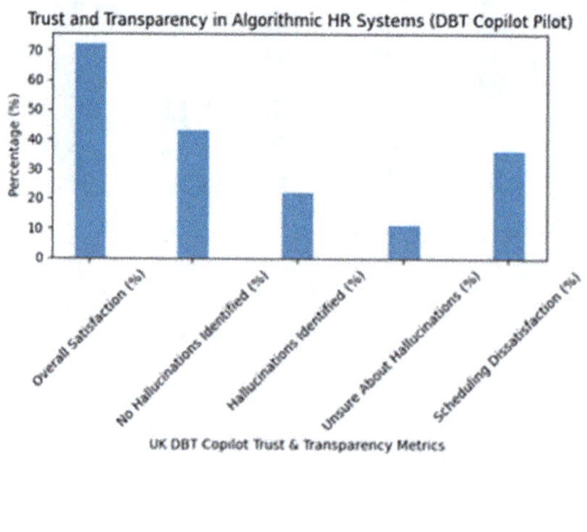

7.3 Sustainability Outcomes in Human–AI Collaboration

Case: Orange-Ericsson 5G network modernization (Apr 2025). Ericsson was selected by Orange to modernize 60% of its 5G network in France with a specified sustainability objective and an increase in the performance. The joint venture has recorded the quantifiable impacts on the environment at the infrastructure level: the modernisation of the sites and equipment will result in a reduction of the energy consumption in the sites by 30% and the embodied carbon emission by more than 20%, compared to the equipment of the older generation. Although the case is not mentioned in the context of HR technology, it can be applied to the human capital and digital sustainability as the efficiency is achieved due to the operational redesign (organized human-AI/ automation-based operation and monitoring and optimization practices) (Ravikumar, 2025a). The case illustrates how outcomes relating to sustainability could be expressed as operational measures that are auditable and explain the importance of governance frameworks that facilitate the provision of environmental returns by the digital transformation without growing the reliability, development of workforce and growth maintenance, or accountability of the effects on a system-level basis. Table 4 A summary of the case studies, AI use cases and measurable outcomes (adoption, efficiency, trust, sustainability metrics) is shown.

Table 4. Summary of Case Studies and Key Performance Indicators

Case	AI Application	Key Outcome	Measured Impact
IBM AskHR	AI-enabled HR services	Process efficiency	94% query containment
UK DBT Copilot	AI decision support	User satisfaction	72% satisfied users
Orange–Ericsson	AI-driven network ops	Energy efficiency	30% energy reduction

8. RESULTS AND DISCUSSION

The conclusions based on the case studies indicate that the implementation of generative AI has multidimensional effects that transcend beyond efficiency benefits to the work design, employee agency, trust, and sustainability. The examples indicate that AI-based systems can enhance the speed, uniformity, and scalability of service provision, especially when the knowledge intensive and personnel-driven scenarios. Nevertheless, such advantages depend on the manner in which AI is implemented in organizational operations and managed. The results show that the perception of control, fairness, and transparency by employees is a decisional factor in influencing acceptance and the proper use of AI systems. Confidence is one of the mediating factors that develop between technological capability and sustainable workforce performance (Chung & Yang, 2025). Further on, the sustainability case demonstrates that human-AI cooperation can bring quantifiable environmental and operation value upon itself in case it is accompanied by strategic governance goals. In general, the findings indicate that the sustainable workforce design of the age of generative AI implies a balance between automation and human control, enhanced trust infrastructures, and the implementation of sustainability concerns in AI-driven organizational transformation.

8.1 Impact on Work and Employee Agency

The case studies demonstrate that the application of generative AI modifies work process considerably and redefines agency of employees. With AI in HR service provision, workload and response times were significantly lowered since many routine and repetitive jobs were automated. This change enabled human professionals to concentrate in activities that gave higher value like advisory services, problem solving that are more complex, and strategic decision support. Efficiency and access by the employees was enhanced, but agency was maintained by well-articulated escalation routes and human-in-the-loop services. Nevertheless, the results are also suggesting that agency of employees may be undermined in cases where AI results are seen as authoritative without much contextualization (Guo & Chen, 2025). Users might leave judgment to algorithms in this situation instead of critical oversight. The findings indicate that generative AI can improve work quality and autonomy, but only when used as an augmentative system and not as a prescriptive system, which reinstates the significance of the conscious work redesign that protects human decision-making potential.

8.2 Trust as a Mediating Mechanism

Trust was an important factor that mediated between AI adoption and the outcomes of workforce. According to the evidence provided in the case, the high levels of satisfaction and adoption went hand in hand with the perceptions of transparency, reliability, and procedural fairness (Awad & Alharthi, 2025). In cases where the employees knew the functionality of AI systems and had guidance on the use of the AI systems, there were significantly high acceptance levels. On the other hand, any doubt about the origin of information, quality of output, and reasonable use was a barrier to forward action and discriminatory participation. Even in cases where there is a strong system performance, perceived inconsistency or hallucinated outputs undermined confidence (Khan et al., 2024). These results support the lack of an automatic link between technology effectiveness and trust as being a social construction by governance practices, communication, and leadership behavior. Trust acts as a balancing tool that allows employees to incorporate AI into the day-to-day workflow without being afraid of losing control, being biased, and unfairly evaluated.

8.3 Implications for Sustainable Workforce Design

The results discussion highlights valuable implications to the designing of sustainable workforce in AI-enabled organizations. As shown in the cases, both social and environmental results of sustainability can be attained when the use of generative AI correlates with long-term human capital policies and governance systems. The development of sustainable workforce design will involve developing AI systems that will be incorporated in a manner that facilitates lifelong learning, inclusive engagement, and accountable decision-making. The models of human-AI collaboration that are balanced between automation and augmentation will help to achieve resilience by maintaining employability and meaningful work. As well, sustainability varies with not only employee results, but also quantifiable decreases in resource usage and operational waste (Jeon, 2025). These results indicate that companies should cease to focus on individual AI applications and resort to systemic strategies of connecting work redesign, trust-building systems, and sustainability goals. Generative AI, when holistically designed, has the capacity to be the facilitator of a sustainable value generation, not the cause of disruption in the workforce. Table 5 Compiles results across cases, showing the effects on sustainability of the work force, the mediation of trust and agency of employees.

Table 5. Impact of Generative AI on Work, Trust, and Sustainability Dimensions

Dimension	Observed Impact	Sustainability Implication
Work Design	Task automation	Role enrichment
Employee Agency	Assisted decision-making	Preserved autonomy
Trust	Transparency-dependent	Adoption stability
Environment	Optimized operations	Reduced energy use

9. FUTURE RESEARCH DIRECTIONS

The fast adoption of generative AI in organizational practices leaves a number of unanswered questions that should be addressed in the long-run. Although literature on the topic provides useful comprehension of the short-term effectiveness and adoption success, little can be found about the long-term consequences of the workforce change due to AI use (Awad, 2025). The future studies should thus go further than short-term performance indicators to look at the long-term impacts of this on employability, trust and organisational resilience. Due to the increased integration of generative AI into the process of decision making, the necessity to develop the solid theoretical and empirical frameworks that reflect the dynamics of human-AI interactions over time increases (HR, 2022). Also, the shifting regulatory and ethical environment related to the implementation of AI provides the possibility to consider innovative governance practices and institution-based structures. The discussion of these knowledge gaps will allow considering the issue of making generative AI a more effective contributor to sustainable, inclusive, and reliable work systems. The subsequent guidelines also outline the important points on which future research can enhance theory, address practice, and facilitate the responsible adoption of AI in workforce settings.

9.1 Long-Term Workforce Sustainability

In future studies, the application of the long-term sustainability of work and employment in AI-enabled organizations is required. Although recent literature tends to focus on productivity and efficiency benefits, there is less information on the overall generative AI effects on career paths, skill refreshment, and employment stability in long-term settings. There should be longitudinal studies on the effectiveness of AI-driven work redesign in facilitating sustained employability or it leads to job polarization and skill erosion. The study of the impact of long-term human-AI cooperation on the well-being, motivation, and workplace identity of employees should also be conducted (Komajwar, 2025). Moreover, industry-specific results may be used to determine the different sustainability results within industries that exhibit different automation and knowledge intensities. A long-term view will enable the future research to inform approaches that can enable the adaptation of generative AI adoption towards inclusive growth, workforce resilience, and social sustainability goals.

9.2 Measurement of Trust in AI Systems

The other important area that future research needs is the aspect of measuring trust on AI-based organizational systems. The available research typically uses general attitudinal measures which are not necessarily sufficient to define the multidimensionality of trust in human-AI interactions. Future research ought to provide instruments that are proved in differentiating trust in technology, trust in organizational governance as well as trust in managerial decision-making using AI. A combination of surveys, behavioral data, and qualitative information can also provide more detailed knowledge on how trust can vary over time and situations (Aldhafeeri, 2025). Moreover, it is essential to research the role of explainability, transparency and perceived fairness regarding trust at various phases of AI adoption. Better measurement systems will allow assessing trust as a mediating variable more accurately and will facilitate the evidence-based design of trustful AI systems in the workplace.

9.3 Emerging Human–AI Governance Models

New human-AI governance frameworks are a good way to develop in further studies. The historical forms of governance might not be adequate as AI systems used to generate work and talent become more significant in deciding what work to do and whom to employ. Researchers ought to consider hybrid systems of governance incorporating technical regulations, ethical principles, regulatory adherence, and participatory systems. Regional and institutional comparative studies can be used to illuminate the impacts of various governance structures on the outcomes of trust, accountability and sustainability. There is also a need to conduct research to determine the role of employee voice, collective representation, and cross-functional AI oversight committees in developing responsible AI use (Ejjami, 2024). Through the promotion of knowledge regarding human-AI governance, the future research can help secure institutional frameworks that would balance innovations and ethical accountability, so that generative AI would assist in sustainable and valid workforce change. Figure 5 is a hierarchical governance model which spans between technical controls to sustainable transformation that is needed to achieve ethical, compliant and participatory AI-enabled organizational systems.

Figure 5. Framework of AI Governance Models

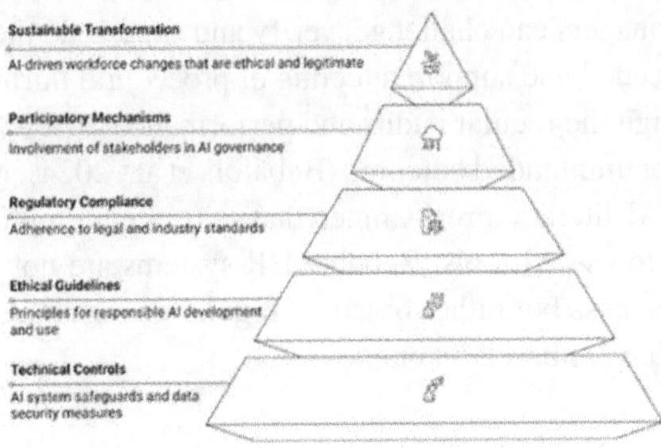

10. MANAGERIAL IMPLICATIONS

The results of this chapter have a number of significant managerial implications to organizations that consider using generative AI in human capital and work systems. Managers can influence the perception, acceptance, and use of AI technologies by the employees significantly. In addition to technical application, the successful implementation of AI must be strategically aligned with organizational values, have clear communication, and continuous focus on the personnel experience. The data indicates that generative AI projects are successful when the managers perceive trust, ethics, and sustainability as essential design factors instead of post-implementation factors. Managerial choices concerning system design, governance systems, and skill development have direct impacts on workforce engagement and value creation in the long term (Ajaero & Anjorin, 2024). By integrating human values within the AI-powered HR systems, leaders can alleviate the resistance, maximize the legitimacy, and make technological innovation a source of organizational resiliency. The implications listed below bring into focus actionable implications on managers who intend to develop reliable AI systems, develop ethical governance and balance automation with meaningful human involvement in AI-based workplaces.

10.1 Designing Trustworthy AI-Enabled HR Systems

Trustworthiness as a design consideration should be at the forefront of the managers in adopting AI-enabled HR systems. This deals with making sure that there is transparency in the way AI devices make recommendations, assessments, or affect recruitment, performance, and development choices. Unambiguous messages regarding the source of data, the criteria by which it will be evaluated, and the limitations of the system are useful in minimising uncertainty and cynicism among the employees. When introducing human-in-the-loop mechanisms, human employees and managers can challenge, verify and supersede the AI outputs in the situations when needed and support a feeling of procedural fairness. Trust can also be enhanced through the regular audits and performance review of AI systems that may include bias or unintended outcome (Babalola et al., 2024). Managers will also have to invest in AI literacy programmes that will allow employees to learn and comprehend how to use AI tools. Reliable HR systems are not just created based on technical correctness but rather based on regular governing, responsibility, and design practices that are based on employees.

10.2 Leadership and Ethical AI Governance

The key to the establishment of ethical AI governance in organizations is leadership commitment. Responsible AI utilization is determined by senior leaders who should establish the ethical principles and translate them into the organizational policy and decision-making processes. The ethical governance frameworks are to deal with such issues as data privacy, bias reduction, accountability, and adherence to the regulatory standards. Leaders should make sure that the responsibilities associated with AI are properly identified and bolstered with cross-functional oversight arrangements (Haque, 2025). Increased involvement of employees and other stakeholders in the governance debate can increase legitimacy and collective ownership of AI initiatives. Continuous monitoring of AI systems and responsiveness towards arising risks or unintended consequences is also an aspect of ethical leadership. Leaders can inspire trust and confidence in AI-enabled practices by exhibiting ethical stewardship and enable sustainable adoption and strengthen the commitments of the organization to social responsibility.

10.3 Balancing Automation and Augmentation

The key idea is to balance automation and augmentation because the managers should make sure that the generative AI supplements instead of supersedes the human input in the workplace. Excessive automation can result in skills being lost, less engagement, and a sense of lack of control, and under-utilization of AI can result in a lack of productivity potential. Good workforce design consists in pinpointing tasks that can be automated by AI so that the employees are not busy with routine jobs but also with complex, creative and relationship work. To accommodate this change, managers are expected to reformulate the job descriptions and performance measurements to address the collaborative results and not necessarily individual or algorithm-driven results (Clark et al., 2024). New reskilling and upskilling programs need to be a constant to train employees in the new positions in AI-enhanced settings. Through a careful balance of automation and human judgment, companies are able to retain meaningful work, enable employability, and create sustainable value by using human-AI interaction. Table 6 Offers practical managerial practices in responsible AI engineering, ethical governance and well-balanced automation-augmentation.

Table 6. Managerial Guidelines for Sustainable Human–AI Workforce Design

Managerial Area	Recommended Practice	Expected Outcome
System Design	Human-in-the-loop AI	Trust and control
Governance	Ethical AI policies	Compliance and legitimacy
Skills	AI literacy training	Workforce resilience
Work Design	Augmentation strategy	Meaningful work

11. CONCLUSION

In this chapter, the author discussed the ever-changing convergence of generative AI, work change, talent management, and trust in the human-centered approach to sustainability. The discussion has revealed that generative AI is not a simple on-demand technological resource with efficiency-enhancing potential, but a socio-technical movement that alters the structure of the work, employee agency, and the relations between employees. It was identified that AI-based systems can have a significant benefit in terms of operational efficiency and service provision in their presence in open, responsible and participatory governance frameworks. Trust proved to be one of the key mediating factors generating impact on employee acceptance, engagement and psychological safety in digitalized workplaces. In the theoretical perspective, the chapter is valuable in the sense that it combines the concept of work, talent, and trust into one conceptual framework that moves the study of the human-AI interaction beyond the fragmented or technology-focused approaches. In practice, the chapter offers useful information to managers and leaders on how to create trustful AI-based HR systems, ethical leadership, and a balance between automation and augmentation to sustain meaningful work and employability. It was also noted during the discussion that sustainable adoption of AI must facilitate the alignment of the workforce change with the broader environmental, social, and governance goals, taking a responsible approach to data stewardship and making innovation inclusive. In future perspectives, the chapter holds that work systems based on sustainable human-AI will rely on a learning curve, dynamic governance, and continuous assessment of the long-term effects of workforce. The chapter highlights how the generative AI can be used in the next decade to build sustainable value by positioning trust as the center of AI-enabled organizational design to enhance ethical, inclusive, and resilient work systems.

REFERENCES

Ajaero, O., & Anjorin, J. B. (2024). Human Resource Management and generative artificial intelligence (ChatGPT): Nexus, Perspectives and Praxis. *Global Journal of Human Resource Management, 12*(5), 19–29. DOI: 10.37745/gjhrm.2013/vol12n51929

Aldhafeeri, F. M. (2025). Governing artificial intelligence in radiology: A systematic review of ethical, legal, and regulatory frameworks. *Diagnostics (Basel), 15*(18), 2300. DOI: 10.3390/diagnostics15182300

Altassan, M. A. (2025). AI-powered HRM and ethical leadership: Balancing efficiency and human-centricity. *International Journal of Innovative Research and Scientific Studies, 8*(4), 2219–2228. DOI: 10.53894/ijirss.v8i4.8358

Arnestad, M. N., Bigman, Y. E., Solberg, E., & Gray, K. J. (2025). Knowing how personnel selection algorithms compare with human recruiters influences their perceived trustworthiness. *International Journal of Selection and Assessment, 33*(4), e70028. Advance online publication. DOI: 10.1111/ijsa.70028

Kulkarni, S. R., & Kulkarni, S. S. (2024). Revolutionizing organizations by technological innovations in HR. *Shodh Sari-An International Multidisciplinary Journal, 03*(01), 03–14. DOI: 10.59231/SARI7650

Awad, A. (2025). The role of universities' social responsibility in enhancing business sustainability: Mediating role of entrepreneurial culture. *Problems and Perspectives in Management, 23*(1), 181–192. DOI: 10.21511/ppm.23(1).2025.14

Awad, A., & Alharthi, B. (2025). The role of digital marketing tools in promoting tourism: An applied study on online marketing strategies. *Innovative Marketing, 21*(2), 14–26. DOI: 10.21511/im.21(2).2025.02

Awad, A., Fathy Aziz, A., & Rashad Shma, T. (2025). Investment behavior in the Egyptian stock market: The impact of social media on investor decision-making. *Investment Management and Financial Innovations, 22*(1), 203–212. DOI: 10.21511/imfi.22(1).2025.16

Babalola, O., Adedoyin, A., Ogundipe, F., Folorunso, A., & Nwatu, C. E. (2024). Policy framework for Cloud Computing: AI, governance, compliance and management. *Global Journal of Engineering and Technology Advances, 21*(2), 114–126. DOI: 10.30574/gjeta.2024.21.2.0212

Bankins, S., Ocampo, A. C., Marrone, M., Restubog, S. L. D., & Woo, S. E. (2024). A multilevel review of artificial intelligence in organizations: Implications for organizational behavior research and practice. *Journal of Organizational Behavior, 45*(2), 159–182. DOI: 10.1002/job.2735

Belghachi, M. (2023). A review on explainable artificial intelligence methods, applications, and challenges. [IJEEI]. *Indonesian Journal of Electrical Engineering and Informatics, 11*(4). Advance online publication. DOI: 10.52549/ijeei.v11i4.5151

Borg, J., Scott-Young, C. M., & Bartram, T. (2025). A review of graduate work readiness literature: A conceptual exploration of the implications for HRM research and practice. *Asia Pacific Journal of Human Resources, 63*(2), e70012. Advance online publication. DOI: 10.1111/1744-7941.70012

Chang, Y.-L., & Ke, J. (2024). Socially responsible artificial intelligence empowered people analytics: A novel framework towards sustainability. *Human Resource Development Review, 23*(1), 88–120. DOI: 10.1177/15344843231200930

Chung, H., & Yang, X. J. (2025). Understanding multi-referent trust in AI-supported evacuations: The role of transparency and altruism. *Proceedings of the Human Factors and Ergonomics Society Annual Meeting. Human Factors and Ergonomics Society. Annual Meeting, 69*(1), 214–217. DOI: 10.1177/10711813251358779

Clark, Q. M., Kanavikar, D. B., Clark, J., & Donnelly, P. J. (2024). Exploring the potential of AI-driven food waste management strategies used in the hospitality industry for application in household settings. *Frontiers in Artificial Intelligence, 7*, 1429477. DOI: 10.3389/frai.2024.1429477

Criado, J. I., Valero, J., & Villodre, J. (2020). Algorithmic transparency and bureaucratic discretion: The case of SALER early warning system. *Information Polity, 25*(4), 449–470. DOI: 10.3233/IP-200260

Ejjami, R. (2024). Ethical Artificial Intelligence Framework Theory (EAIFT): A new paradigm for embedding ethical reasoning in AI systems. *International Journal For Multidisciplinary Research, 6*(5), 28231. Advance online publication. DOI: 10.36948/ijfmr.2024.v06i05.28231

Gama Espinosa, J. C., Leiva Sánchez, L. M., & Fajardo Pereira, M. A. (2024). Benefits of Artificial Intelligence in human talent management. *Multidisciplinar (Montevideo), 1*, 14. DOI: 10.62486/agmu202314

Giri, R., Firdhos, S. H., & Vida, T. A. (2025). Artificial intelligence in anesthesia: Enhancing precision, safety, and global access through data-driven systems. *Journal of Clinical Medicine, 14*(19), 6900. DOI: 10.3390/jcm14196900

Guo, W., & Chen, Y. (2025). Investigating whether AI will replace human physicians and understanding the interplay of the source of consultation, health-related stigma, and explanations of diagnoses on patients' evaluations of medical consultations: Randomized factorial experiment. *Journal of Medical Internet Research*, *27*, e66760. DOI: 10.2196/66760

Haque, A. (2025). Responsible artificial intelligence (AI) in healthcare: A paradigm shift in leadership and strategic management. *Leadership in Health Services (Bradford, England)*, *38*(4), 644–656. DOI: 10.1108/LHS-01-2025-0018

Hu, D., Navas, D. A., Gaube, S., Mozannar, H., Taylor, M. E., Dvijotham, K., & Bondi-Kelly, E. (2025). Human at the center: A framework for human-driven AI development. *AI Magazine*, *46*(4), e70043. Advance online publication. DOI: 10.1002/aaai.70043

Jeon, G. (2025). Leveraging AI for ESG performance: A global analysis of national AI capabilities and sustainability in international business. *Business Strategy & Development*, *8*(3), e70162. Advance online publication. DOI: 10.1002/bsd2.70162

Khan, M. K., Huo, C., Zahid, R. M. A., & Maqsood, U. S. (2024). The automated sustainability auditor: Does artificial intelligence curtail greenwashing behavior in Chinese firms? *Business Strategy and the Environment*, *33*(8), 9015–9039. DOI: 10.1002/bse.3961

Komajwar, S. (2025). Artificial Intelligence in Human Resources: Transforming talent management and workforce efficiency. *International Journal For Multidisciplinary Research*, *7*(2), 39595. Advance online publication. DOI: 10.36948/ijfmr.2025.v07i02.39595

Kumar, S., & Bargavi, D. S. K. M. (2024). Trust's significance in human-AI communication and decision-making. *INTERANTIONAL JOURNAL OF SCIENTIFIC RESEARCH IN ENGINEERING AND MANAGEMENT*, *08*(02), 1–10. DOI: 10.55041/IJSREM28468

Marlapudi, K., & Lenka, U. (2024). Unlocking the potential: Redefining talent and competency mapping for Industry 4.0. *Management Research Review*, *47*(11), 1805–1832. DOI: 10.1108/MRR-07-2023-0496

Milad, A., & Whiba, M. (2024). Exploring Explainable Artificial Intelligence technologies: Approaches, challenges, and applications. *International Science and Technology Journal*, *34*(1), 1–21. DOI: 10.62341/amia8430

Nofal, H. A., Mohamed, A. E., Almadani, N., Mahfouz, R., Bahri, H. A., Ali, H. T., & Elrafey, D. S. (2025). The impact of an artificial intelligence enhancement program on healthcare providers' knowledge, attitudes, and workplace flourishing. *Frontiers in Public Health, 13*(1639333), 1639333. DOI: 10.3389/fpubh.2025.1639333

Nyathani, R. (2023). Preparing for the future of work: How HR tech is shaping remote work. *Journal of Technology and Systems*, *5*(1), 60–73. DOI: 10.47941/jts.1498

Nyathani, R.HR Digital Transformation Architect IL USA. (2022). AI-powered recruitment the future of HR digital transformation. *Journal of Artificial Intelligence & Cloud Computing*, *1–5*(4), SRC/JAICC-145. Advance online publication. DOI: 10.47363/JAICC/2022(1)133

Phd student at Tashkent International University, U., & Qizi, F. M. A. (2025). Artificial intelligence and team effectiveness in management: a transformative impact on decision-making, collaboration, and productivity. *International Journal Of Management And Economics Fundamental, 5*(3), 110–115. DOI: 10.37547/ijmef/Volume05Issue03-16

Prabagar, S., Mothkur, R., Swetha, C. B., Kurian, A., Pavithra, K., & Aarthi, S. (2025). Generative AI for inclusive special education. In *Advances in Computational Intelligence and Robotics* (pp. 205–236). IGI Global Scientific Publishing. DOI: 10.4018/979-8-3373-3745-6.ch008

Rathinavel, P., Ravikumar, R. N., Aarthi, S., Habib, M., Salaeva, N., & Pardaev, J. (2025). Augmenting human capabilities. In *Advances in Computational Intelligence and Robotics* (pp. 1–30). IGI Global Scientific Publishing. DOI: 10.4018/979-8-3373-2372-5.ch001

Ravikumar, R. N., & Aarthi, S. (2025c). Human-AI synergy for organizational resilience. In *Advances in Computational Intelligence and Robotics* (pp. 287–322). IGI Global Scientific Publishing. DOI: 10.4018/979-8-3373-7416-1.ch011

Ravikumar, R. N., & Aarthi, S. (2025d). Integrating machine learning with human decision making in HR. In *Empowering Human Resources Through Human-Computer Interaction* (pp. 115–146). IGI Global Scientific Publishing., DOI: 10.4018/979-8-3373-1676-5.ch005

Ravikumar, R. N., Aarthi, S., Rai, P. K., & Mamadiyarov, Z. (2025). Intelligent code analysis and feedback generation. In *Advances in Computational Intelligence and Robotics* (pp. 137–170). IGI Global Scientific Publishing. DOI: 10.4018/979-8-3373-0598-1.ch006

Ravikumar, & Aarthi, S. (2025a). Cognitive collaboration. In *Advances in Computational Intelligence and Robotics* (pp. 125–158). IGI Global Scientific Publishing. DOI: 10.4018/979-8-3373-7416-1.ch006

Ravikumar, & Aarthi, S. (2025b). Conscious AI Integration in business education. In *Advances in Computational Intelligence and Robotics* (pp. 73–104). IGI Global Scientific Publishing. DOI: 10.4018/979-8-3373-4377-8.ch003

Saad, M., Awad, A., Fathy Aziz, A., & Rashad Shma, T. (2025). Influencer marketing's impact on credibility and purchase intention: A study on University of Bisha students in Saudi Arabia. *Innovative Marketing*, *21*(1), 326–337. DOI: 10.21511/im.21(1).2025.26

Seba, F., Isola, M., Mills, L., Zalake, M., & Krive, J. (2025). Incorporating generative AI into a health informatics curriculum to build 21st century competencies: Multisite pre-post study. *JMIR Medical Informatics, 13*(v13i4e76507), e76507. DOI: 10.2196/76507

Shaheen, A., Khataan, A., Awad, A., Yahia Shams Eldin, A., & Elnour, A. (2025). The role of influencer content value and credibility in purchase intention. *Innovative Marketing*, *21*(3), 14–30. DOI: 10.21511/im.21(3).2025.02

Singh, A., & Pandey, J. (2023). Artificial intelligence adoption in extended HR ecosystems: Enablers and barriers. An abductive case research. *Frontiers in Psychology*, *14*, 1339782. DOI: 10.3389/fpsyg.2023.1339782

Stamate, A. N., Sauvé, G., & Denis, P. L. (2021). The rise of the machines and how they impact workers' psychological health: An empirical study. *Human Behavior and Emerging Technologies*, *3*(5), 942–955. DOI: 10.1002/hbe2.315

Wang, Y.-F., Chen, Y.-C., & Chien, S.-Y. (2023). Citizens' intention to follow recommendations from a government-supported. *Public Policy and Administration.* Advance online publication. DOI: 10.1177/09520767231176126

Wen, Y., Wang, J., & Chen, X. (2025). Trust and AI weight: human-AI collaboration in organizational management decision-making. *Frontiers in Organizational Psychology*, *3*(1419403), 1419403. Advance online publication. DOI: 10.3389/forgp.2025.1419403

KEY TERMS AND DEFINITIONS

Algorithmic Fairness: The extent to which AI systems make decisions without bias or discrimination against individuals or groups.

Augmentation: The use of AI to enhance human capabilities and support decision-making rather than replace human roles.

Automation: The use of technology to perform tasks with minimal human intervention, often focused on routine activities.

Ethical AI Governance: Organizational policies and structures that ensure responsible, accountable, and compliant use of AI technologies.

Generative Artificial Intelligence (AI): AI systems capable of creating new content, insights, or solutions by learning patterns from large datasets rather than following fixed rules.

Human Capital: The collective knowledge, skills, abilities, and experience of employees that contribute to organizational performance and value creation.

Human–AI Collaboration: A work arrangement where humans and AI systems jointly perform tasks, with humans retaining oversight and decision authority.

Human-Centered Sustainability: An approach to sustainability that prioritizes employee well-being, dignity, inclusion, and long-term employability alongside performance goals.

Talent Management: Organizational practices related to recruitment, performance evaluation, learning and development, and workforce planning.

Transparency and Explainability: The ability of AI systems to provide understandable explanations for their outputs and decisions.

Trust in AI Systems: The degree to which employees believe that AI-driven tools are reliable, fair, transparent, and aligned with organizational values.

Work Transformation: Changes in job roles, task structures, and work processes resulting from the integration of digital and AI technologies.

Compilation of References

A. YA Bani Ahmad. (2025). P. Jangra, S. Sood, A. Gupta, A. Namdev, S. Pramanik, Banking Sector's Unification of Culture Following Artificial Intelligence Adoption. In *Real-World Applications of AI Innovation* (pp. 199–212). IGI Global., DOI: 10.4018/979-8-3693-4252-7.ch010

Aarthi, S., Ravikumar, R. N., & Pardaev, J. (2026). Synergizing Multimodal Generative AI and Blockchain for the Future of Digital Media. In Fusion of Multimodal Generative AI and Blockchain Technology in Digital Media (pp. 1-34). IGI Global Scientific Publishing. DOI: 10.4018/979-8-3373-1504-1.ch001

Abbu, H., Khan, S., Mugge, P., & Gudergan, G. (2025). Building digital-ready leaders: Development and validation of the human-centric Digital Leadership Scale. *Digital*, *5*(1), 7. DOI: 10.3390/digital5010007

Acemoglu, D., & Autor, D. (2011). Skills, Tasks and Technologies: Implications for Employment and Earnings. In Card, D., & Ashenfelter, O. (Eds.), *Handbook of Labor Economics* (Vol. 4, pp. 1043–1171). Elsevier., DOI: 10.1016/S0169-7218(11)02410-5

Acemoglu, D., Autor, D., Hazell, J., & Restrepo, P. (2022). Artificial Intelligence and Jobs: Evidence from Online Vacancies. *Journal of Labor Economics*, *40*(S1), S293–S340. Advance online publication. DOI: 10.1086/718327

Acemoglu, D., & Restrepo, P. (2022). Tasks, automation, and the rise in U.S. wage inequality. *Econometrica*, *90*(5), 1973–2016. DOI: 10.3982/ECTA19815

Achar, H.V.B., Prasad, P.S., Rajeshwari, D. *et al.* Federated learning and Neuro-Symbolic AI for botnet classification in IoT-Enabled consumer devices. *Int. j. inf. tecnol.* (2025). https://doi.org/DOI: 10.1007/s41870-025-02993-0

Adilov, Z., Tajibaev, J., Rasul-Zade, L., Tursunov, M., Mamadiyarov, Z., & Abdullayev, D. (2025). Exploring virtual reality and digital twin technologies for sustainable construction training in higher education. E3S Web of Conferences, 680, 00131. https://doi.org/DOI: 10.1051/e3sconf/202568000131

Afreen, J., Mohaghegh, M., & Doborjeh, M. (2025). Systematic literature review on bias mitigation in generative AI. *AI and Ethics*, *5*(5), 4789–4841. DOI: 10.1007/s43681-025-00721-9

Agarwal, S., Gupta, A., & Roshani, P. (2023). Redefining HRM with artificial intelligence and machine learning. In *The adoption and effect of artificial intelligence on human resources management, Part A* (pp. 1–13). Emerald Publishing Limited. DOI: 10.1108/978-1-80382-027-920231001

Agarwal, V., Kaur, S. N. R., Gupta, S., Zaveri, B., Sohal, J., & Shrivastav, A. K. (2024). Adoption of advanced systems for digital resource management in academic institutions. *Evolutionary Studies in Imaginative Culture*, •••, 913–923. DOI: 10.70082/esiculture.vi.1089

Ahmed, S. Y., & Pardaev, J. (2025). Human-AI decision dynamics: How risk propensity and trust impact choices through decision fatigue, conditional on AI understanding. *Decision Making: Applications in Management and Engineering*, *8*(2), 96–113. DOI: 10.31181/dmame8220251484

Aisa, R., Cabeza, J., & Martin, J. (2023). Automation and aging: The impact on older workers in the workforce. *The Journal of the Economics of Ageing*, *26*, 100476. DOI: 10.1016/j.jeoa.2023.100476

Ajaero, O., & Anjorin, J. B. (2024). Human Resource Management and generative artificial intelligence (ChatGPT): Nexus, Perspectives and Praxis. *Global Journal of Human Resource Management*, *12*(5), 19–29. DOI: 10.37745/gjhrm.2013/vol12n51929

Akinlade, I., Balakumar, G. B., Narayan, S., Badami, S., Madineni, U. K., Mittal, T., & Aludogbu, P. (2025). Investigating executive leadership responses to AI-induced structural change in multinational corporations-2025. *International Journal of Science and Research Archive*, *17*(3), 196–207. DOI: 10.30574/ijsra.2025.17.3.3196

Al Doghan, M. A., & Absamatov, A. (2025). Effects of Big Data, Mechanical System Flexibility, IOT and Digital Twin Adoption on Company Resilience and Operational Performance. *Reports in Mechanical Engineering*, *6*(2), 65–79. DOI: 10.31181/rme524

Al Naqbi, H., Bahroun, Z., & Ahmed, V. (2024). Enhancing work productivity through generative artificial intelligence: A comprehensive literature review. *Sustainability (Basel)*, *16*(3), 1166. DOI: 10.3390/su16031166

Alavi, M., & Leidner, D. E. (2001). Review: Knowledge management and knowledge management systems: Conceptual foundations and research issues1,2. *Management Information Systems Quarterly*, *25*(1), 107–136. DOI: 10.2307/3250961

Aldhafeeri, F. M. (2025). Governing artificial intelligence in radiology: A systematic review of ethical, legal, and regulatory frameworks. *Diagnostics (Basel)*, *15*(18), 2300. DOI: 10.3390/diagnostics15182300

Aldossary, M. A., & Pardaev, J. (2025). Leveraging Big-Data Management for Production Excellence: Decision-Making Capabilities, Decision Quality, and the Moderating Effect of Manufacturing IT Infrastructure. *Reports in Mechanical Engineering*, *6*(1), 136–151. DOI: 10.31181/rme499

Alexandro, R. (2025). Strategic human resource management in the digital economy era: An empirical study of challenges and opportunities among MSMEs and startups in Indonesia. *Cogent Business & Management*, *12*(1), 2528436. Advance online publication. DOI: 10.1080/23311975.2025.2528436

Aljohani, A. (2025). Exploring Future Trends and Uncovering Opportunities in AI-Enhanced Financial Technologies. In Gupta, S. K., Rosak-Szyrocka, J., Rena, R., Shieh, C. S., & Erkol Bayram, G. (Eds.), *The Impact of Artificial Intelligence on Finance: Transforming Financial Technologies. Information Systems Engineering and Management* (Vol. 53). Springer., DOI: 10.1007/978-3-031-92916-8_10

Al-Kfairy, M., Mustafa, D., Kshetri, N., Insiew, M., & Alfandi, O. (2024a, August). Ethical challenges and solutions of generative AI: An interdisciplinary perspective. In Informatics (Vol. 11, No. 3, p. 58). MDPI.

Al-Kfairy, M. (2025). Strategic integration of generative AI in organizational settings: Applications, challenges, and adoption requirements. *IEEE Engineering Management Review*, *53*(6), 80–97. DOI: 10.1109/EMR.2025.3534034

Al-kfairy, M., Mustafa, D., Kshetri, N., Insiew, M., & Alfandi, O. (2024b). A Systematic Review and Analysis of Ethical Challenges of Generative Ai: An Interdisciplinary Perspective. Available at *SSRN* 4833030. DOI: 10.2139/ssrn.4833030

Allam, Z., & Cheshmehzangi, A. (2024). Technological Innovation and Sustainable Transitions. In *Sustainable Futures and Green New Deals*. Palgrave Macmillan., DOI: 10.1007/978-3-031-63642-4_3

Alomair, A., Farooq, U., Almulhim, A. A., & Mamadiyarov, Z. (2026, March). Do cultural values matter? The role of national cultural dimensions in shaping female entrepreneurship in ASEAN. In *Women's Studies International Forum* (Vol. 115, p. 103273). Pergamon. DOI: 10.1016/j.wsif.2025.103273

Altassan, M. A. (2025). AI-powered HRM and ethical leadership: Balancing efficiency and human-centricity. *International Journal of Innovative Research and Scientific Studies*, *8*(4), 2219–2228. DOI: 10.53894/ijirss.v8i4.8358

Amazon. (2022). *Machine learning in supply chain optimization*. Amazon Science Publications.

Ammer, M. A., & Sattarov, A. (2025). Enhancing investors' decision-making through financial risk management: Role of corporate governance and financial communication transparency. Decision Making: Applications in Management and Engineering. https://doi.org/DOI: 10.31181/dmame8220251527

Ammer, M. A., & Mamadjanova, T. (2025). Effects of educational digital literacy, educational aspirations, self-directed learning on e-learning motivation and effectiveness. *Educational Sciences: Theory & Practice*. Advance online publication. DOI: 10.12738/jestp.2025.1.18

Ammer, M. A., & Mamadjanova, T. (2025). *Impact of educational quality, educational resource, and educational climate on educational engagement and student intention to attend lectures*. Espacio, Tiempo y Educación., DOI: 10.14516/ete.12208

Arigbabu, A. T., Olaniyi, O. O., Adigwe, C. S., Adebiyi, O. O., & Ajayi, S. A. (2024). Data governance in AI - enabled healthcare systems: A case of the Project Nightingale. *Asian Journal of Research in Computer Science*, *17*(5), 85–107. DOI: 10.9734/ajrcos/2024/v17i5441

Arista, A., Ismail, M. A., Shuib, L., & Herawan, T. (2025). A SYSTEMATIC LITERATURE REVIEW ON ETHICAL FRAMEWORK FOR ADOPTION OF GENERATIVE ARTIFICIAL INTELLIGENCE. *Malaysian Journal of Computer Science*, *38*(Special). Advance online publication. DOI: 10.22452/mjcs.vol38spf.6

Arnestad, M. N., Bigman, Y. E., Solberg, E., & Gray, K. J. (2025). Knowing how personnel selection algorithms compare with human recruiters influences their perceived trustworthiness. *International Journal of Selection and Assessment*, *33*(4), e70028. Advance online publication. DOI: 10.1111/ijsa.70028

Arslan, A., Cooper, C., Khan, Z., Golgeci, I., & Ali, I. (2021). Artificial intelligence and human workers interaction at team level: A conceptual assessment of the challenges and potential HRM strategies. *International Journal of Manpower*. Advance online publication. DOI: 10.1108/IJM-01-2021-0052

Asrifan, A. (2025). Building trust in AI-driven organizations. In *Moral and Legal Aspects of Artificial Intelligence* (pp. 195–228). IGI Global Scientific Publishing., DOI: 10.4018/979-8-3373-3114-0.ch006

Autade, R. (2026). AI-Enabled Blockchain Framework for Detecting Threats in Payment Systems. In Mishra, D., Yang, X. S., Unal, A., & Jat, D. S. (Eds.), *Data Science and Big Data Analytics. IDBA 2025. Learning and Analytics in Intelligent Systems* (Vol. 55). Springer., DOI: 10.1007/978-3-032-05377-0_32

Autor, D. H. (2015). Why are there still so many jobs? The history and future of workplace automation. *The Journal of Economic Perspectives*, *29*(3), 3–30. DOI: 10.1257/jep.29.3.3

Autor, D. H., Levy, F., & Murnane, R. J. (2003). The Skill Content of Recent Technological Change: An Empirical Exploration. *The Quarterly Journal of Economics*, *118*(4), 1279–1333. DOI: 10.1162/003355303322552801

Awad, A. (2024). Artificial intelligence and marketing innovation: The mediating role of organizational culture. *Innovative Marketing*, *20*(3), 170–181. DOI: 10.21511/im.20(3).2024.14

Awad, A. (2025). The role of universities' social responsibility in enhancing business sustainability: Mediating role of entrepreneurial culture. *Problems and Perspectives in Management*, *23*(1), 181–192. DOI: 10.21511/ppm.23(1).2025.14

Awad, A., & Al Ahmari, D. (Eds.). (2026). *Digital resilience in supply chains: Security, governance, and AI innovation*. IGI Global Scientific Publishing., DOI: 10.4018/979-8-3373-8841-0

Awad, A., & Alharthi, B. (2025). The role of digital marketing tools in promoting tourism: An applied study on online marketing strategies. *Innovative Marketing*, *21*(2), 14–26. DOI: 10.21511/im.21(2).2025.02

Awad, A., Fathy Aziz, A., & Rashad Shma, T. (2025). Investment behavior in the Egyptian stock market: The impact of social media on investor decision-making. *Investment Management and Financial Innovations*, *22*(1), 203–212. DOI: 10.21511/imfi.22(1).2025.16

Awad, A., & Ghonim, A. (2025). Data-driven marketing in banks: The role of artificial intelligence in enhancing marketing efficiency and business performance. *International Review of Management and Marketing*, *15*(5), 422–431. DOI: 10.32479/irmm.19738

Ayoub, A. (2026). The Architecture of Intelligent Governance (AIG): A conceptual framework for integration AI, quantum computing, and global resource resilience. *Sustainability (Basel)*, *18*(5), 2312. DOI: 10.3390/su18052312

Azahari, L. M., Ahmad, F. A., & Saniff, S. M. (2026). Connecting Employability and the Future of Work: A Systematic Review of Global Trends, Employer Expectations, and Evolving Recruitment Strategies. *Enhancing Graduate Employability in an Evolving Workforce*, 99-118. DOI: 10.4018/979-8-3373-4450-8.ch005

Babalola, O., Adedoyin, A., Ogundipe, F., Folorunso, A., & Nwatu, C. E. (2024). Policy framework for Cloud Computing: AI, governance, compliance and management. *Global Journal of Engineering and Technology Advances*, *21*(2), 114–126. DOI: 10.30574/gjeta.2024.21.2.0212

Babashahi, L., Barbosa, C. E., Lima, Y., Lyra, A., Salazar, H., Argôlo, M., Almeida, M. A., & Souza, J. M. (2024). AI in the Workplace: A Systematic Review of Skill Transformation in the Industry. *Administrative Sciences*, *14*(6), 127. DOI: 10.3390/admsci14060127

Bakker, A. B., & Demerouti, E. (2017). Job demands–resources theory: Taking stock and looking forward. *Journal of Occupational Health Psychology, 22*(3), 273–285. DOI: 10.1037/ocp0000056

Balamurugan, M., & Roopa, D. K. N., S., Sushma, R., T. C., K., Swetha, G., & Raghu, N. (2026). Late Night Use of Social Media and Sleep Deprivation. In I. Nabila Marzuki, W. Wan Ali, H. Lee, A. Manaf, & M. Sanmugam (Eds.), *Examining the Intersection ofTechnology, Media, and Social Innovation* (pp. 205-236). IGI Global Scientific Publishing. DOI: 10.4018/979-8-3373-5307-4.ch008

Bandura, A. (1986). *Social foundations of thought and action: A social cognitive theory*. Prentice-Hall.

Bankins, S., Jooss, S., Restubog, S. L. D., Marrone, M., Ocampo, A. C., & Shoss, M. (2024). Navigating career stages in the age of artificial intelligence: A systematic interdisciplinary review and agenda for future research. *Journal of Vocational Behavior, 153*, 104011. DOI: 10.1016/j.jvb.2024.104011

Bankins, S., Ocampo, A. C., Marrone, M., Restubog, S. L. D., & Woo, S. E. (2024). A multilevel review of artificial intelligence in organizations: Implications for organizational behavior research and practice. *Journal of Organizational Behavior, 45*(2), 159–182. DOI: 10.1002/job.2735

Barley, S. R., Bechky, B. A., & Milliken, F. J. (2017). The changing nature of work: Careers, identities, and work lives in the 21st century. *Academy of Management Discoveries*, *3*(2), 111–115. DOI: 10.5465/amd.2017.0034

Barney, J. (1995). Looking inside for competitive advantage. *The Academy of Management Perspectives*, *9*(4), 49–61. DOI: 10.5465/ame.1995.9512032192

Barney, J. B. (2021). Resource-based theory: Creating and sustaining competitive advantage. *Journal of Management, 47*(7), 1621–1644.

Barney, J., & Wright, P. M. (1998). On becoming a strategic partner: The role of human resources in gaining competitive advantage. *Human Resource Management, 37*(1), 31–46. DOI: 10.1002/(SICI)1099-050X(199821)37:1<31::AID-HRM4>3.0.CO;2-W

Bautista, Y. J. P., Theran, C., & Aló, R. (2024, May). Ethical considerations of generative ai: A survey exploring the role of decision makers in the loop. In *Proceedings of the AAAI Symposium Series* (Vol. 3, No. 1, pp. 391-398). DOI: 10.1609/aaaiss.v3i1.31243

Baygi, R. M., & Huysman, M. (2025). Generative AI and the social fabric of organizations. *Organization Studies*. Advance online publication. DOI: 10.1177/14761270251385456

Becerra-Fernandez, I. (2000). The role of artificial intelligence technologies in the implementation of People-Finder knowledge management systems. *Knowledge-Based Systems, 13*(5), 315–320. DOI: 10.1016/s0950-7051(00)00091-5

Becker, B. E., & Huselid, M. A. (2022). Strategic human capital management: Where do we go from here? *The Academy of Management Perspectives, 36*(1), 1–15.

Behaghel, L., Caroli, E., & Roger, M. (2014). Age-biased Technical and Organizational Change, Training and Employment Prospects of Older Workers. *Economica, 81*(322), 368–389. DOI: 10.1111/ecca.12078

Belghachi, M. (2023). A review on explainable artificial intelligence methods, applications, and challenges. [IJEEI]. *Indonesian Journal of Electrical Engineering and Informatics, 11*(4). Advance online publication. DOI: 10.52549/ijeei.v11i4.5151

Benbya, H., Davenport, T. H., & Pachidi, S. (2020). Special issue editorial: Artificial intelligence in organizations: Current state and future opportunities. *SSRN, 19*(4), ix–xxi. DOI: 10.2139/ssrn.3741983

Bennett, E. E. (2022). Leveraging technology to design and deliver human resource development. In *The emerald handbook of work, workplaces and disruptive issues in HRM* (pp. 261–276). Emerald Publishing Limited., DOI: 10.1108/978-1-80071-779-420221026

Bentayeb, A., Khoualed, A., & Medjdoub, A. (2026). Artificial Intelligence in Human Resource Management: Applications, Workforce Implications, And Market Trends (2024-2034). *Інститут бухгалтерського обліку, контроль та аналіз в умовах глобалізації*, (3-4), 68-78. **https://doi.org/**DOI: 10.35774/ibo2025.03-04.068

Berardi, C., Antonini, M., Jordan, Z., Wechtler, H., Paolucci, F., & Hinwood, M. (2024). Barriers and facilitators to the implementation of digital technologies in mental health systems: A qualitative systematic review to inform a policy framework. *BMC Health Services Research, 24*(1), 243. DOI: 10.1186/s12913-023-10536-1 PMID: 38408938

Bhatia, R. (2025). Next-Generation Digital Finance: Architecting AI-Driven Financial Systems on the SAP Cloud Ecosystem. In: Awan, I., Younas, M., Ghinea, G., Tor-Morten, G., Şen, S. (eds) The 6th Joint International Conference on AI, Big Data and Blockchain (AIBB 2025). AIBB 2025. Lecture Notes in Networks and Systems, vol 1618. Springer, Cham. DOI: 10.1007/978-3-032-04728-1_8

Bhatti, M. A., & Mamadjanova, T. (2025). From Calling to Performance: The Role of Linguistic and Communicative Competence in Employee Success. *Eurasian Journal of Applied Linguistics, 11*(2), 147–162. DOI: 10.32601/ejal.11212

Bhatti, M. A., & Otamurodov, S. (2025). Job Satisfaction and Employee Commitment: Role of Internal Communication, Language Proficiency, Information Quality and Information Usefulness. *El Profesional de la Información, 34*(2). Advance online publication. DOI: 10.3145/epi.2025.ene.34201

Bhatti, M. A., & Shodiyev, A. (2025). Enhancing Employee Performance: Role of Communication Competence, Internal Communication and Satisfaction with Communication Climate. *International Journal of Operations and Quantitative Management, 31*(2), 216–239. DOI: 10.46970/2025.31.2.11

Bhatt, P. K., & Muduli, A. (2022). Artificial intelligence in learning and development: A systematic literature review. *European Journal of Training and Development, 47*(7/8), 677–694. DOI: 10.1108/EJTD-09-2021-0143

Bi, S., Lian, Y., & Wang, Z. (2025). Research and Design of a Financial Intelligent Risk Control Platform Based on Big Data Analysis and Deep Machine Learning. In: Atiquzzaman, M., Yen, N., Xu, Z. (eds) Proceedings of the 5th International Conference on Big Data Analytics for Cyber-Physical System in Smart City—Volume 1. BDCPS 2023. Lecture Notes on Data Engineering and Communications Technologies, vol 234. Springer, Singapore. DOI: 10.1007/978-981-96-0208-7_37

Bidwell, M. (2011). Paying More to Get Less: The Effects of External Hiring versus Internal Mobility. *Administrative Science Quarterly, 56*(3), 369–407. https://www.jstor.org/stable/41410272. DOI: 10.1177/0001839211433562

Bionicyarn. (2025). Retrieved from https://bionicyarn.com/

Boeri, T., Garibaldi, P., & Moen, E. R. (2022). In medio stat victus: Labor Demand Effects of an Increase in the Retirement Age. *Journal of Population Economics, 35*(2), 519–556. DOI: 10.1007/s00148-021-00871-0

Bommasani, R., Hudson, D. A., Aditi, E., ... (2022). On the opportunities and risks of foundation models. arXiv preprint arXiv:2108.07258.

Bonilla-Chaves, E. F., & Palos-Sánchez, P. R. (2023). Exploring the evolution of human resource analytics: A bibliometric study. *Behavioral Sciences (Basel, Switzerland), 13*(3), 244. DOI: 10.3390/bs13030244

Borg, J., Scott-Young, C. M., & Bartram, T. (2025). A review of graduate work readiness literature: A conceptual exploration of the implications for HRM research and practice. *Asia Pacific Journal of Human Resources, 63*(2), e70012. Advance online publication. DOI: 10.1111/1744-7941.70012

Boyatzis, R. E. (2008). Competencies in the 21st century. *Journal of Management Development, 27*(1), 5–12. DOI: 10.1108/02621710810840730

Bradley, M. (2000). Working Knowledge: How Organizations Manage What They Know20004Thomas H. Davenport and Laurence Prusak. Working Knowledge: How Organizations Manage What They Know. *New Library World, 101*(6), 282–287. DOI: 10.1108/nlw.2000.101.6.282.4

Brandao, P. R. (2025). The Impact of Artificial Intelligence on Modern Society. *AI, 6*(8), 190. DOI: 10.3390/ai6080190

Breque, M., De Nul, L., & Petridis, A. (2021). *Industry 5.0: Towards a sustainable, human-centric and resilient European industry*. European Commission, Directorate-General for Research and Innovation. DOI: 10.2777/308407

Brown, J. S., & Adler, R. P. (2020). Minds on fire: Open education, the long tail, and learning 2.0. *EDUCAUSE Review*.

Brown, O., Davison, R. M., Decker, S., Ellis, D. A., Faulconbridge, J., Gore, J., Greenwood, M., Islam, G., Lubinski, C., MacKenzie, N. G., Meyer, R., Muzio, D., Quattrone, P., Ravishankar, M. N., Zilber, T., Ren, S., Sarala, R. M., & Hibbert, P. (2024). Theory-driven perspectives on generative artificial intelligence in business and management. *British Journal of Management, 35*(1), 3–23. DOI: 10.1111/1467-8551.12788

Brynjolfsson, E., Li, D., & Raymond, L. (2025). Generative AI at work. *The Quarterly Journal of Economics, 140*(2), 889–942. DOI: 10.1093/qje/qjad020

Brynjolfsson, E., Li, D., & Raymond, L. R. (2023). Generative AI at work (NBER Working Paper No. 31161). National Bureau of Economic Research. DOI: 10.3386/w31161

Brynjolfsson, E., Li, D., & Raymond, L. R. (2023). Generative AI at work. NBER Working Paper No. 31161. National Bureau of Economic Research.

Brynjolfsson, E., & McAfee, A. (2022). *The Turing trap: The promise and peril of human-like artificial intelligence*. Princeton University Press.

Brynjolfsson, E., Mitchell, T., & Rock, D. (2018). What can machines learn, and what does it mean for occupations and the economy? *AEA Papers and Proceedings. American Economic Association, 108*, 43–47. DOI: 10.1257/pandp.20181019

Budhwar, P., Chowdhury, S., Wood, G., Aguinis, H., Bamber, G. J., Beltran, J. R., ... & Varma, A. (2023). Human resource management in the age of generative artificial intelligence: Perspectives and research directions on ChatGPT. Human Resource Management Journal, 33(3), 606-659.4

Budhwar, P., Chowdhury, S., Wood, G., Aguinis, H., Bamber, G. J., Beltran, J. R., Boselie, P., Lee Cooke, F., Decker, S., DeNisi, A., Dey, P. K., Guest, D., Knoblich, A. J., Malik, A., Paauwe, J., Papagiannidis, S., Patel, C., Pereira, V., Ren, S., & Varma, A. (2023). Human resource management in the age of generative artificial intelligence: Perspectives and research directions on ChatGPT. *Human Resource Management Journal, 33*(3), 606–659. DOI: 10.1111/1748-8583.12524

Bukartaite, R., & Hooper, D. (2023). Automation, artificial intelligence and future skills needs: An Irish perspective. *European Journal of Training and Development, 47*(10), 163–185. DOI: 10.1108/EJTD-03-2023-0045

Byambaa, O., Yondon, C., Rentsen, E., Darkhijav, B., & Rahman, M. (2025). An empirical examination of the adoption of artificial intelligence in banking services: The case of Mongolia. *Futur Bus J, 11*(1), 76. DOI: 10.1186/s43093-025-00504-y

Cahyani, I., Buriev, K. T., Ngongo, M., Mamadiyarov, Z., Ino, L., Herman, H., Saputra, N., & Baxtishodovich, S. B. (2025). Exploring the use of TikTok application in enhancing the skill of pronunciation: A case on students' perception. *Studies in Media and Communication, 13*(2), 7553. DOI: 10.11114/smc.v13i2.7553

Canas da Costa, L., & Popović, T. (2020). Financing Sustainable Infrastructures in a Smart Cities' Context—Innovative Concepts, Solutions and Instruments. In Planing, P., Müller, P., Dehdari, P., & Bäumer, T. (Eds.), *Innovations for Metropolitan Areas*. Springer., DOI: 10.1007/978-3-662-60806-7_18

Cappelli, P., & Tavis, A. (2024). The talent management revolution: Skills-first hiring and the future of work. *Harvard Business Review, 102*(1), 62–71.

Carmeli, A. (2003). The relationship between emotional intelligence and work attitudes, behavior and outcomes. *Journal of Managerial Psychology, 18*(8), 788–813. DOI: 10.1108/02683940310511881

Casas, P., & Román, C. (2023). Early retired or automatized? Evidence from the survey of health, ageing and retirement in Europe. *The Journal of the Economics of Ageing, 24*, 100443. DOI: 10.1016/j.jeoa.2023.100443

Cascio, W. F., & Montealegre, R. (2016). How technology is changing work and organizations. *Annual Review of Organizational Psychology and Organizational Behavior, 3*(1), 349–375. DOI: 10.1146/annurev-orgpsych-041015-062352

Cascio, W. F., & Montealegre, R. (2021). How technology is changing work and organizations. *Journal of World Business, 56*(1), 101–119.

Çelik Ertuğrul, D., & Bitirim, S. (2025). Job recommender systems: A systematic literature review, applications, open issues, and challenges. *Journal of Big Data, 12*(1), 140. Advance online publication. DOI: 10.1186/s40537-025-01173-y

Chang, Y.-L., & Ke, J. (2024). Socially responsible artificial intelligence empowered people analytics: A novel framework towards sustainability. *Human Resource Development Review, 23*(1), 88–120. DOI: 10.1177/15344843231200930

Chan, S. H., Sutton, S. G., & Yao, L. J. (2009). The paradoxical effects of feedback and reward on decision performance. In *Advances in Accounting Behavioral Research* (pp. 109–143). Emerald Group Publishing Limited., DOI: 10.1108/s1475-1488(2009)0000012008

Chatterjee, S., Chaudhuri, R., & Vrontis, D. (2023). Digital transformation and HR practices: Knowledge sharing via HR blog platforms. *Information Systems Frontiers, 25*(2), 723–742.

Chaudhary, N. S., Banerjee, R., Mathur, G., Sachdeva, L., & Amoozegar, A. (2025). AI and the future of talent management. In *Advances in Computational Intelligence and Robotics* (pp. 297–316). IGI Global Scientific Publishing. DOI: 10.4018/979-8-3373-1270-5.ch017

Chen, F., Lin, Z., & Li, X. (2025). Research on the emerging technological intervention models in design education from a strategic perspective of global design education institutions. *Scientific Reports, 15*(1), 41366. DOI: 10.1038/s41598-025-25272-1 PMID: 41272010

Cheng, M. M., & Hackett, R. D. (2021). A critical review of algorithms in HRM: Definition, theory, and practice. *Human Resource Management Review*, *31*(1), 100698. DOI: 10.1016/j.hrmr.2019.100698

Chowdhury, S., Budhwar, P., Dey, P. K., Joel-Edgar, S., & Abadie, A. (2022). AI-employee collaboration and business performance: Integrating knowledge-based view, socio-technical systems and organisational socialisation framework. *Journal of Business Research*, *144*, 31–49. DOI: 10.1016/j.jbusres.2022.01.069

Chowdhury, S., Budhwar, P., & Wood, G. (2024). Generative artificial intelligence in business: Towards a strategic human resource management framework. *British Journal of Management*, *35*(4), 1680–1691. DOI: 10.1111/1467-8551.12824

Christenko, A. (2022). Automation and occupational mobility: A task and knowledge-based approach. *Technology in Society*, *70*, 101976. DOI: 10.1016/j.techsoc.2022.101976

Chuang, S., Shahhosseini, M., Javaid, M., & Wang, G. G. (2024). Machine learning and AI technology-induced skill gaps and opportunities for continuous development of middle-skilled employees. *Journal of Work-Applied Management*. Advance online publication. DOI: 10.1108/JWAM-08-2024-0111

Chu, C. H., Donato-Woodger, S., Khan, S. S., Nyrup, R., Leslie, K., Lyn, A., Shi, T., Bianchi, A., Rahimi, S. A., & Grenier, A. (2023). Age-related bias and artificial intelligence: A scoping review. *Humanities & Social Sciences Communications*, *10*(1), 510. DOI: 10.1057/s41599-023-01999-y

Chung, H., & Yang, X. J. (2025). Understanding multi-referent trust in AI-supported evacuations: The role of transparency and altruism. *Proceedings of the Human Factors and Ergonomics Society Annual Meeting. Human Factors and Ergonomics Society. Annual Meeting*, *69*(1), 214–217. DOI: 10.1177/10711813251358779

Chung, J., & Lee, C. (2022). Technological Change, Job Characteristics, and Employment of Elderly Workers: Evidence from Korea. Bank of Korea WP 2022-14. http://dx.doi.org/DOI: 10.2139/ssrn.4223940

Ciarrochi, J., Chan, A. Y. C., & Caputi, P. (2001). A critical evaluation of the emotional intelligence construct. *Personality and Individual Differences, 28*(3), 539–561. DOI: 10.1016/S0191-8869(99)00119-1

Cingillioglu, I., & Schoettner, M. (2025). Adapting to AI-mediated workplaces: How STEM trainees navigate new challenges and opportunities. *Information Technology & People*, *38*(8), 251–275. DOI: 10.1108/ITP-02-2025-0163

Clark, Q. M., Kanavikar, D. B., Clark, J., & Donnelly, P. J. (2024). Exploring the potential of AI-driven food waste management strategies used in the hospitality industry for application in household settings. *Frontiers in Artificial Intelligence*, *7*, 1429477. DOI: 10.3389/frai.2024.1429477

Collings, D. G., Mellahi, K., & Cascio, W. F. (2022). Global talent management and performance in multinational enterprises. *Human Resource Management Journal*, *32*(2), 297–315.

Corvello, V. (2025). Generative AI and the future of innovation management: A human-centered perspective and an agenda for future research. *Journal of Open Innovation*, *11*(1), 100456. DOI: 10.1016/j.joitmc.2024.100456

Criado, J. I., Valero, J., & Villodre, J. (2020). Algorithmic transparency and bureaucratic discretion: The case of SALER early warning system. *Information Polity*, *25*(4), 449–470. DOI: 10.3233/IP-200260

Danilova, O., & Belayeva, I. (2019). Economic Efficiency of Using the Electric Grid Complex: Problems of Reserves of Network Power and Development of Intelligent Technologies. In Popkova, E. (Ed.), *The Future of the Global Financial System: Downfall or Harmony. ISC 2018. Lecture Notes in Networks and Systems* (Vol. 57). Springer., DOI: 10.1007/978-3-030-00102-5_26

Darioshi, R., & Lahav, E. (2021). The impact of technology on the human decision-making process. *Human Behavior and Emerging Technologies*, *3*(3), 391–400. DOI: 10.1002/hbe2.257

Davenport, T. H., Guha, A., Grewal, D., & Bressgott, T. (2020). How artificial intelligence will change the future of marketing. *Journal of the Academy of Marketing Science, 48*(1), 24–42. DOI: 10.1007/s11747-019-00696-0

Davenport, T. H., & Miller, S. (2022). Working with AI: Real stories of human-machine collaboration. *MIT Sloan Management Review*.

Deb Biswas, D., & Sengupta, R. (2025). Reimagining leadership for the AI era: A grounded theory of adaptive, ethical and contextually situated practices in workplaces. *Leadership and Organization Development Journal*, •••, 1–22. DOI: 10.1108/LODJ-06-2025-0488

Dell'Acqua, F., McFowland, E., III, Mollick, E. R., Lifshitz-Assaf, H., Kellogg, K., Rajendran, S., Krayer, L., Candelon, F., & Lakhani, K. R. (2023). Navigating the jagged technological frontier: Field experimental evidence of the effects of AI on knowledge worker productivity and quality (Harvard Business School Working Paper No. 24-013). Harvard Business School. DOI: 10.2139/ssrn.4573321

Deloitte. (2022). *Global Human Capital Trends Report.*

Deloitte. (2023). *2023 Global Human Capital Trends: New fundamentals for a boundaryless world.* Deloitte Insights.

Deloitte. (2024). *Global human capital trends 2024.* https://www2.deloitte.com

Derks, D., Bakker, A. B., & Peters, P. (2021). Work-related use of digital communication technologies and emotional demands. *Computers in Human Behavior, 122*, 106817. DOI: 10.1016/j.chb.2021.106817

Dohale, V., Ambilkar, P., Bilolikar, V., Narkhede, B. E., Kumar, A., & Kumar, A. (2025). Evaluating circular economy and smart technology adoption barriers in the Indian textile and apparel industries using neutrosophic ISM. *Annals of Operations Research, 355*(1), 211–251. DOI: 10.1007/s10479-023-05651-5

Doh, W., Goh, Y., & Kim, S.-H. (2025). Beyond overreliance: The human-ai-system concordance (HASC) matrix and the cognitive dynamics of ai-assisted decision-making. *Proceedings of the Human Factors and Ergonomics Society Annual Meeting, 69*(1), 427–432. DOI: 10.1177/10711813251358240

Dutta, S., Mohiya, M., & Caputo, A. (2025). Leadership participation in digital knowledge platforms and employee engagement: Evidence from HR Blog systems. *Journal of Knowledge Management, 29*(1), 112–138.

Dweck, C. S. (2006). *Mindset: The new psychology of success.* Random House.

Dwivedi, Y. K., Hughes, L., & Baabdullah, A. M.. (2023). Artificial intelligence adoption research: A review and future research agenda. *International Journal of Information Management, 70*, 102623.

Dwivedi, Y. K., Kshetri, N., Hughes, L., Slade, E. L., Jeyaraj, A., Kar, A. K., Baabdullah, A. M., Koohang, A., Raghavan, V., Ahuja, M., Albanna, H., Albashrawi, M. A., Al-Busaidi, A. S., Balakrishnan, J., Barlette, Y., Basu, S., Bose, I., Brooks, L., Buhalis, D., & Wright, R. (2023). Opinion paper: 'So what if ChatGPT wrote it?' Multidisciplinary perspectives on opportunities, challenges and implications of generative conversational AI for research, practice and policy. *International Journal of Information Management, 71*, 102642. DOI: 10.1016/j.ijinfomgt.2023.102642

Edmondson, A. C., & Lei, Z. (2014). Psychological safety: The history, renaissance, and future of an interpersonal construct. *Annual Review of Organizational Psychology and Organizational Behavior, 1*(1), 23–43. DOI: 10.1146/annurev-orgpsych-031413-091305

Ejjami, R. (2024). Ethical Artificial Intelligence Framework Theory (EAIFT): A new paradigm for embedding ethical reasoning in AI systems. *International Journal For Multidisciplinary Research, 6*(5), 28231. Advance online publication. DOI: 10.36948/ijfmr.2024.v06i05.28231

El-Kassar, A. N., & Singh, S. K. (2019). Green innovation and organizational performance: The influence of big data and the moderating role of management commitment and HR practices. *Technological Forecasting and Social Change, 144*, 483–498. DOI: 10.1016/j.techfore.2017.12.016

Elkington, J. (2020). *Green swans: The coming boom in regenerative capitalism.* Fast Company Press.

Ellingrud, K., Gupta, R., Sanghvi, S., & Seong, J. (2023). *Generative AI and the future of work in America.* McKinsey Global Institute.

Elmenzhi, Z., Elfassi, S., Jdidou, Y., Aarab, I., & Bakraoui, I. (2025). Recruitment 4.0: A conceptual framework integrating AI and social media for intelligent talent acquisition. In *Proceedings of the 2025 11th International Conference on Optimization and Applications (ICOA).* DOI: 10.1109/ICOA66896.2025.11236940

Eloundou, T., Manning, S., Mishkin, P., & Rock, D. (2024). GPTs are GPTs: Labor market impact potential of LLMs. *Science, 384*(6702), 1306–1308. DOI: 10.1126/science.adj0998 PMID: 38900883

European Commission. (2021). *Proposal for a regulation laying down harmonised rules on artificial intelligence (Artificial Intelligence Act).* European Union. https://ec.europa.eu

European Institute of Applied Science and Management Chez Republic, P., Upreti, P. K., Gangwar, N., & European Institute of Applied Science and Management Chez Republic, P. (2025). Artificial Intelligence and leadership effectiveness: Empirical evidence from multinational corporations in Uganda. *RA Journal of Applied Research, 11*(05). DOI: 10.47191/rajar/v11i5.10

Eurostat. (2024). Digital economy and society statistics — households and individuals. European Commission.

Fazi, L., Zaniboni, S., & Wang, M. (2025). Age differences in the adoption of technology at work: A review and recommendations for managerial practice. *Journal of Organizational Change Management, 38*(8), 138–175. DOI: 10.1108/JOCM-12-2024-0767

Fichman, R. G., Dos Santos, B. L., & Zheng, Z. (Eric). (2014). Digital innovation as a fundamental and powerful concept in the information systems curriculum1. *Management Information Systems Quarterly, 38*(2), 329–354. DOI: 10.25300/misq/2014/38.2.01

Fitas, R. (2025). Inclusive education with AI: Supporting special needs and tackling language barriers. *AI and Ethics, 5*(6), 5729–5757. DOI: 10.1007/s43681-025-00824-3

Floridi, L., & Cowls, J. (2019). A unified framework of five principles for AI in society. *Harvard Data Science Review*. https://hdsr.mitpress.mit.edu

Floridi, L., Cowls, J., Beltrametti, M., Chatila, R., Chazerand, P., Dignum, V., et al. (2020). AI4People—An ethical framework for a good AI society. *Minds and Machines, 30*(4), 689–707. DOI: 10.1007/s11023-020-09530-0

Floridi, L. (2019). *The logic of information: A theory of philosophy as conceptual design*. Oxford University Press. DOI: 10.1093/oso/9780198833635.001.0001

Fosso Wamba, S. (2022). Impact of artificial intelligence assimilation on firm performance: The mediating effects of organizational agility and customer agility. *International Journal of Information Management, 67*, 102544. DOI: 10.1016/j.ijinfomgt.2022.102544

Founder of Filmy AI and Startup Consultant Lubin School of Business Pace University New York USA, T. L. and M. C., & Dedhia, P. (2025). Transformational leadership in the age of AI-driven tech: Inspiring with vision in no code generation. *INTERNATIONAL JOURNAL OF SCIENTIFIC RESEARCH IN ENGINEERING AND MANAGEMENT, 09*(06), 1–9. DOI: 10.55041/IJSREM50924

Fountaine, T., McCarthy, B., & Saleh, T. (2022). Building the AI-powered organization. *Harvard Business Review, 100*(4), 62–73.

Frey, C. B., & Osborne, M. A. (2017). The future of employment: How susceptible are jobs to computerisation? *Technological Forecasting and Social Change, 114*, 254–280. DOI: 10.1016/j.techfore.2016.08.019

Friedberg, L. (2003). The Impact of Technological Change on Older Workers: Evidence from Data on Computer Use. *Industrial & Labor Relations Review, 56*(3), 511–529. DOI: 10.1177/001979390305600309

Gama Espinosa, J. C., Leiva Sánchez, L. M., & Fajardo Pereira, M. A. (2024). Benefits of Artificial Intelligence in human talent management. *Multidisciplinar (Montevideo), 1*, 14. DOI: 10.62486/agmu202314

Garavan, T. N., Carbery, R., & Rock, A. (2021). Mapping talent development: Definition, scope, and architecture. *European Journal of Training and Development, 45*(2/3), 93–112.

Garcia-Arroyo, J., & Osca, A. (2021). Big data contributions to human resource management: A systematic review. *International Journal of Human Resource Management, 32*(20), 4337–4362. DOI: 10.1080/09585192.2019.1674357

Garcia, R. F., & Kwok, L. (2025). Generative artificial intelligence in human resource management: A critical reflection on impacts, resilience and roles. *International Journal of Contemporary Hospitality Management, 37*(9), 3136–3158. DOI: 10.1108/IJCHM-01-2025-0159

Garg, P., Gupta, B., Kapil, K. N., Sivarajah, U., & Gupta, S. (2025). Examining the relationship between blockchain capabilities and organizational performance in the Indian banking sector. *Annals of Operations Research, 348*(3), 1513–1546. DOI: 10.1007/s10479-023-05254-0

Gartner. (2024). HR leaders' 2024 priorities: Building critical skills and competencies. Gartner Research.

Georgieff, A., & Hyee, R. (2022). Artificial Intelligence and Employment: New Cross-Country Evidence. *Frontiers in Artificial Intelligence, 5*, 832736. DOI: 10.3389/frai.2022.832736 PMID: 35620279

Gerber, M., Krause, A., Probst, J., & Heimann, M. (2024). HR analytics between ambition and reality. *Gruppe. Interaktion. Organisation. Zeitschrift für Angewandte Organisationspsychologie, 55*(2), 225–236. Advance online publication. DOI: 10.1007/s11612-024-00743-7

Ghaleb, M. M. S., & Sattarov, A. (2025). *Use of ChatGPT in education and quality of education: Role of student course engagement and regulator support.* Revista Electrónica de LEEME., DOI: 10.58262/LEEME.55.0020

Ghanbaripour, A. N., Talebian, N., Miller, D., Tumpa, R. J., Zhang, W., Golmoradi, M., & Skitmore, M. (2024). A Systematic Review of the Impact of Emerging Technologies on Student Learning, Engagement, and Employability in Built Environment Education. *Buildings (Basel, Switzerland), 14*(9), 2769. DOI: 10.3390/buildings14092769

Ghobakhloo, M., Iranmanesh, M., Mubarak, M. F., Mubarik, M., Rejeb, A., & Nilashi, M. (2022). Identifying Industry 5.0 contributions to sustainable development: A strategy roadmap for delivering sustainability values. *Sustainable Production and Consumption, 33*, 716–737. DOI: 10.1016/j.spc.2022.08.003

Ghonim, A., Awad, A., Shemais, M., Shma, T., & Aziz, A. (2025). Exploring the impact of flexible work arrangements on employee engagement in telecommunications: Case of Egypt. *Problems and Perspectives in Management, 23*(2), 198–207. DOI: 10.21511/ppm.23(2).2025.13

Girdharry, K., & Wynstra, B. (2025). Distributed AI leadership: The Generator as a model for faculty-led innovation. *Journal of Leadership Studies, 19*(2), e70013. Advance online publication. DOI: 10.1002/jls.70013

Giri, R., Firdhos, S. H., & Vida, T. A. (2025). Artificial intelligence in anesthesia: Enhancing precision, safety, and global access through data-driven systems. *Journal of Clinical Medicine, 14*(19), 6900. DOI: 10.3390/jcm14196900

Gmyrek, P., Berg, J., & Bescond, D. (2023). Generative AI and jobs: A global analysis of potential effects on job quantity and quality (ILO Working Paper 96). International Labour Organization. DOI: 10.54394/FHEM8239

Gold, A. H., Malhotra, A., & Segars, A. H. (2001). Knowledge management: An organizational capabilities perspective. *Journal of Management Information Systems, 18*(1), 185–214. DOI: 10.1080/07421222.2001.11045669

Goleman, D. (1995). *Emotional intelligence: Why it can matter more than IQ.* Bantam Books.

Goleman, D. (1998). What makes a leader? *Harvard Business Review, 76*(6), 93–102. PMID: 10187249

Google Health. (2021). *Deep learning for medical image analysis.* Google Research Publications. https://health.google

Gorka, E., Baran, D., Wojak, G., Ćwiakala, M., Zupok, S., Starkowski, D., Resko, D., & Okrasa, O. (2025). The impact of artificial intelligence on enterprise decision-making processes. *European Research Studies Journal, XXVIII*(3), 1126–1147. DOI: 10.35808/ersj/4178

Goštautaitė, B., & Šerelytė, M. (2024). Decreasing employability with age? The role of automation risk, lifelong learning and occupational mobility. *Baltic Journal of Management, 19*(2), 145–162. DOI: 10.1108/BJM-11-2022-0419

Grandey, A. A. (2000). Emotion regulation in the workplace: A new way to conceptualize emotional labor. *Journal of Occupational Health Psychology, 5*(1), 95–110. DOI: 10.1037/1076-8998.5.1.95

Grant, A. M., & Parker, S. K. (2009). Redesigning work design theories: The rise of relational and proactive perspectives. *The Academy of Management Annals*, *3*(1), 317–375. DOI: 10.5465/19416520903047327

Grant, R. M. (1996). Toward a knowledge-based theory of the firm. *Strategic Management Journal*, *17*(S2), 109–122. DOI: 10.1002/smj.4250171110

Gray, K., Slavotinek, J., Dimaguila, G. L., & Choo, D. (2022). Artificial intelligence education for the health workforce: Expert survey of approaches and needs. *JMIR Medical Education*, *8*(2), e35223. DOI: 10.2196/35223 PMID: 35249885

Grimes, M., von Krogh, G., Feuerriegel, S., Rink, F., & Gruber, M. (2023). From scarcity to abundance: Scholars and scholarship in an age of generative artificial intelligence. *Academy of Management Journal*, *66*(6), 1617–1624. DOI: 10.5465/amj.2023.4006

Guimarães, L., & Gil, P. M. (2022). Looking ahead at the effects of automation in an economy with matching frictions. *Journal of Economic Dynamics & Control*, *144*, 104538. DOI: 10.1016/j.jedc.2022.104538

Guleria, N., Sajabul, M., Sharma, N., Yadav, T., & Semwal, R. (2025). The role of emotional intelligence in enhancing employee performance and job satisfaction in hybrid workplaces. *. *International Journal of Environmental Sciences*.

Guo, W., & Chen, Y. (2025). Investigating whether AI will replace human physicians and understanding the interplay of the source of consultation, health-related stigma, and explanations of diagnoses on patients' evaluations of medical consultations: Randomized factorial experiment. *Journal of Medical Internet Research*, *27*, e66760. DOI: 10.2196/66760

Guo, Y., & Wei, L. (2025). AI technology adoption and intergenerational knowledge transfer among older employees. *Frontiers in Psychology*, *16*, 1673730. DOI: 10.3389/fpsyg.2025.1673730 PMID: 41383432

H. V Balachandra Achar and R. N. "The Impact and Future of Artificial Intelligence in Learning," *2025 3rd International Conference on Integrated Circuits and Communication Systems (ICICACS)*, Raichur, India, 2025, pp. 1-6, DOI: 10.1109/ICICACS65178.2025.10967881

Haddad, M. (2024). The paradox of leadership absence in organisational knowledge systems. *Leadership and Organization Development Journal*, *45*(3), 1–18.

Hair, J. F., Jr., Rana, S., Robb, D., & Stroud, M. (2026). The emerging role of AI and social robots in university student recruitment. In *Social robots and artificial intelligence in education: Integrating AI in K-12 and higher education* (pp. 153-183). Cham: Springer Nature Switzerland. DOI: 10.1007/978-3-032-03977-4_7

Hair, J. F., Risher, J. J., Sarstedt, M., & Ringle, C. M. (2019). When to use and how to report the results of PLS-SEM. *European Business Review*, *31*(1), 2–24. DOI: 10.1108/ebr-11-2018-0203

Haldar, A., & Sethi, N. (2022). Environmental effects of information and communication technology: Exploring the roles of renewable energy, innovation, trade and financial development. *Renewable & Sustainable Energy Reviews*, *153*, 111754. DOI: 10.1016/j.rser.2021.111754

Hamid, E. M., & Shodiyev, A. (2025). Role of information needs, information accessibility, information overload and digital literacy in shaping web search self-efficacy. *El Profesional de la Información*, *34*(2). Advance online publication. DOI: 10.3145/epi.2025.ene.34205

Hani, S. (2019). *Entrepreneur's understanding on MSME (micro small medium enterprises) on concept on sharia financial statement*. Center for Open Science. DOI: 10.31227/osf.io/hr92x

Haque, A. (2025). Responsible artificial intelligence (AI) in healthcare: A paradigm shift in leadership and strategic management. *Leadership in Health Services (Bradford, England)*, *38*(4), 644–656. DOI: 10.1108/LHS-01-2025-0018 PMID: 40911384

Helfat, C. E., & Martin, J. A. (2022). Dynamic managerial capabilities: Review and assessment. *Academy of Management Review*, *47*(1), 134–156.

Henseler, J., Ringle, C. M., & Sarstedt, M. (2014). A new criterion for assessing discriminant validity in variance-based structural equation modeling. *Journal of the Academy of Marketing Science*, *43*(1), 115–135. DOI: 10.1007/s11747-014-0403-8

Hernández-Tamurejo, Á., Bužinskienė, R., Barbosa, B., Miceikienė, A., & Saura, J. R. (2025). Generative artificial intelligence use in the workplace: Implications for management practice. *Review of Managerial Science*, •••, 1–33. DOI: 10.1007/s11846-025-00949-z

Heß, P., Janssen, S., & Leber, U. (2023). The effect of automation technology on workers' training participation. *Economics of Education Review*, *96*, 102438. DOI: 10.1016/j.econedurev.2023.102438

Hinds, P., & von Krogh, G. (2024). Generative AI, emerging technology, and organizing: Towards a theory of progressive encapsulation. *Organization Theory*, *5*(4), 26317877241293478. Advance online publication. DOI: 10.1177/26317877241293478

Hindustan College of Arts & Science Tamil Nadu. C., & Sundaram, S. (2025). Innovating for the future: Sustainable corporate strategies for workforce upskilling and reskilling. *International Journal of Research in Entrepreneurship & Business Studies, 6*(3), 33–46. DOI: 10.47259/ijrebs.2025.633

Hossain, M. M., Abdulla, F., & Huq, M. N. (2025). Challenges Faced by Older Employees in the Era of Open Artificial Intelligence and Strategies to Empower Them. *Health Care Science*, *4*(2), 154–157. DOI: 10.1002/hcs2.70011 PMID: 40241985

HSBC. (2021). *Artificial intelligence in financial crime detection*. HSBC Technology Report.

Huang, M. H., Rust, R. T., & Maksimovic, M. (2022). The role of automation in enhancing HR operations. *Journal of Service Research*, *25*(4), 321–335. DOI: 10.1177/10946705221104693

Huang, M.-H., & Rust, R. T. (2021). Artificial intelligence in service. *Journal of Service Research*, *24*(1), 3–14.

Huang, S., Lin, H., Zhou, Y., Ji, H., & Zhu, N. (2022). The influence of the policy of replacing environmental protection fees with taxes on enterprise green innovation—Evidence from China's heavily polluting industries. *Sustainability (Basel)*, *14*(11), 6850. DOI: 10.3390/su14116850

Hu, D., Navas, D. A., Gaube, S., Mozannar, H., Taylor, M. E., Dvijotham, K., & Bondi-Kelly, E. (2025). Human at the center: A framework for human-driven AI development. *AI Magazine*, *46*(4), e70043. Advance online publication. DOI: 10.1002/aaai.70043

Hund, A., Wagner, H.-T., Beimborn, D., & Weitzel, T. (2021). Digital innovation: Review and novel perspective. *The Journal of Strategic Information Systems*, *30*(4), 101695. DOI: 10.1016/j.jsis.2021.101695

Hussain, Z., Mohammad, S. I., Vasudevan, A., Awad, A., & Bansal, R. (2025). Exploring the effect of Industry 5.0 human-centric sustainability and green knowledge automation in enhancing green process adaptability: The mediating role of sustainable human–tech interaction. *Journal of Cleaner Production*, *537*, 147240. DOI: 10.1016/j.jclepro.2025.147240

Hutter, C., & Weber, E. (2023). Labour market effects of wage inequality and skill-biased technical change. *Applied Economics*, *55*(27), 3063–3084. DOI: 10.1080/00036846.2022.2108751

Hwang, J. (2024). Exploring the impact of AI on leadership styles: A comparative study of human-driven vs. AI-assisted decision-making in high-stakes environments. *International Journal of Science and Research Archive*, *13*(1), 3436–3446. DOI: 10.30574/ijsra.2024.13.1.2030

IBM Institutc for Business Value. (2024). *The talent pivot: Skills-first workforce strategies in the age of AI*. IBM.

IBM. (2018). *Augmented intelligence: AI and the future of cognitive collaboration*. IBM Institute for Business Value.

IBM. (2022). *SkillsBuild and workforce transformation report*.

Illeris, K. (2011). *The fundamentals of workplace learning: Understanding how people learn in working life*. Routledge.

ILO. (2025). Workforce 2030 Skills for thriving in the green and digital transitions. International Labour Organization, Geneva. https://www.ilo.org/sites/default/files/2025-12/Workforce%202030_Web_final.pdf

International Labour Organization. (2021). *Skills and lifelong learning in the digital economy*. https://www.ilo.org

Isiaku, L., & Dawud, A. M. (2025). Blockchain and the Smart Circular Economy: Real-World Applications and Insight. In Singh, R., Shafik, W., & Kumar, V. (Eds.), *Blockchain Technologies for Smart Circular Economy and Organisational Sustainability. Environmental Footprints and Eco-design of Products and Processes*. Springer., DOI: 10.1007/978-3-031-89183-0_13

Islamutdinov, V., Akhmetshin, E., Lydia, E. L., & Raja, P. V. K. (2024, April). Implementation of AI in an Ethical and Responsible Manner to Empower Education in Digital Sector. In International Conference on Smart Computing and Informatics (pp. 127-134). Singapore: Springer Nature Singapore. DOI: 10.1007/978-981-96-3939-7_13

Jain, V., Rastogi, M., Ramesh, J. V. N., Chauhan, A., Agarwal, P., Pramanik, S., & Gupta, A. (2023). FinTech and Artificial Intelligence in Relationship Banking and Computer Technology. In Saini, K., Mummoorthy, A., Chandrika, R., Gowri Ganesh, N. S., & Global, I. G. I. (Eds.), *AI, IoT, and Blockchain Breakthroughs in E-Governance*. DOI: 10.4018/978-1-6684-7697-0.ch011

Jaiswal, A., Arun, C. J., & Varma, A. (2022). Rebooting employees: Upskilling for artificial intelligence in multinational corporations. *International Journal of Human Resource Management, 33*(6), 1179–1208. DOI: 10.1080/09585192.2021.1891114

Jarrahi, M. H. (2018). Artificial intelligence and the future of work: Human-AI symbiosis in organizational decision making. *Business Horizons, 61*(4), 577–586. DOI: 10.1016/j.bushor.2018.03.007

Jarrahi, M. H. (2023). Human–AI collaboration in knowledge work. *Business Horizons, 66*(2), 197–206.

Jarrahi, M. H., Askay, D., Eshraghi, A., & Smith, P. (2023). Artificial intelligence and knowledge management: A partnership between human and AI. *Business Horizons, 66*(1), 87–99. DOI: 10.1016/j.bushor.2022.03.002

Jarrahi, M. H., Newlands, G., Lee, M. K., Wolf, C. T., Kinder, E., & Sutherland, W. (2021). Algorithmic management in a work context. *Big Data & Society, 8*(2), 20539517211020332. Advance online publication. DOI: 10.1177/20539517211020332

Jeong, C., Lee, S., Jeong, S., & Kim, S. (2025). A Study on the Framework for Evaluating the Ethics and Trustworthiness of Generative AI. arXiv preprint arXiv:2509.00398.

Jeon, G. (2025). Leveraging AI for ESG performance: A global analysis of national AI capabilities and sustainability in international business. *Business Strategy & Development, 8*(3), e70162. Advance online publication. DOI: 10.1002/bsd2.70162

Jesuthasan, R., & Boudreau, J. W. (2022). *Work without jobs: How to reboot your organization's work operating system*. MIT Press. DOI: 10.7551/mitpress/13930.001.0001

Jha, A. (2025). AI-augmented project management: The rise of the Intelligent Project Manager and the intelligent PMO. *Journal of Advances in Developmental Research, 16*(2), 1616. Advance online publication. DOI: 10.71097/IJAIDR.v16.i2.1616

Jia, J., Ning, X., & Liu, W. (2025). The consequences and theoretical explanation of workplace AI on employees: A systematic literature review. *J. Digit. Manag., 1*(1), 14. DOI: 10.1007/s44362-025-00016-3

Jordan, M. I. (2018). Artificial intelligence—The revolution hasn't happened yet. *Harvard Data Science Review*. https://hdsr.mitpress.mit.edu

Kabudi, T., Pappas, I., & Olsen, D. H. (2021). AI-enabled adaptive learning systems: A systematic mapping of the literature. *Computers and Education: Artificial Intelligence, 2*, 100017. DOI: 10.1016/j.caeai.2021.100017

Kanbach, D. K., Heiduk, L., Blueher, G., Schreiter, M., & Lahmann, A. (2023). The GenAI is out of the bottle: Generative artificial intelligence from a business model innovation perspective. *Review of Managerial Science, 18*(4), 1171–1197. DOI: 10.1007/s11846-023-00696-z

Kassa, B. Y., & Worku, E. K. (2025). The impact of artificial intelligence on organizational performance: The mediating role of employee productivity. *Journal of Open Innovation, 11*(1), 100474. DOI: 10.1016/j.joitmc.2025.100474

Katiraee, N., Berti, N., Das, A., Zennaro, I., Aldrighetti, R., Dimovski, V., Peljhan, D., Dobbs, D., Glock, C., Pacheco, G., Neumann, P., Ogawa, A., & Battini, D. (2024). A new roadmap for an age-inclusive workforce management practice and an international policies comparison. *Open Research Europe, 4*, 85. DOI: 10.12688/openreseurope.17159.1 PMID: 38933690

Kato, M., & Choi, S. (2022). Digital learning ecosystems and future education. *Computers & Education, 182*, 104463.

Katta, V., & Padhy, P. C. (2026). Gamification of HRM and green behaviour: Understanding the relationship between reciprocal benefits and engagement. *International Journal of Procurement Management, 25*(1), 1–20. DOI: 10.1504/IJPM.2026.150261

Kellogg, K. C., Valentine, M. A., & Christin, A. (2020). Algorithms at work: The new contested terrain of control. *The Academy of Management Annals, 14*(1), 366–410. DOI: 10.5465/annals.2018.0174

Khaliq, R., & Saritha, B. (2023). Benefits and challenges of adopting HR analytics: A comprehensive review. *Journal of Economics. Management and Trade, 29*(11), 24–33. DOI: 10.9734/jemt/2023/v29i111159

Khan, M. I., Parahyanti, E., & Hussain, S. (2024). The role generative AI in human resource management: Enhancing operational efficiency, decision-making, and addressing ethical challenges. *Asian Journal of Logistics Management, 3*(2), 104–125. DOI: 10.14710/ajlm.2024.24671

Khan, M. K., Huo, C., Zahid, R. M. A., & Maqsood, U. S. (2024). The automated sustainability auditor: Does artificial intelligence curtail greenwashing behavior in Chinese firms? *Business Strategy and the Environment, 33*(8), 9015–9039. DOI: 10.1002/bse.3961

Kodagoda, T. (2026). Generation Y Employees' Understandings on Artificial Intelligence (AI): Interventions at Workplace. In *Communication and Knowledge in Organizations: Approaches from Positivist and Interpretivist Paradigms* (pp. 19-32). Singapore: Springer Nature Singapore. https://doi.org/DOI: 10.1007/978-981-95-0622-4_2

Komajwar, S. (2025). Artificial Intelligence in Human Resources: Transforming talent management and workforce efficiency. *International Journal For Multidisciplinary Research*, *7*(2), 39595. Advance online publication. DOI: 10.36948/ijfmr.2025.v07i02.39595

Kong, H., Yuan, Y., Baruch, Y., Bu, N., Jiang, X., & Wang, K. (2021). Influences of Artificial Intelligence (AI) awareness on career competency and job burnout. *International Journal of Contemporary Hospitality Management*, *33*(2), 717–734. DOI: 10.1108/IJCHM-07-2020-0789

Kshetri, N. (2021). Evolving uses of artificial intelligence in human resource management in emerging economies in the global South: Some preliminary evidence. *Management Research Review*, *44*(7), 970–990. DOI: 10.1108/MRR-03-2020-0168

Kulkarni, S. R., & Kulkarni, S. S. (2024). Revolutionizing organizations by technological innovations in HR. *Shodh Sari-An International Multidisciplinary Journal*, *03*(01), 03–14. DOI: 10.59231/SARI7650

Kulmanov, T., Dadabaev, U., Qulmetov, M., Ulashov, A., & Eshboyev, M.. (2025). Global services market transformation: Digitalization export trends and future forecasts. *ACM International Conference Proceeding Series*. DOI: 10.1145/3726122.3726245

Kumar, R., Gupta, P., Singh, S., & Jain, D. (2021). Human empowerment by Industry 5.0 in digital era: Analysis of enablers. In *FLAME 2020: 2nd International Conference on Future Learning Aspects of Mechanical Engineering* (pp. 401–410). Springer. DOI: 10.1007/978-981-33-4320-7_36

Kumar, S., & Bargavi, D. S. K. M. (2024). Trust's significance in human-AI communication and decision-making. *INTERANTIONAL JOURNAL OF SCIENTIFIC RESEARCH IN ENGINEERING AND MANAGEMENT*, *08*(02), 1–10. DOI: 10.55041/IJSREM28468

Kuzmin, E., Bondareva, V. S., Shodiyev, A., & Ochilov, I. (2025). Digitalization, Innovation, and Competitiveness: Insights from a Cross-Country Analysis of Labor Productivity Effects. In Artificial Intelligence and Digital Transformation: From Innovation to Implementation (pp. 307-329). Cham: Springer Nature Switzerland. DOI: 10.1007/978-3-032-00118-4_17

Labib, N. M., & Alarabi, N. I. (2022). A Proposed Framework to Apply Secured Mobile Banking in Egypt. In Magdi, D. A., Helmy, Y. K., Mamdouh, M., & Joshi, A. (Eds.), *Digital Transformation Technology. Lecture Notes in Networks and Systems* (Vol. 224). Springer., DOI: 10.1007/978-981-16-2275-5_22

Laker, D. R., & Powell, J. L. (2011). The differences between hard and soft skills and their relative impact on training transfer. *Human Resource Development Quarterly, 22*(1), 111–122. DOI: 10.1002/hrdq.20063

Lee, Z. (2023). The Skill-Specific Automatability of Aging Workers and Its Impact on Retirement Decisions, Work, Aging and Retirement. https://doi.org/DOI: 10.1093/workar/waad008

Lee, C. C., Czaja, S. J., & Sharit, J. (2009). Training Older Workers for Technology-Based Employment. *Educational Gerontology, 35*(1), 15–31. DOI: 10.1080/03601270802300091 PMID: 20351795

Lee, I. S. (2023a). Economic Effects of Industrial Automation in Aging Workforces. *Intersect: The Stanford Journal of Science. Technology in Society, 17*(1), 1–15.

Leippold, M. (2023). Sentiment spin: Attacking financial sentiment with GPT-4. *Finance Research Letters, 55*, 103957. DOI: 10.1016/j.frl.2023.103957

Lenka, R., Gupta, R., Pabalkar, V., & Chitranshi, J. (2026). Ensuring privacy and data integrity in payroll systems using blockchain and IPFS. In *Lecture Notes in Networks and Systems* (Vol. 1652, pp. 300–311). DOI: 10.1007/978-3-032-06691-6_29

Lesener, T., Gusy, B., & Wolter, C. (2020). The job demands–resources model: A meta-analytic review. *Journal of Occupational Health Psychology, 25*(4), 261–277. DOI: 10.1037/ocp0000162

Li L. (2022). Reskilling and Upskilling the Future-ready Workforce for Industry 4.0 and Beyond. *Information systems frontiers: a journal of research and innovation*, 1–16. https://doi.org/DOI: 10.1007/s10796-022-10308-y

Liang, W., Yuksekgonul, M., Mao, Y., Wu, E., & Zou, J. (2024). GPT detectors are biased against non-native English writers. *Patterns (New York, N.Y.), 4*(7), 100779. DOI: 10.1016/j.patter.2023.100779 PMID: 37521038

Li, N., Yan, Y., Yang, Y., & Gu, A. (2022). Artificial intelligence capability and organizational creativity: The role of knowledge sharing and organizational cohesion. *Frontiers in Psychology, 13*. Advance online publication. DOI: 10.3389/fpsyg.2022.845277

LinkedIn Learning. (2023). *Workplace learning report 2023.* https://learning.linkedin.com

Longo, F., Padovano, A., & Umbrello, S. (2020). Value-oriented and ethical technology engineering in Industry 5.0: A human-centric perspective for the design of the factory of the future. *Applied Sciences (Basel, Switzerland), 10*(12), 1–25. DOI: 10.3390/app10124182

Lozano, R., Merrill, M. Y., Sammalisto, K., Ceulemans, K., & Lozano, F. J. (2022). Connecting competencies and sustainability. *Journal of Cleaner Production, 366*, 132993.

Lu, Y., Zheng, H., Chand, S., Xia, W., Liu, Z., Xu, X., & Bao, J. (2022). Outlook on human-centric manufacturing towards Industry 5.0. *Journal of Manufacturing Systems, 62*, 612–627. DOI: 10.1016/j.jmsy.2022.02.001

Lynn, T., Rosati, P., Conway, E., & van der Werff, L. (2023). Introducing the Future of Work: Key Trends, Concepts, Technologies and Avenues for Future Research. In Lynn, T., Rosati, P., Conway, E., & van der Werff, L. (Eds.), *The Future of Work.* Palgrave Studies in Digital Business & Enabling Technologies. Palgrave Macmillan., DOI: 10.1007/978-3-031-31494-0_1

M., B., N., R., L. N., D., Sahoo, S. K., Ankanahalli Shankaregowda, S., Kannanugo, N., M., D., & M., V. K. (2024). AI-Enhanced Leadership Decision Support System Using ChatGPT for Ethical Learning. In A. Agnihotri, R. Agarwal, A. Maurya, M. Sinha, & B. Balusamy (Eds.), *Impact of New Technology on Next-Generation Leadership* (pp. 137-161). IGI Global Scientific Publishing. DOI: 10.4018/979-8-3693-1946-8.ch008

Mainhagu, S., Grima, F., & Defiebre-Muller, R. (2018). Career stability despite mobility norms: Work identification as a source of both dependence and free will. M@n@gement, 21(3): 994-1031

Makhmudov, S., Maqsood, M., Musaev, U., Urazmetov, M., & Shahzadi, A. (2025). Foundations of agentic AI redefining autonomy in learning environments. In *Multidisciplinary Perspectives on Agentic AI in Educational Systems.* IGI Global., DOI: 10.4018/979-8-3373-4621-2.ch001

Makhmudov, S., Otakhonova, D., Kulmanov, T., Shamshiyeva, N., Juraev, U., Ruziev, G., & Sabirova, U. (2026). The Impact of Digital Marketing and Mobile Applications on Service Innovation in German Companies. *International Review of Management and Marketing, 16*(1), 210–217. DOI: 10.32479/irmm.22052

Malik, A., Budhwar, P., & Kazmi, B. A. (2023). Artificial intelligence (AI)-assisted HRM: Towards an extended strategic HRM framework. *Human Resource Management Review, 33*(1), 100940. DOI: 10.1016/j.hrmr.2022.100940

Mariani, M., & Dwivedi, Y. K. (2024). Generative artificial intelligence in innovation management: A preview of future research developments. *Journal of Business Research, 175*, 114542. DOI: 10.1016/j.jbusres.2024.114542

Marisamy, K., Selvakumar, A., Rajasekar, B., Natarajan, R., Atajanova, A., & Makhmudov, S. (2026). Smart logistics integrating AI, IoT, blockchain, and Robotics for a sustainable Future. In *Emerging Trends in Smart Logistics Technologies* (pp. 73–104). IGI Global Scientific Publishing., DOI: 10.4018/979-8-3373-2434-0.ch003

Marlapudi, K., & Lenka, U. (2024). Unlocking the potential: Redefining talent and competency mapping for Industry 4.0. *Management Research Review, 47*(11), 1805–1832. DOI: 10.1108/MRR-07-2023-0496

Maslach, C., & Leiter, M. P. (2016). Understanding the burnout experience: Recent research and its implications for psychiatry. *World Psychiatry; Official Journal of the World Psychiatric Association (WPA), 15*(2), 103–111. DOI: 10.1002/wps.20311 PMID: 27265691

Mattingly, V., & Kraiger, K. (2019). Can emotional intelligence be trained? A meta-analytical investigation. *Human Resource Management Review, 29*(2), 140–155. DOI: 10.1016/j.hrmr.2018.03.002

Mayer, J. D., & Salovey, P. (1997). What is emotional intelligence? In Salovey, P., & Sluyter, D. J. (Eds.), *Emotional development and emotional intelligence: Educational implications** (pp. 3–31). Basic Books.

McCartney, S., & Fu, N. (2022). Promise versus reality: A systematic review of the ongoing debates in people analytics. *Journal of Organizational Effectiveness: People and Performance, 9*(2), 281–311. DOI: 10.1108/JOEPP-01-2021-0013

McCartney, S., & Fu, N. (2023). Enacting people analytics: Exploring the direct and complementary effects of analytical and storytelling skills. *Human Resource Management, 62*(2), 129–148. DOI: 10.1002/hrm.22194

McIntosh, T. (2020). The Impact of Technological Advances on Older Workers. doctoral dissertation. Walden University. https://scholarworks.waldenu.edu/cgi/viewcontent.cgi?article=10679&context=dissertations

McKinsey & Company. (2023). *The state of AI in 2023: Generative AI's breakout year*. McKinsey Global Institute. https://www.mckinsey.com

McKinsey & Company. (2023).The state of AI in organizations. https://www.mckinsey.com

McKinsey & Company. (2025). *Superagency in the workplace: Empowering people to unlock AI's full potential.* https://www.mckinsey.com/

McKinsey Global Institute. (2021). The future of work after. *COVID, 19*, •••. https://www.mckinsey.com

McKinsey Global Institute. (2023). *The economic potential of generative AI: The next productivity frontier*. McKinsey & Company.

Mecocci, F. B., & Maghssudipour, A. (2025). Is aging in the regional labor market wiping out localized external economies? Evidence from European manufacturing firms. *Industrial and Corporate Change, 34*(4), 831–854. DOI: 10.1093/icc/dtaf006

Meister, J. (2021). The future of work: How AI is transforming HR. *Harvard Business Review*. https://hbr.org

Miao, C., Humphrey, R. H., & Qian, S. (2020). Emotional intelligence and job performance: A meta-analysis. *Human Performance, 33*(2), 1–24. DOI: 10.1080/08959285.2019.1683374

Microsoft. (2023). *AI copilots and human-centered productivity systems*. Microsoft Official Blog. https://www.microsoft.com

Microsoft. (2024). *2024 Work Trend Index Annual Report: AI at work is here. Now comes the hard part*. Microsoft.

Mikki Ewim, C. P., Omokhoa, H. E., Ogundeji, I. A., & Ibeh, A. I. (2021). Future of work in banking: Adapting workforce skills to digital transformation challenges. *International Journal of Multidisciplinary Research and Growth Evaluation, 2*(1), 663–676. DOI: 10.54660/.IJMRGE.2021.2.1.663-676

Milad, A., & Whiba, M. (2024). Exploring Explainable Artificial Intelligence technologies: Approaches, challenges, and applications. *International Science and Technology Journal, 34*(1), 1–21. DOI: 10.62341/amia8430

Minbaeva, D. (2021). HR analytics and value creation. *Human Resource Management Journal, 31*(2), 361–374.

MIT Sloan Management Review. (2021). *Expanding AI's impact with organizational learning*. MIT Sloan Research Report. https://sloanreview.mit.edu

Moen, P., Kojola, E., & Schaefers, K. (2017). Organizational Change Around an Older Workforce. *The Gerontologist, 57*(5), 847–856. DOI: 10.1093/geront/gnw048 PMID: 27048706

Mola, R. (2025). Strategic alignment of Workday talent & performance modules with organizational leadership competencies. *International Journal Management and Organizational Research, 4*(5), 123–127. DOI: 10.54660/IJMOR.2025.4.5.123-127

Mollick, E. R., & Mollick, L. (2023). Assigning AI: Seven approaches for students, with prompts. SSRN Electronic Journal. DOI: 10.2139/ssrn.4475995

Mollick, E., & Mollick, L. (2023). Using AI to implement effective teaching strategies in classrooms: Five strategies, including prompts. SSRN Electronic Journal. DOI: 10.2139/ssrn.4391243

Mooney, A., Earl, J., Gerrans, P., Wijeratne, C., & Mooney, C. (2025). Integrating career, health, and finance in a holistic retirement planning intervention for Australian older workers. *Work, Aging and Retirement, 11*(1), 28–46. DOI: 10.1093/workar/waad029

Motasem Alrfai, M., Kamal Bani Yaseen, O., Khairo Issa Al Daabseh, T., Ismail Noori Al.Blaushi, H., & Bataineh, M. (2025). The role of HR digital competence in enhancing FinTech-based information security and risk management: Evidence from Smart PLS modeling. *EDPACS*. DOI: 10.1080/07366981.2025.2586479

Murire, O. T. (2024). Artificial Intelligence and Its Role in Shaping Organizational Work Practices and Culture. *Administrative Sciences, 14*(12), 316. DOI: 10.3390/admsci14120316

Muthuswamy, V. V., & Absamatov, A. (2025). *Determinants of students engagement and their role in boosting students' academic performance among higher education institutions*. Revista Electrónica de LEEME., DOI: 10.58262/LEEME.56.13

Nag, R. (2018). Strategic HR in the digital age: Rethinking capability development. *International Journal of Human Resource Management, 29*(12), 1856–1878.

Nahavandi, S. (2019). Industry 5.0—A human-centric solution. *Sustainability (Basel), 11*(16), 4371. Advance online publication. DOI: 10.3390/su11164371

Napoli, G., Barbaro, S., Giuffrida, S., & Trovato, M. R. (2021). The European Green Deal: New Challenges for the Economic Feasibility of Energy Retrofit at District Scale. In Bevilacqua, C., Calabrò, F., & Della Spina, L. (Eds.), *New Metropolitan Perspectives. NMP 2020. Smart Innovation, Systems and Technologies* (Vol. 178). Springer., DOI: 10.1007/978-3-030-48279-4_116

NASA. (2022). *Artificial intelligence for climate modelling and space research.* NASA Technical Reports. https://www.nasa.gov

Nedeljko, M., Gu, Y., & Bostan, C. M. (2024). The dual impact of technological tools on health and technostress among older workers: An integrative literature review. *Cognition Technology and Work, 26*(1), 47–61. DOI: 10.1007/s10111-023-00741-7

Neumark, D., Burn, I., & Button, P. (2019). Is It Harder for Older Workers to Find Jobs? New and Improved Evidence from a Field Experiment. *Journal of Political Economy, 127*(2), 922–970. Advance online publication. DOI: 10.1086/701029

Nguyen, T. H., Dinh, V. H., Nguyen, H. M., Do, H. M. H., Luong, M. D., & Nguyen, H. H. A. (2026). AI-analytics capabilities and knowledge assimilation: Driving innovation in SMEs. *International Journal of Innovation Science*, 1–25. DOI: 10.1108/ijis-07-2025-0338

Nigar, M., Juli, J. F., Golder, U., Alam, M. J., & Hossain, M. K. (2025). Artificial intelligence and technological unemployment: Understanding trends, technology's adverse roles, and current mitigation guidelines. *Journal of Open Innovation, 11*(3), 100607. DOI: 10.1016/j.joitmc.2025.100607

Nithya, B., Krishnan, K., Chachithanantham, A., & Ravikumar, S. (2026). Optimizing digital talent management with AI: Analytical approaches and innovations. In *Artificial Intelligence for Digital Talent Acquisition and Management* (pp. 23–53). Emerald Publishing Limited., DOI: 10.1108/978-1-83708-884-320251002

Noe, R. A., Clarke, A. D. M., & Klein, H. J. (2021). Learning in the twenty-first-century workplace. *Annual Review of Organizational Psychology and Organizational Behavior, 8*, 245–275.

Nofal, H. A., Mohamed, A. E., Almadani, N., Mahfouz, R., Bahri, H. A., Ali, H. T., & Elrafey, D. S. (2025). The impact of an artificial intelligence enhancement program on healthcare providers' knowledge, attitudes, and workplace flourishing. *Frontiers in Public Health, 13*(1639333), 1639333. DOI: 10.3389/fpubh.2025.1639333

Nonaka, I., & Takeuchi, H. (1995). *The knowledge-creating company*. Oxford University PressNew York., DOI: 10.1093/oso/9780195092691.001.0001

Noy, S., & Zhang, W. (2023). Experimental evidence on the productivity effects of generative artificial intelligence. *Science, 381*(6654), 187–192. DOI: 10.1126/science.adh2586 PMID: 37440646

Nunes, A. (2021). Automation Doesn't Just Create or Destroy Jobs — It Transforms Them. https://hbr.org/2021/11/automation-doesnt-just-create-or-destroy-jobs-it-transforms-them

Nunnaguppala, M., Meenakshisundaram, K. S., Desetty, A. G., Venkteshwar, A., Bora, B., & Khudayer, K. (2025). Multimodal AI-integrated performance monitoring system for global team management. In *Proceedings of the 2025 International Conference on Recent Innovation in Science, Engineering and Technology (ICRISET)*. DOI: 10.1109/ICRISET64803.2025.11251788

Nwokolo, S. C., Singh, R., Khan, S., Kumar, A., & Luthra, S. (2023). Africa's awakening to climate action. In *CSR, sustainability, ethics & governance* (pp. 299–310). DOI: 10.1007/978-3-031-44514-9_9

Nyathani, R. (2023). Preparing for the future of work: How HR tech is shaping remote work. *Journal of Technology and Systems*, *5*(1), 60–73. DOI: 10.47941/jts.1498

Nyathani, R.HR Digital Transformation Architect IL USA. (2022). AI-powered recruitment the future of HR digital transformation. *Journal of Artificial Intelligence & Cloud Computing*, *1–5*(4), SRC/JAICC-145. Advance online publication. DOI: 10.47363/JAICC/2022(1)133

Odia, J. O. (2026). The Ethical and Managerial Implications of Integrating Generative Artificial Intelligence Into Knowledge Management Processes.4

OECD. (2006). Ageing and Employment Policies. https://www.oecd.org/content/dam/oecd/en/publications/reports/2006/02/live-longer-work-longer_g1gh607a/9789264035881-en.pdf

OECD. (2009). OECD Employment Outlook 2009. https://www.oecd.org/content/dam/oecd/en/publications/reports/2009/09/oecd-employment-outlook-2009_g1ghb2df/empl_outlook-2009-en.pdf

OECD. (2019). *OECD principles on artificial intelligence*. Organisation for Economic Co-operation and Development. https://www.oecd.org

OECD. (2019). *OECD skills outlook 2019: Thriving in a digital world*. OECD Publishing.

OECD. (2023). *OECD Employment Outlook 2023: Artificial Intelligence and the Labour Market*. OECD Publishing., DOI: 10.1787/08785bba-

OECD. (2023). *OECD skills outlook 2023*. https://www.oecd.org

OECD. (2023). *Retaining Talent at All Ages, Ageing and Employment Policies*. OECD Publishing., DOI: 10.1787/00dbdd06-

OECD. (2024). *Promoting Better Career Choices for Longer Working Lives: Stepping Up Not Stepping Out, Ageing and Employment Policies*. OECD Publishing., DOI: 10.1787/1ef9a0d0-

OECD. (2025). *OECD Employment Outlook 2025: Can We Get Through the Demographic Crunch?* OECD Publishing., DOI: 10.1787/194a947b-

OECD. (2025). *OECD Skills Outlook 2025: Building the Skills of the 21st Century for All.* OECD Publishing., DOI: 10.1787/26163cd3-

OECD. (2025a). *Education Policy Outlook 2025: Nurturing Engaged and Resilient Lifelong Learners in a World of Digital Transformation.* OECD Publishing., DOI: 10.1787/c3f402ba-

Open, A. I. (2023). *GPT-4 technical report.* OpenAI Research Publications. https://openai.com

Özdemir, V., & Hekim, N. (2018). Birth of Industry 5.0: Making sense of big data with artificial intelligence, "the internet of things" and next-generation technology policy. *Omics : A Journal of Integrative Biology*, *22*(1), 65–76. DOI: 10.1089/omi.2017.0194 PMID: 29293405

Paesano, A. (2021). Artificial intelligence and creative activities inside organizational behavior. *The International Journal of Organizational Analysis.* Advance online publication. DOI: 10.1108/IJOA-09-2020-2421

Pai, R. Y., Shetty, A., Shetty, A. D., Bhandary, R., Shetty, J., Nayak, S., Dinesh, T. K., & D'souza, K. J. (2022). Integrating artificial intelligence for knowledge management systems – synergy among people and technology: A systematic review of the evidence. *Economic Research-Ekonomska Istraživanja*, *35*(1), 7043–7065. DOI: 10.1080/1331677x.2022.2058976

Pandey, D., Singh, G., Joshi, L., Polyakova, O., Sungatullina, D., & Singh, R. (2024). Organizational preparedness for navigating disruption towards sustainability: Strategies' analysis. E3S Web of Conferences. DOI: 10.1051/e3sconf/202457407001

Pan, X. (2023). Online Learning Environments, Learners' Empowerment, and Learning Behavioral Engagement: The Mediating Role of Learning Motivation. *SAGE Open*, *13*(4), 21582440231205098. Advance online publication. DOI: 10.1177/21582440231205098

Parker, S. K., & Grote, G. (2022). Automation, algorithms, and beyond: Work design in the future. *Annual Review of Organizational Psychology and Organizational Behavior*, *9*, 1–28.

Peng, S., Kalliamvakou, E., Cihon, P., & Demirer, M. (2023). The impact of AI on developer productivity: Evidence from GitHub Copilot. arXiv preprint. https://doi.org//arXiv.2302.06590DOI: 10.48550

Pfeifer, Y., Murnane, E., & Schwede, D. (2024). Cognitive load and decision fatigue in AI-augmented workplaces: Evidence from longitudinal field research. *The Journal of Applied Psychology*. Advance online publication.

Phd student at Tashkent International University, U., & Qizi, F. M. A. (2025). Artificial intelligence and team effectiveness in management: a transformative impact on decision-making, collaboration, and productivity. *International Journal Of Management And Economics Fundamental, 5*(3), 110–115. DOI: 10.37547/ijmef/Volume05Issue03-16

Plekhanov, D., Franke, H., & Netland, T. H. (2023). Digital transformation: A review and research agenda. *European Management Journal, 41*(6), 821–844. DOI: 10.1016/j.emj.2022.09.007

Policepatil, S., Sharma, J., Kumar, B., Singh, D., Pramanik, S., Gupta, A., & Mahabub, B. S. (2025). Financial Sector Hyper-Automation: Transforming Banking and Investing Procedures. In *Examining Global Regulations During the Rise of Fintech* (pp. 299–318). IGI Global., DOI: 10.4018/979-8-3693-3803-2.ch012

Popkova, E. G., Bogoviz, A. V., Tikhomirov, Y. A., Arupova, N. R., & Aghabekyan, E. V. (2026). Sustainable management of human resources in smart transport systems as an advanced infrastructure of the digital economy. In *Lecture Notes in Intelligent Transportation and Infrastructure* (Part F1434, pp. 257–264). DOI: 10.1007/978-3-032-12181-3_26

Porter, M. E., & Kramer, M. R. (2021). Creating shared value. *Harvard Business Review*.

Prabagar, S., Mothkur, R., Swetha, C. B., Kurian, A., Pavithra, K., & Aarthi, S. (2025). Generative AI for inclusive special education. In *Advances in Computational Intelligence and Robotics* (pp. 205–236). IGI Global Scientific Publishing. DOI: 10.4018/979-8-3373-3745-6.ch008

Prabha, K. R., Mabel, B. R., Isaev, F., Mamadiyarov, Z., Raxmatullayevich, K. U., & Erkinjon, T. (2026). A Multi-Layer Artificial Intelligence–Enabled Governance Framework for Integrating Information Security Management, Quality Management, and Strategic Human Resource Analytics: An Empirical Study on the Role of Corporate Social Responsibility in Sustainable Organizational Performance. *Quality - Access to Success, 27*(210). Advance online publication. DOI: 10.47750/QAS/27.210.45

Pramanik, S. (2024). AI-Powered Hospital Accounting: Towards Sound Financial Management. In *Exploring Global FinTech Advancement and Applications* (pp. 121–142). IGI Global. DOI: 10.4018/979-8-3693-1561-3.ch005

PwC. (2023). *Upskilling for shared prosperity*. https://www.pwc.com

PwC. (2024). *27th Annual Global CEO Survey: Thriving in an age of continuous reinvention*. PricewaterhouseCoopers.

Qadeer, A., & Awad, A. (2025). Generative AI in advertisements: A conceptual framework based on the technology acceptance model. In Wahid, A., & Awad, A. (Eds.), *Impacts of AI generated content on brand reputation* (pp. 109–127). IGI Global., DOI: 10.4018/979-8-3373-4327-3.ch004

Raghavan, M., Barocas, S., Kleinberg, J., & Levy, K. (2020). Mitigating bias in algorithmic hiring: evaluating claims and practices. In Proceedings of the 2020 Conference on Fairness, Accountability, and Transparency (FAT* '20). Association for Computing Machinery, New York, NY, USA, 469–481. https://doi.org/DOI: 10.1145/3351095.3372828

Raghu, N. V. N., T., L. N., D., Kumar B. M., H., & Shankaregowda, S. A. (2025). Enhancing Critical Thinking Through Problem-Based Learning: A Comprehensive Approach to Modern Education. In M. Lytras, P. Ordóñez de Pablos, & T. Aldosemani (Eds.), *Fostering Teacher Skills and Critical Thinking in Modern Education* (pp. 259-282). IGI Global Scientific Publishing. DOI: 10.4018/979-8-3373-1692-5.ch011

Raina, K., Sharma, G. D., Taheri, B., Dev, D., & Chavriya, S. (2026). Artificial intelligence-driven management: Bridging innovation, knowledge creation, and sustainable business practices. *Journal of Innovation &amp. Knowledge (Beverly Hills, Calif.), 11*, 100860. DOI: 10.1016/j.jik.2025.100860

Raisch, S., & Krakowski, S. (2021). Artificial intelligence and management: The automation–augmentation paradox. *Academy of Management Review*, *46*(1), 192–210. DOI: 10.5465/amr.2018.0072

Rajeswari, M., Vanitha, C. L., Xudoynazarova, S., Mamadiyarov, Z., Naveen, S., Nematovich, K. I., & Isaev, F. (2026). Design and Validation of an Explainable Artificial Intelligence–Based Decision Intelligence Model for Cyber Risk–Aware Quality Systems and Ethical Human Resource Management: Investigating the Moderating Influence of Corporate Social Responsibility in Digitally Transformed Organizations. *Quality - Access to Success*, *27*(210). Advance online publication. DOI: 10.47750/QAS/27.210.46

Rambhau Patil, L. (2024). AI IN WORKFORCE PLANNING AND PERFORMANCE MANAGEMENT. In *AI-Powered HR Finance: Transforming Workforce Management and Financial Strategies in the Digital Age* (pp. 128–137). Iterative International Publishers, Selfypage Developers Pvt Ltd. DOI: 10.58532/nbennurptch12

Ranasinghe, T., Grosse, E. H., Glock, C. H., & Jaber, M. Y. (2024). Never too late to learn: Unlocking the potential of aging workforce in manufacturing and service industries. *International Journal of Production Economics*, *270*, 109193. DOI: 10.1016/j.ijpe.2024.109193

Rane, N. (2023). Role and challenges of ChatGPT and similar generative artificial intelligence in business management. Available at *SSRN* 4603227. DOI: 10.2139/ssrn.4603227

Rane, N. (2024). Role and challenges of ChatGPT, Gemini, and similar generative artificial intelligence in human resource management. *Studies in Economics and Business Relations*, *5*(1), 11–23. DOI: 10.48185/sebr.v5i1.1001

Rašticová, M., Šácha, J., Lakomý, M., & Mishra, P. K. (2025). Technostress Among Older Workers: A Central European Perspective. *Psychology Research and Behavior Management*, *18*, 1211–1225. DOI: 10.2147/PRBM.S508500 PMID: 40438320

Rathinavel, P., Ravikumar, R. N., Aarthi, S., Habib, M., Salaeva, N., & Pardaev, J. (2025). Augmenting human capabilities. In *Advances in Computational Intelligence and Robotics* (pp. 1–30). IGI Global Scientific Publishing. DOI: 10.4018/979-8-3373-2372-5.ch001

Ratnam, D. S., & Devi, V. R. (2023). Addressing impediments to HR analytics adoption: Guide to HRD professionals. *Human Resource Development International*, *26*(2), 237–247. DOI: 10.1080/13678868.2023.2195986

Ravikumar, & Aarthi, S. (2025a). Cognitive collaboration. In *Advances in Computational Intelligence and Robotics* (pp. 125–158). IGI Global Scientific Publishing. DOI: 10.4018/979-8-3373-7416-1.ch006

Ravikumar, & Aarthi, S. (2025b). Conscious AI Integration in business education. In *Advances in Computational Intelligence and Robotics* (pp. 73–104). IGI Global Scientific Publishing. DOI: 10.4018/979-8-3373-4377-8.ch003

Ravikumar, & Aarthi, S. (2026). Synergizing innovation. In *Advances in Computational Intelligence and Robotics* (pp. 59–90). IGI Global Scientific Publishing. DOI: 10.4018/979-8-3373-7620-2.ch003

Ravikumar, R. N., & Aarthi, S. (2025b). Human-AI synergy for organizational resilience. In *Advances in Computational Intelligence and Robotics* (pp. 287–322). IGI Global Scientific Publishing. DOI: 10.4018/979-8-3373-7416-1.ch011

Ravikumar, R. N., & Aarthi, S. (2025c). Towards collaborative intelligence. In *Advances in Computational Intelligence and Robotics* (pp. 1–32). IGI Global Scientific Publishing. DOI: 10.4018/979-8-3373-5747-8.ch001

Ravikumar, R. N., Aarthi, S., & Mamadiyarov, Z. (2026). Building the foundations of augmented organizations through AI empowerment. In *Advances in Computational Intelligence and Robotics* (pp. 101–130). IGI Global Scientific Publishing. DOI: 10.4018/979-8-3373-8607-2.ch006

Ravikumar, R. N., Aarthi, S., & Mamadiyarov, Z. (2026). Mitigating Risks Through AI-Powered Fraud Detection Systems in Digital Banking. In Innovating Cost-Efficient and Scalable Business Models in the Digital Era (pp. 343-376). IGI Global Scientific Publishing. https://doi.org/DOI: 10.4018/979-8-3373-2120-2.ch011

Ravikumar, R. N., Aarthi, S., Atamuratova, Z., Ashirova, A., Jurayev, K., & Hayitova, M. (2026). Comprehensive Evaluation of AI-Driven Systems in Modern Hospital Environments. In Evaluation and Assessment of AI-Driven Systems in Hospitals (pp. 61-88). IGI Global Scientific Publishing. DOI: 10.4018/979-8-3373-2787-7.ch003

Ravikumar, R. N., Aarthi, S., Rai, P. K., & Mamadiyarov, Z. (2025). Intelligent code analysis and feedback generation. In *Advances in Computational Intelligence and Robotics* (pp. 137–170). IGI Global Scientific Publishing. DOI: 10.4018/979-8-3373-0598-1.ch006

Ravikumar, R. N., Aarthi, S., Ruzimova, F., & Mamadiyarov, Z. (2026). Training and Development in AI-Driven Education Scaling Solutions: K-12 to Workforce. In Transforming Education with Data Science in the AI Era (pp. 267-298). IGI Global Scientific Publishing. DOI: DOI: 10.4018/979-8-3373-2185-1.ch010

Ravikumar, R. N., Aarthi, S., Usmani, M. A., Rai, P. K., Jumaniyozova, M., & Narboshova, M. (2026). Advancements in Multilingual Speech Technologies for Human-Computer Interaction. In Advancements in Speech Processing for Human-Computer Interaction (pp. 101-132). IGI Global Scientific Publishing. DOI: 10.4018/979-8-3373-3048-8.ch004

Ravikumar, R. N., & Aarthi, S. (2025d). Integrating machine learning with human decision making in HR. In *Empowering Human Resources Through Human-Computer Interaction* (pp. 115–146). IGI Global Scientific Publishing., DOI: 10.4018/979-8-3373-1676-5.ch005

Ray, C. (2023). Internal Mobility: A Review and Agenda for Future Research. *Journal of Management*, *50*(1), 264–306. DOI: 10.1177/01492063231180826

Redchuk, A., Walas Mateo, F., Pascal, G., & Tornillo, J. E. (2023). Adoption Case of IioT and Machine Learning to Improve Energy Consumption at a Process Manufacturing Firm, Under Industry 5.0 Model. *Big Data and Cognitive Computing*, 7(1), 42. Advance online publication. DOI: 10.3390/bdcc7010042

Romeo, G., & Conti, D. (2025). Exploring automation bias in human–AI collaboration: A review and implications for explainable AI. *AI &amp. Society*, *41*(1), 259–278. DOI: 10.1007/s00146-025-02422-7

Russell, S. (2019). *Human compatible: Artificial intelligence and the problem of control*. Viking.

Saad, M., Awad, A., Fathy Aziz, A., & Rashad Shma, T. (2025). Influencer marketing's impact on credibility and purchase intention: A study on University of Bisha students in Saudi Arabia. *Innovative Marketing*, *21*(1), 326–337. DOI: 10.21511/im.21(1).2025.26

Sætra, H. S. (2022). The AI ESG protocol: Evaluating and disclosing the environment, social, and governance implications of artificial intelligence capabilities, assets, and activities. *Sustainable Development (Bradford)*. Advance online publication. DOI: 10.1002/sd.2438

Sambamurthy, V., Bharadwaj, A., & Grover, V. (2003). Shaping agility through digital options: Reconceptualizing the role of information technology in contemporary firms1. *Management Information Systems Quarterly*, *27*(2), 237–263. DOI: 10.2307/30036530

Samorodov, A. (1999). *Ageing and labour markets for older workers*. Employment and Training Department International Labour Office Geneva.

Sapayev, V. O., Hayat, N., Mamadiyarov, Z., & Ahmad, M. (2026). Inside the Black Box: How Generative AI Creates Digital Synthetics. In Digital Synthetic Data and Outputs (pp. 409-434). IGI Global Scientific Publishing. https://doi.org/DOI: 10.4018/979-8-3373-2277-3.ch016

Schmelzer, P. (2011). Unemployment and occupational mobility at the beginning of employment career in Germany and the UK. *IAB-Discussion Paper 25/2011*. https://doku.iab.de/discussionpapers/2011/dp2511.pdf

Schmidpeter, B., & Winter-Ebmer, R. (2021). Automation, unemployment, and the role of labor market training. *European Economic Review*, *137*, 103808. DOI: 10.1016/j.euroecorev.2021.103808

Schwab, K. (2016). The Fourth Industrial Revolution. World Economic Forum.

Seba, F., Isola, M., Mills, L., Zalake, M., & Krive, J. (2025). Incorporating generative AI into a health informatics curriculum to build 21st century competencies: Multisite pre-post study. *JMIR Medical Informatics, 13*(v13i4e76507), e76507. DOI: 10.2196/76507

Shabat, M. E. (2020). Early retirement incentive programs as a human resources restructuring strategy in public sector: Theoretical perspective. *Review of Economics and Political Science*, *5*(1), 69–90. DOI: 10.1108/REPS-06-2019-0087

Shaheen, A., Khataan, A., Awad, A., Yahia Shams Eldin, A., & Elnour, A. (2025). The role of influencer content value and credibility in purchase intention. *Innovative Marketing*, *21*(3), 14–30. DOI: 10.21511/im.21(3).2025.02

Shams Eldin, A. Y., Elnour, A., Omer Ahmed Hassan, R., & Awad, A. (2025). The role of technological and environmental factors in creating business value from social media dynamic capabilities for SMEs in Saudi Arabia. *Humanities & Social Sciences Communications*, *12*(1), 1431. DOI: 10.1057/s41599-025-05784-x

Sharma, P., Hussain, S. S., & Gwal, R. (2026). Harmonizing intelligence: AI integration, workforce development, and ethical governance for future of work. In *Human 2.0* (pp. 143–162). Emerald Publishing Limited., DOI: 10.1108/978-1-83708-166-020251008

Sharma, R., & Gupta, H. (2025). Exploring Industry 5.0 hurdles and strategies to support sustainable development and realize future growth aspirations: A comprehensive analysis. *Benchmarking*, •••, 1–27. DOI: 10.1108/BIJ-07-2024-0573

Shen, Y., & Zhang, X. (2024). The impact of artificial intelligence on employment: The role of virtual agglomeration. *Humanities & Social Sciences Communications*, *11*(1), 122. DOI: 10.1057/s41599-024-02647-9

Shen, Y., & Zhou, P. (2024). Technological anxiety: Analysis of the impact of industrial intelligence on employment in China. *Zhongguo Renkou Ziyuan Yu Huanjing*, *22*(3), 343–355. DOI: 10.1016/j.cjpre.2024.09.013

Sherehiy, B., Karwowski, W., & Layer, J. K. (2007). A review of enterprise agility: Concepts, frameworks, and attributes. *International Journal of Industrial Ergonomics*, *37*(5), 445–460. DOI: 10.1016/j.ergon.2007.01.007

Sherov, A., Rakhimov, T., Hajiyev, H., Zelinskaya, M., & Khidirova, G. (2025). Evaluating class-imbalanced data handling for enhanced financial distress prediction using an attention-based deep neural network and heuristic optimization algorithms. Engineering. *Technology and Applied Science Research*, *15*(6), 13372. DOI: 10.48084/etasr.13372

Shi, L. (2025). Global perspectives on AI competence development: Analyzing national AI strategies in education and workforce policies. *Human Resource Development Review*, *24*(4), 447–476. DOI: 10.1177/15344843251332360

Shiri, R., El-Metwally, A., Sallinen, M., Pöyry, M., Härmä, M., & Toppinen-Tanner, S. (2023). The Role of Continuing Professional Training or Development in Maintaining Current Employment: A Systematic Review. *Healthcare (Basel), 11*(21), 2900. DOI: 10.3390/healthcare11212900 PMID: 37958044

Shneiderman, B. (2022). *Human-centered AI*. Oxford University Press. DOI: 10.1093/oso/9780192845290.001.0001

Shreha, S. A., Ravikumar, R. N., & Aarthi, S. (2025). Neuro-symbolic AI and Behavioral Intelligence. In *Advances in Computational Intelligence and Robotics* (pp. 121–152). IGI Global Scientific Publishing. DOI: 10.4018/979-8-3373-5012-7.ch005

Shreha, S. A., Ravikumar, R. N., & Aarthi, S. (2026). Precision medicine, genomics, and health equity challenges and opportunities. In *Advancing Equity in Global Healthcare Systems* (pp. 321–354). IGI Global Scientific Publishing., DOI: 10.4018/979-8-3373-1330-6.ch012

Shrestha, Y. R., Ben-Menahem, S. M., & von Krogh, G. (2023). Organizational decision-making structures in the age of artificial intelligence. *California Management Review, 61*(4), 66–83. DOI: 10.1177/0008125619862257

Shukla, T., Nirban, V. S., Das, M., Nadig, R. S., & Buttan, D. (2025). Cultural negotiations of digital transformation: Womenpreneurs and social media in rural india's domiciliary enterprises. *Journal of Cultural Analysis and Social Change*, 2619–2633. DOI: 10.64753/jcasc.v10i4.3297

Shukla, S. S., Bajpai, S., Pankajam, A., Gupta, A., Veeraiah, V., Pramanik, S., & Bag, S. (2024). The Central Bank of India as an Example of the Green Revolution in the Banking Sector. In *Recent Developments in Financial Management and Economics* (pp. 166–184). IGI Global., DOI: 10.4018/979-8-3693-2683-1.ch010

Siemens Healthineers. (2022). *AI-driven medical imaging and diagnostics systems*. Siemens Healthcare White Paper.

Siemens, G. (2020). Connectivism: A learning theory for the digital age. *International Journal of Instructional Technology*.

Siemens. (2025). *Sustainability at Siemens*. https://www.siemens.com/in/en/company/sustainability.html

Sindhwani, R., Afridi, S., Kumar, A., Banaitis, A., Luthra, S., & Singh, P. L. (2022). Can Industry 5.0 revolutionize the wave of resilience and social value creation? A multi-criteria framework to analyze enablers. *Technology in Society, 68*, 101887. DOI: 10.1016/j.techsoc.2022.101887

Singh, R., & Khan, M. Z. (2025). 'AI cannot eliminate an entire occupation', say experts on future of jobs. https://www.business-standard.com/specials/bs-events/ai-job-displacement-automation-employment-growth-125022801028_1.html

Singh, A., & Pandey, J. (2023). Artificial intelligence adoption in extended HR ecosystems: Enablers and barriers. An abductive case research. *Frontiers in Psychology, 14*, 1339782. DOI: 10.3389/fpsyg.2023.1339782

Sir C R Reddy College AP, E., & Yalamarthi, V. R. S. B. (2025). Artificial Intelligence in recruitment: Transforming talent acquisition practices. *International Journal of Innovations & Research Analysis, 05*(03(II)), 01–11. DOI: 10.62823/IJIRA/5.3(II).7946

Skubis, I. (2025). Humanoid robots CEOs and leaders in project management: Decision-making, human oversight, team dynamics and ethics. *International Journal of HR; Humanoid Robotics, 22*(06), 2550008. Advance online publication. DOI: 10.1142/S0219843625500082

Söllner, M., Arnold, T., Benlian, A., Bretschneider, U., Knight, C., Ohly, S., ... & Wendt, D. (2025). ChatGPT and Beyond: Exploring the Responsible Use of Generative AI in the Workplace: M. Söllner et al. Business & Information Systems Engineering, 67(2), 289-303.4

Somasundaram, R., Varalakshmi, S., Sanadi, H., Saini, R., Chinnusamy, S., & S., B. (2024). Entrepreneurship in emerging markets and intrapreneurship within organizations. In *Advances in Business Strategy and Competitive Advantage* (pp. 291–322). IGI Global. DOI: 10.4018/979-8-3693-3100-2.ch011

Sposato, M. (2025). Synthetic ethics: posthuman leadership in algorithmically governed organizations. *Journal of Information Communication and Ethics in Society*, 1–16. DOI: 10.1108/JICES-05-2025-0096

Sposato, M. (2026). Leading hybrid intelligence systems: A general systems theory approach to organizational leadership in hybrid intelligence knowledge ecosystems. *VINE Journal of Information and Knowledge Management Systems*, •••, 1–22. DOI: 10.1108/VJIKMS-06-2025-0220

Sreeram, A., Mehra, R., Parashar, K., Rao, B. U., Mohapatra, C. K., Jabbar, M. A., & Malagi, V. (2025). Ethical Leadership in managing AI-integrated library environments. *Indian Journal of Information Sources and Services, 15*(3), 131–139. DOI: 10.51983/ijiss-2025.IJISS.15.3.15

Sriharan, A., Kuhlmann, E., Correia, T., Tahzib, F., Czabanowska, K., Ungureanu, M.-I., & Kumar, B. N. (2025). Artificial Intelligence in healthcare: Balancing technological innovation with health and care workforce priorities. *The International Journal of Health Planning and Management, 40*(4), 987–992. DOI: 10.1002/hpm.3927 PMID: 40075189

Sroufe, R. (2020). *Integrated management: How sustainability creates value for any business*. Emerald Publishing.

Stamate, A. N., Sauvé, G., & Denis, P. L. (2021). The rise of the machines and how they impact workers' psychological health: An empirical study. *Human Behavior and Emerging Technologies, 3*(5), 942–955. DOI: 10.1002/hbe2.315

Stanford University. (2023). *Artificial intelligence index report 2023*. Stanford Institute for Human-Centered AI. https://aiindex.stanford.edu

Stypinska, J. (2023). AI ageism: A critical roadmap for studying age discrimination and exclusion in digitalized societies. *AI & Society, 38*(2), 665–677. DOI: 10.1007/s00146-022-01553-5 PMID: 36212226

Subramanian, Y. R., Riya, R., & Rajendran, R. (2024). Revolutionizing workforce education. In *Integrating Generative AI in Education to Achieve Sustainable Development Goals* (pp. 282–299). IGI Global., DOI: 10.4018/979-8-3693-2440-0.ch015

Sufyan Ghaleb, M. M., & Pardaev, J. (2025). Effects of Advertisement Language, Communication Style, Information Seeking Behavior and Information Source Credibility on Customers' Intentions towards International Products via Brand Trust. *El Profesional de la Información, 34*(2). Advance online publication. DOI: 10.3145/epi.2025.ene.34203

Sundstrup, E., Meng, A., Ajslev, J. Z. N., Albertsen, K., Pedersen, F., & Andersen, L. L. (2022). New Technology and Loss of Paid Employment among Older Workers: Prospective Cohort Study. *International Journal of Environmental Research and Public Health, 19*(12), 7168. DOI: 10.3390/ijerph19127168 PMID: 35742416

Sutton, J., Arcidiacono, A., Torrisi, G., & Arku, R. N. (2023). Regional economic resilience: A scoping review. *Progress in Human Geography, 47*(4), 500–532. DOI: 10.1177/03091325231174183

Tabata, M., Wildermuth, C., Bottomley, K., & Jenkins, D. (2025). Generative AI integration in leadership practice: Foundations, challenges, and opportunities. *Journal of Leadership Studies, 18*(4), 41–54. DOI: 10.1002/jls.70005

Taherdoost, H., & Madanchian, M. (2023). Artificial intelligence and knowledge management: Impacts, benefits, and implementation. *Computers*, *12*(4), 72. DOI: 10.3390/computers12040072

Tambe, P., Cappelli, P., & Yakubovich, V. (2019). Artificial intelligence in human resources management: Challenges and a path forward. *California Management Review*, *61*(4), 15–42. DOI: 10.1177/0008125619867910

Tang, Q. (2025). Emerging Technologies, Sustainability and Carbon Accounting. In *Carbon Accounting and Sustainability* (Vol. II). Palgrave Macmillan., DOI: 10.1007/978-3-031-90636-7_6

Tarafdar, M., Pullins, E. B., & Ragu-Nathan, T. S. (2021). Technostress: Negative effect on performance and well-being. *Journal of Information Systems, 35*(1), 1–24. DOI: 10.1080/0960085X.2020.1868891

Tata Power. (2025). *Green energy and smart grid initiatives*. https://www.tatapower-ddl.com/corporate/smart-grid-index/green-energy

Teece, D. J. (2007). Explicating dynamic capabilities: The nature and microfoundations of (sustainable) enterprise performance. *Strategic Management Journal*, *28*(13), 1319–1350. DOI: 10.1002/smj.640

Teece, D. J., Pisano, G., & Shuen, A. (1997). Dynamic capabilities and strategic management. *Strategic Management Journal*, *18*(7), 509–533. DOI: 10.1002/(sici)1097-0266(199708)18:7<509:aid-smj882>3.0.co;2-z

Tenakwah, E. S., & Watson, C. (2025). Embracing the AI/automation age: Preparing your workforce for humans and machines working together. *Strategy and Leadership*, *53*(1), 32–48. DOI: 10.1108/SL-05-2024-0040

Tenakwah, E., & Otchere-Ankrah, B. (2024). Future of work and workforce capabilities: Navigating post-pandemic disruptions. *International Journal of Manpower*, *45*(1), 45–68.

The Economic Times. (2024). *AI adoption in Indian IT sector and its impact on jobs and productivity*

Tursunbayeva, A., Pagliari, C., Di Lauro, S., & Antonelli, G. (2021). The ethics of people analytics: Risks, opportunities, and recommendations. *Personnel Review*, *51*(3), 900–921. DOI: 10.1108/PR-12-2019-0680

Ulrich, D., & Dulebohn, J. H. (2021). HR competencies and the future of work. *Human Resource Management Review*, *31*(2), 100–112.

Umair, A., Conboy, K., & Whelan, E. (2023). Examining technostress and its impact on worker well-being in the digital gig economy. *Internet Research, 33*(7), 206–242. DOI: 10.1108/INTR-03-2022-0214

UNESCO. (2021). *Recommendation on the ethics of artificial intelligence*. United Nations Educational, Scientific and Cultural Organization. https://www.unesco.org

UNESCO. (2021). *Reimagining our futures together: A new social contract for education.*

Unilever. (2024). *Annual Report and Accounts 2024*. https://www.unilever.com/files/unilever-annual-report-and-accounts-2024.pdf#page=262

Unilever. (2025). *Reducing plastic use and improving recyclability*. https://www.unilever.com/sustainability/plastics/

United Nations Environment Programme (UNEP). (2019). *Global Environment Outlook – GEO-6: Healthy Planet, Healthy People*. Cambridge University Press., DOI: 10.1017/9781108627146

United Nations. (2022). *Sustainable development goals report 2022*. https://unstats.un.org

University, W. G., Khair, M. A., Shaheen, N., University, W. G., Khair, M. M., University, W. G., Jain, S., & University, M. A. H. G. (2025). HCM AI agents and data-driven decision making. *International Journal of Research in Modern Engineering & Emerging Technology, 13*(3), 36–54. DOI: 10.63345/ijrmeet.org.v13.i3.3

Vaishnav, L., Singh, S., & Cornell, K. A. (2024). Transparency, security, and workplace training & awareness in the age of generative ai. arXiv preprint arXiv:2501.10389.

Valle-Cruz, D., & García-Contreras, R. (2025). Towards AI-driven transformation and smart data management: Emerging technological change in the public sector value chain. *Public Policy and Administration, 40*(2), 254–275. DOI: 10.1177/09520767231188401

Varouchas, E. (2026). Executives' perspectives on the impact of generative AI in business: a qualitative study of strategic, ethical and organizational transformations. *Journal of Science and Technology Policy Management*, 1–34. DOI: 10.1108/JSTPM-10-2025-0493

Vial, G. (2019). Understanding digital transformation: A review and a research agenda. *The Journal of Strategic Information Systems, 28*(2), 118–144. DOI: 10.1016/j.jsis.2019.01.003

Vial, G. (2021). Understanding digital transformation. *MIS Quarterly Executive, 20*(1), 13–27.

Vrontis, D., Christofi, M., Pereira, V., Tarba, S., Makrides, A., & Trichina, E. (2022). Artificial intelligence, robotics, advanced technologies and human resource management: A systematic review. *International Journal of Human Resource Management, 33*(6), 1237–1266. DOI: 10.1080/09585192.2020.1871398

Wamba, S. F., Queiroz, M. M., Randhawa, K., & Gupta, G. (2025). Generative artificial intelligence and the challenges to adding value ethically. *Technovation, 144*, 103235. DOI: 10.1016/j.technovation.2025.103235

Wamba-Taguimdje, S.-L., Fosso Wamba, S., Kala Kamdjoug, J. R., & Tchatchouang Wanko, C. E. (2020). Influence of artificial intelligence (AI) on firm performance: The business value of AI-based transformation projects. *Business Process Management Journal, 26*(7), 1893–1924. DOI: 10.1108/bpmj-10-2019-0411

Wang, B., Liu, Y., Qian, J., & Parker, S. K. (2023). Achieving effective remote working during COVID-19: A work design perspective. Applied Psychology, 72*(1), 16–59. DOI: 10.1111/apps.12391

Wang, K.-H., & Lu, W.-C. (2025). AI-induced job impact: Complementary or substitution? Empirical insights and sustainable technology considerations. *Sustainable Technology and Entrepreneurship, 4*(1), 100085. Advance online publication. DOI: 10.1016/j.stae.2024.100085

Wang, X., Chen, M., & Chen, N. (2024). How artificial intelligence affects the labour force employment structure from the perspective of industrial structure optimisation. *Heliyon, 10*(5), e26686. DOI: 10.1016/j.heliyon.2024.e26686 PMID: 38434398

Wang, Y.-F., Chen, Y.-C., & Chien, S.-Y. (2023). Citizens' intention to follow recommendations from a government-supported. *Public Policy and Administration.* Advance online publication. DOI: 10.1177/09520767231176126

Wang, Y., Liu, H., & Zhu, Y. (2022). Knowledge sharing behaviour in digital work environments: A social exchange perspective. *Journal of Knowledge Management, 26*(5), 1223–1245.

Wang, Z., Fu, J., & Bai, W. (2024a). Public management approaches to an aging workforce: Organizational strategies for strategies for adaptability and efficiency. *Frontiers in Psychology, 15*, 1439271. DOI: 10.3389/fpsyg.2024.1439271 PMID: 39131863

Warner, M. E., Zhang, X., & Guillemot, J. (2025). Demographic ageing: An opportunity to rethink economy, society and regions. *Cambridge Journal of Regions, Economy and Society*, *18*(1), 79–92. DOI: 10.1093/cjres/rsae031

WEF. (2025). Future of Jobs Report 2025. https://reports.weforum.org/docs/WEF_Future_of_Jobs_Report_2025.pdf

Wei, H., Trepanier, S., Wei, T., Marshall, D., Wiley, R. D., & D'Agostino, D. (2025). The philosophy of Artificial Intelligence in healthcare: Facilitating a human-centered paradigm to optimize healthcare outcomes. *Forum Gestion Des Soins de Sante [Healthcare Management Forum]*, (08404704251394950), 8404704251394950. DOI: 10.1177/08404704251394950

Wen, Y., Wang, J., & Chen, X. (2025). Trust and AI weight: human-AI collaboration in organizational management decision-making. *Frontiers in Organizational Psychology*, *3*(1419403), 1419403. Advance online publication. DOI: 10.3389/forgp.2025.1419403

Westover, J. (2024). Preparing the workforce for ethical, responsible and trustworthy AI. *Human Capital Leadership Review*, *13*(4). Advance online publication. DOI: 10.70175/hclreview.2020.13.4.7

World Bank. (2022). *Skills for jobs in the digital age*. https://www.worldbank.org

World Economic Forum. (2020). *The future of jobs report 2020*. World Economic Forum. https://www.weforum.org

World Economic Forum. (2023). Future of Jobs Report 2023. WEF.

World Economic Forum. (2023). *Responsible AI governance: Frameworks for ethical deployment*. World Economic Forum. https://www.weforum.org

World Economic Forum. (2023). *The future of jobs report 2023*. https://www.weforum.org

Xu, F., Hou, J., Chen, W., & Xie, K. (2025). Generative AI and organizational structure in the knowledge economy. *SSRN*. https://doi.org/DOI: 10.2139/ssrn.5242296

Yadav, M. Minakshi, Choudhury, T., & Dewasiri, N. J. (2026). The smart HR cloud: Automating workforce planning and skill mapping. In *Automating Intelligence With Cloud-Native AI Tools* (pp. 385–394). DOI: 10.4018/979-8-3373-7442-ch025

Yamashita, T., Narine, D., Chidebe, R. C. W., Kramer, J. W., Karam, R., Cummins, P. A., & Smith, T. J. (2024). Digital Skills, STEM Occupation, and Job Automation Risks Among the Older Workers in the United States. *The Gerontologist*, *64*(8), gnae069. Advance online publication. DOI: 10.1093/geront/gnae069 PMID: 38835197

Yang, J., Amrollahi, A., & Marrone, M. (2024). Harnessing the Potential of Artificial Intelligence: Affordances, Constraints, and Strategic Implications for Professional Services. *The Journal of Strategic Information Systems, 33*(4), 101864. DOI: 10.1016/j.jsis.2024.101864

Yin, H., Huang, S., & Chen, G. (2022). Emotional labor and emotional exhaustion: A meta-analysis across occupations. *Frontiers in Psychology, 13*, 845678. DOI: 10.3389/fpsyg.2022.845678

Yi, Y., Wang, D., Li, J. Y., Lee, Y., & Tao, W. (2025). Be ethical then proficient: Navigating employees' ethical adoption of generative AI in the workplace. *Journal of Communication Management (London)*. Advance online publication. DOI: 10.1108/JCOM-10-2024-0206

Yong, J. Y., Yusoff, Y. M., Fernando, Y., Lin, W. L., Chong, S. C., & Pek, C. K. (2026). Generation Green: Navigating ESG in Generation Z's Job Search Landscape. In *Stimulating Economic Growth Through Cultural and Societal Transformations* (pp. 83-100). IGI Global Scientific Publishing. https://doi.org/DOI: 10.4018/979-8-3373-0603-2.ch004

Yorke, M. (2006). *Employability in higher education: What it is, what it is not.* Higher Education Academy.

Yousaf, M., Latif, M., Aslam, S., & Saddiqui, A. (2022). Impact of digital learning tools on employee skill development: Moderating role of leadership support. *Sustainability, 14*(8), 4567.

Zack, M., McKeen, J., & Singh, S. (2009). Knowledge management and organizational performance: An exploratory analysis. *Journal of Knowledge Management, 13*(6), 392–409. DOI: 10.1108/13673270910997088

Zakrzewska, A. (2025). OECD Employment Outlook 2025: Can We Get Through the Demographic Crunch? https://www.oecd.org/en/publications/2025

Zambia, U. (2026). Re-engineering the Botswana civil service with human-AI augmentation: A grounded theory of organizational transformation for a Fourth Industrial Revolution-ready public sector. *International Review of Social Sciences Research, 6*(1), 87–106. DOI: 10.53378/irssr.353309

Zayniddinov, R., Jumaev, N., Irgasheva, G., Asadov, A., & Makhmudov, N.. (2025). The influence of the digital economy on economic development: Evidence from Uzbekistan. *ACM International Conference Proceeding Series*. DOI: 10.1145/3726122.3726242

Zhang, H., Hou, X., & Rao, Z. (2025). Can fintech improve total factor energy efficiency? Evidence from China's listed companies. *Climatic Change*, *178*(8), 145. DOI: 10.1007/s10584-025-03994-5

Zhang, S., Guo, P., Yuan, Y., & Ji, Y. (2025). Anxiety or engaged? Research on the impact of technostress on employees' innovative behavior in the era of artificial intelligence. *Acta Psychologica*, *259*, 105442. DOI: 10.1016/j.actpsy.2025.105442 PMID: 40834779

Zhao, H., & Xie, H. (2025). Workplace Intelligent Technology Use and Health of Older Remote Workers. *Journal of Occupational and Environmental Medicine*, *67*(7), 469–476. DOI: 10.1097/JOM.0000000000003402 PMID: 40165527

Zhao, J., Ragmoun, W., Dong, Z., Nawaz, M. A., & Sattarov, A. (2025). Circular economy implementation through AI adoption, CSR and green finance: The mediating role of green product innovation and green supply chain. *Corporate Social Responsibility and Environmental Management*. Advance online publication. DOI: 10.1002/csr.70289

Zheng, H., Ou, M., Luo, C., & Zeng, Y. (2026). Unpacking generative AI adoption in the workplace: The roles of algorithmic ethics and intellectual humility. *Aslib Journal of Information Management*, •••, 1–25. DOI: 10.1108/AJIM-06-2025-0377

Zhong, L., Ady, S. U., & Indrasari, M. (2026). AI in strategic management and organizational agility of SMEs: Leadership, policy environment, and adaptive capability. *Future Technology*, *5*(2), 1–12. DOI: 10.55670/fpll.futech.5.2.1

Zirar, A., Ali, S. I., & Islam, N. (2023). Worker and workplace Artificial Intelligence (AI) coexistence: Emerging themes and research agenda. *Technovation*, *124*, 102747. DOI: 10.1016/j.technovation.2023.102747

Zuboff, S. (2019). *The age of surveillance capitalism*. PublicAffairs.

Zwick, T. (2015). Training older employees: What is effective? *International Journal of Manpower*, *36*(2), 136–150. DOI: 10.1108/IJM-09-2012-0138

About the Contributors

Abdelrehim Awad is a faculty member in Business Administration (Marketing and Supply Chain Management) at the University of Bisha (Saudi Arabia). His scholarship spans digital transformation, AI-enabled marketing, customer knowledge management, and sustainability-oriented decision-making. He has served as editor of multiple IGI Global volumes focused on AI and sustainability and contributes to international peer review and editorial activities.

Amr El Daba is Regional Dean at the Arab Academy for Management, Banking, and Financial Sciences (AAMBFS). He has extensive academic and administrative leadership experience across undergraduate and postgraduate programs, with research and training interests spanning economics, governance, and development-oriented strategy. He has supervised postgraduate research and supported digital transformation initiatives in higher education.

***

Elena Akhunova is an Associate Professor in the Department of Finance and Financial Technologies at Tashkent State University of Economics, Tashkent, Uzbekistan. She specializes in financial systems, digital finance, and emerging financial technologies, with a strong focus on integrating theoretical frameworks with practical financial applications. With extensive academic and teaching experience, she contributes to the development of modern finance curricula aligned with global industry trends. Her research interests include fintech innovations, financial analytics, investment strategies, and digital transformation in financial services. She actively engages in scholarly research, academic publications, and collaborative projects, contributing to advancements in finance and financial technology. Through innovative teaching methods, including case-based learning and technology-driven instruction, she supports the development of analytical and professional skills among students. Her work reflects a commitment to academic excellence and the advancement of finance education in a rapidly evolving global financial landscape.

Asheetu Bhatia Sarin is an Assistant Professor (Senior) in Management at Vivekananda Institute of Professional Studies-Technical Campus, affiliated with GGSIPU, Delhi. She has over 12 years of teaching experience in the fields of Commerce and Management. She has done a Ph.D. in Behavioral Finance, did her post-graduation (MBA) from ICFAI Business School in Finance and Marketing, and earned her graduate degree in B.Com (H) from Delhi University. She is a lifetime member of the Indian Commerce Association and has to her credit many national and International publications.

Deeksha Gupta Ganguly is an Assistant Professor, School of Business & Management. She is a Post-graduate in Commerce & Management (Human Resource Management & Marketing). She has also cleared UGC NET in Management. Prof. Ganguly has a rich academic & industry experience of 15 plus years and worked for various Educational institutions & universities in Delhi NCR and Chennai. She is very much involved in academic research and has extensively published research papers in various Scopus-indexed academic journals.

Deepak Gupta is a distinguished academician with over 20 years of teaching experience and expertise in Computer Science and Engineering. He holds a Ph.D. in Computer Engineering and has an extensive research portfolio, including many international journal papers, multiple conference proceedings, and several books. His research interests span machine learning, artificial intelligence, and data mining. Currently, Dr. Gupta serves as an Associate Professor and Head of Department of CSE (Emerging Branches) at ITM Gwalior, MP, India. He has also contributed significantly to the field through patents and copyrights and actively engages as a reviewer, conference chair and editor.

Vishal Jain currently serves as a Professor and Dean of Accreditation, Statutory Compliances & Institutional Development at the School of Engineering & Technology, Vivekananda Institute of Professional Studies - Technical Campus, New Delhi. His previous roles include Professor at Sharda University, Greater Noida, and Associate Professor at Bharati Vidyapeeth's Institute of Computer Applications and Management (BVICAM), New Delhi. Dr. Jain has actively participated in various academic governance bodies, including the Faculty Board, Board of Planning and Management, Executive Council, Academic Council, Curriculum Development and Review Committee, and Academic Audit across multiple higher education institutions. He collaborates with Kuala Lumpur University of Science and Technology (KLUST), Malaysia, Lincoln University College, Malaysia and the Research Institute of IoT Cybersecurity at National Kaohsiung University of Science and Technology in Taiwan for research initiatives. He has supervised three Ph.D. candidates, with two additional scholars currently pursuing their degrees under his guidance.

Nodir Jumaev is a faculty member in the Department of International Finance at Tashkent State University of Economics (TSUE), Tashkent, Uzbekistan. His teaching and research focus on international finance, investment policy, capital markets in emerging economies, and regional economic development. He has authored and co-authored scholarly works on investment climate assessment, foreign direct investment attraction, and financial sector reforms, and has contributed to policy dialogues and professional trainings for public and private institutions. At TSUE, he supervises student research, develops practice-oriented coursework, and collaborates with industry and government stakeholders on applied finance projects. Dr. Jumaev holds advanced degrees in economics/finance and brings extensive academic and leadership experience to advancing TSUE's internationalization and research agenda.

Sadirdin Khudoykulov is affiliated with the Department of Finance and Tourism at Termez University of Economics and Service, Termez, Uzbekistan. He is actively involved in academic teaching and research, contributing to the interdisciplinary domains of finance and tourism. His work focuses on integrating financial principles with tourism management practices, enabling students to understand both economic and service-oriented perspectives. He supports the development of analytical, managerial, and decision-making skills through practical and case-based learning approaches. His academic interests include financial management, tourism economics, and sustainable development within the service sector. In addition to teaching, he participates in research activities, academic collaborations, and scholarly initiatives aimed at addressing contemporary challenges in finance and tourism. His contributions reflect a commitment to enhancing educational quality and preparing students for dynamic industry environments.

Saidjanova Madinabonu is affiliated with the Department of Biomedical Engineering, Biophysics, and Informatics at Bukhara State Medical Institute, Bukhara, Uzbekistan. She is engaged in interdisciplinary academic and research activities that integrate principles of biomedical engineering with biophysics and medical informatics. Her work focuses on applying computational and technological approaches to healthcare challenges, including data analysis, medical systems, and bio-signal processing. She contributes to teaching and academic development by delivering courses related to biomedical technologies and informatics, fostering both theoretical understanding and practical skills among students. Her research interests include healthcare data analytics, medical imaging, and the application of artificial intelligence in biomedical systems. She actively participates in scholarly research and collaborative projects aimed at improving healthcare solutions through technology-driven innovations. Her academic efforts reflect a commitment to advancing biomedical education and supporting the development of modern, technology-enabled healthcare systems.

Chandan Maheshkar is one of the founders of the East Nimar Society for Education (2019), dedicated to quality improvement in higher education and the development of educator competencies. As a Senior Consultant, he has served the Centre for Internal Quality Assurance (CIQA), Madhya Pradesh Bhoj (Open) University, Bhopal, India. He is associated with several management institutes in central India, including the University of Indore, India, in various academic roles. Dr. Maheshkar earned his MBA and Ph.D. from the University of Indore, India. In 2014, the University of Indore awarded him the Golden Jubilee Research Fellowship on the occasion of its successful 50th anniversary. Business education, HRD, cross-cultural business, and organizational behavior are his core areas of research interests. His research papers and book chapters have been published in the journals of international repute and edited collections by Springer, Taylor & Francis, Emerald, Sage, IGI Global, Vernon Press, and others, respectively.

Yogesh Mehta is a Professor specializing in entrepreneurship, business analytics, and innovation, with extensive experience in teaching, research, and academic content development. He mentors student startups and institutional teams, contributes to global entrepreneurial ecosystems, and actively engages in curriculum design, publications, and capacity-building initiatives across higher education institutions.

Nitish Kumar Minz is a researcher in the field of Human Resource Management with a focus on Artificial Intelligence, digital transformation, and sustainable organizational systems. His research agenda is centeredSchool, Vellore Institute of Technology, India, and serves as the Managing Editor of the International Journal of Convergent Research (IJCR). He has authored and co-authored 50+ research publications in reputed and indexed journals, with an H-index of 8, reflecting his growing scholarly impact. His research primarily examines AI-driven HRM, workforce diversity and inclusion, digital HR practices, and sustainable business models in emerging economies. His work employs advanced analytical and interdisciplinary approaches, including fuzzy logic modeling and bibliometric analysis, to explore complex organizational and societal challenges. He has also contributed to ICSSR-supported research projects and interdisciplinary studies linking technology with human-centric management practices. His research agenda is centered on developing inclusive, ethical, and future-ready workforce frameworks, integrating technological innovation with sustainability and socio-cultural perspectives.

Xolmirzayev Furqatbek Muxtarjonovich is a Senior Teacher in the Department of Finance at Alfraganus University, Tashkent, Uzbekistan. He is actively engaged in teaching and academic development within the field of finance, focusing on strengthening students' understanding of financial systems, management principles, and economic analysis. His teaching approach integrates theoretical knowledge with practical applications, enabling learners to develop critical thinking and decision-making skills relevant to the financial sector. His academic interests include corporate finance, financial management, and emerging trends in financial technologies. In addition to teaching, he contributes to curriculum development and participates in research and scholarly activities aimed at advancing finance education. He also supports students through interactive and case-based learning methodologies, fostering both academic excellence and industry readiness.

Raghu N has Ten years of experience in Academic and Research. He received the Ph.D. (2020) in Electronics Engineering from Jain University, and B.E. in Electronics and Telecommunications Engineering from VTU University, Karnataka. His research interests were in RF Communication and Image Processing. He has published his research findings in various Scopus indexed Journals and International conferences. He is a member of various professional bodies.

Tarika Nanadedkar is research scholar with experience of 10 years. She is faculty of statistics and mathematics with special inclination towards research. She is having many national and international publications.

Nazokat Panjieva is affiliated with the Department of Economics at Termez University of Economics and Service, Termez, Uzbekistan. She is actively involved in teaching and research in the field of economics, with a focus on economic development, policy analysis, and applied economic studies. Her academic work emphasizes the integration of theoretical economic concepts with real-world applications, supporting students in developing analytical and decision-making skills. She contributes to curriculum delivery and engages in scholarly research aimed at addressing contemporary economic challenges at both regional and global levels. Her areas of interest include macroeconomic trends, sustainable development, and economic policy frameworks. She is also involved in academic collaborations and knowledge dissemination through publications and conferences. Her ORCID identifier (0009-0009-4774-5505) reflects her commitment to maintaining a recognized academic research profile and contributing to the broader research community.

Sabyasachi Pramanik is a professional IEEE member. He obtained a PhD in Computer Science and Engineering from Sri Satya Sai University of Technology and Medical Sciences, Bhopal, India. Presently, he is an Associate Professor, Department of Computer Science and Engineering, Haldia Institute of Technology, India. He has many publications in various reputed international conferences, journals, and book chapters (Indexed by SCIE, Scopus, ESCI, etc). He is doing research in the fields of Artificial Intelligence, Data Privacy, Cybersecurity, Network Security, and Machine Learning. He also serves on the editorial boards of several international journals. He is a reviewer of journal articles from IEEE, Springer, Elsevier, Inderscience, IET and IGI Global. He has reviewed many conference papers, has been a keynote speaker, session chair, and technical program committee member at many international conferences. He has authored a book on Wireless Sensor Network. He has edited 8 books from IGI Global, CRC Press, Springer and Wiley Publications.

Ravikumar R. N. is currently a Postdoctoral researcher at Universiti Malaysia Perlis, Malaysia. Also, working as an Assistant Professor in the Department of Computer Engineering at Marwadi University, Rajkot, Gujarat. He has 14 years of national and international teaching experience. He completed his PhD at Amity University, Rajasthan, M.E at VMRF Deemed University, B.E at Anna University, Chennai. He is the co-founder of the Research Activities Club at Marwadi University and trains students on research activities, which leads to the various publications. He has published numerous research articles in Scopus, SCI journals, Book chapters, and Conference papers. Also, he hold several patents and authored books. His specialization is ML, DL, Federated Learning, Recommendation Systems, and Optimization Techniques.

Aarthi S is a dedicated Assistant Professor in Computer Science with over six years of teaching experience. She is currently pursuing her Ph.D. at Marwadi University, Gujarat, and holds an M.Phil. and MCA from Bharathiar University, Tamil Nadu. Throughout her academic career, Aarthi has specialized in programming languages such as C++, Java, and C, and contributed to research in recommender systems and AI-related data privacy. She has published journal articles, contributed to book chapters, and actively participated in technical workshops. Known for her student mentorship and engagement in academic events, Aarthi remains committed to fostering innovation and excellence in computer science education.

Valisher Sapayev is an academic professional associated with the Department of General Professional Subjects at Mamun University, Khiva, Uzbekistan.

He is engaged in teaching and academic development across foundational and interdisciplinary subjects that support diverse professional programs. His areas of interest include curriculum design, higher education pedagogy, and the integration of modern teaching methodologies to enhance student learning outcomes. Dr. Sapayev contributes to fostering academic excellence by promoting practical knowledge, critical thinking, and skill-based education among students. He is also involved in institutional initiatives aimed at strengthening educational quality and aligning academic programs with industry and societal needs. Through his teaching and academic contributions, he supports the development of competent graduates equipped with essential professional and analytical skills.

Puja Sareen is a Doctorate in the area of Human Resource Management with 17 years of industry and academic experience. She has expertise in teaching OB/HRM subjects. She has been certified by IICA, Ministry of Corporate Affairs as a Master Trainer for their Certificate Programme in CSR. A University Topper in B.Com (H) and MBA, she has extensive experience in curriculum development. Conducting soft skills training is her forte. She has published several papers and case studies in international and national journals and conference proceedings.

Ilxom Sayfiddinov is affiliated with the Department of Bank Accounting and Auditing at Tashkent State University of Economics, Tashkent, Uzbekistan. He is an academic professional engaged in teaching, research, and scholarly activities in the areas of banking, accounting, and auditing. His work supports the development of students' knowledge of financial reporting, banking operations, audit procedures, and the role of accounting systems in modern economic institutions. He is committed to promoting academic excellence through a balanced approach that combines theoretical understanding with practical relevance. His academic interests may include bank accounting, financial analysis, auditing standards, corporate governance, and financial management. Through his role at Tashkent State University of Economics, he contributes to creating a strong learning environment that encourages analytical thinking, ethical awareness, and professional competence among students. His professional profile reflects dedication to quality education, research engagement, and the broader advancement of accounting and auditing studies in Uzbekistan.

Fakhritdin Turdialiev is a faculty member in the Department of Economics at Termez University of Economics and Service, Uzbekistan. He is actively engaged in teaching and research in the field of economics, with a focus on economic development, policy analysis, and applied economic studies. His academic interests include macroeconomic and microeconomic analysis, regional economic development, and the application of modern analytical tools to evaluate economic trends and decision-making processes. He contributes to curriculum development and student mentoring, fostering critical thinking and practical skills among learners. Turdialiev participates in academic research, publications, and collaborative initiatives that promote innovation and knowledge dissemination. His work emphasizes the integration of theoretical concepts with real-world economic challenges, contributing to the advancement of economic education and sustainable development.

Davronov Shaxbos is a researcher and academic affiliated with the Department of Biomedical Engineering, Biophysics, and Informatics at Bukhara State Medical Institute, Bukhara, Uzbekistan. His work focuses on the interdisciplinary integration of biomedical engineering and computational informatics to address modern healthcare challenges. His research interests include medical data analysis, health informatics systems, biomedical signal processing, and the application of artificial intelligence in clinical diagnostics and decision support. Dr. Davronov has contributed to academic teaching and research activities, supporting the development of innovative solutions for patient monitoring and healthcare optimization. He is actively involved in guiding students and participating in collaborative research initiatives aimed at improving healthcare technologies and digital medical systems. His contributions reflect a commitment to advancing biomedical sciences through technology-driven approaches and fostering academic excellence in the field of biomedical engineering and health informatics.

Monika Yadav is currently associated with K.R. Mangalam University, Gurugram as Assistant Professor. She has earned her PhD from BMU University, Rothak, Haryana in Strategic management. Besides having consistently, a meritorious academic background, she has experience in academic administration, teaching and research. She has chaired 2 conferences and filed 1 Patents. She has published several research papers in National and International Journals and has several national and international conferences, a patent, book chapters, a book (fiction) and case studies to her credit. She has awarded by various national and international Awards.

Index

A

B

C

D

E

F

G

H

I

J

K

M

O

P

R

S

T

U

W

www.ingramcontent.com/pod-product-compliance
Lightning Source LLC
LaVergne TN
LVHW062331300926
849161LV00007B/1648
9798260027264